NIXON'S
SHADOW

NIXON'S
SHADOW

The History of an Image

David Greenberg

W. W. NORTON & COMPANY • NEW YORK • LONDON

Since this page cannot legibly accommodate all
the copyright notices, page 435 constitutes
an extension of the copyright page.

For information about permission to reproduce selections from
this book, write to Permissions, W. W. Norton & Company, Inc.,
500 Fifth Avenue, New York, NY 10110.

Manufacturing by The Haddon Craftsmen, Inc.
Book design by Mary McDonnell
Production manager: Andrew Marasia

Library of Congress Cataloging-in-Publication Data

Greenberg, David, 1968–
    Nixon's shadow : the history of an image / David Greenberg.—1st ed.
    p. cm.
Includes bibliographical references (p.) and index.
    ISBN 0-393-04896-9 (hardcover)
    1. Nixon, Richard M. (Richard Milhous), 1913—Public opinion. 2. Presidents—United
States—Biography. 3. Public relations and politics—United States—History—20th century.
4. Political culture—United States—History—20th century. 5. Public opinion—United
States—History—20th century. 6. United States—Politics and government—1969–1974.
I. Title.
    E856.G747 2003
    973.924'092—dc21

                                                                                          2003008421

W. W. Norton & Company, Inc., 500 Fifth Avenue, New York, N.Y. 10110
www.wwnorton.com

W. W. Norton & Company Ltd., Castle House, 75/76 Wells Street, London W1T 3QT

To my parents,
Maida and Robert Greenberg

Between the idea

And the reality . . .

Falls the shadow . . .

—T. S. Eliot, "The Hollow Men"

Contents

Preface

When you're writing a book, people expect you to be able to sum it up in a phrase or sentence. Inquisitive friends often want to know—briefly—what your book is "about." Over the last few years, I've given a variety of answers to this question: "A history of Nixon's image in American culture and politics". . ."A cultural history of Nixon". . ."A study in political image making that focuses on Nixon." People generally seemed content with these answers, but I was never perfectly satisfied. None did justice to the entirety of this project.

I still don't have a single phrase of explanation, but I'm going to try to sum it up in a few pages. First, let me say what the book is not. *Nixon's Shadow* is not a biography of Nixon. It covers the span of his life, and it includes a lot of biographical information. I touch on the critical episodes in his career and sometimes explore them in depth. But the work lacks both the structure and the approach of a conventional biography. Besides, there's much more about Nixon that I would have included had I been trying mainly to tell the story of his life.

Rather, *Nixon's Shadow* tells the story of how Nixon was perceived and understood by different groups of people throughout his career and afterward. In this sense, it is the history of his image. As I explain in the Introduction that follows, I believe that history consists not only in what important people did and said but equally in what they symbolized—what they meant—to their publics. I'm as interested in understanding these publics as I am in understanding Nixon, as keen to pinpoint what qualities of theirs shaped their images of Nixon as to discern what Nixon brought to the equation. My usual short answer, therefore, is to call this book a history of Nixon's image.

The reason I sometimes describe this book as a "cultural history" of Nixon is that the meanings of a figure as rich and controversial as Nixon are found not just in high politics but also in the culture. So I have examined, along with "political" groups of Nixon-watchers such as conservatives, liberals, radicals, and Nixonian loyalists, various "cultural" constituencies, including reporters, psychoanalysts, foreign policy pundits, and historians. The materials I consulted comprised both political archives, newspapers, opinion journals, and memoirs and plays, songs, movies, and TV shows. "Culture" here refers not simply to the arts but (in its anthropological meaning) to the ways a society makes meaning.

These first two definitions suggest that this book's purpose is to shed light on Nixon. That's certainly one goal; I hope readers will learn about Nixon's life, his character, his politics, his significance. But I also want to trace a story of how American political culture in the last half century has become consumed by concerns about image making and authenticity. We now live in a culture that's hyperaware of the construction and manipulation of images in politics. Nixon provides a vehicle for tracing the rise of this new hyperawareness, since, perhaps uniquely among late twentieth-century politicians, he both reflected and contributed to it. Indeed, his historical importance lies partly in having helped to foster our current image-obsessed political culture. Hence, this book is also a study in political image making.

The title is meant to touch on all these aspects. A shadow is, first, an image, a semblance of a person as distinct from the person himself. In Plato's allegory, cave dwellers mistake shadows on the wall for reality itself, until they step out into the daylight and learn otherwise. Although I have a rather un-Platonic view of images and shadows—I argue that they are expressive of reality, yet also rooted in individual perceptions—the ancient themes of image, reality, perception, interpretation, and meaning are at the heart of this book.

A shadow, secondly, is an aura; sometimes it refers to a ghost. Nixon's shadow haunts our landscape in that he so influenced our thoughts about politics and leaders that ours is, as many observers have called it, an Age of Nixon. There are well-known ways in which Nixon influenced the culture that I don't dwell on here precisely because they're so well known:

most obviously, his unique violations of the Constitution, his unmatched abuses of power, his deliberate direction of a criminal conspiracy from the White House, and his calculated cover-up all helped to shatter public faith in the president, the presidency, and the government (a faith that the Vietnam War had already weakened). Beyond that direct blow to public trust, however, Nixon also influenced our political culture through his relentless image craft, which bolstered the belief that politics is little more than a contest of images—a belief that, in its own way, has given rise to popular cynicism about politics.

Then, too, there's no denying that Nixon was a shadowy figure. Even if you reject those dark, malign images whose creation and evolution are traced in the following chapters—Nixon as Machiavellian, Nixon as paranoid, Nixon as conspirator—there's no getting around the fact that Nixon fascinates people because of his dark side. Just as the shining, heroic face of Franklin Roosevelt dominated an earlier, optimistic era of triumph through depression and war, Nixon's dour and shadowy profile beclouded the years that followed. For the epoch of the Cold War, the Red Scare, Vietnam, Watergate, and malaise, Nixon—as opposed to the Kennedy of Camelot or the Reagan of "Morning in America"—seems the most fitting avatar. Just as presidents since the New Deal have toiled "in the shadow of FDR" (in William Leuchtenberg's phrase), so Americans watching, thinking about, or participating in postwar politics have journeyed in Nixon's shadow.

Finally, of course, the shadow refers to Nixon's own trademark five-o'clock shadow, immortalized by the legendary *Washington Post* cartoonist Herblock and by Nixon's own sweaty, furtive demeanor in the first 1960 presidential debate against John F. Kennedy. That stubble was Nixon's signal physical trait, and for many it evoked his shadowy personality. But it also represented, even for his admirers, something else: the notion, ascendant in the postwar television age, that political success hinged on the image a politician projected, that to thrive, leaders would have to master not just the old arts of rhetoric and retail politics but the newer tricks of conveying the impression—no matter how honestly or accurately—of unmistakable, twenty-four-carat authenticity.

Introduction

Portraying Nixon demands a *Rashomon*-like approach if one
is to understand those varied images he projected and the
society and constituencies that stimulated and responded to
him.

—*Stanley Kutler,* The Wars of Watergate[1]

This is a man of many masks, but who can say they have seen
his real face?

—*Adlai Stevenson*[2]

He is not listed in the credits, but Richard Nixon plays a key part in Ang
Lee's 1997 film, *The Ice Storm*. Set in Greenwich, Connecticut, in 1973, the
film tells the story of an upper-middle-class family of four, the Hoods,
who are wracked by secrets, resentments, and an inability to communi-
cate. The teenage son, Paul, who has been shipped off to prep school, covers his dorm-room wall with a poster of Nixon and Vice President Spiro
Agnew dressed in striped prisoners' uniforms. Later, as Paul and two of
his classmates get drunk and stoned in a parentless Park Avenue apartment, they see Nixon's memoir *Six Crises* on the coffee table and have a
laugh at the president's expense. "You ought to read this, Hood," says
Paul's friend Francis. "Nixon, our leader, all ye need to know about the
travails of life." The boys prepare their marijuana between the book's
pages. In contrast to Paul's cool contempt for Nixon, his sister, Wendy,
harbors white-hot anger. Throughout the film, she watches news about
Watergate nonstop on television, exclaiming periodically to her blasé family that Nixon is a "liar" or "should be shot."[3]

Nixon's most memorable turn comes when Wendy and a neighbor's son engage in some groping in the neighbor's TV room. As the teenagers approach sexual contact, Wendy discovers a Nixon mask on the floor and puts it on. The sight of two forlorn teenagers fumbling through a sexual initiation is unsettling, but by hiding behind Nixon's grotesque visage, Wendy makes the scene almost too eerie to watch. A tender rite of passage becomes an ordeal of awkwardness, alienation, and human coldness, one of the icy movie's iciest moments. Even the film crew was disturbed by it; after each take, everyone on the set broke out into peals of laughter. The scene wasn't supposed to be funny.[4]

Although Nixon has always been an evocative symbol, in this scene it's the Nixon *mask* that's compelling. Other films have also used the former president to represent the materialism or malaise of the Nixon years. Hal Ashby's *Shampoo* (1975), for example, is set on Election Day, 1968, and features Nixon's image flickering across television screens as an omen of America's darkening future. But *Shampoo*'s use of Nixon is obvious, almost heavy-handed. In contrast, the mute, inscrutable artifact of the Nixon mask in *The Ice Storm* is a beginning, not an end, to interpretation. It invites a range of readings. Reminding us of Nixon's criminal acts, it represents corrupted authority in a world where parents carry on affairs while preaching to their kids. Recalling Nixon's awkwardness, it highlights the characters' incapacity for closeness. And the patent phoniness of the disguise—the fact that its wearer couldn't possibly be mistaken for Nixon—speaks to the inauthenticity of these suburbanites' lives, the sense conveyed throughout the film that Americans have become estranged from their political environment, their communities, their families, even themselves.

Not any mask would have worked so well; the Nixon mask is powerful because it's redundant—the mask of a man who seemed to be wearing a mask already. Perhaps for this reason, it has long captured the American imagination. As of October 2000, it remained the top-selling political costume at Halloween. Protesters have always loved it: in October 1972, fifty feminists staged a "kiss-off" in front of Nixon's campaign headquarters in New York City, many wearing rubber Nixon faces. At an April 1974 rally for Nixon's impeachment, five protesters streaked through the crowd as

Tricky Dicks. In the movie *Where the Buffalo Roam* (1980), a buddy of the journalist Hunter S. Thompson wears a mask to make mischief in a hotel restaurant. In recent years, thieves with a taste for irony have worn them too, not only in the forgettable films *Best Seller* and *Point Break*, but also in real-life holdups from Marlborough, Massachusetts, to Omaha and from Bloomington, Minnesota, to Seattle.[5]

When burglars don the disguise, they allude to Nixon's burglaries. Usually, however, the mask has lacked an explicit referent. It connotes something more obscure—something like obscurity itself. It reminds us of Nixon's instinctive concealment of his true self. "Any letting my hair down, I find that embarrassing," Nixon said in 1958, when he was vice president. "If you let down your hair, you feel too naked. . . . I can't really let my hair down with anyone, . . . not even with my family." Not wanting to feel naked, Nixon covered up: his feelings, his illicit activities, his secret diplomacy. He hid behind his public personae.[6]

Nixon's labors to conceal, to control the impression he made on others, did not always work. He often ended up conveying only the sense of a man behind a mask. "Great care has gone into the construction of the shadow which declares itself to be Richard Nixon," the *New York Post* columnist Murray Kempton wrote in 1956. Forty years later, the critic Daniel Aaron called Nixon "a cipher, because he seems somehow synthetic, invented, abstract, a fiction embedded in history." The judgment wasn't confined to Nixon's detractors. "Nixon remains the most enigmatic of American presidents," the conservative British polemicist and Nixon admirer Paul Johnson noted. ". . . His character is elusive; the inner man is almost totally inaccessible."[7]

The elusiveness of Nixon's true self has made him a rich symbol, well suited for a study of political image making. Nixon's longevity and prominence in postwar American life render that elusiveness all the more striking. Nixon stood at or near the center of American politics for fifty years, as a congressman, senator, vice president, president, ex-president, and dead president; for this reason alone, the political journalist Theodore H. White ranked him with FDR as "the most enduring American politicians of the twentieth century." Nixon galvanized debates over the Red Scare, negative campaigning, Vietnam, the Great Society, the media's role in politics, and Watergate. Even after his death in 1994, his shadow hovered over American culture, manifesting itself in a widespread cynicism toward leaders and politics. After his resignation in 1974, the *New York Times* columnist Anthony Lewis called the years since World War II "the Age of Nixon." Since then, many historians have expanded that label to cover the last quarter century as well.[8]

Important and inscrutable, Nixon was also controversial—easily the most controversial president, according to a 1983 poll of historians. The debates in which he figured were not fleeting skirmishes but grand struggles about power and trust, truth and democracy. Uncommonly divisive even among politicians, Nixon relished combat, nourished suspicions, and polarized citizens during his many crises. No one was more admired (he was the most respected man in America four years in a row, Gallup reported), no one more loathed (for six years he ranked among the world's most hated men in one poll, twice edging out Hitler as number one). One of his editors, Michael Korda, called him "the one American president of [the twentieth] century about whom it is absolutely impossible to be indifferent."[9]

Over the years, Nixon's importance as a political actor, his controversial nature, and his inscrutability have occasioned a search for the "real" Nixon. For different groups of Americans, Nixon has embodied starkly divergent values and meanings. *Nixon's Shadow* explores some of these groups—conservative businessmen, liberal intellectuals, New Left radicals, Washington reporters, political loyalists, psychoanalytic biographers, foreign policy pundits, and academic historians—and the images of Nixon that they developed and disseminated over the last half century. As much as anything Nixon did or said, it is these responses to him—the ways people experienced his tenure, the feelings toward him they harbored, the pictures of him they formed—that speak to his importance.

These responses to Nixon shed light not just on what he meant but also on the constituencies themselves. History consists not just of the doings of great figures but of the experiences and activities of the members of society. Since national politics—and especially a president as prominent and controversial as Nixon—matter to almost everyone, people's images of Nixon reveal their own concerns and ideas. Together, they provide a window into the postwar history of American culture.

The debates about Nixon's image and meaning disclose the diversity of political viewpoints in postwar America; collectively, they also limn a growing concern in the years after World War II with images in politics. Nixon both contributed to and reflected this heightened image-consciousness. He helped foster an awareness—which could manifest itself as either mature realism or corrosive cynicism—that politics depends on the construction and manipulation of images. Through the debates about Nixon's image, Americans awakened to the centrality of image making in politics, and this awakening proved to be among his most lasting legacies.

In *The Image, Or What Happened to the American Dream* (1961), the historian Daniel Boorstin addressed what he took to be "the most important question in our lives: namely, what we believe to be real." Boorstin observed that the rise of mass media, including the attendant apparatuses of advertising and public relations, had helped create an alternate sham reality, where celebrities replaced heroes, credibility superseded truth, invention eclipsed discovery, and personality was vaunted over character. Coining a term that would increase in use over the years, Boorstin identified a new phenomenon he called the "pseudo-event": a staged happening that becomes news not for intrinsic reasons but because those who cover the news deem it so. As pseudo-events proliferated, Boorstin said, few zones remained—sports and crime were two—where one could still find an "authentic, uncorrupted, spontaneous event." This demise of the authentic extended to people, too. Instead of admiring heroes, Americans worshiped celebrities, who were human pseudo-events, well known for their well-knownness, as Boorstin quipped.[10]

These changes undermined democratic politics, Boorstin argued. Television and media manipulation had become so pervasive that "more important than what we think of the presidential candidate is what we think of his 'public image.'" A perfect example, he said, was the 1960 presidential debates between Nixon and John F. Kennedy. Cooked up in an unholy collaboration between the news networks and the candidates, the debates offered "specious" drama that did not reflect "which participant was better qualified for the presidency." They raised the peripheral matters of lighting, makeup, and Nixon's five-o'clock shadow to prominence while "reducing great national issues to trivial dimensions" and squandering "this greatest opportunity in American history to educate the voters." At stake, Boorstin said, was representative government itself. Lincoln's maxim that "you can't fool all of the people all of the time," he suggested, was "the foundation-belief of American democracy." It implied, first, that the citizenry can distinguish "between sham and reality," and second that "if offered a choice between a simple truth and a contrived image, they will prefer the truth." But in the face of mass culture and its illusions, he claimed, this assertion no longer held. The cornerstone of the American temple was shaky.[11]

Boorstin wasn't alone in 1961 in criticizing the rise of images. He spoke for many who worried that mass culture and media were subverting traditional Enlightenment ideals. According to then-fashionable ideas, mass society—technological gains, corporate growth, the bureaucratization and routinization of life—was making people feel alienated from one another. People's knowledge of the world now reached them not directly but through representations transmitted via the mass media, especially television. Consumer capitalism bred an unhappiness with the tawdriness and disposability of so much cultural fare. These critics and the millions whom they influenced decried a crisis of authenticity: a fear that society would lose touch with real feelings, the honest pursuit of needs and wants, genuine connections with others, a sense of being true to oneself, and other intangibles that made human experience authentic.

Of these analyses, Boorstin's has been among the most lasting. It has provided a lens for innumerable scholars and journalists to critique American culture. "The landscape now seems Boorstinian," historian Stephen Whitfield wrote in 1991. ". . . The emerging and exasperating phenomena that he traced have continued to spread like an oil slick across the American scene." Critics have also echoed Boorstin's lament that the rise of the image threatens democratic politics. Despite their differences, the conservatives, liberals, radicals, reporters, loyalists, psychoanalysts, pundits, and historians that this book discusses have all sought to blow away the froth of image crafting, spin, and obfuscation and recover the nucleus of authenticity at the system's core.[12]

Yet before swallowing the criticism of our culture as thoroughly inauthentic, we should specify precisely what Boorstin identified that was novel. Political image making, for instance, is hardly new. Leaders have always superintended their images as mindfully as they have run the affairs of state. In 1485, Henry Tudor of England, eager to shore up his power after assuming the throne, drew a new crest that melded the symbols of the York and Lancaster families into a Tudor Rose and had it engraved on buildings and embossed on papers. In American politics, image making permeated William Henry Harrison's 1840 presidential campaign, in which the aristocrat remade himself as an earthy, log-cabin-born, cider-swilling rustic. As Machiavelli noted, image craft has always been intrinsic to politics—important and even valuable. Not even the pseudo-event is as recent an innovation as Boorstin suggested. Nothing better embodies the concept than the newspaper publisher William R. Hearst's purported remark to the artist Frederic Remington, whom Hearst had sent to Cuba to illustrate a war that Remington couldn't find. "You furnish the pictures," Hearst alledgedly said, "and I'll furnish the war."[13]

All the same, Boorstin was onto something. Times have changed. Politicians today certainly devote more attention and develop more sophisticated strategies for shaping their images than they used to: think of Nixon's "Game Plans," Ronald Reagan's daily TV shots, or Bill Clinton's spin cycles. Boorstin's key insight, however, which often gets lost amid the easy laments about inauthenticity, was his realization that people educate themselves about the process of image construction around them. "The stage machinery, the processes of fabricating and projecting the image, fascinate us," he noted. "We are all interested in watching a skillful feat of magic; we are still more interested in looking behind the scenes and seeing precisely how it was made to seem that the lady was sawed in half."[14]

Americans turned out to be adept at seeing through the technological, psychological, and political tricks of the image culture. They adapted. What makes today's landscape Boorstinian, then, isn't simply the proliferation of pseudo-events; it's our identification of pseudo-events everywhere about us—our frequent allusions to Boorstin and his cultural discovery; our signals that we're hip to what's going on backstage; our need to be what David Riesman in *The Lonely Crowd* (1950) called an "inside dopester," someone never "taken in by any person, cause or event," who "know[s] the political score." Before television, David Halberstam has recounted, Franklin Roosevelt could on a hot day stop a radio address, ask for a drink of water, apologize to his listeners for the interruption, and come off as seeming more human than the average pol. The gimmick could never work today. Now the reverse is true: so great is our suspicion of politicians and their devotion to image craft that when Vice President Al Gore spontaneously kissed his wife at the Democratic Convention in August 2000, the gesture was derided as staged. What changed in the intervening years was that America developed a culture in which the acknowledgment of the role of constructed images—indeed, a belief that images are everything in politics—came to underpin discussions of public events.[15]

This awareness has in turn changed politics. "Since the advent of television as the primary means of communications and source of information," one expert on image craft has written,

> modern presidents must have specialized talents at once more superficial and more complicated than those of their predecessors. They must try to master the art of manipulating the media not only to win in politics but in order to further the programs and causes they believe in; at the same time they must avoid at all costs the charge of trying to manipulate the media. In the modern presidency, concern for image must rank with concern for substance.[16]

This quotation from Richard Nixon's memoirs has been seized upon by his detractors to show that Nixon was obsessed with his image—which he was. But the comment also shows an appreciation of Boorstin's insight: Nixon understood that successful image craft requires staying one step ahead of the voters and their canny decoding of the representations before them. Voters aren't passive. They grow wise to the ruses and sleights of modern politics. They retain confidence that they can spot a phony. Thus, as politics became increasingly staged—with makeup and lighting in the 1950s, refined polling methods in the 1960s, slick campaign ads in the 1970s, sound bites in the 1980s, focus groups in the 1990s—public awareness kept pace, incorporating each innovation into its storehouse of knowledge. In this upward spiral of sophistication, the authentic appeared to recede, like the earth as seen from a space capsule hurtling skyward.[17]

Those who wish to restore authenticity to politics have set out to debunk the contrivances of politicians like Nixon who have seemed to be proffering false images. After Nixon's 1968 campaign, a landmark in media manipulation, scholars began studying the art of political "packaging," while reporters filled their stories with accounts of the behind-the-scenes image craft.[*] These debunkers hoped that exposing the politicians' contrivances would light a path back to a more straightforward politics. But their revelations only whetted the public appetite for a more elaborate show, as Boorstin anticipated. The public's greater knowledge forced the professionals to innovate further, feeding a cycle that confirmed voters in their suspicion that the backstage artifice is what counts.[18]

Recent politics, then, is distinguished most notably by the embeddedness of image craft in our *understanding* of politics—the heightened awareness that so much of it is predicated on constructed and manipulated symbols. Even the least reflective observer is aware of polling, advertising, marketing, packaging, spin control, and the press—the layers of mediation that come between the citizen and what Boorstin called (quaintly) "plain fact." A 1992 cartoon in *The New York Times* pointed up this condition, depicting a backwoods old-timer on the porch of a general store saying to a friend: "I like Buchanan's sound bites, but Clinton and Tsongas have slicker production values." Consequently, politics has come to be seen as an illusion, a superficial contest of images, that, like the pseudo-event, has no intrinsic meaning.[19]

Cynicism stems from the belief that appearances regularly misrepresent reality. It is, according to one definition, "the universally widespread way in which enlightened people see to it that they are not taken for suckers . . . the stance of people who realize that the times of naïveté are gone." Hyperaware of the manipulation in politics, people have no recourse but

---

[*] In separate studies, Kiku Adatto and Daniel C. Hallin compared the coverage of the 1968 and 1988 campaigns. Both found that the 1968 coverage barely mentioned the candidates' media and image-making strategies, whereas the 1988 coverage did so relentlessly.

cynicism if they want to guard against continual disappointment. (No matter how cynical you get, a joke goes, it's never enough.) Cynicism becomes the rational position when credence in authenticity has ebbed: If genuine ideals, straight talk, and honest portrayals have given way to provisional beliefs, double talk, and fakery, then it's natural to believe that politicians are seeking solely to win a contest, not to represent the constituents who elected them.[20]

The upshot of these developments, as Boorstin predicted, was to call the American experiment into question. If leaders aren't really representing their constituents, if instead they're cynically crafting their appearances to present voters with a false front, then representative government turns out to be an illusion. That conclusion, once radical, has now become widespread. Though it isn't always stated quite so dramatically, the notion that our politicians regularly mislead us with manufactured and manipulated images is an underlying premise of much political commentary today.

The suspicion of political image craft rests on a common misperception of what images are. Although politics today is surely guided too much by concerns about appearance and reputation, the baleful warnings about the inauthenticity of our system are exaggerated. Instead of denouncing or resisting the importance of images, we would do well to study them as a part of history, as vehicles that convey important meanings and ideas about the world. To lament that "image" has triumphed over "substance" is, as Daniel Bell once wrote of similar laments about mass society, to embrace "an ideology of romantic protest against contemporary life." It shows an unwillingness to reckon with the realities of modernity.[21]

Fears of image making and jeremiads against inauthenticity rest on the faulty assumption that images are distinct from reality. They aren't. Images reflect substance, if sometimes through the fun-house mirrors of individual minds. They're the way we understand reality. Images can be false or misleading, and people aren't immune to politicians' phony self-presentations. But the pictures we hold of politicians are rarely just manufactured and foisted upon us. They emerge from a dialectical or collaborative process between politicians and their audiences. We filter the images that politicians project through our own political, cultural, intellectual, professional, and psychological lenses.

The ways that we respond to public figures, the feelings they evoke, the interpretations they invite, the meanings they embody—these aren't shadows cast upon a cavern wall but the stuff of political experience itself. "In the last analysis, it is human consciousness which is the subject matter of history," wrote Marc Bloch. "The interrelations, confusions and infections of human consciousness are, for history, reality itself." Citizens invest in their leaders strong feelings about their world. The images they form of public figures or events shape and spur political action. Recovering the past means recapturing the pictures and interpretations that people have had about their political worlds and how those worlds are reshaped by people's changed sensibilities.[22]

In American culture, few symbols carry greater meaning than the president. Starting in childhood, we regard the president as the personification of politics and the nation. He is the first official of whom we're typically aware and about whom we have feelings. Adults use particular presidents as metonymy for an era ("the Age of Jackson"), a philosophy ("Reaganism"), or a style ("Kennedyesque"), even though academic scholars renounced the so-called presidential synthesis of history long ago. People invest so much psychic energy in the chief executive that when presidents die, reports of psychosomatic illness tend to rise. Associations with the president—even the idea of the president—guide our behavior. Nixon's White House counsel John W. Dean III wrote that during Watergate, "[I] debated with myself how I could . . . deal with [Watergate burglar Howard] Hunt's extortion and protect the President at the same time. The *President.* I felt myself rising instinctively in salute. I thought of aircraft carriers, battles, strong men reverent at the mention of his name, a communications network that flashed each utterance around the world." The president's symbolic power exerts material force.[23]

These beliefs about the value of political symbols, especially the president, have shaped this book in several ways. First, I chose to write not just about what Nixon *did* but also about what he *meant.* I selected events based on how much they mattered not to Nixon but to the people who responded to him. An episode like the 1970 rumor that Nixon planned to cancel the

1972 elections would receive scant mention in a conventional biography but merits exploration here because it loomed large for the all-important student left. Second, I have examined not just the standard sources of political history—newspapers, opinion journals, memoirs, the papers of key figures—but also cartoons, novels, films, plays, operas, memorials, and rituals. Cultural artifacts shed light on the meanings that people impart to public figures, especially with one who has inspired as much artistic creation as Nixon.* Third, highly charged symbols don't evoke just one set of associations; they are contested and ever-changing. Accordingly, instead of identifying a single dominant image of Nixon at each point in the past, I have tried to honor the multiple perspectives on him that have existed, the clashing views that made him so controversial.[24]

Nixon is an especially good candidate for a study of political images. Not only was he the dominant politician of the age of image-consciousness—prominent, enduring, controversial, inscrutable—but he was himself exceptionally implicated in questions about authenticity. He didn't single-handedly change the way people understood their political world; the advent of mass society and mass culture, especially television, mattered more. But no postwar politician did more to educate Americans to the primacy of images in politics. Nixon embraced the new tools of political artistry and used them to his advantage. Ironically, he also used them, quite often, ineptly—exposing, if inadvertently, how much artistry was at work. And Nixon served as a vehicle through which various groups struggled to make sense of this emerging image-ridden political culture.

* Nixon, for one, knew that people's impressions are shaped by popular culture. He monitored how comedians, filmmakers, and television personalities portrayed him. In August 1959, his aide Charles McWhorter filed a report from the Playboy Jazz Festival detailing the Nixon jokes told by comic Mort Sahl ("Nixon returned from Russia and found that Eisenhower was running the country"). McWhorter wrote that "The guy, in my opinion, is sick, sick, sick, but he does have a following." As president, Nixon placed a watch on the Smothers Brothers variety show on CBS and ordered letters be sent to the producers if the mockery became too nasty. Nixon also had aides investigate the left-wing documentarian Emile de Antonio, the director of *Millhouse: A White Comedy* (1971), and keep tabs on a presidential look-alike and satirist who called himself "Richard M. Dixon."

The most memorable episodes from Nixon's career endure as examples of his devotion to image craft. In the Checkers speech of 1952, he saved his place as the Republican vice-presidential nominee with a winning televised presentation. In 1968, he brought new media techniques to bear on his comeback presidential campaign. His well-scripted trip to China unfolded before television audiences. Even his post-resignation years were marked by a purposeful struggle to rehabilitate his image. His losses, too, represented failures of media politics. In the 1960 election, his defeat was ascribed to his poor showing in the televised debates. The release of the Watergate tapes in 1974 hurt him partly because he failed to see that people would recoil from the exposure of unattractive traits that he had concealed for so long. Even the joke that dogged Nixon—"Would you buy a used car from this man?"—spoke to his relentless yet clumsy attempts at salesmanship.[25]

Nixon insisted he had no use for image making. "A lot of people have told me, what you need is a public relations expert," he said in 1958. But he never used one, he claimed, because "I don't want to seem artificial." He made similar boasts in March 1971, during an interview on NBC's *Today* show. "When presidents begin to worry about images . . . do you know what happens? They become like the athletes, the football teams and the rest, who become so concerned about what is written that they don't play the game well. . . . I don't worry about images. . . . I never have." Just before that appearance he had implored H. R. Haldeman, his chief of staff until 1973, to hire a "full-time PR man to really convey the true image of a president to the nation." Nixon knew that image craft is a key part of the job. As he later wrote, "The leader necessarily deals to a large extent in symbols, in images."[26]

Nixon's vehement disavowals of image making were a classic case of protesting too much. His preoccupation with his image actually ran so deep that, according to his domestic policy aide John Ehrlichman, he "seemed to believe that there was no national issue that was not susceptible to public-relations treatment." He has been credited with creating the "image-is-everything presidency" and with making polling a guiding presidential concern. More than any predecessor, Nixon drew his aides from advertising and public relations.* His White House staff monitored press coverage with unrivaled vigilance. For five and a half years, his communications team churned out 15,000 pages of news summaries—daily briefs, laced with acid commentary, of what the press said about the president—which Nixon marked up diligently. A "Five O'Clock Group," considered shadowy by some, planned public relations strategy, with the president offering ample input. Nixon drafted memoranda detailing "Game Plans" for shaping perceptions of him. Once, he told Haldeman he needed a full-time adviser who could coach him on "how I should stand, where the cameras will be," even "whether I should [hold] the phone with my right hand or my left hand." Given "the millions of dollars that go into one lousy thirty-second spot advertising deodorant," he wrote, it was "unbelievable" that his own image didn't receive equal attention.[27]

If this story were just a tale of Nixon's attempts to dupe others into accepting his pictures of himself, it would hold limited interest. By now we know too well the constructed nature of our politics. But Nixon's permanent campaign has a Faustian twist. If he is a sorcerer using the black arts of mass communications to shape his public identity, he is a second-rate one. Few leaders can simply foist their self-portraits on a passive public, and Nixon was not among those so gifted. "Nixon was a man obsessed with maintaining what he perceived to be a correct public image," Haldeman wrote. He "took pains with his public image; he dressed neatly and conservatively, handled himself calmly in public . . . and yet, no matter what he did, he seemed to come across as flat, unattractive, unappealing." Nixon's image craft regularly backfired. The newscaster Walter Cronkite recalled that during the 1968 campaign, he was asked to meet with the candidate in his hotel room. When he arrived, Nixon was stretched out on the couch, his shoes off, his feet up. Over drinks, Nixon chatted uninhibitedly, using profanities. The Nixon that Cronkite saw was so unlike the prim and awkward cardboard man he knew that he concluded not that he was see-

---

* As early as 1957, *Printer's Ink*, "the magazine of advertising, selling, marketing,"identified the vice president as the administration official friendliest to their cause—because of his closeness with men such as "Robert [sic] Halderman [sic], with the J. Walter Thompson office in Los Angeles" and his "grasp of marketing matters and . . . generally sympathetic attitude toward business."

ing the "real" Nixon but that the event was staged to make Nixon seem like one of the boys.* Better known is the ill-conceived photo-op in which Nixon sought to appear Kennedyesque by having his picture taken as he strolled on the beach. After weeks of planning, reporters and photographers were summoned to a picturesque San Clemente bluff. Yet the resulting shots—of Nixon stiffly walking the sands in trousers and wing tips—conveyed the image only of someone *trying* to look Kennedyesque.[28]

Nixon couldn't control his public identity not only because of his own shortcomings but because it was inevitably shaped by the culture around him. Millions of Americans interacted with and interpreted Nixon, and their concerns as much as his own determined his image—or, rather, his images. Although any politician is, to some degree, a mirror or a Rorschach test, Nixon was exceptionally protean. Enemies and allies alike observed that he presented different faces to different audiences. Haldeman called his boss "a multifaceted quartz crystal. Some facets bright and shining, others dark and mysterious. And all of them constantly changing as the external light rays strike the crystal." Haldeman praised this adaptive quality, but others saw it as an intrinsic penchant for misrepresenting what, if anything, was at his core. "Where other public figures present a pattern, Nixon presents a kaleidoscope," wrote a *Nation* correspondent in the 1950s. ". . . One can oppose a Nixon only as one boxes a shadow." In 1971, the folk rocker Country Joe McDonald sang about Nixon as "the genuine plastic man":

> Late last night I was watchin' the tube
> When I saw the most incredible thing
> They built a new mechanical man
> Looked just like a human being.
> I started to become terrified,
> Good God it was makin' me sick
> And then I began to realize
> It was no one but Tricky Dick.

---

* When Cronkite heard the Watergate tapes six years later, he decided he had seen the real Nixon after all.

The psychoanalysts who diagnosed Nixon concluded that because he lacked a secure sense of himself, he adopted multiple personae—leading to "disturbing speculation," wrote Bruce Mazlish, his first psychobiographer, "about who the 'real' Nixon is." Uncovering the real Nixon became the raison d'être of biographies and profiles bearing the titles *In Search of Nixon*; *The Nixon Nobody Knows*; *Richard Nixon: The Man Behind the Mask*; and *The Real Nixon*. The historian William Appleman Williams believed it was a trick question, calling the search for the real Nixon "a shell game without a pea."[29]

Nixon's capacity for reinvention gave rise to a curious concept: the "New Nixon." Generally, the term meant a softer Nixon, one who had renounced the hard-hitting ways of his early career. But it also came to refer to any one of Nixon's identities. The first known use of the term "New Nixon" occurred on July 9, 1953, when the Montgomery, Alabama, *Advertiser* praised the vice president after having criticized his Checkers speech a year earlier: "We have found ourselves dissolving our previous conception . . . the New Nixon rejoices us." The notion resurfaced in 1955, as *New York Times* columnist James Reston noted Nixon's "carefully planned and well executed performance" to recast himself "as the noble and romantic substitute for the leading man." Before the 1960 campaign, the liberal group Americans for Democratic Action asked its members, "Is There a New Nixon?", hoping to disabuse them of the notion. The most convincing "New Nixon" arrived in 1968, when the once skeptical pundit Walter Lippmann heralded the appearance of "a maturer, mellower man who is no longer clawing his way to the top." Lippmann would change his mind again.[30]

During Nixon's presidency, his true nature was debated more strenuously than ever. With Watergate the question seemed—to most, anyhow—to be settled. Art Buchwald joked that a high-level White House source ("Deep Toes") confessed to him, as if it were a mind-bending revelation, that "there is no New Nixon and there never was. . . . It was the old Nixon with makeup on." But even after his disgrace Nixon wouldn't be defined so easily, and his resignation created more opportunities for reinvention.[31]

Any attempt to arrange these many Nixons into a strict chronology will be imperfect, since at any moment different images competed for primacy. Rather than recount Nixon's life chronologically, *Nixon's Shadow* considers a handful of them roughly in the order that they appeared on the scene. One New Nixon did not succeed the next like floats passing in a parade; they were superimposed on one another, each colored by its predecessors. The images overlapped, mingled, coexisted. Each was a response to or modification of earlier Nixons, a new contribution to an ongoing argument.[32]

In his early career, Nixon's conservative supporters saw him as a populist everyman—a navy veteran, family man, and fighter for the American Dream. By the 1950s, liberal intellectuals challenged that image and proffered another interpretation: that of Tricky Dick, an unprincipled opportunist. In the 1960s more New Nixons emerged. Young radicals reinterpreted him as a dark conspirator. White House reporters who covered his administration saw an enemy of the First Amendment. Loyal aides and supporters considered him a victim of liberal enemies. And to psychoanalytic historians, Nixon was a case study in paranoia. After Watergate, foreign policy hands (along with Nixon himself) promoted the image of the former president as an elder statesman. And later still, revisionist historians argued that Nixon was, improbably, a liberal steward of the Great Society.

None of these groups invented its image of Nixon out of thin air. Each detected real qualities in the man: his populist rhetoric, his conspiratorial designs, his devotion to high-stakes diplomacy. And each filtered those qualities through its own traditions, interests, ideologies, and assumptions. What's more, although each portrait had its champions, none remained confined to a single pocket of society; each coursed through the arteries of mass culture to gain credence among other segments of the public. Nor were these images mutually exclusive; people believed in more than one simultaneously. Nixon's image was constantly changing, always contested.

Nixon's Shadow doesn't suggest that every image of Nixon has an equal measure of truth, or that every group's perspective is equally valid. This book is not an idealist argument that truth consists solely in our perception of it. But the task of assessing the validity of the various Nixons is one I assume only when necessary; instead of adding another voice to the debate over the "real" Nixon, I try to understand how and why each of these groups formed and disseminated its interpretations of Nixon in the first place. These interpretations themselves, whatever their accuracy, mattered to postwar history. Thoughts about Nixon affected people's lives, prompted them to act, and lastingly altered their attitudes toward the world. Cumulatively, through their experiences with Nixon, Americans came to believe that politics revolves around the construction and manipulation of images—a shadow that Nixon still casts upon our age.

NIXON'S

SHADOW

1

The California Conservatives: Nixon as Populist

Richard M. Nixon Is One of Us.
—*Campaign advertisement, 1946*[1]

"Richard Nixon Is Returning to Whittier"—so said the banner that decked the streets of the young naval officer's Southern California hometown. It was Thursday, November 1, 1945. Nixon, a thirty-two-year-old lieutenant commander back from the South Pacific and doing legal work for the U.S. Navy, had flown in from his post in Middle River, Maryland. A throng of some forty supporters turned out at Whittier's Dinner Bell Ranch to launch his bid to become their next congressman.[2]

Lean and smart in his navy uniform, Nixon stepped forward to speak. Close to six feet, with a thick head of dark hair and a strong jaw, he looked earnest, confident, and handsome. Before him sat a crowd of Republican leaders from California's 12th district: Roy Day, an advertising salesman for the *Pomona Progress-Bulletin*; State Representative Tom Erwin; Harry Schuyler, a rancher and former Rotary Club president. They sat rapt as Nixon delivered a sharp rebuke to the New Deal. He told the audience that he and his fellow returning servicemen had grown tired of government paternalism, frustrated with "standing in line" while the federal bureaucracy, which had swollen over twelve years of Democratic dominance, lumbered to meet their needs. Veterans, he said, "don't want the dole, nor do they want a governmental employment or bread lines. They want a fair chance at the American way of life."[3]

The local businessmen swooned. This boyish, clean-cut orator exhibited all the requisite traits for a successful political career: churchgoing parents; good schools (Whittier College, Duke Law School); a local legal practice; navy service; a poised, pretty wife and a family sure to follow. His words displayed an understanding of others like him—young, ready to work, and seeking a shot at the American Dream. He was devoted, too, to the principles of patriotism, church, and the free market to which these Californians had long subscribed. He seemed, in short, an authentic emblem of the promise of the budding postwar age.

Nixon's speech was a success, but the next day he had more auditioning to do. He had flown to California at the urging of an ad hoc body called the "Committee of 100," a group of in fact 104 local activists who had taken it upon themselves to vet Republican candidates for the upcoming congressional race. On Friday afternoon, Nixon lunched with key committee members at Los Angeles's posh University Club. Then, that night, he gave his formal audition before the whole group at Whittier's William Penn Hotel. Appearing after five other hopefuls, Nixon said he wanted to help young families enjoy the fruits of America's victory, and he again attacked Washington liberalism as the impediment to progress. In the lucid, methodical style that would become his trademark, he sketched a landscape divided into two camps. "One advocated by the New Deal is government control regulating our lives," he said. "The other calls for individual freedoms and all that initiative can produce. I hold with the latter viewpoint. I believe the returning veterans, and I have talked to many of them in the foxholes, will not be satisfied with a dole or a government handout. They want a respectable job in private industry, where they will be recognized for what they produce, or they want an opportunity to start their own business."[4]

Nixon called this program "practical liberalism." The content of the speeches, however, made it clear that he opposed the philosophy of Franklin Roosevelt and Harry Truman, with which the term "liberalism" had been increasingly associated since the 1930s.* Although Nixon sought to attract more than just ultraconservatives, he did not lack for ideological vigor. Indeed, some committee members voiced satisfaction that they had found a solid "conservative" to take on five-term incumbent Jerry Voorhis, a classic New Deal liberal.[5]

As important as Nixon's program was his demeanor. "He was neatly dressed. He was serious. He replied to questions in short, crisp terms," recalled Murray Chotiner, the politico who later became Nixon's top strategist. "This young fellow was not trying to put on a show. . . . He seemed intelligent, forceful, and with a capacity for growth." Moreover, after the lackluster, hedging performances of his rivals, some of whom had blanched at a full-throated attack on the incumbent, Nixon came across as "an electrifying personality," as one committee member said. Nixon was a fighter, too. He told Herman Perry, the Whittier banker who had first encouraged him to run, that he would "tear Voorhis to pieces," and pledged before the group to "put on an aggressive and vigorous campaign." When the committee reconvened later that month, Nixon won 63 votes from the seventy-seven members who attended. A second ballot made it unanimous.[6]

The mood during Nixon's visit was caught by Roy Day, the committee's founder, who exulted: "This man is salable merchandise!" An advertising salesman, Day was speaking in the idiom of his trade. But he was also recognizing that politics involved the traffic of images and that Richard M. Nixon projected a winning one, especially within this Southern California world of rising affluence and resentment toward Washington. From the start of his career, Nixon, even among politicians, was viewed as emblematic of larger currents in society—in this case, as representative of notions of a burgeoning conservative populism, but in other situations as

---

* It was in using the modifier "practical" that Nixon meant to distinguish himself from his would-be opponent, Jerry Voorhis, whom he saw as a woolly-minded idealist. Nixon meant the term "liberalism" in its older sense, to signify a creed of limited government and economic freedom. He avoided "conservative" because at the time it evoked the right-wing extremism, and in recent elections avowedly conservative candidates had repeatedly failed to vanquish Voorhis.

representative of darker forces as well. A central reason for this tendency was Nixon's character. Intensely private yet hungry for approval, he had always been both protective of his feelings and eager to convey a positive impression. These inclinations produced an enthusiasm for the craft of political image making and an intuitive grasp of the symbolism of politics—traits that were on display in 1945.

Besides his character, however, Nixon's affinity for image craft was also rooted in the distinct political culture of twentieth-century California, where, before the rest of the country, the cultivation of a candidate's image was a key to electoral success. Progressive Era reforms in the Golden State had allowed for "cross-filing" in elections, permitting candidates to run in both parties' primaries at once. Designed to weaken party bosses, the policy meant that a candidate could clinch victory by winning both primaries, as happened more often than not. As a result, California journalist Carey McWilliams noted, "candidates must depend upon individual political merchandising, that is, they must 'sell' themselves as candidates . . . they must maintain a general aura of non-partisanship."[7] In addition, California was home to a vanguard of professional image consultants, notably the team of Clem Whitaker and Leone Baxter, who revolutionized campaigns in the 1930s and 1940s. Trained in public relations, drawing on the culture of nearby Hollywood, they devised cutting-edge techniques to "sell" candidates' personae in a mass media age. As Whitaker told a local public relations society in 1948, winning the vote of "Mr. and Mrs. Average Citizen" in the modern era meant playing to their love of "a good hot battle" or their wish "to be entertained"—either putting on a fight or putting on a show. Either approach had to use simple, clear themes that would remain linked to the candidate.[8]

Nixon self-consciously embraced the task of crafting a winning image. In the 1946 campaign and throughout his early career—culminating in his famous Checkers speech of 1952—he would expertly burnish the self-portrait he had put forward at Whittier's Dinner Bell Ranch and Los Angeles's William Penn Hotel in November 1945. It was a portrait that transcended ideology, one of a clean-cut, upright avatar of the hopes of Americans who looked forward to a new era of opportunity and ease after the depression and the war. Ideology wasn't absent: Nixon struck his backers as an eager, articulate voice for the conservative agenda they believed would usher in prosperity. But the image went beyond ideology; it built on the sympathy that Nixon displayed for those who were struggling, the fight he showed in taking on the Washington bureaucracy. It blended conservative nostrums and pioneer mythology to fashion Richard Nixon as an authentic, ordinary American—the personification, quite literally, of his supporters' values. Long before the right-wing ascendancy of the 1980s, Nixon used populist imagery* to extend conservatism's appeal beyond its upper-class base and to reach success by reviving, in his person and persona, the dream of the self-made man.[9]

Nixon-watchers have long debated whether the candidate's man-of-the-people self-portrait was genuine or a cynical contrivance. To his critics, who didn't emerge as an identifiable bloc until some years later,† Nixon's presentation was thoroughly phony, a guise assumed by a lackey of oilmen and fat cats. His defenders have argued otherwise, seeking to show that his advocates were not plutocrats but "small-business men" or "entrepreneurs." The answer, of course, depends on your perspective and definitions, and can be endlessly debated. As with most debates about the "real" Nixon, it's finally less important than the indisputable allure he held for California voters. Whatever your judgment about the purity of Nixon's common-man persona, the image itself mattered. It launched Nixon's career; it signaled the potency of conservative populism; and it nourished a culture in which the traffic in imagery was a constant and overriding concern.[10]

Although Richard Nixon ranks among the most prominent postwar Republicans, historians of American conservatism have never been sure

---

* "Populism" once denoted the ideas of the old People's Party. Some historians stingily reserve the term for them alone. Other writers now use it, as the journalist Michael Kinsley has said, as nothing more than a synonym for "popular." Between these extremes, Kevin Phillips, Michael Kazin, and others have defined it to mean a set of symbols that appeals to an ostensibly noble common folk against a privileged elite. This sense of the word, which I am using, has become commonly accepted in recent years.

† See chapter 2.

what to do with him. Between the 1940s and the 1980s, conservatism transformed itself from an elitist and dated doctrine of the rich into a governing philosophy that united wealthy businessmen, middle-class professionals, and disaffected wage earners under a populist banner. In tracking this shift, historians, taking their cues from the right's own official chroniclers, have refined a familiar narrative: Originally a besieged remnant of lonely believers, the postwar American right proceeded, through F. A. Hayek's manifesto *The Road to Serfdom* and William F. Buckley's flamboyant *National Review*, to fashion a cogent challenge to the reigning New Deal orthodoxy. By the 1960s, the story goes, the Republican Party shook the grip of its Eastern Democrat wannabes and embraced unadulterated conservatism in the person of the rugged Arizona senator Barry Goldwater, its 1964 presidential nominee. Although Goldwater lost, the grassroots organizers he inspired labored for a decade to harness popular frustration with taxes, big government, and liberalism—a struggle that bore fruit with Ronald Reagan's election as president in 1980.

These narratives typically cast Nixon as a bit player with a peripheral or even detrimental role. His precocious emergence in the 1940s as a leader of the right is discounted because as vice president he adopted Dwight Eisenhower's moderate "modern Republicanism," whereupon many ultraconservatives concluded he wasn't truly one of them. Meanwhile, his recruitment, as president, of socially conservative Democrats and independents into the GOP fold is dismissed as a latecomer's rip-off of third-party candidate George Wallace. Several factors account for this downplaying of Nixon's role. The relatively liberal slant of his presidential policies has led some historians to view his administration as a continuation of the Great Society rather than the start of its undoing. The short-term damage that Watergate inflicted on the GOP lent a certain logic (and satisfaction) to the decision to write Nixon out of the story. Historians consequently have viewed his presidency as an interruption of, rather than a chapter in, conservatism's postwar rise.[11]

The main reason Nixon has been overlooked in the rise of the right, however, is one of historical focus. In 1955, the political scientist Clinton Rossiter defined "the contemporary right" as "those who now admit to distaste for the dominant political theory and practice of the twenty years between Hoover and Eisenhower." Within that spectrum, Rossiter identi-fied four different groups (between which, he stressed, there existed not lines but only "imperceptible gradation"): "the lunatic right" of "profes-sional haters" such as Gerald L. K. Smith and John Birch Society founder Robert Welch; the "ultraconservatives" such as Buckley, Goldwater, and Senator Joe McCarthy; "middling conservatives" such as Nixon, Herbert Hoover, and editorialists at *Life* and the *Saturday Evening Post*; and "liberal conservatives" such as Earl Warren and Nelson Rockefeller. Of these groups, historians have written overwhelmingly about the ultraconserva-tives and even the so-called lunatic fringe: the McCarthy acolytes, *National Review* aficionados, Goldwater enthusiasts, and hard-core Reaganites. Indeed, sometimes the terms "conservatism" and "the right" are used to refer *only* to the Republican Party's extremists. This focus ignores those mainstream, middling conservatives—the businessmen and housewives, realtors and shopkeepers, bankers and doctors—who were critical to the right's successes. To these "Middle Americans," as Nixon called them, the Whittier congressman was as important as Goldwater or Reagan. [12]

Like all successful parties in the United States, the Republican Party has triumphed only when it articulated a philosophy that inspired its base while also attracting Americans who lie closer to the center. In the late twentieth century, Republicans reached this goal by shedding their old image as the defenders of the rich and recasting themselves as the tribune of the people, winning the loyalties of middle-income Americans who had once flocked to the Democrats' belief in state-sponsored largesse. The Republicans did so through conservative populism: a fusion of old anti-statist principles with the symbols and language of identification with the common man. Conservative populism rewrote the New Deal equation: Instead of protecting the citizen from the depredations of big business and safeguarding individual rights, government itself, piloted by decadent liberal elites, became the oppressor. Free-market economics and a minimal state became the people's salvation.

Nixon pioneered the use of populist language and imagery in the service of free-market economics long before the Reagan revolution, before the much-celebrated "backlash" against the liberal indulgences of the 1960s, even before McCarthy became a household name. When Nixon spoke about "the forgotten man" in 1968, he was not cribbing from George Wallace. He was cribbing from his own speeches in 1946.

Nixon began to refashion conservatism as early as that first campaign. At the time, analysts were writing off conservatism as an atavistic creed. But Southern California was ripe for a Republican revival. Fourteen years of New Deal regulations and wartime restraints had brought unprecedented federal control over how Americans could conduct their business, and nowhere did that control provoke greater resentment than in the havens of pioneer capitalists along the lower Pacific Coast.[13]

The state of California in its short life had come to epitomize for many the American Dream. The discovery of gold at Sutter's Mill near San Francisco in 1849 was like a Big Bang, generating an ever-expanding universe of wealth from nothing in a blink. Overnight, the Gold Rush drew hordes of fortune-seekers to the West Coast. In two years the sleepy territory became the nation's thirty-seventh state. For the next century, the Golden State's promise of sunshine, ocean, and abundant land lured settlers— some yearning for riches, others for just a fresh start. Some got wealthy in real estate, oil, manufacturing, farming, ranching, the movies, or new retailing ventures such as supermarkets. Others did not, yet still fed, by their sheer numbers, robust markets that attracted more newcomers, further swelling California's ranks. The state's population climbed almost 45 percent per decade. In the 1940s, thanks to droves of arrivals seeking wartime manufacturing work (coming on the heels of the Dust Bowl migration), it soared past Ohio in residents and nearly passed Pennsylvania as the second most populous state in the country.[14]

In particular, the region known as the Southland, stretching from Santa Barbara through Los Angeles and Orange County down to San Diego, provided a Mecca for plucky migrants. Most hailed from towns in Michigan and Indiana, Illinois and Kansas, and elsewhere in the Midwest. John Gunther dubbed Los Angeles "Iowa with palms" in his travelogue *Inside U.S.A.* (1947); tens of thousands would drive their Chevys and Dodges to eat fried chicken and hard-boiled eggs at Iowa State Society picnics in Long Beach's Bixby Park. California teemed, in the words of journalist Willard Huntington Wright, with "leading citizens from Wichita, honorary pallbearers from Emmetsburg, Good Templars from Sedalia, honest spinsters from Grundy Center—all commonplace people."[15]

From the Heartland to the Southland these migrants brought provincial values and Old Guard loyalties. Families staked out communities concentrated on Protestant churches and civic clubs. They championed prohibition, banned public dancing, restricted beachfront dress. The Ku Klux Klan enjoyed a heyday in the Southland, as its members won elected office in numerous Orange County towns. So did evangelical cults and enthusiasms, including the following of the celebrated preacher Aimee Semple McPherson. Nixon's Whittier was just one of many towns that recoiled at what its citizens considered Hollywood's corrupting influences and kept its cinemas closed on Sundays.[16]

The displaced Midwesterners brought a Main Street trust in laissez-faire economics, and the possibilities for profit afforded by California's ample land and resources fortified such predilections. Real estate developers, speculators, tourism promoters, ranchers, and growers developing large-scale farming ventures—all saw opportunities to make fortunes in the still sparsely settled territory, free of governmental interference. But while powerful railroad magnates and canny speculators locked up future wealth during the land-grab years, striving workers watched their fantasies wither in the sun. Class conflict rocked the Southland, resulting in strikes and pitched labor battles. In 1910, two syndicalists, John and James McNamara, dynamited the Los Angeles Times Building, owned by the baronial publisher Harrison Gray Otis, searing an antipathy to labor into the minds of California businessmen for decades to come.[17]

But if California's businessmen resembled their eastern counterparts in their enmity toward labor, their politics also differed from capitalist countrymen. The West's frontiersmen relied heavily on Wall Street financiers and powerful railroad companies, and that dependency bred resentment. Californians, consequently, were receptive to reforms that targeted oppressive monopolies and corrupt politicians. During the depression, a series of grass-roots movements emerged to fight the stark economic inequity. Francis Townsend, a Long Beach doctor, won a national following with his call for a federal guarantee of old age pensions; a crusade known as "Ham and Eggs" nearly secured passage of a similar pension measure on the state ballot; and the muckraker Upton Sinclair ran for governor in 1934 on a bold, socialistic program called End Poverty in California, which brought on the combined assault of the state's most entrenched forces—and Sinclair's rout.[18]

Where dependency on banks and railroads fueled an anti-corporate impulse, the growing presence of the federal government fed a hatred of Washington during the 1930s and 1940s. Struggling workers might be grateful for a federal safety net. But those who had secured a foothold and were eager to start climbing felt the federal government held them back. Given the development of public works projects and the wartime boom in military spending (increasingly central to the Southland's economy), there was much to resent.[19] Projects like the development of the Central Valley infused millions of dollars into the state. Vital industries—oil, power, communications—came under Washington's watch; the federal bureaucracy more than tripled between 1940 and 1945 to encompass an unheard of 3.5 million employees. New corporate taxes helped pay for it all. Businessmen believed that FDR was exploiting the Depression and the war to enact oppressive taxes and regulations, out of either a deluded faith in central planning or a sinister plot to install a dictatorship. Conservatives routinely compared New Deal programs to those of Soviet communism. They called Roosevelt's liberalism "creeping socialism," a first step in the creation of a leviathan state. In Whittier, city leaders had even refused a Works Progress Administration jobs program because it smacked of "Bolshevik" politics.[20]

The antagonism toward anything that resembled collectivism showed up in the apocalyptic language that Southland Republicans used. "The combination of great political and economic power in the hands of New Deal government threatens to destroy those processes upon which the Republic is founded," declared a 1946 brochure issued by the Los Angeles County Republican Central Committee. "Under the guise of public welfare the American people are being subjected to the will of multiple bureaucratic agencies and personalities." This program had taken hold, Republicans believed, because "special minority groups and blocs" had imposed their agenda from above, using "the most voluminous propaganda hand-outs in American history."[21]

Yet conservatives also glimpsed grounds for hope. Roosevelt was gone. The inexperienced Truman seemed a feckless substitute, likely to be toppled soon. Peace held out the prospect of deregulation, and Americans were waking up to the Communist threat. California's Republicans eyed a chance to regain national power for the first time in decades. They could envision a new era, bright and full of opportunity. In this climate, rife with both hope and fear, Richard Nixon began his lifelong career in politics.

As early as the spring of 1945, Whittier Republicans had been training their sights on Jerry Voorhis. A Yale-educated patrician with a liberal voting record, Voorhis was the scourge of local insurance firms, oil drillers, agribusiness, and banks. He had always been an anomaly in a district that tilted to the right, but he had held onto his seat, even thrived, by playing to the district's deep distrust of remote, centralized power. During the New Deal, that power had been embodied in the Eastern businesses and financial houses—an equation that favored the Democrats. Voorhis had benefited, too, from the Republicans' recent choice of candidates, whose unreconstructed capitalism had seemed anachronistic and whose racial and religious bigotry (in some cases) had proved unpalatable. Most prominent among the GOP activists was Roy Day, the advertising man, who sensed that 1946 might be the Republicans' year and set about assembling a team to find a new—conservative—congressman.

The Committee of 100 that Day put together sometimes referred to its membership as "the amateurs," since they weren't officially part of the Republican Party. Yet many of the group's members had served as assemblymen, local committeemen, and officials in low-level campaigns of years past. Though not of statewide repute and not powerful industrialists (as some of Nixon's critics later alleged), they commanded, as Day recalled, "a following." The group included, he said, not just "the big shots" and "the presidents of the bank" but a wide sampling of local power brokers from the Scout movement, women's clubs, and civic groups. White, middle-aged, Protestant, mostly male, and of what historian Herbert Parmet called "Rotarian character," they included bankers and insurance men, realtors and ranchers, oilmen and salesmen and cor-

porate attorneys. Nixon remembered these early backers as "typical representatives of the Southern California middle class," which in fact
entailed some affluence, as Los Angeles County had by 1946 become the
wealthiest county in the United States.[22]

Ideologically, the group was decidedly conservative, even if that term
was not always embraced. The members were, said committee member
Gerald Kepple, a telephone company vice president, "people who believed
in individual enterprise and believed that we had, under the New Deal,
gone too far afield." One committee member, Herbert Spencer, joked that
"my friends all say I am a hidebound reactionary," yet insisted that he
merely wished to preserve the capitalist system under which he had pros-
pered so that "young people starting out with nothing may once again
have the chance to establish themselves and get ahead in the world."
Many feared that socialism, or communism, or collectivism—what you
called it didn't matter much—might be on its way to world domination.
The Cold War was beginning; with Nazism vanquished, many feared
communism would now conquer the globe. Roy Day was not just practic-
ing his rhetoric when he proclaimed to his Committee of 100: "We must
win in 1946 and do our part to preserve a Constitutional form of government in this country, a government responsible to the people, and free
from bureaucratic control." The stakes, he believed, really were that high.[23]

From the southern Los Angeles border to the San Gabriel Mountains,
the committee members combed the district, looking for a candidate with
the right combination of distaste for the New Deal and appeal to Voorhis
voters. They even publicized the search with a press release that made
front-page news in twenty-six of the mostly Republican-run local papers:

> WANTED, Congressman candidate with no previous experience to
> defeat a man who has represented the district in the House for ten
> years. Any young man, resident of the district, preferably a veteran,
> fair education, no political strings or obligations and possessed of a
> few ideas for betterment of country at large, may apply for the job.
> Applicants will be reviewed by 100 interested citizens who will guar-
> antee support but will not obligate the candidate in any way.

For many months, the dragnet proved fruitless. But in September, Herman Perry, the manager of the local branch of the Bank of America, sub-

mitted Nixon's name. Perry attended the same Quaker church as Nixon's family and had befriended the young lawyer when they shared an office building during Nixon's years in Whittier after law school. Nixon had flirted with politics in those years and had almost run for state assembly. He "had been 'noticed,'" recalled committee member McIntyre Faries, an attorney from Pasadena and national GOP activist, "as a good speaker and a man of promise." Having since served in the war and witnessed the regulatory state up close as an official at the Office of Price Administration, Nixon possessed, as Perry put it, "the personal appeal, the legal qualifications. He had been in Washington and around the world. In my mind he was a natural." Perry wrote to Nixon, who jumped at the chance. In November, he flew to Whittier for his audition.[24] After getting the nod, he took a couple of months to extricate himself from his navy obligations, then returned to Whittier in January 1946 to begin his campaign.

Nixon's 1946 campaign has been remembered mostly for his use of anti-communism. That issue, however, became prominent only in the fall. During the winter and spring before the Republican primary, Nixon made a name for himself by fashioning an image as the embodiment of this new conservative populist creed. He sought to rid the Republican Party of its taints and to reach voters struggling during the difficult reconversion to a peacetime economy and a Cold War.

Nixon was hardly the only veteran coming home that winter. Of 12 million Americans in the military on V-J Day, some 10 million were trading in their uniforms for work clothes. The reconversion from a wartime to a peacetime economy brought trepidation. Without military exigencies forcing the full-tilt production that had more than doubled the gross national product since 1940, the economy, it was feared, was now poised to collapse. A *Fortune* magazine survey found leading executives foretelling another depression. The rejuvenated economy, combined with rationing of goods and price controls, had amassed $136 billion in unspent savings by the war's end; now pent-up demand for meat and cigarettes, tires and nylon stockings, threatened to loose a torrential inflation. To smooth the transition, Truman in his 1946 State of the Union address called for another year of controls—a prescription that drew fusillades from the Chamber of Commerce and the National Association of Manufacturers, who feared that production would be throttled and long-deferred profits would stay low. They wanted the Office of Price Administration abolished altogether.[25]

Workers had grievances of their own. Freed of its wartime pledge not to agitate, labor undertook a series of actions to demand higher wages and workplace control. Starting with the United Automobile Workers strike of November 1945, 4.5 million steelworkers, electricians, dockworkers, railroad employees, coal miners, and others walked off the job in the year that followed—in the greatest one-year eruption of strikes in U.S. history. Some 116 million days of work were lost. For veterans, anxieties centered on finding good jobs and homes. In California the situation was acute, since so many military employees there had worked in aircraft and shipbuilding, where job cutbacks were high. Washington's solution was to extend benefits for education and home ownership, notably in the 1944 GI Bill of Rights and Veterans Administration–assisted mortgages. But to Southland businessmen, the key was to remove the artificial controls on rent that made housing scarce and regulations that kept businesses from creating jobs.[26]

Nixon was aware of the issues on voters' minds. But as he plunged into retail politics, he at first refrained from offering a concrete platform. In a letter to Roy Day on November 29, 1945, he spoke vaguely of a "progressive and constructive program designed to promote industrial peace," of a foreign policy "responsive to the will of the people," and of "positive action" to address "the needs of the district." As for his economic philosophy, he stressed his desire for minimal government, although he stopped short of endorsing his supporters' calls to roll back New Deal staples such as Social Security. He was more content to state that "the inventive genius and industrial know-how which have made America great must not be stifled by unnecessary bureaucratic restrictions." At other times he echoed Day's shrill prophecies, warning of "economic dictatorship by irresponsible government agencies."[27]

After winning over the Committee of 100, Nixon knew that core Republican activists would stand behind him. He next had to appeal to primary voters, who had weaker partisan attachments. He explained to

Day, who was preparing to assume the role of campaign manager, that "we definitely should not come out on issues too early. . . . We thereby avoid giving Voorhis anything to shoot at." (As he would throughout his career, Nixon managed his campaign more than his campaign manager did.) Instead of staking out controversial stands, Nixon toured the district and listened to voters. At small gatherings, coffee klatches, and civic clubs, he modestly introduced himself to likely voters. "He would ask them what they wanted," Day remembered, "and he would let them speak their piece." Dozens of small towns dotted the district, and each had chapters of one club or another—an Elks or Kiwanis or Rotary Club—where citizens met to hear talks and hold dinners. Starting in January, Nixon made the rounds, garnering daily write-ups in local papers. On January 14, he visited the Whittier Optimist Club; the next day he spoke at Post 51 of the American Legion; and so on, every day, throughout the winter and spring. Escorted by Day and Frank Jorgensen, a Metropolitan Life insurance executive and Committee of 100 leader, he crisscrossed the district, building a base. He made a strong impression. With his healthful, youthful aura and innate "magnetism," said Whittier lawyer Wallace Black, Nixon seemed "a kind of fair-haired boy around Whittier . . . [a] natural choice for political office." "He was always the type of fellow that rose to the top and was the president of this and the president of that," Gerald Kepple agreed, "and always had a sense of leadership."[28]

At first, Nixon listened more than he lectured. Unlike a previous candidate, Roy Day recalled, who put off voters by "telling everybody what *he* was going to do for *them*," Nixon "would ask people what they would like to have from their government." Voters told of their battles with regulations. Builders resented federal rent controls that cut their profits; chicken farmers protested price limits on meat; entrepreneurs fumed at the shortage of ready capital; consumers fretted at the shortages they blamed on government regulations. Nixon integrated these comments into his speeches. He praised "small business," which he called "the hope of America." He sketched out an economic program: dismantling the bureaucracy, removing price controls, fighting inflation by paying off the national debt, curtailing the "lavish spending of government money," and other laissez-faire nostrums that sounded newly promising during the reconversion.[29]

This constellation of ideas was already recognizable in 1946 as modern conservatism. Yet Nixon shunned the label. He still hoped to reclaim the term "liberal," which Roosevelt had appropriated. "Conservative," Nixon realized, smacked of the obeisance to corporate power that many thought had characterized the Republican Party since the days of the robber barons. "We cannot talk of being conservative. That is bankers' talk," he asserted, knowing full well that bankers and self-proclaimed conservatives were among his most ardent boosters. Yet it was against not conservatism but Voorhis's impractical, socialistic "idealism" that Nixon juxtaposed his own "practical liberalism." "The liberal's first task," he noted, ". . . and the mark by which you can tell a true one, is to remind men that only good individuals, whether rich or poor, can make a good society." Nixon was groping for language that would rally the Committee of 100 and other regulars and also reach beyond the party's base. To win a majority in a district that had elected Voorhis five times, he realized, preaching to the choir was not enough. "We need every Republican and a few Democrats to win," he told Day, prodding his campaign manager to "bring in the liberal fringe Republicans."[30]

Nixon also appreciated the Southland's independent voting habits and image-centered politics. As was common, he registered in the Democratic primary as well as the Republican contest, and cultivated an aura that would not only attract fence-sitters but transcend partisan categories altogether. Doing so meant steering clear of negative associations with the GOP. A Gallup poll taken in February 1946 showed that the public viewed his party as "the party of privilege and wealth." Only one fifth of voters thought the party cared about "men and women of average income." Nixon confronted the charge head-on, courting those who remained leery of Republican orthodoxy. "The Republican party has been labeled the party of big business and privilege," he said at a Lincoln Day speech in Pomona. "The charge is not justified by the record. Republicans live on both sides of the tracks." Nixon pried loose from the New Deal fold voters with weak ideological allegiances who wanted practical answers to everyday problems.[31]

Yet Nixon didn't run as a man of the left. On a few issues, his positions did place him closer to the center than to the right: he talked of extending Social Security, which was still anathema to the far right, and he rejected his party's isolationism on foreign affairs. On other issues, Nixon masked his conservative positions through finely phrased arguments. In offering what he called a "New Labor Policy," for example, he attributed the state's labor strife to tyrannical union bosses, violent labor radicalism, and the "undemocratic" closed shop. But he took pains not to castigate the workers themselves. If his policy was anti-labor, it was not anti-laborer.[32]

The heart of Nixon's campaign, however, wasn't his occasional centrist position or passing gesture to Democratic constituencies. The key was the populist cast he gave to his conservative beliefs. He styled himself a champion of the Southland's unprivileged, industrious men on the make. "Our national growth has been due to the fact that men of all classes, creeds and races had an opportunity in America to make individual contributions to the national community and to be rewarded," Nixon told audiences. "Emphasis was on freedom for the individual, private enterprise."[33]

His favorite populist device was to invoke what he called "the forgotten man." The phrase was first coined by the nineteenth-century Social Darwinist William Graham Sumner and then became part of Roosevelt's vocabulary in the 1930s. Reclaiming the term for conservatism, Nixon painted the forgotten man as one who worked hard, maybe had fought for his country, and now, in trying to provide for his family, faced a stifled economy and an unresponsive bureaucracy. He built up a roster of average citizens, sprinkling the list, as he recited it in speeches, with details gleaned from his conversations: "the vet," the "rabbit grower," "chicken men," the "grocer forced to buy mustard to get mayonnaise," the "butcher dealing in [the] black market against his will," the "housewife," the "small contractor," "the vet [again] trying to get a loan under a ridiculous plan which is unworkable." An elastic category that could include the working class, the bourgeoisie, and even the well-to-do who resented Washington's power, "the forgotten man" was central to Nixon's appeals in 1946 and was a forerunner to the "Middle Americans" and the "Silent Majority" to whom he would appeal decades later.[34]

. . .

To advance his message of conservative populism, Nixon touted his own biography, painting himself as a latter-day Horatio Alger. First, he underscored his status as a Navy veteran. At the civic clubs, he recounted his experiences in the South Pacific, on Bougainville and Green Island in the Solomon Islands, where he had (once) come under enemy fire. Rather than boasting about his standing as an officer, Nixon presented himself as one of the guys in the foxholes. As if describing scenes from a Hollywood war movie, he told of how he and his comrades—"a typical American melting pot crew" of rich and poor, Texan and New Yorker, Mexican and Indian—put aside differences to fight a common foe.[35] He recalled how they bathed in fungus-filled tidepools and faced sweltering humidity and water shortages. The experiences, he said, gave him an appreciation for the plight of the young soldiers and sailors, the war's unsung heroes. "GIs are mighty good kids," Nixon told his audiences, "and it is up to us to help them and give them the opportunities they deserve."[36]

In 1946, political aspirants around the country (including John F. Kennedy in Boston) were parlaying their battle stars into national office. In the 12th district, the Committee of 100 had made military experience a sine qua non. Service was a sign of the patriotism that the Southland's conservatives prized and would counter the recent inclination of veterans, as beneficiaries of the New Deal's largesse, to vote Democratic. Nixon's veteran status also highlighted Voorhis's lack of wartime service, which Roy Day argued was "a weak point" that made the incumbent seem effete and even un-American. Day urged local campaign chairmen to "secure a well-known returned service man" to head a Veterans-for-Nixon Committee in every community, and recruited a local car dealer to write and distribute "a non-partisan appeal from veteran to veteran to send a veteran to Congress."[37] Nixon's advertisements proclaimed: "He knows what it means to sleep in a foxhole—exist on K rations—'sweat out' an air raid. As a veteran he knows firsthand the problems of other veterans." The campaign biographies released by Murray Chotiner, the campaign's part-time public relations consultant, touted the candidate as a "clean, forthright young American who fought in defense of his country in the stinking mud and jungles of the Solomons." Nixon joined the American Legion and the Veterans of Foreign Wars.[38]

Religion, too, constituted a key to Nixon's conservative populism. Southland conservatives thought nothing of praising a candidate as a "fine Christian"; churchgoing meant integrity. Herman Perry had lobbied for Nixon because he came "from good Quaker stock"—an important selling point in towns like Whittier, a Quaker redoubt.* Given Voorhis's own reputation as a churchgoer, Roy Day argued, it was "imperative that we crack into Voorhis' church following, and NIXON can do it." He instructed campaign workers to arrange afternoon teas for Nixon to attend, "sponsored by some prominent lady in the community, preferably with good church connections." Nixon's old law partner, Tom Bewley, drafted a letter to a local clergyman, assuring him that Nixon "has taken part in the church's activities and given of his time and talents to church work. He is a firm believer in our doctrine." Bewley also praised Nixon as a believer in temperance. Campaign ads told voters that Nixon "typified the American way of service to God" and embodied "the solid heritage of the Quaker faith."[39]

Lastly, Nixon presented himself as an exemplary young family man. His wife, Pat, worked full time on the campaign, attending events with Nixon or on her own, despite being many months pregnant. When she delivered a baby girl, Tricia, on February 19, Nixon's backer John Cassidy alerted the local papers, gaining the candidate free, and fawning, coverage. The *Whittier News* ran a photograph of the joyous parents and baby— the model postwar family. Under a three-column headline, an article clucked over the "perfect young lady" and "her lovely mother," and quoted Nixon, who used the occasion to speak about "the grave responsibilities for all of us" at this moment of American crisis. Afterward, Nixon praised Cassidy for his "excellent job in getting out the publicity on Mrs. Nixon and our new baby." Nixon said it was "the best and most effective piece of publicity which has been sent out."[40]

---

* California Quakerism differed from the Eastern liberal-pacifist variety. Influenced by fundamentalist Protestantism, it placed more of a stress on emotion. This difference has been used to suggest how Nixon could reconcile his faith with his pugnacious campaign style.

Voters grew familiar with an assortment of Nixon's life experiences. "Richard M. Nixon Is One of Us," declared a newspaper ad that reviewed the highlights. Having been raised on a farm, it said, "he has a working knowledge of farm problems . . ." Having pumped gas at his father's service station, "he knows what it means to earn a dollar—the problems of the working man." Having done contract work for the U.S. Navy, he possessed a "practical knowledge of business problems." And having become a father, the ad asserted, "he wants his child and your child to live and work in a free country, with the chance to advance."[41]

Later in his career, many would see this portrayal of Nixon as nothing but marketing. But the record of his first campaign shows little doubt among Southern Californians that he embodied their values. Nixon's self-presentation stirred many voters. Describing herself as the wife of an orange grower, one Lillian Amberson wrote Nixon that he had been a smash at the Alhambra–San Gabriel Women's Republican Study Club. "We are still receiving reports from people who were at the meeting . . . everyone is so enthusiastic." Nixon's schedule grew crowded as solicitations poured in. Hector M. Powell, after hearing Nixon at the South Pasadena Kiwanis Club, asked the candidate to speak again before his Masonic Lodge. "We will be happy to have you use the same talk that thrilled our Kiwanis Club, 'A Service Man Looks to the Future.'"[42]

Editors and publishers joined the cheerleading. Upon meeting Nixon in May, the *Los Angeles Times*'s political editor Kyle Palmer—known throughout California as a fount of political information, a wheeler-dealer, and a kingmaker—judged him "serious, determined . . . an extraordinary man." Publisher Norman Chandler, a local titan, liked Nixon's "fight and fire," his "forthrightness, and the way he spoke," and urged Palmer to endorse him. Herb Klein, a friendly editor for the *Alhambra Post-Advocate* and later a Nixon aide, remembered that Nixon handily sewed up the "enthusiastic editorial support" of the mostly conservative editors and publishers of the area's papers.[43]

Nixon also spoke directly to the concerns of local business interests. By May, his team had arranged its mailing lists by profession, the better to target each group. "Thousands of letters are being sent out continually from Realtors, Insurance Men, Automobile Dealers, Doctors, Dentists and others" to members of their own professions, Roy Day told his staff. Later, Nixon's men created such paper committees as Ranchers for Nixon and Physicians for Nixon. These bodies, which consisted of a mere handful of supporters, placed ads or sent out letters under their official-sounding names. Kenneth Spencer, a pro-Nixon dentist, warned colleagues about "the increasing threat of socialization," while Ron Stevens told fellow insurance men to back Nixon because "our business success depends upon the continuation of private enterprise."[44]

Nixon's strategy paid off on June 4, when he not only won the Republican primary but fared well against Jerry Voorhis in the combined results of both primaries, in which both candidates had run, as allowed by the state's cross-filing provision. Although Voorhis garnered a majority of the overall primary vote, his total margin was his thinnest since 1936—a fact that heartened Nixon. "Wherever Mr. Nixon has appeared he has made a most favorable impression," Day wrote proudly to the campaign staff. "His sincerity, determination and natural ability as a leader has made a deep niche in the hearts of all those who have been privileged to work with him in this campaign." When Nixon and Pat set off for a vacation in British Columbia to rest up for the fall campaign, they did so knowing he had found a potent message and image for the new era.[45]

By the fall of 1946, the contours of a national Republican revival could be dimly discerned. On the home front, fears about reconversion seemed to be coming true. The lifting of price controls in June, forced on Truman by his Republican opposition, led to the biggest one-month jump in prices in American history. Food shortages intensified—by September the supply of meat was one fifth of its August level—and exacerbated ideological divisions: the left faulted cattlemen for cutting production, while the right, more successfully, pinned blame on the incumbent party's management. Black markets flourished. Labor militancy surged.[46]

As domestic tensions rapidly increased, foreign threats mounted. A bellicose speech by Joseph Stalin in February 1946 was followed by Winston Churchill's admonition in March, given with Truman at his side, that an "iron curtain" now cordoned off Eastern Europe from the free world.

Relations between the former Allies deteriorated. When in September Commerce Secretary Henry Wallace criticized Truman's intransigence toward the Soviet Union, the president fired him, though that did not stop Republicans from coloring Truman and the Democrats as too soft on the Communist threat. In San Francisco on September 30, FBI head J. Edgar Hoover warned that Communists were infiltrating the government and labor unions. The combined weight of these events helped the Republicans frame the upcoming elections as a contest, in party chairman Carroll Reece's phrase, between "communism and Republicanism." GOP congressional hopefuls invoked the Red menace from Massachusetts to Wisconsin to Southern California.[47]

Nixon saw anti-communism, said Committee of 100 member McIntyre Faries, as "a good issue, a gut issue." Nixon was now entering the general election campaign and would be competing head to head against Voorhis for uncommitted voters. Harrison McCall, a Pasadena business owner and GOP activist, had taken the reins as campaign manager, and a modified message, to go with the new boss, was needed for the fall fight. More than in the primaries, anti-communism played, since it was an issue on which Nixon thought Voorhis vulnerable.[48]

Nixon's attacks have long provoked controversy. Critics later charged that he introduced the issue opportunistically. Voorhis, although a former socialist, had long since joined the camp of anti-Communist liberals. He had even served on the House Un-American Activities Committee and sponsored the Voorhis Act, which forced groups with foreign allegiances to register with the government. Nixon's critics also suggested that the Red issue shifted attention from voters' bread-and-butter concerns.[49]

Nixon's intimates believed otherwise. "It wasn't just a political thing with him," Frank Jorgensen insisted, not just a crude, tangential scare tactic. On the contrary, anti-communism grew naturally from the Southlanders' anti-collectivist ideology. Rent control, price controls, the power of organized labor, high taxes, the prospect of a national health care system—these were the harbingers, they believed, of full-blown socialism. If Voorhis was carrying water, even unwittingly, for radical groups, he might undermine the Southlanders' way of life. Anti-communism and opposition to the New Deal, as they saw it, were interlocked. By showing himself to be tough on communism, Nixon was not changing the topic; he was augmenting his patriotic image.[50]

Nixon had consistently made his own belief in free-market capitalism central to his platform. And in the spring, he and his surrogates had gently begun to invoke the corollary: that Voorhis—the son of a millionaire, schooled at Yale, sympathetic to the unions—had no such priorities. Roy Crocker, a Committee of 100 member and Nixon's campaign chairman, launched the first salvo in April, assailing Voorhis for receiving the endorsement of the "PAC." Most voters took this shorthand phrase to refer to the CIO-PAC, a radical political action committee formed in 1944 by the Congress of Industrial Organizations and its left-wing (but anti-Communist) leader Sidney Hillman. In fact, the group that had endorsed Voorhis was the National Citizens Political Action Committee (NCPAC), a different entity, not tied to labor. Comprising anti-Communist liberals as well as Marxists, NCPAC stressed civil rights for blacks and cooperation with the Soviet Union but hardly toed the Kremlin line. Still, Nixon argued that since some Communists belonged to NCPAC, and since the two PACs shared some board members, "the question of which PAC endorsed him was a distinction without a difference."[51]

The anti-communism issue, as Nixon and his supporters saw it, stemmed naturally from his imprecations about New Deal regulations and too-powerful labor unions. They were part of the same overarching ideology. A Nixon campaign memo made this connection clear. Enumerating the campaign's key themes, it included "state socialism versus free enterprise," "a PAC endorsed candidate versus an independent," and "Pro-Russian policy versus American policy," tying together in a neat bundle economics, foreign affairs, and Nixon's self-styled image as an underdog fighting weak-kneed idealists. In speeches that fall, Nixon chided "the people who front for un-American elements . . . by advocating increasing federal controls." He contrasted the philosophy "supported by the radical PAC and its adherents [that] would deprive the people of liberty through regimentation" with his own worldview, which would "return the government to the people under Constitutional guarantee." Far from a diversion, the PAC issue echoed Nixon's other positions such as abolishing the Office of Price Administration ("shot through with extreme left-wingers . . . boring from within, striving to force private enterprise into bankruptcy") or ending public housing ("a conspiracy among the social housers to discredit private enterprise as represented by the home-building industry"). Other national issues—meat shortages, labor strife, Henry Wallace—buttressed this same message.[52]

Nixon's aggressive use of the PAC issue also bolstered his patriot image. His tenacity appeared not only legitimate but a heroic response to an emerging crisis. "It was good politics at that time," said Wallace Black, the local attorney and Nixon supporter. "I would describe it as a pretty hard-fought campaign by a young, up-and-coming political leader." Using a line that would become a staple of his rhetoric for years to come, Nixon had pledged a "rocking, socking campaign," and at the candidates' first joint appearance, in September, Nixon had a chance to showcase his hard-hitting style.[53]

Almost one thousand Californians turned out at the South Pasadena–San Marino Junior High School on September 13, a balmy Friday night. Nixon, having scheduled another event right before, was running late, and inside the auditorium Voorhis mounted the dais alone. Unprepared for verbal fisticuffs, the incumbent rambled over the issues, oblivious to the audience's boredom. Then, just as he finished, Nixon strode from the wings to a roar of applause. Poised and practiced, he briskly recited his well-rehearsed anti–New Deal litany, chiding the federal government for food shortages and attacking the left-wing San Francisco labor leader Harry Bridges for threatening a strike that might imperil the availability of sugar. "The time is at hand in this country when no labor leader or no management leader should have the power to deny the American people any of the necessities of American life," Nixon boomed. His comments elicited the longest cheers he could remember.[54]

With Roy Day having made sure that "we had questions planted in the audience," the PAC issue was certain to arise. As it turned out, a Democrat broached the topic, asking Nixon why he was falsely charging that Voorhis had CIO-PAC support. Perfectly prepared, Nixon pulled from his pocket a copy of NCPAC's endorsement. Confidently, he marched across the stage and handed it to a flustered Voorhis. Voorhis meekly stammered that this was a different group, but the crowd hooted and shouted, while Nixon listed the groups' shared board members. "It's the same thing, virtually, when they have the same directors," he parried. For the rest of the night, Voorhis fumbled while the audience laughed or booed and Nixon fired off pithy responses. "From then on," recalled Lyle Otterman, a Nixon supporter who worked for Herman Perry, "he proceeded to take Voorhis apart piece by piece, and toss him around the audience."[55]

Otterman considered the debate decisive for Nixon. "He was definitely in the minority when he started his speech," he recalled. ". . . But I could pick up around me the feeling that 'this guy's not so bad after all, is he? He seems to have something on the ball.'" Committee of 100 member Herbert Spencer judged the incumbent "scared and nervous" and the challenger simply "splendid." The enduring impression, wrote the *Los Angeles Times*, was that "Voorhis was at particular pains to clear himself of any implications that he was pro-Russian." Voorhis's camp agreed. "Jerry," said his adviser Chet Holifield, later himself a congressman, "he murdered you."[56]

Nixon ran with the issue. Campaign manager Harrison McCall ordered thousands of plastic thimbles that said: "Nixon for Congress— Put a Needle in the PAC." Advertisements drummed the message home. "A vote for Nixon is a vote against Socialization of free American institutions, . . . the PAC . . . and its communist principles," said one. Another assailed not only the PAC, "its communistic principles and its gigantic slush fund," but also Voorhis himself, claiming that of 46 votes in the past four years, "43 times Voorhis voted the PAC line!" A third claimed that Voorhis voted "to provide luxuries for the minority without a fair return of work at the expense of the hardworking majority of Americans," while depicting Nixon as "the clean-cut, forth-right, patriotic and American candidate for Congress in the 12th district." District newspapers, friendly to Nixon, helped out. Herb Klein's *Alhambra Post-Advocate* speculated coyly on "just why Jerry got the CIO Political Action Committee endorsement" and ran an editorial entitled "How Jerry and Vito Voted," likening Voorhis's record to that of New York's Vito Marcantonio, a far-left New York congressman.* As it turned out, the votes included approval of school lunches, soil conservation, and a ban on poll taxes.[57]

---

* Nixon would use the same tactic four years later in his Senate race against Helen Gahagan Douglas.

Another debate had been scheduled, but Murray Chotiner, eyeing an advantage, called for still additional contests. Rejecting his advisers' counsel, Voorhis acquiesced to three more exchanges. Across the district, excitement mounted. With television still in its infancy, and politics still relying on retail events, the debates took on the feel of season-ending high school football games, replete with marching bands, fanfare, and crowds of more than a thousand. By the final event, held at the San Gabriel Mission near Los Angeles, the audience was spilling out of the building and the organizers had to set up audio speakers outside so that the latecomers, encamped on the lawn, could hear. If Nixon did not raise the PAC issue at these debates, the audience invariably did; during the question-and-answer periods, Faries recalled, it arose more than any other topic.[58]

Nixon's sharp performances cemented his reputation as a local hero. His forensic skills—"very convincing, very smooth, very glib, very fast," as one admirer said—drew raves. "As far back as I can remember, a political meeting was usually made up of inarticulate speakers who just threw mud around, and you could hardly get a baker's dozen to come," said Gerald Kepple. At the Nixon-Voorhis match-ups, however, "you would have thought that you were back in the days of the Lincoln-Douglas debates. There was no mudslinging; there was just straight-from-the-shoulder debating." Locals began discussing the election as never in recent memory, at lunch counters, taverns, and weekly card games.[59]

Nixon basked in the adulation of strangers. "This is really a fan letter," gushed Sara Morelock of El Monte in one of the many letters Nixon received after the final debate, "for after that magnificent debate last night at San Gabriel I feel I must tell you how proud we in this district are of you." She and others "really beat their hands off in applause for everything you said." Volunteers turned up at Nixon campaign headquarters to help with door-to-door campaigning and stuffing envelopes. "In all the different towns and communities that make up the 12th district," recalled Kepple, "I have never seen such enthusiastic support of people getting out and working as there was in that campaign."[60]

On November 5, Nixon won, with 57 percent of the vote. Across the country, Republicans drove out New Dealers in what the news media heralded as a changing of the guard. The GOP captured both houses of Congress for the first time since 1928, "far beyond its most sanguine hopes," *Time* magazine reported. The Republicans took all six Senate seats that were up for grabs in the populist states of the West and Northwest, which had long voted Democratic. Independent voters, who had also been supporting New Dealers, turned out in significant numbers for the GOP. The main reason, according to *Time*: "The majority of Americans no longer feared to be on their own in free markets."[61]

Certainly, Nixon's boosters felt this way. The day after his victory, the leader of the Whittier Chamber of Commerce led a flock of businessmen to Nixon's law office to extend congratulations. The next week, Gerald Kepple, Harrison McCall, and other business leaders fêted the new congressman at a banquet. Congratulatory letters arrived by the hundreds, especially, the campaign noted, from groups like insurance men, realtors, and doctors. "We will no longer be shackled by government controls," exulted one local contractor. "To have the 'New Deal' stranglehold in this area at last broken is like some form of emancipation," echoed another citizen.[62]

Nixon, exhibiting what Wallace Black called his "uncanny sense of timing," had picked the right moment to run. "Roosevelt's era was fading," Kepple felt. "All of the various government agencies that had been created were having their problems and the government . . . was flailing in the air." Nationally, the Republicans used the slogan "Had Enough?" to play upon what Black called "this swing, following the war, over to the more conservative view. Dick happened to hit it right." Voorhis agreed. Political races, he said, boiled down to battles not between left and right but "between the 'outs' and 'ins'"; Nixon won in California, he said, because he had aligned himself with the people and Voorhis with the federal bureaucracy. The members of California's 12th district who had rallied to Nixon finally felt that they had in Congress a representative who was truly one of them.[63]

Nixon arrived in Congress in January 1947 to begin what would be six years of service in the House and the Senate, culminating in his election as vice president, at age thirty-nine, in 1952. During this time, he refined the conservative populism and all-American image that had endeared him to California voters and made him the Republican Party's brightest young star. What has generally been remembered from these years is Nixon's focus on fighting communism. His role in exposing Alger Hiss as a Soviet spy and his aggressive 1950 Senate race against Helen Gahagan Douglas helped define his persona as a Cold Warrior with a national profile. But although his supporters cheered his vehement anti-communism and praised him as a fighter, his Red-hunting, as in 1946, was just one element of a more fully rounded identity as a heroic American everyman.

Almost as soon as Nixon arrived in the capital as a freshman representative, he found that his populist persona resonated beyond California's 12th district. Just one month into his term, he was standing out among his class. "He looks like the boy who lived down the block from all of us," a reporter for the *Washington Times Herald* gushed; "he's as typically American as Thanksgiving." After he debated a CIO official on a network radio broadcast in March, citizens from around the country wrote to praise his attack on big labor. Nixon distinguished himself, too, with his legislative work. He helped lead the fight for the Taft-Hartley Bill that outlawed the closed shop, and he made headlines back home when he called for a neutral "czar" to arbitrate labor union disputes.[64]

But Nixon's signal issue was anti-communism. Like Voorhis before him, he was given a seat on the House Un-American Activities Committee (HUAC), where he co-authored with South Dakota's Karl Mundt a bill that barred Communist Party members from appointed office and forced them to register with the government. Though the bill didn't pass until two years later, it earned Nixon plaudits.* To Kyle Palmer of the conservative *Los Angeles Times*, a booster since 1946, Nixon had already proved himself "one of the ablest and most fearless of the younger generation in Congress." The U.S. Junior Chamber of Commerce named the new legislator one of the nation's "ten most outstanding young men."[63]

Nixon's greatest fame accrued from his role in the most celebrated espionage case that came before HUAC: the case of Alger Hiss. In August 1948, Whittaker Chambers, a stout, rumpled, wild-eyed editor at *Time*, tes-

---

* Later reintroduced and renamed for Nevada senator Pat McCarran, it became law in 1950.

tified that Hiss, a courtly, blue-blooded ex–State Department official with a seemingly impeccable reputation, had been a Soviet agent. Nixon seized the issue. He brought Hiss before the committee for interrogation, eventually helping to land him in prison for perjury. Nixon and his supporters saw the Hiss case in populist terms, with the liberal diplomat representing the corrupt elite and Nixon (and Chambers) embodying the virtuous common folk. Although Nixon later recalled that he had little support during the Hiss case, in fact his aggressiveness throughout the affair impressed Americans as proof of the pure, patriotic spirit of his pursuit. Chambers himself recalled that to his children Nixon was known as " 'Nixie,' the kind and the good, about whom they will tolerate no nonsense." Intending to underscore Nixon's noble motives, Chambers added: "I have a vivid picture of him, the blackest hour of the Hiss case, standing by the barn [on Chambers's farm] and saying in his quietly savage way (he is the kindest of men): 'If the American people understood the real character of Alger Hiss, they would boil him in oil.'"[66]

The Hiss case crystallized Nixon's image as a crusader against Communists. In October 1948, he barnstormed the West and Middle West, refining his speeches about "Cold War treason and other communist dangers." One advertisement, designed with all the subtlety of a cover from the era's potboiler paperbacks, proclaimed Nixon, in screaming letters, "AMERICA'S GREATEST ENEMY OF COMMUNISM." Setting Nixon's earnest visage starkly against a black background, it luridly exhorted locals in bold paintbrushlike strokes to come hear "THE INSIDE FACTS ON THE RED THREAT! TOO HOT TO PUBLISH! TOO INFLAMATORY TO BROADCAST!" Back in California's 12th district, the South Pasadena Republican Club passed resolutions honoring their hometown hero, part of a continuing chorus of huzzahs.[67]

Riding high, precocious as ever, Nixon set his sights on the Senate, capitalizing on his reputation as a champion of ordinary folks. His opponent, Representative Helen Gahagan Douglas—a Barnard-educated actress, ardent New Dealer, and friend of Eleanor Roosevelt—made a perfect foil. Nixon picked up an attack that had been used against her in the primary, comparing her votes to those of Vito Marcantonio (as Nixon's supporters had done to Voorhis's in 1946). He juxtaposed the two representatives' records on a pastel flyer that became known as the "Pink Sheet." Many liberals were outraged by this tactic; thereafter they fumed about Nixon's too-ready use of the communism issue and pronounced him a cheap-shot artist nonpareil. But, again, as important as Nixon's barbs against "the Pink Lady" was his rendering of Douglas as an elitist, a captive to Eastern interests, and a feminist career woman. In contrast, Nixon styled himself the family man who shared Californians' kitchen-table concerns. He toured the state in a ramshackle, wood-paneled station wagon, with Pat or his daughters in tow. His background, wrote Carl Greenberg of the *Los Angeles Examiner*, was "so average American that, unless you found it out for yourself, it would smack of a campaign man-ager's imagination." Throughout these years, newspapers adoringly pro-filed Nixon (the "tall, dark and—yes—handsome freshman"), while glossy middlebrow magazines displayed photographs of the Nixon fam-ily sitting together in their cheerful living room or on their idyllic front lawn. "He lives modestly [and] avoids the flamboyant side of Washington social life," ran a typically rapturous piece in the *Saturday Evening Post*. California's voters ratified their belief in this image of Nixon in the 1950 election, giving him 59 percent of their 3.7 million votes and a seat in the U.S. Senate.[68]

Within a year, he became the Republican Party's most sought after speaker and the vessel for hopes of a conservative revival. "He was dark and erect, a still youthful Navy veteran of World War II," recalled the Pulitzer Prize–winning biographer Margaret L. Coit upon seeing Nixon in Worcester, Massachusetts, in 1952. "He gave a wonderful speech. It was exciting; it got us all enthused. I couldn't put it out of my mind. I still remember it as one of the best speeches I ever heard." Others compared him to Jack Armstrong, the "All-American boy" of radio and children's books. In the Southland particularly, a new generation of activists coa-lesced around Nixon and his message. Pat Hillings, Nixon's aide and suc-cessor in Congress, called it "a bona fide Republican movement." "We belonged to the new postwar crop; many of us were converted Democrats, moving into the Republican ranks," Hillings said. "Nixon became in those days the champion of this younger group, and as a result, we were able to build around him a very active political organization."[69]

Among those excited by this new star was General Dwight Eisenhower, the favorite for the 1952 Republican presidential nomination. Eisenhower had met Nixon twice before and admired his air of integrity and statesmanship. Ike saw Nixon's behavior in the Hiss case not as vicious or crude but as an actual asset. "The feature that especially appealed to me," the general wrote in his memoirs, "was the reputation that Congressman Nixon had achieved for fairness in the investigating process. Not once had he overstepped the limits prescribed by the American sense of fair play or American rules applying to such investigations. He did not persecute or defame. This I greatly admired." At the Republican Convention in Chicago in July 1952, Eisenhower chose Nixon as his running mate, hoping the vigorous, youthful Californian would complement the older general's staid persona.[70]

Nixon's selection sent his hometown crowd into raptures. "Your nomination . . . created such a high pitch of excitement in the Gibbons household," Committee of 100 member Boyd Gibbons wrote, "that we really haven't calmed down as yet." Like a proud parent, Gibbons waxed rhapsodic about Nixon's "fresh, clean, 'young American' personality" and his "'Lincolnish' qualities and . . . deep convictions and the need for such a man 'someday,' to be at the helm of this great country." No less adoring was the national press. *U.S. News* lauded Nixon as "the fighting member of the Republican team," blessed with "youthful stamina" and "skill as a debater." Magazine profiles cheered the "5-foot, 11½-inch Californian with his curly dark hair and his flashing white smile" and his "brown-eyed blonde" wife. "The average Nixon day begins soon after sunup," went one piece. "Pat dresses the children and feeds them first. At around seven o'clock Nixon comes down for his breakfast and before eight o'clock he has kissed his womenfolk and gone to his office . . . often until 11 o'clock at night." The controversy Nixon had generated in the past—in the Hiss case and the Voorhis and Douglas races—was buried under the avalanche of adulation.[71]

Then came the Checkers speech. Years later, it would be remembered by his critics as the ultimate expression of his phoniness, as the moment that turned many of them into lifelong Nixon-haters on the spot. In Emile de Antonio's documentary *Millhouse: A White Comedy* (1971), made by and for left liberals, long stretches of the Checkers speech are excerpted in toto and played deadpan, for laughs. Antonio assumed that Nixon's theatrics, which seemed primitive in hindsight to a hip 1970s filmgoer, would strike his audience as patently comical. Antonio wasn't wrong—audiences roared at Nixon's earnest delivery—but in going for cheap laughs, he forsook historical understanding.

Only by clearing away the various images of Nixon that have developed over the years is it possible to understand how most Americans saw the speech: as the quintessential expression of Nixon's populist image. To the large majority of those who watched or heard it in 1952, it demonstrated Nixon's affinity for ordinary, middle-class families, his capacity for straightforward talk, his authenticity. If it was the spark that ignited the wildfire of Nixon-hating, it was also the capstone of Nixon's populist self-presentation.

The trouble for the vice-presidential aspirant began on September 18, when the *New York Post* reported the existence of a private fund, totaling some $18,000, that Nixon's Southland backers had raised to cover his expenses. The news, reeking of favor-trading, sent the news media into a frenzy and jeopardized Nixon's place on the Republican ticket. Leading Eastern Republicans, including the influential *New York Herald Tribune* and (privately) many of Eisenhower's closest advisers, joined Democrats in calling for him to resign from the ticket. As Ike pondered changing running mates, Nixon prevailed on the general to let him defend himself before a national television and radio audience. On Tuesday night, September 23, Nixon spoke from the El Capitan Theater, converted by NBC into a television studio, to the largest audience any politician had ever enjoyed.

His words did more than dispel doubts about the fund. They painted, in the most vivid colors he had yet found in his rhetorical palette, a portrait of himself as an American everyman. Only the first portion of the speech addressed questions about the fund. The balance was straight autobiography: a sepia-toned recounting of the trials of a self-made man, adorned with emotional touches to make Nixon's plight feel familiar.

Nixon recalled the "modest circumstances" of his boyhood, in which his entire family toiled in his father's grocery store to make ends meet, and, later, the "rather difficult time" he and Pat had faced, "like so many of the young couples who may be listening to us." He mentioned, too, as he had so often in 1946, his war service. "I got a couple of letters of commendation," he said, "but I was there when the bombs were falling." Then came the 1946 campaign, into which he had sunk his savings. He lived a frugal lifestyle like most middle-class Americans. "It isn't very much but Pat and I have the satisfaction that every dime we've got is honestly ours." Alluding to the Truman administration scandals in which furs had been given as bribes, he added: "I should say this, that Pat doesn't have a mink coat. But she does have a respectable cloth coat. And I always tell her she'd look good in anything." As a crowning touch, he invoked his daughters and a gift they'd been given, "a little cocker spaniel dog . . . black-and-white spotted. And our little girl, Tricia, the six-year-old, named it Checkers. And the kids love the dog and . . . regardless of what they say about it, we're gonna keep it."

Nixon had instructed viewers to telegram the Republican National Committee to vote on whether he should stay on, and they supported him overwhelmingly. "The telephone is lit up like a Christmas tree," Ted Rogers, Nixon's television consultant, crowed. Millions of letters and telegrams poured in—to Nixon, to Eisenhower, to the RNC, to NBC, to countless news outlets. Heavily pro-Nixon, they expressed admiration that he had courageously bared his soul, and his finances, before the public; they praised him as honest, sincere, humble. Young couples professed to have faced the exact same hardships. Republicans who had been thinking about defecting, as well as self-described lifelong Democrats, claimed that Nixon had won them over. The most important endorsement came on a West Virginia airstrip. Greeting Nixon in the cool night, a beaming Eisenhower assured his number two, "You're my boy!"[72]

Like a good politician, Eisenhower was simply heeding the popular will. Nixon had turned himself into a national hero. In particular, the mail from his home state—six hundred letters from Whittier alone—dripped with pride. "We were overwhelmed by the sincerity of your speech last night," wrote Jeanne Wells of Artesia, California, who mailed a letter because the telegraph offices were backed up for more than an hour. "Your honesty and sincerity are unquestionable," echoed Bill Hanna of Metro-Goldwyn-Mayer Productions on stationery decorated with Tom-and-Jerry cartoons. "Count my Democratic vote for 'Ike and Dick.'" Banged out on rickety typewriters or scrawled in longhand, stated in one-sentence slogans or argued in minor treatises, jotted on flowered notecards or authored jointly by like-minded office workers on official stationery—whatever the form, reams of letters extolled Nixon's television performance. One young Southern Californian, a moderate conservative, stood outside the TV studio the night of the speech and then volunteered to work in the campaign. It would be another four years, however, before Bob Haldeman joined Nixon's team. (He went into advertising first.)[73]

The applause came from beyond California, too. Editorial pages and commentators weighed in with accolades on behalf of small-town Americans everywhere. More than thirty years later, a Texas-born writer named Lawrence Wright recalled Nixon's populist image for a culture that had all but forgotten it. Wright remembered that his father, a local bank vice president in Abilene, "had no real idea who Nixon was" until the speech. Watching it, he wrote, "was an arresting moment in my father's life"; afterward, "Daddy was a Nixon man." For millions of God- and country-loving people like his parents, Wright argued, who came from poverty and were rising into middle-class life during the postwar years, Nixon "began to personify certain attitudes they endorsed . . . yearning for dignity and status. . . . Nixon became their angry representative, their score-settler."[74] Six weeks after the speech, Eisenhower and Nixon reclaimed the White House for the GOP, championing a conservatism that embraced not only business growth and anti-communism but also a resentment of liberal elites.

In *Nixon Agonistes*, the writer Garry Wills called the Checkers speech Nixon's classic attempt to assert that "He is just like all the rest of us, only more so." Like others for whom the speech inspired venom or ridicule, Wills judged the attempt a failure. He had caught glimpses, he said, of "the private Nixon," a man "who thinks of himself as a Wilsonian intellectual," suggesting that the common-man adornments amounted to phony image making; Nixon, he said, was the "least authentic man alive."[75] Wills in effect posited a "real" Nixon behind this mask. The suggestion was understandable. From Wills's vantage point in 1969, it was hard to make out, through the layers of interpretation that had accrued over the years, Nixon's original everyman persona. But in 1952, that Horatio Alger rendering from the Voorhis race and the Checkers speech resonated with millions who hadn't yet learned to view their politics with Wills's sardonic detachment.

Just how much truth existed in this image of Nixon matters less, finally, than the credence it demonstrably enjoyed. Nixon's successful self-presentation launched his career and made him a leader of the Republican Party for twenty years. It inspired a generation of activists like Pat Hillings and Bob Haldeman, who saw dividends in forging a conservative populism to appeal beyond the GOP's well-to-do base. And the success of Nixon's everyman image ushered in a new candidate-centered politics, in which old dichotomies between image and reality would cease to have anything like the purchase they had in earlier times.

2

The Fifties Liberals: Nixon as Tricky Dick

The Fifties were not the Eisenhower years but the Nixon years. That was the decade when the American lower middle class in the person of this man moved to engrave into the history of the United States, as the voice of America, its own faltering spirit, its self-pity and its envy, its continual anxiety about what the wrong people might think, its whole peevish, resentful whine.

—*Murray Kempton*, America Comes of Middle Age[1]

"He has, probably, more enemies than any other American," the *Saturday Evening Post*'s Stewart Alsop wrote of Richard Nixon in 1958. Nixon had fairly earned, Alsop explained, through his combativeness and unctuous style, the spite of Democrats everywhere. But, he added, "Sometimes the dislike of Nixon is pure bile, undiluted by rational content, as in the case of the elderly lady in Whittier, Nixon's hometown in California, who telephoned this reporter to say, 'I know it's against religion to hate anybody, but I just can't help hating that Nixon.'"[2]

It may not need proving that Richard Nixon was the most despised American politician of his time. But the testaments of his adversaries support Alsop's idea that in the 1950s a new and distinct phenomenon called Nixon-hating emerged. With liberal Democrats blazing the way, many

Americans came to regard Nixon as a singularly dark and dangerous presence in national life. And while the hatred had an ideological component,
there was far more to it. Nixon's detractors viewed him as categorically different from other partisan foes. "All the time I've been in politics," Harry
Truman told his biographer, "there's only two people I hate, and he's one."
Adlai Stevenson said Nixon was the sole public figure he ever "really
loathed" and once, upon hearing Nixon's name at a party, exclaimed,
"Please! Not while I'm eating!" Eleanor Roosevelt, a biographer wrote,
considered Nixon "the politician she most detested." Dean Acheson
thought just two or three others as odious. Averell Harriman once stalked
out of a swanky Georgetown dinner party—the kind where Democrats,
Republicans, and reporters normally mixed with ease—because he spied
Nixon sitting nearby. "I will not break bread with that man!" the diplomat
boomed before exiting. And John F. Kennedy, speaking to *The New Yorker*'s
Washington correspondent Richard Rovere, called his 1960 presidential
opponent a "son of a bitch" and a "bastard."[3]

Nixon-hating wasn't confined to politicians. In the pages of the
nation's liberal newspapers and magazines, intellectual journalists—Murray Kempton, Max Lerner, and William Shannon of the *New York Post*,
William Lee Miller and Meg Greenfield of *The Reporter*, others at *The
Nation*, *The New Republic*, and *The Progressive*—dissected with numbing
frequency the peculiar nature of Nixon's odiousness. "A ruthless partisan," said columnist Walter Lippmann. "The West's streamlined
McCarthy," said historian Arthur M. Schlesinger, Jr. "If he did wrestle
with his conscience," japed *New Republic* contributor William Costello,
"the match was fixed." These barbs brought nods and echoes from their
readers—intellectuals, academics, and other well-educated members of
the arts and professions who voted Democratic and joined groups like
Americans for Democratic Action and the American Civil Liberties Union.
These writers and readers were known as the "eggheads," a term coined
by Stewart Alsop and his brother Joe. Nixon hated the eggheads, along
with the press and the "Eastern establishment" generally, for their influence and social grace. They returned the sentiment in spades. In the 1950s
they collectively forged a new picture of Nixon that would soon join, and
later supersede, the populist image that he had previously enjoyed.[4]

If one has to strain, after fifty years, to retrieve the portrait of Nixon as Horatio Alger, picturing the malevolent Nixon takes little work. Vividly rendered in the cartoons of *The Washington Post*'s "Herblock," summed up in the nickname affixed to Nixon during his 1950 race for the Senate— "Tricky Dick"—the notion of Nixon as America's consummate political villain lasted through his vice presidency, his presidency, his post-presidency, and into the present. "Like more than a few Americans of my generation," wrote Frank Rich of *The New York Times* in 1994, a baby boomer, "I learned to despise Richard Nixon around the time I learned to recite the Pledge of Allegiance." Whether in the fiction of Robert Coover (whose *Public Burning* depicts the young Nixon arranging to immolate the Rosenbergs in Times Square) or offhand references from Woody Allen (whose film *Sleeper* gibes that when Nixon left the White House, the Secret Service would count the silverware), this dastardly Nixon has thrived. For all the images of Nixon that have come along since, Tricky Dick remains indelible and ubiquitous in American culture. As William F. Buckley, Jr., wrote after Watergate, "The enemies of Richard Nixon have totally succeeded in their mission of making Nixon the most despised figure in America." Nixon, he added, "turned out to be [their] principal accomplice."[5]

Demonic portraits of Nixon proliferated during his presidency, but they took root in American culture as early as the 1950s. The liberals' dark view of Nixon suffused descriptions of even his physical appearance. In the 1940s and early 1950s, Nixon's admirers had described the young politician as fresh-faced, boyish-looking, clean-cut, handsome. But beauty lay with the beholder: Nixon's foes noted only his dour demeanor, as if it provided a window onto his soul. "He had," said Sam Rayburn, the Democratic Speaker of the House in the 1950s, "the meanest face I've ever seen." The thick curls of black hair, the bushy eyebrows, and the five-o'clock shadow enveloped Nixon in an aura of gloom. He scowled and frowned, prematurely creasing his forehead and cheeks. Few profiles of him failed to note his "ski-jump" nose, which poked out, Pinocchio-like. His eyes, beady and dark, darted as he spoke, adding to the air of suspicion; "shifty eyed," Truman called him. The heavy jowls, which grew more pronounced as he aged, made him seem, Kempton wrote, as though "a great wad of unmelting butter [was] stuffed next to his lower jawbone." Liberals just didn't like the looks of him.[6]

The unflattering descriptions of Nixon's appearance only begged the question of what, besides his perpetual stubble, gave rise to this deep animus in the first place. "Why," as *The Reporter's* William Lee Miller asked searchingly, "is there such a widespread distaste for Nixon?"[7] Starting with his advent as a national figure in 1952, liberals expended much thought and energy trying to articulate the answers. At first they resorted to the stand-by categories in which they had placed political enemies before: He was a right-winger, they said, a shill for business, a demagogue, an anti-Semite. But in the course of the Fifties, they honed their analyses, trying to do justice to Nixon's complicated nature.

The new picture was a photographic negative of the conservatives' all-American hero. What Southern Californians saw as fighting spirit, the eggheads saw as below-the-belt viciousness. The patriotic anti-communism admired by conservatives struck liberals as cynical Red-baiting. The everyman stylings were seen as phony populism. Nixon, liberals concluded, was not a right-wing ideologue but an opportunist who exploited the new tools of television, advertising, and public relations to project a false image. He remained popular, they argued, by hoodwinking middle-class voters with these black arts. Nixon posed a threat to democracy itself.

The image of Tricky Dick would haunt Nixon his whole life. Although Fifties liberals were its main creators and proponents, it informed the views of Nixon held by other constituencies as well. It lay at the core of the hatred toward him that made his presidency an ordeal for both Nixon and the country. Without it, perhaps, Nixon might have weathered the crises that forced him in August 1974 to resign.

But the popularity of this image in intellectual circles also revealed the liberals' own prejudices and constraints. In demonizing Nixon for his appeals to the middle class, the liberals acknowledged their own growing distance from, and even scorn for, those Americans like the Texas journalist's parents who saw Nixon as their earnestly striving spokesman. At times the liberals wondered whether Nixon might indeed speak for ordinary citizens, whether they might be the ones who were out of touch.

Their diatribes against Nixon as a manipulator of the masses showed a lack of trust in the people's judgment, a retreat from their once adamantine faith in democracy's health. Propounding this portrait of Tricky Dick marked a step toward an elitist politics that would eventually leave their own reputations damaged, in many people's eyes, almost as much as that of the man they loved to hate.

Nixon came to fame at a moment of uncertainty for liberals. On the one hand, they were enjoying new prestige in a "postindustrial" society that valued intellectual expertise as never before. This sense of security helped them retain faith in American democracy as an authentic, well-functioning system. Rejoicing in the victory over fascism, confident that skilled management of the economy and an active program of social relief and civil rights safeguards could counter capitalism's injustices, they expected the country could finally deliver on its promises of equality and justice. But Truman's Fair Deal fell victim to newly powerful congressional Republicans, the South blocked civil rights legislation, and liberals had to take comfort in preserving what remained of the New Deal. When the Republicans nominated Eisenhower for president in 1952, many liberals resigned themselves to a Republican ascent, realizing that the general's benign demeanor would appeal to Americans content with the postwar equilibrium.[8]

Complicating matters, the Red Scare placed liberals in a bind. They struggled to walk the vanishing line between fighting communism and defending civil liberties. Liberals supported a foreign policy of containing Soviet expansion but also understood that the anti-Communist mania sweeping the country represented anti–New Dealism by other means. Nixon and other politicians were winning headlines—and elections—by charging their liberal opponents with socialist leanings or naïveté in the face of Soviet designs. Amid blacklists and witch-hunts, upholding an inflexible anti-Communist stance was hard to reconcile with a commitment to civil liberties. Liberals tried to make sure that anti-Communist strictures operated within procedural safeguards, and they tried to contrast their own positions with those of Nixon, Joe McCarthy, and the Red-baiters. But in the decade's early years, at least, liberals were clearly losing the fight, as even a moderate position was likely to bring on accusations of being "soft on communism."

The Red Scare's irony was that American capitalism was actually in great shape. Despite early fears, the economy had in fact adjusted to peacetime superbly. Truman's Keynesian policies of fine-tuning the economy kept production high and unemployment low. A GI Bill granted a college education to returning veterans, many of whom took steady jobs with blue-chip corporations. Scientists and engineers perfected new technologies that showered consumers with a cornucopia of goods. In automatic-transmission Chevrolets, along newly paved ribbons of highway, families migrated to prefabricated suburbs, where in their split-level houses they enjoyed the fruits of American ingenuity. Conformity and alienation became the new perils of modern, mass society. In *The Lonely Crowd*, the Harvard sociologist David Riesman contended that Americans in the 1950s were becoming "other-directed," slavishly emulating the behavior and tastes of their peers. In *The Organization Man* (1956), William H. Whyte bemoaned an ethos of managerial harmony and conflict-averse teamwork that was supplanting an earlier era's do-it-yourself entrepreneurialism.

Technology, especially, brought discontents. One of the most popular inventions, the television, also generated a special set of concerns. In 1948, there were 172,000 TV sets in the United States; by 1952, there were 15.3 million, in one third of all homes. Thrilling as entertainment, television united the country as neither radio nor magazines had; a powerful marketing tool, it brought sales pitches for Colgate toothpaste and Campbell's soup into living rooms. But many intellectuals scoffed: TV, they warned, degraded the culture by targeting mass tastes and, through its advertising, nourished the era's materialism. The Democrats' standard-bearer Adlai Stevenson claimed he never watched it and during his 1952 campaign refused to run TV ads because he felt that to hawk candidates like "Ivory Soap versus Palmolive" insulted people's intelligence.

Television, which used staging, lighting, and camera tricks to create illusions, fed concerns about propaganda and manipulation. So too did the developing fields of advertising and public relations, which used market research and psychological tricks to drum up enthusiasm for a company's products. In *The Hidden Persuaders* (1957), a best-seller, the journalist Vance Packard, with the mischievous glee of a magician divulging his secrets, described how ad men used "motivation research" to get people to buy goods whether they wanted them or not. Advertising, already ubiquitous on billboards and buses and in glossy magazines, now also penetrated the political arena. The methods of Leone Baxter and Clem Whitaker, the California politicos who had transformed that state's elections with their statistically sophisticated opinion polls and cutting-edge PR, came to influence national candidates and elections as well.[9]

Liberals developed a deep ambivalence toward the public that readily fell prey to these tricks. In the 1930s, when they were part of a broad left-liberal coalition that supported a program of social change, most liberals professed faith in the people's commonsense judgment. But the horror of Nazism and the Holocaust, and their echoes in the Red Scare, fueled a fear of the mob and a distrust of ordinary people's capacity for rationality in the face of propaganda and demagoguery, especially when they were yoked to technology and the mass media. "The unhappy truth is that the prevailing public opinion has been destructively wrong at the critical junctures," Walter Lippmann wrote. "Mass opinion . . . has shown itself to be a dangerous master of decisions when the stakes are life and death." Having discovered the power of the irrational, intellectuals now saw the populace, in the economist Joseph Schumpeter's phrase, as "an indeterminate bundle of vague impulses playing about given slogans and mistaken impressions." Even more than in politics, liberals set themselves apart from their countrymen in the cultural sphere, where they prized humanistic education, artistic sophistication, and a cosmopolitan outlook. Critics such as Lionel Trilling extolled the virtues of complexity, sophistication, ambiguity; they deplored, with Dwight Macdonald, the "midcult" vulgarization of standards enabled by the mass production of culture. Together, these strains of political and cultural elitism led liberals to believe that America's problems would be best solved if tackled by people like themselves.[10]

Liberals found a hero in Stevenson, the eloquent governor of Illinois and the Democrats' presidential nominee in 1952 and 1956. Stevenson seemed the rare political creature who was above politics, who could elevate the whole messy business to a higher plane. Though he was, on the issues, more conservative than Truman, he struck intellectuals as one of their own—"so charming and cultivated, so witty and so . . . well, *somewhat* weary," the critic Irving Howe provocatively wrote, and so well suited "to represent and speak for them." In their letters, Stevenson's supporters called for a politics of "faith, not fear," for "forward-looking speeches," for someone to tell "the whole truth." The candidate responded with a vision of a refined, upright America in which light and reason would be restored to politics and "freedom . . . made real for all without regard to race or belief or economic condition."[11]

No one posed a greater threat to this vision, in the liberal intellectual view, than the menacing figure of Richard Nixon. In an era when analysts decried the "personalization" of politics, Nixon seemed hateful not just as a politician but as a person. His most obvious failings, liberals felt, were but "surface indications," as August Hecksher wrote, of intrinsic flaws in his character.[12] His hard-hitting and cagey rhetorical style combined with his lack of grace to create a man who seemed false and dishonest to his core. The liberals' Nixon was a mirror image of the conservatives' Nixon: not an authentic hero of the postwar age but a paradigmatically inauthentic man for anomic modern times.

More than other leading Republicans such as Senator Robert Taft or House Speaker Joe Martin, Nixon was perceived as nasty, aggressive, and heedless of normal restraints. What supporters admired as mettle, enemies saw as ruthlessness—a trait that always remained the first count in the liberals' bill of indictment against Nixon. "Certain charges are not made," wrote *The New Republic*'s Richard Strout, in his "TRB" column; "there are unwritten rules in the great game of politics. But the lethal young Nixon does not accept these rules. He is out for the kill and the scalp at any cost." Contrary to later lore, few liberals pointed out Nixon's virulence during his 1946 race against Voorhis, which went mostly unnoticed outside California (although after 1952, liberals retrospectively found in that race proof of Nixon's viciousness).* Nor was the charge heard much during the Hiss case (when, contrary to Nixon's later recollections, many liberals and journalists had sided with him).† Rather it was amid his high-profile 1950 Senate race against Helen Gahagan Douglas that liberals gave Nixon his hostile makeover. The brainy, glamorous Douglas was just the sort of liberal Nixon loved to attack. Reporters covering the campaign relayed tales of Nixon's street fighting that became notorious in liberal circles: not only the "Pink Sheet" that compared her to the Communist congressman Vito Marcantonio, but other dirty tricks as well; flyers appeared, for example, boasting fake endorsements of Douglas from the "Communist League of Negro Women." The Nixon who struck much of California's petit bourgeoisie as a family man and fighting patriot appeared to liberals as a deft master, as *The Nation's* Carey McWilliams wrote, of "petty malice" and "brazen demagoguery." The veteran muckraker Drew Pearson called Nixon's 1950 operation "one of the most skillful and cut-throat campaigns . . . I have ever seen." At the root of this viciousness was Nixon's character, many critics asserted. "He is hard and inflexible," wrote William Costello of the Mutual Broadcast System, Nixon's first critical biographer, "with few of the saving graces of tenderness, humor, generosity toward the fallen."[13]

Even when Nixon muted his vituperative style after 1954, liberals found other traits to despise or scorn: a crippling social awkwardness, a lack of ease and grace, an overweening earnestness. Sometimes these complaints

---

* Voorhis was among the few who castigated Nixon soon after the 1946 race both for what he considered Nixon's distortions of the PAC issue and for advertisements that painted the Democrat as "subversive" and "pro-Russian." Voorhis alleged in 1947 that Nixon's minions had bullied shopkeepers, workers, and newspaper editors into suppressing their support for him. "Merchants were warned that if they dared to sign newspaper statements in my support, as they had done in previous campaigns, their line of credit would be cut off at the bank. One large banking institution sent the word 'down the line' that its employees were not to vote for Jerry Voorhis." The sole editor in the district who had previously supported him, Voorhis added, "was informed the next morning by his landlord that he had read the editorial and the editor would have to 'get out.' " Yet for all the alleged foul play, Voorhis said he bore no grudge against Nixon. He wrote Nixon a friendly note afterward, and the two met and "parted . . . as personal friends."

† Typifying the liberal attitude, William V. Shannon wrote of Nixon in 1955: "The prestige of his participation in the unmasking of Alger Hiss for example is untarnished and not in dispute, but he cannot live on that forever." Nixon scarcely appears in books about the Hiss case written before he became vice president.

seemed like little more than intellectual snobbery. In the *New York Post*, William Shannon wrote that Nixon lacked "skepticism, detachment, humor, irony, tolerance—qualities generally considered hallmarks of a civilized mind." Richard Rovere said he had "no gift for bonhomie." Seeing Nixon at a party, Stewart Alsop's wife, Patricia, compared him to a high school hall monitor, "wooden and stiff . . . terribly difficult to talk to," and "a terrible dancer" to boot. These descriptions made Nixon sound like an unappealing guest but hardly a menace to the republic. Indeed, a *New Republic* reader complained that the magazine's attacks on Nixon "smack of personal prejudice or snobbism," adding: "We may not like his ungentlemanly tactics, nor his shallow-seeming background. He is not the sort of man one would care to ask for dinner. But we have nothing that adds up to a real case."[14]

Yet beneath the hauteur, liberals did have a legitimate and complicated critique of Nixon's style. Nixon's strained efforts to appear reasonable, they felt, were not just coarse but baleful. His studied air of thoughtfulness may have played in the Rotary clubs, but to media-wise liberals it was condescending and insulting and cheapened political debate. Then, too, his innate uptightness, worse than a social failing, indicated an underlying deceptiveness; whenever he tried to project casualness or candor, he seemed only to be donning a false front. "It is the style of Nixon," wrote Evelyn Houston, "or to be more painfully exact, the lack of one—that pervasive and alchemic falsity . . . a veritable Midas touch for making ersatz of the real—that has made many of us wince."[15]

When Nixon told a reporter that "a good off-the-cuff informal speech takes more preparation than a speech you read" or otherwise admitted that he worked at molding his public profile, liberals seized on the remarks as proof that his common-man portrait was a facade. Arthur Schlesinger Jr. mocked the spate of stories in which Nixon claimed he liked hamburger or didn't like champagne—clumsy bids to make himself seem average; he joked about one newspaper headline that read: "Nixon's Aim: To Portray Himself as a Regular Guy." To liberals, Nixon's image crafting always backfired: the spontaneity invariably seemed planned, the naturalness artificial. If sincerity is everything, and being able to fake it means you've got it made, then Nixon's problem was that he couldn't.[16]

To liberals, Nixon wasn't just unrefined. He was deliberately, dangerously deceptive. "Since nothing about him is spontaneous," wrote Murray Kempton, "it is somehow impossible to forgive him that smallest transgression, because he knows exactly what he is doing." Behind his mask of fair-mindedness, liberals saw a deft practitioner of "innuendo, half-truths, and downright distortion"—even, some claimed, alluding to the Nazi propagandists, "the Big Lie." Nixon could dodge a question expertly and level accusations so carefully that he could later deny that he had spoken ill of anyone. In 1952, for instance, he labeled Truman, Dean Acheson, and Adlai Stevenson "traitors to the high principles in which many of the nation's Democrats believe"—and then innocently insisted he could not understand the outcry since he had never charged anyone with treason.[17]

Cataloguing and exposing these ruses with Aristotelian precision became a favorite liberal pastime. The best minds of their generation devoted their analytical prowess to explaining, in an endless procession of articles throughout the 1950s, the maddening success of Nixon's political and rhetorical style. In one of the more famous of these efforts, Meg Greenfield parsed "The Prose of Richard M. Nixon" in *The Reporter*, identifying such devices as "The Straw Men," "The Slippery Would-Have-Been," and "The Short Bridge from (a) to (b)" (professing, in a single sentence, to believe both a statement and its opposite).[18] These exegeses sought to prove, if only to the converted, that Nixon was fooling the public with his sly rhetoric and self-presentations. And while liberals howled when he did it, they congratulated themselves when they caught him, suggesting their own sense of superiority to the public they believed was so easily fooled.

None of Nixon's critics had articulated such a fine analysis when he mounted the podium in Chicago in July 1952 to accept his party's nomination as vice president. The Hiss case and Douglas race notwithstanding, on a national level Nixon's image remained relatively uncontested. The press praised his selection as likely to help Eisenhower's already good chances, and even the liberals at first said little. They too were still getting to know him. "Who Is Richard Nixon?" was the headline of pieces in *The Reporter* and *The New Republic*. A profile in *The Progressive* had hardly a mean word for Nixon; it dispassionately described his "routine Republican voting record" and depicted "the clean-cut, flashing-eyed, dark-haired Nixon" in language reminiscent of the flattering profiles of the *Saturday Evening Post*.[19]

For those nursing grudges from the 1950 Senate race, however, Nixon fast became a lightning rod. Lacking a deep familiarity with this relative newcomer to the scene—Nixon was all of thirty-nine—they drew reflexively on familiar types that they associated with their worst enemies: right-wing thug, demagogue, bigot, crook. Eventually, liberals formed more complicated pictures of Nixon, but these stock personae provided a starting point.

What liberals knew best about Nixon was his strident anti-communism and his hardball campaigning. Accordingly, they lumped him with such angry ultraconservative Senate colleagues as John Bricker, William Jenner, Kenneth Wherry, and Joe McCarthy. These Old Guard stalwarts, unreconciled to the New Deal even into the 1950s, were known for their unceasing crusade against all federal programs. Liberals, scrambling to size up Nixon's brief career in July 1952, latched onto how neatly his record matched his right-wing peers': votes to cut income taxes, to enact the anti-labor Taft-Hartley Act, to reduce public housing, to block the expansion of Social Security. What Nixon's conservative boosters saw as devotion to capitalist principles struck liberals as the sort of reactionary thinking the nation had supposedly left behind with Herbert Hoover. The pugilistic rhetoric and tactics that Nixon used against Douglas also reminded liberals of the Old Guard's intemperate language and Red-baiting. A Stevenson campaign poster portrayed Nixon as part of a cabal of right-wing extremists. The sketch, entitled "Watch out for the Man on a White Horse!", showed a clueless Eisenhower atop a Trojan horse, while McCarthy, Jenner, and Taft scurried inside the belly and Nixon grabbed the reins.[20]

A second image styled Nixon an old school anti-Semite in the manner of Gerald L. K. Smith, Huey Long's more intemperate associate, or Father Charles Coughlin, the demagogic radio broadcaster.* Fifties liberals,

---

* Decades later, the image of Nixon as an anti-Semite would reappear after the release of some of his White House tapes. As the National Archives released tapes and White House memos over the years, evidence of Nixon's anti-Jewish slurs and actions mounted. In one case, Nixon ordered his aide Fred Malek literally to count the Jews who were employed by the Bureau of Labor Statistics, which he believed was rigging unemployment data to make him look bad. The news of the count forced Malek to resign his position in George Bush's 1988 presidential campaign. In other contexts, Nixon made comments that were indisputably anti-Semitic.

many of whom were Jewish, remembered the far right's unvarnished anti-Semitism of the 1930s—attacks on the "Jew Deal," delusions that Jewish bankers caused the depression—and were sensitive to undercurrents of Jew hatred in the McCarthy movement. When Nixon emerged as a national figure, they began hearing troubling stories from his past campaigns. During Nixon's race against Douglas, for example, the Louisiana rabble-rouser Gerald Smith had caused a furor by asking voters to "help Richard Nixon get rid of the Jew-Communists." Although Nixon repudiated Smith's support, suspicions lingered. Later in the race, anonymous operatives reminded California voters through phone calls and advertisements that Helen Douglas's husband, the actor Melvyn Douglas, was Jewish and had been born with the conspicuously Semitic last name Hesselberg. Occasionally, some claimed, Nixon himself would "slip" during a stump speech and call his rival "Helen Hesselberg," only to hastily "correct" himself.[21]

Days after Nixon's nomination as vice president in 1952, these stories resurfaced. Murray Chotiner, who had been advising Nixon since 1946 and served as his campaign manager in 1950 (and who was himself Jewish), moved to stanch the damage. He drew up a public relations strategy, which he sent to Mendel Silberberg, Nixon's liaison to Hollywood. But the story persisted. During August and September, inquiries flooded the Anti-Defamation League (ADL), Jewish newspapers, and the campaign. In October, Baltimore's leading African-American newspaper reported that in July 1951 Nixon had bought a home whose deed contained a restricted covenant barring its resale or rental to "any person of the Semitic race, blood, or origin," defining Semitic as including "Armenians, Jews, Hebrews, Persians and Syrians." Panicky, Chotiner stepped up his response. He recruited the ADL to vouch for Nixon's tolerance and fed to the Jewish press a list of occasions when Nixon had aided various Jewish causes. The staff even drafted memos arguing that since the Supreme Court's 1948 ruling *Shelley v. Kraemer*, covenants were unconstitutional and inoperative and thus did not reflect on Nixon in any way. Nixon himself got involved in the replies. "I want to thank you for . . . your courtesy in calling my attention to the false rumor that I am anti-Semetic [sic]," he wrote to Edgar L. Strauss of Los Angeles, among other voters. "We have received a number or inquiries regarding this unfounded rumor."[22]

Whether due to Chotiner's damage control or simply a paucity of evidence, the Jew-hating image failed to gain fatal traction. But despite the assurances of the ADL, individual Jews kept watch. Nixon's old ally McIntyre Faries informed Chotiner that the owner of the Los Angeles eatery Sternberger's had switched his vote from Eisenhower to Stevenson when he heard about Nixon's covenant, a decision that was surely replicated in Jewish homes elsewhere. And the story evinced more staying power than its light coverage would suggest: In his 1956, 1960, and 1962 campaigns, Nixon had to squelch "whispering campaigns," rebut criticisms in Jewish papers, and field constant queries to his office. During the 1960 race, Raymond Moley, the former Democrat turned Nixon booster, felt it necessary to deny the anti-Semitism charges in his *Newsweek* column.* For Fifties liberals concerned about anti-Semitism, the steady trickle of allegations, however thin, deepened their suspicion and hatred of Nixon.[23]

Yet another dark image of Nixon also drew on old-time liberal demonology: Nixon as a corrupt stooge of big business. In the 1950s, political scandal usually meant graft, the exchange of favors, or lining one's pockets for political gain; until Watergate, the Harding administration's Teapot Dome fiasco loomed as the benchmark for scandal. In the fall of 1952, liberal journalists scoured Nixon's career for traces of financial misdoing. Early profiles in *The New Republic* and *The Reporter* raised questions about the role of the underworld figure Henry Grunewald in delivering Nixon a $5,000 donation in 1950. They noted, too, that the Nixon campaign's official expenditures that year came in suspiciously low for such a high-profile race, and alleged that shadowy corporate interests had secretly made up the difference. Meanwhile, Truman's Justice Department pursued a story that back in 1945, while a navy lawyer, Nixon had shaken down a client for a loan. The Democratic National Committee charged that the Nixon family held a quarter of a million dollars' worth of ill-gotten real estate.[24]

The most dogged investigator of Nixon's dealings was the seventy-two-year-old columnist Drew Pearson, an enemy since the Douglas race.

---

* In the 1960 campaign, press secretary Herb Klein compiled a list of "Celebrities for Nixon-Lodge" on which he underlined the names of Jewish stars Ray Bolger and Jerry Lewis in red pencil. Next to the name Efrem Zimbalist he placed a question mark.

An old-style fedora-wearing gumshoe, Pearson earned his stars exposing financial shenanigans of the powerful. He commanded a wide following, both in his popular syndicated column, "Washington Merry-Go-Round," and on his weekly radio broadcasts. In the 1952 campaign, Pearson and his assistant Jack Anderson (who later took over the column) unearthed a slew of thinly substantiated reports about Nixon's shady transactions, which they fired at Nixon like grapeshot. The accusations came one after the next: that Nixon had interceded with the Justice Department to secure a tax break for Pasadena attorney Dana Smith, the keeper of Nixon's expense fund; that he had rescued Smith from gambling debts incurred at a Havana nightclub; that he had helped Nicola Malaxa, a disreputable Romanian industrialist, gain entrance to the United States to undertake business ventures with Nixon's old law partner; that Nixon took bribes from oil moguls; that he falsified his property value to get a tax break; that he illegally hired a Swedish maid. Nixon grew enraged, unable to keep pace with the accusations, frantically firing off denials and demanding retractions. Again, no hard proof of corruption emerged to tarnish Nixon irreparably, and by election day Pearson's once powerful cannonades faded into background noise. But although Nixon didn't go the way of Harding's Teapot Dome cronies, an air of venality hovered around him, casting suspicion on his every move thereafter.[25]

Corruption did not turn out to be the defining piece of the Nixon-haters' portrait of their foe. But the probes of Nixon's finances in the fall of 1952 did produce the outstanding moment of his early career: the Checkers speech. The address not only crystallized the conservatives' image of Nixon as an all-American hero but proved seminal for liberals as well. Their reaction, indeed, established the outlines of the picture of Nixon that they would flesh out in the years ahead, as they transformed Nixon from another corrupt, business-friendly right-winger into a uniquely sinister operator of the machinery of modern politics.

Drew Pearson, among others, had heard whispers over the summer about the expense fund that Nixon's California backers had created to cover personal expenses. When word leaked that Pearson was snooping around, Jack Anderson recalled, Nixon enlisted William Rogers, a mutual friend of his and Pearson's (and later a member of the Eisenhower and Nixon cabinets) to help. Rogers told Anderson, the reporter wrote, that if they published the story, Nixon would brand Pearson a Communist spy. Undaunted, Pearson disclosed Nixon's intimidation tactics on TV and resolved to probe deeper. In the end, however, it was not Pearson but the *New York Post*, the newspaper run by James Wechsler and Dorothy Schiff and beloved of liberal intellectuals, that broke the story on September 18, blaring news of the "Secret Rich Men's Trust Fund" across its front page.[26]

This story marked the real start of Nixon's troubles. The day after the *Post* story appeared, Nixon was delivering a speech from his campaign train in Marysville, California. A carload of Young Democrats, recruited by Adlai Stevenson's California campaign manager, hurried to the depot to meet him, and arrived just as the train was pulling away for the next town on the whistle-stop tour. "Tell 'em about the $16,000," one heckler jeered.* Stopping the train, Nixon launched into an angry retort from the outdoor platform. He blamed "communists and crooks" for spreading the story and warned the agitators to relent. But the next day in Eugene, Oregon, Charles Porter, a member of Americans for Democratic Action and a local Democratic Party activist, rounded up a group of University of Oregon students for another protest, replete with signs and banners. "Shh! Anyone who mentions $16,000 is a Communist!" one said. "Will the Veep's salary be enough, Dick?" asked another. That evening, in Portland, it got even nastier. A crowd—"the ugliest we had met so far," Nixon recalled—staked out Nixon's hotel, dressed up as blind beggars, sporting dark glasses, rattling their tin cups and mocking: "Nickels for poor Nixon." They threw pennies into Nixon's car and blockaded the hotel's front door, bumping up against Nixon and Pat as they elbowed their way past. Within days, calls arose for Nixon to resign from the ticket, from liberal Republicans and pro-Eisenhower papers as well as Democratic regulars.[27]

Leading the charge were the liberals in the news media, who at first

---

* The *Post* initially reported the sum as $16,000. The expense fund actually contained $18,235.

sounded a good-government cry against corruption. "The man who the people of the sovereign state of California believed was actually representing them," thundered the *Sacramento Bee*, "is the pet and protégé of rich Southern Californians. . . . Nixon is their subsidized front man, if not, indeed, their lobbyist." On the stump, Nixon had been decrying scandal in the Truman administration, but now, as *Newsweek* wrote, the fund imbroglio "cast a shadow on his crusade." Liberals attacked his hypocrisy. "Nixon is a kept man," *The New Republic* huffed. "He is also a phoney."[28]

Had Nixon not then proceeded to deliver the Checkers speech, Eisenhower probably would have dropped him from the ticket. He also might have remained, in liberals' eyes, just another crooked politician. Instead, the speech, with its common-man touches, did more than just revive Nixon's fortunes; it became a rallying point for anti-Nixon sentiment, a touchstone for a new image more complicated than the stock figures that liberals had previously batted around.

Liberals recoiled at the speech. Nixon, they said, dodged key questions about the fund. He had failed to persuade them that he wasn't on the take from his "millionaire's club." He was self-righteously defensive, speaking in what Stewart Alsop later called a "high moral tone, [with an] air of injured innocence."[29] And they cried foul at Nixon's attempt to paint himself as an average American. Just a week earlier reporters were admiring "the Horatio Alger tradition of Richard Nixon's rise," noted *The New Republic*. "Now the bubble has burst." The speech, they said, had made clear that the reputation was bogus. "In describing his personal financial history Nixon offered the impression that [his] family is just barely remaining afloat," the *New York Post* editorialized, ". . . but we do not detect any desperate impoverishment in a man who has bought two homes, even if his Oldsmobile is two years old." Sarcastic references to "Poor Richard" abounded.[30]

Worst of all, the populist persona was doused in sentimentality, which liberals felt was cheap, mass-produced, and false. At a time before politicians routinely used their family members as props, liberals faulted Nixon for showcasing his wife and trumpeting details of his personal life in the service of his ambition—a habit of "cultivating irrelevant emotions," as Arthur Schlesinger, Jr., later wrote, that "corrupts the political dialogue." (George Washington, Schlesinger sniffed, did not go around saying,

"Martha and I . . .") Liberals had to concede, of course, that the emotionalism worked. "On the level of political soap opera, there can be no question of the effectiveness of the Nixon performance," the *New York Post*'s Max Lerner wrote. ". . . The pretty and adoring wife, the mortgages on the houses, the saga of a poor boy who became Senator—these were sure-fire stuff." But Lerner professed faith that people would be able to "strip away the phony from the real."[31]

Finally, the medium—television—was part of the message, and liberals distrusted it, too. In 1952, TV was still a novelty; that year's election was the first in which it played a large role. It was also still something of a bugbear, a repository for fears about the technological future. Although the trappings of the medium remained crude, Nixon's televised appeal made them wary. Even the primitive stage set and effects he used—the Los Angeles studio he spoke from was amateurishly decked out to resemble a suburban den, with draperies and a bookcase that barely disguised the soundstage—struck liberals as dangerously deceitful gimmickry, as state-of-the-art technology that might insidiously influence viewers. "What Nixon owed the American people was a straightforward answer to the question of ethical wrongdoing," Max Lerner wrote. "What he gave them instead was a slick and glossy job of television art."[32]

Most of the public disagreed. Millions praised the speech as, of all things, sincere. Eventually, the outpouring of support for Nixon and Eisenhower's embrace of his running mate would force liberals to confront their own position as a minority. But at first, reluctant to blame their compatriots for accepting Nixon's everyman portrait, liberals faulted the high-tech staging, the power of television, even "the genius of American advertising agencies," as *The New York Times* reported. A dejected Max Lerner struggled to account for the raves Nixon received. "Ask yourself whether you are fool enough to fall for one of the slickest and sleaziest fake emotion routines that ever gulled a sentimental people," he challenged his readers. ". . . In its earlier phase, it [the scandal] pointed up the hypocrisy of public officials who preach morality and practice the double take. But the lesson of the Nixon case now is how a cynical group of men, using money and the new communication arts and the tried and true techniques of the propaganda masters, can stand an issue of morality on its head and make the faker appear the martyr." Despair gripped the liberal camp. Faced with masters like Nixon, they privately wondered if the public could be brought around to support a progressive agenda again.[33]

Publicly at least, most intellectuals reaffirmed their faith in democracy, and some dimly perceived the elitism implicit in their critique of the Checkers address. "On many occasions during the last few days," the *New York Post* editorialized, "we have heard the same remark from a lot of journalists, scholars and gentlemen: '*I* know the Nixon speech was strictly soap opera, but you can't expect the ordinary guy to see through it.'" Such self-congratulation troubled the *Post's* editors. It suggested that the distance between them and their former New Deal allies was widening. While acknowledging the alarming popularity of "demagogues" such as McCarthy, the *Post* nonetheless wishfully affirmed that "most of the people"—they did not say where they got their statistics—"know the difference between a slick press agent's mind and a responsive human heart."[34]

The reaction to the Checkers speech—and the reaction to the reaction—held the seeds of a dilemma that would flower later in the 1950s. Still frightened by the European experience with fascism, by the Continental masses' susceptibility to irrational racist appeals, liberals questioned their own compatriots' essential goodness. Americans too, they saw, accepted crude stereotypes, bought into personalized pitches, showed impatience with complex problems. But the liberals stopped short of writing off the middle class; the hand-wringing over Checkers previewed, but hardly resolved, an ongoing conundrum about whether "most of the people" would succumb to emotional appeals and high-tech trickery. Indeed, the liberal predicament only worsened in the ensuing years. As Eisenhower and Nixon's election victory in November showed, and their reelection in 1956 confirmed, liberal ideals no longer commanded support from a majority of Americans as they had under FDR. Shielding themselves from such an admission, liberals found it easier to chalk up the masses' defection to the villainous powers and artful deceptions of Richard Nixon.

"I have spent God knows how many unproductive hours asking myself if I was really put on this earth to write about the likes of Richard Nixon and

Joe McCarthy," reflected Richard Rovere late in his career. Rovere grouped the two men together as "transparent demagogues and frauds," and like many of his peers believed that Nixon's villainy was best exhibited in the Red-baiting that he fomented alongside McCarthy. Like the headstrong Wisconsin senator, Nixon struck liberals as a vicious smear artist, and his anti-Communist drumming would long be remembered as McCarthyism's backbeat. Yet unlike Rovere, many liberals drew sharp distinctions between the two men, contrasting McCarthy's tail-gunner nihilism with Nixon's stiletto attacks. Not just a comrade but also a foil to Nixon, McCarthy made Nixon seem less like a crude reactionary than a frighteningly deft operator.[35]

Many casual observers, it was true, viewed Nixon and McCarthy as partners in grime, mud-slinging bullies who magnified the Communist threat for partisan gain. Friends and colleagues, both arrived in Congress in 1947—McCarthy in the Senate, Nixon in the House—and won renown for their full-throated attacks on Communists in government and their effete sympathizers. Where Nixon trained his fire on Hiss, Douglas, and Stevenson, the darlings of the intellectuals, McCarthy targeted, more idiosyncratically (if not randomly), policy hand Owen Lattimore, Senator Millard Tydings, and General George Marshall. And where McCarthy bounded to notoriety with sensational charges that garnered banner headlines starting in 1950, Nixon had paved the way. Whether or not one agreed with Drew Pearson and Jack Anderson, who contended that Nixon's use of "guilt by association" in the Voorhis campaign was "the real birth of McCarthyism," it is true (as the historian Fawn Brodie later discovered) that McCarthy's famous Wheeling, West Virginia, speech, which launched him into the headlines, drew heavily from—even plagiarized from—the speech Nixon had given weeks earlier on the House floor about Alger Hiss's conviction. Nixon continued to share McCarthy's rhetoric into the 1952 campaign, mixing fears of communism with suspicion of the eggheads. He branded Stevenson "Adlai the Appeaser . . . who got a PhD from Dean Acheson's College of Cowardly Communist Containment."[36]

Despite superficial resemblances, however, Nixon and McCarthy had their differences. After the Republicans won the White House in November, McCarthy's nightmare scenarios about the enemy within began to harm his own party. Eisenhower, on cool terms with the senator, tasked Nixon with controlling his renegade friend. Gingerly, Nixon tried to dissuade McCarthy from targeting the new administration, but despite repeated promises McCarthy wouldn't cooperate. By March 1954, McCarthy was blasting the U.S. Army for promoting a dentist who had refused to sign a loyalty oath, and his allies feared he was going to bring down the whole party. Sensing a moment to strike, Adlai Stevenson, priming himself for another White House bid, assailed the GOP in a Lincoln Day speech as "divided against itself, half Eisenhower, half McCarthy."[37]

With the president skittish, it fell to Nixon to deliver a televised response. His address, aired on NBC and CBS, marked his biggest public moment since Checkers. Studiously omitting McCarthy's name, Nixon condemned those who despite their "effective work exposing communists" now by their "reckless talk" and "questionable methods" jeopardized the anti-Communist project. Slamming previous (Democratic) administrations—and taking another potshot at former Secretary of State Dean Acheson: Nixon concluded in his familiar tone of exaggerated thoughtfulness: "I have heard people say, 'Well, why all of this hullabaloo about being fair when you're dealing with a gang of traitors? . . . After all, they're a bunch of rats.' . . . Well, I agree they're a bunch of rats, but just remember this. When you go out to shoot rats, you have to shoot straight, because when you shoot wildly, it not only means that the rat may get away more easily, you make it easier on the rat."[38]

Afterward, the press construed Nixon's speech, with its painfully extended metaphor, as a break with McCarthy. The senator considered it a betrayal. Again, the liberals saw it differently. By continuing to skewer the Democrats, the *New York Post* wrote, "Nixon proceeded again to practice the thing he had denounced . . . undocumented and unsupported hearsay and innuendo." In fact, said Arthur Schlesinger and James Doyle on behalf of ADA, Nixon "embraced McCarthyism as the Republican Party's major political program." They agreed that the vice president's rhetorical style hadn't matured since Checkers. *The Washington Post* called the speech "melodramatic," and Max Lerner derided its "homey phony touches [and] its too slick sophisms."[39]

A few months later, McCarthy self-destructed as a result of his assault on the army and slid swiftly into disrepute. But Nixon, touring the country on behalf of Republican congressional candidates, seemed to be picking up the mantle McCarthy had just put down. He accused the Democratic Party of being beholden to its left wing and dangerously soft on communism. Privately backed by Eisenhower, cheered on by top Republicans, Nixon recounted breathlessly that on entering the White House in 1953, "we found in the files a blueprint for socializing America," and tossed barbs at Acheson and Truman, as well as Stevenson, whom he accused of "spreading pro-Communist propaganda as he has attacked with violent fury the economic system of the United States and praised the Soviet economy." Stevenson, who was doing his own stumping in the fall of 1954, quipped that the vice president was embarking on an "ill-will tour."[40]

A variety of Nixon-haters responded, not just in word but in image. Walt Kelly, the cartoonist who drew the strip *Pogo*, introduced a character named "Indian Charlie," modeled after Nixon, to be an ally of his McCarthyesque bobcat Simple J. Malarkey. Victor Arnautoff, a Stanford art professor, painted a work called *Dick McSmear* that was accepted in the 1955 San Francisco Art Festival but then ordered removed. Yet without question no one captured—or defined—the image of Nixon as McCarthy's successor better than the cartoonist Herbert Block (known as Herblock) of *The Washington Post*.[41]

Herblock had joined the *Post* in 1945, and by the decade's end was syndicated in more than 250 papers. He drew such memorable Nixon images that the two men's names would forever be linked. The consumer activist Ralph Nader, recalling the cartoons of his youth, once said, "I can't think of Nixon without thinking of Herblock," and many of his generation concurred. Zeroing in on a few key features—the five-o'clock shadow, the scowl, the pointy nose—Herblock captured Nixon exactly as the liberals saw him: mud-slinging, opportunistic, and ugly. In 1952, he had drawn a muck-splattered McCarthy and Nixon side by side, having just defaced an Adlai Stevenson poster, as a smiling Eisenhower gently chided: "Naughty, naughty." Now, two years later, the cartoonist drew a fallen McCarthy, his trademark bucket of tar toppled over, passing his black brush to Nixon, who raced to finish the smear job. Nixon's campaign travels—to ninety-five cities that fall—further inspired the cartoonist's acid wit. "While Nixon went from city to city and state to state smearing reputable and responsible legislators," Herblock wrote, "it occurred to me that he was figuratively criss-crossing the country by sewer." On October 29, the cartoonist sketched his most stinging Nixon yet: a drawing of the vice president clambering out of a manhole, his suitcase stamped with a dozen airport stickers, while a local booster shouted to a welcoming party: "Here he comes now!" No image better caught what Democratic Party chairman Stephen Mitchell was calling the vice president's "gutter campaign." The drawing scarred Nixon: He promptly canceled his subscription to the *Post*, and six years later, when he was asked why he wasn't attacking his presidential rival John Kennedy with his usual gusto, the candidate remarked, "I have to erase the Herblock image first."[42]

There was an element of the thug in this rendering of Nixon, but the liberals recognized, too, that the cunning Nixon was more refined than the barroom-brawling McCarthy. As the liberals saw it, McCarthy barged through the corridors of power hurling outlandish slurs; Nixon carefully deployed his rhetorical techniques—the "innuendo," "guilt by association," and similar methods that they detailed in their analyses—against choice targets. "McCarthyism in a white collar," Stevenson labeled him. Irving Howe caught the contrast when he wrote about Nixon's so-called break with McCarthy. "Nixon never ventured . . . a moral judgment of McCarthyism," Howe wrote. "His only complaint, and how revealing it is of his small-minded shrewdness, was that Joe was 'inept.' And by comparison, Joe was." It was Nixon's use of specific techniques, not just anti-Communist bombast—a sinister sophistication, not a double-barreled crudeness—that liberals said made him dangerous.[43]

McCarthy's demise left Eisenhower's number two as the liberals' enemy number one. As the president remained popular with the 1956 elections approaching, Nixon stood out all the more as a favorite whipping boy. For the first time in history, a vice president became a central target in the opposing party's campaign for the White House.

If his differences with McCarthy accented Nixon's deadly sophistication, the contrast with Eisenhower underscored his anything-to-win unscrupulousness. (Irving Howe called Nixon "a well-oiled drawbridge between McCarthyite barbarism and Eisenhower respectability.") Although intellectuals mocked Eisenhower as a dullard who read cowboy novels and lazed on the golf course, he commanded reverence as Europe's liberator. Not so Nixon. "Mr. Nixon is cynical," wrote August Hecksher, "whereas Mr. Eisenhower has been singularly pure and disinterested in motive." "Eisenhower unites the country and heals its divisions," echoed Walter Lippmann, while Nixon "divides and embitters." The president's sunny congeniality made Nixon's dark combativeness all the more unpalatable.[44]

Protective of his avuncular image, Eisenhower assigned Nixon his dirty work, whether reining in McCarthy or playing hatchet man in the '52 and '54 campaigns. The roles elevated Nixon's public profile, if not always for the better. Nixon also played a more substantive role in the administration than any vice president before him, helping to make him, pollster Louis Harris found, "a focal point of expressed concern."[45] When Eisenhower suffered a heart attack in September 1955 and a bout of intestinal disease nine months later, the succession question became no mere parlor game. Journalists ran articles asking, "Would he be a good president?" as *Life*'s Robert Coughlan put it, presenting the pros and cons with predictable even-handedness.[46] The preferred adjective for Nixon was "controversial"; like the celebrity well known for his well-knownness, Nixon at times seemed controversial because of his controversiality.

Republicans as well as Democrats saw how Nixon polarized Americans, and one GOP cadre, led by Harold Stassen of Minnesota, lobbied Ike to "Dump Nixon" from the ticket in 1956. First behind the scenes, then at the Republican Convention, administration insiders and party chiefs jockeyed for Nixon's dismissal, while loyalists sported pins saying, "Stick with Dick." In airing their worries about Nixon, Republicans handed their opponents an irresistible issue. Nixon's foes made his status as "the nation's life insurance policy," in the words of TRB, a focus of their 1956 campaign.[47]

Liberals cast the 1956 election as a referendum on Nixon. At *The New York Times*, John Oakes, the editorial-page editor, sent publisher Arthur Sulzberger a ten-page report called "The Case Against Richard Nixon."

The *Times* was more of an establishment paper than its liberal rival, the *Post*. It had backed Eisenhower in 1952. But the liberal Oakes hoped to sway Sulzberger not to repeat the error, and he thought Nixon's voting pattern, unsavory political style, and checkered past were the key. Portraying Nixon as a cutthroat opportunist whose "eye is on the main chance, irrespective of principle," Oakes pleaded with Sulzberger to endorse Stevenson. Ultimately, however, the paper endorsed Ike again, albeit unenthusiastically.[48]

More public in its anti-Nixon campaign was Americans for Democratic Action. In November 1955, ADA chairman Joseph Rauh declared, perhaps in a fit of wishful thinking, that Nixon's noxiousness would prompt independents and moderates to vote Democratic. His group compiled a scalding booklet called *Nixon: The Second Man*, which it released in July as the campaign geared up. Noting Eisenhower's frail health, the pamphlet spoke of "deep anxieties as to Mr. Nixon's fitness to succeed him," and recounted the litany of Nixon's transgressions, from the Voorhis campaign through his over-the-top rhetoric of 1954. Reliable Nixon-hating organs advertised the brochure. Getting ahold of Nixon's itinerary, ADA political secretary Violet Gunther wrote to members in towns from St. Petersburg and Louisville to Phoenix and Spokane, inviting them to buy copies to distribute when Nixon came to town. Nixon-haters across the country signed up. "We will be ready and waiting for our 'illustrious' visitor Nixon," responded Franklin A. Moss of the New Jersey ADA as he ordered 150 pamphlets. One ADA member wrote a song called "The Ballad of Richard Nixon," which he performed at the group's annual Roosevelt Day Dinner, prompting an investigation by Nixon's office for possible Communist sympathies. (Also investigated was "some fellow named Jack Purcell," who, Republican Party aide and Nixon loyalist Robert Humphreys was told, "turns up at the Press Club to play Commyish songs which are diatribes against the Vice President.")[49]

The Democratic Party followed ADA's lead. "Everyone, we believe, is in agreement that the possibility of Vice President Nixon succeeding to the Presidency is an important issue in the 1956 campaign," the party's advertising agency, Norman, Craig & Kummel, set out in a memo. ". . . We are fortunate in the fact that an amazingly large segment of the population, and even of his own party, seems to dislike and mistrust him instinctively. . . . It is best to start with the assumption that Nixon as President of the United States is an extremely distasteful idea to millions of Americans . . . without wasting valuable time in establishing his undesirability." The Democrats compiled a dossier on Nixon's transgressions and set up a "Chamber of Smears" showcasing Nixon's dark side. At the party's presidential convention in Chicago, speakers spit out Nixon's name like an epithet. "From the first bang of the gavel until the final balloon fell to earth," *Newsweek* reported, "Nixon was the target, skewered as 'the vice hatchet man,' 'the White House pet midget,' a traveler of 'the low road.'" A *New Republic* cover by illustrator Robert Osborn depicted a huge, smiling Eisenhower effigy with Nixon lurking behind it, pulling the strings. Accepting that people "liked Ike," grammatically fastidious advertisements in *The New York Times* warned that "No matter whom you like, the Republican Party is firmly controlled by the young and ambitious Richard Nixon." Brochures mailed by New York City Democrats predicted disaster "if Fate promoted Nixon to the White House." "Nixon" and "Ike's health" climbed to the top of *Newsweek* readers' election-year concerns.[50]

Stevenson, who had sparred with Nixon during the 1954 midterm races, now placed the vice president at the center of a broad critique of America in the 1950s. Taking heart from his party's off-year gains, he told a New York audience in April 1956 that "the 1954 rejection of the Vice-President's campaign appeal about communists in government, the election of a Democratic Congress, and the censure [of McCarthy] . . . marked the turning of the tide against the high point of the flood of hate, hysteria and fear." He painted a tableau of a "New America" of decency, respect, and neighborliness. Then, as the campaign heated up, he gave a special assignment to his adviser John Kenneth Galbraith, the Harvard economist. "Ken," Stevenson told Galbraith, "I want you to write the speeches against Nixon. You have no tendency to be fair." Accepting the "notable compliment," Galbraith wrote a brutally hard-hitting diatribe that Stevenson delivered in Los Angeles on October 27, late in the campaign. The election ahead, it said, marked "a fork in the political road." One path led to a bright future, the other to "a land of slander and scare; the land of sly innuendo, the poison pen, the anonymous phone call and hustling, pushing, shoving; the land of smash and grab and anything to win." This land, Stevenson asserted, "is Nixonland. But I say to you this is not America." Stevenson had also by 1956 accepted the need for television ads. The Democrats aired a spot that showed a sketch of Nixon dwarfed by a presidential chair as a voice-over asked, "Nervous about Nixon? President Nixon?" Another planned commercial spoofed the show *This Is Your Life*, dredging up people from Nixon's past to deliver scathing testimonials. But Stevenson, fearing that it signaled desperation, scuttled the ad.[51]

Most controversially, Stevenson linked Nixon's untrustworthiness to rising fears of nuclear war. In November 1955, the Soviet Union had exploded its first hydrogen bomb, and by the following fall Stevenson was warning of a debilitating arms race. Max Lerner tied the issue to Eisenhower's health and Nixon's character: another heart attack and it would be Nixon's finger on the button. Stevenson followed, tying Nixon, the H-bomb, and Ike's heart condition together into what Lerner called the "triple issue." In a nationally televised speech on the eve of the 1956 vote, he broached the "distasteful" likelihood that Eisenhower wouldn't finish his term and called Nixon's probable ascension "the central truth about . . . [tomorrow's] most fateful decision." Stevenson put it bluntly: "As a citizen more than a candidate . . . I recoil at the prospect of Mr. Nixon as custodian of this nation's future, as guardian of the hydrogen bomb, as representative of America in the world, as Commander-in-Chief of the United States armed forces."[52]

To Schlesinger and fellow Stevenson adviser John Bartlow Martin, the attack sounded desperate. By indecorously predicting Eisenhower's demise, they thought, Stevenson had "tarnished his reputation" for fairness—exactly what distinguished him from the likes of Nixon. The conundrum was a familiar one for Fifties liberals, who seesawed over how to counter Nixon's jabs. When Stephen Mitchell, the Democratic chairman, proposed retaliating in kind, intellectuals balked. If victory were achieved on such terms, asked William Lee Miller in *The Reporter*, "then whose is the victory?" On the other hand, he cheerfully ventured, "if we stick by what we believe, we may not win as often, but when we do we shall know what the victory means." Miller's prescription, like Stevenson's hyper-dignified, above-it-all posture, offered the luxury of consistency but not the necessity of victory. Like the *New York Post*'s commentary after Checkers, it bespoke an abiding faith that playing by the rules would be its own reward, and that in the long run the people's better angels would prevail. But that faith was coming to seem like self-delusion.[53]

While liberals weighed the cost of descending to Nixon's level, Nixon tried to remake himself as more mature and less combative—the first of what would be many "New" Nixons. Some establishment journalists, including Stewart Alsop and *The New York Times*'s James Reston, believed him; conservative supporters, meanwhile, felt saddened at his mellowing or betrayed by his apostasy. Liberals, however, dismissed any possibility that he was turning over a new leaf. "Is there a New Nixon?" they joked. "Absolutely: The old Nixon was sly and opportunistic. The new Nixon is just the opposite: opportunistic and sly." If anything, they felt, the vice president's reinvention underscored his lack of a core identity. Anyone who donned a new persona so casually, they reasoned, must be a synthetic and artificial creature of public relations men. Liberals concluded that Nixon was, as William Shannon wrote, "the outstanding product of the new synthetic politics in America . . . [of] the science of conditioning and manipulating men's minds."[54]

As early as 1954, when Nixon first forswore his feisty campaigning, observers wondered about his capacity to change. Conversations centered on whether Nixon had evolved into a statesman—or, as Stevenson gibed in 1956, whether he had simply "put away his switchblade and assumed the aspect of an Eagle Scout." Liberals believed they knew the answer: the new guises were just more proof of Nixon's Machiavellian nature. When a dinner guest gushed to Dean Acheson about Nixon's changed manner, he replied, "Madam, for five million dollars you can change the public impression of almost anyone." To liberals, the appearance of the New Nixon suggested only that the old, expedient Nixon would remake his image whenever the old one no longer worked.[55]

Herblock, as always, caught the change in his cartoons. In place of the sewer-dwelling smear artist, he now drew the vice president as an opportunist trying to shed his past. In one 1956 sketch, Nixon answered the door on Halloween to see, standing before him with their buckets of tar, "Nixon 1954," "Nixon 1952" (in a cocker spaniel mask), "Nixon 1950," and "Nixon 1948"—as the "New Nixon" yelled: "Now you kids beat it!" In another 1956 image he captured Nixon's ability to don and doff his various personae. Examining his wardrobe, Nixon wondered, "What'll I wear today?" as he chose among street clothes labeled "Dead-End Gang," a varsity sweater marked "All-American Boy," formal wear saying "Look, Folks—I'm a Statesman," and a garish plaid coat stamped "Political Pitchman."[56]

Nixon's self-reinvention did force liberals to reassess him in one sense. Previously, many judged him a right-winger with a record of "almost unbroken subservience to the most reactionary elements of the business community," as William Shannon wrote. Now, looking at a career riddled with stands along the Republican spectrum, he appeared, as Rovere phrased it, "innocent of doctrine," an opportunist who "would rather be President than be Right." The new liberal consensus held that Nixon adopted his positions, even his supposedly inveterate anti-communism, from expedience. He was, Stevenson said, "the kind of man who would cut down a redwood tree, and then mount the stump and make a speech for conservation." His lack of convictions, they said, betrayed an essential hollowness, flexibility in the service of self-advancement. Although liberals held fast to a picture of America as an authentic democracy, Nixon—devoid of beliefs, willing to do anything to win—seemed the quintessentially inauthentic man who might undermine it all.[57]

The Nixon-haters used various metaphors to describe his artificiality. First, noting his youthful dabbling in high-school and community theater, they called him a Hollywood actor who "memorize[d] his lines" and played any part required. His Checkers performance marked only the most successful in a series of portrayals. "He has been understudying so many different roles and reciting so many different scripts," *The Reporter* noted in contemplating a Nixon presidency, "that it is impossible to say how he would act as protagonist." Murray Kempton noted the "pleasure of the actor" as Nixon managed to "contrive the pitch of proper scorn" in responding to attacks. When his eyes filled with tears after getting Eisenhower's vote of confidence in 1952, his old drama teacher, watching on TV, was said to comment: "Here goes my actor." Liberals felt that said it all.[58]

A second trope also drew on Nixon's adolescent activities: Nixon as the "bright young debater." Lacking core convictions, his detractors said, Nixon could advance any argument with equal facility. His boyhood success in forensics, they surmised, shaped his principle-free view of politics, and besting Voorhis in the 1946 debates convinced him of the virtues of his style. But because liberals thought Nixon assumed his various stands provisionally, for reasons of the moment, they distrusted his every profession of belief. He was, argued William Lee Miller, "under a bit of a shadow . . . [since] one is never sure just where the conviction ended and sheer artistry began."[59]

Finally, critics snidely recalled Nixon's adolescent stint as a carnival barker. After the Checkers speech—which one critic dubbed "as slick a performance as ever devised on Madison Avenue for soap or cereals"—liberals portrayed Nixon as a "salesman" and a "huckster." His speeches were compared to "advertising copy," his facial expressions to "a Pepsodent smile,"[60] his ideas to "slogans for a thorough sales campaign," his manner to that of "the television pitchman . . . cogently explain[ing] the benefits of life insurance one evening . . . frenziedly shouting the dubious virtues of a headache nostrum" the next. *The Reporter* read profound meaning into Nixon's acceptance of the Los Angeles Sales Executive Club's "Salesman of the Year" award in 1954.[61]

These metaphors suggested a man who had reached the top through his skill with Hollywood and Madison Avenue techniques. Indeed, the notion of technique itself infused the liberal view of Nixon. In the unsettling quality of "a sales 'pitch' too glib and too simple," opined the ADA *Second Man* pamphlet, "lies the origin of the diffuse, unfocussed, yet steadily mounting distrust of Richard Nixon. He has become identified with a method, a technique of selling himself or his party rather than clarifying issues or arguing them." Liberals had already flagged the dirty tricks—the anonymous phone calls and deceptive flyers—that marked Nixon's early campaigns. Likewise, they had grown wise to his rhetorical tools—the Red-baiting ruses and verbal ploys that they ritually deconstructed in their magazines. But now in the mid-Fifties, they awakened to the power of modern techniques of manipulation in the political sphere. Liberals spoke darkly of "professionals" such as Nixon's mentor Murray

Chotiner who were using breakthroughs in technology and psychology to turn the age-old art of politics into a cold science. This state-of-the-art demagoguery that Nixon practiced was more fearsome than any imprecations hurled from behind a podium or any handbill tacked to a tree.[62]

Even as Stevenson and his egghead followers reconciled themselves to television's growing importance, they remained wary of it. In his 1956 acceptance speech, Stevenson called political advertising "the ultimate indignity to the democratic process," and insisted that "the minds of Americans can [not] be manipulated by shows, slogans and the arts of advertising." Beneath the protestations of faith in the people, liberals watched nervously as Nixon and the Republicans embraced the new politics, from the Checkers speech onward. "Nixon's arrival in the Vice-Presidency coincided with the full flowering of television," Douglass Cater wrote in *The Reporter* in 1958, "and he has applied many of TV's techniques to develop the potential of his office. He has demonstrated that the Vice-President, if he is skillful, can manipulate the fade-in and the fade-out, the filters and the cropping devices familiar to the cinematographer." Since Nixon was at home "in the realm of artifice," liberals felt, he proved an easy master of this dangerous medium.[63]

Advertising and public relations exacerbated the potential for electronic-age deception. In *The Hidden Persuaders*, Vance Packard's exposé of the ad men's subliminal manipulations, the journalist noted how Chotiner and Republican operatives grafted newfangled techniques onto national political campaigns, producing "spectacular strides in changing the traditional characteristics of political life." Much more readily than the Democrats, the Republicans, Packard wrote, set out to "merchandise" their candidates through unconscious appeals to the instincts and emotions instead of reason. "The man who benefited from many, if not all, these techniques," the single figure who "has been described by perceptive observers as a new breed of American politician," Packard added, was none other than Richard Nixon.[64]

Reflecting liberal thinking, Packard saw these innovations as an assault on the Enlightenment notion that reason should guide human decisions. Bypassing rationality, they threatened the American ideal of the citizen as "thoughtful voter, rugged individualist . . . [and] flowering of twentieth-century progress and enlightenment" by stripping him of his capacity for intelligent choice. "Disturbing Orwellian" implications followed: Without the bedrock assumptions that individuals could reliably interpret information and make judgments that reflected their will, democracy took on a different character. Cunning, self-serving leaders could, without the public's free consent, dupe them into following their own agenda. Transparency of meaning and individual autonomy were supposed to provide a check on would-be dictators. Such suppositions, Packard feared, were losing purchase. Nixon, some said, was to blame. "He is the only major American politician in our history," Schlesinger claimed, "who came to prominence by techniques which, if generally adopted, would destroy the whole fabric of mutual confidence on which democracy rests."[65]

The liberal intellectuals of the Fifties, of course, were confident that they themselves would never be gulled by Nixon's hidden persuasion. But they feared he would prey upon an ignorant and malleable public. That was why they felt compelled to rebut Nixon's populist self-portrait, debunking his common-man pretensions, demystifying his cons. Without their smarts and vigilance, they implied, Nixon would dupe voters and ruin America.

But if liberals sometimes claimed that they needed to awaken the public to Nixon's deceptions, at other moments they betrayed another fear: that Nixon might indeed speak for an American middle class that, as liberals saw it, basked uncritically in the postwar materialism. Having proved distressingly receptive to McCarthyism, the people now showed themselves, intellectuals felt, to be irresponsibly indifferent to social concerns. Galbraith, in *The Affluent Society*, his critique of a society in which "the bland lead the bland," bemoaned the average family's numbness to "public squalor," its complicity in the neglect of poverty, public health, and the environment. David Riesman's comfort- and status-seeking "other-directed" citizen epitomized the problem, hiding his ambitions and drives behind a facade of complaisance. When Eisenhower beamed that "Americans are 'a happy people' doing exactly what they choose," liberals thought that was precisely the problem.[66]

By the mid-1950s, liberals were depicting the protean Nixon as the personification of the other-directed striver. The vice president's self-promoting image-consciousness and anti-intellectual posturing struck them as embodying and encouraging the worst of the middle class. "If it were possible to take a photograph of his brain," Kempton gibed, "it would show the single sentence, 'What will people think?'" Nixon was "the 'other-directed' man in politics," agreed Schlesinger, ". . . obsessed with appearances rather than the reality of things, obsessed above all with his own appearance, his own image, seeking reassurance through winning, but never knowing why he is so mad to win or what he will do with his victory." Irving Howe added that Nixon "seems to represent a potential in American life . . . of a fairly prosperous, politically besieged, emotionally tight-lipped, rigidly conformist suburban America in which all values are transvalued into salability, all techniques have become devices for persuasion, and persuasion itself is indistinguishable from a hidden bludgeon." Ironically, these versions of Nixon conceded that there was some truth in Nixon's populist portrait. Nixon *did* represent the common folk, they seemed to be saying, and like them he was shallow and petty.[67]

Though superficially at odds, the portraits of Nixon as a hidden persuader and a middle-class striver both fed liberal fears that something like fascism might come to American shores. The demagoguery and the use of "the Big Lie," the high-tech propaganda, even the lingering whiffs of corporatism and anti-Semitism—these traits suggested, if as a distant and unlikely scenario, the makings of an authoritarian who would prey upon a docile public. No one called Nixon a Nazi in the Fifties (though in time they would), but the implications hovered beneath the surface of references to Nixon's "dark" side and the "danger" he posed to democracy. And a few liberals toyed with the verboten epithet: William Costello noted "fascist tendencies" in the man and "an insinuation that Big Brother is watching" in his utterances. Brooding about the prospect of a Nixon presidency—an increasing likelihood as the decade closed—Costello predicted that "anyone running afoul of policy . . . could expect only the swiftest and most merciless reprisals," for Nixon "understands the use of power but not the unwritten restraints on its use." Drew Pearson and Jack Anderson also feared that Nixon, if elected president, would "revert to type," "purge innocent[s]," and order his "personal goons" to impose his fiats.[68]

Whether Nixon actually harbored this potential was a question that the balance of his career would complicate rather than resolve. His presidency, as perceived by not just liberals but others, became a battleground for fights over power and its restraints. But whatever its validity, the portrait of Nixon as a dangerous manipulator served as a powerful political symbol. For the moment, as Nixon began his 1960 presidential run, his villainous image galvanized his enemies, who worked furiously to stave off their worst political nightmare.

Talk of political image making suffused the 1960 election. While Nixon easily won his party's nomination, the Democrats chose Senator John F. Kennedy of Massachusetts, who struck liberals as witty and glamorous but not terribly weighty or progressive. Some charged that the two nominations represented the triumph of style over substance. "They are junior executives on the make, political status seekers, end products of the Age of Public Relations," scoffed Eric Sevareid of CBS. ". . . The 'managerial revolution' has come to politics, and Nixon and Kennedy are its first completely packaged products." Critic Dwight Macdonald, too, alienated from the new prefabricated politics, shrugged at liberals' desperate "Keep Nixon out of the White House" campaign and trumpeted his decision not to vote.[69]

At first some liberals had looked to the twice-defeated Stevenson, but he lacked both the support and the will. The prospect of losing to his arch foe deterred him too. "I despise Nixon so much that I couldn't be trusted not to say something absolutely terrible about him in the course of the campaign," he told Schlesinger, defensively. Instead, Schlesinger, Galbraith, and their cohort warmed to Kennedy, who radiated the qualities Nixon lacked: charm, wit, respect for intellectuals. To those who lumped the two candidates together, Schlesinger responded with a book called *Kennedy or Nixon: Does It Make Any Difference?* (it did to him), which became a *summa* of Nixon-hating. Rehearsing the view of Nixon as unprincipled and manipulative, Schlesinger wrote that the vice president had "no ideas, only methods . . . He cares about winning . . . he cares about the 'image' (in one of his own favorite words) that the public has of him;

he cares about appearances. But he does not care much about what is intellectually or morally the right or wrong position to take on questions of public policy." JFK, in contrast, was serious and confident in his identity, sharing none of Nixon's obsession with externals. Increasingly, intellectuals joined Schlesinger in the cause. On university campuses and in highbrow circles, Nixon-bashing rose to new heights, as comedy troupes such as Chicago's Second City, nightclub comics including Mort Sahl, and a Broadway play by Gore Vidal turned satirizing the Republican candidate into sport.[70]

Image talk peaked that fall with the first ever televised general election debates. With TV sets now in nine of ten American homes, as many as 120 million people watched Kennedy and Nixon square off on September 26. As historians would oft retell, viewers saw a sharp contrast: Kennedy, standing calmly in a dark suit, projected unflappability. Handsome, relaxed, he answered questions crisply. Nixon, recovering from a knee infection and a cold, looked terrible. Sweat streaked the pancake makeup that had been applied to his five o'clock shadow, and his gray suit blended in with the walls. Afterward, the press, declaring Kennedy victorious, blamed Nixon's appearance for his loss. "Fire the make-up man," Nixon's aide Herb Klein was told. "Everybody in this part of the country thinks Nixon is sick. Three doctors agreed he looked as if he had just suffered a coronary."[71]

If a consensus held that Kennedy had bested Nixon on image, some critics felt that the whole concern with televised appearances debased politics. When Daniel Boorstin derided the so-called Great Debates for sullying an important democratic rite, he was but one voice in a chorus of liberals and intellectuals. With their fears of PR and TV and slick advertising, they worried that a new culture of manufactured images, of Boorstin's pseudo-events, would drive reason and authenticity from the political sphere altogether. The debates, Boorstin said, were hastening the collapse. "If we test presidential candidates by their talents on TV quiz performances, we will, of course, choose presidents for precisely these qualifications. . . . Reality tends to conform to the pseudo-event."[72]

Indeed, whether or not Kennedy outdebated Nixon, reality conformed to that perception. In November, Nixon lost, it might be said, by a whisker. With a margin of just 0.2 percent of the vote, Kennedy won, in the analysts' telling, on the strength of his image. Nixon, so skilled with TV during the Fifties, ironically now fell victim to an increasingly image-conscious culture. Once the savvy expert, he now came across as flat-footed, behind the times. In 1958, *The Reporter*'s Douglass Cater had predicted that "in this age of fast and fleeting publicity, the merchants of modern mass communications are ready to discard the old and faded figure for someone who is fresh and interesting," and that Nixon faced his toughest job yet, to "achieve the highest form of art—the art that appears artless." In 1960 (and again in 1962 when Nixon lost his bid to become governor of California), Tricky Dick failed to pull it off. For the time being, liberals could believe that Americans were able to see through the scrim of appearances that Nixon draped before them and could glimpse the heavy hand of the petty striver pulling the strings.[73]

In their celebration, however, liberals forgot that Nixon's defeat was almost a triumph, and in their glee they failed to foresee that his retirement would prove short-lived. When Nixon surprised them all by winning the presidency six years after his political career had been declared finished, liberals reached back into the Fifties for their images of Tricky Dick. It took little time for the old image to be adapted to new conditions and become a cultural touchstone all over again.

Watergate, of course, represented cultural triumph for the image of Tricky Dick; if the image had been pronounced before Nixon's presidential crisis, it became indelible thereafter. Yet even at their moment of vindication, liberals still filtered Nixon through their ideological and cultural lenses. When Nixon delivered his farewell address in August 1974 from the White House East Room, in which he dwelled on his parents and his boyhood, many heard only mawkish echoes of Checkers. When Nixon shook hands with the White House staff, they shook their heads that he was pursuing his cynical image making right until the end. James Taylor's song "Line 'Em Up," written some years later, captured these feelings. In rhyming couplets, Taylor recalled how the president, in a false show of sadness, wallowed in self-pity while privately relishing the political opportunity his resignation speech presented. Even as he hit bottom, the cagey Nixon, in Taylor's telling, looked forward to pressing the flesh one last time with those who had served him in the White House, so that he might publicly display his affinity for ordinary Americans. Meg Greenfield, who had moved from *The Reporter* to *The Washington Post* a few years earlier, recalled hearing such sentiments from her liberal friends at the time. "Did you hear that performance?" they asked. "Would you believe he's still trying that stuff?" Greenfield herself—the self-professed "last unreconstructed Nixon critic on earth"—had heard the speech on her car radio and sympathized with the president and his "unendurable shame." But her fellow Nixon-haters, she wrote, couldn't grasp what she was talking about. "Live by the image, die by the image," she concluded. "They saw Nixon's speech merely as evidence of further faking. . . . I thought this reaction said something not about Nixon, but about us."[74]

Greenfield had a point. Even as liberals saddled Nixon with a permanent image as Tricky Dick, they also revealed their distance from the Americans who shared his values. During Nixon's years, liberals adopted an elitist politics that relied upon executive branch bureaucrats and unelected federal judges to administer justice where the democratic masses could not be counted on to do so. The liberals could take pride in their noble and often brave positions. But those positions came at the price of distrusting the masses, Nixon's cherished Middle Americans. Their battles with Nixon forever tarnished their nemesis, but in isolating themselves politically, they hurt their own cause a lot as well.

3

The New Left Radicals: Nixon as Conspirator

> Richard Nixon, the main villain of my political conscious-
> ness, . . . was finally biting that bullet he's been talking
> about all those years. . . . The truth was turning out to be
> even worse than my most "paranoid ravings" during that
> painful 1972 election.
>
> —*Hunter S. Thompson*, The Great Shark Hunt[1]

Nixon was sworn in as the nation's thirty-seventh president on January 20, 1969, amid chilly winds, roiling skies, and disorder in the streets. In the sanctums of the White House, Lyndon Johnson's aides, having long struggled to contain urban riots and a restive anti-war movement, left the new president a sheaf of executive orders declaring martial law, with only the date and the name of the city in question omitted. At the Capitol, Nixon joylessly delivered the speech he had waited eight years to give. He grimaced at the turmoil of the times, lamented a nation "torn by division, wanting unity," and expressed hope that his inauguration could start the healing.[2]

Many Americans, viewing Nixon as their populist spokesman, cheered him heartily, such as the teenagers of the Whittier High School marching band, who had flown in from Nixon's hometown. Others, including Democratic leaders, distrusted Nixon yet mustered respectful words for the occasion. But the inaugural was hardly placid. Radicals on the political left, determined to stop the Vietnam War, lacerated Nixon as they had his predecessor. The *Berkeley Barb*, the irreverent bible of Northern California's hippie culture, caricatured the new president dressed in a policeman's suit and wielding a "Law 'n' Order" billy club. Anti-war leaflets chided that "the unity Nixon talks about is evasion, the peace Nixon talks about is a hoax."[3]

For peace activists, whether iconoclastically absurdist or solemnly political, Nixon's inauguration boded a dark future of continued war abroad and increased repression at home. Determined to resist, they organized what they billed as the "Counter-Inaugural." The National Mobilization Committee to End the War in Vietnam (or "Mobe"), an umbrella group for the proliferating array of anti-war bodies, planned a slate of protests over the long weekend to provide an antidote to the charade of good cheer and to warn Nixon that they would hold him to his peacemaker rhetoric. Through activist networks and alternative newspapers a call went out to protest. By Saturday, January 18, ten thousand activists had poured into Washington. Stew Albert of the Youth International Party (or "Yippies") wrote that he came "to denounce the war and the phony democracy that produced it." Steve Lerner of *The Village Voice* said he didn't want to miss "the beginning of an historic slaughter, the coming of the great Repression." Hunter S. Thompson, the "gonzo" journalist whose colorful prose riffs voiced the young radicals' fury, attended "mainly to be sure it wasn't a TV trick. It seemed impossible that it could actually happen: President Nixon." Fueled by these motives, radicals made Nixon, Albert claimed, "the first president whose very inauguration was met with organized opposition in the streets."[4]

The events began Saturday with a Counter-Inaugural Parade—"spirited and noisy," as its leaders described it—followed Sunday night by a Counter-Inaugural Ball that featured light shows and rock bands. Rain had turned the lawn into mud, but scruffy students and hippies crammed under a green-and-white circus tent, dancing, eating, drinking, and smoking marijuana. At midnight, actors staged an inaugural playlet: One man wearing a judge's robe climbed atop a truck and, holding a *Reader's Digest*, swore in another man, who was wearing a pig mask. In a bow to the prevalent fear of assassination, the pig-president was instantly gunned down.[5]

Inauguration Day revealed the mutual distrust between Nixon and the left that would characterize the next six and a half years. As the president's entourage rolled along Pennsylvania Avenue with the customary pep and pomp—marching bands, VIP-filled sedans, a float of well-scrubbed carolers singing "Up with People"—caution filled the air. In one section of the parade route stands, where the Mobe had bought a block of tickets, demonstrators waved signs. Thousands more protesters lined the streets below. Longtime pacifists such as Mobe leader Dave Dellinger had forsworn violence, but the Secret Service was taking no chances. It ordered the roof and windows of Nixon's limousine fastened shut, while soldiers with rifles and bayonets milled about the crowd.[6]

As Nixon's car approached 12th Street, heading from the Capitol to the White House, the president spotted a cluster of signs. "Nixon's the One," read one, playing off his campaign slogan, ". . . the No. 1 War Criminal." Next came an onslaught of shouted epithets. "Ho, Ho, Ho Chi Minh!" "Four more years of death!" Then a fusillade of sticks and stones, bottles and cans, forks and spoons, tinfoil balls and smoke bombs, raining down on the motorcade. A few errant protesters ran off to smash store-front windows, bait policemen, and burn hand-held American flags, which earlier had been distributed to pageant-watchers free of charge by well-meaning Boy Scouts.[7]

Dellinger and the Mobe condemned the violence. Mirroring the government's suspicion of the left, they charged that FBI provocateurs had staged the disturbances. The claim was not far-fetched. The government often used such unethical tricks in these years. Trying to arrange the Counter-Inaugural Ball, Mobe organizer Rennie Davis had taken to using pay phones because the FBI kept canceling whatever arrangements he made. One suspicious-looking Mobe volunteer named Irwin Bock seemed determined to get the organization into trouble. Bock pressured Dellinger and Davis to devise violent schemes, and at one point during the weekend he even heckled a speaker whom Dellinger described as "a disfigured, badly wounded veteran who had sneaked out of his [hospital] bed" to participate. (Actually an undercover Chicago policeman, Bock later testified in the trial of Dellinger, Davis, and the rest of the "Chicago Seven," the movement leaders who had led protests at the Democrats' 1968 convention.) It was later learned that FBI and army intelligence officers had also burgled a left-wing Washington newspaper seeking information on the Counter-Inaugural. But agitators from the movement's militant fringes did initiate some of the weekend's violence, and it was hard to tell a home-grown radical from an FBI mole. The left, like the man about to take power, hovered between legitimate distrust and delusional paranoia.[8]

In the crucible of Vietnam, the left forged a lasting image of Nixon distinct from the sly "Tricky Dick" of liberal demonology. Their Nixon was worse than a ruthless political manipulator. He was a shadowy conspirator, a repressive dictator, and, in the words of the radical journalist I. F. Stone, a "moral monster" who thought nothing of slaughtering civilians in the Vietnam War for his own advantage.[9] In one sense, of course, the left was correct: Nixon directed malign plots, for which he eventually resigned the presidency. But his actions alone cannot account for the shrill descriptions of him as a war criminal, a Hitleresque tyrant, and a cold-blooded murderer. Those exaggerated portraits stemmed also from the fevered climate of the times, in which the bonds of political authority were eroding, and from the "conspiracist" ideology or "paranoid style" that much of the left embraced.[10] Indeed, conspiracism—a tendency to explain political events as the work of high-placed secret plotters—would infuse American political culture during the 1960s and early '70s, finding expression in political discourse, film, literature, and the fabric of everyday experience. If its main adherents remained on the political margins, it still colored the views of those in the mainstream.

The left's portrait of Nixon as conspirator in chief reinforced a sense among radicals, and those who imbibed their ideas, that democracy was no longer working. It encouraged a view of politics as a dead end. It isolated the left from Americans who found conspiracist modes of thought outlandish or frightening. Finally, despite this resistance, the left's conspiratorial image of Nixon seeped into the wider culture and became a powerful force in hastening the president's resignation.

.   .   .

Much had changed by 1968 since Nixon's presidential bid eight years earlier. The country was now split asunder by race, sex, social issues, and especially the Vietnam War. An increasingly radical "movement"—part
political protest, part generational rebellion—turned its anger on Lyndon
Johnson, who amid mounting body counts could not or would not end the
war. The carnage galvanized radicals and cost Johnson the goodwill of the
left, which broke off from the Democratic Party to challenge him. In 1967,
the historian Gabriel Kolko, the journalist Robert Scheer, and the linguist
Noam Chomsky were among those backing a "Peace and Freedom Party,"
one of many short-lived splinter groups, which circulated pamphlets bearing Johnson and Nixon's pictures and proclaiming: "You can do better than
this." Radicals took heart momentarily when in March Johnson declined
to seek reelection—it was "like driving an evil King off the throne,"
Hunter S. Thompson crowed—but when they realized the Democrats
would nominate Johnson's chief water-carrier, Hubert Humphrey, hopes
fizzled. "It would have felt like the height of masochism," wrote movement
activist and chronicler Todd Gitlin, "for anyone in the movement orbit to
vote for Hubert Humphrey." George Wallace, the segregationist Alabama
governor whose populistic appeals to working-class whites fed up with
liberal policies and values were bringing him unforeseen support, was
even less palatable.[11]

This breach created an opening for Nixon, who had engineered a stun-
ning comeback. Though Nixon is often described as having spent the mid-
1960s "in the wilderness," he was quietly rebuilding his career. Having
repaired to a Wall Street law firm, he cultivated wealthy businessmen and
Republican leaders and in 1968 claimed his party's presidential nod on the
first ballot.[12] His platform of "peace with honor" abroad and "law and
order" at home rallied both longtime admirers and the so-called Middle
Americans whose disenchantment with the war was outstripped by their
dislike for the anti-war movement. Just as Nixon had offered a softer version of McCarthyism in the 1950s, his 1968 message contained echoes of
Wallace's rhetoric—though of course Nixon himself had pioneered conservative populism long before Wallace appeared on the scene.

To the left Nixon was "an impossible alternative," as anti-war organizer David Mixner said. "Richard Nixon represents the dark side of the

American spirit," declared Robert F. Kennedy, who despite his late conversion to the cause had become the anti-war left's last great hope to win
the presidency in 1968. Radicals turned out at Nixon's speeches to taunt
him. In Akron, Ohio, that October, hundreds of members of Students for a
Democratic Society (SDS), the leading left-wing campus association,
packed an auditorium balcony, where they chanted: "Ho, Ho, Ho Chi Minh,
the NLF is going to win!" and "Sieg Heil!" over Nixon's remarks. But the
inability to stomach Humphrey left few options. "Nobody for President,"
concluded one rally-goer's plaintive sign. The Mobe, calling the election a
"fraud," urged citizens to boycott the ballot box and "register a vote of
repudiation of the Presidential choices and the system that imposes these
choices on us." Others backed protest candidates. "Humphrey lost that
election by a handful of votes—mine among them," wrote Hunter Thompson afterward, "and if I had to do it again I would still vote for Dick Gregory." The political comedian or the Black Panther Eldridge Cleaver or
"Pigasus," the pig nominated for president by Yippies Abbie Hoffman and
Jerry Rubin, seemed to many the only conscionable choices.[13]

When Nixon prevailed, anger vied with resignation on the left. Mobe
leader Arthur Waskow wrote organizers that "millions of people who
were deeply upset by Chicago . . . feel themselves wholly excluded from
the government, with scarcely a smidgeon of hope. . . . Ditto for the black
communities." In San Francisco, Todd Gitlin attended a rally where no
speaker mentioned Nixon's victory. He described the omission as "a
shrug of despair and fatalism, as if to say: *Of course* Richard Nixon has just
been elected President of the United States; we always knew it would
come to this." Nixon's ascent confirmed their dread that democracy was
in disrepair.[14]

Nixon's worries ran just as deep. Possessed by his own account of
"paranoiac" tendencies, he saw his critics—student radicals, political
reporters, and longtime Nixon-hating liberals—as a monolithic adversary.
"We're up against an enemy, a conspiracy," he told his chief of staff, H. R.
Haldeman. "They're using any means. We are going to use any means. Is
that clear?" Persuaded of the threat, Nixon concluded that he had to quash
the movement. His aides compiled "Enemies Lists" that included leading
leftists. His Justice Department used the catch-all charge of "conspiracy"

to prosecute political opponents. His security agencies spied on dissenters. His IRS used tax audits to retaliate against foes. His staffers, obsessed like their boss with public relations, sought to discredit the left with the public. Nixon's sweeping efforts amounted to a conspiracy all their own. Not for nothing was he the only president to be named by a grand jury as an "unindicted co-conspirator," as he was in 1974 during the Watergate prosecutions.* His abuses of power, most historians agree, though not wholly unprecedented, were manifestly greater, more far-reaching, and more damaging than other presidents'.[15]

Yet even paranoids have enemies, as it is said, and Nixon's conspiratorial view of the movement found an exquisite complement in activists who saw Nixon as their persecutor. Radicals maintained a drumbeat of vicious criticism throughout his presidency, creating an image of him as a would-be dictator and—well before Watergate emerged—demanding his impeachment. Hence the fearful symmetry: Nixon and the left each inflated the other's hostility into a full-blown conspiracy; each validated the other's fears by coordinating assaults in what each believed was a last-ditch attempt to save democracy.

Like Fifties liberalism, the radical movement known as the New Left arose in reaction to postwar conformity. These young radicals, however, demanded more thoroughgoing remedies than did their liberal elders. Indeed, the New Left took liberalism as its chief adversary. In the early Sixties, the fledgling New Left aimed to restore authenticity to people's lives through grass-roots reform. But soon the government's unresponsiveness led many to redirect their energies into personal pursuits or to dismiss politics as a sphere ruled by conspiracies and immune to any reform but revolution. Such thinking, though far from universal, permeated New Left culture. Given the left's influence in these years, it infused the broader zeitgeist as well.

Born of a fusion of old-line Marxists and newly radicalized students,

* The grand jury recorded that it concluded, by a vote of 19–0, "that there is probable cause to believe that Richard M. Nixon (among others) was a member of the conspiracy to defraud the United States and to obstruct justice."

the New Left challenged the stultifying, homogenizing power of what SDS president Carl Oglesby called "corporate liberalism." Situated in high posts of government, business, academia, and the military, corporate liberals, the New Left believed, created a repressive society that snuffed out individuality and authentic experience. To inject meaning back into politics, the New Left promoted what its early leader Tom Hayden called "participatory democracy": a grass-roots politics that bypassed bureaucracy to restore authenticity in an anomic world. Working in the civil rights movement, in ghettoes, with community organizing, New Leftists believed they could effect radical social change.

As the Sixties progressed, however, and grass-roots experiments failed, many came to see politics as a rigged game. This determinism had roots in the New Left's foundational theorists. The sociologist C. Wright Mills introduced the idea of a "power elite" of corporate, political, and military leaders who tailored policy to their own interests. The historian William Appleman Williams portrayed America's globalism as an expression of its imperialistic desire to open markets, with corporations controlling foreign policy. Others argued that U.S. capitalism bred a "national security state" that used repression against alleged subversives to maintain the status quo. By Nixon's presidency, many wondered whether all political action in the face of entrenched power was doomed.[16]

Not all radicals subscribed to the conspiracist corollaries of New Left thought. But in the tumultuous Nixon years, even rationalists had to acknowledge the possibility of high-level intrigues. The government's use of electronic surveillance against domestic enemies, which had been going on since the 1940s but had become common in the 1960s, conjured images of Big Brother. Eventually, through legal challenges, the Supreme Court in 1972 curtailed the state's powers somewhat, with Justice William O. Douglas bemoaning that a "national seizure of paranoia" had permitted far too many civil liberties violations under the bogus claim of national security. But only after Nixon's departure would the paranoia subside.[17]

That paranoia escalated in a vicious cycle, as Nixon and the left reinforced each other's fears. Four months into his term, Nixon and his national security adviser, Henry Kissinger, ordered the first of seventeen taps to be placed on the phones of newsmen and officials they thought had discussed information about the war, thus launching the administration's headlong plunge into criminality.* Kissinger's taps remained secret until 1973, but the exposure of similar surveillance scandals much sooner nourished a distrust of the government, especially among radicals. In January 1970, an army captain disclosed a military intelligence program that targeted political activists; in March 1971, a raid by radicals of an FBI office "liberated" files detailing government spying on black radicals and student groups. With the 1973 Watergate Hearings, the dam broke, flooding public consciousness with knowledge of not just the wiretapping but also the aborted "Huston Plan" to bring federal intelligence gathering under White House control; the establishment of a White House "Plumbers' Unit" to stop leaks through break-ins and buggings; Nixon's taping of his own White House conversations; and of course the break-ins at the Democratic Party's headquarters that led directly to Nixon's demise.[18]

Nixon's paranoia led him to increase surveillance; the surveillance fueled popular paranoia, as New Leftists attested. David Mixner, at the time a closeted homosexual, let down his guard to a seemingly sympathetic lover who then tried to blackmail him into becoming an informer; distraught, Mixner contemplated suicide. Activists feared that their phones were tapped, their movements tracked. A government agent explained how the spying heightened the radicals' fears. "Our inside information has caused SDS to get more conspiratorial in a lot of places," he told *The New York Times*. "They make their plans at the last minute now to fool us."[19]

Each side fed the other's fears of violence, which was fast becoming a tool of everyday politics. Black Power champion H. Rap Brown declared violence "American as apple pie," as riots, protests, and assassinations

* Kissinger's role in the taps has been especially controversial. According to most standard accounts, a May 9, 1969, article by William Beecher in *The New York Times* divulging the administration's secret bombing of Vietcong sanctuaries in Cambodia infuriated Nixon and Kissinger. In consultation with J. Edgar Hoover, Nixon decided to place taps on the phones of officials he suspected of leaking. Kissinger agreed with the decision and helped choose the targets. On the day the bombing story appeared in the *Times*, Kissinger spoke to Hoover four times. Similar taps to stop leaks were soon placed on journalists as well. In his defense, Kissinger admitted that "my office" selected some targets and that FBI summaries of the monitored conversations "were sent to my office." Although the Supreme Court ruled in 1972 that the warrantless taps were illegal, Kissinger maintained that they therefore weren't illegal *until* June 1972. Of course, the Court did not create a new law banning warrantless taps; it merely affirmed that they had been illegal all along.

(including little-remembered plots to murder Nixon), occurred with numbing frequency. According to a presidential panel that decried a national "crisis of violence," 41,000 bombings or bomb threats occurred in the United States in the fifteen months after Nixon took office. At times, the extreme left's activities were genuinely menacing and even murderous—and warranted government investigation and surveillance—as in August 1970, when a homegrown left-wing terrorist bombed a University of Wisconsin research center, killing a thirty-three-year-old graduate student. At other times, the administration used the specter of violence to silence legitimate dissent.[20]

Quickly, Nixon and his staff whipped themselves into what aide Jeb Magruder called "a permanent sense of crisis." In March 1970, White House "domestic security coordinator" Tom Huston cautioned Haldeman about revolutionary violence. "While you may think I'm paranoid, I want to . . . warn with deadly seriousness that this threat is terribly great," he wrote; ". . . the most logical target at some point in time for these people is the President and the White House . . . [and] innocent people are going to be killed." Not only hard-liners talked this way. Daniel Patrick Moynihan, Nixon's professorial policy guru, voiced similar warnings: "We have simply got to assume that in the near future there will be terrorist attacks on . . . members of the Cabinet, the Vice President, and the President himself," he told Haldeman. ". . . What we are facing is the onset of nihilism in the United States." Moynihan told the president he had sent his family into seclusion after SDS members threatened to torch his Cambridge home and added that ten-year-old John Moynihan thought his father would be assassinated.* Nixon and his aides believed these threats legitimized their own use of violence, even if that meant skirting the law. They talked of

---

* Other administration figures feared violence from *Nixon*. Vice President Spiro Agnew, when evidence of his corrupt practices as governor of Maryland emerged in 1973, wrote that he was urged to "Go Quietly . . . Or Else." He said a Nixon aide warned him, "The President has a lot of power—don't forget that." Agnew took it as a dark hint that if he did not comply, he "might have a convenient 'accident.' " White House counsel John W. Dean, when he spoke to prosecutors in 1973, also worried for his life. His lawyer Charles Shaffer, Dean said, was "concerned about my life, afraid someone might like to eliminate me from the scene." Confidants of Dean's told him of "serious rumors that there may be attempts to rub you out." U.S. marshals moved into Dean's house.

getting "thugs" from the Teamsters' Union to beat up anti-war protesters. Haldeman wrote himself reminders to "Get a goon squad to start rough-ing up demo's, VFW or Legion—no insults to P., use hard hats."* [21]

Given such talk, leftists (and others)† naturally feared violence from the state, which they believed used disorder as a pretext for repression.[22] In the *Berkeley Barb*, a writer identified as "David" riffed:

> The wiretapping snooping gestapo FBI taking pictures and lurking behind trash cans of the alley as they watch your every move and who you talk to and who you visit and fat jowls of Hoover as he directs his legions and tells you there is a communist under every woodpile and that the world needs more lawandorder as he points the gun barrel right at your eyes and tells you to watch your step. . . .

---

* On May 8, 1970, New York City construction workers, known as "hard hats," angry at the anti-war crowd, brutally beat up protesters near City Hall. New York policemen watched; some abetted or cheered the assaults. Nixon rewarded the hard-hat leaders by inviting them to the White House and later naming one of them, Peter Brennan, secretary of labor. To what extent, if any, the White House conspired in the hard-hat rally and violence has never been settled.

† Journalists included. Reporters who covered Nixon, including Dan Rather and Marvin Kalb of CBS and Tad Szulc of *The New York Times*, had their apartments burgled. Szulc fingered the government, which had also tapped his phone. Katharine Graham, publisher of *The Washington Post*, was told by a trusted friend, financier André Meyer, to stay vigilant. "I'm serious," he told her cryptically. "I've talked to them, and I'm telling you not to be alone." *Post* editor Howard Simons, convinced his house was bugged, went outside when he wanted to talk about Nixon. In May 1973, Graham's star Watergate investigators, Bob Woodward and Carl Bernstein, were informed by Woodward's famed source "Deep Throat": "Everyone's life is in danger."

Most distressingly, White House "Plumber" G. Gordon Liddy, as he recounted in his memoir, contemplated assassinating columnist Jack Anderson if given the green light by legitimate higher-ups. Liddy has always worn his tough-guy, military-man persona with such conviction that it can be difficult to tell when he is joking. It is hard to imagine that he seriously considered murdering a journalist, but he has insisted, without any hint of unseriousness, that he did. In *Will*, he recounted a conversation with Howard Hunt and a former CIA agent "introduced to me as Dr. Edward Gunn." In the conversation—couched, Liddy recalled "in the hypothetical terms usually employed in such circumstances"—Hunt reported that Anderson, in a column he published, had compromised the safety of a U.S. intelligence officer. Liddy proposed killing Anderson, and, according to his account, the others endorsed the idea and discussed how it should be done. Liddy and Hunt agreed to enlist the Cubans working for CREEP. Liddy justified his willingness to kill Anderson as necessary to save the lives of American officials. Hunt eventually told Liddy not to go through with the plan—although even after that instruction Liddy pretended to CREEP officials Robert Reisner and Jeb Magruder that he was willing to do the deed.

> When people cry out against the idiocy and the madness they are
> gunned down like dogs in the streets or hit on the head or thrown in
> the dungeons to rot.[23]

Black radicals woke and slept in dread, particularly after Chicago Black
Panther Fred Hampton was killed in a police raid on December 4, 1969,
when the FBI gave the floor plan of his residence to local cops. For black
and white alike, Nixon seemed to make everything worse. However
severe the previous crackdowns, anti-war leader Fred Halstead recalled,
"The Nixon administration was different. . . . Suddenly, you were covered
like a blanket." Yippie historians Stewart and Judy Albert agreed:
"Nixon's program of political repression was qualitatively different from
anything American protest movements had recently experienced. The
assaults were concerted, coordinated, well financed, and thorough."[24]

Admonitions of Nixon's malign intentions filled the pages of the
underground press, with counterculture scribes using a hip, iconoclastic
argot, as if conventional language could not convey the situation's
urgency. "President Nixon wants your cock, cats," wrote one Muhammad
Khan I in the *Berkeley Barb*, about the military draft. "The whole fucking
system of the military is geared to cut it off at the short hairs and deliver it
on the platter of your soul to Tricky Dick." In an article called "Nixon's
Plan for Amerikkka" (with a swastika in place of the "x," a favorite underground press flourish), a *Philadelphia Free Press* writer asked: "Can the liberals continue to believe that capitalist amerika can be changed through
electoral campaigns or by reform measures? . . . [T]he only way to change
this system is by forceful overthrow of a government which cannot meet
the needs of the people."[25]

Liberals shared the radicals' worry over the corrosion of civil liberties
but scorned their conspiracist worldview. "'Repression' is one of those
imbecile catchwords of our era like 'genocide' and 'imperialism' that have
had all the meaning washed out of them," the Columbia University historian Richard Hofstadter sighed to *Newsweek*. Hofstadter agreed that "a
terrible new phase of reaction" posed a starker threat than did the revolutionary left, but to believe that horrors like Fred Hampton's killing were
premeditated, he felt, showed a break with reality. To liberals, a U.S. gov-

ernment of murderers remained unthinkable. To radicals, it was becoming an article of faith.[26]

Hofstadter's interest in this strain of thought, which he shared with many colleagues, reflected the culture's obsession with paranoia and conspiracies. In his 1965 essay "The Paranoid Style in American Politics," Hofstadter had argued that McCarthyite anti-Communists, John Birch Society members, and similar right-wing groups viewed politics through a lens that "distorted" their judgment. Removing contingency from the sweep of events, they blamed all misfortune on enemies of liberty. Hofstadter and other historians traced conspiracism back through time, whether among leaders of the American Revolution or antebellum abolitionists and anti-abolitionists. The parallels to New Left thought were obvious. Historian James Hitchcock saw resemblances between the New Right and the New Left, including an antipathy to rationalism and a belief in "The System . . . as a coordinated whole." David Brion Davis explained the popularity of conspiracy theories among his students by suggesting that "it was less frightening to believe in hostile conspirators than it was to face the fact that no one was in control."[27]

Literature and film exhibited concerns similar to those of historical scholarship. The American fiction of the period, observed critic Tony Tanner, revealed "an abiding American dread that someone else is patterning your life, that there are all sorts of invisible plots afoot to rob you of your autonomy of thought and action." In the novels of Kurt Vonnegut, Norman Mailer, Joseph Heller, and Don DeLillo, individuals found themselves consigned to the role of unwitting pawns in the designs of unknown powers. Nixon himself often figured in these scenarios as an emblem of conspiratorial forces. In Thomas Pynchon's *Gravity's Rainbow*, a character named Richard M. Zhlubb, described as "fiftyish and jowled, with a permanent five o'clock shadow . . . and a habit of throwing his arms up into an inverted peace sign," takes the reader on a hallucinatory ride along the Santa Monica Freeway, apparently resulting in catastrophe. In Ishmael Reed's "D Hexorcism of Noxon D Awful," a Voodoo sorcerer enters the dreams of "Noxon," a presidentlike figure who swims through the sewers to work and cracks down on unruly students, discontented tenants, and people "threatening to go to Chicago."[28]

Purveyors of pulp fiction, too, spun conspiracist webs. In the 1950s, journalists-turned-novelists Allen Drury and Fletcher Knebel popularized the genre of the political thriller in which high-stakes Washington intrigue unfolded against a backdrop of Cold War hostilities. By the Seventies, these novels had taken a left-wing turn.* Favorite villains included money-hungry executives or (as in Knebel's *Seven Days in May*) right-wing generals plotting a coup. One 1974 novel, Lou Rossetto's *The Take-Over*, featured a President Richard Nixon who, facing removal from office, uses an "attempted coup" by his enemies as an excuse to impose censorship and appropriate all power to his office; the sole staffer to resist, press secretary Ron Ziegler, assassinates Nixon on national television. Philip K. Dick's *Radio Free Albemuth* revolves around the efforts of a repressive, Communist-hunting Nixon-like president, Ferris Fremont, who recruits conservative youths for a spy agency to persecute left-wingers he suspects are spreading anti-American sentiments in their writings or music. At a time when political truth seemed stranger than fiction, fiction was racing frantically to catch up.[29]

Cinema best expressed the conspiracist grip on the imagination. Earlier thrillers such as John Frankenheimer's adaptation of *Seven Days in May* were broadly drawn nightmares that dispensed with any pretense to believability. In the conspiracy films of the 1970s, the line between fantasy and reality faded. *The Parallax View, Three Days of the Condor*, and *Network* purported not to provide escapism but to suggest parallels between the unsettling stories on the screen and those in contemporary politics. Unsatisfied with the left's description of the Nixon administration as totalitarian, Irving Howe found a "more useful analogy" in Constantin Costa-Gavras's *Z* (1969). The thriller portrayed "a country where some of the externals of democracy survive," including a legal opposition, but the

---

* Many Nixon aides later wrote such novels. John Ehrlichman, after serving time for Watergate, wrote *The Company* (New York: Simon & Schuster, 1976), *The Whole Truth* (New York: Simon & Schuster, 1979), and *The China Card* (New York: Simon & Schuster, 1986). Agnew tried his hand with *The Canfield Decision* (Chicago: Playboy, 1976).

regime, "through a systematic use of gangs of hoodlums working in close collaboration with the police," rendered "the opposition . . . politically helpless and the nation morally inert." Nixon, Howe believed, was working toward a system like Z.[30]

Nixon himself turned up in these conspiracy films too, typically to symbolize the sabotage of democracy. In Alan J. Pakula's *Klute* (1971), a psychotic stalker of prostitutes who bears a resemblance to Nixon is undone by the tapes he makes of his telephone conversations. In Pakula's next film, *The Parallax View* (1974), Joe Frady, a reporter probing a string of assassinations, applies to work for a mysterious firm involved in the killings. To join, he must watch a fast-paced montage of violent images in which Nixon's face appears repeatedly; Nixon's recurring visage in the montage links the president, if indistinctly, with secret murders committed by a conspiratorial elite. In Costa-Gavras's *Missing* (1982), based on the plight of a left-wing American journalist killed in Chile in 1973 by a right-wing junta (which, in actuality, enjoyed U.S. support), a large official portrait of Nixon hangs prominently in the climactic scene, as the U.S. ambassador baldly lies to the missing journalist's father. Nixon serves as a token of the dishonesty—and worse—of American officialdom. As Nixon ascended from fame into iconhood in these movies and books, he typically represented the dark fears of the conspiratorial left.[31]

Repression at home was second only to Nixon's prosecution of the war on the radicals' lists of Nixon's sins. When Johnson waged the war, its merits were still debatable, but by Nixon's presidency, the left felt, any remaining moral issues had resolved themselves. More than Nixon's unctuous style or opportunism, the urgency of ending the war united young radicals in their anti-Nixonism. Wrote the poet Bruce Wiegl:

> Everyone hated him
> and that brought us all together . . .
> Nixon
> whom we had seen
> in all of his flesh,

standing on the White House balcony,
Apollonian
above the half million citizens
who had come to stop his killing; he
even waved to us . . . [32]

At each flashpoint of the home-front war—the historic "Moratorium" protests in October and November 1969, the Ohio National Guard's killing of Kent State University students in May 1970, Nixon's reelection campaign in 1972—radicals unleashed increased fury at Nixon. Vietnam was for Sixties radicals what the Red Scare had been for Fifties liberals: a crisis of American democracy that set the terms for their perception of Nixon, in this case as a murderous war criminal and a would-be dictator.

As the Counter-Inaugural had shown, radicals granted Nixon no honeymoon. While his liberal critics fell silent in early 1969, the left held demonstrations demanding immediate withdrawal from Vietnam. Half measures won Nixon no gratitude. In June, the president began his plan of "Vietnamization," under which American-trained South Vietnamese soldiers replaced American troops. The policy placated many Middle Americans concerned about body counts. But radicals, who saw the whole war as an imperialist enterprise, disparaged the plan as merely "changing the color of the bodies."[33]

In their eyes, Nixon became another Lyndon Johnson, stubborn and callous—and perhaps also susceptible to being forced from office. Left-wing publications, from the peace movement's *Liberation* to *The New York Review of Books*, from the New Left *Ramparts* to countercultural alternative papers, painted Nixon as LBJ reincarnate. I. F. Stone discerned "a clear continuity between the Johnson and Nixon Administrations." *Village Voice* cartoonist Jules Feiffer sketched Nixon uttering pieties about "meeting our responsibilities abroad," as his face morphed into Johnson's. By fall it was "becoming more obvious" each day, wrote *Washington Post* columnist David Broder, "that the men and the movement who broke Lyndon Johnson's authority in 1968 are out to break Richard Nixon in 1969." White House aides read Broder's column with distress.[34]

The autumn marked a turning point. Anti-war liberals finally banded with radicals to mount the largest demonstrations in history. In October and again in November 1969, day-long protests called "Moratoriums" drew hundreds of thousands to Washington, San Francisco, and other cities, and marked the movement's zenith. Nixon countered with an unprecedented public relations blitz to discredit the left, a detailed "Game Plan" of strategies including a televised speech on November 3. In that speech Nixon reproached dissenters for undercutting negotiations, thereby prolonging the war, and appealed to the "great silent majority" of Americans for their support. At least temporarily, the speech and the Game Plan roused the Silent Majority and deflated the movement.

Although the speech pleased most Americans, peace activists thought it "ugly, belligerent," in David Mixner's words, a veiled threat "to crack down on dissent." I. F. Stone felt it showed "how committed he is ideologically and emotionally to this war." At a press conference just after the speech and just before the November Moratorium, Mobe organizer Sidney Lens, questioned about rumors of impending violence, lashed out at the press's misplaced priorities: "Why the hell don't you ask the man who is really committing violence, Richard Nixon, whether he intends to continue the massacres in Vietnam? If all of us on this podium lived a thousand years we couldn't perpetrate as much violence as Nixon does in one day." For radicals, the speech proved only that Nixon was a dedicated warmonger.[35]

A stalemate set in that lasted until the spring. Then, on April 30, 1970, Nixon announced that the United States was invading Cambodia. Almost instantaneously, students at five hundred campuses went on "strike" to force their schools to shut down. On May 4, National Guardsmen, summoned to control disturbances at Ohio's Kent State University, fired on and killed four students. Nixon was thrown on the defensive. His callous reply—"This should remind us . . . that when dissent turns to violence it invites tragedy"—sent activists to new heights of outrage. Anti-war literature railed against the "immoral killing and destruction" wrought by "Nixon and the military establishment." When thousands of protesters converged on Washington the following weekend, they vilified the president without restraint, chanting, "Fuck Nixon!" between the rally's speeches.[36]

A siege mentality gripped the White House, as Nixon's men exhibited Nixonian paranoia. Anticipating mayhem, five thousand soldiers donned

battle gear and massed in government building basements. Henry
Kissinger took refuge one night in a bomb shelter beneath the East Wing.
Admiral Thomas Moorer, the chairman of the Joint Chiefs of Staff,
indulged conspiracist fantasies, insisting that Berkeley agitators had
"masterminded" the Kent State killings and taunted the National Guardsmen so that innocent students would get shot and win sympathy for the
doves. Nixon himself, distraught, took an impromptu walk to the Lincoln
Memorial one night at 4:00 A.M., where he rambled about football, surfing,
world travel, and other topics before dumbstruck students.[37]

The rolling out of troops, at Kent State and in Washington, crystallized
images of Nixon as a symbol of militarism. The rock group Crosby, Stills,
Nash, and Young sang of "Tin soldiers and Nixon coming" in its bitter
lament "Ohio," recorded May 21 and rushed onto radio stations. The song
eulogized the Kent State victims as the casualties of the president's
domestic war. Radicals now spoke routinely of "the murders" and "the
slaughter" at Kent State (and Mississippi's Jackson State, the site of more
student killings days later), as if the question of motive was beyond
debate. An anti-war poster showed Nixon's mug shots, fingerprints, and
vital statistics, declaring him WANTED for "conspiring to murder tens of
thousands of American soldiers and at least one million Vietnamese. He is
also wanted in connection with the murders of twenty-eight Black Panthers, four Kent State students, and two Jackson State students." Cartoonist David Levine of *The New York Review of Books* drew Nixon as leading a
firing squad, proclaiming the victims "bums," as he had labeled campus
protesters days before.[38]

Amid this vilification, some radicals balked at singling Nixon out.
Liberal Democrats might have thought him qualitatively different from
LBJ, but the farther left one traveled, the more one heard sentiments like
The Nation's claim that "whether Johnson or Nixon [is president] makes no
appreciable difference." Wade Myers, a student who spoke with Nixon at
the Lincoln Memorial, refused to hold him responsible. "It's just not the
man's fault," he told a reporter for *Rolling Stone*. "It has something to do
with the system. Personally, attacks just aren't right." In his own untheo-
retical way, Myers was expressing the New Left's power elite critique. Far
from a lone individual thwarting the democratic will, Nixon was a

dummy figurehead who represented vast, systemic forces over which radicals could scarcely imagine effective popular restraint.[39]

Even so, as the war festered for three more years, Nixon the warmonger remained a target. In 1972, the left made the GOP convention, and Nixon's renomination, the target of its protest, as radical priest Daniel Berrigan vowed to "take the joy out of Nixon's death game" and "line Highway One with admissible evidence against war criminals." The turnout was relatively weak, but those who heeded the call and came to Miami, convention-watcher Norman Mailer observed, were "divided by every idea but one: that Richard Nixon is a war criminal."* Meanwhile, American intellectuals discussed with the utmost seriousness how war crimes trials for Nixon and Kissinger might proceed.[40]

Even after Watergate and Nixon's resignation, many leftists considered Vietnam Nixon's cardinal sin. The Oscar-winning anti-war documentary *Hearts and Minds* (1974) laid the carnage at Nixon's feet. In one scene, a North Vietnamese farmer whose children were killed by American bombs calls Nixon a "murderer of civilians." He tells the camera crew, "I'll give you my daughter's beautiful shirt. Take it back to the United States. . . . Throw this shirt in Nixon's face. Tell him she was only a little schoolgirl." At the film's end, Nixon laughs it up at a formal dinner for returned POWs, callous toward the plight of the Vietnamese. For the filmmakers and other anti-war activists, such cruelty was far worse than Watergate. Daniel Ellsberg, who had incurred Nixon's wrath for leaking the Pentagon Papers to the press, claimed the government's violations of his rights bothered him less than the continuation of the war. Nixon and Kissinger, he said, were "mass murderers . . . people who, without any justifiable excuse, killed hundreds of thousands of people with no good reason."[41]

.   .   .

---

* The American support for the right-wing coup in Chile in 1973 added another count to the bill of indictment. As the Chilean poet Pablo Neruda wrote in his *A Call for the Destruction of Richard Nixon and Praise for the Chilean Revolution:* "I call on all people to wipe out/this blood-covered leader, this liar/who, by sea and air, ordered/that entire nations should live no more . . . /that distant and unconcerned jackal." For many American leftists, too, Chile outranked Watergate among Nixon's offenses.

Having adopted symbiotic siege mentalities during May 1970, the administration and the New Left now found themselves in a self-perpetuating *folie à deux*. Nixon's men believed the left capable of brutal mob violence, while the left came to view Nixon as capable of once unthinkable usurpations of power. Nothing better illustrated this tendency than two bizarre rumors that took hold in 1970.

It's impossible to say when radicals began whispering about Nixon's plans to cancel the 1972 presidential election, but the rumor first appeared in print on April 5 in the *Portland Oregonian*, the *Staten Island Advance*, and other Newhouse-owned newspapers. According to the item, the administration had asked the RAND Corporation, a defense-industry think tank, to study whether "rebellious factions using force or bomb threats would make it unsafe to conduct an election" and how the president might respond. Ron Rosenbaum, a reporter for *The Village Voice*, heard about the article from a Staten Island cab driver and investigated. He reported in the *Voice* on April 16 that RAND and the administration denied that any such study existed, but then playfully pointed out that they would surely deny it if it were true. Rosenbaum added that the country would just have to wait until 1972 to see.[42]

Soon publications from the alternative *Los Angeles Free Press* to *The Nation* picked up the story. Some treated the tale as established fact. In the springtime ether, the rumor spread fast and took on sinister connotations. A group called the Urban Coalition claimed Nixon had commissioned a *second* study, from MIT, to survey how voters would react to an announcement of suspended elections. Another version held that Nixon, to ensure he had pretext for the move, was arranging for provocateurs to instigate frightful acts of violence, to create an American Reichstag fire. "The burning of government buildings in Germany, though first blamed on Communist arson, has since been exposed as the act of Hitler himself," the comedian and activist Dick Gregory wrote in the *Freedom News*. Nixon, he intimated, was about to do the same.[43]

Administration officials realized the rumor was gaining strength. To squelch it, Pat Moynihan, in a Fordham University commencement address, said he knew the story had reached "just about every campus in the nation" and chalked up its currency to students' "growing distrust of

all social institutions." Moynihan reassured his audience that the report
was "not so," but then, either playing for a laugh or falling victim himself
to the pervasive mistrust, he added: "Or at least I *think* that it is not so."
Moynihan failed to put the concerns to rest. Then, in July, a left-wing magazine called *Scanlan's Monthly* obtained one page of a memo allegedly written by an aide to Vice President Spiro Agnew. The memo, which *Scanlan's*
printed in its August issue, was dated March 11, 1970, and alluded to three
administration schemes: to cancel the elections; to orchestrate seemingly
spontaneous pro-administration rallies by labor groups;* and, eventually,
to "repeal" the Bill of Rights. *Scanlan's* advertised its "scoop" heavily, and
at a press conference a *New York Times* reporter asked Agnew about the
memo. The vice president denounced it as "completely false," as did Attorney General John Mitchell a week later, and Nixon went so far as to order
an audit of the magazine. (As a brand-new publication, however, it had yet
to file a tax return.)[44]

It is doubtful that many people expected Nixon to suspend the election, let alone repeal the Bill of Rights. Even some countercultural journalists who inspected the document judged it a hoax. But the memo's
authenticity mattered less than the fact that so many people thought it
plausible that Nixon might entertain a power grab at all. *The Nation*, while
stopping short of accepting the rumor, grouped it with such recent "internal security" measures as stepped-up wiretapping and infiltration. "As an
old-time Red-hunter, [Nixon] is, in fact, inclined by temperament in that
direction himself," the editors argued. Ron Rosenbaum, in a follow-up to
the *Village Voice* pieces he wrote the previous spring, maintained that "the
Rand rumor is metaphorically and cosmically true, even if proven mun-
danely false." During the Nixon era, he argued, indulging paranoid fantasies made sense. Given that a few years later the world would learn of
Nixon's very real tampering with the 1972 election, Rosenbaum's argu-

---

* Such rallies did occur. After Kent State, the White House quietly worked with labor groups
to plan anti-anti-war activities. As noted, at a May 8 rally in New York City, so-called hard
hats pummeled peace protesters. Some of this information was already known when *Scanlan's* printed the memo. Presumably, the inclusion of this item, with its apparent foretelling of
the anti-radical labor violence, was meant to lend credence to the backdated document's
authenticity.

ment had a certain logic. While itself fictional, the canceled-election rumor sprang from an accurate sense that Nixon was willing to push democracy's limits. The rumor had a literary, if not literal, integrity.

Rosenbaum ended his follow-up report by describing, only half in jest, "a more demoralizing rumor than the RAND report: . . . that the '72 elections will be held and that the candidates will be Richard Nixon, Hubert Humphrey and George Wallace." The point was not just that one couldn't know if the scotched-election rumor was true or false; it was that it did not *matter* whether it was true or false because metaphorically it had already come to pass. Reality and fantasy had already merged in a system where, as in Z, democratic forms persisted absent democratic content.[45]

Alongside the canceled-election rumor, another incident in the fall of 1970 fed the left's dim view of the state of American democracy: the assault upon the president by a crowd of anti-war protesters during his trip to San Jose in October 1970. The episode was a classic *Rashomon* case, with each side viewing it as proof of the other's sinister designs. William Safire, voicing the administration view, called it "the most serious mob attack on a national leader in American history." Radicals, in contrast, believed it constituted a sham excuse for a crackdown, Nixon's Reichstag fire.

The trouble occurred on Thursday, October 29, days before the midterm elections, when Nixon delivered a campaign speech at San Jose's municipal auditorium. Having risen to power in 1968 on his themes of law and order, Nixon was again styling himself and his party the protectors of the public order, the reliable authorities who would stop the left-wing hooliganism that they blamed for sundering and endangering the country. After his speech, and others by Governor Ronald Reagan and Senator George Murphy, Nixon exited the building via the rear door. He was met by two thousand anti-war protesters, cordoned off by police barricades, chanting and hoisting signs. The mood was nasty. Protesters shouted obscenities, and one sign, tacked to a tollbooth roof, read: "Stop Nixonism" (with the now de rigueur swastika in lieu of the "x"). Having previously baited hecklers to profitable effect, Nixon leapt on the hood of his limousine and flung his arms in his trademark double-V. Suddenly, a refrigerator's worth of projectiles sailed through the air—eggs, tomatoes, vegetables—and a hail of rocks. Nixon hurried into the car as the Secret

Service called for an emergency evacuation. On the staff bus, Safire watched as stones smashed the windows, spewing glass, while the motorcade sped to the airport. Bob Haldeman panicked for a moment after a rock hit his car, which stalled and was rear-ended, though to his relief, "we caught up and all got out" safely. In the fall of 1970, Safire wrote, anti-war protests had become so common that they were "more a drag than a dread." But, he added pointedly, "San Jose was different."

The administration viewed the incident, Safire wrote, as "more proof, if any more were needed, of the deep-seatedness of the hatred of Nixon by the lunatic fringe." It also presented an opportunity to win favor with those Americans who saw the president as a brave patriot. On October 31, in Phoenix, Arizona, Nixon gave a speech denouncing "the wave of violence and terrorism by the radical anti-democratic elements in our society." Playing the role of the strong authority, he insisted that "the answer to bluster is firmness . . . the strong application of fair American justice." The audience cheered wildly. Emboldened, Nixon and Haldeman decided to rebroadcast the remarks the night before the election.[46]

The left, not surprisingly, saw the event differently. At first it fought rhetoric with rhetoric: an organizer of the protest insisted Nixon was the criminal—a war criminal—and said that whatever had been lobbed at the president paled beside the tonnage of bombs he had strewn across Indochina. Soon, however, activists were in the grip of a new conspiracy theory and took to calling the episode "the Nixon Hoax." Nixon, they claimed, abetted by a compliant press corps, had magnified or even concocted the whole episode to tarnish the left. Far from uncontrollable mob violence, it amounted to a run-of-the-mill protest in which no one got hurt. Tom DeVries, a Bay area TV reporter, surveyed journalists in the crowd and reported that none saw objects hurled or violence threatened (though even some underground journalists reported that rocks and bottles were thrown). A few intimated that the White House had recruited members of the conservative Young Americans for Freedom or other paid goons to pose as anti-Nixon demonstrators and provoke the entire incident.[47]

The news media were caught in the middle. At first, they had reported the story more or less according to the administration's view, as an organic mob assault. Soon, however, many newspapers, including *The Washington*

Post, ran stories questioning Nixon's version of events. In the *Columbia Journalism Review*, Mel Wax, a colleague of Tom DeVries, agreed that the rock-throwing was, if not nonexistent, then at least wildly exaggerated. (No one was arrested for rock-throwing, he noted, and no one was known to have been injured by a rock.) Wax suggested that the media had been used to create an impression of an endangered Nixon and bolster his law and order campaign. But this self-scrutiny—which was becoming routine for a press corps wary of government manipulation—brought perils of its own. Where the left thought reporters had overhyped the incident, the White House was troubled by the press's readiness to allow "that perhaps the whole thing was a pseudo-event," Safire wrote. ". . . The apparent willingness of much of the media to minimize this contributed to the isolation of the men around the president" and reinforced their paranoia.[48]

The truth lay somewhere in the middle. On the one hand, the more outlandish rumors about provocateurs were never borne out, and some members of the crowd clearly acted violently. On the other hand, it was known that the White House welcomed and on some occasions had even abetted unruly dissenters at the president's appearances; Nixon wanted them there because he knew that, in the eyes of most Americans, the radicals made him look good by contrast, especially when he dramatically scolded those who were chanting, heckling, or shouting him down. Bill Gulley, a member of Nixon's Secret Service detail, later wrote that "knowing how the Nixon advance team worked . . . it [was] well within the realm of possibility" that the San Jose incident was "rigged." More concretely, Haldeman recorded in his diary, also published long afterward, that the White House had deliberately contributed to the violence. "We wanted some confrontation and there were no hecklers in the hall, so we stalled departure a little so they could zero in outside," he wrote. Haldeman found the ensuing outburst "rather scary . . . as rocks were flying. . . . Bus windows smashed, etc." But he also plainly relished the event: It "made a huge incident and we worked hard to crank it up," he noted, predicting that it "should make [a] really major story and might be effective." After arriving in San Clemente, Haldeman said, Nixon "kept calling with ideas about how to push the line." What dictated how one viewed the event, then, was not so much the facts of what happened but the lenses through which it was viewed. Both sides interpreted the situation through their familiar prisms of paranoia, allowing the administration to come away feeling more besieged and the movement to come away newly fearful of Nixon's intentions.[49]

One outgrowth of this paranoia was the tendency to portray Nixon, in rhetoric and in illustrations, as a potential monarch, tyrant, or dictator who, like Hitler, needed only the right occasion to seize complete power. The image caught hold at a moment of rare vulnerability in the system, when the ballasts of authority were collapsing. The mix of systemic weakness, tyrannical imagery, and Nixon's own misdeeds fostered a climate in which a president's impeachment, once almost unthinkable, became suddenly possible.

For a decade, the bonds of political authority had been eroding. The left's assault on social hierarchies created a vulnerability in the once stable American system. Within a few years a string of bold challenges to the nation's leadership unfolded. President Johnson was all but forced to abdicate. One Supreme Court Justice (Abe Fortas) was forced to step down and another (William O. Douglas) faced an abortive impeachment drive. In 1973, Agnew became the first vice president to resign since the early nineteenth century. And the drive to impeach Nixon, the first such proceeding in a century, hastened the only presidential resignation in history. Political assassination, too, became chillingly routine, feeding a sense that authority was up for grabs.

If political instability made calls for Nixon's ouster newly credible, the picture of him as a would-be tyrant gave them urgency. In the national mythology, the defense of freedom against high-placed conspirators had always inspired would-be revolutionaries. Foes of strong presidents—Jackson, Lincoln, FDR—used monarchical imagery to argue that their nemeses were wielding power illegitimately. Each year, Nixon's actions, large and small—arranging to streamline power in the executive branch; cracking down unilaterally on dissent; outfitting White House Secret Service agents in tunics, epaulets, and Beefeater hats reminiscent of British Empire royal guards—reinforced the picture of an aspiring dictator or monarch.

Long before Watergate—indeed, from the start of his presidency—radicals maintained that Nixon's law and order agenda betrayed the soul of a tyrant. The image and language of tyranny, monarchy, and despotism were ubiquitous, turning up not just in political commentary but in cartoons, novels, and poems. In May 1969, the Beat poet Lawrence Ferlinghetti published "Tyrannus Nix?", a poem that united the old 1950s portrait of Nixon as the avatar of middle-class banality ("the face we all love in the Geritol ads/the face of the nation facing the nation on color TV") with the New Left's demonic view of him ("your yahoo cohorts now conducting the nazification of California and other campuses/I heard you plainly tell them to get a little tougher on campus and the next day they murdered one of us"). It was hard to tell whether Ferlinghetti's poem was an act of deliberate, mischievous sloganeering or genuine political extremism. The ambiguity was probably intended; the left's tyrannical renderings of Nixon typically blurred the line between impish provocation and out-and-out zealotry.[50]

Satirical images of Nixon as a monarch proliferated. Cartoonist Garry Trudeau endorsed the cries heard at the 1972 Republican Convention that Nixon was turning the event into a "coronation." In Trudeau's strip *Doonesbury*, the hippie character Zonker, writing for his campus newspaper, calls a Nixonite to interrogate him about "the Nixon monarchy," only to be reassured that "it's going to be a constitutional monarchy." Later in the week, when Walter Cronkite reports that the rumors are unsupported, Zonker yells at his TV, warning that under the "new order" he will be "Walter Cronkite, serf!" Edward Sorel, who began drawing for *Ramparts*, *The Realist*, and *The Village Voice* before being discovered by the mainstream press, drew Nixon as Louis XVI, holding a scepter and bedecked in ermine and regalia, and as Milhous I, Lord of San Clemente, scowling under his heavy white wig.[51]

The most extreme versions of the dictator image turned Nixon into a fascist, a Nazi, or an American Hitler. Under Lyndon Johnson, it had been de rigueur on the left to compare the U.S. government to the Third Reich. Even *The Nation* lamented that the "extreme Left" had drained the meaning from the overused term "Fascist." But with Nixon, Hitler comparisons gained new meaning and power. Nixon-as-Hitler cartoons filled underground newspapers weekly and adorned anti-war posters. The *Los Angeles Free Press* showed Hitler holding a Nixon mask that fit snugly over his face. Outrages from Fred Hampton's killing to Kent State to the canceled-election rumors to the carpet-bombing of Indochina invited Nazi analogies. An anti-war flyer from May 1972 showed a flagpole waving both the Nazi banner and Old Glory, with a vaguely Ginsbergian "poem" underneath:

HITLER NIXON! HITLER NIXON!
BOMBING THE VIETNAM JEW
BURN THE BABIES, RAPE THE WOMEN
GAS THE MEN, HONEYWELL DO IT AGAIN
HITLER NIXON! HITLER NIXON!

After the 1972 election, the *Berkeley Barb* put Hitler on its cover, asking: "Guess Who Won?"[52]

Unlike the leftists, the liberal flank of the movement—the national politicians, leading magazines, and high-profile movement chiefs—typically shied away from inflammatory analogies, though occasionally one made an exception: When the administration rounded up ten thousand protesters in a preventive mass detention in May 1971, New York congresswoman Bella Abzug condemned the "Gestapo maneuver." A year later, news of the Watergate burglars' links to the White House prompted Senator George McGovern, the Democrats' presidential nominee, to call the break-in "the kind of thing you expect under a person like Hitler." (He also labeled the bombing of Cambodia "the most barbaric thing . . . since the Nazis were in power.") But those comments brought McGovern more grief than support, as Nixon officials accused him of "character assassination" while reporters browbeat him. In 1972 most of the country was busy reelecting Nixon, not branding him an American Führer.[53]

But if Nazi imagery remained controversial, less inflammatory monarchical metaphors enjoyed wider use. Any Nixonian usurpation of power validated the left's concerns of the impending demise of democracy. Nixon's commandeering of the public airwaves for his speeches led anti-war patron Cyrus Eaton to proclaim, in the staid *New York Times*, the advent of "a presidential dictatorship sustained by the greatest propaganda machine in history." Left-liberal voices, from *The Nation* to the

Times's Tom Wicker, explicated why Nixon was genuinely coming to resemble "an American sovereign" or "emperor." The notion of Nixon as a monarch would last beyond his presidency: during the American bicentennial, the poet Robert Lowell compared him to the tyrant whose rule the nation's founders had originally rejected:

George—

once a reigning monarch like Nixon,
and more exhausting to dethrone . . .

Could Nixon's court,
could Haldeman, Ehrlichman, or Kissinger

blame their king's behavior
on an insane wetnurse . . .[54]

If Nixon truly was a potential monarch, then deposing him, as Lowell implied, became imperative for the republic's survival. The most innocent way to oust Nixon was electoral politics. In March 1971 Allard Lowenstein, the New York congressman who had led the "Dump Johnson" movement, started (what else?) a "Dump Nixon" movement. Lowenstein was no one-man band. In October 1971, the People's Coalition for Peace and Justice—a successor umbrella group to the Mobe—planned, under Rennie Davis's direction, five days of "Evict Nixon" activities. "The crimes of this government must be exposed and those who are responsible driven from power," Davis declared in announcing the campaign. "Richard Nixon can be endured no longer." Peace activists channeled their energies into electing a Democrat who would end the war. Even a small number of anti-war Republicans rallied behind GOP congressman Paul McCloskey of California, who entered his party's 1972 primaries on an anti-war plank.[55]

At the other end of the range of options for removing Nixon was assassination. No one ever came as close to harming Nixon as did those who fired upon George Wallace or Gerald Ford, but there were scares. Several days after Nixon's election in 1968, New York police arrested three

Yemeni men for plotting to kill the president-elect. In August 1973, the Secret Service canceled a motorcade through New Orleans's French Quarter after discovering a "possible conspiracy" to assassinate Nixon.[56] While these incidents were destined to become historical footnotes, at the time they made front-page headlines and reinforced a sense of the system's fragility.

The prevalent fear of assassination confounded clear-eyed distinctions between genuine and rhetorical threats. Radicals exploited the uncertainty to nettle the authorities, while authorities used it to harass radicals. At the November 1969 Moratorium, Black Panther leader David Hilliard warned hyperbolically, "We will kill Richard Nixon," for which he was summarily arrested. Hilliard had made the statement amid a fiery condemnation of the government's campaign against the Panthers, in which he vowed, with panache common among militants, "We will kill any motherfucker who stands in the way of our freedom."* Whether to play it safe or simply to crack down on a movement leader, the government kept Hilliard detained for eighteen months. Hilliard insisted that he clearly had no intention of murdering the president, that he was simply "talk[ing] the language of Nixon and Mitchell," who were "Hitler's helpers" and "tyrants, paying professional gunmen to kill my comrades in early-morning attacks." Ultimately, his case was thrown out because the government had used inadmissible evidence that it had gained from illegally tapping Hilliard's phone.[57]

Manifestly playful assassination talk also stoked New Left fantasies. In May 1971, editors of the underground paper *Flash* interviewed Groucho Marx. "I think the only hope this country has is Nixon's assassination," the comedian commented off-handedly. Mischievously, the editors highlighted the quote in syndicating the piece to underground papers, which had a field day. "MARX (the one we all love) SAYS 'NIXON'S ASSASSINATION IS THE COUNTRY'S ONLY HOPE,'" read one headline. When no one came to

---

* Hilliard's full quote: "Richard Nixon is an evil man. This is the motherfucker that unleashed the counter-insurgent teams upon the Black Panther Party. This is the man that sends his vicious murderous dogs out into the black community and invades our Black Panther Party breakfast programs. Destroys food that we have for hungry kids and expects us to accept shit like that idly. Fuck that motherfucking man. We will kill Richard Nixon. We will kill any motherfucker that stands in the way of our freedom. Peace!"

arrest Groucho, Paul Krassner, the puckish editor of *The Realist*, face-tiously complained to the government about the double standard applied to Hilliard. When a U.S. Attorney sent back a letter that showed no trace of irony, Krassner published the response in his next issue.[58]

Between the extremes of voting Nixon out and taking him out lay a more legitimate, if unfamiliar avenue: impeachment. The presidential impeachment mechanism was, in historian Stanley Kutler's analogy, like the atom bomb: Just once had it been used (in 1868, against President Andrew Johnson) and to do so again was almost inconceivable. By the time Representatives Ron Dellums, Bella Abzug, and left-wing associates were throwing their "Impeachment Ball," in January 1974, few remembered that they had first oiled up the creaky machinery of impeachment quite early in Nixon's presidency, when the war still raged and Watergate was just an apartment complex along the Potomac. Indeed, the left had called for impeachment almost as soon as Nixon took office. Sidney Lens of the Mobe raised the possibility at the November 1969 demonstrations; the National Student Association and sixty-eight Cornell University professors, among others, did so after the 1970 Cambodia invasion; and Abzug and Representative Paul McCloskey considered an impeachment resolution over Vietnam in 1971.[59]

Abzug and four colleagues on the Democratic Party's left wing plunged ahead in 1972. On May 10, they submitted an impeachment bill. More an anti-war *cri de coeur* than a serious bid to remove Nixon, it charged the president with violating the provisions of the Constitution that assigned warmaking powers to Congress. (While not without merit, the charge was clearly political; after all, if waging the war were unconstitutional, then Lyndon Johnson would have been equally deserving of impeachment.) Working with a group of lawyers and academics called the National Committee for Impeachment, Abzug's group placed a two-page ad in *The New York Times* on May 31. Still, in May 1972 they had relatively little popular support. Indeed, *The New York Times*'s pressmen, considering the ad "traitorous" and Nixon an honorable man, initially refused to operate the presses unless the ad were pulled.[60]

Confined as they were to a handful of representatives, left-wing professors, and radicals, calls to impeach Nixon for continuing the war cut little ice. By October 1972, moreover, Kissinger was announcing that "peace is at hand" in Vietnam. Although his proclamation proved premature—many thought it was a ploy to help Nixon win reelection the next month—in January 1973 a deal was struck. Suddenly, Vietnam, the issue that along with repression had most vexed radicals, was off the table. Even though Nixon had been now deeply associated with the face of a fascist and a conspirator, he was standing tall.

In a matter of weeks, all that would change.

With the break-in of Democratic headquarters on June 17, 1972, and the tracing of the crime to the White House, Nixon's presidency unraveled. Liberals, once loath to describe Nixon as a literal despot, now signed on to something akin to the radicals' view of him. For radicals, though, Watergate raised a dilemma: It validated their worst fears of Nixon as a conspirator; yet it also bolstered their view of the whole system as a conspiracy, in which case (in contrast to the liberals) they could not see Nixon as unique. Where liberals congratulated themselves during Nixon's dying days that "the system worked," radicals saw only business as usual.

Watergate corroborated the radicals' worst suspicions about Nixon's dictatorial designs. From the start, the radical press proclaimed to all who would listen that the break-in was proof of their conspiratorial fears. Like the proverbial stopped clock, this time they turned out to be right; three days after the break-in, Nixon engaged in a conspiracy to obstruct justice by having the CIA tell the FBI to curtail its investigation of the break-in on the false grounds that it would uncover national security operations. This was the single act that, when confirmed by Nixon's White House tapes, did the most to force his ouster. Yet during the summer of 1972, before information surfaced linking Nixon's closest aides to the crimes, Nixon's cover-up worked. The mainstream press (apart from a small contingent of reporters) saw the left's agitation about Watergate as hysterical conspiracism. The public generally accepted White House claims that only low-level campaign employees were involved. In November, Nixon was reelected overwhelmingly.

During the first few months of 1973, however, a series of shocking revelations changed public opinion: the Watergate burglars were convicted; defendant James McCord revealed to Judge John Sirica details of a cover-up; L. Patrick Gray admitted in his FBI confirmation hearings that the White House had monitored the Justice Department's Watergate investigation; a Senate committee opened an inquiry; and prosecutors found evidence that Nixon's top aides, including Haldeman, Ehrlichman, and Dean, had been involved. In short order, the nation learned volumes about the White House's dirty tricks and "Enemies Lists," the burglars and the Plumbers, the taps and the tapes.

Enjoying "a warm sense of poetic justice," Hunter Thompson confessed to "getting a daily rush out of watching the nightmare unfold. . . . The word 'paranoia' was no longer mentioned except as a joke or by yahoos in serious conversations about national politics." Bo Burlingham, an editor of *Ramparts,* agreed that Watergate had forced the mainstream to take the left seriously, to give credence to what had once been dismissed as "paranoia—the catch-all term used for critics unable to take America at its word." Some former skeptics told radicals they had been at least partly right. Addressing a Berkeley audience, Bob Woodward of *The Washington Post* faulted the press, himself and his paper included, for not heeding the left's complaints sooner. "The underground press was largely right about governmental sabotage," he said, as glowingly reported in the *Berkeley Barb,* "but the country didn't get upset because it was the left that was being sabotaged. The country got upset when it was the broad center, with its political institutions, that was attacked."[61]

Watergate allowed liberals to join in the view of Nixon as an aspiring tyrant and to press for his ouster. For liberals, Watergate was a much easier case to argue than Vietnam. Under Johnson, it was liberals themselves who had prosecuted and supported the war, and for Democrats to have sought Nixon's impeachment over warmaking would have smacked of hypocrisy. Besides, the constitutional grounds for doing so were murky. Watergate, in contrast, was a relatively straightforward matter for them. Before Watergate, historian Herbert S. Levine noted in *The Nation,* "The use of the Nazi-Fascist analogy to describe the American political system was . . . restricted almost entirely to the radical left, and never developed beyond the level of sloganeering." But now Levine urged that the old term be dusted off for Nixon. In 1972, the press had vilified McGovern for making the most attenuated comparisons between Nixon and Hitler. Now Sam Ervin, the head of the Senate Watergate Committee, bluntly denounced the Huston Plan—the aborted effort in 1970 to unite federal intelligence operations under Nixon's direct control—as reflecting a "Gestapo mentality." When on October 20, 1973, Nixon fired Attorney General Elliot Richardson, deputy Attorney General William Ruckelshaus, and Watergate Special Prosecutor Archibald Cox, the "Saturday Night Massacre," as it quickly became known, instantly changed people's assessments of Nixon. Few quarreled with Senator Ed Muskie's claim that the firings "smack[ed] of dictatorship," or with Senator Robert Byrd's blasts at Nixon's "Brownshirt operation." Once shy about such comparisons, leftist and liberal intellectuals alike now soberly explained why Nixon could historically be classed as a fascist or how his presidency amounted to a "brush with tyranny." Cartoonists increasingly sketched him sitting on a throne, bedecked in regalia, or hunched and misshapen like Richard III. From far left to moderate center, a consensus formed that Watergate was a near coup d'état, a step toward despotism.[62]

With Watergate, liberals also accepted the New Left's arguments about the rise of the national security state, albeit without the conspiratorial flourishes. In March 1973, *New York Times* reporter John Herbers wrote a four-part series tracing the growth of an "imperial presidency" that culminated with Nixon's unprecedented usurpations of power. Reflecting what he found to be "almost unanimous opinion" among experts that Nixon was expanding the power of his office as no predecessor had done, Herbers argued that Nixon excluded Congress from key decisions and reorganized the executive branch to concentrate power in the White House. "In so many ways I think Mr. Nixon has gone far beyond any previous presidents in our history," the historian Henry Steele Commager was quoted as saying in the article. Nixon was annoyed when he read the series. "This is really nonsense," he wrote to Ehrlichman, asserting, as he often did, that Kennedy and Johnson had done worse. But the label stuck. That fall, Arthur M. Schlesinger, Jr., published *The Imperial Presidency*, which argued that presidents of both parties (Kennedy pretty much excepted) had expanded the executive warmaking powers under "the all-purpose invocation of 'national security.'" Schlesinger, too, singled out Nixon as "a genuine revolutionary," who had uniquely sought to "import subversion into domestic politics." Concluded the historian: "Watergate was potentially the best thing to have happened to the presidency in a long time," because it provided a chance to halt the presidency's growth before any worse disasters occurred.[63]

Still, liberals and radicals saw the situation differently. For radicals, the war and Nixon's repressiveness were what made him a brutal despot. Questions about the balance of powers troubled them less. Liberals focused on the subversion of the political process in Watergate. Though it far exceeded Nixon's skullduggery against Helen Douglas, they felt, it showed essentially the same old Tricky Dick at work, a man who would stop at nothing for electoral success.

As the impeachment process began, radicals and liberals argued over these differences. To the left, the political crimes of Watergate could never match the horror of prolonging the carnage in Vietnam. To liberals, the Vietnam War was a disaster, a geopolitical and even moral mistake. But it "lay within a range of [permissible] executive decision," as Schlesinger put it. When the House Judiciary Committee excluded Nixon's bombing of Cambodia from its impeachment counts, radicals were furious. George McGovern was among those who thought the committee had missed the big picture. "If John Ehrlichman deserved five years in prison" for ordering the break-in of Daniel Ellsberg's psychiatrist's office, McGovern later wrote, "one can only wonder what other policy makers deserved for the senseless expeditions against the people of Indochina. . . . The secret, unconstitutional bombing of [Cambodia] was the clearest ground for a Nixon impeachment. It was a vastly more serious crime than the break-in at Watergate." Nabbing Nixon for Watergate was, Noam Chomsky said, like jailing gangland murderers for income tax fraud.[64]

The left's subordination of Watergate to Vietnam meshed with its cynicism about liberal politicians. Noting the liberals' *Schadenfreude* at Nixon's downfall, radicals argued that Democrats were just happy to regain power. Chomsky mocked the political scientist Hans Morgenthau for carping that Nixon had "broken the rules of the political game"—a key liberal complaint against Nixon since the 1950s; Chomsky believed the whole game was broken. Likewise, *Ramparts* belittled Eric Sevareid for claiming that the scandal "touches the heart of the democratic system," because, its editors retorted, "the heart of the democratic system was cut out long ago and no simple transplant operation . . . will return the patient to good health."[65]

Radicals argued that both liberals and conservatives wanted to suppress the New Left and its revolutionary potential. Anti-war leader Dave Dellinger wrote that liberals were planning to decide Nixon's fate based not on whether "they think he is guilty or innocent of major crimes against Indochinese or Americans, but . . . [on an] estimate that it is the best way to head off popular initiatives to probe the workings of the system and to make it significantly more democratic." The liberals' stake in keeping the waters calm could be seen, he added, by their rush, following Agnew's resignation in October 1973, to confirm Gerald Ford as the new vice president. Senators, he said, should have probed Ford's service on the controversial Warren Commission, which, in reporting John Kennedy's assassination to have been a lone gunman's work, amounted to "a far greater cover-up than Nixon's cover-up of Watergate."[66] Chomsky agreed that the post-Watergate attack on Nixon served "to restore the familiar system in which the wealthy and the privileged control American politics."[67]

Thus, while many liberals sighed in relief when Nixon's Watergate crimes were exposed, radicals insisted it was foolish to think that the system worked. The conditions that had bred Watergate predated Nixon and would persist after his ouster. "Anyone who thinks that the type of activity partially revealed to the public in the Watergate disclosures began with Richard Nixon or will end with his departure has not been around the movement very long," Dellinger asserted. Cointelpro (the FBI campaign to spy on, harass, and discredit leftist and liberal activists begun in 1956) and other espionage programs had thrived under Democratic presidents after all. Like Wade Myers, the college student who blanched at blaming Nixon for Vietnam and Kent State because "it has something to do with the system," many radicals thought the demonization of Nixon obscured structural problems. The result was that even as the left rendered Nixon as a murderous villain, it could not delight unequivocally in his removal.[68]

· · ·

The paradox of reviling Nixon while downgrading his culpability was most apparent in one strain of post-Watergate New Left thought. For some radicals, Watergate snapped the last restraints on what they could imagine of their leaders. They had already judged Nixon a mass murderer. Now some supposed him capable of crimes more ghastly still: traffic with cold-blooded killers, the plotting of individual murders, even participation in the greatest conspiracy of them all, the Kennedy assassination. In the late Nixon years, these radicals devoted themselves to research into far-fetched conspiracies surrounding Nixon, Watergate, and Kennedy's death, founding assassination-related organizations and publishing anthologies of conspiracist essays. In plunging headlong into conspir-acism, in slipping the last bonds of rationalism, these radicals effectively gave up on politics. The quest for authenticity, once pursued through participatory democracy, seemed no longer attainable through a system that was itself a total sham. Instead, the radical search for truth became the vehicle for rediscovering the authentic.[69]

One favorite fantasy held that Nixon was in league with organized crime. The claim surfaced in the underground paper *Sundance* in 1972. Probing Nixon's friendship with the enigmatic service station mogul Bebe Rebozo, a reporter named Jeff Gerth alleged nebulous financial links among Nixon, Miami's Cuban-American community, and the mobsters Meyer Lansky and Jimmy Hoffa. Reciting a litany of shady business deals, Gerth proved only that Nixon had entered into one or two arrangements with some businessmen who may also have had separate dealings with Mob-related men or outfits. But this relatively benign charge was concealed behind breathless claims that with Nixon, "organized crime . . . put its own man in the White House." Gerth's story was snapped up by alternative newspapers, and after Nixon's fortunes plummeted, Gerth reworked his article for publication in *Penthouse* magazine and in two anthologies of New Left conspiracism.[70]

Despite its thinness, Gerth's article—republished with a Hiss-era photo of Nixon in trench coat and fedora—fostered a picture of a thuggish, criminal Nixon at home in the world of casino owners, drug runners, and Saturday Night Specials. With the first Watergate disclosures—the discovery, for example, that the burglars carried walkie-talkies, surgical gloves, and lock picks—the Mafioso image of Nixon gained currency. In July 1972, just after the break-in, *The Nation* (pleading that it meant no "smear against persons of Italian descent") maintained that "Mafia" provided "an apt metaphor" for the Watergate crimes. Over the next two years, cartoonists and commentators compared Nixon and his aides to a gang of low-life crooks, riding around in a Model T with tommy guns waving in the air. Gerth just made the metaphorical literal.[71]

If Nixon could be viewed as a mobster, it was a short step to casting him as a murderous boss, capable of plotting others' deaths. Some radicals wondered about Nixon's role in the death of Dorothy Hunt. The wife of Watergate burglar Howard Hunt, Dorothy Hunt was aboard a flight from Washington to Chicago on December 8, 1972, that crashed upon landing, killing her and forty-four other passengers. She had been carrying $10,000 in hundred-dollar bills, "hush money" meant for the burglars. A National Transportation Safety Board investigation found that the crash was an accident. But conspiracy theorists construed the government's verdict as proof of a cover-up. A Chicago-based "independent investigator" named Sherman Skolnick, claiming to have been tipped off by a Federal Aviation Administration whistle-blower, combed the flight's passenger list and the autopsy reports for clues. Random pieces of "evidence"—cyanide traces in the pilot's blood; the presence on the flight of businessmen who allegedly knew that John Mitchell was colluding with their competitors; the suspiciously quick arrival of FBI agents at the crash scene—convinced Skolnick that the government engineered the disaster. Many New Left pamphleteers agreed. One, Barboura Morris Freed, rehearsed the arguments in an essay for the anthology *Big Brother and the Holding Company*, noting that after the crash several White House staffers conveniently relocated to new jobs where they could monitor the investigations.* Freed also cited a private detective who claimed that Nixon's political adviser Chuck Colson thought the CIA was responsible. She concluded with a call for "an accounting, a new investigation"—a call that could be repeated until what conspiracists considered the awful truth finally came to light.[72]

---

* Egil Krogh went to the Transportation Department, Alexander Butterfield took over the FAA, Dwight Chapin became a United Airlines executive, and Herb Kalmbach, Nixon's lawyer, had long represented United.

Only another short step remained to implicating Nixon in the grand-daddy of New Left conspiracies, the Kennedy assassination. From the day he was shot in November 1963, Kennedy's murder had been a magnet for conspiracists. Indeed, the inquiry into the various alleged assassination plots had become, *Ramparts* wrote, "a social and political affair, aligned in spirit with the anti-war movement." It was not that radicals adored Kennedy. On the contrary, most considered him a corporate liberal and mocked the intellectuals' romance with Camelot. Rather, rejecting the Warren Commission's explanation that gunman Lee Harvey Oswald acted alone became a mark of heroic skepticism, a defiance of sanctioned, spoon-fed answers and official authority. Moreover, the left's explanations blamed the killing on powerful forces in American society—the CIA, organized crime, LBJ, big oil, the military-industrial complex, anti-Castro crusaders, or all of the above—that came straight from the New Left's rogues' gallery.[73]

Open-ended by their nature, the left's assassination theories easily accommodated Watergate, crossing a new frontier of Nixon-related imagery. Their imaginations rekindled by Watergate, assassination buffs set about linking Nixon to Kennedy's murder, seizing on each newly dis-covered coincidence. It turned out, for example, that Nixon was visiting Dallas the day before the assassination because his law firm represented Pepsi-Cola, whose bottlers were meeting there; conspiracists took his presence as evidence of his involvement. Eyebrows were raised too when it emerged that the Watergate burglars had participated in the failed 1961 Bay of Pigs invasion, a key event in assassination lore; Nixon's statement, heard on his Oval Office tapes, that Howard Hunt might "blow the whole Bay of Pigs thing"—by which he likely meant the post–Bay of Pigs CIA plots to kill Castro—fueled suspicions of a Dallas-Watergate link. And when Ford pardoned Nixon in September 1974, conspiracists recalled Ford's service on the Warren Commission and argued that the new presi-dent was seeing to it that the truth would remain hidden.[74]

The books and articles that these buffs wrote formed, within the volu-minous Kennedy assassination literature, a small corpus all their own. One author, Professor Peter Dale Scott of the University of California at Berkeley, first aired his Dallas-Watergate hypothesis in an article for *Ram-*

parts in November 1973 and over the next two decades published book after book on the subject, revising his theory to accommodate new facts. Another champion conspiracist—a legend in some leftist circles—was Mae Brussell, a California homemaker who spent eight years cross-referencing the Warren Report into a 27,000-page concordance. According to the countercultural satirist Paul Krassner, Brussell noticed eerie parallels between Nixon's rise to power and Hitler's, including the prevalence of assassinations. Upon hearing about the Watergate break-in in June 1972, Brussell hammered out a twenty-one-page article for Krassner's magazine, *The Realist*. It claimed that a "hidden, clandestine government" of "military and industrial fanatics" had killed Kennedy because he would not wage war with the Soviet Union; this secret government, Brussell continued, had then installed President Nixon, who ordered the break-in to protect his power. To Krassner, the appeal of Brussell's home-cooked fabulism lay more in its unabashed iconoclasm than in any polemical rigor. But some leading New Left voices were coming to believe that the Dallas-Watergate connection held the key to postwar American politics.[75]

These extreme notions of Nixon's supposed boundless capacity for evil—gangsterism, sabotage, assassination—came together in the thinking of Carl Oglesby, a former SDS president and a leading voice of the New Left in the late Sixties. Once passionately engaged with urgent political issues, Oglesby had by 1972 turned his attention entirely to a Cambridge-based group he founded called the Assassination Information Bureau, organized, he wrote elliptically, "to politicize the question of John F. Kennedy's assassination." Oglesby's journey from New Left theorist to full-time assassination buff was emblematic of the trajectory of one segment of the New Left. Where some erstwhile radicals abandoned politics in the Seventies to take up personal searches for meaning, from Zen Buddhism to organic farming, a small brigade of people like Oglesby sought answers in sorting out the disaster-ridden history of recent times. Oglesby found purpose in reaffirming, through baroque conspiracy theories, the notion that a power elite deliberately blocked all avenues for radical change.[76]

While with SDS, Oglesby had been a cogent analyst of corporate liberalism, and he lost none of his intelligence or zeal in shifting his attention to assassinations. First in a series of articles for the *Boston Phoenix*, then in a book called *The Yankee and Cowboy War* (1976), he presented a single octopuslike conspiracy to explain the whole gamut of catastrophes from the assassination through Watergate. "Dallas and Watergate," he wrote "are intrinsically linked conspiracies in a drama of coup and countercoup which represents the life of an inner oligarchic power sphere . . . a clandestine American state, perhaps an embryonic police state." As the younger Oglesby had married diverse strands of New Left thought into an overarching critique of corporate liberalism, now the older, jaded man provided a unitary explication of all the New Left's woes. Oglesby tied together the Kennedy assassination, opposition to the Vietnam War, fears of surveillance, violence and repression, and Watergate into a mind-boggling theory as impressive in its scope as it was ridiculous.[77]

Oglesby never met a conspiracy theory he did not like. Jeff Gerth's claims about Nixon's Mob links found their place in *The Yankee and Cowboy War*, as did conjecture about CIA plans to kill Castro. Sherman Skolnick's theory about Dorothy Hunt's plane crash made a cameo appearance too, even though Oglesby derided Skolnick as given to "wild raving." When a critic rebuked Oglesby in *The Nation* for nonetheless endorsing Skolnick and "a style of political thinking which turns assumptions into conclusions and hunches into facts," Oglesby responded:

> [E]ven wandering at his most hysterical through dismal swamp, as perhaps with the cyanide question (and perhaps not), Skolnick still makes more sense and does more good teaching than those who use modest rhetoric to tell us there is nothing wrong. Something in fact may be quite wrong, the wrong may be of Satanic magnitude . . . [But] the standard statistic-ridden, political-sociology models employed in conventional federal-academic discourse . . . give us a lone madman here and a lone madman there, as though our time's violent assault on presidential figures were the purest contingency, purest acts of God, unstructured, random events lying outside the events constitutive of "politics" proper.

Whether right or wrong about the murder of a planeload of innocents, Oglesby was arguing, "hysterical" skeptics like Skolnick offered a surer route to knowledge than did liberals with their faith in the "baseless reas-surances" of government agencies and liberal experts. Whizzing through a litany of recent horrors—the Kennedy and King assassinations, Fred Hampton's killing, CIA and FBI repression of dissenters, Kent State, Jack-son State, Watergate—Oglesby concluded that the imputation of sabotage in the Dorothy Hunt case, however "lurid" and "monstrous," was in fact warranted.[78]

The Mob and Dorothy Hunt were for Oglesby just players in a grand drama that unfurled over the postwar era. The larger protagonists were two cabals of business elites, once allied in promoting the Cold War con-sensus, who had gone to war with each other over whether to pursue a "détentist" or "militarist" foreign policy. One group, which Oglesby called the "Yankees," consisted of old-money Northeastern businessmen—the corporate liberals of New Left thought. Internationalists on foreign policy, the Yankees had come by the late 1960s to oppose American involvement in Vietnam and soften their hostility toward Castro's Cuba. Oglesby's other group, the "Cowboys," comprised the new-money real estate and oil moguls of the Southwest who wished to keep expanding America's eco-nomic frontiers in Asia. Extreme anti-Communists, they despised Castro and supported the Vietnam War, from which they profited. Secretly run-ning the country, both groups employed clandestine means and violence to work their will. The Cowboys killed Kennedy because of his timidity over Cuba and Vietnam, installed their front man Nixon in power, and funded his dirty tricks against the Yankee-friendly Democrats. Eventually, however, the Yankees, including top CIA operatives, came to consider Nixon too dangerous, so they deliberately botched the Watergate break-in to bring him down.

Needless to say, most leftists rejected Oglesby's theories. But a good many others, including the journalist and historian of SDS Kirkpatrick Sale, gave them some credence. What resonated was Oglesby's assertion that Watergate represented not a unique event but just the latest instance of an ongoing struggle within an entrenched establishment that average Americans were powerless to change. "Watergate cannot be reduced to a question of Nixon's personal psychology," asserted Oglesby, mocking "the fashion for psychohistory" then in vogue. Rather, Kennedy's assassi-

nation, Vietnam, and Watergate—the whole era's violence and chaos—
stemmed from larger forces in American life. Radicals had taken to the
streets in protest, written devastating critiques of American politics, politi-
cized the young. But the government seemed less responsive than ever to
the popular will.[79]

Where democratic theory collapsed, conspiracy theory filled the void.
For the left, Watergate did not represent a new failure of democracy
because democracy had already failed. In an earlier incarnation, New Left
thought had interrogated the authenticity of American democracy by
exposing a power elite–dominated system in which two status quo parties
offered voters no real choice. But the continuing war and repression made
the notion that even a radical politics could right things seem jejune. Looking back at the string of horrors over the last decade, some leftists noticed
that it all benefited one man: Richard Nixon. It made sense to ask whether
he might be the one who somehow was behind it all.

By the 1980s and 1990s, conspiracy theorists like Oglesby had with-
drawn into a small but hardy subculture. At the same time their cause
found a spokesman as influential as any activist or historian. By 1995
Oliver Stone had become, arguably, America's top film director, and his
movie *Nixon* that year, launched on a riptide of Hollywood hype, put the
recently deceased president back in the public eye. Stone's previous political film, *JFK* (1991), had irritated historians by popularizing the discredited assassination theories of former New Orleans district attorney Jim
Garrison. *Nixon* extended *JFK*'s vision, fitting Watergate and Nixon's
career into one grand conspiratorial scheme. Sharing the worldview that
made *JFK* a *cause célèbre*, *Nixon* functioned as a sequel, focusing on postwar America's most symbolically fraught villain instead of its most fabled
hero.

Although a box-office disappointment by Hollywood standards—it
grossed "only" $26 million in its American theatrical release—*Nixon* gen-
erated a hue and cry. Like *JFK*, it drew rebukes for botching various matters of historical detail. (Nixon, for example, did not use the phrase "Big
Mo"; Herb Klein objected that he was not "short and dumpy," as Stone
depicted him.) But more interesting than this nitpicking was Stone's prop-
agation of the left-conspiracist image of Nixon. Like the New Left, Stone

took pride in his anti-liberalism, deriding liberal "Nixon-haters" in publicity interviews. Stone's worldview was most apparent in the film itself.
In his *JFK* phase, Stone had consumed the writings of conspiracy buffs
Peter Dale Scott and former air force colonel L. Fletcher Prouty, written an
introduction for one of Prouty's books, and had retained Carl Oglesby as
a consultant to the film. *Nixon* also drew from Scott and Oglesby's works,
and its annotated screenplay contained footnotes to their books mixed in
among more standard works. Stone's footnotes in fact provoked charges
of intellectual dishonesty, with at least one scholar, historian Stephen
Ambrose, alleging that the director had twisted his work to make it support conclusions that he rejected.[80]

True to his New Left sympathies, Stone made Vietnam the key to
Nixon. He inserted battle scenes amid the biographical drama, and the war
shaped his narrative choices. His rendition of Nixon's presidency jumped
straight from the candidate's 1968 convention speech to the 1970 decision
to invade Cambodia—a foreshortening that betrayed a view of which
events mattered most. Stone's portrayal of the invasion decision featured
a bloodthirsty Nixon overriding the counsel of moderate cabinet officials
in favor of Kissinger's call for an "incursion." "Exactly!" Nixon exclaimed.
"We've got to take the war to them," adding, in a sacrifice of verisimili-
tude for drama, "More assassinations, more killings!" Documentarylike
footage of Cambodia's strafing followed.[81]

Throughout the film Stone laced intimations about Nixon's murderous past. In one invented scene, Howard Hunt (whom Nixon didn't know
in real life) tells John Dean that Nixon is "the darkness reaching out for the
darkness. . . . Look at the landscape of his life and you'll see a boneyard."
Stone's Nixon was in thrall to the left's stock villains: Texas oilmen, the
anti-Castro right, government spooks, the Mob. He even had a hand in
Kennedy's assassination, appearing in Dallas before the murder to consort
with a shadowy group of businessmen. Elsewhere in the film, Nixon says
that the assassinations of both Kennedys "cleared a path through the
wilderness for me. Over the bodies. . . . " Stone said as much in talking to
the press: "Nixon," he claimed, "was at the very beginning a founder of
political murders in this country."[82]

Yet even while demonizing Nixon, Stone reflected the left's view that

he was just the figurehead of a more sweeping conspiracy. In his rendering of Nixon's late-night Lincoln Memorial visit, Stone included a fictional
exchange that echoed Wade Myers's comments to *Rolling Stone*. In the
film, a student protester surprises Nixon by expressing empathy for his
Vietnam predicament. "You can't stop it, can you?" she says. "Even if you
wanted to. Because it's not you. It's the system. And the system won't let
you stop it." Later in the film, Nixon repeats this analysis. "She understood something it's taken me twenty-five fucking years in politics to
understand," he says. "The CIA, the Mafia, the Wall Street bastards. . . .
'The Beast.' . . . She understands the nature of 'the Beast.'" This "Beast"
represented, according to screenwriter Christopher Wilkinson, "the dark-
est organic forces in American Cold War politics: the anti-communist crusade, secret intelligence, the defense industry, organized crime, big
business." The villainy of these forces overwhelms even Nixon. Like the
New Left, Stone's Nixon is hateful and vindictive, angry and murderous,
but also, in his way, a victim.* [83]

Where some radicals retreated into conspiracism as the only sane
response to Nixonian politics, others embraced a savage form of satire. In
the new freewheeling and unbridled culture, humor became increasingly
wild, nasty, sexually explicit, and violent in ways that were once unthinkable. Quite often Nixon, the ultimate symbol of authority, became the target of this anti-authoritarian wit and venom.

　　As early as the 1950s, Nixon had inspired the so-called sick humor of
Mort Sahl and other comedians, and he even had his staffers attend Sahl's
performances to monitor him.† But Sahl's raillery was tame next to the anti-
Nixon humor that arose from the 1960s counterculture. Alternative papers,

---

* Stone was not the only 1990s artist to place Nixon at the center of conspiracy theories in late
twentieth-century America. Chris Carter, the creator of the television series *The X-Files*, said
that his show drew inspiration from Nixon (indeed, some episodes made reference to
Nixon and Watergate): "If there is a ghost animating the machinery of *The X-Files*, it is
Richard Nixon, the icon of paranoia whose career virtually defined the golden age of American conspiracy theory."

† See p. xxvi.

which had no qualms about using obscenities in their headlines, publishing nude photographs, or otherwise defying the norms of the "straight" press, printed extreme and grotesque renderings of Nixon. They depicted him not just as a murderer or as Hitler—common tropes—but as a hideous and evil beast. As always, it was left deliberately ambiguous as to whether the savage attacks were meant to be taken playfully or literally. In their pages, scatology and profanity abounded. "My God! I seem to have tapeworms!" shouted a frightened-looking Nixon in a May 1974 cartoon in the *Berkeley Barb*, as he expelled a huge pile of audiotape. In Gilbert Shelton's popular alternative press comic strip *The Fabulous Furry Freak Brothers*, a "Tricky Pricky" ordered rookie drug enforcement agents, "When dealing with hippies, radicals and niggers, shoot first and ask questions later. Above all, don't let them get to their Jewish lawyers." Again, when Nixon caught wind of such mockery, he had the offenders (including filmmaker Emile de Antonio and the Smothers Brothers) investigated.[84]

One such episode occurred when Haldeman caught wind of a 1971 film called *Tricia's Wedding*. A soft-porn film of thirty minutes, it starred a San Francisco troupe of transvestites and other performers called the Cockettes and depicted the president's daughter's marriage to Ed Cox in drag. The chief of staff convened a secret screening of the film for White House aides to decide what action to take, though, as John Dean noted, none was necessary, since the film "died a natural death." Nonetheless, director Mark Lester followed it up during Watergate with *White House Madness*. In this sequel, Nixon hides damning recordings of his conversations in a stuffed and hollowed-out Checkers, whom he keeps in a closet and with whom a sexual relationship is strongly implied. The plot centers on Bebe Rebozo's kidnapping of the taxidermied dog and Nixon's use of Haldeman, Ehrlichman, and Mitchell to retrieve it, but they end up torching the room where Checkers is held and the animal is consumed by flames. Later, at a White House banquet, Nixon wears a Hitler mustache, says, "If you can't fool all the people all the time, fuck 'em," and has his guests chant, "Heil Nixon!" The film, alas, fared no better than its predecessor, though it got renewed attention two decades later when one of its investors was unmasked as the conservative Texas senator and aspiring presidential candidate Phil Gramm.[85]

Sexual ribaldry and related themes were common to counterculture send-ups of Nixon, playing off the president's straitlacedness. In the spirit of *Tricia's Wedding*, *The Realist* ran a short story, "My Affair with Tricia Nixon" ("Leaping on me, we roll, she grabs at my crotch . . ."). A handful of satirists managed to lift the vulgarities to a truly artistic or creative level. The artist Philip Guston, who began his career as a peer of Jackson Pollock in the New York School of abstract painting, was inspired, and egged on by his friend Philip Roth—then refining his own scabrous Nixon satire, *Our Gang*—to draw a series of Nixon caricatures portraying the jowly, sloped-nosed president as a penis and testicles. (Puns on "Dick" were a counterculture staple, but none other was quite so ingenious.) In one sketch, possibly inspired by Nixon's Lincoln Memorial visit, an upright (not to say erect) Nixon in suit and tie stiffly puts his arm around a shaggy, fringe-wearing hippie. In another, he dresses up as a policeman, with badge and nightstick. Despite his own vulgar appearance, Nixon is shocked in another drawing to see in a public bathroom a wall covered in graffiti, including a crude drawing that looks rather like himself.[86]

Another of the wittier satirists of the era was Paul Krassner of *The Realist*. In the 1960s, Krassner had stirred up controversy by writing a grotesque spoof in which Lyndon Johnson sexually penetrated the slain John Kennedy's bullet wound. In August 1974, Krassner did himself one better with a piece that he called "A Sneak Preview of Richard Nixon's Memoirs." Capturing Nixon's manner of speech perfectly, he imagined Nixon and Haldeman during Watergate's dark days. When Haldeman asks if there's anything he can do, Nixon responds, as Krassner wrote, "'Oh, *sure*'—and I certainly did not intend for this to be taken literally—'why don't you try sucking my cock, maybe *that*'ll help.'" Krassner continues, in Nixon's voice:

> To my utter astonishment, Haldeman unzipped my fly and proceeded to do exactly what I had *facetiously* suggested, with what can only be described as extreme efficiency. He must have had some practice in his old prep school days. But neither of us said a word—before, during, or after. It occurred to me that this misunderstanding was comparable to the time that Jeb Magruder remarked how convenient

it would be if we could get rid of Jack Anderson, and G. Gordon Liddy assumed this was a direct order and rushed out to accomplish the act. . . . As for my own motivation, here was an exercise, not of homosexuality but of power. I realized that if I could order the Pentagon to bomb Cambodia, it was of no great consequence that I was now merely permitting my chief of staff to perform fellatio on me. . . . When the incident was over, I simply returned to my desk and . . . said in a normal tone of voice, "What's on the agenda?"

Krassner and Guston both walked a line between the vicious humor of the radical left and the softer attacks of mainstream liberals, mixing *Berkeley Barb* venom with Rothian subtlety.[87]

Yet a difference certainly existed. Tony Hendra was a writer and editor of the young, countercultural *National Lampoon* humor magazine and a member of its performance troupe, which in the Watergate years was staging a popular revue called *Lemmings*. In the fall of 1973, a group of well-to-do New Yorkers who had made Nixon's Enemies List threw an anti-Nixon party and asked the *Lemmings* troupe to perform. The socialite hostess of the evening condescended to the troupe, treating them like hired help instead of the local celebrities they had become. Hendra remembered that "these Enemies weren't exactly our friends" and wondered if perhaps Nixon had been onto something. With Hendra's blessing, performer Gary Goodrow announced that he would conclude the show with his "impersonation" of Nixon, whereupon, after receiving hearty applause, he dropped his pants and waved his behind in front of the mortified audience. The hostess called it "filth," but the performers considered it the cutting edge of satire, flouting the standards of not just the Nixonites but also their own liberal hosts.[88]

The anarchic spirit of *National Lampoon's Lemmings* went mainstream two years later in the surprise-hit television show *Saturday Night Live*, whose cast included *Lemmings* alumni John Belushi and Chevy Chase. One night in 1976, *SNL* writers Al Franken and Tom Davis took LSD and wrote an inspired parody of the recently published book *The Final Days*, an account of the last weeks before the president's resignation. Dan Aykroyd, playing Nixon for the first time, exquisitely mimicked his defensive self-pity as he talked to portraits of former presidents. "Well, Abe, you were lucky," he said to Lincoln. "They *shot* you." To Kennedy he fumed, "They're gonna find out about you, too. The president having sex—with women—within these very walls. That *never* happened when Dick Nixon was president."[89]

Despite his slight physical resemblance to Nixon and minimal makeup job, Aykroyd would reprise his role in the future, becoming one of the great Nixon imitators. Within a few years, *Saturday Night Live*'s satire would become apolitical and toothless, like Johnny Carson's, lacking the countercultural political edge of the Aykroyd-Belushi years. It came to rest content with uncanny imitations in the tradition of Rich Little, bolstered by elaborate cosmetics and costumes, devoid of bite. Like Oglesby's retreat into full-blown conspiracism, or other counterculturalists' embrace of self-fulfillment, the adulteration of *Saturday Night Live*'s satire reflected the culture's gradual abandonment of the political engagement that characterized the embattled Nixon years. But in its early years the show had represented the successful mainstreaming of the anarchic comic energies of the counterculture, inhabiting the narrow swath between offensive, vitriolic savagery and vacuous family-room jokes. Nixon was an ideal target.

Before he could be turned into a laughingstock, however, Richard Nixon had to leave office, and he did not do so eagerly. Because Nixon considered the drive to impeach him a vendetta, he would not give his enemies the satisfaction of his compliance until he realized resignation was his best option. Even then, he did not leave the White House before offering radicals—and other Americans—one last occasion to spin nightmare scenarios about his capacity for villainy and the precariousness of American democracy.

By midsummer 1974, a fever had been rising along the Potomac, as the showdown between Nixon and his would-be impeachers entered its endgame. On July 13, Sam Ervin's Senate Watergate Committee issued the last volume, 2,200 pages, of its report; on July 24, a unanimous Supreme Court forced Nixon to surrender tapes that showed him obstructing the FBI's Watergate inquiry; on July 27, the House Judiciary Committee reported the first of three counts of impeachment; on August 5, Nixon released the tape that showed his early involvement in the cover-up; and two days later, congressional Republicans told the president he had lost their support. Nixon's ouster was now a foregone conclusion.

Aware of the president's tenacity, observers speculated about his next move. Rumors reminiscent of the 1970 canceled-election scenarios surfaced. If impeached and convicted, people wondered, might Nixon summon the military to prevent his removal? In the past, others had entertained the thought. In July 1973, Philip Roth published in *The New York Review of Books* (alongside a Philip Guston cartoon) a parody of a speech Nixon might give after a Senate vote to remove him from office:

> . . . according to the doctrine of the separation of powers, the Executive Branch has an equal voice in the management of government. . . . the President, which I am, has the sole responsibility for safeguarding the security of the nation. That responsibility is spelled out in the oath of office, which, as you all know, every President takes on Inauguration Day. . . . And that is why I have decided tonight to remain in this office. My fellow Americans, though I respect the sincerity and the integrity of those Senators who voted earlier in the day for my removal, I find after careful study and grave reflection that to accept their decision would be to betray the trust placed in me by the American people.

Roth's Nixon goes on to explain that he understands that some in Congress won't "respect" his decision, will try to attack it for political reasons, or "may attempt to use force to remove me from Office," but that since his administration "will not tolerate lawlessness of any kind," he was placing the army on alert to ensure that such force wouldn't be used against him.[90]

After the Saturday Night Massacre, the idea evolved from a joke into a fear. In late 1973, Congressman Fortney "Pete" Stark of California suggested that Nixon might attempt a coup to keep power. Soon after, Jack Anderson reported that in May 1969 Nixon had approved an "Interdepartmental Action Plan for Civil Disturbances" in case he declared a state of emergency that, as the radical press claimed, would allow him to "suspend the Constitution." By May 1974, the possibility was being discussed as a realistic scenario. The *New York Post*'s Pete Hamill wrote a column exhorting the governor and mayor to "begin planning a program of self-defense in the event of a military coup." Hamill added, "Two years ago, such a thought would have been preposterous. But Nixon's contempt for the law is now a large dark fact." He suggested that the National Guard be enlisted to defend New York, along with citizen brigades to serve as "block defense committees and defenders of bridges, tunnels, airports [and] . . . the supply of food and water."[91]

The concerns troubled men in the highest tiers of government as well. Henry Kissinger, promoted to secretary of state a year earlier, and General Al Haig, who succeeded the ousted Haldeman as chief of staff, traded notes about Nixon's talk of calling out the army's 82nd Airborne Division to "protect" him. Defense Secretary James Schlesinger, concerned that Nixon might bypass the chain of command and contact military units directly, instructed military personnel to follow White House orders only if the secretary personally approved them. That Nixon did not actually call up the troops gave skeptics little comfort afterward. William Shannon, a Nixon-hating *New York Post* reporter in the 1950s who had since moved to the *Times*, compared the scenario to the movie *Seven Days in May*. "The United States was lucky in August," he said—"lucky" because had the situation been slightly different, Nixon might well have tried a coup. "Next time," he wrote, ". . . the Secretary of Defense might be feeble and compliant."[92]

Ron Rosenbaum, the *Village Voice* correspondent who investigated the canceled-election rumors in 1970, recalled that days before Nixon's resignation, journalists were milling about the White House press room when suddenly Secret Service men locked the doors. For the next half hour the security men stood stonily by the exits as the trapped reporters hollered and shook the doors. Knowing Nixon's hatred for the press, knowing that the moment had no historical precedent, the reporters bruited about scenarios. "Were generals arriving to administer a state of emergency?" Rosenbaum wondered. "Had the president done something . . . bizarre, dangerous, or self-destructive?" Had Nixon imprisoned them in order to mount a coup? The truth turned out to be far more benign. Nixon, it emerged, had wanted to take one last walk around the White House grounds unmolested and unobserved by the press.[93]

Two decades later, Rosenbaum offered a mea culpa. "He didn't do what we feared in our dark fantasies he'd do," Rosenbaum admitted. "He didn't bring in the generals, call up the troops . . . defy the Supreme Court . . . or rip up the Constitution (well, not after he got caught trying). He didn't live up to the paranoid vision of Richard Nixon we, some of us, were guilty of holding, or hoping he'd fulfill." In the years after Watergate, as what Rosenbaum called the "inflamed paranoia of the moment" subsided, other leftists similarly recanted their warnings. "An excess of paranoia blinded the movement to that even more fierce paranoia, Nixon's, which drove him to violate liberal democracy's own rules," wrote Todd Gitlin a decade after Watergate, the former SDSer having himself softened over time. Tom Hayden, a founder of SDS and a Chicago Seven defendant, likewise stated in 1987 that the left was wrong to have predicted that the United States "would eventually become a police state," misguided in cultivating "a paranoid style of our own." It was not the Chicago Seven, he noted, but "people like John Mitchell" who ultimately went to jail. Though Hayden still shuddered at "Watergate with all of its dread implications," in the end, he felt, "the democratic process worked more than we could have imagined, and more than our ideology would permit us to imagine. . . . It took me almost a decade to acknowledge that forthrightly."[94]

Not all New Leftists admitted to excessive paranoia. Carl Oglesby clung to his stance that Watergate proved that "the 'paranoias' of the Sixties fascist-criers like myself were based on rather clear-eyed judgments of Nixon" and of the American system. In 1975, in the pages of *Ramparts*, Oglesby sparred with David Horowitz, the magazine's former editor who was beginning an ideological journey from far left to far right. Mocking Oglesby's Yankee-Cowboy theory, Horowitz accused his former ally of keeping alive "the assumptions that buried the New Left under a wave of sectarian paranoia." Oglesby welcomed the charge. Watergate, the exposure of Cointelpro, and similar revelations, he noted, vindicated the radicals' alarms; what was more, those alarms "opened mass consciousness . . . and made it possible for western media collectivities to see truths formerly seen only by their victims." But so long as the "class structure" and "strains" that created Watergate continued, radical paranoia was not just warranted but necessary.[95]

Horowitz, then still a man of the left, happily disavowed the liberal nostrum that Watergate proved "the system works" and agreed that Nixon should have been tried for "war crimes" instead of the "dirty tricks . . . that have been common devices of the presidency while extending America's imperialist frontiers." But he also offered what sounded like a liberal's defense of democracy. While acknowledging the government's repression, Horowitz stressed the difference between that repression, which occurred within a democratic framework, and fascism, which denied democratic rights altogether. Nixon, he argued, while "malevolent," never approximated fascism or planned a coup. "The commitment to the two-party system and the Bill of Rights is still a powerful force in the determination of ruling-class strategy," he said, and it would likely remain so.[96]

The debate between Oglesby and Horowitz underscored the New Left's delicate position as the era of superheated paranoia drew to a close. Horowitz was correct that Oglesby's octopus theories were out of touch with reality and that events couldn't justify calling America "fascist," even under Nixon. But he failed to address the irony that without the left's warnings and hyperbole, the press corps and the president's liberal critics would have been slower to pursue Nixon's removal. For while reporters first brought Watergate to light, and liberals carefully laid out how Nixon was subverting democracy, radicals helped create the conditions that made impeachment possible. Radicals first directly challenged authority, first sounded alarms about illegal surveillance, first promoted suspicion about covert activities, first pegged Nixon as a conspirator. Although absurd when followed to their conclusions, their paranoid fears—as writers from Oglesby to Rosenbaum to Hunter S. Thompson noted—wound up hitting the mark. If some became unmoored, that was partly because reality had caught up to their skepticism and pushed them farther toward the extremes.

Regardless of the validity of the left's images of Nixon, those images and the currents underlying them had important ramifications. For Nixon, the dictator imagery animated not just radicals but others who came to share it, galvanizing them to press for impeachment. The left, for its part, felt confirmed in its desperation with an unresponsive politics. The radi-

cals' retreat from politics in the 1970s—whether by plunging into conspiracism or by wearily abjuring the political arena as meaningless—contributed later to the overall weakening of the left. Nixon's resignation
coincided with their own sense of resignation. Finally, the culture's absorp-
tion of conspiracist thought would nourish in the years ahead a general,
offhand indifference among Americans. Politics no longer seemed a realm
in which we could expect to find anything authentic at all.

4

The Washington Press Corps:
Nixon as News Manager

> The air was thick with lies, and the president was the lead liar.
>
> —*Ben Bradlee*, A Good Life[1]

Senator Sam Ervin, Democrat of North Carolina, banged his gavel, silencing the Senate Caucus Room. A fervent civil libertarian, given to quoting Shakespeare, the Bible, and America's founders, the crusty, graying Ervin had called a round of committee hearings because Richard Nixon's recent abuses of power had made him fear that "the Constitution's guarantee of a free press" might be "on its deathbed." Over the next weeks, a parade of famous figures came before Ervin's Subcommittee on Constitutional Rights, speaking of the administration's failed lawsuit to stop the publication of the Pentagon Papers and Vice President Spiro Agnew's lacerating attacks on the news media. One witness after another echoed Ervin's worry that American freedom was in jeopardy.[2]

The now forgotten hearings that Ervin held in the fall of 1971 on Nixon's crusade against the media failed to bring him the fame he later achieved as the head of the Senate's Watergate investigation. But he did attract a flurry of attention with his procession of journalists, news executives, and First Amendment experts, including NBC president Julian

Goodman, CBS president Frank Stanton, and even the most trusted man in America, Walter Cronkite, whose appearance packed the caucus room.[3] And although Ervin's hearings proved inconsequential, the mere fact that in September 1971 an influential senator was investigating—or at least grandstanding about—this issue meant that presidential press relations had reached a point of crisis.

Ervin's witnesses voiced a growing sense among Washington journalists that Nixon was waging an unprecedented war against them. In a slew of articles, books, and public and private comments, reporters bemoaned the president's campaign of evasions, attacks, propaganda, and abuses of power designed to control the news.[4] These reporters struggled with a range of administration offensives, from routine wrangles with the notoriously evasive White House press secretary Ron Ziegler to the secret tapping of their telephones. From these daily fights, they formed a picture of Nixon as a consummate manager of the news. Leading newsmen said as much. Accepting the "Broadcaster of the Year" award in 1971, Cronkite labeled Nixon's anti-press campaign "a grand conspiracy." On *The Dick Cavett Show, Washington Post* editor Ben Bradlee charged that "the First Amendment is in greater danger than any time I've seen it." The National Press Club convened a blue-ribbon panel, which ultimately found Nixon guilty of "an unprecedented, government-wide effort to control, restrict and conceal information" and "discredit the press." All of this happened before Watergate.[5]

Some Nixon aides later owned up to their zealotry. "We used to watch the news broadcasts and go up the walls at what we thought was unfair coverage of Nixon," recalled Chuck Colson, who described his efforts to strong-arm CBS executives into gentler treatment. "We did often lie, mislead, deceive, try to use [the press], and to con them," wrote speechwriter Ray Price, "and I could appreciate their resentment." William Safire recalled that Nixon told him often that "the press is the enemy . . . to be hated and beaten"—an attitude Safire called "neither justifiable nor defensible." Nixon, too, admitted to his belligerence, even as he justified it. "I was prepared to have to do combat with the media," he wrote in his memoirs, "in order to get my views and my programs to the people."[6]

Not everyone considered the press the victim in the fight. Nixon and his aides saw themselves as the ones under attack. Nixon had long believed that reporters hated him and treated him unfairly. He considered his actions, however draconian, to be reasonable responses to their distortions. (In fact, until Watergate, Nixon received no worse, and sometimes better, coverage than other candidates or presidents.)[7] The president's lieutenants agreed, as did many of his constituents. Nixon struck political gold when he, Agnew, and other officials decried the media as a biased, out-of-touch, liberal elite.[8]

Reporters wavered over how to respond. Beholden to a professional code that taught them to prize objectivity, they often bent over backward to be fair. Concerned about their credibility, they flaunted their new penchant for self-criticism. But reporters realized, too, that their pursuit of objectivity had in the past left them vulnerable to government manipulation; now, touched by the tenor of the times, many hearkened instead to a competing tradition—muckraking—which dictated that they distrust official answers and stake out an adversarial stance. White House correspondents took it upon themselves, as one put it later, to "compel the government to explain and justify what it's doing," to serve as "the permanent in-house critics of government"—although typically this adversarialism manifested itself not in productive reporting but simply in a snide, captious tone.[9] Throughout Nixon's presidency, journalists seesawed between these approaches, sometimes bathing Nixon in flattery, sometimes riding him mercilessly.

The reporters' image of Nixon as a nefarious manager of the news was forged in the daily struggles of their work. It was also shaped by their own professional (as opposed to ideological) assumptions. In recent years their power had made them what Douglass Cater called "the fourth branch of government"—independent of the state, yet part of the nation's governing class, with an important role to play in American democracy.[10] Jealous of their status, they read Nixon's attacks as an assault on the First Amendment.

The reporters' picture of Nixon as a news manager at first produced just inside-the-profession squabbling. But during Watergate, their critique of Nixon deepened. As his comments became harder and harder to explain except as deliberate falsehoods, Nixon the scourge of the press turned into Nixon the liar, and then into Nixon the crook. These images, building on existing images of Tricky Dick and Nixon the conspirator or tyrant, eventually became permanently attached to the president. The triumph was ironic, since it suggested that, despite Nixon's efforts to control the news, reporters were much less vulnerable to manipulation than they claimed or perhaps realized. It was their views of Nixon and of the events of his presidency, not Nixon's, that came to be shared by most Americans. For all their protests about Nixon's manipulation of the media, their interpretations of the president ultimately proved far more influential and enduring than his own.

That the White House press corps had swollen into a bloated institution by Nixon's presidency was evident to everyone who traveled on his first overseas trip. In February 1969, Nixon left for Europe with a retinue of two hundred journalists, all clamoring and clambering after the same few shards of information. At more than $2,000 per person for the eight-day excursion (almost $10,000 today), the newspapers and networks were bound not to get their money's worth. No breakthroughs were about to happen, and few chances arose to report original stories. The gaggle of regulars simply tailed Nixon from one capital to another, relaying the gist of the administration's press releases. This was exactly what Nixon wanted.[11]

The European trip showed in microcosm what had become a reporter's occupational hazard since the White House press corps had become an institution. Washington-based correspondents had covered the president ever since the capital was established in 1800, but only toward the end of the nineteenth century did they congeal into a profession, founding societies like the Gridiron Club in 1885 and the National Press Club in 1908 to certify their identity. With the twentieth-century explosion of government, the White House press corps became an entity unto itself. Theodore Roosevelt opened a White House press room and invited correspondents to hear him hold forth during his afternoon shave. He feuded with reporters too, lashing out at "the man with the muckrake," thus baptizing an era and a genre of journalism.[12]

Professional routines emerged. Most important was the press conference, which Woodrow Wilson introduced and which underscored the new
institutionalized nature of the relationship between president and press.
FDR turned it into a regular duty for reporters, and Truman held parleys
in the Executive Office Building once a week, having moved them from
the Oval Office to accommodate a corps that had grown to 150 scribes.
Eisenhower recognized the importance of television and filmed his press
conferences for broadcast (after editing). Kennedy pioneered the live conference, with spectacular success.[13]

As part of the power structure, political reporters found that their
own role in shaping events became "the object of curious scrutiny," as
Douglass Cater wrote in 1959. Much of this scrutiny centered on how they
could resist governmental efforts to control them. Journalists had always
denounced attempts to restrict the news, but after World War II technological innovation and the government's growth made the worry into an
obsession. Echoing the era's intellectuals, reporters feared not censorship
but manipulation that might render them unwitting conduits for propaganda. They viewed Eisenhower's ungrammatical obfuscations as
Orwellian doublespeak, and his press secretary James Hagerty's insinuat-
ing charm as a narcotic that numbed them to the restriction of news. Joe
McCarthy's exploitation of their commitment to objectivity was even
more troublesome. They saw how the senator leveled wild charges, which
they, feeling obliged to be neutral, would publish uncritically and thus
vest with legitimacy. Rules of reporting, far from serving truth, abetted falsity. Reporters ended up giving "the lie the same prominence [as] truth,"
Eric Sevareid wrote, and elevating "the influence of fools to that of wise
men . . . the evil to the level of the good." Such fears led to congressional
hearings in 1955, at which *The New York Times*'s James Reston warned of
"the growing tendency to manage the news"—making "news management" a buzzword for the age.[14]

The Vietnam War occasioned more introspection, as journalists pon-
dered how to contend with routine lying from the government. Lyndon
Johnson's "credibility gap" yawned wide. "It was not that President Johnson tried to manage the news: all politicians try to do that," wrote *Washington Post* columnist David Broder, then emerging as the dean of

Washington journalism. "It was that in a systematic way he attempted to close down the channels of information . . . so that decisions could be made without public debate." Reporters saw themselves as embattled truth-seekers fighting the president's vast public relations machine. In 1968, one society of journalists proclaimed in a report that "secrecy, lies, half-truths, deception" had become their "daily fare" and charged Johnson with "perhaps the worst record for credibility . . . in our history." Nixon, whose devotion to secrecy and enthusiasm for public relations dwarfed even Johnson's, would surpass that dubious achievement.[15]

Reporters were responding to more than deception. The very development of mechanisms for handling a burgeoning press corps in a complex society troubled them. By the late 1960s a reporter's daily schedule encompassed, as the White House reporter and frequent press critic Jules Witcover described it, "an endless round of press conferences, . . . a dreary buffet of routine announcements and elaborately fortified justifications." News came packaged, and the demands of deadlines made it tempting to sign for the parcel. Reporters rarely felt good about such compromises and strained at the strictures of their trade. They were influenced, too, by the 1960s spirit of defiance of authority. Journalism had always vaunted inquisitiveness, impertinence, and doubt, but the Sixties gave those values added cachet.[16]

Some critics crudely ascribed this adversarialism to politics. Nixon speechwriter Patrick Buchanan, like the president himself, believed journalism was teeming with liberal Democrats whose biases skewed their reports. Slightly more nuanced was the view of the administration's other Pat, Daniel Patrick Moynihan, the president's adviser for urban affairs and all-purpose policy guru. Moynihan argued that Washington reporters, once the products of working-class backgrounds, now hailed from the liberal intellectual elite. Raised in well-to-do communities, schooled at liberal-arts colleges, they inhabited, Moynihan said (using Lionel Trilling's phrase), an "adversary culture" that aimed "to judge and condemn, and perhaps revise" society.[17]

Cultural differences undeniably divided the press corps from administration aides, especially after Nixon took office. The clash, wrote the *Post*'s Meg Greenfield, was "more traumatic" than any "since Pizarro first dropped in on the Incas." Nixon's staffers mostly came from conservative regions, had careers in advertising and business, and favored short hair and dark suits. Reporters were self-consciously urbane, and each side viewed the other with curiosity if not contempt. Still, Moynihan and Buchanan were wrong to see a bald political agenda at work. As journalists attested, professional goals—getting a scoop, asking a revealing question, writing a talked-about column—mattered more to them than political goals.* Although reporters did tend to be liberal Democrats and an ideological bias could sometimes be detected their coverage, partisan loyalties couldn't explain the similar drubbing that Lyndon Johnson had endured, and countercultural sympathies certainly didn't extend to the older reporters and editors who still called the shots in newsrooms. Moreover, while some talked of jettisoning hoary values like objectivity, few did so. ("Take out the goddamn editorializing!" *The New York Times*'s managing editor A. M. Rosenthal was known to howl.) Instead, they tried to reconcile unpoliticized reporting with skepticism toward officialdom. A more knowing and opinionated tone resulted. Journalists now sought to convey the motives behind an act, the likely impact of a proposal, an occasional value judgment.[18]

Experiments in news writing emerged: the virtuosic innovations of the "New Journalism," which tossed out the reporter's well-thumbed rulebook in favor of brash subjectivity and chatty or stylized language;[19] investigative reporting—adopted at *Newsday, The Washington Post*, and CBS's *60 Minutes*—which assigned teams to long-term stories to overcome official deceptions;[20] and "advocacy journalism," a hybrid of the two that produced such exposés as a *Ramparts* report on the CIA's funding of a national student group or Seymour Hersh's account of the My Lai Massacre in *The New York Review of Books*.[21] Soon the young Turks were winning praises and prizes. Fitfully, the Washington press corps was

---

* David Halberstam: "In the give and take and scrambling for status among their peers, liberalism, do-goodism and bleeding-heartism are really not deeply admired. Tartness, skepticism, irreverence, fatalism are much more valued among reporters . . . the sense at least of partial alienation." David Broder: "The evidence I have seen—and the personal experience of thirty years' political talk with other journalists—makes me think the charge of ideological bias in the newsroom laughable. There just isn't enough ideology in the average reporter to fill a thimble."

shedding its clubbiness and coziness as front-line reporters increasingly confronted officials head-on.

Partly as a result of their new posture, journalists too were now suffering from the distrust of institutions. Polls showed record lows in esteem for the Fourth Estate. Much of the public doubted the press's objectivity, complaining of biased reporting during the riots at the 1968 Democratic Convention in Chicago. Reporters, in response, embraced self-criticism as never before. If Americans viewed the press not as neutral messengers but as self-interested political actors—as a fourth branch of government— then the press had to be written about critically. Journalism reviews proliferated, and newspapers hired in-house ombudsmen tasked with second-guessing their reporters' and editors' decisions.[22]

"It was Nixon's misfortune to be in office when both 'advocacy journalism' and the notion that the media should be 'adversary' to the government enjoyed their greatest modern-day vogue," wrote Ray Price.[23] Price was partially correct. The press corps was embracing its position as an adversary; but that embrace, though vigorous at times, was at other times quite reluctant. Facing public criticism, reporters wished to preserve their reputation for integrity even as they sought to escape the confines of workaday journalism. In their erratic treatment of Richard Nixon—sometimes fawning, sometimes hostile—this seesawing, ambivalent response would make itself felt.

Suspicious by nature, Richard Nixon always distrusted the press. But the press, contrary to his assertions, did not hate him, at least not as much as he thought. Early in his career, reporters lauded him as an ascendant star. Local California papers, notably the *Los Angeles Times*, hastened his rise. As a congressman, he soaked up the press corps' flattery. Coverage of the Hiss case generally portrayed him, contrary to his later recollections, as a hero. *Time* magazine's Hedley Donovan, typical of his peers, remembered the early Nixon as "swift and coldly analytical" in his intelligence and "many cuts above Joe McCarthy" in his anti-communism—though Donovan added, in an understatement, "I was not captivated aesthetically." Apart from muckrakers like Drew Pearson or die-hard liberals like those at the *New York Post*, the press in the 1950s remained balanced in writing about Nixon.[24]

Members of the Washington press corps, after all, believed their job wasn't to advocate but to report. They prided themselves on keeping ideology out of their copy. *The New York Herald Tribune*'s Earl Mazo recalled that when he began a biography of Nixon, he "despised" the man and set out "to cut him up." But he was a reporter first and foremost, Mazo added, and "I wanted to do it honestly. So I started researching. . . . I found out that so much of what I knew to be total fact, had rated as fact, even written as fact, was just total horseshit. And this alarmed me as a political reporter. . . . I ended up . . . having an enormous amount of respect for the guy." Mazo's final product reflected his admiration for Nixon, even as it also acknowledged his enemies' complaints.[25]

Nixon, alas, couldn't distinguish between a skeptical news item motivated by legitimate journalistic concern and a political (or personal) attack. "He took everything critical as a personal blast at him," William Safire wrote. The scrutiny he received during the 1952 fund crisis confirmed his view of "the press" as a monolithic foe. Although most papers applauded his Checkers speech, his roughing-up led him to conclude that the press had inflated the crisis. Thereafter, he nursed a grudge. When reporters were late for the campaign bus or plane, his adviser Ted Rogers remembered, Nixon would say, "Fuck 'em, we don't need them," and start the engine.[26]

Nixon held reporters at arm's length. His lingering anger kept him resentful, while his awkwardness made it hard for him to befriend all save a few ideological kinsmen. Hence a self-fulfilling prophecy: Few reporters felt any warmth from Nixon, and the discomfort, not any political disagreement, fostered a distrust. This was an altogether different kind of aversion from the liberals' hatred—even if Nixon never understood the distinction. "My dislike had nothing to do with ideology and everything to do with the kind of guy he was," recalled Jack Germond, who covered Nixon from 1954 through his presidency. "He was not someone with whom a reporter would choose to have a friendly jar at the end of the day. He was always posing." Columnist Carl Rowan recalled that during his first interview with Nixon in 1960, "He kept crossing and uncrossing his

legs. He almost never looked me in the eye, acting as though he were reading answers to my questions off the wall or ceiling."[27]

Throughout the 1960 presidential race, Nixon shut himself off from
reporters, who discovered it was more fun to travel with Kennedy's
entourage anyway. On Kennedy's plane they sang songs and told jokes,
often at Nixon's expense. "We want Quemoy/ We want Matsu/ We want
Nixon/To be *their* president," went one riff on a Nixon campaign jingle.
Nixon's resentment burst forth two years later after losing yet another
race, to Pat Brown for governor of California. In November 1962, in what
he called his "last press conference," Nixon sneered at "all the members of
the press [who] are so delighted that I have lost," and berated them for
slanted coverage.* Although that speech was more subdued than many
would later recall, Nixon's bluntness etched in their memories the image
of a man who regarded them as an implacable foe.[28]

From his experience with the media, Nixon might have drawn either of
two lessons. He might have inferred that it behooves politicians to curry
favor with reporters, as Roosevelt and Kennedy did, and that his strong-
arm approach only created bad press. Instead, he concluded the opposite:
that shutting out the media worked. The Checkers speech succeeded
because, as he wrote in *Six Crises*, he opted "to tell [his] story directly to
the people rather than funnel it to them through a press account."[29] He
liked the televised speech, in which he could decide how he appeared. He
ran his 1968 campaign accordingly.

Nixon expected to face hostility in 1968. Early campaign notices, however, were sympathetic. Reporters assigned to him were too young to harbor grudges; older ones, as Nixon perceived it, "had a guilt complex about
their inaccuracy" in the past and repented through softer coverage. John
Herbers of *The New York Times* found Nixon to be pleasant and effective.
"In one story I began, 'You couldn't find a nicer man in North Dakota
today then Richard M. Nixon,'" he recalled with self-mocking disbelief

---

* Nixon praised one reporter, Carl Greenberg of the *Los Angeles Times*, for covering the campaign "fairly" and "objectively," adding that editors had "the responsibility . . . to put a
few Greenbergs on the candidate they happen to be against."

years later. Early in his 1968 bid, Nixon acknowledged to Jules Witcover that since 1962, reporters had been "generally accurate and far more respectful" toward him.[30]

Nixon reciprocated with attempts, however inept, at small talk. The newsmen rewarded these game efforts. They declined to interrogate him about, among other things, his unspecified plan to end the Vietnam War. Later, they would rue their generosity. "In retrospect, I find our failure mind-boggling," Germond wrote. "Nonetheless, at the time it seemed to be a natural evolution of our general feeling that Nixon had been treated harshly in the past, if not by us then by others in our role, and was entitled to a fresh start."[31]

Meanwhile, old hands decreed that Nixon had learned humility. Talk of a "New Nixon," common in the late Fifties, resurfaced. "I believe that there really is a 'new Nixon,'" wrote Walter Lippmann, using the standard adjectives, "a maturer and mellower man who is no longer clawing his way to the top." Theodore H. White, whose *Making of the President 1960* had tapped a public appetite for behind-the-scenes reporting, seconded the idea: "One heard a 1968 Nixon quite different from the 1960 Nixon. The snarl and self-pity . . . were gone . . . what was left was genuine and authentic, true to the inner man." Even the adversarial Norman Mailer agreed. Having loathed Nixon since the Checkers speech, Mailer now professed that the battle-scarred veteran had earned his respect. Admiring the candidate's fielding of questions at a press conference, Mailer saw in Nixon "the sure, modest moves of an old shortstop. . . . His modesty was not without real dignity."[32]

Most striking was the discovery of Nixon's sense of humor. Known for his seriousness—Hunter Thompson once wrote that he couldn't imagine Nixon laughing "except maybe [at] a paraplegic who wanted to vote Democratic but couldn't quite reach the lever"—Nixon was now said to be able even to laugh at himself. When he appeared on *Laugh-In* during the campaign to say, "Sock it to me," the gesture was applauded as proof of his newfound capacity for self-deprecation.[33]

Perhaps the most significant endorsement came from *The New York Times*'s Nixon man, Robert Semple, Jr. A buttoned-down Republican who had graduated from Andover and Yale, Semple was a rising star at the paper. He subscribed to "the rules" at the *Times* that demanded objectivity—"they're good rules," he insisted—and, unlike his scrappier colleagues, balked at introducing opinion into his pieces. "I think there's such a thing as being too critical," he said in response to suggestions he went easy on his subjects. Semple asserted that since he was too young to remember Nixon's early, contentious races, he could "look at this man dispassionately and do a good job." Put on the Nixon beat in 1967, when the candidate's chances seemed slim, Semple wrote a long feature for the *New York Times Magazine* in January. The piece claimed that the McCarthy-era Nixon had "vanished," that "in his place stands a walking monument to reason, civility, frankness." Although Semple acknowledged his "great trepidation" in pronouncing Nixon reformed, since he knew that "the search for the 'real Nixon' has been a popular but fruitless pastime," he still heralded a New Nixon who displayed "candor" and a sense of humor.[34]

Soon, however, Nixon's openness gave way to cloistering and control. Even Semple protested that the staff "became kind of secretive, and you couldn't get beyond a certain point with them." In June 1967 H. R. Haldeman, who shared Nixon's suspicion of the press, urged the candidate to gear his campaign techniques and strategies to television, "to move out of the dark ages and into the brave new world of the omnipresent eye." Having failed to exploit TV in 1960, Nixon vowed not to repeat his error. He hired advisers, including advertising executive Harry Treleaven, CBS's Frank Shakespeare, and Roger Ailes, a young producer of *The Mike Douglas Show*. Nixon shielded himself from the gaze of reporters. Before the New Hampshire primary he filmed a series of question-and-answer sessions made to look spontaneous, only with handpicked audience members, and no reporters allowed. When Haldeman joined the campaign full time that summer, Nixon shuttered what remained of the openness. He allowed TV reporters few chances to film him, sometimes just one a day, ensuring only flattering images for the nightly news.[35]

Two decades later, media strategies like Nixon's would draw ample, even excessive attention from the reporters they aimed to co-opt. But in 1968 editors were loath to inject analysis into news articles, and the press scarcely mentioned Nixon's designs. Articles that spoke of Nixon's image making were straightforward and uncritical. A June 1968 Semple piece that profiled the media advisers Harry Treleaven and Frank Shakespeare was typical. Calling the staged forums "a stately, dignified effort," designed to "emphasize Mr. Nixon's long experience in government," the article betrayed not a hint of the anger that reporters felt about being excluded. "The shows were never rehearsed but Nixon was never stumped," Semple quoted Treleaven as saying, a self-serving remark to which Semple, bound by journalistic convention, added neither his own qualifier nor a dissent from an opposing candidate's camp.[36]

Reporters who objected to the dwindling access did little more than grouse, mostly in private. John Osborne, a longtime AP writer who had recently joined *The New Republic*, was among the critics. Osborne's background and position gave him a rare perch: he had old-fashioned reportorial skills, but writing for an opinion journal, he was expected to comment. Osborne commanded respect from Nixon's men for what Ray Price called his "rigorous intellectual integrity" and willingness to "meticulously separate . . . what he knows from what he surmises." His peers liked him because he often voiced their collective feelings—as he did near the close of the 1968 campaign:

> Like other wearers of the Nixon press badge, pampered and cosseted and served as no campaign reporters have ever been before, I keep waiting for Mr. Nixon to show himself. . . . As of this writing, the fourth week of travel just behind him (not really "with him," as we like to think), I know that I and my companions wait in vain. . . . [Nixon] is not going to . . . tell us anywhere near as much as we need to know about him and the presidency he proposes to give us.[37]

David Broder, who was also unusually positioned, writing both an opinion column and news stories, charged that Nixon was skirting a discussion of issues. Broder faulted a Nixon commercial that showed domestic rioting and Vietnam carnage while promising peace—but without mentioning any solutions. Broder called the spot "a classic example of 'image' over 'meaning,'" and warned that if politicians continued with such misleading image making, "a system of government like ours may no longer be operable." If the admonition was hyperbolic, Broder was merely reflecting his colleagues' fears that in bypassing the fourth branch of government, Nixon was undermining a cornerstone of democracy. Yet despite such occasional cries, the public learned little of Nixon's media strategy in 1968. Although the press was forming a picture of Nixon as a pioneer of image management, they felt the rules of objectivity still obliged them to relay Nixon's own preferred view of himself instead of the one that they had formed.[38]

Nixon thus enjoyed positive treatment into his first year as president. Reporters, happy to be rid of the dissembling Johnson team, placed hope in Nixon's rhetoric of healing. They trusted his genial communications secretary Herb Klein when he pledged, in words that would come to haunt him, that "truth will be the hallmark of the Nixon administration." Nixon did some courting himself. With *The Washington Post*, soon to become his *bête noire*, relations were "if not cordial," reporter Chalmers Roberts wrote, "then at least workable." Nixon sent *Post* writers thank-you notes for favorable stories; to publisher Katharine Graham, he called himself an "admirer." Attorney General John Mitchell, for his part, wrote to her: "Now you can see why I say the *Post* is the best paper in the country."[39]

The affection was requited. Setting the tone, Herblock drew a sketch in which he promised the new president a "free shave." Jack Anderson claimed he "honestly tried to understand" Nixon and "bored in with no more or less zeal" than he had with his predecessors. "I was determined to keep an open mind on Nixon and his administration," echoed CBS's David Schoenbrun, "for reasons of professional integrity [and] out of respect for the presidency." Teddy White sent the president a copy of his latest book, apologizing for his earlier, harsher coverage, which, he wrote, "must have hurt." The new book, White pleaded, depicted "a man of courage and of conscience . . . and the respect [that Nixon's campaign] wrung from me—which I hope is evident—surprised me as I went along."[40]

In Nixon's first year, he drew positive notices—for reforming the draft, for planning to revamp the welfare system, and for a global tour that took him to the Far East and Europe. Nixon-hater Mary McGrory of the *Washington Star* was effusive to Herb Klein after the president's first press conference: "Your man was great. . . . Maybe he's different now that he's president." "Like most of my colleagues and competitors," wrote Jack

Germond, "[I] was impressed by the 'new Nixon' we were seeing. He was advancing interesting and innovative ideas on domestic policy, and the White House was relatively open." Nixon was faulted on a few counts—mainly his ill-advised Supreme Court nominations and his failure to end the war—but year-end assessments in 1969 were kind. Robert Semple declared that Nixon had closed the credibility gap: "So far no major chasms have appeared between what the administration has said and what it is in fact doing." Semple's boss, Max Frankel, was just as enthusiastic, as seen in a passage that he later called "embarrassingly generous, if not naïve":

> He is trying to be a temperate president in intemperate times, a moderate man coping with extravagant problems, a modest figure upon a gigantic stage. . . . For the most part, he has lowered his voice, just as he promised at the inaugural a year ago. . . . After a lifetime of sly and aggressive partisanship, he is slipping into the habits of a judge, presiding over policy debates . . . and resolving them—plausibly, practically or even compassionately.

Overall, Nixon enjoyed better press in his first year than any other twentieth-century president except Theodore Roosevelt.* "We all wanted to believe," explained *Newsweek*'s John Lindsay, "in a New Nixon."[41]

By August 1969, signs had already appeared that Nixon's wasn't going to be an "open administration." Although the press hadn't yet learned that Nixon and Kissinger were wiretapping journalists, *Newsweek* did report that the national security adviser's mania about leaks was instilling fear among his staffers.[42] Still, not until the winter did the tension escalate. Although certain controversial decisions—on Vietnam especially—were in part responsible, the new adversarialism also had a lot to do with the publication of a book: *The Selling of the President 1968* by a twenty-six-year-old *Philadelphia Inquirer* columnist, Joe McGinniss.

---

* According to one political scientist's study, Roosevelt's coverage in his first year was 88.8 percent positive, Nixon's 81.2 percent.

The book, published in October, created a sensation. An account of Nixon's image-making efforts in 1968, it won plaudits from liberal reviewers, who recognized in McGinniss's portrait of Nixon the old Machiavellian they knew. Murray Kempton led the chorus, calling the book a "masterpiece." British journalist Alistair Cooke cheered that McGinniss had exposed Nixon's "fraud."[43]

McGinniss's book clearly owed a debt to Teddy White's *Making of the President, 1960*, which had shown the significance of the previously neglected role of campaign strategy. But McGinniss's work was less a sequel than a rebuttal to White, evincing disdain for White's romantic view of politics as America's civic religion. In contrast to White's insiderly authoritativeness, McGinniss's tone was sassy and brassy, the outsider exposing the insiders'"con game." If White was the voice of the liberal consensus, with its sonorous, even-keeled wisdom, McGinniss was an emissary from the New Journalism, with his countercultural accents, youthful iconoclasm, and nonchalant willingness to bare his left-leaning political views. Where White gained access to the candidates by virtue of his senior status, positioning himself as the official campaign chronicler, more sober and detached than the riffraff of the press pack, McGinniss sneaked in under the radar screen, presenting himself to Nixon's men as such an insignificant fly on the wall that they never thought to swat him away.[44]

Following Nixon's media men into sessions from which other reporters were barred, joining them in casual chats and cafeteria planning sessions, McGinniss gathered the goods for a taut exposé of campaign image making. McGinniss claimed that since Nixon's natural personality was so unappealing, his campaign aides concocted a new persona they projected through TV ads and tightly guarded performances. Both unscripted debates like the 1960 encounters with Kennedy and outbursts like the 1962 "last press conference" were shunned. He quoted from memoranda, including the following meditation on image by Ray Price: "We have to be very clear on this point: that the response is to the image, not to the man, since 99 percent of the voters have no contact with the man. It's not what's there that counts, it's what's projected—and, carrying it one step further, it's not what he projects but rather what the voter receives. It's not the man we have to change but the received impression." McGinniss also drew cursorily from Marshall McLuhan ("The medium is the massage," he quipped, "and the masseur gets the votes") and from Daniel Boorstin, whose themes about authenticity echoed throughout *The Selling of the President*. Like Boorstin and other 1950s liberals, McGinniss decried the "insidious" trickery of those who maneuvered public perceptions for political ends. Like Boorstin, he implicated the public for its outsized expectations. "'We have become so accustomed to our illusions that we mistake them for reality,'" he quoted Boorstin as saying. Devious politicians and undiscriminating citizens conspired to create a political world rife with inauthenticity.[45]

But although McGinniss reprinted the campaign's memos, he subjected them to little analysis. He failed to explore the most original memo, written by William Gavin, a thirty-one-year-old Nixon speechwriter. A closer reader of McLuhan than was McGinniss, Gavin emphasized the idea that TV involves the audience in completing a process as print does not; it is, to use a later era's jargon, interactive. Nixon's linear style of painstakingly spelling out his arguments, Gavin wrote, played poorly on the screen. To "the TV generation," Nixon seemed to be trying too hard, whereas Bobby Kennedy's "screaming appeal" stemmed not from any "logical persuasion" but from "a total experience, a tactile sense—thousands of little girls . . . [wanting to] run their fingers through the image of his hair." Nixon had to craft a TV image, Gavin said, in a way that wouldn't be seen as phony by a television-savvy generation. "It's got to appear noncalculated, incomplete, the circle never squared," Gavin wrote.[46]

Read decades later, *The Selling of the President* would seem somewhat superficial and obvious, undeserving of the outcry that attended its publication. But that loss of luster was itself a result of the book's impact. For where liberals treated the work as proof of the Old Nixon's immutability, reporters read it through their own professional lens. Just as *The Making of the President* had taught them to focus on behind-the-scenes campaign drama, McGinniss's book made it clear that media strategy—run by masters not just of makeup and lighting but also of speechwriting, advertising, polling, and television—now demanded coverage too. In 1968 Leonard Garment, the sole member of Nixon's media team without a media background, had commented, as Nixon policy aide Richard Whalen wrote, that "the issues men were now superfluous"; with McGinniss's book, reporters caught on. "All of a sudden everybody said, 'Oh I get it. They're trying to sell candidates the way they sell soap,'" recalled ABC's Ted Koppel, then a campaign reporter. "From that moment on, we had emerged from the Garden of Eden. We were never able to see candidates or campaigns quite the same way again."* *The Selling of the President* thus made reporters more self-conscious, since they realized that media strategies were meant to box them into a fixed role; now they had to try to observe the very process in which they were implicated.[47]

For similar reasons, McGinniss's book heightened the tension between Nixon and those who covered him, because only increased vigilance could guarantee that they wouldn't be caught off guard. As *Rolling Stone*'s Timothy Crouse observed in his own campaign book four years later (which centered, appropriately, on the journalists covering the 1972 race), reporters felt embarrassed about their passivity in 1968. "They thought it made them look like fools," Crouse wrote. ". . . Nixon fed reporters a phony campaign, and many of the reporters ate it up." More than that, they were angry that McGinniss had shown them up. As AP reporter Walter Mears noted, "McGinniss made it look like he had discovered the TV thing," when in fact "we knew what was happening and we all wrote stories about it." Indeed, Mears, Semple, and Teddy White had. But as Semple's article showed, the strictures of hard-news reporting kept the regulars from presenting the Nixon media strategy with the same bluntness and critical edge that animated McGinniss. The institutionalized role of the established press prevented an overarching New Journalistic critique like McGinniss's.[48]

Perhaps because they didn't want to be burned again, most reporters accepted McGinniss's conclusion that Nixon engaged in an "unprecedented image-management campaign." But while McGinniss was right that Nixon brought an improved professionalism to his efforts, candidates

---

* Others made similar comments. "The packaging is important, and Joe McGinniss's book was the first time a lot of us thought about that. . . . [Newspeople are] still coming to grips with that," said TV producer Tom Bettag. "That changed the way everybody covers campaigns to a degree," agreed Don Irwin of *The Los Angeles Times*. And Don Oberdorfer of *The Washington Post*: "The press became much more conscious of political advertising."

had been using television to shape their images since at least 1952, as the occasional Nixon defender, such as William F. Buckley, noted. Indeed, after Adlai Stevenson's fatal failure to exploit TV, no candidate dared deem it beneath him to do so. Only because so many reporters had fallen for Nixon's efforts did they conclude that it was uniquely insidious.[49]

Besides, no one actually knew if Nixon's machinations redounded to his benefit. He won the election, but it's not clear that the media strategy was decisive. Garment recalled that after Nixon's lead over Hubert Humphrey began shrinking in October 1968, none of the media team's efforts could counteract it; fortunately for them, the lead never dissipated altogether. What was more, many reporters had remained unpersuaded of Nixon's professed reinvention. John Osborne, who already considered Nixon a chameleon, huffed that McGinniss's book held no revelations. "Essentially the same Richard Nixon whom I followed in person around the country came across to the country through the tube."[50]

Just possibly, the conclusion to be drawn from *The Selling of the President* was that Nixon's image making *didn't* work. Despite Nixon's ruses, McGinniss and others had no trouble forming their own picture of him. Without even trying—without even realizing it—they formed an impression of Nixon different from the one he promoted: that of a dissembling manager of the news. "We as a group," Osborne wrote, ". . . share a sense that Richard Nixon ought to be faulted for a fundamental lack of political honor, for what he is doing to the political process with his tactics of concealment and pseudo-disclosure." The problem wasn't that reporters were taken in; the problem was that they couldn't "establish a just and factual basis" for calling Nixon a manipulator in cold print. They felt obliged to show Nixon as he presented himself. McGinniss's book, then, didn't exactly reveal something they hadn't known. But it did tap into the tension they felt between wanting to brandish their toughness, lest they fall prey to manipulation, and fearing that they would seem biased if they did so. By pointing up their docility, it prompted them to stiffen their spines.[51]

Along with Nixon's policies and McGinniss's blockbuster, another event also heightened tensions between the president and the press in late 1969:

Vice President Spiro T. Agnew's attacks on the media. Called "Nixon's Nixon" by Democratic senator and sometime presidential aspirant Eugene McCarthy, Agnew lambasted the media in a pair of high-profile speeches in November that set Washington abuzz. Behind the scenes, Nixon had been moving against the press all year; in the spring, he and Kissinger had begun wiretapping reporters; in the fall he had orchestrated a "Game Plan" of media manipulation to undercut the anti-war protests. But Agnew's speeches commenced what Herb Klein deemed "full-fledged open warfare between the news media and the Nixon administration." Where McGinniss's book pushed reporters toward a more adversarial position, Agnew's attack tugged them the opposite way, prodding them to mute their critical tone in order to preserve their credibility.[52]

Nixon ordered the attacks after his televised address of November 3, when he summoned the "great silent majority" of Americans to rally behind his Vietnam policy. After the speech, reporters gathered in the TV studios to analyze it. Having expected Nixon to announce a diplomatic overture, most thought it newsworthy that he hadn't. "Nothing of a substantial nature or a dramatic nature that is new," said CBS's Eric Sevareid. "No new initiative, no new proposal, no announcement of any troop withdrawals," said ABC's Frank Reynolds. Others, such as Reynolds's colleague Bill Lawrence, were more scathing, their analysis shading into anti-war advocacy. "There wasn't a thing new in this speech that would influence anybody to vote . . . in a different way," Lawrence said. "A good politician would have taken the momentum of the election and the inauguration and come forward with a program of some kind. He wouldn't be explaining Vietnam now. . . . He would have done that in February." By the end of his comment, Lawrence was editorializing. "In his campaign he said he had a plan that would end the war and win the peace. He said that again tonight. I still don't know where it is."[53]

Lawrence and the others thought they were doing their job: describing the speech, analyzing it, judging Nixon's performance, and perhaps providing the public with a corrective to Nixon's one-sided presentation. Nixon heard only potshots. He had hoped to "go over the heads of the reporters"—he'd told Haldeman the previous morning that he was hoping to "circumvent" the "hostile press"—but the commentary, he felt (especially Lawrence's and Marvin Kalb's on CBS), blocked his direct channel to the public. The next morning, at a meeting of top White House aides, Herb Klein reported that the next-day telegrams (some of them generated by the White House) showed that viewers, too, disliked the after-speech punditry. The president moved to strike back. "Unless the practice were challenged," he wrote, "it would make it impossible for a president to appeal directly to the people, something I considered to be of the essence of democracy." He assigned the job to Agnew, who had weeks earlier caused a stir, and sent Americans scrambling for their dictionaries, by branding anti-war activists "an effete corps of impudent snobs who characterize themselves as intellectuals." Now Pat Buchanan drafted a speech, which Nixon personally edited—barely able to stifle his glee, Haldeman noted, as he imagined the media's reaction. As Nixon remembered it, he "toned down some of Buchanan's rhetoric"; William Safire recalled that the president "toughen[ed] it up." Either way, Safire said, "it retained its white-heat vitality."[54]

Delivered in Des Moines on November 13, Agnew's diatribe—and especially a few choice alliterations—entered political lore. Decrying the "instant analysis and querulous criticism" that followed Nixon's talk, the vice president blasted the networks as biased, sensationalist, and irresponsible. "A tiny, enclosed fraternity of privileged men elected by no one," he said, decided what information millions received each day. These men, he continued in the conservative populist vein that Nixon often mined, didn't represent the nation. They came from elite, Ivy League backgrounds, favored liberal viewpoints, and showcased controversial developments. Invoking the will of the people, Agnew called for a return to "straight and objective news."[55]

The journalist David Halberstam once discerned two different strains of anti-press thinking in Nixon: "Haldemanism," which believed in shutting out the press and using direct, televised speeches; and "Buchananism," which favored attacking the press head-on for its liberal agenda. In 1968 and 1969, Nixon had followed a program of Haldemanism; now came Buchananism. For some years, conservatives had reaped gains by attacking the press. Dwight Eisenhower derided "sensation-seeking columnists and commentators" at the 1964 Republican Convention, and more recently such themes had become a theme of the Republican National Committee's newsletter. With polls showing that most people believed the press was at least sometimes biased, the president knew his adversaries were vulnerable. Agnew's speech thus had two (related) goals: tarnishing any anti-Nixon commentary and providing a rallying point for the president's supporters.[56]

Calls came in to the White House two to one in support of Agnew, and an ABC survey found 51 percent of viewers endorsing his position. Buoyed, Agnew prepared a second blast for the next week, targeting *The New York Times* and *The Washington Post*. The follow-up caused a "huge problem" within the White House, Haldeman recorded. Noting that the speech was "pretty rough" and believing Agnew was going "too far," the staff chief tried to get the vice president to soften his rhetoric. He didn't get very far, and Agnew's speech, on November 20 in Montgomery, Alabama, lived up to expectations. The vice president accused the newspapers of having grown "fat and irresponsible" as they accrued power, singling out the Washington Post Company, which owned *Newsweek* and several TV and radio stations, as embodying the trend toward debate-stifling monopoly. Agnew intimated that the government might use its regulatory power against these conglomerates, threatening to turn Nixon's rhetorical war on the press into a legal one.[57]

Agnew's back-to-back speeches, wrote NBC's Reuven Frank, "shook every broadcasting official." They amounted, said CBS's Martin Plissner, to a "declaration of war." The threat of new regulation was especially troubling, and reporters soon found evidence to conclude that a crackdown was imminent. Dan Rather of CBS reported that after Nixon's Silent Majority speech, Federal Communications Commission chairman Dean Burch had requested from the networks transcripts of their post-address analyses—a sign, many concluded, that retaliation was in the offing. Then Herb Klein, the Nixon aide most respected by the press, said on CBS's *Face the Nation* that the media's failure to modify its coverage would "invite the government to come in"—an unfortunate choice of words that Klein later insisted he didn't mean as a threat. The accumulation of such omens antagonized reporters. When Klein appeared before White House correspondents the next Friday, they shoved and shouted in a small room—

"mass chaos," Klein recalled—vying to interrogate him. The behavior suited a war or a national emergency, not a vice-presidential speech.[58]

The press took to denouncing Agnew as a menace to freedom. With their own considerable power, they made sure viewers heard their perspective. Walter Cronkite delivered a rebuttal to a local chamber of commerce in his hometown of St. Joseph, Missouri, which 60 Minutes aired as a special. The outrage was not unmerited. Agnew's speeches were shrill, misleading, and cynically designed to fan public anger. Some journalists genuinely felt intimidated. Although the editorial page of The New York Times hardly seemed to ease up on Nixon after the speech, the page's editor, John Oakes, claimed he and others were unconsciously softening their attacks.[59] What was more, Nixon did move to wrest the Washington Post Company's local broadcasting affiliates from its control—although his efforts were halfhearted and soon abandoned.*

On the whole, however, the initial outrage smacked of overreaction. Notwithstanding the moves against the Post Company—along with the genuinely nefarious but still concealed wiretaps—Agnew wasn't really seeking to apply government pressure to the press; it was public pressure he wanted to mobilize. Nixon and Agnew were hoping to harness the rage of socially conservative Middle Americans and make the media heel to their concerns. Agnew's speech contended that journalists were ignoring public sentiment—which could only make them seem irresponsible. The press's howls meant to make it seem that they were resisting government pressure—in which case they could only look heroic.

But Agnew's points weren't just conservative demagoguery. With a few alterations, his addresses could have been given by a liberal journal-

---

* In January 1970, a corporation headed by Nixon's friend Bebe Rebozo applied to the FCC to take over the license of the Post's Miami station. Three years later (after the Post began investigating Watergate), other Nixon allies challenged the license of the Post's Jacksonville affiliate. In a White House conversation on September 15, 1972, with Haldeman and Dean, Nixon fumed over the paper's Watergate disclosures: "The main thing is the Post is going to have damnable, damnable problems out of this one. They have a television station . . . and they're going to have to get it renewed. Does [the radio station] come up too? . . . The game has to be played awfully rough." And on January 2, 1974, the Justice Department asked the FCC to deny license renewal requests to stations owned by the St. Louis Post-Dispatch and Cowles Communications, which had been critical of Nixon during Watergate.

ism-school dean. (Much of the first speech in fact drew from the *Columbia Journalism Review*.) Liberals had long championed broadcast regulation as a price for private control of the public airwaves. They had fretted that newspaper chains were extinguishing independent papers and narrowing public debate. And they had warned of television's power to sway impressionable viewers—pointing to Nixon's Checkers speech, no less, as a prime example. Like Nixon's original critics, Agnew suggested that televised images evoked raw feelings rather than considered judgments and wondered about television's "effect on a democratic society." If charitably interpreted, Agnew had simply joined an argument about democracy in a mass media age.[60]

Nor was the public as credulous as reporters feared. Although many Americans agreed generally with Agnew's comments, only a minority believed that the press had a vendetta against the president. Most wanted the networks to keep offering "instant analysis." Like Agnew, the public wanted a greater range of viewpoints than the mainstream press offered. This belief suggested, however, not that they were being duped, but the reverse: that they felt competent to sort out fact from opinion for themselves. Given all this, it was clear that the press's reaction stemmed in part from its own position of power as an entrenched, influential institution. Its reaction contained more defensiveness than actual fear.[61]

Some journalists soon agreed that they had overreacted. After previously envisioning imminent repression, Dan Rather conceded that the speeches contained "a few truths"—a widely echoed sentiment. Ben Bradlee said Agnew's attack "probably had a good effect overall because they've made the intelligent editor be self-critical and examine the decision-making process." The speech helped convince Bradlee to appoint an ombudsman at *The Washington Post*; and Richard Harwood, who got the job, found that many of the paper's reporters also endorsed parts of the vice president's critique. "We are, for the most part, a collection of Easterners, middle- and upper-middle class, well-educated, relatively sophisticated, generally liberal," went one typical comment. "This shows in our reporting." Katharine Graham told the journalism fraternity Sigma Delta Chi the next November that Agnew's charge had "some validity." It

became a point of pride for journalists to own up to their own (or their colleagues') shortcomings, to decry their own uniformity of background,
opinion, and instinct.[62]

Such self-flagellation irked others. Increasingly feisty, Walter Cronkite
fumed that he was "somewhat sick and mighty tired of broadcast journalism being constantly dragged into the operating room and dissected,
probed, swabbed, and needled to see what makes it tick." John Osborne
called the ostentatious introspection "masochistic drivel." When Agnew
appeared on Face the Nation in February 1970, Osborne noted, panelists
treated him with kid gloves. One newsman, after a mildly confrontational
exchange, obsequiously apologized, "I'm sorry, I didn't mean to put you
on the spot." Ironically, this rash of self-criticism displayed the same
groupthink that the reporters were deploring in the first place. By collectively mulling over the "germ of truth" in Agnew's attacks, the media
tamed themselves more than the government did. Eager to ward off
charges of bias, reporters resolved to be fairer.[63]

McGinniss and Agnew notwithstanding, the tensions between Nixon and
the press remained rooted in the president's own penchant for secrecy and
isolation. Nixon rarely gave interviews, background sessions, or informal
chats, and he liked to work at his homes outside the capital, in San
Clemente, Key Biscayne, or Camp David. Haldeman and Ehrlichman
formed what reporters called a "palace guard" or "Berlin Wall" around
him, insulating him even from his own staff. At a remove, reporters
couldn't deepen or complicate their image of the president. "Nixon was to
me," John Herbers wrote, "a distant and enigmatic figure as seen backwards
through a telescope." Ben Bradlee defended himself against accusations of
Nixon-hating by noting that he barely knew the man. "It's not a question
of disliking him personally," he said. "We never got close enough—I certainly never did." "We—the press corps—seldom saw much of Nixon,"
agreed Dan Rather, "not even at the start, when the slate should have been
clean." Marvin Kalb felt an air of remoteness about Nixon, who shunned
the journalists' social world and "lived so lonely a life that it seemed as if
he had converted the Oval Office into an underground bunker."[64]

The film of *All the President's Men* (1976), directed by Alan J. Pakula of *The Parallax View* and *Klute*, memorably rendered Nixon as inaccessible to reporters except via their TV screens. "One of our big problems," said Robert Redford, the film's producer and star, was "dramatizing an opposition that had become almost invisible." Pakula explained that the solution they devised was to make sure "you don't see the president except on television." At the opening, Nixon is seen addressing Congress after his triumphant Moscow summit. In the closing sequence, he is sworn in for a second term, pledging to "preserve, protect, and defend the Constitution," as Robert Redford and Dustin Hoffman, playing Bob Woodward and Carl Bernstein, doggedly clack away on their typewriters. Nixon's absence except as a TV image served as a rebuttal to his claims that he liked to speak "directly" to the public via television; as the film demonstrates, the televised address could be an *indirect* form of self-presentation, compared to press reports based on direct personal contact. Nixon is perceived as a flickering shadow, not a flesh-and-blood person—which was how most reporters experienced him in real life.[65]

To show the faceless "power of the administration," Pakula laced his film with shots of the imposing facades of the White House and other stony Washington structures. Indeed, under Nixon, the White House became a symbol for the reclusive president. Garry Trudeau depicted Nixon by drawing the White House front with the president's words floating above the building. Reporters, unable to speak knowledgeably about Nixon personally, increasingly used "the White House" as a synonym. So common did such references become that Art Buchwald joked about a conversation he had with the building. "The other night I heard Dan Rather say on television that the White House planned to stonewall the House Judiciary Committee," the edifice complained. "I've never stonewalled anyone in my life. . . . All I've ever done is hold receptions, entertain tourists, and pose for pictures." The word "stonewall"—the administration's phrase for stalling by withholding information—poetically captured the concrete obstructions that Nixon threw in the path of investigators. Jules Feiffer drew a strip of a brick wall bearing Nixon's face, with the bricks crumbling in each successive panel as Nixon declares: "I have not yet begun to stonewall."[66]

Reporters glimpsed dark designs in Nixon's remoteness. The creation of a new White House press room in 1970, which was necessary to deal with the burgeoning press corps, struck correspondents as "a subtle part of the Nixon war against the press," Helen Thomas of UPI wrote, since it ended their freedom to roam the West Wing halls. Also troublesome to reporters was the infrequency of Nixon's press conferences, of which he held fewer (thirty-nine) than any president since Herbert Hoover. Max Frankel lamented that reporters enjoyed "no chance to measure [Nixon's] changes of view or mood [or] . . . to remind him of what he said or did a year ago. It is not just the event that is lapsing but a whole process of communication and, indeed, government." The National Press Club chided the president for shunning "an integral part of government," for flouting a vital tradition of accountability; if he persisted, "The main casualty [would be] the American people and their confidence in the openness of their government." Of course, as such commentary showed, Nixon himself paid a price for his isolation, as they painted him as secretive, sinister, and bent on dictating the news.[67]

In a 1972 television interview, John Ehrlichman commented that Nixon avoided press conferences because reporters ask "a lot of flabby and fairly dumb questions, and it really doesn't elucidate very much." The press corps pounced, branding the remark another shot in Nixon's anti-media war, and Ehrlichman recanted. Yet in all likelihood it was the messenger, more than the message, that offended the reporters. Had the rebuke come from the *Columbia Journalism Review*, they probably would have voiced amens.[68] Indeed, when White House reporters weren't groaning about the paucity of press conferences, they complained how pointless the parleys were. In *The Atlantic* in 1970, Hedrick Smith of *The New York Times* chided his colleagues for the "hectic superficiality" of their performance at one recent session. "Nixon held the assembled reporters at bay as easily as Cassius Clay dabbling with a clutch of welterweights," he wrote. ". . . Nothing caught Mr. Nixon off guard or prodded him to acknowledge a shred of responsibility for the turmoil that was rolling over the country." Jules Witcover also thought the conferences had become "a controlled showcase for [Nixon's] considerable talents as a semantic shadow-boxer." Both reporters called on their peers to shed what Witcover called their "excessive deference to the president"—to show, Smith said, more "daring and tenacity . . . without sliding into malevolent heckling or the rasping cross-examination of a district attorney." John Herbers went further, claiming that the ritual had become "staged and plastic," "show business and a device for the president to promote himself," rather than "a session of inquiry to uncover news"—a classic pseudo-event. This evolution of the press conference, its loss of spontaneity, was a long-term cultural development, a response to a larger and more complex press corps and government. But the reporters blamed Nixon, since he had orchestrated his conferences so that they wouldn't produce any surprises.[69]

In a more subtle way, Nixon's detachment may have also generated negative press. When previous presidents socialized with reporters or talked to them off the record, they helped persuade the correspondents that they were seeing the "real" man behind the presidency (whether it was true or not). This firsthand knowledge not only created an affection that served to brake criticism; it also made reporters feel that they could understand the man. It made them, however unconsciously, more willing to cut the president some slack. But few reporters ever felt they knew the chimerical "real" Nixon. This lack of intimacy, in the long run, made it easier to believe that Nixon was engaging in shadowy deceit.

Nixon's hostility to the media surfaced in ways far more troubling than his reclusiveness. Reporters saw sinister designs in Nixon's efforts to monitor what was said about him and a threat to democracy in his use of his power to suppress the news. Collectively, they concluded that these actions amounted to a war against them.

Nixon devoured the news. Each day, he plowed through his "News Summaries"—thick sheaves compiled by staffers that distilled the day's stories from all the major media, often in snide or caustic language. Nixon added his own usually intemperate marginalia. Although the White House said the summaries showed the administration's efficiency, reporters wrote about them in a scandalized tone, as proof of Nixon's image obsession and his unabating need to keep track of critical reporters to exact retribution.[70]

Reporters glimpsed malice in Nixon's public relations apparatus as well. Nixon was the first president to make the presentation of his image his dominant goal; his papers brim with notes on tailoring his public persona, strategic memos on projecting that persona, and directives on handling compliant or hostile journalists. He created the White House office of communications and a White House office for dealing with television. He was the first president to hire what he called a "full-time PR director," advertising executive Jeb Magruder. He established dedicated White House councils to figure out how best to present the administration's work. "We tried to devise an imaginative, aggressive publicity program," explained Magruder. "We did the trivia and the dirty tricks when we had to, but we also tried to explore every possible means to reach the public with a program that we all believed to be excellent." Strategies included drumming up phony pro-Nixon letters to news outlets, devising "Game Plans" for promoting initiatives, and rewarding reporters who wrote kindly about the administration. As with the News Summaries, reporters detailed these efforts in a tone of outrage—even as those exposés showed their ability to see past such ploys.[71]

Another count in the bill of indictment against Nixon was that his reclusiveness forced them to rely so much on Ron Ziegler. Where previous press secretaries had usually come from the ranks of the Fourth Estate itself, Ziegler was a twenty-nine-year-old USC graduate, Haldeman protégé, and former advertising man. Like the president he served, he was tight-lipped with information and disrespectful of the reporters with whom he sparred. Lacking the charm or the skills to put reporters at ease, he struck them as self-satisfied and imperious, "a small-bore man," in the words of Ben Bradlee, "over his head, and riding a bad horse."[72]

The contempt, which was mutual, flared up at Ziegler's daily briefings, which became sophomoric games of charges and evasions. On the average day, a throng of sixty or seventy reporters, most hoping to salvage a tidbit of news from a tedious round of unenlightening exchanges, gathered in the briefing room for an 11:00 A.M. conference. Typically, Ziegler showed up late, since wire-service reporters had to file stories before noon and the truncated hour meant that much less time he had to stall. The session that followed resembled a substitute teacher facing down a roomful of teenagers. Ritualistically, the correspondents tried to pin Ziegler down on questions they knew he wouldn't answer. Ziegler offered opaque, business-world twaddle. "I am completed on what I had to say," he would remark, or, "This is getting to a point beyond which I am not going to discuss beyond what I have said." Reporters dubbed these gems "Zieglerisms," "zigzags," or "ziggies." Even Nixon joked about Ziegler's obfuscation; at a White House Correspondents Dinner, he said that when he asked Ziegler for the time, the aide responded: "Could I put that on background?" Toward the end of Nixon's presidency, one reporter vented the press corps' feelings by trashing Ziegler in the *Columbia Journalism Review*. In an article reminiscent of those once written about Nixon, he listed eight Zieglerian strategies for ducking reporters' questions, ranging from "the broad and meaningless statement" and "the I'll-try-to-find-out ploy" to "the carefully constructed deception" and, worst of all, "the lie."[73]

If the administration's daily evasions elicited overwrought alarmism, its acts of retribution sparked legitimate worry. Not returning reporters' phone calls or denying them access to trips or events paled next to real abuses of law enforcement agencies to probe, intimidate, or punish journalists. The wiretapping and the abortive efforts to strip the Washington Post Company of its broadcasting licenses were but two examples. Others included the use of the Internal Revenue Service to harass journalists the president didn't like and the launching of anti-trust suits against the TV networks. One of the most serious cases was the harassment of CBS's Daniel Schorr. In August 1971, reporting on Nixon's promise to aid Catholic schools, Schorr quoted a source who said the pledge was "made for political or rhetorical effect." Enraged, Nixon ordered Haldeman to have the FBI investigate "that bastard. And no stalling." An FBI agent showed up in Schorr's office, and when word of the investigation spread among the press corps, the administration implausibly claimed it was considering Schorr for a job. Only during the Senate Watergate investigation did the full story emerge.[74]

Most distressing to the newspeople were the government's June 1971 lawsuits to stop *The New York Times* and *The Washington Post* from publishing the Pentagon Papers. When Nixon picked up his Sunday *New York Times* on June 13, he saw, alongside the coverage of Tricia's wedding, a long

article based on a secret Defense Department study of American involvement in Vietnam; former government official Daniel Ellsberg had given the
study to *Times* reporter Neil Sheehan. Egged on by Kissinger, who told
Nixon he would be seen as a "weakling" if he didn't respond, the president instructed John Mitchell to sue the *Times* to force it to stop publishing
classified information. (Fatefully, he also had Ehrlichman establish a special White House unit, the "Plumbers," to stop leaks; their first job was to
break into the office of Ellsberg's psychoanalyst, Lewis Fielding, in search
of harmful information about him.) Although Nixon won a temporary
injunction against the *Times*, first *The Washington Post* and then other
papers obtained copies of the study and began disclosing its contents. Then
the administration lost its bid to enjoin the *Post* from publishing, the
restraint on the *Times* was overturned on appeal, and on June 30 the
Supreme Court rejected the claim that national security warranted the sup-
pression of the information. The press rejoiced.[75]

Though a victory for the press, the case reinforced the notion that
there were no lengths to which Nixon would not go to control the news.
No previous administration had ever attempted to impose outright prior
restraint—that is, censorship. With the Pentagon Papers, the antagonism
between Nixon and the press metastasized. "The Nixon administration
now entered the ring with a particularly deliberate gusto," Katharine
Graham later wrote. "By sending the Justice Department into court
instead of merely using the vice president as a mouthpiece, they had
changed the character of the fight." Halfway through his first term,
reporters were convinced that Nixon was hostile to the First Amendment.
The episode cemented fears that Nixon's assault was assuming unprecedented proportions.[76]

Faced with these attacks, the White House press corps felt compelled
to react. That reaction, however, consisted mostly of indignation, not
inquiry. On June 26, 1972, the board of governors of the National Press
Club commissioned a "full-scale investigation of the Administration's
relationship with and to the press." The committee tasked with the job
included some of the White House press corps' leading lights: Dan Rather,
Jack Germond, Adam Clymer of the *Baltimore Sun*, Alan Otten of the *Wall
Street Journal*. Under the guidance of an American University professor, a

team interviewed reporters, presidential aides, and media critics, and issued a report the following year. The press club came down hard on the president for a range of offenses. It rallied journalists to "muster all of the resources at [their] command to resist any and all forms of intimidation and control." Such judgments were echoed in a spate of studies of Nixon's treatment of the press. In *The Boys on the Bus* (1973), Timothy Crouse wrote that Nixon "was different" from his predecessors. "Nixon felt a deep, abiding, and vindictive hatred for the press that no president, with the possible exception of Lyndon Johnson, had ever shared. . . . No other president had ever worked so lovingly or painstakingly to emasculate reporters." "Under the Nixon Administration, there has been an unprecedented effort," former *Herald Tribune* reporter David Wise agreed in *The Politics of Lying* (1973), ". . . to downgrade and discredit the American press. . . . It was a terribly dangerous policy." The perception of an "unprecedented" war on the media was virtually universal.[77]

But the press club report said as much about the press corps' mentality as about Nixon, whose anti-media stratagems were after all a matter of public record. It reflected the frustrated correspondents' need to register their displeasure with Nixon in some official way. If they couldn't stop the administration's news management, they could state for the record that they weren't going to be cowed. Perhaps the most telling part of the report was its lament that news organizations weren't "moving smartly . . . to give people a better picture of the workings of the system. While they fend off critiques by self-interested politicians, news executives have only timidly reached out for suggestions for improving reporting on government so that the public achieves a better grasp of what is going on." Although the reporters, with this passage, shifted responsibility for their neglect onto their bosses, they tacitly acknowledged that they weren't engaging in the muckraking revival that so many were heralding. Instead, they were lashing out defensively.[78]

Reporters also failed to grasp that the fact that they viewed Nixon as they did suggested he wasn't really so effective. Whatever Nixon's public relations skills, reporters had no trouble formulating a different impression of him than the one he wished to convey. Presidential image making, after all, was as much a matter of their control as of Nixon's.

. . .

Nixonites remember Watergate as the ultimate paroxysm of Nixon-hating by the liberal media. They note the barrage of attention that Watergate received in the sixteen months before the president's resignation. Reporters remember it differently. As they recall the months after the June 1972 break-in, they see an embarrassing indifference to a huge story. For all the lessons they had supposedly learned, White House correspondents in 1972 proved remarkably docile. As Max Frankel observed in a year-end *New York Times* retrospective, "The president pursued the image of a man who addresses problems and does things dramatically. . . . How can you . . . not feel that the president ultimately came across to the country more or less as he wanted to be portrayed?" From the White House, Chuck Colson agreed that Nixon in 1972 came "as close to managing the news as you can do."[79]

Within a few days of the Watergate break-in, two young *Washington Post* metro reporters, Bob Woodward and Carl Bernstein, had linked the burglars to the White House, tugging the string that would unravel Nixon's presidency. Despite this connection, however, most reporters paid Watergate little heed. When the break-in was first reported on the nightly news, it was covered lightly. Reports emphasized Ziegler's description of it as "a third-rate burglary . . . nothing the president would be involved with, obviously." NBC's John Chancellor smirked as he recounted the "exotic" episode, which most news outlets called a "caper." When reporters had their first chance to ask Nixon about Watergate on June 22, they posed just one question, retreating quickly when he reiterated that his men weren't involved. A week later, at Nixon's first televised press conference in a year, they skipped Watergate altogether. Reporters believed the administration's denials and focused on seemingly more pressing matters like Nixon's diplomacy, the conventions, and the fall campaign. Of more than twelve hundred Washington correspondents, only about twenty pursued the Watergate story that summer, some briefly. Nixon, ahead in the polls, declared a cease-fire in his war with the press. Agnew, Buchanan, and others promised to make nice for what Safire called a "period of phony peace." Warily, reporters softened their tone.[80]

Unlike in 1968, the early failure to pursue Watergate took place amid full awareness of Nixon's anti-media efforts. "Everyone was mindful of Joe McGinniss's *Selling of the President 1968*," Jules Witcover noted. The *Times* even assigned a reporter, Warren Weaver, to a media-strategy beat. Reporters grasped that the 1972 Nixon was reprising his 1968 strategy: making few appearances, refusing to debate his opponent, stiff-arming the press. Yet they did little but rail about his invisibility. At one event, the president forbade all cameras except his own from filming his speech and forced reporters to watch it on closed-circuit TV in another room. "You can't cover this guy," fumed the *Philadelphia Bulletin*'s John Farmer as he typed away, screens flickering. "They won't let you." Suddenly, the *Washington Star*'s Jim Doyle, who would later serve as press secretary to the Watergate Special Prosecutor, burst out: "This is terrible! This is awful shit. I just want to be able to take a look at him! Is he alive?" Other reporters, weary and jaded, jotted down Nixon's words. David Broder, Jules Witcover, and a few others again warned that Nixon was using the press as a propaganda conduit and turning the campaign into a mere "contest of images." But few reporters did anything to deter such practices. Nixon's coverage remained positive.[81]

Reporters were complicit in their own manipulation—perhaps fearful, after years of browbeating, that they would be seen as biased. Nixon exploited the press's vulnerability. Reporters, he told Haldeman in 1970, "have a fetish about fairness, and once they are caught being unfair, they are very sensitive about it and try to compensate it from time to time." (At all other times, he added, "they have no intention whatever to be fair.") During the 1972 campaign, reporters noted this trait in themselves. *The Washington Post*'s Stephen Isaacs said his peers were "over-compensating" with gentle treatment of Nixon because they didn't want readers to think they were "'in the tank' for McGovern." Also playing into Nixon's hands was a professional consensus that frowned on any indecorous breach of routine. Once, in October 1972, before the full extent of the connection between Nixon's campaign team and the Watergate break-in emerged, Ziegler let it slip to Clark Mollenhoff of the *Des Moines Register*—a veteran reporter who had briefly worked for Nixon and then quit to return to his beat—that the burglars had been paid from the president's reelection funds. After Mollenhoff reported the item, Ziegler denied it. At the next White House briefing, Mollenhoff tried to pin him down, but Ziegler just robotically repeated the phrase, "I have issued a statement on that and I will stand by it," as Mollenhoff fired off questions. The amusement of Mollenhoff's colleagues shaded into impatience and then contempt, as they itched to move on. No one helped him out. Finally, one reporter huffed, "Ron, may I change the subject?" to the others' relief. Reporters knew Ziegler's games and appreciated Mollenhoff's grievance. But they wouldn't disrupt their business to indulge a colleague they viewed as eccentric.[82]

Direct intimidation also contributed to the press's early neglect of Watergate. The threats to discontinue television licenses, the freezing out of reporters, the investigations into Schorr, Newsday, and others—all had a chilling effect. Most notorious was the case of CBS, the lone television network to pursue Watergate seriously in 1972. Although White House aides told reporters—and reassured themselves—that the break-in was of no interest to most Americans, Dan Rather featured the story prominently. Both Rather and Daniel Schorr worked the story throughout the summer. In October, Walter Cronkite agreed to air a special report, scheduled to consume most of two nightly newscasts. The first segment, which relied heavily on Woodward and Bernstein's Post coverage, aired October 27 and won much attention, not least because it took up fourteen of the program's twenty-two minutes of news—a radical departure from the standard format. The segment made Watergate a national story.[83]

Nixon was furious. "That finishes them," he told Haldeman. Colson, whose job included bullying network officials at the president's behest, phoned CBS chairman William Paley and dressed him down in an obscenity-laced rant, claiming the show amounted to McGovern propaganda. Paley said that he too considered the Watergate segment excessive and sent word that the second installment was to be scaled back. Producer Stanhope Gould was forced to trim it to eight minutes, "cut[ting] the guts out" of a piece, he felt, that could have riveted attention on the scandal.[84]

Such out-and-out intimidation, however, was not the norm. More typical was the case of The New York Times. "The Times bureau was made up of well-established men who were not inclined to drop everything, their home life, their wives and children and hang onto a story night after night no matter how late or how much effort it took," said James Naughton, who came to the paper from the *Cleveland Plain-Dealer*. "There were no hungry reporters in the *Times'* Washington bureau in 1972." One well-qualified reporter assigned to Watergate, Tad Szulc, was misled by his own extensive experience reporting on U.S. efforts to overthrow Cuba's Fidel Castro. On learning that several right-wing Cubans were among the burglars, Szulc guessed anti-Castro forces were behind the whole plot—a theory that, unfortunately for Szulc, dovetailed with Nixon's initial cover story. Another potential sleuth for the *Times*, Seymour Hersh, hadn't yet joined the paper, but even he didn't consider Watergate significant at first. On the White House beat, Bob Semple couldn't fathom how high up the involvement ran. "It was hard to believe that a national administration, a president, would stoop to something like this," Semple said. "Maybe there was a belief all around that it just couldn't have happened." Senior editors were blinded by their competition with the *Post*. "I was so envious of the *Post*'s lead [on Watergate] that I allowed myself to be skeptical of some of its revelations," Max Frankel said, even though he granted that the rival paper turned out to be wrong "only once or twice that fall." This attitude was widespread. White House reporters, Jack Germond noted, arrogantly dismissed these "two unknown young punks . . . Bob Woodward and Carl Bernstein, whoever the hell they were." The beat men told themselves, Germond said, that "the story is old stuff or it's exaggerated or it's just plain horseshit. . . . There was a lot of that going around when we were getting our brains beaten out during the summer of 1972."[85]

Underneath was a systemic problem. CBS, the *Times*, and the established organs of the press were too entrenched in their ways to get the story. "It was not gullibility that kept many of us from grasping the significance of Watergate," Henry Grunwald of *Time* magazine explained, ". . . it was sophistication"—a blasé attitude, born of years in elite circles, that made it hard to imagine that Nixon's men had done anything so unusual. White House beat reporters fell victim to their routines. Their daily tussles with Ziegler, their lunchtime gossip with sources, and their felt duty to report the White House line all militated against breaking stories like Watergate. "The White House press room," John Herbers ruefully noted, "is the last place from which to launch a journalistic investigation of crime and corruption." "The brutal truths of the Watergate story continued to be broken not by television or by the White House press corps," Dan Rather noted, "but by a pair of mavericks from the police beat: Woodward and Bernstein."[86]

The story of how Bob Woodward and Carl Bernstein and *The Washington Post* blazed the lonely Watergate trail long ago passed into legend. Three decades later, it's still hard to dispute the judgment of former *Post* editor and longtime press critic Ben Bagdikian, who called it "the most spectacular single act of serious journalism [in the twentieth] century." Watergate made the reputations of Woodward, Bernstein, and the *Post*, inspired generations of young journalists, and established a benchmark for investigative reporting. Some have argued that Woodward and Bernstein have reaped too much credit, since they brought to light information that was already in the hands of government investigators. Such a claim, while a useful corrective, fails to consider how press coverage itself influences political actors, like judges or congressional investigators. In Watergate, it was unclear at first whether the FBI would pursue crimes beyond the break-in itself. If the *Post* hadn't kept Watergate alive, it's not certain that the bureau, or the Senate, would have kept digging. Woodward and Bernstein's work shaped the way Watergate unfolded.[87]

Yet it doesn't diminish their accomplishments to note that their story has also become enshrined as what Ben Bradlee himself later called "mythology." As others realized that Woodward and Bernstein were onto something big, a David-and-Goliath storyline emerged: two cub reporters, armed with skepticism and determination, uncovering the scandal of the century and forcing a president to resign. The magazine profiles of Woodward and Bernstein, the success of their book *All the President's Men*, and the award-winning film based upon it all fostered this mythology—as did the behavior of colleagues like Bradlee, who was heard around the *Post*'s newsroom hollering, "The White Hats win!" The film furthered the theme of light and truth against darkness and evil. When Pakula filmed the Washington structures that he intended to convey the administration's faceless power, he showed the buildings shrouded in shadows, to suggest a hidden menace. In contrast, he shot the *Post*'s newsroom in all its fluorescent vividness. The workspace's "incredibly harsh, tough poster colors," Pakula said, symbolized the often-unsettling light of truth. "You can hide nothing in that room," he explained.[88]

Because of the book and the film, the Watergate story itself has come to be known from the *Post*'s point of view. The highlights are familiar but still dramatic: When the paper's editors heard about a break-in at the Democratic Party headquarters at the Watergate complex on June 17, 1972, they treated the case as a local crime story and assigned it to Bob Woodward, a recent hire. At the burglars' arraignment, Woodward learned that one of them, James McCord, had worked for the CIA, and he soon discovered that someone listed in a burglar's address book, Howard Hunt, worked for the White House. Woodward was joined by another young reporter, Carl Bernstein, his stylistic opposite: Woodward was moderate in his politics, Midwestern, and WASPish; Bernstein, a Jewish Red-diaper baby, had almost gone to work for *Rolling Stone*. Their differences introduced a creative tension as the reporters rushed in where senior colleagues feared to tread. Running on instinct and shoe leather, they pursued leads the old-fashioned way: knocking on doors, combing phone books, assembling the puzzle piece by piece, with occasional help from Woodward's high-level source known as "Deep Throat." After enduring barbs from the administration, Woodward and Bernstein were vindicated when confirmations of the administration's corruption spilled forth, Ziegler publicly apologized to them, and Nixon resigned.[89]

As commonly presented, this story is divorced from the context of the press's love-hate relationship with Nixon. But the story's significance lies partly in the contrast between Woodward and Bernstein and most of their peers. The film, of course, engages in some dramatic license, compressing certain incidents and omitting others. City editor Barry Sussman's real-life role is folded into that of other *Post* editors, and Woodward and Bernstein are often shown laboring in a newsroom that's emptier than it really was. But for all the altered details, the film remains true to the way the reporters experienced Watergate. "If there were ever a movie that had to be authentic," the screenwriter William Goldman noted, "it was this one." Goldman knew he couldn't reproduce the book with absolute fidelity to facts, but he tried to obey what he considered "the most important rule of adaptation . . . you *must* be totally faithful to the *intention* of the source material."[90]

Although the film didn't show rival reporters carping about the *Post*'s coverage, throwaway lines of banter among the paper's editors did capture the skepticism with which some first viewed the story. One scene showed editors talking avidly about McGovern's hardships in picking a vice president while paying Watergate little heed. "No one cares about the Dahlberg repercussions," one editor says about a Woodstein story linking cash solicited by Nixon fund-raiser Kenneth Dahlberg to the burglars. Another editor speaks of "lunch at the Sans Souci"—a high-end insider restaurant in the 1970s—where administration sources assured him Watergate was a minor matter. This resistance from the upper tiers (with some important exceptions) tracked with actual events. According to Roger Wilkins, Walter Pincus, and others at the *Post*, veterans of the national desk assumed that Nixon administration higher-ups couldn't have been involved. "If the national staff of the *Washington Post* had handled [Watergate]," one press corps regular said, ". . . even if it had been men like David Broder and Haynes Johnson"—two of the paper's best reporters—"I don't think they would have picked it up." It wasn't just Woodward and Bernstein's talent that served them well but also their position in the Washington order.[91]

Also accurate is the film's portrayal of the reporters' methods. As Woodward, Bernstein, and Bradlee have said, their work was mundane and apolitical. "The reporting we did was not that extraordinary," Bernstein said. "We used the most basic empirical reporting techniques similar to what you first learn when you go down to police headquarters. We knocked on a lot of doors. . . . What was extraordinary, however, was the information that these rather simple and basic techniques yielded." Nor were they motivated by politics; theirs was not advocacy journalism. Woodward said he "never detected any political motivation" in himself or his colleagues. ". . . We tried to do our job and, in fact, if you look at it, our coverage was pretty conservative." If anything, Bradlee added, "we started worrying about the question of the perception of some that we had an animus against Nixon [and] bent over backward the other way."

Bradlee remembered times when "we had stories ready to write and I held back and said, 'No. We have to go another mile. We have to get another source.' I felt we might be accused of being motivated by animus rather than fact."[92]

The movie's scenes of ringing doorbells and phoning sources captured the legwork that contrasted with the normal press corps rituals of attending briefings or riding the press bus. *All the President's Men* also underscores the reporters' empirical methods, which differed from the newly faddish opinion-mongering of the era. Early in the film, Bernstein leaps to unsupported conclusions about what "must have" happened: someone must have financed the Watergate break-in, he says, because the burglars carried so much equipment; Howard Hunt must have been investigating Ted Kennedy because of the books he checked out of the library. Although Woodward lets Bernstein's inferences guide their questions, he tells his partner that they can't print surmises without evidence. (Later in the film, the roles get reversed, as Bernstein reins in the speculations of an impatient Woodward.) Bradlee, too, presses the reporters for "harder information," relegating a story to the inside pages because they "haven't got it," postponing another one because "there's not enough fact."

The film dramatizes the idea that Woodward and Bernstein cracked Watergate because they shunned attitudinizing and advocacy and strove for objectivity. Woodward has acknowledged that the reporters' pursuit of Watergate "became a form of combat"; yet he also made an important distinction. "We didn't go after the president," he said. "We went after the story." The two reporters were skeptical, but constructively so. Their doubts about Nixon's claims arose not from any worldly-wise cynicism but from curiosity. Yet unlike some of their peers, they didn't let fairness and balance translate into a wishy-washy capitulation to the administration's line. Woodward and Bernstein thus found a solution to the dilemma of reconciling objectivity and toughness. They took an adversarial stance toward authority while preserving a reputation for fairness. It was this feat—much more than the toppling of a president—that won the reporters the admiration of their peers.[93]

. . .

What allowed this circle to be squared was not just Woodward and Bernstein's methods but also the realization that Nixon was lying. If Nixon was a liar, then being objective wasn't inconsistent but synonymous with being adversarial. Reporting just "the facts," as the administration had long demanded, no longer meant accepting White House spoon-feeding; it meant countering White House falsehoods. Pitting oneself against authority could be understood not as an act of rebellion but as a venerable professional mandate.

It took reporters a while to label Nixon a liar. By mid-1973, journalists had no choice but to give the scandal massive attention. Without their knowledge, Nixon was committing many of the acts that would drive him from office: meeting with aides to prolong the cover-up, suborning perjury, authorizing payments of hush money, talking about offering clemency to the defendants. But as damaging to him as those secret crimes were his public statements. Under mounting pressure to explain his and the White House's role, Nixon made a series of spoken and written remarks that reporters who were sifting through the facts could only regard as highly dubious at best.

On May 22, 1973, for example, the president put out a long account in which he claimed: "I took no part in, nor was I aware of, any subsequent efforts that may have been made to cover up Watergate." He insisted he'd had no role in any of the specific activities, whether the hush money payments or the bogus CIA directive to thwart the FBI's probe of the June 17 break-in. But as his chief of staff Al Haig later admitted, six of the seven denials in the statement were knowingly false. After John Dean implicated Nixon during his five days of testimony before Sam Ervin's Senate Committee in June, Nixon went farther out on a limb by denying the charges. "Not only was I unaware of any cover-up," the president said on August 15, "I was unaware there was anything to cover up." In other similar statements, Nixon would assert the White House's innocence, claim that he wanted to get to the bottom of Watergate, or state that he would punish any obstruction of justice.[94]

"Watergate joined the issue of credibility," wrote *The Washington Post*'s Ben Bradlee and Howard Simons, "as it had never been joined before." So stark were the daily contradictions between what Nixon said and what journalists were discovering that many concluded he was something much worse than a wily news manager; he was a liar, they believed, whose need to control the news overrode ethical compunctions and even legal limits. To be sure, many Americans, not just reporters, had for a long time thought that Nixon was dishonest. But during Watergate it was the working press, which sorted through Nixon's statements day after day, that kept this image in the forefront of the culture. The administration's ongoing attacks on the media and its claims that reporters were manufacturing an issue "forced the reader and the listener," Bradlee and Simons noted, "to choose between the White House and the press."[95]

For a while, reporters, not wanting to seem biased, avoided inflammatory labels. "When it's Richard Nixon," Clark Mollenhoff of the *Des Moines Register* explained, "you restrain yourself and do not call him a liar." But the accumulating evidence that Nixon had deliberately misled the public tested the reporters' restraint. The release of the damning tape transcripts on April 30, 1974, was the final straw. Some friendly columnists, such as Joe Alsop, now turned on Nixon ("sheer flesh-crawling repulsion," he wrote), while other reporters at last said publicly what they had suspected privately: Nixon was incorrigibly dishonest. Helen Thomas maintained good relations with Nixon before Watergate, but during the scandal, when asked when she first knew Nixon was lying, she cuttingly replied: "In 1946." "He lied to the people. . . . He lied to his lawyers. He lied to the press," wrote the conservative columnist James J. Kilpatrick the day after Nixon resigned. "My president is a liar." Nixon's mendacity became, for reporters especially, his defining trait. "For more than two years he looked the nation in the eye . . . and lied," Meg Greenfield wrote in 1977. "Tonight, he would say, he wanted to talk to us 'from my heart' . . . and there would be more lies, ever more elaborate lies that brought down people and dirtied institutions as he sought frantically and recklessly to hide."[96]

Nixon's liar reputation caught hold, of course, far beyond the press corps. Even loyalists endorsed it. "Lies," Chuck Colson noted years later, "brought Nixon down." "Nixon had no compunction about lying to the press," concluded David Gergen. *Philadelphia Inquirer* cartoonist Tony Auth drew Nixon dressed in Revolutionary garb holding an ax amid a plain of fallen trees, declaring, "I cannot tell the truth. . . ." A Watergate-era bumper sticker called him "Richard the Lyin' Hearted." Even the dishonesty of his successors was seen as derivative of his own. Well after his resignation, Johnny Carson was still joking that "whenever anyone in the White House tells a lie, Nixon gets a royalty."[97]

Among its other consequences, the mounting evidence that Nixon was lying prompted a change in attitude among the Washington press corps. It forced reporters to own up to their earlier neglect of the issue. It also led them to pursue the story with a vengeance. Although the reporting in Watergate's later stages was mostly responsible and valuable, it also showed an unseemly side that belied later myths of the press corps' unmitigated heroism.

With the breaking of the Watergate dam in 1973, some reporters engaged in self-rebuke. John Osborne wrote that when Nixon first denied White House involvement in Watergate, "I stood within ten feet of him and didn't even try to ask [the] simple and obvious question" of whether he knew who ordered the break-in. Osborne chalked up his failure to "respect for the presidency" and a feeling of weariness, rooted in "the futility of trying to make this president say anything he doesn't want to say." Dan Rather offered a similar mea culpa. "I'm angry with myself for not having worked harder at bringing it out," Rather declared in late 1973 (despite being labeled "the reporter the White House hates"), ". . . I think a beat man at the White House could have done more." The colleagues who had dismissed Woodward and Bernstein now fêted them at the White House Correspondents Dinner and honored them with a slew of awards.[98]

In contrast, other reporters distributed credit to "the press" as a collective entity, thus claiming a piece of glory for themselves. "It was the press, and essentially the press alone," asserted the National Press Club's 1973 report, "that unearthed the most scandalous misuse of the powers of government in this century." As Carl Bernstein noted, this "orgy of self-congratulation" was a bit much. It not only slighted the roles of Congress and the courts in exposing Watergate; it also ignored the fact that those reporters who did the unearthing were few, and unlikely to be found conducting studies of presidential press relations. But now every reporter wanted a piece of the action.[99]

It was in this last year and a half of Nixon's presidency that the notion of a braying press pack emerged. Between April 1973 and August 1974, *Newsweek* ran thirty-five covers featuring Watergate, and another four on Agnew's scandal. *Time* ran more than thirty. Although the coverage of Nixon's early presidency had been no more negative than what other presidents endured, his treatment in 1973 and 1974 was decidedly more critical than any of his twentieth-century predecessors. "There was a feeling in the White House press corps, which I had just joined and didn't share so much," said Lou Cannon of the *Post*, "of how we had been betrayed and lied to. If you are looking at that, Watergate did change everything." Once friendly reporters felt violated. Joseph Kraft, a Georgetown society regular and Kissinger lunch companion, had been by his own admission "on reasonably good terms with the Nixon Administration." But Kraft was "caught off guard," he said, when he learned that Nixon had tapped his phone. By October he came to share the view, once the province of the radical left, that Nixon was making the country "very close to something like a police state." Even William Safire had a change of heart. In his first column for *The New York Times* in April 1973, he called Watergate "a tempest in a Teapot Dome," confirming the fears of liberal readers who considered him a Nixon apologist. By the end of 1973, however, Safire recanted, saying he had been "grandly, gloriously, egregiously wrong." Nixon's anti-press efforts had turned allies into enemies.[100]

With knowledge of Nixon's complicity in Watergate, it is hard to recall the impassioned debates that raged in 1973 over whether he was guilty or innocent, over what he knew and when. The involvement of his top aides, his defenders claimed, didn't necessarily implicate the president. He may have been no worse than negligent, some said. But Nixon's continued lack of candor led reporters to conclude that he was concealing abuses of power and serious crimes. At *Time*, erstwhile Nixon enthusiasts Hedley Donovan and Hugh Sidey became convinced of Nixon's criminal guilt. So did John Herbers, Dan Rather, and Helen Thomas, among other press corps regulars. Again, plenty of people outside the press corps were coming to similar conclusions; Nixon made his November 1973 declaration, "I am not a crook"—probably the most famous thing he ever said—at precisely the moment that millions of Americans were concluding he was exactly that. Only the revelation of the contents of key tapes in mid-1974 would confirm Nixon's criminality for citizens and reporters alike. But among the press corps, the view of Nixon as a criminal became increasingly popular, and was decisive in changing their coverage from deferential to antagonistic.[101]

The new suspicion that the president was a criminal had some unwholesome consequences. Reporters, swept up in the chase, made mistakes that they failed to correct. In May 1973, Walter Cronkite opened the CBS Evening News with an item erroneously implicating a Bethesda bank run by Pat Buchanan's brother in Watergate money-laundering. The AP falsely reported that Ehrlichman was present at a key cover-up meeting among Nixon, Haldeman, and Dean. ABC's Sam Donaldson wrongly asserted that James McCord had implicated departed aide Harry Dent in the White House sabotage efforts; Donaldson apologized. News outlets overplayed trivial items, as *The New York Times* did by placing on the front page a three-column story about the possibility that Nixon's campaign had received gambling money from the Bahamas. As *Post* editor Robert Maynard conceded, there was "a lot of fast and loose stuff being printed."[102]

More pervasive was the snide and pugnacious attitude many journalists struck. Not all reporters channeled their adversarial spirit into productive investigation. Often the result was sarcasm and churlishness. Ziegler, always a target, became a piñata. "We felt we'd been shown up by a pair of kids," one press corps veteran confessed, "so some people tried to prove their manhood by bellowing at old Ron." In March 1973, Ziegler fielded, by one count, some 478 Watergate questions and grew visibly exasperated. On April 17, he told the press that new information about White House involvement had come to light and that all his previous statements were "inoperative" (which essentially meant, as David Gergen later said, "We have been lying from the start"). At the next day's briefing, Clark Mollenhoff, now one of Nixon's most dogged pursuers, verbally assaulted the press secretary. His voice oozing contempt, Mollenhoff asked how Ziegler could unabashedly "stand up there and lie and put out misinformation and then come around later and say it's all 'inoperative.'"

The press secretary, Mollenhoff asserted, was "not entitled to any credibility at all." Thereafter, Ziegler was jeered at the briefings, as reporters "crossed the line," the battered functionary complained, ". . . from aggressiveness to belligerence." Explained Helen Thomas, "The evasion we accepted before we will never accept again. We realize that we did a lousy job on Watergate. We just sat there and took what they said at face value." Now, unanswered questions prompted reporters to editorialize creatively about Ziegler's evasions while technically sticking to accounts of the facts. "For the third day in a row, White House Press Secretary Ron Ziegler refused to answer questions about how that 18½-minute gap appeared on the tape of the President's conversations of June 23, 1972," read one lead, a statement that, while wholly factual, clearly meant to convey the reporter's scorn for the press secretary's circumlocutions.[103]

If some reporters felt they were just belatedly doing their job, others discerned a new insolence. Nixon certainly saw it that way. "It was as if a convulsion had seized Washington," he recalled in his memoirs. "Restraints that had governed professional and political conduct for decades were suddenly abandoned. . . . In reporting the story the members of the Washington press corps . . . felt that they had embarrassed themselves by uncritically reporting the months of White House denials, and so they frantically sought to reassert their independence by demonstrating their skepticism of all official explanations." Some regulars agonized over their new tenacity, just as they had rued their earlier passivity. Daniel Schorr said that in 1973 "a new kind of journalism developed," in which, during the absence of disclosures, "the press began to try men in the most effective court in the country . . . the media." ABC's Harry Reasoner singled out *Time* and *Newsweek* for "pejorative pamphleteering [rather] than objective journalism." The *Chicago Daily News*'s Peter Lisagor, a press corps regular, saw a "sadistic quality" in the battering of Ziegler. John Osborne described his peers as "dogs who have scented blood and are running the fox right down to his death"; Joseph Kraft, despite having warned of a Nixonian police state, now argued that since the machinery of government was functioning, reporters' skullduggery had become unnecessary.[104]

Some reporters were still doing important work. Though the revelations of Nixon's financial improprieties paled next to his abuses of power—indeed, they became sideshows in the grand Watergate spectacle—on their own they might well have crippled Nixon's presidency. During Nixon's last year in office, reporters discovered that he had illegally backdated the donation of his vice-presidential papers to claim a bigger tax deduction; that he had paid barely any income taxes in some years; and that he improved his properties with federal funds. Notably, these exposés came from writers who worked at small papers or floated outside the White House press corps nucleus. John Blackburn of the *Santa Ana Register* first reported that Nixon acquired the Western White House at San Clemente with shady financial help and renovated it with public funds. John White of the *Providence Journal-Bulletin* exposed Nixon's minuscule income tax payments. Others who broke fresh ground, such as Jack Anderson, were once scorned as eccentrics but now celebrated as mavericks. That the high-profile Washington correspondents reverted to pack journalism during Watergate's climactic months reflected not any dearth of information to be unearthed about Nixon but rather a reassertion of old, enduring habits.

Nixon's own press conferences from January 1973 until his resignation in August 1974 allowed the public to see the mounting antagonism. At the start of his second term, the president set the relationship off on the wrong foot. Before the election, he had been relishing the thought of punishing hostile journalists, and Colson and others had been less than subtle in communicating those intentions to the press. But no one was prepared for Nixon's taunts at his January 31, 1973, press conference announcing the peace settlement in Vietnam. Proudly declaring that he had reached his goal of "peace with honor," Nixon sneered at the journalists. "I know it gags some of you to write that phrase," he said, "but it is true, and most Americans realize it is true." "It was the first of a sparse, infrequent series of press conferences," commented ABC's Howard K. Smith, "that could aptly be called carnivorous."[105]

  With the springtime Watergate revelations, Nixon again withdrew into isolation. Only after an extended hiatus did he return, on August 22, to face the press, when he announced Kissinger's appointment as secretary of state. By this point Watergate had sprouted multiple subplots, and reporters were backlogged on questions. The tension was thick, especially when noted Nixon antagonists, such as Dan Rather, took the floor. "I want to state this question with due respect to your office," the reporter said, unintentionally doing just the opposite. Nixon shot back: "That would be unusual."* "I would like to think not," Rather replied, and he proceeded to ask Nixon about John Ehrlichman's *ex parte* contacts with Pentagon Papers judge Matt Byrne. Nixon dodged the question. For the next half hour, tough interrogation followed, until Nixon erupted and chastised the reporters for neglecting "the business of the people." Two weeks later, at another press conference, the parties reenacted the drama. Nixon began talking about policy, but reporters badgered him about Watergate; the president then lashed out at the press's attacks "by innuendo, by leaks, by, frankly, leers and sneers of commentators."[106]

After the Saturday Night Massacre, the need for yet another press conference became apparent, as public opinion was crystallizing in favor of Nixon's ouster. Adding to the call were mainstream media, including *Time* magazine, which ran its first ever editorial to urge Nixon to step down. Weakened, Nixon twice postponed the crucial press conference, finally going before the correspondents on October 26, at 7:00 P.M., in the White House East Room. It was, Helen Thomas judged, "the most excruciating news conference, and the lowest point ever between the president and the press in such a venue."[107]

Nixon came out fighting. "Cronkite's not going to like this tonight, I hope," he muttered before heading out to face the crowd. He opened with a discussion of the Middle East, but the first question, from Dan Rather, raised the question of resignation. "Well, I am glad we don't take a vote of this room," the president sniped. Responding to another question, Nixon began calmly but then segued into an attack on the "outrageous, vicious, distorted . . . frantic, hysterical reporting" that he said had shaken public confidence. ("I'm not blaming anyone for that," he added.) CBS's Robert

---

* Nixon was angry at Rather in part because CBS had recently aired footage of the president shoving Ron Ziegler before a speech in New Orleans, an incident discussed in chapter 6.

Pierpoint asked why Nixon was angry with the press. "Don't get the impression that you arouse my anger," Nixon said tersely. "You see, one can only be angry with those he respects."[108]

Reporters were flabbergasted. Some, like Hugh Sidey, thought the press had embarrassed itself. The reporters, he charged, "could not or did not ask the right questions for a public that cries out more each day for some answers." He described the East Room as "a bear pit" of reporters, "shrieking and roaring for attention, jostling each other as they leaped up and down signaling frantically for the president's attention, ignoring the previous questions and the incomplete answers to press their own divergent points." Others, like Pierpoint, were "in a bit of a state of shock," as he said two days later when he and Rather interviewed Pat Buchanan on the CBS Morning News. Noting Nixon's "vitriolic attack on the news media," Pierpont said he would assume "it wasn't directed at me personally, although I happened to be the immediate object of it." Buchanan blamed the press. "The mood there was really like Sunday afternoon in the Tijuana bullring," he said. When Rather replied that the tension was "mostly of the president's own creation," Buchanan countered with a description of "the jumping up, the shouting, the screaming of questions" that he said forced a fair-minded reporter like Sidey to leave the room. Buchanan's view was echoed in *National Review*, which described the press as "sweating, jumping and shouting, hair matted, eyes glazed—wondering about *Mr. Nixon's* emotional stability."[109]

Though chastened, Pierpoint and Rather were arguing that the testy clashes showed only that the press corps was doing its job. *New York Times* columnist Tom Wicker agreed. With the recent news conferences, he claimed, "for the first time in my experience, the press has suddenly become what it has touted itself to be all these years—an adversary." Others were downright gleeful, not because they hated Nixon, as the president claimed, but because they seemed now to have a role in history. Reporters thrilled to the thought that they were important players in a momentous event. "I am not proud of this, but I enjoyed Watergate," Hedley Donovan later wrote. "To a journalist, it was a stupendously exciting story, fascinating in its complexity and fecundity, new sensations constantly leading onto more sensations. Beyond the sensations, however, I thought in the spring and summer of 1974 I was also seeing a majestic republican drama."[110]

Nixon, for his part, had been exploiting the press's excitement to paint himself as the victim of a lynch mob. When Nixon scheduled time on March 19, 1974, to field reporters' questions after an appearance before an audience of media executives whom he expected to be friendly, Dan Rather and others wondered if the session was meant as an ambush. Rather vowed to hold his tongue. Yet when Nixon falsely said in his talk that he was cooperating fully with the Special Prosecutor, the newsman felt obliged to speak up. As Rather rose to his feet, audience members, who had seen the reporter's chilly exchanges with Nixon and watched his hard-edged reporting, cheered and booed. Picking up on Rather's obvious notoriety with the crowd, Nixon fired off a barb whose meaning was obscure but whose sarcastic tone was unmistakable: "Are you running for something?" he asked. Caught off guard, Rather lost his composure. "No, sir, Mr. President," he said, adding just as opaquely, "Are you?"[111]

If the literal meaning of the exchange was murky, the hostility between the two men was clear. The White House considered it a victory for Nixon, who pointed to the incident as proof of the press's hostility. When Rather saw Pat Buchanan the next day, the speechwriter was grinning triumphantly. Journalists were divided. Some praised Rather's gutsiness. "It's obvious that there is tension between Rather and the president," James Reston said, "but . . . he is doing his job." Owners of many CBS affiliates, who tended to be conservative local businessmen, were angry with Rather and began an abortive bid to have the network formally censure him. Some Washington journalists also said the newsman had overstepped his bounds. *The Washington Post*'s Phil Geyelin thought Rather's rejoinder to Nixon was "gratuitous" and served only "to confirm in the public mind what the president says about TV newscasters." John Chancellor thought that whatever jabs Nixon took at reporters, it was wrong to reciprocate. Rather himself regretted the remark instantly, realizing it diverted attention from the substance of Nixon's reply to the dynamic between president and reporter.[112]

If Rather had crossed the line into gratuitous adversarialism, he behaved differently when he was assigned, along with CBS's other leading newsmen, to provide instant analysis of Nixon's resignation statement on August 8, the night before his East Room farewell. Nixon's speech was dodgy and defiant enough that, had the commentators been the unstinting opponents that Nixon imagined, they surely could have picked apart his performance. But almost everyone at CBS, from the executives to the on-air analysts, was reluctant to kick Nixon when he was down. During the day, Washington bureau chief Sanford Socolow had urged Daniel Schorr not to appear "vindictive" in his reporting—and told Schorr the word was going out to all correspondents. Executives also decided not to show a "political obituary" of Nixon that reviewed the history of Watergate.[113]

Far from vindictive, CBS's newsmen gushed with praise. Eric Sevareid claimed that "few things in his presidency became him as much." "It certainly was a conciliatory speech," agreed Walter Cronkite. Rather had been in Lafayette Park, enjoying his celebrity as "thousands of people" mobbed him, as Hugh Sidey enviously recalled, excited "to see Dan Rather in the flesh." But Rather, too, disappointed the Nixon-haters with his analysis, judging it Nixon's "finest hour." The president invested the moment, he said, with "a touch of class" and "a touch of majesty." Only Roger Mudd, Rather's rival to succeed Cronkite, was critical, noting that Nixon had refused to accept blame for the ordeal of the last two years.[114] Even as Nixon departed, the press was still torn between its competing impulses.

The press's relationship with Nixon had consequences. For the press, the initial result seemed to be salutary. The investigative reporter became "a new American folk hero," as New York magazine wrote, seen as a fearless truth-seeker, and record numbers of students enrolled in journalism schools and joined newspapers. Beat reporters now reflexively adopted an adversarial posture. Any act of news management could be the tip of an iceberg of concealment; any hint of deceit could justify an investigation. After Watergate, Joseph Kraft wrote in 1979, "there has been no holding us. The more august the person, the hotter the chase." By 1996, the media critic James Fallows was writing that "The working assumption for most reporters is that most politicians and handlers will mislead them most of the time."[115]

This zeal for exposure was a mixed blessing. As always, when channeled into hard reporting it provided an indispensable check on official dishonesty, a proper function of the government's fourth branch. But too often post-Watergate journalists set themselves up as the nation's guardians of political morality and joined in what came to be called "feeding frenzies." In learning from Watergate, they too often emulated not the trailblazers whose skepticism had produced fruitful inquiries but the latecomers who jumped on Watergate only as it was becoming a media spectacle. When distrust of authority spurred investigation, it remained a cherished trait; but when cynicism fed easy opinion-mongering and bandwagon journalism, it was bound to be superficial and fickle—and could easily revert to its mirror image, an equally shallow pose of credulous appreciation.

Compared to this mixed legacy for reporters, the repercussions for Nixon of his battles with the press were less ambiguous. His image as a spin doctor remained (only in later years it was historians, not newsmen, he was said to be spinning). And although his news management came to be viewed as his mildest sin—no different from the incorrigible PR work of his successors—the images of him as a liar and criminal continued to mark him as a uniquely blameworthy president, in the eyes of many groups in society other than just the press. The images of Nixon as liar and crook built upon and commingled with his other menacing images—the liberals' manipulator, the radicals' dictator—to form a portrait of America's chief political villain that endured long after.

The durability of this revised Tricky Dick image itself had a double legacy. For while it fed a distrust of all politicians and a taste for scandal, it also served as a benchmark, a reminder of the singular severity of Nixon's crimes. Even in the fog of the post-Watergate scandal culture, in which crimes were often lumped together with peccadilloes, Nixon's dark image served as a bright beacon for the discriminating. Memories of Nixon's abuses helped Americans decide when their fourth branch of government was onto a real scandal and when it was working itself into a lather simply because of its ingrained adversarial attitude.

Like most post-Watergate representations of Nixon in film and television, the movie *Dick* (1999), directed by Andrew Fleming, reaffirmed the former president's image as a liar and a criminal. The film, a comedy, supposes that two dizzy teenage girls, Arlene and Betsy, who live across the street from the Watergate building, are the real but uncredited heroes who brought Nixon's crimes to light. Meeting Nixon by accident on a school field trip to the White House, they become his official dog walkers and soon begin, unwittingly, to unravel the Watergate conspiracies. They feed their discoveries to Woodward and Bernstein, calling themselves, of course, "Deep Throat."

A broad satire, *Dick* is less scathing in its portrayal of Nixon than was the humor of the Watergate era; Nixon is portrayed as a bumbler, incompetent to run his own cover-up. But the film is far from the sort of anodyne non-ideological political satire of a Jay Leno monologue or the later years of *Saturday Night Live*. "Ultimately, our goal was to personalize Nixon's betrayal of the country," explained Andrew Fleming. His portrait of Nixon's deception of Arlene and Betsy stamps the president as a genuine, if comic, villain—ranting about Jews, lying to the country, and even kicking his dog, King Timahoe, whom he absent-mindedly continues to call "Checkers."[116]

If in many respects *Dick* could have been made by Watergate-era Nixon-haters, in one important way it bears the imprint of its own time: its portrayal of the press. Indeed, the film is largely a spoof of *All the President's Men* and its main characters; even the actors who play Woodward and Bernstein resemble Redford and Hoffman more than the real-life reporters. In place of the earlier film's heroic depiction of the journalistic sleuths, *Dick* offers a pair of Keystone Kops—petty, vain, and as incompetent and bumbling as Nixon himself. Woodward is parodied as humorless and plodding, Bernstein as a hypercompetitive runt. When Betsy and Arlene call the reporters, the men fight like schoolboys for control of the telephone, and they insult each other with sophomoric taunts. More pointedly, they are shown to be utterly dependent on the scraps of information that the teenage girls toss their way. Left to their own devices, the film implies, they never would have cracked the case.

Twenty-five years after Watergate, *Dick* spoke to the cultural perceptions of both Nixon and the press. Where Woodward and Bernstein were hailed as heroes in the 1970s, their 1990s emulators became objects of public scorn. Nixon's image as a liar was indelible. But the moment of revival and heroism for American journalism was all too fleeting.

5

The Loyalists:
Nixon as Victim

> Watergate was bullshit, pure and simple. They framed
> Nixon and they killed him politically. I don't care what *he*
> did. It's disgraceful what *they* did to the country—the press
> and Congress and the protesters. . . . I loved Nixon for loving
> the country.
>
> —*Member of the Italian-American League of Canarsie*[1]

Like millions of other Americans, Baruch Korff of Rehoboth, Massachusetts, watched the Senate Watergate Hearings on television in the spring
of 1973. The select committee, formed in January after the new Senate convened, began holding televised sessions on May 17 amid daily bombshells. As a parade of witnesses disclosed the baroque details of the White
House's clandestine political operations, television audiences swelled.
But where others looked on with fascination, glee, or a sense of betrayal,
Korff felt waves of anger. A fifty-nine-year-old Ukrainian-born rabbi who
had recently retired as the head of a local congregation, Korff had
opposed Nixon in 1960 and 1968 but switched sides in 1972 after the president took up the cause of oppressed Soviet Jews. Now loyal to Nixon,
Korff believed the hearings were a partisan attempt to overturn the president's recent re-election. The interrogation of Nixon's men and the bar-

rage of commentary predicting his doom fed the rabbi's fury. "I've got to do something or I'll explode," he told his wife.[2]

On July 1, Korff wrote a letter to *The New York Times* venting his rage toward the Democrats and the media. Like most letters to the *Times*, it wasn't published. So Korff decided to buy his way into the paper. With $1,000 of his own cash, a loan, and contributions from friends, he placed an advertisement in the *Times* on July 29, 1973. Titled "An Appeal for Fairness," it declared that the hearings were a charade:

> Witness after witness has been paraded before the cameras in what has become a perfect amalgam of circus performance and popularity contest. Viewing the proceedings, one thinks more of 1789 than of 1973. The noisy claque that makes up the caucus room audience resembles nothing more than the Parisian mob cheering and shouting as the tumbrels deposit their victims before the guillotine. For them, the verdict is already in.

The ad bore a few hallmarks of an amateur, if not a crackpot—the hyperbole, the generous use of capital letters (in passages besides the one above), the dense blocks of prose that would daunt all but the most determined readers. Despite its independent origins, though, its message mimicked the one Nixon himself was fashioning: blaming the break-in on "overzealous and irresponsible White House aides"; condemning the Ervin Committee and the media for a "lynch-mob mentality" and tactics reminiscent of Joe McCarthy; insisting that Watergate mattered less than "the historic accomplishments of the president's first term." Nixon could take comfort in knowing that even as his popularity plummeted, Korff and others saw Watergate from his perspective.[3]

The response to Korff's ad over the next three days overwhelmed the local activist: three thousand letters, hundreds of phone calls, donations totaling close to $30,000, six times the cost of the ad. He gathered a few volunteers and devoted himself full time to running a group he called the National Citizens' Committee for Fairness to the Presidency, or "Fairness." The self-described "small-town rabbi" was himself transformed into a minor celebrity. Korff was no more a stranger to politics than Sam Ervin was a simple country lawyer; he had written speeches for congressmen since the 1930s, and in 1947 was arrested (and acquitted) for aiding a plot by militant Zionists to bomb Buckingham Palace. Korff had even met with Nixon before, in 1967, when the candidate was courting Jewish leaders.[4]

But Korff had never been in such demand as in the weeks after his *Times* ads. In the last five months of 1973, he made five hundred appearances in the president's defense. He spoke at rallies. He sparred with Gore Vidal on *The Dick Cavett Show*. He raised cash (some $5.5 million in all), placed ads (in five hundred papers, with such titles as "THE ASSASSINS" and "THE RAPE OF AMERICA"), and promoted the idea that Nixon was being persecuted by sore-loser Democrats and out-for-the-kill journalists. Two million Americans, Korff claimed, joined his efforts.[5]

During the Ervin hearings, it had emerged that the White House secretly used right-wing networks to drum up shows of support for Nixon that it pretended were spontaneous. As Korff grew prominent, skeptics wondered whether his outfit, too, was a White House front. Technically, it wasn't; it had sprung up as a grass-roots organization. But the group did fall under the White House's purview, if not its actual control. Along with other pro-Nixon groups, the Committee for Fairness was monitored and contacted by White House aides and the president himself. At one point they flew the rabbi to New York to meet Nixon's friend Donald Kendall, the head of Pepsi-Cola, who sought to subsume the committee under a larger, well-financed and star-studded (and White House–backed) pro-Nixon campaign. Jealous of his independence, Korff refused to cede control of his group. But throughout 1974 he worked with Kendall's group—which went by the supremely inoffensive name "Americans for the Presidency"—in placing ads and staging events starring the likes of Bob Hope and Norman Vincent Peale. Korff himself was not immune to the blandishments of power, as he visited the White House with growing frequency.[6]

The symbiotic relationship between Korff and Nixon peaked on Monday, May 13, 1974, when the rabbi interviewed the president in the Oval Office for ninety minutes. The colloquy was, in Korff's words, a "collaboration" with the White House.[*] After failing to interest New York publish-

---

[*] The interview was initiated by administration staffer Bill Baroody and launched by Nixon aide Bruce Herschensohn. Frank Gannon of the press office helped write Korff's questions, and Nixon's old friend Ralph de Toledano worked on the final text.

ing houses in the transcript, Korff issued it with committee funds. *The Personal Nixon: Staying on the Summit* read like a White House public relations effort, only less professional. Korff asked Nixon loaded questions; Nixon offered stock defenses. "Has there been a wholesale smear of the president's men in the Watergate affair?" Korff asked. Nixon replied that he respected Leon Jaworski, Archibald Cox's successor as Special Prosecutor, but that "eager-beaver staffers" had created "an abusive process" that would have gotten Joe McCarthy "ridden out of town on a rail." What did Nixon think of the coverage? Korff asked. The liberal media, Nixon responded, were inflating the "thinnest scandal in American history. . . . If it hadn't been Watergate, there probably would have been something else." So the exchange went, for forty-six pages. Korff's questions were so obsequious, his defense of Nixon so unstinting, that even Nixon's defenders squirmed. But Korff took pride in his pains to set the record straight, as did his fevered legions. They pressed on into the summer of 1974, even as Nixon's ouster appeared inevitable, holding gala luncheons and urging Nixon not to capitulate to the calls for his removal. Even the release of the June 23, 1972, tape revealing Nixon's early role in the cover-up led the rabbi only to joke (paraphrasing Ron Ziegler) that his faith in Nixon's innocence had been "rendered 'inoperative'"—not to change his mind about Nixon's duty to resign.[7]

Korff's loyalist position always remained a minority one. But what he and his cohorts lacked in numbers they made up for in stridency. For more than two decades after Nixon's resignation, a diverse group of indefatigable loyalists and Watergate buffs promoted a picture of Nixon as the victim of vengeful foes. The most brazen of them declared that the president had been framed as part of a dark plot, that he was an innocent undone by treacherous underlings. Outside this small nucleus, a larger circle of sympathizers held fast to their Watergate-era view of the scandal as what the conservative polemicist Paul Johnson called a "maelstrom of hysteria . . . a witch-hunt . . . run by liberals in the media."[8] In a third, outer circle, others still—journalists, historians, and politicians beyond the loyalist cadre—came to see Nixon not as an innocent but nonetheless as a victim: they agreed that the president, though guilty of grievous wrongs, had been judged too harshly. Though hardly the redemption

Nixon sought, this modest change in mainstream sentiment was not without significance.

The claim that Richard Nixon was "rehabilitated" after Watergate is mistaken.* But over time the intense conviction that his transgressions were unique faded. Americans showed a greater willingness to treat Nixon as a victim, thanks in part to loyalists like Korff. In tirelessly championing Nixon's innocence, the loyalists fed a cycle that redounded to Nixon's favor: on occasion they convinced ostensibly neutral authorities of their claims, and these authorities' repetition of those claims allowed the loyalists to declare vindication. In 1977, for instance, the journalist Victor Lasky, a friend of Nixon's since the 1940s, wrote a best-selling book called *It Didn't Start with Watergate*. He argued that the wrongs committed by Lyndon Johnson, John Kennedy, and others should mitigate history's judgment of Nixon. "Granted that two wrongs don't make a right," Lasky wrote, "but in law and politics, two wrongs can make a respectable precedent." Fourteen years later, Stephen Ambrose, who has been called Nixon's "definitive" biographer because of his reliable, moderately sympathetic three-volume work, picked up the line. Ambrose didn't agree that Nixon had been railroaded, but he echoed Lasky's key point. "Two wrongs do not make a right, not even in politics," wrote Ambrose, modifying his predecessor slightly, "but they do make a precedent." And when Korff wrote his memoir in 1995, he quoted that same line—but attributed it to "biographer Stephen Ambrose," rather than to Nixon's friend, Lasky. Korff used Ambrose's weight to bolster his own view that "the justification for defending Nixon is all the stronger given . . . what we now know other presidents did"—a view that he, like Lasky, had held all along.[9]

The picture of Nixon as a victim was hard to square with the documentary record. Congressional committee reports, FBI and Special Prosecutor investigations, White House tapes and papers, personal diaries—all proved that Nixon broke laws and directed the Watergate cover-up. But to confirm the general wisdom isn't news, and after the appearance of several excellent studies of Watergate, few scholars had much to add.[10] In the

* See chapter 7 for a fuller discussion.

silence of the many, the few who saw Nixon as Watergate's victim could be heard louder. Through their persistence, their image of him grew more prevalent as memories of Watergate faded.

To many, the idea of Nixon as a victim is probably hard to fathom. But when set in its historical context, it becomes more explicable. During the upheaval of the late Sixties and early Seventies, millions of Americans believed that their time-honored values were being swept away by an insurgent left. Impeaching a president, still a strange novelty in 1973 and 1974, was to Nixon's supporters a metaphor for the larger, equally strange effort to replace old social codes with new ones. To them, the attack on Nixon was an attack on their mores and way of life.

During Nixon's presidency, America was in the throes of the 1960s. Established strictures of propriety were being jettisoned; social norms, sexual norms, the norms that governed acceptable political protest and journalism were shifting. In the midst of this turmoil, in both 1968 and 1972, Nixon sought and won the support of traditionalists. Speaking, as he had in 1946, on behalf of "forgotten Americans," Nixon pledged to quell the riotous campuses, to reassert law and order against crime and unrest. In these years he assailed drug use, pornography, school busing, judicial activism, and the student radicals he called "bums." He championed religion, duty, and patriotism; inspired by the film *The Candidate* (1972), his staff wore American flag pins in their lapels. Influenced by voting-behavior analysts Kevin Phillips and Richard Scammon and Ben Wattenberg, who placed the "social issue" at the center of a winning Republican coalition, Nixon sought the allegiance of the "forty-seven-year-old Dayton housewife" of Scammon and Wattenberg's analysis, the voters who resided in what columnist Joseph Kraft labeled "Middle America." Nixon's strategy of "positive polarization" mobilized the heartland's social conservatism against elites on campuses, in the press, and in Washington—those whom Spiro Agnew dubbed "radiclibs." For daring to defend traditional values, Nixon won the loyalty of millions.[11]

A typical member of Nixon's coalition was Frank Trotta, an Italian-American resident of New Rochelle, New York. Trotta, whose story the

journalist Samuel Freedman tells in his book *The Inheritance* (1996), was
born in 1954 to working-class parents who in the 1960s broke from their
Democratic roots over what they considered the liberals' refusal to confront the escalating social chaos. As the Vietnam War raged, Frank Trotta
embraced his parents' uncomplicated patriotism, deeming the peace
movement to be un-American. On the day of the October 1969 Moratorium, the 15-year-old Trotta wore an American-flag armband proclaiming:
"These Colors Don't Run"; when Nixon proclaimed July 4, 1970, "Honor
America Day," Trotta organized a local rally with veterans and churchgo-
ers. Pat Buchanan, an advocate of exploiting the "social issue," wrote in
his 1972 book *The New Majority* that Nixon's loyalists were "visibly patriotic and [willing to] applaud the president for holding out for 'peace with
honor'"; Nixon's foes, he said, "view flag-waving as a fetish of the simple-
minded." By Buchanan's lights, Trotta was a loyalist. During Trotta's first
year in college, Nixon's presidency began collapsing, and amid the delight
on campus—the anti-Nixon posters, the pro-impeachment demonstrations, the Nixon masks at Halloween—Trotta identified ever more
strongly with the beleaguered president. His grandfather, a Democrat,
gloated, "I told you that your Tricky Dicky was no good," but Trotta saw
Nixon's plight as a coup perpetrated by the media, Congress, and John
Dean. He resolved never to watch Dan Rather again.[12]

The view of Nixon as a victim—shared by Frank Trotta, the hypothetical Dayton housewife, and Rabbi Korff's brigades—drew upon an earlier
image of Nixon: the fighting populist. Just as the young Nixon presented
himself as a defender of American values against subversive New Dealers, so during his presidency he pledged to uphold national pride against
the radiclibs. He rallied voters by casting his presidency in populist terms,
with his everyman-patriot fighting a powerful, degenerate elite. His triumph in 1972, said Buchanan, represented "a victory of traditional American values and beliefs over the claims of the 'counterculture,' a victory of
Middle America over the celebrants of Woodstock Nation." When Watergate hit, Nixon and his aides hoped the drama could be similarly cast.[13]

Nixon's victim image also built on the left's portraits of him. The liberals' Tricky Dick image was by now prevalent, and many Americans realized that the image said as much about the liberals' enmity toward Nixon

as about his own wiliness. Prone to blame his troubles on the machinations of others, Nixon assumed instinctively during Watergate that he was being persecuted. His defenders, aware of the ancient feud, instinctively agreed. Making matters worse, the newly unbuttoned, no-holds-barred culture of the 1970s gave the attacks on Nixon an unparalleled savagery, handing loyalists more evidence that Nixon's enemies were out to get him.

The eminently square Nixon not only voiced but embodied the embattled values of these loyalists. "Vietnam being now off the agenda," editorialized *National Review* in 1973, the media were seizing on "this objectively trivial Watergate affair . . . to launch a broad and fierce counterattack . . . against the embryo[nic] 'new majority' that has been forming . . . and that threatens to oust the old establishment and its New Left allies from their traditional dominance." Although many of the magazine's editors would soon change their minds about the "objectively trivial" nature of the scandal, most continued to agree that a left-liberal-media putsch was underway. Besieged by a fast-changing culture and a robust opposition, adherents of this view needed only a short imaginative leap to see their president as the target of a "Parisian mob cheering and shouting as the tumbrels deposit their victims before the guillotine," in Korff's purple prose. That imaginative leap was made easier when such a grim picture was reinforced daily by White House spokesmen themselves making the case for Nixon's victimhood.[14]

As the stories of Rabbi Korff and Frank Trotta illustrate, the image of Nixon as an innocent victim wasn't simply issued from the White House and lapped up by credulous supporters. Nixon's loyalists jumped to his defense. Yet no one believed in the image more fervently than Nixon himself. During Watergate, Nixon's aides brought groups like Fairness into the White House orbit. They planted column ideas with friendly journalists (it was later reported that Victor Lasky had secretly been on the payroll of Nixon's Committee to Re-Elect the President). White House communications director Ken Clawson set up a "surrogates" program under which Nixon's friends, family members, and aides were trotted out to mouth White House–issued talking points. Not infrequently, these arguments trickled down to Nixon's citizen defenders. Sometimes, then, Nixon's ordinary admirers, media friends, and Republican colleagues purposefully coordinated their messages; sometimes they reached similar arguments through an indirect mutual influence. By both design and simple confluence, the loyalists collectively proffered another New Nixon: the victim of a witch-hunt and a double standard, a good man besieged by opportunistic foes.[15]

This image of Nixon reached its peak, perversely, during the depths of Watergate. The more the rest of society maligned Nixon, the more vociferously his stalwart defenders proclaimed his innocence. Yet Nixon's self-conception as a victim whose troubles stemmed from the designs of vengeful enemies was hardly new. In 1948, he had perceived that the press and the liberal intelligentsia were arrayed against him because of his lead role in going after Alger Hiss, even though most of them actually believed he was in the right. In 1952, he had blamed Communists, liberals, and the media for inflating the fund scandal into a national brouhaha—and noted sourly that Adlai Stevenson's political expense fund generated no similar outrage. In the California gubernatorial race, he had lashed out at the press for hewing to a double standard and covering him more critically than it did his Democratic opponent, the incumbent Pat Brown.

Perhaps most significantly, Nixon felt he had been cheated out of the presidency in 1960 and had spread the unproven charge that electoral fraud cost him the election. Some fraud indeed occurred in Cook County, Illinois, where Chicago mayor Richard Daley ran a tight and corrupt machine, and fraud likely occurred in Texas, too. But it was unclear and unlikely that the number of doctored votes in those places was larger than Kennedy's margins of victory—9,000 in Illinois, 46,000 in Texas. Nixon and his campaign team, however, felt they had been robbed, and they swiftly launched court challenges to Kennedy's victories in eleven states.* Nixon himself offered a conditional and grudging concession to JFK ("If

---

* The other states were Delaware, Michigan, Minnesota, Missouri, New Jersey, New Mexico, Nevada, Pennsylvania, and South Carolina. Kennedy's people countered and asked for a recount in Hawaii. None of the Kennedy states ended up being awarded to Nixon; but, ironically, Hawaii's recount did lead to that state's falling into Kennedy's column. Hawaii's vote was not settled until December 28, 1960, after the Electoral College convened but before Congress met to certify the Electoral College results.

this trend does continue and he does become our next president . . .") and met with his rival to promise he would make no trouble. He publicly distanced himself from the challenges, knowing, as he later wrote, that "charges of 'sore loser' would follow me through history and remove any possibility of a further political career." Meanwhile, his aides Bob Finch and Len Hall, along with Republican National Committee chairman Thruston Morton and General Counsel Meade Alcorn, waged battle. They filed lawsuits, secured recounts, had the government empanel grand juries, formed a "Nixon Recount Committee" that raised at least $100,000, and stoked the fire with inflammatory comments to the press. ("The more we dig into this election, the clearer it becomes that fraud was widespread," Morton said on December 1.) After stringing out the election through mid-December, however, they lost two critical court cases and had to close up shop.[16]

Despite the failure to establish Kennedy's victory as illegitimate, Nixon nursed a grudge. At a Christmas party that he and Pat threw, the outgoing vice president was heard to greet guests with, "We won, but they stole it from us." The narrow loss—Kennedy had prevailed by less than 120,000 ballots nationwide, 0.2 percent of the overall vote—gnawed at Nixon; losing to a man whom he already resented for his wealth, charm, good looks, and sexual prowess only compounded Nixon's conviction that men like Kennedy got the breaks while he always lost out. Nixon's belief that Kennedy won the office illegally may also have emboldened him to view the Watergate tactics he sanctioned before the 1972 election as legitimate.[17]

Another result of Nixon's predisposition to see himself as a victim was that when Watergate broke, he continued to believe his actions had been justified. He wasn't able to think of the emerging scandal, he wrote, as anything but "a public relations problem that only needed a public relations solution." When he met with Haldeman three days after the fateful break-in, he was, his staff chief noted, "concerned about what our counterattack is, our PR offensive." Later in the day, Nixon was still fretting about the message. "My God, the [Democratic National] Committee isn't worth bugging, in my opinion," he said. "That's my public line." Again with Haldeman on September 11, 1972, he was still "mainly concerned about the Watergate, wanting to know . . . what our thorough game plan is, our PR plan on how to handle the whole thing, the need to take the offensive, develop a line, and so forth." According to the "line" that they developed, the Watergate probe was a witch-hunt by Nixon's enemies who wanted to defeat his reelection—or, as they argued after the election, to overturn it.[18]

Though conceived as PR, the idea that Democrats were going after Nixon for political reasons wasn't entirely cynical, or fanciful. Indeed, it would have been surprising if, after the June 17 break-in, Democratic leaders hadn't tried to keep Watergate alive. After the burglars were linked to the Committee to Re-Elect the President (or CREEP, as it was often called), Larry O'Brien, chairman of the Democratic National Committee, demanded an investigation. He charged that the crime "raised the ugliest questions about the integrity of the political process," and announced a $1 million lawsuit. George McGovern also played up the issue. With his presidential campaign moribund, hemorrhaging support from Southerners and urban ethnics, the Democratic nominee hoped the corruption issue would boost his prospects. Flitting from one city to the next, he dumped "the whole ugly mess of corruption, of sabotage, of wiretapping right squarely in the lap of Richard Nixon." The emerging scandal represented, McGovern said, "a moral and Constitutional crisis of unprecedented dimensions." On election eve he bought television time to warn that Nixon was aiming to destroy the two-party system. But McGovern, widely perceived as far to the left, was the wrong messenger. His manifest desperation, Teddy White noted, made his charges sound like "hysterical moralizing." Nixon, meanwhile, distanced himself from the crimes—"No one in this administration, presently employed," he said in August 1972, "was involved in this very bizarre incident"—and people believed him.[19]

By depicting Watergate inquiries as a partisan witch-hunt, Nixon and his supporters inverted the roles of culprit and victim. They made McGovern's use of a legitimate issue seem like a smear. The Democrats, the victims of the burglary, were said to be engaging in "character assassination," while Nixon and his men, the culprits, were painted as innocents. The president railed throughout the fall that he was the victim of "the dirtiest campaign ever waged against a president." After the election he had aides compile a memo that he hoped would show the attacks on him, Watergate included, to be a slander of historic proportions.[20]

At first the tactic succeeded. In the fall of 1972, the Republicans stymied a potentially harmful investigation of Watergate. Texas Democratic congressman Wright Patman convened hearings on CREEP's illegal procurement and use of campaign funds. But Nixon, judging the move an "unabashed partisan" effort to tar him, told his aides to "put the screws on Congress to turn off the Patman hearings." They did. Assistant Attorney General Henry Petersen, who was overseeing the indictments in the Watergate burglary, warned Patman that hearings would jeopardize the prosecution. The White House then ensured that the hearings *would* be partisan by having House Republicans refuse to cooperate with the chairman's agenda.* It required only some "arm-twisting and back-room politics," John Dean recalled, to deny Patman's committee subpoena power and render it toothless. Patman summoned a host of White House and CREEP officials anyway, but none showed up, leaving the congressman to grandstand before a row of empty chairs.[21]

Apart from the Democrats, Nixon also thought that the media's attention to the scandal—such as it was in 1972—stemmed from a vendetta. His old suspicion of the media colored his view. *The Washington Post* especially aroused his ire. When in October 1972 the *Post* implicated White House appointments secretary Dwight Chapin—he would later serve time—Nixon wrote in his diary that the charges represented "McCarthyism at its worst." He sniffed that when Democrats committed crimes they were seen as "good clean fun," but Nixon's men's deeds were judged "grim and

---

* The role of House Minority Leader Gerald Ford came under scrutiny during his 1973 hearings to be confirmed as vice president. Nixon had told aides to have Ford enlist GOP congressmen in thwarting Patman. "He's [Ford's] got to know that it [the order] comes from the top," Nixon said, "and he's got to get at this and screw this thing up." Although Ford apparently didn't take his marching orders directly from the White House, he and other Republicans hardly needed prodding. "Because of the political overtones of this matter," Ford wrote to one GOP committee member, "I think it would be imperative for all Republican members to be present at the Committee meeting to assure that the investigative resolution is appropriately drawn." When questioned, Ford denied any collusion with the White House, and in 1976 the Watergate Special Prosecutor, Charles Ruff, rebuffed Democratic requests to pursue obstruction-of-justice charges against Ford.

vicious espionage and sabotage of the worst type." This *idée fixe* never left Nixon's mind: he voiced it in private comments, in memos, in press conferences. Of course, if journalists and Democrats were persecuting Nixon in 1972, they failed miserably, as his landslide reelection showed.[22]

Some Americans who expected partisanship from the Democrats joined Nixon, especially in 1973, in regarding the press corps as the leaders of the witch-hunt. Whether because of the cynical tone of much reporting or simply because journalists bore the bad news, the press came in for attack on the letters pages of small papers, in the dinner conversations of Republican bastions, in the columns of editorialists. Sacks of hate mail bombarded White House reporters. "If you have wives and children, how very proud they must be of the notches in your guns and the scalps in your tepees of the lives you wrecked," one Kansas City woman wrote *The New York Times*'s John Herbers, in a letter he singled out for its vitriol. "You dog every footstep of President Nixon, spying and searching for a minor incident to pump up into a printed lie." At one Korff rally, a mob circled the reporters and demanded they transcribe the rabbi's words verbatim, causing Sarah McClendon, one of the press corps's few women, to fear for her safety.[23]

Attacking the press played into the demonology of the hard right, which had long cheered the anti-media jeremiads of Spiro Agnew and Pat Buchanan. Archconservatives were uneasy about Nixon: they had supported him early in his career, fallen out with him in the late 1950s, returned to the fold in 1968, and again grown leery when Nixon began toasting the Soviet and Chinese Communists. Watergate, however, rebuilt the bond, as they rushed to defend the president from the liberal onslaught. Even conservatives unsure about his innocence agreed he was being tried in the press. At *National Review*, an otherwise divided editorial staff spoke with near unity when lambasting "the media's daily spasms of moral indignation," its efforts "to undo the results of the 1968 and 1972 elections."* Conservatives weren't always pro-Nixon, but they were consistently anti-anti-Nixon.[24]

---

* The magazine's Washington correspondent, George F. Will, dissented, insisting that the press's "prolonged scrutiny of Watergate" stemmed from a sense of professional duty. This independence from conservative orthodoxy helped Will to become a columnist for *Newsweek* and brought him national fame.

What elicited the right's own spasms of indignation was its perception that liberals were trying to impose an agenda that Americans had rejected at the ballot box. For all their gripes, archconservatives appreciated that Nixon was building a Republican majority, which they believed the liberals wanted to overturn. "Since 1968 the liberal establishment and its allies in the media have been on the defensive," *National Review* noted. The target of "the media storm" was "not really Nixon himself or this or that aide, but, rather, that 'new majority.'" In the face of such an insurrection, once lukewarm Nixonites became ardent supporters. William Loeb, publisher of the far-right *Manchester Union-Leader*, had for some time wanted Nixon to resign—"not because of Watergate," he explained, but because of "incompetence." After Agnew's resignation in October 1973, however, Loeb changed his mind. It was now evident, he said in Agnewian language, that "a small group of arrogant self-appointed rulers"—journalists—were trying to hand over the presidency to the Democratic Speaker of the House, Carl Albert, who was constitutionally next in line after the vice president. It didn't matter to Loeb that Democratic congressional leaders had sworn that they would wait until Agnew's replacement was picked before considering impeachment; the power of Loeb's fantasy—mirroring the left's earlier delusions of a Nixonian plot to cancel the 1972 elections—popularized archconservatives' belief in an imminent liberal coup.[25]

In January 1974, the Jacksonville-based rock group Lynyrd Skynyrd was earning a following with its bluesy guitar-heavy music and Confederate flag motif, but it had yet to record a hit single. Lead singer Ronnie van Zant had written a song called "Sweet Home Alabama," a response to Neil Young's anti-segregationist "Southern Man." In a populist voice, van Zant sneered at Young and other liberals who denigrated Nixon, George Wallace, and the folkways of the white South. The song took a withering view of Nixon's latest crisis: "Now Watergate does not bother me/Does your conscience bother you?" Overriding concerns from the band's producer and record company executives who thought the song was too regional in its appeal, Lynyrd Skynyrd released "Sweet Home Alabama" in June 1974.

Amid controversy over its politically incorrect lyrics, it rocketed to No. 8 on the Billboard chart. The defiant Watergate couplet captured a widespread belief that Nixon was under fire only because liberal arbiters of opinion hewed to a double standard.[26]

This idea was central to Nixon's victim persona. The claim that others had committed crimes similar to Watergate—sometimes against Nixon—was one that Nixon voiced often and enthusiastically. It allowed him to tap into a perdurable American distrust of politics and to downplay his crimes as routine behavior. Since the American Revolution, a powerful strain of popular political thought had held that all elected officials were prone to corruption. Nixon's imputations that "everyone does it" traded on this widespread suspicion of politicians as a class.

These arguments also helped Nixon to justify retaliating against his rivals. Surprisingly for someone who steadfastly maintained his innocence, Nixon actually admitted to having done much of what he was accused of; where he differed with his critics was in claiming that those actions were warranted. Nixon said in his memoirs, for example, that he told Haldeman and others, "I wanted the leading Democrats annoyed, harassed and embarrassed—as I had been in the past." Yet he simultaneously maintained that he was guilty of only political "mistakes." That Nixon could hold such contradictory views speaks to the power of his image of himself as victim, the depth of his conviction that he was entitled to break laws or harass others because others had done so against him.[27]

Finally, the everyone-does-it line let Nixon believe he was being singled out. "If I were a liberal," he told Rabbi Korff, "Watergate would be a blip." He compiled a private catalogue of behaviors by others that he believed excused his own. On the basis of comments J. Edgar Hoover made to him, he frequently claimed, not quite accurately, that Lyndon Johnson had bugged his campaign plane in 1968.* When Nixon was chided for spying on political opponents, he shot back that John and Robert Kennedy had done the same. And as precedents for his 1972 pro-

---

* In fact, the FBI monitored the conversations of Anna Chennault, a Nixon loyalist with ties to the South Vietnamese. Chennault was urging Saigon—treasonously, Johnson felt, and possibly at Nixon's bidding—to reject his peace proposals so as to secure a better deal after Nixon took office.

gram of political sabotage, he regularly cited the pranks of Democratic operative Dick Tuck, who had hounded Nixon since his 1950 Senate race. During the Watergate Hearings, Haldeman testified that "dirty tricks" maestro Donald Segretti was hired to be a "Dick Tuck for our side."[28]

Within the White House, this sense of injustice fed Nixon's anger; it also inspired a "counteroffensive." Like the witch-hunt line, the double-standard theme originated in Nixon's June 1972 damage-control sessions. When he and Haldeman plotted their PR offensive on June 20, the president felt that "we have to hit the opposition with their activities," the chief of staff noted.[29]

The first example of the double standard that leapt to Nixon's mind was the hubbub over Daniel Ellsberg's decision to leak the Pentagon Papers. "Do they justify this [the Watergate break-in] less than stealing Pentagon Papers, [Jack] Anderson Files, etc.," Nixon mused, according to Haldeman's paraphrase. ". . . We should be on the attack—for diversion."* To Chuck Colson, Nixon joked that someone should sarcastically suggest awarding a Pulitzer Prize to the Watergate burglars. Colson pumped this idea through the White House communications channels, noting that while the June 17 break-in had produced "4 or 5 days straight of front-page headlines," Ellsberg's act had produced a Pulitzer. Pat Buchanan, asked to "entice Bill Buckley to write something along these lines," countered with "a better idea": turning the issue against McGovern. "We should . . . say, this SOB is raising hell about a couple of Cubans stealing papers from Larry O'Brien's office, when George McGovern himself personally urged Daniel Ellsberg, the thief of secret Government documents, to fence those documents with the *New York Times*." The Ellsberg analogy went nowhere, though Nixon continued to urge it on his audiences for years afterward.[30]

Ellsberg's case was but one grievance in an endless catalogue. In his memoirs, Nixon wrote that he told Haldeman on June 21, 1972, "It seemed that the Democrats had been doing this kind of thing to us for years and *they* never got caught" (italics his), perhaps thinking of the 1960 election.

---

* This is the conversation whose secret recording was marred by the mysterious (but deliberate) erasure of a crucial 18½ minutes. The "Anderson Files" probably refers to columnist Jack Anderson's publication in December 1971 of classified information about Nixon's policy toward the feuding nations of India and Pakistan.

Haldeman agreed that "the press just never went after them the way they went after us." Likewise, during his September 15, 1972, cover-up conversation with Haldeman and Dean, the president claimed: "Goldwater put it in context [when] he said, 'Well, for Christ's sake, everybody bugs everybody else.' . . . We were bugged in '68 on the plane and in '62 even running for governor." Indeed, practically whenever the Watergate bugging was mentioned, Nixon insisted that others had done worse to him with impunity.[31]

Nixon used the argument not just to try to sway public opinion but to cover up Watergate. When in early 1973 Senate Democrats convened the Ervin Committee, Nixon hoped to handcuff it as he had Patman's inquiry. He tried to get the Senate to probe wrongdoing by both parties, taking heat off himself. But Senate Republicans, confined to the minority, failed to expand the committee's mandate. Instead, Nixon tried to hamper the committee's proceedings secretly while professing that he would cooperate. "A behind-the-scenes media effort would be made," John Dean testified, to make the hearings seem partisan. By publicizing misdeeds by JFK and LBJ, Dean said, the White House could "discredit the hearings and reduce their impact by . . . show[ing] that the Democrats . . . engaged in the same type of activities." The cumulative weight of the bipartisan disclosures might lead the public to conclude that "'They are all bad down there!'" and "change the atmosphere of the whole Watergate hearings."[32]

In this early 1973 period, in which Dean met often with Nixon, the president focused on "his desire to launch a counterscandal against the Democrats" and "his determination to find a strategy to handle the upcoming Ervin hearings," Dean recalled. The administration conscripted aides to dredge up information from 1964 and 1968 to impugn the Democrats. Attorney General Richard Kleindienst was to order the FBI to "get the fullest possible information" about the supposed bugging of Nixon's campaign plane in 1968. John Mitchell was to have Donald Kendall at Pepsi-Cola extract information from his assistant Cartha "Deke" DeLoach, a former associate of J. Edgar Hoover. When DeLoach proved reticent, Dean turned to William Sullivan, another Hoover man, for evidence of how other presidents misused the FBI; Sullivan delivered a memo, focusing on FDR and LBJ, that made its way into the newspapers that summer. Nixon, though, was "never satisfied," Dean noted, "with the evidence I brought him of buggings and surveillance by previous administrations, even though I thought it was impressive in a grisly way."[33]

Nixon and his loyalists made the double-standard argument long after it ceased to persuade anyone new. In May 1973, the president ranted to Ron Ziegler, as if his press secretary had never heard such claims before, that Watergate was "chicken shit. . . . It's what Bobby Kennedy did to me in '60 and '62, what Johnson did to Goldwater. . . . My God, the Kennedys and Johnson used the FBI, Hoover told me, in a shameful way. We didn't do that." Two months later, his senior staff decimated by resignations, Nixon found a fresh receptacle for his fulminations in his new chief of staff, Al Haig. He wrote Haig of the need for "an all-out offensive" that enlisted "friendly commentators and columnists . . . the party people . . . the Congress" and sympathetic Watergate committee members. He wanted "a concerted public relations campaign" to "re-emphasize" that Kennedy's wiretapping was more extensive than his own. White House memoranda and transcripts of Nixon's conversations in 1973 and 1974 showed the president railing about the Kennedys, Johnson, and even McGovern to Haig, Kissinger, and, apparently, anyone else willing to listen.[34]

In August 1973, Nixon took to the bully pulpit to make the comparison himself. Previously, in his April 30 speech, in which he announced the departures of his top aides, Nixon had spoken elliptically of "campaign excesses . . . on all sides." But at his August 22 press conference, his first in five months, he bluntly accused his Democratic predecessors of sanctioning burglaries. "In the three Kennedy years and the three Johnson years through 1966, when burglarizing of this type did take place, . . . there was no talk of impeachment," he needled the reporters. ". . . I shall also point out that when you ladies and gentlemen indicate your great interest in wiretaps, and I understand that, that the height of the wiretaps was when Robert Kennedy was Attorney General in 1963. I don't criticize it, however. He had over 250 [taps] in 1963, and of course the average in the Eisenhower Administration and the Nixon Administration is about 110." Nixon attributed the double standard to the refusal of "most of the members of the press corps" to "accept the mandate of 1972" or to embrace "the strong America that I want to build." "If it weren't Watergate," he said, they would use "anything else—in order to keep the president from doing his job."[35]

Nixon's suggestion that the press was trying to undo the 1972 election results led critics to charge him with megalomania. But Nixon's comments also prodded reporters to investigate. *Time* finally disclosed the contents of William Sullivan's memo to Dean about LBJ's FBI abuses, and other publications followed suit. Newspapers ran stories about FBI and National Security Agency programs (in existence from Roosevelt's administration until 1966) that involved breaking and entering, mail opening, and surveillance. But although those stories may have lowered public regard for presidents past, they didn't help Nixon. *The New York Times* argued that Nixon's "blunderbuss intimation" would serve only "to undermine public confidence in the integrity of government" as a whole. Nixon's thrust, the *Times* concluded, was that "the only thing the Watergate plotters did wrong was to get caught."[36]

Just how many people saw Nixon as the victim of a double standard is hard to discern. Although it was a minority, the number was not insignificant. Hunter S. Thompson, for one, feared the "ominous tide of public opinion that says that whatever Nixon and his small gang of henchmen and hired gunsels might have done, it was probably no worse than what other politicians have been doing." Thompson added that "anybody who believes this is a fool," yet he noted that "a lot of people seem to." Man-on-the-street opinion surveys included remarks like that of a New Jersey businessman who told *Time*, "If Nixon gets out, we'll just be giving some other burglar a chance"—showing that America's deep cynicism about politicians was reviving.[37]

To be sure, these same surveys showed most interviewees unwilling to agree that Nixon's only crime was getting caught. On the contrary, the everyone-does-it arguments were widely seen, as Michael Schudson has written, as "stock dodges for Nixon defenders." Art Buchwald offered a list of "instant responses for loyal Nixonites" to carry around for "when they are attacked at a party" ("What about Daniel Ellsberg stealing the Pentagon Papers?", "LBJ used to read FBI reports every night," and of course, "Everybody does it"). Garry Trudeau drew Al Haig presenting Pat Buchanan with a draft of a resignation speech that declared: "I am an innocent public servant being hounded by a partisan pack of wolves off on a witch hunt!"—only to back off from what Haig recognizes to be absurd hyperbole and tell the speechwriter, "You can change the wording a little if you like." Don Novello, a comic actor known for his character Father Guido Sarducci on *Saturday Night Live*, published a book of fawningly supportive letters from a fictional character named Lazlo Toth (who rather evoked Rabbi Korff) to Nixon, Bebe Rebozo, Korff, and other Nixonites; the silliness of such staunch devotion to the president was presumed to be self-evident. By 1974 Nixon's hard-core loyalists had dwindled to a derided minority, while their image of Nixon as a victim was taken as a lame expression of denial.[38]

Since mid-1973 Nixon had been urging the press to "move on," as he said in his August 22 press conference, to allow him to proceed with "the business of the people."[39] But it wasn't just the press that stopped him from doing so. Watergate divided Nixon's supporters. One contingent, comprising roughly a quarter of the populace, stood fast in its support for him, in part because of the intensity and the provenance of the calls for his removal. But others, devastated by the Saturday Night Massacre, the 18½-minute gap, and the release of the tape transcripts, found that, whatever their feelings toward the press, they were coming to see Nixon as a liar or a criminal. More than the hatred of his inveterate foes, it was these defectors' changed assessments of Nixon that broke his presidency. From Main Street to Pennsylvania Avenue, an exodus from the loyalists' ranks pulled out from under Nixon's tottering presidency the props that had held it aloft.

The defectors included, first, members of the Silent Majority who had made Nixon's landslide possible. Typical was Abbie Hoffman's father, a blue-collar worker from Worcester, Massachusetts. During the Ervin Hearings, the elder Hoffman, who had always scorned his son's radicalism, sat transfixed in front of a small black-and-white TV, concluding, his son Jack recalled, that "the things he had believed in—our government leaders, and the American Way of Life—weren't worthy of his trust. Abbie had been right all along." Other Middle Americans told similar stories:

a Cleveland mechanic realized "something was terribly wrong" when Agnew resigned; a Presbyterian minister from Beaver Falls, Pennsylvania, became suspicious when Nixon wouldn't surrender the tapes; a Lexington, Virginia, secretary inched toward backing impeachment in November 1973 "to demonstrate that we as a people insist upon ethical government." Between Nixon's second inaugural in January 1973 and November, Gallup found Nixon's approval ratings had plummeted by 41 points, to 27 percent. The left's opposition may have hampered him, but without the middle he was doomed.[40]

Also decisive was the apostasy of conservative journalists and activists—some of whom had previously rallied to his side only because they had considered him a media scapegoat. "At the beginning, all of us assumed Watergate was . . . what Ron Ziegler told us it was:" wrote William F. Buckley, "nothing more than a third-rate burglary." But all that changed. In December 1973 activist Howard Phillips, still pro-Nixon, had written an article in the far-right *Human Events* entitled "The Plot to Get Nixon"; a few months later, convinced "there was no principle to which Nixon was really committed," Phillips began organizing "Conservatives for the Removal of the President."* By May, even such stalwart Republican organs as the *Chicago Tribune* were calling for the president's resignation.[41]

Most crucially, the withdrawal of his own party mates' support ensured Nixon's ouster. The attrition occurred slowly. In 1973, when the Senate Watergate investigation began, most Republicans were happy to help the president. Republican members of the Ervin Committee, notably Florida's Edward Gurney, gamely argued the White House line. But Republicans too had reputations and careers to protect. In April 1974, Ohio's William Saxbe, who had been blasting the Ervin Committee as partisan, set off a row when he publicly compared Nixon's protestations of ignorance to those of a piano player in a whorehouse. More momentous was Barry Goldwater's shift. At first, despite his deep-seated distrust of Nixon, the Arizonan considered the break-in and dirty tricks to be insignificant; he believed that the liberal media were inflating the issue.

---

* Phillips insisted his change of heart "had nothing to do with Watergate," which he called "a means that was used by the left to derail significant policy changes."

But as 1973 progressed, Goldwater declared himself "disgusted" by the White House's behavior and, while stopping short of supporting resignation until the end, he grew surer of Nixon's guilt. In March 1974, New York senator James Buckley, William's brother, became the first Republican to call for Nixon's departure on the Senate floor, making it safe for the far right to break with the president.[42]

The critical defections came amid the summer heat, as the House Judiciary Committee took up impeachment. In July, key committee Republicans, including Maine's William Cohen and Illinois's Tom Railsback, stepped off the fence to the side of impeachment. With that, only Nixon's fate in the Senate remained unclear. But after the Supreme Court forced him to surrender the "smoking gun" tape, his support dwindled there as well. GOP leaders pressured Nixon to abdicate. On August 7, Senator Goldwater, Senate Minority Leader Hugh Scott, and House Minority Leader John Rhodes visited the White House to inform the president of the extent of the defections—Nixon's Senate supporters numbered "ten at most," Goldwater said—signaling that he was finished.[43]

As evaporating congressional support doomed Nixon politically, the turnabout of his own aides dashed his credibility. Chuck Colson, for one, had considered Nixon a patriot and stood by him into 1973. After leaving the White House, he sent his old boss notes of moral support, including polls showing that the public wasn't all that agitated about Watergate. Yet when the president summoned Colson in December 1973 to talk strategy, Colson realized that "Nixon, flag and country were no longer one and the same to me." And when the tape transcripts were released in April 1974, Colson further revised his view. Now he saw a new Nixon, "indecisive, vacillating and shallow," quite unlike "the leader I had heard making courageous decisions." Colson continued to promote theories that pinned Watergate on the CIA and later effused that his old boss would be remembered as "a towering figure whose strategic genius changed the world for the better." But he never renounced his view of Nixon as a "sinner" who deserved to be impeached.[44]

Even Pat Buchanan, a staffer since 1966, the most steadfast of Nixonites, eventually turned. For most of the Watergate ordeal, Buchanan was the administration's most aggressive pit bull. But his loyalty was not blind. Following the Supreme Court's tapes ruling, Nixon's lawyer Fred Buzhardt had listened to the June 23 "smoking gun" recording and turned to Buchanan, a barometer of bitter-ender opinion, for an assessment. When Buchanan heard the evidence of Nixon's early role in the cover-up, which the president had long denied, he too concluded that Nixon had to go.[45]

In sum, although Nixon's support remained firmest in Republican strongholds, neither ideology nor party identification nor personal fealty alone determined how he was viewed. More significant was how cynically one viewed those who were leading the presumed witch-hunt. Most defectors still criticized the media but felt that the president's own actions ultimately had to determine their judgment. Die-hard loyalists, in contrast, thought the liberal "putsch" was always the central issue, that Watergate was about something larger than Nixon's misdeeds. As William F. Buckley argued, conservatives who stood by Nixon did so "because Nixon is the target of . . . Eastern Seaboard liberalism, . . . because the alternative is to wake up in the morning and find that they are in agreement with a particular conclusion reached by the *New York Times*." Breaking with these "wildly pro-Nixon" loyalists, Buckley maintained that in calling for Nixon's resignation he was not tolerating a liberal coup but merely refusing "to be dominated by the thought and analysis" of his adversaries.[46]

More striking, in retrospect, than the stampede of defections was the steadfast devotion of those who preferred Nixon, Watergate and all, to waking up in agreement with *The New York Times*. "Nixon, Now More than Ever" had been the president's bumper-sticker slogan during his 1972 campaign, and during Watergate Nixonites invested it with new meaning, brandishing it with pride. Local newspaper editors, conservative columnists, White House aides, and legions of Americans like Rabbi Korff spent the better part of 1973 and 1974 trying to convince their countrymen that the president was being scapegoated. Emerging evidence of Nixon's guilt did little to shake their faith; on the contrary, the attacks on Nixon enhanced his appeal. "I felt more warmly toward our doomed chief" during Watergate, Henry Kissinger wrote, "than at any previous time."[47] The more he was pilloried, the more he seemed a victim, and the stronger their affection grew. They identified with Nixon as the target of decadent liberal elites. For such bitter-enders—proportionately few, yet still numbering in the millions—Watergate was not a shameful defeat but an Alamo, a Custer's Last Stand, that served to rally the faithful for another day.[48]

As defections mounted, Ken Clawson of the communications office struggled to find spokespeople to fire up the troops. One who needed no prodding was deputy special assistant John McLaughlin, who would later achieve fame as the ringleader of a talk show on which journalists interrupted and yelled at each other. A Jesuit priest, McLaughlin went before the press corps during the May 1974 outcry over the tape transcripts, which were condemned for their amoral tone. McLaughlin defended Nixon's foul language as a "good, valid" form of "therapy" and called the president "the greatest moral leader of the last third of this century" (which was then only seven years old). "The more he suffers," McLaughlin said, "the more he becomes believable to me." Such statements baffled the press and mortified even some Nixon allies ("My God, he's a monster, and I created him," said White House aide Dick Moore). But they gratified those who saw in Nixon's persecution a symptom of the left's ruthlessness. For them, the blunt-talking priest injected into the debate a dose of righteous outrage they felt had been missing from his spokesmen's legalistic, mealy-mouthed defenses.[49]

One reason McLaughlin may have lacked his colleagues' hesitancy was that he had joined the White House recently and had known no Nixon but the man under fire. The same was true of Bruce Herschensohn, another deputy special assistant with a taste for inflammatory charges. He called the impeachment drive "an attempted coup d'état of the U.S. Government through well-measured steps . . . by a non-elected coalition of power groups." McLaughlin and Herschensohn joined Clawson in a public relations battle in the spring of 1974. Clawson fed reporters a diet of materials that, as John Herbers of *The New York Times* wrote (displaying the press's heightened inside-dopester tone), sought "to depict a president who is maligned unfairly." They monitored the Judiciary Committee hearings, drafting rebuttals to Nixon's critics and firing them off to friendly congressmen to parry attacks. "We had immediate responses to the president's enemies down to a science," Clawson recalled. When committee chairman Peter Rodino, mistakenly thinking he was speaking off the record, prematurely told reporters that the panel was going to vote to impeach, Clawson and McLaughlin assailed the committee as a "partisan witch hunt" and Rodino as "a crude political tactician." A month later, Ron Ziegler branded the committee a "kangaroo court," while even the most soft-spoken staffers, like speechwriter Ray Price, "quietly cheered." Yet as the summer wore on, Price recalled, demoralization set in. On Saturday, July 27, the speechwriter was in San Clemente with the president and chose not even to watch the committee vote on the first impeachment article. "I said to hell with it and went to the beach instead," preferring, he said, "embeachment" to impeachment. Price returned to the San Clemente sands the next day, too, where he lost track of time and almost missed the plane back to Washington.[50]

As the White House mood grew funereal, Nixon's citizen defenders remained energetic. While Price gazed into the Pacific, spirited College Republicans, led by George Mason University student Karl Rove, circulated memos from the faux-grass-roots Americans for the Presidency, urging phone calls to the Judiciary Committee; congressmen, they warned, were getting "swept up by the lynch-mob atmosphere created in this city by the *Washington Post* and other parts of the Nixon-hating media." Supporters swarmed on Capitol Hill wearing pins that said: "Get off the president's back." One accosted Tom Railsback of the Judiciary Committee in the Rayburn Office Building elevator and warned him not to "convict the president on circumstantial evidence."[51]

Such zeal had been visible among the Silent Majority—now a vocal minority—for months. Local Republican bodies, business lobbies, grass-roots groups like Rabbi Korff's "Fairness"—all turned out in droves when Nixon spoke, even as his approval ratings nose-dived. A rally in Phoenix, Arizona, on May 3, 1974, was typical. Staged at a cost of $20,000 to the Republican National Committee, requiring more than a week's preparation, it was held at a sports arena full of thirteen thousand cheering supporters. Upon his arrival, Nixon was greeted by three thousand balloons, five hundred pounds of confetti, and a round of "Hail to the Chief." Flanked by synthetic foam elephants adorned with flowers, Nixon insisted again that it was time "to get Watergate behind us." But these appearances didn't always help. Demonstrators crashed them, taunting Nixon with hoots and placards.[52]

When they weren't attending rallies, the famous and the anonymous alike gathered in kitchens and living rooms to write letters, sign petitions, and even pen pro-Nixon songs. Besides the hit "Sweet Home Alabama," there was jazzman Lionel Hampton's anthem "We Need Nixon," which he played at Rabbi Korff's fund-raisers. Nixon's friend Dana Smith, the Pasadena attorney who had administered the 1952 fund, kept the sheet music to "Hang in There, Mr. President!", a 1973 song full of clichés and simple rhymes intended to be sung "bright, with spirit." Tennessee Republicans scripted a paean to the tune of "Okie from Muscogee," which they belted out during a March rally at the Grand Ole Opry:

> Stand up and cheer for Richard Nixon,
> For he's the president of our great land.
> We said we wanted peace and we got it,
> He brought our soldiers home from Vietnam.
> I've been hearing talk about impeaching
> The man we chose to lead us through these times
> But talk like this could weaken and defeat us.
> Let's show the world we're not the quitting kind.

Other songs—issued on records or sheet-music folios—included such classics as "We're Fixin' a Date with Nixon" and "I'm a Democrat for Nixon." The White House cultivated these loyalists, albeit more for their enthusiasm than for their creative talents. In 1974, Herschensohn ushered Nixon's citizen defenders through the White House, where they delivered suitcases and cartons of petitions. Nixon's support, these efforts meant to show, came not just from Republican bigwigs but from the Good Templars from Sedalia, honest spinsters from Grundy Center, and other Middle Americans who understood Nixon's plight.[53]

What united these Americans, suggested John Herbers, who interviewed them extensively, was "a sense of alienation and of outrage that has increased as President Nixon's troubles have worsened." They were watching troubling events over which they had no control. As GOP leaders grew silent, they worried that the whole Washington establishment was deaf to the concerns and passions of people like themselves. In contrast to the official reticence, theirs was an unofficial clamor—"aggressive, highly partisan, and loyal," Herbers noted. Among Italian-Americans in Brooklyn's Canarsie neighborhood, sociologist Jonathan Rieder found, fealty to Nixon—who had stuck up for their "square" values of patriotism and tradition—overrode any censorious judgments. "Watergate was bullshit, pure and simple," said a local Italian-American League member. "They framed Nixon and they killed him politically. I don't care what *he* did. It's disgraceful what *they* did to the country—the press and Congress and the protesters. . . . I loved Nixon for loving the country."[54]

The values of plainspokenness, unpretentiousness, duty, and uncritical patriotism informed the thinking of working-class Nixonites. They shared the president's scorn for liberal elites, who seemed not to have to work hard for what they earned; they identified with Nixon as a fighter who had risen from his plain background to great heights. His persecution was a front in a cultural class war, waged by left-wingers who thought themselves better than the average Americans they felt Nixon represented. In his novel *Rabbit Is Rich*, John Updike depicts the late father-in-law of Rabbit Angstrom as a consummate Middle American who felt liberal cultural commissars were targeting Nixon because of the square values he embodied. "You know, I think it broke Fred's heart . . . Watergate," comments the dead man's widow, Bessie Springer. "He followed it right to the end, when he could hardly lift his head from the pillows, and he used to say to me, 'Bessie, there's never been a president who hasn't done worse. They just have it in for him because he isn't a glamour boy. If that had been Roosevelt or one of the Kennedys,' he'd say, 'you would never have heard "boo" about Watergate.' He believed it, too." Like many real-life bitter-enders, Fred Springer never deviated from the double-standard claim.[55]

To this core contingent, no evidence could shake the perception of Nixon as a victim because the perception wasn't ultimately a rational matter. "Don't confuse me with the facts," growled Illinois congressman Earl Landgrebe on the *Today* show on August 8, 1974, shortly before Nixon resigned, adding that he would back the president even if "I have to be taken out of this building and shot" (something NBC News crews were not known to do very often). A Californian from Nixon's old 12th District wrote the president that he had no wish to hear any news that might upset his view of Nixon as a man besieged. "I can no longer watch the newscasts for fear of having a severe case of apoplexy," he noted. A restaurant owner sent Nixon $10,000 to help pay his income taxes, declaring, "I love Richard Nixon—he is the greatest president this country ever had." Many voters stayed loyal even after their representatives defected. Virginia congressman Caldwell Butler, a right-winger who earned a zero rating from Americans for Democratic Action, was jokingly warned that his constituents would load up their pickups with rifles to descend upon him when they learned he was going to vote to impeach.

When on the morning of August 9 Nixon delivered his emotional farewell, loyalists mourned. The speech that had struck liberals as Nixonian fakery moved his admirers to tears; in Updike's *Memories of the Ford Administration*, a "down-the-line liberal" character says of the speech, "The only sad thing is it puts that idiot Ford in office," whereas her husband, Alfred, is filled with a "dim, black-and-white haunted hollow feeling." As in *Rabbit Is Rich*, Updike tapped into the Silent Majority's sensibility, as real-life Nixonites recalled similar pangs of emptiness. Frank Trotta of New Rochelle, the proud young Republican who thrilled to Nixon's patriotism, watched the resignation speech alone in a sparsely furnished room at the local GOP headquarters, wallowing in his misery as Democrats partied across the street. In the East Room of the White House, Colonel Jack Brennan's introduction of Nixon inspired thunderous applause and a standing ovation that lasted for four minutes. Sidling up to the lectern, an American flag pin in his lapel, Nixon quieted the crowd, only to bring them to gasps and sobs with his uncharacteristically personal talk. Rabbi Korff, Herb Stein, and others in the audience broke down and wept. They also ingested the president's concluding words—"others may hate you, but those who hate you don't win unless you hate them, and then you destroy yourself"—without irony. "That's probably the real Nixon," Herschensohn said, deeply moved. "It's a shame he couldn't have been like that more often."[56]

.   .   .

The presidential helicopter that whisked Richard Nixon from the White House lawn to his post-resignation life did not remove him from the public eye. Between Ford's pardon, the Watergate prosecutions, and his own debilities, the former president lingered in the headlines. He remained in the comic strips too. In October 1974, *Doonesbury* teased at a gnawing fear that the dogged Nixon wasn't going anywhere. "Since my pardon will keep the full story from coming out," the deposed president tells Pat excitedly from behind the facade of his San Clemente estate, "millions of Americans will continue to believe I was hounded from office! . . . Do you know where that leaves us, little girl? . . . ON THE COMEBACK TRAIL!" "Oh no, Dick!" Pat replies. "God, no!"[57]

Nixon was already known as a comeback artist. In 1952, he saved his job as Eisenhower's running mate. In 1968, he won the presidency after others had written his "political obituary." In 1972, he achieved a landslide reelection after a rocky start. And so, even as cartoonists mocked the idea, Nixon began his final Houdini act. A long and many-faceted campaign, it included lawsuits to control his papers and tapes, overtures to repair friendships, and, not least, efforts to refashion his image. But initially, Nixon remained so widely reviled that he could barely poke his head above the San Clemente parapets. He relied instead on a band of loyalists to keep alive the picture of him as a casualty of liberal wrath.

Those who stumped most fervently on Nixon's behalf were not his closest aides. Colson, Ehrlichman, Haldeman, and others had changed their views of Nixon after concluding he had mistreated or lied to them. They also knew that they had to reckon with anti-Nixon sentiment if they were ever to regain public credibility themselves. In his memoir, *The Ends of Power* (1978), Haldeman, who had spent his career crafting and selling Nixon's image, declared himself done with the task. Although he claimed to feel "as loyal today to the president I served as I ever have," that loyalty had limits. He called Watergate "a disaster without parallel in presidential history" and "a result—and an expression—of the dark side of President Nixon." The former staff chief reminded his readers about other presidents' offenses, and he indulged some Watergate conspiracy theories. But he insisted that Nixon's crimes were "inexcusable," and that whoever else may have had a hand in Nixon's downfall, the president was no innocent.

"There were many players in the Watergate drama," he wrote, "and behind them all lurks the ever-present shadow of the president of the United States."* As their anger faded, Haldeman and others later found warm words for Nixon. But initially they refused to help rehabilitate the man who had brought them into ignominy.[58]

If cheerleading was scarce among Nixon's old lieutenants, it was more evident among those who had avoided Watergate's taint. Friends who hadn't personally been burned found it easier to keep arguing that Nixon's only crime was being hated. The indefatigable Rabbi Korff lobbied in vain to have the Republican Party praise Nixon's China overture in its 1976 platform. A more successful advocate was Victor Lasky, whose book *It Didn't Start with Watergate* (1977) was an *omnium gatherum* of arguments in Nixon's defense that described his friend's ouster as "the political assassination of a president." An encyclopedia of liberal hypocrisies and double standards, the book was heavy on examples of wrongdoing by Kennedy, Johnson, Ervin Committee investigators, and Watergate reporters. And although no different from the old loyalist line—simply more comprehensive—it was greeted more warmly than such claims had been three years earlier. *It Didn't Start with Watergate* sold 119,000 copies and made the best-seller lists, even if, as Lasky said, most buyers were Nixon voters seeking reasons not to feel guilty anymore.[59]

Fighting alongside Lasky—and flacking his colleague's "blockbuster" in his own newspaper column—was William Safire, ensconced since March 1973 at *The New York Times*. Safire's perch was different from Lasky's. Where Lasky could preach to the converted, Safire addressed a largely liberal *Times* readership, and even if he wanted to provoke them, he had his credibility to maintain. He was wary of seeming like Nixon's mouthpiece. What was more, although he had defended Nixon during Watergate, Safire eventually apologized for his apologias. Thereafter, he didn't assert Nixon's innocence so much as give equal time to the neglected offenses of others. "Nothing angered me more" in those years, he later

---

* As time passed and passions cooled, Haldeman and others backpedaled. After the publication of *The Ends of Power* and his release from prison, Haldeman reconciled with Nixon and repudiated some of the criticisms of Nixon in his memoir as the work of his co-author, Joseph DiMona. DiMona insisted that the book accurately reflected Haldeman's views at the time.

wrote, "than the double standard of political morality applied to Richard
M. Nixon." Thus: "Who Else Is Guilty?" read a headline on a January 1975
column that facetiously called for investigations into the surveillance of
Martin Luther King, Jr., and Anna Chennault. "Nixon Never Did" declared
another column six months later, which enumerated acts committed by the
Kennedys and Johnson that Safire argued were worse than Nixon's.[60]

If Safire agreed that it didn't start with Watergate, he made sure it
didn't end with Watergate either. In succeeding administrations, Safire
played up scandals or would-be scandals. During Jimmy Carter's presidency, he won a Pulitzer Prize for his writings about what he dubbed
"Lancegate," a conflict-of-interest flap involving budget director Bert
Lance. He also attacked Carter for "Koreagate" and "peanutgate"—fleeting, now forgotten episodes which Safire sought to inflate to Nixonian
proportions by appending the "gate" suffix. Into the Bush and Clinton
years, Safire monitored scandals large and small, tailgating them avidly,
quick to lean on his Watergate horn.[61]

Ironically, Watergate itself helped make the culture more receptive to
the arguments of Safire and Lasky. The Nixon scandals had nurtured an
already growing culture of investigation and validated fears of secret government activity. A cycle took hold: popular distrust of authority spawned
inquiries into government misdeeds; and the wave of exposés, in turn,
amplified the distrust. Journalists, enticed by the prospect of Woodstein-
like renown, pounced on any morsel of political wrongdoing, while Congress launched investigations. In 1975, the so-called year of intelligence,
congressional probes into pre-Watergate misdeeds—including the CIA's
domestic spying and plots to kill foreign leaders—cast Nixon's predecessors in a newly unflattering light. With the left criticizing such activities as
undemocratic and the press on alert to any whiff of scandal, Nixon's loyalists no longer felt so alone. Writing in 1976 about the abuse of the FBI, a
satisfied Safire endorsed the claims of the far-left Noam Chomsky, who
had recently argued that FBI operations under JFK and LBJ were "incom-
parably more serious" than the charges against Nixon—conceding, to
Safire's delight, that "Nixon's defenders do have a case."[62]

Liberals also now conceded the point, even as they refused to exonerate Nixon. Meg Greenfield, while insisting that Nixon's crimes were

"unique," nonetheless granted that "'horrors' . . . were perpetrated in our time by a lot of people who were *not* Richard Nixon"—including Johnson and the Kennedys. If the portrait of Nixon as having been hounded from office still seemed like blind partisanship, the suggestion that Americans hadn't shown due concern over others' crimes was persuasive. By 1990, when the former *Times* columnist Tom Wicker published his study of Nixon, *One of Us*, he wrote that "Watergate was a live possibility in any postwar administration, [since from FDR onward] . . . the federal government engaged in eavesdropping, illegal entry, mail covers and openings, payoffs and other surreptitious, often illegal, means of investigating enemies and opponents, real or imagined." He drew no flak for making what was no longer a controversial claim.[63]

Only true believers argued that because everyone had done it, Nixon was therefore a victim. But others inched toward the cynical view that all politicians were corrupt. This sentiment had a double, even contradictory, effect. As noted, it fostered an obsession with scandal in American politics. Yet, as the former Nixon speechwriter Ben Stein argued ten years after the president's resignation, that same cynicism also produced an unusual *indifference* to scandal. Stein noted that Ronald Reagan had lied to the American people about the deaths of U.S. Marines in Lebanon and about his campaign's theft of Jimmy Carter's debate briefing books but that his falsehoods had failed to arouse much outrage. Stein intended his essay as a defense of Nixon, an argument that Watergate wasn't "really such a big deal." But the column's logical conclusion was the reverse: that while the press might be running wild over third-rate Watergates, the public— inured by Nixonism and subsequent scandals—no longer expected consistency or even integrity from its leaders.[64]

While old friends argued on his behalf, Nixon himself crept back into public life. In 1977, he emerged from a prolonged exile for a series of videotaped interviews with the British talk-show host David Frost. From the start, controversy ensued over the question of whether Nixon deserved a platform (not to mention $600,000, which Frost's syndicate paid him) to paint himself as a victim. But Nixon's critics and supporters alike failed to realize how complex the process of revising an image could be. Tuning in to watch Nixon wasn't the same as giving him another chance.

The interviews were staged amid great hype. Newspaper accounts chronicled the details of the negotiations and preparations. *Sixty Minutes* had its star reporter Mike Wallace interview Frost—an interview of an interviewer. The week the first program was to air, *TV Guide*, *Time*, and *Newsweek* featured it on their covers, with the newsweeklies' stories consuming a dozen pages each. More than 150 stations signed up to carry the syndicated shows.[65]

A theme of the coverage was that Nixon was out to present himself in a new light. Frost was known for inoffensive patter and gentle questioning, and Nixon-haters worried that the interviewer would provide Nixon with a soapbox. But Frost, leery of being manipulated, prepared intensively. A team of researchers compiled four 100-page tomes, including advice on how to interrogate the former president. To hone Frost's questioning, they held rehearsals with the researchers playing Nixon. By "N-Day," as Frost called it, he was steeped in Watergate arcana, confident he could "prove" that Nixon had arranged the CIA's interference with the FBI's Watergate inquiry, endorsed clemency offers, and authorized blackmail payments. Frost didn't intend to let a New Nixon appear unchallenged.[66]

In the interview, Frost asked blunt questions: What did Nixon say to Haldeman during the 18½-minute gap? Why did Nixon speak about "the Cubans" if not to refer to the burglars caught at Watergate? At one point he reeled off sixteen quotations from the tapes showing that Nixon had considered paying hush money.

Nixon's responses were hesitant, vague, inconsistent. Although he admitted for the first time that his old defense—that "national security" justified his effort to halt the FBI probe—was "untrue," he still portrayed himself as a victim. He allowed only that he had "let down" the country, confessed only to "bad judgments" and "mistakes." Statements that others considered lies Nixon described as "misleading in exaggerating" the facts but justifiable given the "enormous political attack I was under. It was a five-front war." He had slipped up, he said, and his enemies had pounced. "I gave them a sword," he said, "and they stuck it [in], and they twisted it with relish." Although his words didn't admit guilt, Frost felt, his manner did. At the end of the session, the interviewer judged, "I had scored more heavily than [my assistants] had dared hope."[67]

The first program, which aired on May 4, 1977, was a hit. It drew 45 million viewers, or 42 percent of the TV audience, the same as that year's number one show, *Happy Days*. But as would be true for Nixon's entire post-presidential career, the fascination didn't translate into favor. Interest was a sign only of interest. Significantly, the most watched show was the first one, which focused on Watergate. The Watergate segments also provided the shows' most lasting moments, including Nixon's rationalization, soon to enter *Bartlett's*, that "When the president does it, that means that it is not illegal." Far from changing minds, Nixon's victim pose elicited mostly scorn. Garry Trudeau parodied the president as serving up to Frost his hoary line, "I was hounded from office by a partisan pack of witch-hunting jackals." Even loyalists were stinting. "It takes more than four interviews to properly rehabilitate Richard Nixon," sniped Senator Bob Dole, who had chaired the GOP under Nixon. Ehrlichman judged the performance a "maudlin rationalization that will be tested and found false." Haldeman stated at a press conference that his old boss had twisted the facts; in his memoir published that fall he fumed at Nixon's statement that he should have fired Haldeman and Ehrlichman sooner—calling it "vintage 'dark' Nixon," an effort "to rehabilitate himself over the prostrate bodies of his aides." In Nixon's defense, Safire assailed the Nixon-haters' "hypocrisy and exquisite selectivity" and declared it time to welcome Nixon back to public life. His was a lonely voice.[68]

The public also scoffed. Several polls found no improvement in Nixon's standing. *Newsweek* discovered that the interviews actually hurt Nixon's reputation: 30 percent of respondents to its survey lowered their estimation of Nixon, while 22 percent raised theirs. The magazine's writers were no more charitable. The interviews, *Newsweek* concluded, "revealed the former president as he was and as he remains—careless of the record, heedless of the proper limits of power, unable to plead guilty to anything much worse than 'screwing up' and coming no nearer to that final absolution in history he seeks."[69]

.   .   .

Whatever sympathy Nixon had won by 1977, it was rooted not in revived respect but in pity. So low had Nixon's reputation sunk that he now seemed a sorry case. "The first Frost interview," wrote his antagonist Anthony Lewis of *The New York Times*, "made this dreadful creature seem pathetic."[70] A New Nixon had emerged after all: fallen, humanized, no longer threatening, but a pitiable figure. This was hardly the image that Nixon wished to promote, yet it was, for now, the best he was going to get.

Pity for Nixon was natural in the months after Watergate as Americans glimpsed him in an abject state, recovering from phlebitis and depression. In 1976, Simon & Schuster published *The Final Days*, Woodward and Bernstein's follow-up to *All the President's Men*, which offered a close-up account of Nixon's last weeks in office. Based on interviews with Nixon's aides and, apparently, family members, the book showed Nixon withdrawing into isolation, forlorn and unstable as his presidency crumbled. When the journalists' agent David Obst met Robert Redford that April at the premiere of *All the President's Men*, the actor complained that Simon & Schuster had released *The Final Days* too early. "Everyone's going to be feeling sorry for Nixon now," Obst remembered Redford saying.[71]

Months later, reportedly after reading the book, Pat Nixon suffered a stroke. Nixon's tearful reaction garnered more pity, sometimes from unlikely quarters. Neil Young, the rock star who sang bitterly about the martial, unsparing Nixon in the 1970 Kent State song "Ohio," released a bittersweet dirge called "Campaigner." Young wrote it after watching a TV report about a watery-eyed Nixon shuffling into the hospital to visit his stricken Pat. Originally titled "Requiem for a President," the song didn't treat Nixon as a victim but did paint him as pitiable and excessively demonized. Shifting between Nixon's own voice and the third person, Young's warbled lyrics evoked the former president's self-image as a lonesome battler, toiling in splendid isolation, always seeking the next great political prize. Young's Nixon is a man who privately confesses his own tireless, remorseless campaigning. Without quite petitioning for forgiveness, he nonetheless seeks to reclaim some dignity in his devastated life. A poignant portrait, at once condescending and compassionate, "Campaigner" mercifully finds a kernel of integrity and humanity in a once-ferocious, now-vanquished predator.

Nixon's strivings, once seen by liberals as the worst of bourgeois America, were rendered pathetic, forgivably human. David Frost, too, for all his hardball posturing, knew he could generate a memorable moment by asking Nixon about Pat's stroke. Nixon's struggle to control his sadness moved many viewers. *Time* expected that the Frost interviews, by presenting "the spectacle of such a once proud man being so humbled in public," were "certain to create sympathy." Although Nixon's standing remained low after the interviews, 44 percent of Americans did claim to feel more compassion for him.[72]

Another telling statistic was the percentage of Americans who thought Gerald Ford had been right to pardon Nixon. When Ford issued the pardon in September 1974, 53 percent of Americans, according to Gallup, opposed the decision. "The son of a bitch pardoned the son of a bitch!" Carl Bernstein screamed at Bob Woodward after hearing the news. The move helped ensure Ford's defeat in the 1976 presidential election. Over the years, however, the percentage who supported the pardon grew steadily—to 46 percent in 1982, and 54 percent in 1986. In 2001 Ford was rewarded for his act with a "Profile in Courage" from the John F. Kennedy Presidential Library. Overall public opinion of Nixon, in contrast, climbed only slightly between 1974 and 2001—a discrepancy that suggested not a belief in Nixon's innocence but a lessened vindictiveness, a diminished wish to see him suffer. Far from power, Nixon no longer seemed threatening.[73]

Within a few years, the defanged Nixon was transformed further. For some, he became an object of contrarian admiration. Because the image of Tricky Dick was lodged so securely in the public consciousness, self-styled conservative rebels who reveled in thumbing their noses at liberal norms began admiring Nixon for his very unpopularity. One of the most popular television shows of the 1980s was *Family Ties*. The sitcom, which ran from 1982 to 1989, starred Michael J. Fox as Alex Keaton, a tie-wearing teenage conservative who rebels against his parents' countercultural values by embracing Reaganism. Nixon was a recurring joke on the show. Alex's first word as a baby was said to have been "Nixon," and the teenager kept by his bedside an autographed picture of the former president. *Family Ties* was conceived from a liberal viewpoint: the animating premise was to explore how a liberal 1960s couple grappled with the trauma of having a conservative son. But Fox emerged as the show's star and his character blossomed into a good-hearted contrarian whose conservatism rendered him annoying but hardly villainous. His support for Nixon, too, was thus perverse, provocative, or amusing—but never truly threatening.

A similar desire to flout the dominant wisdom helped fuel interest in the work of a handful of eccentrics whose elaborate theories about Watergate painted Nixon as an unwitting victim of others' secret machinations. The theories of these eccentrics differed from those of Nixon and supporters like Lasky or Korff, which blamed the president's fall on the all too visible work of Democrats and the media. The new school of conjecture, in contrast, faulted shadowy conspirators, usually the CIA or Nixon's underlings, who supposedly framed the president for their own misdeeds.

Although adherents to these theories were sometimes called "revisionists," the term was as misplaced as it was when applied to those who claimed the label in denying the occurrence of the Holocaust. In the context of Watergate, revisionism might properly apply to mainstream conservative historians like James A. Nuechterlein, who, writing in *Commentary* in 1979, agreed that using terms like "McCarthyism" and "witch-hunt" to describe Watergate was "simply perverse," but also argued that there were *"occasions* when the affair took on . . . a 'Roman circus atmosphere,'" and that too many Americans thought that *"everything and everyone* associated with the Nixon administration were irredeemably corrupt" (italics added). The term "revisionism" could also legitimately apply to the work of those historians who in the 1990s rediscovered Nixon as the champion of Great Society liberalism.* In contrast to these debatable but responsibly argued schools of thought, proponents of the conspiracy theories represented something far more extreme. In holding that Nixon and most of his top aides had had only trivial or unwitting roles in the White House horrors, these writers would be better described as Watergate deniers.[74]

* See chapter 8.

The comparison to Holocaust deniers must be qualified. The gravity of Watergate cannot be compared to the enormity of the Holocaust, and the effort to deny the two events is categorically different. Nor, of course, were the Watergate deniers' motives demonstrably hateful. In their methods, however, the two groups were disturbingly similar. Both argued that history—or, as they would have it, "official" history—was a lie. Both ignored mountains of evidence and used a few unanswered questions or errors to impugn the very existence of real events. Both built their cases on faulty logic and tenuous evidence but argued with enough passion and relentlessness to win themselves a hearing.

What the Watergate deniers denied was the whole inventory of Nixonian abuses of power apart from the June 17, 1972, break-in of the Watergate building itself. Their work implied that this bungled break-in alone was the reason for Nixon's fall, and that without it, the president would not have been impeached. Historically, the arrest of the Watergate burglars lit the fatal fuse, but what forced Nixon to resign was a whole series of burglaries, buggings, wiretaps, abuses of executive authority, and lies in the service of obstructing justice. The deniers focused only on the break-in, and on the fact that its specific purpose—if a single specific purpose existed—was never conclusively established. (Many historians believe that Nixon's men wanted to know what DNC chairman Larry O'Brien, who had done work for the aircraft mogul Howard Hughes, knew of Hughes's past dealings with Nixon. Others think the mission involved general intelligence gathering, not a single aim.) This lacuna in the record created an opportunity for speculation—speculation that led to suppositions about Nixon's ultimate innocence. Indeed, so confusing were some of Watergate's subplots that in November 1973 *Esquire* magazine published an article playfully laying out forty-three different theories of what really happened.[75]

The most popular theory of the deniers was that the CIA, not CREEP, had instigated the June 17 break-in. To understand why this claim had such purchase, it's necessary to go back to the first days after the crime. In the absence of the information that later emerged, the notion of CIA involvement was a reasonable hypothesis. After all, Watergate burglars Howard Hunt and James McCord had worked for the agency, and even

after retiring Hunt kept working for the Robert Mullen Company, a public relations firm with CIA ties (it also did work for Howard Hughes). The
Cuban burglars whom Hunt hired had also done CIA work, notably during the Bay of Pigs invasion. Indeed, when early reports linked the burglars to the CIA, many people—including the veteran *New York Times*
reporter Tad Szulc—began chasing the false lead.[76]

Nixon and his aides seized on the CIA links to build a cover story.
Because the CIA story had a surface plausibility, Colson, Dean, Haldeman,
Mitchell, Nixon, and others believed it could be used to ward off the FBI
from investigating too deeply. "I think that we could develop a theory as
to the CIA if we wanted to," Colson told Nixon on June 21, four days after
the break-in. "We know that he [Hunt] has all these ties with these people"—although, of course, Colson also knew that he himself had hired
Hunt, an old friend, to do clandestine work that included the Lewis Fielding break-in (designed to find dirt on Daniel Ellsberg) and the forging of
documents to falsely implicate John Kennedy in the 1963 assassination of
South Vietnamese leader Ngo Dinh Diem. But neither Colson nor Nixon
was deterred by Hunt's traceable links to the White House. On the contrary, Nixon endorsed Colson's idea, adding that the involvement of the
Cubans was a "plus" that made it more believable. Colson followed
through. When FBI agents interviewed him the next day, he told them the
affair was "a CIA thing," Haldeman reported to Nixon June 23. The staff
chief added that he now expected that "the CIA turnoff will play."[77]

In that same historic conversation—recorded on the "smoking gun"
tape whose Supreme Court–mandated release hastened Nixon's resignation—the president green-lighted using the CIA cover story. He approved
a plan to have the CIA thwart the FBI's Watergate inquiry by falsely warning that such a probe would unearth material harmful to the agency and
to national security. As Haldeman explained during that conversation:
"Mitchell came up with [the idea] yesterday, and John Dean analyzed very
carefully last night and concludes, concurs now with Mitchell's recom-
mendation that the only way to solve this . . . is for us to have [Deputy CIA
Director Vernon] Walters call [Acting FBI Director] Pat Gray and just say,
'Stay the hell out of this—this is, ah, business here we don't want you to

go any further on it.'" Nixon, perhaps playing devil's advocate, noted that prosecutors had already traced the burglars' financing to CREEP—a connection that undermined the CIA cover story. But Haldeman lobbied for the plan, and Nixon assented. Seizing on Hunt's Bay of Pigs connection, the president began scripting lines himself. "Look, the problem is that this will open the whole . . . Bay of Pigs thing," he imagined Walters telling the FBI chief.[78]

What happened next helped seal Nixon's fate. He ordered Haldeman to call Vernon Walters, who dutifully told Pat Gray to back off. Within a few days, however, CIA colleagues insisted to Walters that the agency was not involved, and the deputy reversed himself. Gray delayed the FBI's interrogation of key sources, but then he too waffled. He decided he needed a letter from Walters formally telling him to desist, but Walters refused. Gray then asked Nixon for clear instructions. "Dick, Walters and I feel that people on your staff are trying to mortally wound you," Gray explained to the president, "by using the CIA and FBI and by confusing the questions of CIA interest in, or not in, people the FBI wishes to interview." After a pause, Nixon backed down. "Pat, you just continue to conduct your aggressive and thorough investigation," he said, giving the lie to the CIA-involvement story. (Had the "national security" claim been true, Nixon would have had no reason not to tell that to Gray; his reversal showed he didn't really believe the cover story.) Haldeman was worried. "Walters has apparently finked out and spilled the beans to Pat Gray," he wrote in his diary, "which complicates the issue substantially." The president's gambit failed, and in attempting it he had committed an impeachable offense.[79]

Nixon and his men knew that the CIA story was a sham. At one point in July 1973, Nixon, Haig, and Kissinger betrayed their awareness of the story's spuriousness when Kissinger said that he had spoken with Norman Mailer, who, he reported, "wants to write that it's all a CIA conspiracy against you because you were on *détente*." "That's a little weird," Haig replied, and all had a laugh. Still, the notion of CIA responsibility remained alive. McCord was urged to use it during his trial, and even after he told Judge Sirica that the CIA claim was bogus—a White House "ploy," he said—it stayed in circulation.[80]

Unanswered questions about the break-in, after all, remained, and conspiracy-theory rumors like those Norman Mailer purveyed cropped up as they are wont to do. The adherents of these theories were few, but they were energetic and resourceful. The mailboxes of journalists and government officials filled up with manifestos from citizens claiming they alone had deduced the hidden truth of Watergate. One such letter writer, Trevor Swoyer of Knoxville, Tennessee, badgered a whole mailing list of influential figures—Howard Baker, Leon Jaworski, Peter Rodino, Theodore White, and others—explaining why the president was "completely innocent" and had been framed by Howard Hunt. Not only random fantasists endorsed these theories. CIA officer Miles Copeland speculated in *National Review* that McCord, still loyal to the agency despite his employment by CREEP, "took Hunt and Liddy into a trap . . . putting the White House's clowns out of business." Supported by just a few lingering mysteries, such guesswork never went far in any congressional committee or courtroom. But it did furnish ammunition to those who wished to diminish the White House's Watergate role.[81]

Nixon's loyalists fastened onto elements of these conspiracy theories to fashion hypotheses that would mitigate their own guilt. Some endorsed the idea of McCord or Hunt as a double agent. Others, including Haldeman, and Nixon's secretary Rose Mary Woods, imagined that White House aide Alexander Butterfield, the man who told the Ervin Committee about Nixon's taping system, was a CIA "mole." Nixon himself had floated the CIA trap theory during the Frost interviews, although he downplayed it. "I don't go with the idea that what brought me down was a coup, a conspiracy," he told Frost, only to qualify the comment by adding that "there may have been. I don't know what the CIA had to do [with it]. Some of their shenanigans have yet to be told." Later reports said that privately he and Pat both gave the idea some credence. Even the level-headed Ray Price, Nixon's loyal speechwriter, suggested that Hunt may have been a renegade who arranged the break-in to get back into the CIA's good graces. Price realized, he added, that "None of this, . . . if true, excuses the White House or the Committee to Re-Elect the President. The break-ins and the buggings did take place, and at one level or another they were approved by our people."* Colson and Haldeman, too, used the suspicions of CIA double-dealing to argue for their own partial innocence, even while granting Nixon's guilty and central role.[82]

After Watergate, some reporters vetted the CIA theory and found it wanting, or at best unproven. In a 1976 book on clandestine government activities, *New York Herald Tribune* veteran David Wise gathered the evidence of CIA involvement and set forth the "tantalizing facts and lingering unanswered questions" while responsibly asserting that no "hard persuasive evidence" existed to assume a CIA plot. Meanwhile, Nixon loyalist Victor Lasky put a more lurid spin on essentially the same details in *It Didn't Start with Watergate*, imputing a stronger hand to the CIA. Theories implicating the agency also attracted a following among left-wing radicals such as Carl Oglesby who distrusted official explanations. Believing that Watergate stemmed from deep flaws in the American system, rejecting the liberal nostrum that "the system worked" in Watergate, left-wing critics applauded efforts to probe beyond established accounts, to unearth buried secrets—especially when it seemed the government was concealing information. But because CIA theories depicted Nixon as a victim, they were hard to reconcile with portraits of the former president as a dark schemer. Some writers on the left saw Nixon as both villain *and* victim, believing that the White House Watergate conspiracy was real but that behind it lay another, more terrible plot sheltered from view. Hence, the idiosyncratic lawyer and journalist Renata Adler speculated that

---

* The most surprising enthusiast of the CIA theory was Senator Howard Baker. The ranking Republican on the Watergate Committee, Baker had an uneasy relationship with Nixon. At the start of the hearings, he secretly met with Nixon, who wanted the senator to do his bidding. But in time Baker deviated from the White House line, infuriating the president. At one point a frustrated Nixon called Baker a "simpering asshole" who was betraying the White House because he "loves the adulation of the Georgetown set." He barred the senator from the White House. Still, Baker and his counsel, Fred D. Thompson, later a Tennessee senator, devoted their energies to probing CIA theories. When the Watergate Committee wrapped up its work in July 1974, Baker presented his findings in a minority report that, while not exonerating Nixon or CREEP, cast suspicion on the CIA, Hunt, and McCord. The report established that the CIA had known more about some of the burglars' activities than it had disclosed. It found, for example, that a CIA official, Lee Pennington, had visited McCord's home shortly after the June 17 break-in and had watched or helped in the burning of documents. Although the report stopped short of endorsing any theories, Baker continued to press for an inquiry into the CIA's role after Nixon resigned.

Nixon had been concealing a crime worse than all his dirty tricks: the fact that he had taken bribes from the South Vietnamese to prolong the war.[83]

The most radical left-winger revisionist—or denier—was neither Renata Adler nor Carl Oglesby but a lesser known writer named Jim Hougan. The Washington editor of *Harper's* magazine, Hougan was a self-described "left-liberal" who shared the New Left's interest in government intrigue and clandestine intelligence. In 1984, he published *Secret Agenda: Watergate, Deep Throat and the CIA*, which dismissed the received version about Watergate as "counterfeit history" and argued for the veracity of some of the long-standing rumors.[84] It would spawn a new generation of Watergate deniers.

Drawing from previously unreleased FBI documents, Hougan found that bureau officials believed that, contrary to popular belief, Larry O'Brien's phone had not been tapped before June 17. If those officials were correct—and it's not clear that they were—this fact would vitiate the long-standing presumption that the main purpose (or at least one of the purposes) of the burglary was to fix a faulty tap installed during a previous entry.* Hougan found other loose ends in the Watergate record as well, including the fact that burglar Eugenio Martinez, when arrested, was carrying a key to the desk of DNC secretary Ida "Maxie" Wells—an artifact that Hougan called "quite literally, the key to the break-in." Hougan hypothesized that the burglary was actually related to a CIA-run call-girl ring that used Wells's phone to arrange assignations. Picking up threads of earlier conspiracists, he argued that McCord sabotaged the break-in to protect the agency, for which he was secretly working.[85]

Published by Random House, *Secret Agenda* made a bid for the respectability that had eluded such theories before. As reviewers noted,

---

* The FBI did not find a tap on the phone until September 1972. Hougan credits FBI speculation that the Democrats might have planted the tap themselves. However, Earl Silbert, the U.S. Attorney investigating Watergate, had written to Assistant Attorney General Henry Petersen at the time that the FBI was probably trying to account for its own failure to have discovered the tap sooner. Silbert held this opinion in 1984 when asked about *Secret Agenda*'s claims. He noted that the Watergate defendants were charged with illegal electronic surveillance, and none ever denied that they had tapped the DNC's phones, which surely would have been their first line of defense.

The Nixon mask scene is one of *The Ice Storm's* iciest moments. A favorite trope for decades, the mask stands for corrupted authority, the inscrutability of our inner selves — and the patent phoniness of so much of postwar American life.

National Archives Records Administration

HE WALKS!

HE TALKS!

HE
MOVES HIS
ARMS UP AND DOWN!

HE
CHANGES
EXPRESSIONS!

THE
NEW
IM-
PROVED
DICKIE DOLL!

YOU'D ALMOST THINK HE'S REAL
(BATTERY OPERATED)

Jules Feiffer © Jules Feiffer

In 1970, Nixon staged a photo-op, walking on the beach (above) in hopes of seeming Kennedyesque. He ended up — in his wingtips and trousers — looking only like a man *trying* to seem Kennedyesque. Below, Jules Feiffer captured Nixon's stiffness and inauthenticity.

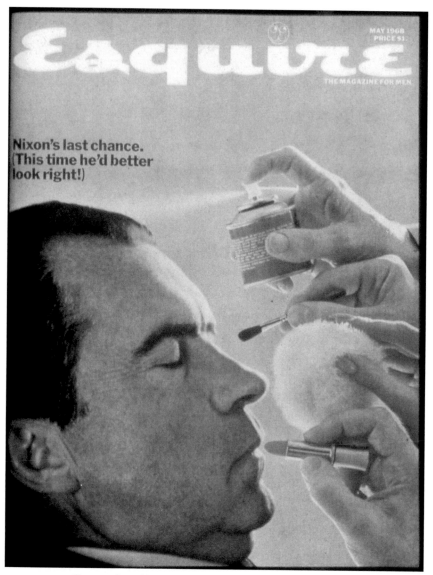

The 1968 campaign heralded the arrival of the latest "New Nixon." But as an *Esquire* magazine cover showed, many believed the makeover to be just so much election-year image-making.

YOUR VETERAN CANDIDATE

Dick Nixon is a serious, energetic individual with a high purpose in life—to serve his fellow man. He is a trained scholar, a natural leader and a combat war veteran. He has acquired the "human touch" the hard way—by working his way through college and law school; by sleeping in fox-holes, sweating out air raids; by returning from war confronted with the necessity of "starting all over again."

There is in Richard Nixon's background much that is typical of the young western American. There are the parents from the mid-west, the father who has been street car motorman, oil field worker, citrus rancher, grocer. There is the solid heritage of the Quaker faith; the family tradition of Work—and Service.

The effects of this background show in Richard Nixon. He has worked in a fruit packing house, in stores, as a gas station attendant. He has made an outstanding success of his law practice. He played college football ("not too successfully," he says); maintains an intensive interest in sports.

Of course, the No. 1 Nixon-for-Congress enthusiasts are Mrs. Richard Nixon, born Patricia Ryan on St. Patrick's Day, and six-months-old baby daughter Pat. Mrs. Nixon is a public servant in her own right, having worked for the government as an economist while her husband was fighting for his country in the South Pacific. Like so many other young "war couples," the Nixons resumed civilian life on a financial foundation comprised solely of War Bonds purchased from the savings of the working wife and sailor husband.

Mr. and Mrs. Richard Nixon have been very busy this year. Individually or jointly, they have (1) been looking for a place to live; (2) practiced law; (3) been taking care of their little girl; (4) been active in veterans' affairs, particularly those relating to housing for Whittier College veteran-students and their families; (5) been looking for a place to live again; and (6) they have been campaigning to ELECT RICHARD M. NIXON TO CONGRESS.

For New, Progressive, Representation in Congress

VOTE FOR

RICHARD M. NIXON

ON NOVEMBER 5

MR. AND MRS. RICHARD M. NIXON AND PATRICIA

"I pledge myself to serve you faithfully;

To act in the best interests of all of you;

To work for the re-dedication of the United States of America as a land of opportunity for your children and mine;

To resist with all my power the encroachments of foreign isms upon the American way of life;

To preserve our sacred heritage, in the name of my buddies and your loved ones, who died that there might endure;

To devote my full energies to service for you while appearing representative of you;

To remain always humble in the knowledge of your trust in me."

Richard M. Nixon

ELECT

RICHARD M.

NIXON

WORLD WAR II VETERAN

YOUR CONGRESSMAN

Richard M. Nixon Library and Birthplace

In his 1946 campaign, before anyone had heard of Tricky Dick, Nixon struck California voters as a hard-working, honorable veteran and the embodiment of their traditional values. In a Christmas card mailing (right), he appears as a committed family man.

Richard M. Nixon Library and Birthplace

Richard M. Nixon Library and Birthplace

In the fall of 1948, Nixon won admirers as the scourge of Communists (above). Four years later, in the "Checkers" speech, he painted an all-American image of himself to save his place as Dwight Eisenhower's vice presidential running-mate.

George Silk/ Timepix

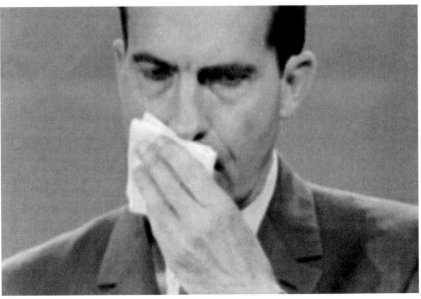

Talk of image-making suffused the 1960 campaign. In the first-ever televised presidential debates, Kennedy looked handsome and unflappable, while the sweaty Nixon couldn't hide his five o'clock shadow. Kennedy won by a whisker.

"Here He Comes Now"

Herblock Estate

---from *Herblock: A Cartoonist's Life* (Times Books, 1998)

Some liberals who came of age in the Fifties can't hear Nixon's name without recalling Herblock's cartoons. Above, Nixon clambers out of a manhole, as if conducting his campaign tour via the sewers. By the 1960s, the left's imagery had grown vicious, with Nixon seen as an American Führer.

Oliver Stone's Nixon was straight out of New Left demonology: a president who reveled in bombing Cambodia and conspiratorially recorded every word spoken in the White House.

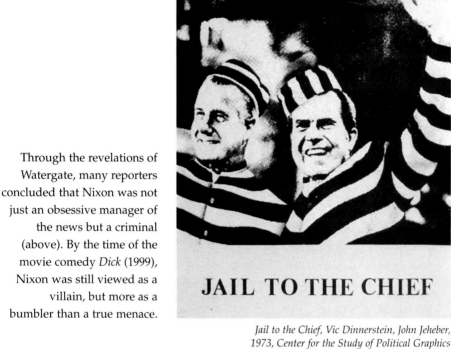

Through the revelations of Watergate, many reporters concluded that Nixon was not just an obsessive manager of the news but a criminal (above). By the time of the movie comedy *Dick* (1999), Nixon was still viewed as a villain, but more as a bumbler than a true menace.

JAIL TO THE CHIEF

Jail to the Chief, Vic Dinnerstein, John Jeheber, 1973, Center for the Study of Political Graphics

Photofest

Above, Nixon faces reporters in the White House East Room — "Sunday afternoon in the Tijuana bullring," Pat Buchanan said. The worse Watergate got, the more his diehard supporters (below) saw Nixon as a victim.

The newly fashionable field of psychobiography made peering into the president's mind a national pastime. Armchair analysis was hard to resist with Nixon, especially when, as in August 1973, he publicly lost his temper — captured here on video shoving his press secretary Ron Ziegler.

Used by permission of New York Magazine

The image of Nixon as madman took hold in magazine cover stories and in plays and films, like Robert Altman's *Secret Honor*.

Photofest

Nixon's own preferred self-image was that of the foreign policy statesman, solving the world's problems with fellow great men like Russia's Leonid Brezhnev. Nixon knew how that image would play for the cameras.

In the 1990s, historians promoted the most improbable "New Nixon" of all — Nixon as a steward of the Great Society and a liberal on race (right). Nixon's farewell address from the East Room on August 9, 1974 (below) was seen in strikingly divergent ways by his different audiences.

Hoover Institute

National Archives Records Administration

National Archives Records Administration

The Comeback Artists

HERE LIES
RICHARD M. NIXON
1913   1994

THE FINAL COVERUP

Hougan's research raised some perplexing questions. But, as many also noted, his own theories were themselves far less tenable than those he was trying to debunk. He extrapolated from unanswered questions to form radical conclusions about Watergate. On one page he would propose a speculative theory and a few pages later he would be calling his own conclusion "inescapable." Hougan seemed not to appreciate that all crimes—and all historical investigations—produce unanswerable questions. Why Martinez was carrying the key to the secretary's desk would probably never be known; but the failure of Judge Sirica's courtroom, the Ervin Committee, and a generation of reporters and historians to answer the question did not therefore render all of their other conclusions suspect. Nor did it make Hougan's conjecture a safe basis for further speculations.[86]

Hougan insisted that his findings didn't "exonerate Nixon in any way," and technically he was correct. He did not make excuses for Nixon's payment of hush money or his attempt to enlist the CIA in blocking the investigation. Still, he painted Nixon as a victim. For Hougan explained Nixon's ouster as resulting from the liberals' refusal to pursue legitimate leads that might have exculpated him. To pursue the CIA angle, Hougan wrote, "was considered almost subversive," because it meant granting credence to the very "smokescreen" that Nixon had ordered his aides to take to Pat Gray. The irony, said Hougan, was that Nixon's ploy backfired; the disclosure that Nixon pushed the CIA cover story deterred others from ever probing whether it was actually true, as Hougan believed it was. "No matter what evidence was found [of CIA sabotage], it could be—and often was—deprecated as a diversion designed to provide the president with an undeserved escape hatch," Hougan wrote. Thus, Hougan's Nixon was the casualty of liberal ire. "Nixon and the CRP were, in some sense of the word, victims of the affair," he concluded, adding ambivalently, "however culpable they may have been in other areas."[87]

Interest in Hougan's book, strong at first, faded quickly. But it never vanished. Some Nixon loyalists, such as onetime economic adviser Martin Anderson, brashly trumpeted its claims, hoping to cast the former president in a better light. But the main way in which *Secret Agenda* helped promote Nixon's victim image was by inspiring others—in particular, a pair of Watergate buffs named Len Colodny and Robert Gettlin. Colodny, a newspaper reporter, and Gettlin, a liquor wholesaler, had set out to write a book about Bob Woodward, which they intended to be critical. But when they read *Secret Agenda*, they changed their focus. Hougan had asserted that as a young navy officer Woodward had once briefed Al Haig on top-secret matters. Although his evidence for the claim was weak and Woodward and Haig both denied it, Colodny and Gettlin were enchanted. Haig became a central player in their conspiracy.[88]

The book that they published in 1991, *Silent Coup*, resembled *Secret Agenda* in key respects. Most basically, it shared a conspiracist approach to the study of history. It began with the premise that the "truth" about the past could be ascertained not by studying official records but by seeking out what remained hidden—which, in conspiracist thinking, was always hidden deliberately. With Watergate, this meant the truth could be divined only by solving such riddles as the exact purpose of the June 17 break-in, the content of what was erased by the 18½-minute gap, and the identity of Deep Throat. The problem with such thinking is that those details, though interesting to buffs and potentially enlightening to historians, don't alter the vast number of facts that are known about Watergate—on the basis of which certain undeniable conclusions have been reached.

Specifically, *Silent Coup* borrowed from *Secret Agenda* in placing a call-girl ring at the center of the conspiracy. Having interviewed a disbarred lawyer and caddish figure of the 1970s Washington demimonde named Phillip Mackin Bailley, Colodny and Gettlin pushed the idea further than had Hougan. They alleged that John Dean had targeted DNC headquarters for burglary because he wanted to retrieve (from Maxie Wells's desk) evidence of his wife's connection to the ring. In other details, *Silent Coup* diverged from Hougan's conjectures. Most notably, it omitted the CIA theory. Instead, it pinned Nixon's undoing first on Dean, who, it said, ran the cover-up until his April 1973 departure from the White House; and then, starting in May 1973, on Al Haig and Fred Buzhardt, Dean's successor as White House counsel.* Dean's motive, they said, was his wife's connection to the prostitution ring. Haig, for his part, supposedly wanted to conceal

* Dean and Haig were not alleged to be in cahoots with each other. The commencement of one man's plot to frame Nixon, in their telling, just happened to begin when the other man's plot to frame Nixon ended.

his own role in the so-called Moorer-Radford scandal—another episode of Nixonian skullduggery, which surfaced in 1974, in which Joint Chiefs of Staff Chairman Thomas Moorer was caught using a liaison officer, Charles Radford, to spy on Henry Kissinger at the National Security Council. Their differences aside, both *Secret Agenda* and *Silent Coup* depicted Nixon not as a cagey schemer but as an unwitting victim, done in by other, abler conspirators who made him the fall guy.

Silent Coup made a bigger splash than *Secret Agenda*. It became a best-seller. Yet its influence remained strongest among buffs and Nixon loyalists, not historians. The book's veracity was immediately impugned. Reviewers pointed out errors of fact, logic, and method. Charging defamation, Dean and his wife sued the authors, their publisher (St. Martin's Press), and Gordon Liddy, who was promoting *Silent Coup*'s theories on his radio show. (The suit was settled separately with each of the parties.)* In subsequent years, others examined the book's theories and rejected them. A British reporter, Fred Emery, and documentarians Brian Lapping and Norma Percy began an investigation on the premise that *Silent Coup* was correct, but their research convinced them otherwise. Anthony Summers, a journalist normally partial to conspiracy theories, rejected *Silent Coup* as groundless after investigating its claims for his mammoth anti-Nixon tome, *The Arrogance of Power: The Secret World of Richard Nixon*.[89]

Nonetheless, for all the battering it took, *Silent Coup* remained in circulation, if at the fringes of debate. One set of boosters included New Left alumni such as journalists Robert Scheer and Robert Sherrill. Indiana University historian Joan Hoff, who was working on her own revisionist book *Nixon Reconsidered*, also lent *Silent Coup* scholarly cover; she faulted the book's "evidentiary gaps" but extravagantly declared that it "surpassed other books about the origins of Watergate." So too did Roger Morris, a former Kissinger aide whose masterly 1990 biography of Nixon's early years had won rave reviews. Although the hapless, guileless Nixon of *Silent Coup* scarcely resembled the manipulative striver of Morris's own work, the biographer nonetheless wrote a fulsome introduction to the

---

* The suit against Liddy was dismissed when both parties agreed to a settlement proposed by the judge.

Watergate book, endorsing its view of Nixon as undone by a coup d'état. "No other portrayal has provided us such a gritty, authentic montage of the tottering ruler, the old predator at bay," Morris wrote. For the first time, Nixon was seen as not crafty but gullible. "He is usually portrayed as paranoid," Herbert Parmet noted in a review, "whereas the Nixon of *Silent Coup* is a victim of misplaced trust."[90]

Where a small platoon of loyalists had championed *Secret Agenda*, an army rallied behind *Silent Coup*. The few scholarly or semi-scholarly endorsements enabled Nixon's allies to deploy *Silent Coup* in the campaign for Nixon's rehabilitation. Nixon himself had no wish to read it (or so he told his assistant in his final years, Monica Crowley), but others did. Besides Liddy, several Nixon loyalists who fared well in the book's telling—including Ehrlichman and Colson—endorsed its hypotheses.[91]

Jonathan Aitken, a British member of Parliament and a friend of Nixon's since the 1970s, endorsed *Silent Coup*'s claims in his biography, *Nixon: A Life* (1993). For a book of its length (633 pages), *Nixon: A Life* barely dealt with Nixon's term as president at all (Aitken spent 155 pages on the presidency). But where it did so, it was adulatory. Aitken wrote forgivingly that because his friend had been "at the sharp end of the campaigning ethics of John F. Kennedy and Lyndon B. Johnson," Watergate seemed to him like "routine hardball." Although Aitken stipulated that Nixon was "by no means an innocent victim," he agreed that it was "the 'good' side of his nature"—his trust in others, his wish to protect underlings—that precipitated his fall. More brazenly, Aitken based his account of Watergate mainly on what he called the "important new research" of *Silent Coup*. Making scant reference to the extensive documentary record—the House and Senate hearings, the criminal trials, Nixon's tapes and papers—the biographer disingenuously presented *Silent Coup*'s account as if it enjoyed the same legitimacy as others. "The righteous certainty that Nixon got what he deserved has, until recently, been the authorised version," Aitken wrote. The statement was doubly coy. It implied first that the standard view of Watergate was "authorized," as if it had been sanitized to conceal hidden truths; second, it implied that this view had "recently" been dethroned, which it had not. And although Aitken added that "the judgement of history on Watergate is a long way from being final," he narrated the rest of the chapter as if a final verdict—exonerating Nixon—had indeed come in. *Nixon: A Life* was recognized, in the gentle words of one reviewer, as "a partisan's book," but it nonetheless fueled a virtuous cycle of pro-Nixon opinion making.* Just as Rabbi Korff had used Stephen Ambrose's authority to validate the rhetorical claims of Victor Lasky, Nixon's defenders cited Aitken's book, and Joan Hoff's support for *Silent Coup*, as supposedly impartial and reliable judges in the debates over Nixon's culpability.† 92

Like Holocaust denial, the far-fetched Watergate theories seemed unlikely to sway more than a few impressionable minds. To most historians, Nixon's offenses were documented well enough that rebutting conspiracy theories seemed like a waste of time—if they were aware of those theories at all. Nixon himself, whatever his private suspicions about the CIA, showed little interest in the deniers' work. When his assistant Monica Crowley read *Silent Coup* in 1991, she wrote to Colodny and Gettlin to praise what she called "their even-handed approach in exploring new theories about Watergate." Colodny telephoned her to say thank you, which she reported to Nixon. The ex-president couldn't match her excitement. "No matter what anyone comes up with," he said, "the Watergate story is over." 93 Nixon was prone to such confessions, even if he still also blustered about double standards and witch-hunts. In this late-in-life sigh of despair, Nixon—dejected, coming to face his mortality—was simply acknowledging reality.

---

* Aitken's credibility soon suffered, à la Nixon, when, in an episode unrelated to the biography, he was sentenced to eighteen months in prison for perjury.

† For example, in his 1997 best-seller *A History of the American People*, Paul Johnson, a well-known British journalist, used *Nixon: A Life* to support conclusions he had already reached fourteen years earlier. Johnson was friends with Aitken, who in fact had introduced Johnson to Nixon himself; and Johnson gave Aitken's biography a rave review. When he published *A History of the American People*, Johnson footnoted his friend's book extensively, even though Johnson's discussion of Nixon's presidency—"Watergate and the Putsch Against the Executive"—was little more than a near-verbatim excerpt from his own previous work *Modern Times*. In the 1997 book, Johnson did not see fit to include the labyrinthine details of *Silent Coup*. He stuck with his focus on Nixon's predecessors' misdeeds and on the "hysteria" of the Watergate-era press. But he did insert a laudatory mention of *Silent Coup* in the book's footnotes, along with a summary of the call-girl theory, which he falsely implied had originated with the academically pedigreed Hoff.

The Watergate deniers never convinced more than a fraction of buffs and loyalists of Nixon's innocence. Nonetheless, with no one actively rebutting them, they attracted for their theories, through fervor and determination, a degree of attention disproportionate to their numbers. The publicity they secured marked a small first step in turning Watergate into a story of a successful cover-up instead of a failed one and Nixon into a victim instead of a crook.

In 1975 John G. Schmitz, a former congressman from Southern California and a member of the John Birch Society, was seeking to regain his Orange County seat. The society, always strongest in Nixon's home territory, was long a haven for what Clinton Rossiter had called the "lunatic right"; in the 1950s its members considered Eisenhower a Communist, and during Nixon's presidency *détente* convinced them he was soft on the Reds as well. But in 1975, with Saigon having just fallen to the North Vietnamese, with the untrustworthy Kissinger still shaping foreign policy and the loathed Nelson Rockefeller installed as vice president, the group's leaders began describing Nixon as a "victim, not [a] dupe" of left-wing internationalists. Schmitz sensed enough sympathy for Nixon in his district that he sought to win support with speeches on Nixon's behalf—suggesting that "double agents" in the White House had engineered Nixon's downfall because they feared "he would not have stood by while Vietnam went down to defeat."[94]

The conversion of the John Birch Society reflected, *in extremis*, the right's gradual re-embrace of Nixon after Watergate. To be sure, many who felt that Nixon had betrayed them never had a kind thought toward him again. Leading Republicans, including Nixon's successors as president, considered him politically toxic and kept their distance. He was never invited to speak at a Republican National Convention after he resigned. Chronicles of the history of the right airbrushed him out of the story. Before public audiences, Ronald Reagan was the party's hero, Nixon an embarrassment whom it wished to forget.

With the passage of time, however, Nixon was welcomed back to the fold, especially in fraternities of Republican die-hards. Nixon's themes and strategies—his conservative populism, his support for law and order, his insistence that the United States not be seen internationally as a helpless giant—became central to Republican electoral successes. He never enjoyed the adulation that Reagan attained, but he scored smaller successes. *National Review* wrote about him favorably again, as did new conservative organs like the Reverend Moon's *Washington Times*. Over time, some on the right came to see Nixon as a fallen martyr in conservatism's long and ultimately triumphant battle with liberalism, and a new generation of conservatives took Alex Keatonesque pride in defending him. GOP operative Bill Kristol, for one, liked to share with reporters his fond memories of his undergraduate days during Watergate, when as "one of five Nixon supporters" at Harvard, he relished taunting liberals with his contrarian views. Besides Monica Crowley, Nixon's posthumous amanuensis, the most prominent of the younger Nixon defenders was John Taylor. Taylor served as an assistant to Nixon in the post-resignation years and went on to become the Nixon Library's director. In that job, he promulgated the notion that Nixon's impeachable acts were defensible in the name of national security, since America was at war and facing violent dissent at home. Only because of the hatred Nixon incurred as a result of Vietnam, Taylor argued, was he singled out for impeachment. "To a great extent our passions about Nixon tell us about us more than they do about him," he noted. "I wonder if there's a term for that kind of historical figure. Scapegoat, maybe."[95]

Since the 1990s, those who embraced Nixon's victim image were mainly rank-and-file Republicans, many of whom had always had a soft spot for him throughout a long career as a committed party man. With the exception of his own tenure as president, when he thought he no longer needed the party's support, the relationships he forged with state and local GOP officials had been crucial to his success. After his resignation, they were the ones who turned out to applaud him. Reciprocally, Nixon felt a continuing loyalty to the GOP, cheering on Republican candidates and sniping at Democrats as he discussed presidential politics on the sidelines.[96]

Sometimes the right's new embrace of Nixon caused problems within the ranks. When an Ohio state senator invited Nixon to speak at a 1981 Republican fund-raiser, some top GOP officials, including the governor, stayed away. "It's like inviting your former mistress to your family Christmas dinner," said one. But the event was a sellout and raised $100,000. As Watergate's stigma faded, the boycotts and protests diminished and the rubber-chicken-dinners multiplied. Before a 1984 fund-raiser for Indiana Republicans, state party chairman Gordon Durnil worried about whether to invite Nixon. But the ex-president drew five hundred guests and favorable coverage in the papers.[97]

Although Nixon was banished from Republican conventions and similar high-profile forums, it was a different story when party leaders were courting the GOP base. Republicans found they could win points from the die-hards by embracing Nixon. In 1988, several primary candidates visited Nixon in Saddle River, New Jersey. In 1996, after Nixon's death, Bob Dole made a pilgrimage to his gravesite at Yorba Linda. In 1990, Nixon drew a warm welcome when he made his first trip to Capitol Hill since his ouster to meet with Republican congressmen. Dole, who had earlier scoffed at declarations of Nixon's rehabilitation, now pronounced the recovery complete; House Minority Leader Newt Gingrich raved; Senate pages and congressional aides barely out of college came to take photographs.[98]

Fittingly, the event of Nixon's post-resignation career that garnered the most attention was also a partisan one: the July 1990 opening of the Richard M. Nixon Library and Birthplace in Yorba Linda, California. Unlike most presidential libraries, which were run by the National Archives, Nixon's library was entirely private. (It also housed no presidential papers, which remained under government care in Washington.) As a result, Nixon and his loyalists could do everything just to their liking. The dedication had the feel of a campaign event, with brass bands, red, white, and blue balloons, and banquets. Loyalists turned out in droves. "I would give my life to be here," said Lloyd Johnson of Michigan, who had raised funds for Nixon's defense in 1976. "I was ready to leave this country 16 years ago. I thought my countrymen had been brainwashed." Nixon's three Republican successors came to celebrate. The only Democratic president to have served since Watergate, Jimmy Carter, stayed away.[99]

Partisanship had its price. Just before the opening, library director Hugh Hewitt said that researchers wishing to use the archives would be screened, and he singled out Bob Woodward for exclusion. "He's not a responsible journalist," Hewitt said. Citing Nixon's lifelong Republicanism, Hewitt said it would "taint" his legacy "to let the premises be used indiscriminately by groups who oppose everything he worked for." Under pressure from scholars and the press—"It's the old enemies-list mentality," Woodward pointed out—the library relented, with Nixon's agreement. Then the library announced that reporters would be banned from the ceremony, only to ease up again after protests. Eliciting the most howls was the library's selective presentation of the June 23, 1972, "smoking gun" tape, which omitted some of the more incriminating parts.[100]

The exhibits at the Nixon Library depicted Nixon as both a great statesman and a victim of liberal vengeance. All presidential memorials sanitize the histories of the men they honor, but the Nixon Library's treatment of Watergate was egregious. It blamed the break-in on John Mitchell and the cover-up on John Dean. It described Nixon as the casualty of "political opponents who ruthlessly exploited those misjudgments as a way to further their own purely political goals." Seizing on a remark that Bella Abzug had made, it wrongly stated that Democrats had planned to force out Nixon and Agnew and install Carl Albert as president. It falsely accused Woodward and Bernstein of trying to bribe sources. And it minimized the importance of the smoking gun tape, saying that "no obstruction of justice, no Watergate cover-up occurred as a result of that conversation." But Nixon's loyalists defended both the library's Watergate presentation and the celebratory tone. For those who saw him as a martyr to the cause, the library was a chance to correct the record, and its opening a moment of redemption. Nixon, basking in the encomiums, called it one of the happiest days of his life. Yet he soon came to a more cold-eyed view and accepted the limits of the library's persuasiveness. At the dedication, he told Jonathan Aitken ruefully, he had been simply "playing before the home crowd."[101]

Still, among that crowd, Nixon's victim image endured. Even though the country had moved decisively rightward since 1968, many conservatives still fancied themselves an embattled minority. Many still wished to undo the changes of the 1960s and decried liberal permissiveness, divorce, drug use, and the decline of "family values." The fallen Nixon, unfairly driven from his seat of power by radiclibs, remained a metaphor for those notions of family, tradition, patriotism, and propriety that were also driven from their position of dominance in the early 1970s.

6

The Psychobiographers: Nixon as Madman

> I cannot help think[ing] that if an American president had a staff psychiatrist, perhaps a case such as Watergate might not have had a chance to develop.
> —Dr. Arnold A. Hutschnecker[1]

The president couldn't sleep. Long afflicted by insomnia, Nixon had special reason for distress on the night of May 8, 1970. He was being pilloried in the press and by the anti-war movement, first for ordering the invasion of Cambodia, then for reacting coldly to the killing of four Kent State students by National Guardsmen. Now protesters had descended on Washington and the capital was in a state of siege.

At 9:22 P.M. Nixon began a five-hour marathon of fifty-one telephone calls, to Henry Kissinger, his daughter Tricia, Bob Haldeman, the Reverend Norman Vincent Peale, John Ehrlichman, Bebe Rebozo, Pat Buchanan, and dozens of others. He dozed for an hour. He then went to the Lincoln Sitting Room, listened to a Rachmaninoff record, made more phone calls. Finally he asked his valet, Manolo Sanchez, to go with him for a predawn stroll on the mall. With only Secret Service agents in tow, Nixon and Sanchez drove to a spot near the Lincoln Memorial where throngs of young demonstrators had encamped. Learning of Nixon's departure,

White House aides Egil "Bud" Krogh and Ron Ziegler hurried to join him, bringing White House doctor Walter Tkach with them.

On the mall, Nixon struck up fragmented conversations with random students, on subjects from college football and surfing to arms control and his desire to end the Vietnam War. "I'm a devout Quaker," he assured them. "I'm against killing as much as you are, and I want to bring the boys home." The concerned staffers pressured Nixon to leave, but the president insisted on lingering. When he finally got back in his limousine, he directed it to the U.S. Capitol, where, befriending a cleaning woman, he spoke about his late mother, whom he called "a saint." Nixon capped the evening with a breakfast of hash and eggs at the Mayflower Hotel before returning to the White House at 7:30 A.M.[2]

Nixon's peregrinations, front-page news the next day, prompted a range of reactions. Many of the students on the mall complained that he had been indifferent to their demands as he lamely made small talk, though at least one saw the president as captive to systemic forces that were prolonging the war. Thirty-year-old White House aide Bud Krogh thought the incident revealed Nixon's heroic dedication to leading the country through trying times. Some reporters read the event as a publicity stunt. Yet all agreed that something highly unusual had happened to make this most private of presidents plunge into the most public of situations. It was deliberate hyperbole when the Berkeley Barb headlined its story NIXON'S MIND SNAPS. But more measured assessments came from Henry Kissinger and Daniel Patrick Moynihan, who both believed that the president was "on the edge of a nervous breakdown." Clearly, some sort of psychological explanation was called for.[3]

Conveniently, a new group of experts was at the ready with a set of answers. In recent years, historians, political scientists, and psychoanalysts had been applying the insights of psychoanalysis*—the exploration of

---

* "Psychology" refers to the study of how the mind works; "psychiatry" to a medical specialty—psychiatrists have MDs. "Psychoanalysis" refers to a school of psychology, derived from the ideas of Freud and since modified, that stresses the role of the unconscious and of early childhood experiences. Many psychologists and psychiatrists practice "psychodynamic" therapy, which uses psychoanalytic theory but not necessarily the same intensive methods.

unconscious motives, the study of how childhood experiences shape people's character—to politics and public figures. The terms "psychohistory"
and "psychobiography" were being heard in academic and even popular
discourse. In the wake of the Lincoln Memorial visit, psychobiographers
focused on Nixon. Bruce Mazlish, a historian at MIT and author of the first
Nixon psychobiography, suggested that the president, "as a basically
peaceful man" who aspired to be like his pacifist mother, blamed his own
anger for the Kent State killings, and wanted absolution. David Abrahamsen, a psychiatrist who later wrote *Nixon vs. Nixon* (1977), thought the president's behavior "abnormal," speculating that the last few weeks' events
had made him face the prospect of defeat in Vietnam, "which unconsciously
he took as his own personal, emotional defeat." Noting Nixon's awkwardness with the students, Duke University political scientist James David
Barber stressed the president's narcissistic "preoccupation with himself,"
which translated into an inability to achieve intimacy with others.[4]

The Lincoln Memorial stroll marked neither the first nor the last time
that Nixon's psyche became the subject of public analysis. More than any
other president, Nixon invited—even demanded—psychoanalytic interpretation. With his alternating bouts of caged-in restraint and explosive
anger, Nixon was a textbook case of the psychoanalytic precept that
repressed feelings affect people's behavior in unplanned ways. His
Freudian slips alone were legendary: When he said in the 1960 debates,
"We can't stand pat," he drew titters from observers who had seen his cool
exchanges with his wife. When he said in his 1962 California gubernatorial bid that he was running for "governor of the United States," it was
hard not to wonder if his heart was in the race. Other traits, too—visible
anger toward his enemies, stray comments that smacked of paranoia,
labored gestures designed to conceal his true self—cried out for psychological readings. From Dan Rather to Arthur Miller, Nixon-watchers who
insisted they normally eschewed the psychoanalytical found themselves
resorting to it when trying to explain Nixon.[5]

The president realized that people viewed him as a psychological
curiosity. One of his ideas for forcing concessions from the North Vietnamese, as he revealed to Haldeman, was predicated on perceptions of his
instability. "I call it the Madman Theory, Bob," he told his top aide one day

in 1969. "I want the North Vietnamese to believe I've reached the point where I might do *anything* to stop the war. . . . We'll just slip the word to them. . . . 'We can't restrain him when he's angry, and he has his hand on the nuclear button'—and Ho Chi Minh himself will be in Paris . . . begging for peace!"[6]

Nixon's army of analysts included not only professionals but also reporters, filmmakers, novelists, even his friends and colleagues, who looked to his upbringing and to repressed events to explain him. "I don't know what happened to him as a teenager with his mother or father," mused his Attorney General Richard Kleindienst, "whether someone caught him masturbating, or something that scarred his character." Asked Henry Kissinger: "Can you imagine what this man would have been had somebody loved him? . . . I don't think anybody ever did, not his parents, not his peers." Press aide Ken Clawson found the key to Nixon in a comment the ex-president made after resigning: "What starts the process really are laughs and slights and snubs when you are a kid. . . . But if you are reasonably intelligent and if your anger is deep enough and strong enough, you learn that you can change those attitudes by excellence, personal gut performance, while those who have everything are sitting on their fat butts."[7]

Those who probed Nixon's psyche most deeply were the newly ascendant scholars known as psychobiographers. From the outset of his presidency, Nixon served as the subject of a raft of studies that sought to understand him—and his era—by putting him on the couch. Collectively, these works found in Nixon a man whose political behavior bubbled up from wellsprings deep in his character: aching insecurities, a furious drive for power, an insatiable hunger for love. They traced those traits to formative childhood influences: his violent father, his controlling mother, the premature deaths of two of his brothers. And they suggested that Nixon suffered from peculiarities, if not deformations, of character—rage competing with suppressed guilt, paranoia that bred secrecy and vindictiveness, a sense of injury. Almost uniformly, Nixon's psychobiographers saw him as a narcissist with a frail ego who lashed out when he felt wounded.[8]

During and just after Nixon's presidency, these psychobiographers led an unprecedented national seminar on the hidden workings of the incumbent president's mind. Like other interpreters of Nixon, the psychobiographers sought a greater purchase on the authentic in a world dominated by political image making and obsessed by exteriors. Psychobiographers believed that the true self was to be found by stripping away externals and getting to the unconscious motivations behind behavior. "Political leaders have both a public and a private 'face,' image, identity or self," wrote Bruce Mazlish. One had to uncover the private to understand the public. The judicious application of psychoanalytic theory, these scholars agreed, was the best means of doing so. It could take them beyond politics and ideology to a deeper level of motivation. If for the New Left the personal was political, for the psychobiographers the political was personal.[9]

The psychobiographers' studies of Nixon, and of politicians in general, unquestionably enriched public understanding. Their projects, however, never resolved a key dilemma. Psychoanalysis has two different aims: first, to diagnose the mentally disturbed; second, to help healthy but troubled people to understand their own behavior. When it came to analyzing public figures, the blurry line between the two goals was further obscured: What began as an unobjectionable effort to interpret the actions of a powerful but secretive figure became a sensationalistic study in pathology. As Nixon's behavior grew erratic under Watergate's strains, the psychobiographers' judicious explorations of Nixon's mind devolved into breathless speculations over whether he posed a danger to the nation—over whether he was going crazy. Instead of operating with clinical distance and providing dispassionate interpretations, the psychobiographers and their followers created an image of the president that, far from a finely grained study in personality, was a reductive portrait of a madman in the throes of a nervous breakdown.

The psychoanalysis of Richard Nixon marked a neat convergence of man and moment. In the early 1970s, just as the nation had elected as president a man so well suited for psychological inquiry, the ideas and practice of psychoanalysis were exerting an unprecedented influence on American society. Once, psychiatric treatment had been deemed a medical process reserved for the mentally ill. But by the 1970s that perception had fallen away. People now saw psychotherapy as useful for the relatively well adjusted. "Never before has the mental health of so many Americans been so dependent on the ministrations of a relatively small number of psychiatrists and psychoanalysts," wrote the political scientist Arnold Rogow in 1970. Rogow estimated that 1 million Americans were then receiving psychiatric care while residing in hospitals or private clinics, and that another 1 million visited psychiatrists as outpatients. By 1975, 6 million Americans saw a mental-health professional. Insurance plans including Blue Cross and Medicaid expanded to cover psychotherapy, both reflecting and encouraging the trend.[10]

The embrace of psychology was part of a larger cultural turn toward inwardness. "After the political turmoil of the Sixties, Americans have retreated to purely personal preoccupations," wrote Christopher Lasch in *The Culture of Narcissism* (1978). Picking up a phrase from the sociologist Philip Rieff, Lasch noted that "Economic man . . . has given way to the psychological man of our times." In detecting this pervasive self-involvement, Lasch had much support. Pollster Daniel Yankelovich described a new "psychoculture" characterized by a search for "self-fulfillment"; sociologist Edwin Schur saw "self-awareness [as] the new panacea" and lamented that it distracted people from political involvement. Along with a host of other crazes—physical fitness, health food, Eastern religions, communes, sexual experimentation—the psychotherapy boom helped make the 1970s the so-called "Me" Decade.[11]

Much of the therapy that Americans embraced in the 1970s was not, strictly speaking, psychoanalytic. Within the therapeutic professions, psychoanalysis was actually losing influence, challenged by behaviorists, feminists, and biological determinists. Faddish New Age therapies and cults with such mystical-sounding names as Esalen, EST, and Synanon dispensed with the clinical distance between doctor and patient, the long-term nature of the treatment, and the rigor that were part of psychoanalysis. Americans who sought "actualization" through the new pop psychologies considered psychoanalysis fusty, hierarchical, and outdated.

Still, as the progenitor of these bastard therapies, psychoanalysis retained pride of place in the public imagination. When people thought about "seeing a shrink," they still conjured up images of a bearded Viennese doctor. Since the late Fifties and early Sixties—what one historian called its "golden age of popularization"—psychoanalysis had informed Hollywood movies, mainstream novels, journalism, advertising, and academic study. Freudian ideas drenched the culture. Newspapers and magazines published celebrity psychologists; television shows featured them on the air. On the *Tonight* show, Woody Allen joked about psychotherapy; in *The Bob Newhart Show*, psychiatry got its own sitcom. In a 1967 film, *The President's Analyst*, James Coburn played a psychiatrist who held top-secret sessions with a fictional chief executive. By the 1970s, people were invoking psychoanalytic ideas so routinely—an Oedipal complex, a death wish, a Freudian slip—that it was easy to forget just how recent or radical the ideas were.[12]

Among intellectuals in particular, psychoanalysis was appealing not just as a mode of therapy but as a theory for interpreting the human condition. Psychohistory and psychobiography were not new to the 1970s; since the early twentieth century, when Freud introduced millions to the power of the unconscious, the nature of sexual and aggressive instincts, and the importance of infantile and childhood experiences, biographers had joined the bandwagon. (Freud himself wrote a life of Leonardo da Vinci and collaborated with the American diplomat William C. Bullitt on a biography of Woodrow Wilson—a book that Richard Nixon, in one of his many slaps at psychoanalysis, judged "so outlandish as to be downright silly.")* But into the 1950s, historians hesitated to embrace Freud. Although psychoanalysis was "recognized as a theory basic to the study of the human personality," American Historical Association president William L. Langer said to the group's members in December 1957, historians remained afraid of it. "How can it be that the historian, who must be as much or more concerned with human beings and their motivation than with impersonal forces and causation, has failed to make these findings?" The next year, the psychoanalyst Erik Erikson published his seminal *Young Man Luther* about the Reformation leader, and Erikson's example and Langer's summons together inspired scholars to blaze a trail in the underexplored field. By 1970, psychobiography had become a hot topic of inquiry and debate. In April 1971, Arthur Schlesinger convened forty lead-

---

* Scholars believe that the work was much more Bullitt's than Freud's; Bullitt published it in 1966, well after the psychoanalyst's death, as psychohistory was coming into vogue.

ing historians and analysts for a weekend symposium on the subject,[13] and the ensuing years saw a slew of books and articles attacking and defending psychohistory.[14] In historical journals such as *The American Historical Review* and general intellectual magazines such as *The Atlantic, Commentary,* and *The New York Review of Books,* the debate raged.[15]

To its critics, psychohistory took a clinical practice—and, some felt, a dubious one at that—and recklessly applied it to figures to whom the analysts had no sustained private access and of whom they had no chance to ask questions. It crammed the inconclusive data, the critics said, into ready-made categories without sensitivity to political or cultural concerns. Proponents responded that a psychobiographer usually had access to diaries, letters, and accounts from the subject's intimates—often more resources than a psychotherapist could consult. Others acknowledged the danger of leaping to conclusions, but pointed out that all historians made inferences based on partial evidence and that it wasn't the field of psychohistory but its shoddy practitioners who should be faulted. The unattainability of an ironclad psychoanalytic interpretation should not deter historians, they argued, from attempting the approach, especially in cases—like those of political leaders—where the consequences mattered.

Paralleling the rise of psychohistory as a professional field was the popular and journalistic exploration of political psychology. In the hands of journalists, or even of psychoanalysts who had studied their subjects only cursorily, psychohistory and psychobiography became a parlor game. Nuanced readings were rare, sensational pronouncements common. Popular psychological readings of presidents had also been going on since Freud's day—Teddy Roosevelt and Woodrow Wilson were favorite subjects*—but again, only in the 1950s did the attention given to the president's mental health intensify. With the advent of nuclear weapons, the image of

---

* In May 1912, a *New York Times Magazine* article entitled "Roosevelt as Analyzed by the New Psychology" tried to reconcile inconsistent comments that Theodore Roosevelt, by then the former president, had made about supporting the reelection of his successor, William Howard Taft. It concluded that TR harbored an unresolved, repressed wish to run again himself (which TR did later that year). Wilson attracted psychoanalytic speculation (and not just from Freud and William Bullitt) after White House aides announced in September 1919 that the president had suffered a nervous breakdown. In fact, he had suffered a stroke, but in Wilson's day it was thought more acceptable to succumb to a psychological ailment than to a physical one, and so the truth was concealed.

a deranged commander in chief suddenly occupied popular fantasies, as stability became the watchword not just in geopolitics but psychopolitics too.[16]

Nixon was the first major politician whose psychological fitness was called into question during the nuclear age; during the 1956 campaign, Max Lerner and Adlai Stevenson used the "triple issue" of the Soviet development of the hydrogen bomb, Eisenhower's frail health, and the vice president's irascibility and immaturity as an argument against reelecting Ike and Dick. Similarly, Lyndon Johnson raised doubts in 1964 about his rival Barry Goldwater's short fuse and militaristic posture, notably in the once-aired "Daisy" television commercial that showed a little girl plucking a flower before being decimated by a nuclear blast. The same year, a magazine called *FACT* used a haphazard survey of American Psychiatric Association members to conclude that Goldwater was paranoid. (Goldwater successfully sued for libel.)[*] But the issue of presidential stability knew no partisan bounds. Soon LBJ himself fell victim to questions about his emotional fitness, as critics painted him as a dangerous narcissist who was prolonging the Vietnam War to salve his own ego. In 1972, more Democrats succumbed to similar doubts. Before the New Hampshire primary, Senator Edmund Muskie dashed his presidential hopes when he appeared to cry while denouncing a scurrilous attack on his wife, though he later insisted (and shamefaced reporters agreed) that the "tears" were really just melting snow.[†] Five months later, Senator

---

[*] *FACT*'s findings were based on questionnaires filled out only by those APA members who chose to respond (about 20 percent), a degree of self-selection considered unreliable in polling. The survey required no familiarity with Goldwater's private or even public behavior. Many responses were transparently political. ("Goldwater's insecurity and feelings of inadequacy cause him to reject all changes and to resent what he considers to be excessive power by the Federal government. His rejection may in fact reflect a threat by a father-image, namely someone who is stronger than he, more masculine and more cultured.") The editor, Ralph Ginzburg, also doctored quotations. Still, *FACT* ran two articles in its September–October 1964 issue based on the survey, one of which claimed that Goldwater displayed "unmistakable signs of paranoia." The APA denounced the articles, though it added that more "reliable" psychological assessments of candidates might be useful.

[†] Nixon's campaign operatives were indirectly responsible for Muskie's troubles. Muskie's allegedly tearful reaction came after a difficult few days before the 1972 New Hampshire primary in which the conservative *Manchester Union-Leader* attacked him for referring to Americans of French-Canadian descent as "Canucks"; the charge, it was later revealed, stemmed from a bogus letter that Nixon operatives had sent to the paper.

Thomas Eagleton stepped down as the Democratic vice-presidential nominee when reporters learned he had hidden the fact that he'd once
received electroshock therapy for depression. The Eagleton affair, while
sparking debates about the stigma of receiving treatment, also elevated
questions about the stability of candidates for high office.[17]

Above all, it was Nixon's ascension to the presidency that brought concerns about the mental condition of leaders to the fore. "With Richard
Nixon there [was] a burst of activity" among psychobiographers, wrote
Bruce Mazlish. "His compulsion to put himself on the couch in public, his
obviously 'psychological' character, his heavily personalized policies . . .
convinced many otherwise skeptical people of the importance of personality in politics." In 1968 Mazlish had resolved to study the next president
psychoanalytically, and after the election he started in on Nixon. James Barber, too, who was writing a comprehensive study of presidential character,
predicted on the eve of Nixon's inaugural that the new president's superego would lead him to cover up any "scandal and/or corruption" that might
arise during his term. With Nixon's election in 1968, man and moment came
together: In the new president, the resort to psychological explanations found
a seemingly perfect vehicle. Psychobiographers, professional and amateur,
could look to Nixon's character for the key to the era's political riddles.[18]

Richard Nixon got angry when psychoanalysis was discussed. Besides
belittling Freud and Bullitt's Woodrow Wilson biography, he regularly
denigrated psychiatrists, psychoanalysis, and psychohistory. "People go
through that psychological bit nowadays," he told reporter Jules Witcover in 1966. "That sort of juvenile self-analysis is something I've never
done." Once in 1968, his aide Roger Ailes was scolded after placing a psychiatrist on a panel of "average citizens" who were supposed to quiz
Nixon for a campaign commercial. "Nixon hates psychiatrists!" Ailes was
told. ". . . Apparently Nixon won't even let one in the same room." On a
1971 Oval Office tape, Nixon berated "soft-headed psychiatrists" who
favored legalizing marijuana "because they're probably all on the stuff
themselves." Some psychobiographers even suggested that the order to
burgle the office of Lewis Fielding, Daniel Ellsberg's psychiatrist, repre-

sented a projection of Nixon's own fear that a psychotherapist might be keeping incriminating notes about the president himself.[19]

Nixon's extreme reactions struck many observers as overly defensive. In the mid-1960s, he had told his law partner (and later presidential aide) Leonard Garment that he would do anything to return to public life—anything, he said, "except see a shrink." Having himself spent many hours on an analyst's couch, Garment took Nixon's protestation as "a sure sign, in Nixon-speak, that despite himself he had seen a shrink."* Others shared the suspicion. For decades, questions dogged Nixon over whether he had ever received counseling. In particular, observers speculated about Nixon's relationship with one Arnold A. Hutschnecker, M.D., of 829 Park Avenue, New York.[20]

An Austrian-born physician who specialized in psychosomatic illnesses, Hutschnecker was always cagey about his dealings with Nixon. On the one hand, he held to the official line that he saw Nixon "simply for occasional checkups and to discuss how to deal with the stresses of his office." But as that carefully worded statement made clear, he never denied that the two men discussed Nixon's psychological troubles. Over the years Hutschnecker shifted in his emphasis—sometimes peremptorily dismissing gossip about being "Nixon's shrink," sometimes hinting slyly at a psychotherapeutic relationship—but never denying outright the psychological component of Nixon's visits. Ultimately, of course, the question of whether Nixon saw Hutschnecker for physical or psychic afflictions rested on a false distinction, since the very notion of the psychosomatic supposes that physical symptoms can have psychic roots. Whether one interpreted Nixon's visits as routine treatment or a scandalous indication of dangerous instability turned not on the facts of what occurred between the two men but on how one regarded psychotherapy in the first place. In any event, Nixon relied on Hutschnecker heavily. A letter from the doctor was among the articles in Nixon's desk drawer when he resigned, and two decades later, when Pat Nixon died, Hutschnecker came to the funeral and held Nixon's hand as the ex-president cried.[21]

---

* "Those who are lying or trying to cover up something generally make a common mistake—they tend to overreact, to overstate their case," Nixon once wrote, showing an intuitive Freudian bent.

Nixon and Hutschnecker met in 1951 after Sheridan Downey, Nixon's predecessor in his Senate seat, gave the junior politician a copy of Hutschnecker's *The Will to Live*, a layman's guide to psychosomatic illness. A chronic sufferer from insomnia, Nixon read the book and admired it greatly (as president, he was still recommending it to aides). For four years, Nixon saw Hutschnecker every few months and called his office at moments of crisis, including during the 1952 fund scandal. Then, in 1955, the gossip columnist Walter Winchell reported that Nixon was seeing a psychiatrist, and, though the report was technically imprecise—Hutschnecker never did a psychiatric residency—Nixon curtailed the visits, thereafter seeing the doctor, apparently, only on social calls.[22]

The vice president's polarizing personality ensured that his psychic health remained an issue of public discussion, fueled by whispers about "Nixon's shrink." Occasionally a journalist stumbled onto Hutschnecker. An Associated Press reporter telephoned the doctor the Saturday evening before the 1960 election asking about Nixon's mental health. Hutschnecker refused to comment.*

Late in the 1968 campaign, the rumors surfaced again. The columnist Drew Pearson, never loath to investigate Nixon, tried to confirm them. Like those who warned in the 1950s of Nixon's unreliability as the custodian of the peace in the atomic age, Pearson believed that "the public has a right to know about [the] medical past" of someone "who has his finger on the nuclear trigger." Pearson tracked Hutschnecker down, but again the doctor insisted he had treated Nixon only as an internist. Unable to corroborate the story, Pearson refrained from publishing it.

After the election, however, Pearson's calculus changed. On November 13, the columnist gave a lunchtime talk to journalists at Washington's National Press Club. During the question-and-answer period, he was asked how he decided whether to publish a rumor. By way of a response, he recounted his efforts to confirm the Nixon-Hutschnecker relationship. At that point, correspondents who had previously deemed the rumor unfit to print had an excuse to pursue the story—which they immediately did.[23]

---

* Hutschnecker later told psychobiographer Blema Steinberg that his failure to publicly give Nixon a clean bill of health in 1960 may have cost him the election.

A minor feeding frenzy ensued. At Nixon's presidential transition headquarters at the Hotel Pierre in New York, reporters converged on Ron Ziegler. Denying that Nixon had ever undergone psychiatric treatment, Ziegler attacked Pearson, who he said routinely wrote things that were "totally untrue." Pearson shot back a week later, musing provocatively about why, as vice president, "Nixon should go all the way to New York to consult a well-known psychotherapy specialist concerning his internal medical problems when some of the best internists in the U.S. are located at Walter Reed Hospital and Bethesda Naval Hospital." Pearson admonished that "a president or candidate for president should make all the facts public regarding his health, mental or otherwise. . . . There should be no covering up of the facts or blatant denials such as issued by Ron Ziegler." *Time, Newsweek,* and other publications ran articles about the flap.[24]

A few months later, Hutschnecker himself joined the debate. In a *Look* magazine article carrying the headline, PRESIDENT NIXON'S FORMER DOCTOR WRITES ABOUT THE MENTAL HEALTH OF OUR LEADERS, Hutschnecker said that in the nuclear age, "the survival of the human race" depended on the "emotional stability" of the U.S. president. He warned of "hostile-aggressive" leaders in whom ambition "can reach a degree of madness." Although he hastily assured readers that he "detected no sign of mental illness" in Nixon, he urged them to weigh a presidential aspirant's "drive for power, his personality, emotional makeup, motivation and goals" in deciding how to vote. First Mazlish and Barber, then Drew Pearson, and now the president's doctor—all were calling for scrutiny of the president's psyche. Under this pressure began the inquiry into the mind of Richard Nixon.[25]

A brigade of psychobiographers set to work. They included psychoanalysts, psychiatrists, historians, political scientists, and journalists, and their work ranged from the scrupulous to the sloppy. They differed, too, in their approaches: Fawn Brodie, for example, hewed to a Freudian model of analysis, while James Barber worked with categories and concepts of his own devising. But for all their differences of method and interpretation, their readings of Nixon did not differ fundamentally from one another. Each painted Nixon as an insecure, narcissistic personality whose childhood injuries instilled a drive to achieve, a sense of guilt over his success, and a frail ego to which small injuries triggered angry outbursts.[26]

Nixon's psychobiographers looked first to his childhood to understand him. In Frank and Hannah Nixon, they found two strong personalities who molded their son. Frank Nixon, a wayfaring jack-of-all-trades and a ladies' man, had dropped out of school at sixteen, and drifted about Ohio and Colorado before moving to Southern California in 1907. He struggled with a series of go-nowhere jobs and failed enterprises before opening in 1924 (when Richard was eleven) a moderately successful gas station and grocery in Whittier. Fawn Brodie, probably Nixon's best known psychobiographer, described Frank as short-tempered, "punishing and often brutal," a man who used his fists and thrashed his children when they crossed him. "Dad was very strict and expected to be obeyed under all circumstances," Nixon once recalled; if not, he said, "I got the strap." Richard, his psychobiographers observed, emulated his father's violence; Frank's punishments fostered "an identification with his aggressive father," the psychobiographer Blema Steinberg wrote, along with "a deep-seated wish to avenge himself on his authoritarian father by administering equivalent humiliations." According to one story, at age seven Nixon so desperately wanted a friend's jar of polliwogs that he clobbered the boy on the head with a hatchet. As he got older, he sublimated his anger into more acceptable activities such as politics and debating, where, Mazlish noted, "he could release his aggressive feeling successfully"—the start of his trademark hard-hitting campaigning. Still, Nixon's unappeased rage erupted whenever he felt wronged.[27]

Hannah Milhous, born in 1885 and married to Frank in 1908, was a foil to her husband: quiet where he was boisterous, modest where he was flamboyant, self-possessed where he was violent. A committed Quaker who prevailed on her Methodist husband to adopt her faith, she exuded an admonishing air. Richard referred to her often as a saint, attributing to her a standard of righteousness that mortals like himself could never hope to match. Although Hannah admired her son's achievements, her tendency to mute her approval devastated him. Worse than Frank's beatings, Nixon recalled, was her "silent punishment," in which "she would just sit you down and she would talk very quietly . . . when you got through, you had been through an emotional experience." From Hannah, Nixon's psychobiographers wrote, the boy also learned to work hard and to plan things out methodically—"a persistent bent toward life," Barber wrote, "as painful, difficult." Seeking her favor, he applied himself industriously to his schoolwork, and in law school he earned the nickname "Iron Butt" for his ability to study for hours on end.[28]

Along with the fear of Frank's anger, Hannah's pious example taught Richard to suppress his feelings, to keep things to himself, and soldier on in the face of adversity. "From his mother Nixon learned . . . the art and necessity of denial," observed Brodie. The need to control his emotions left little room for humor or spontaneity. Always a loner, Nixon donned an aspect of imperturbability. "He always carried such a weight," his mother recalled, using a Quaker expression "for a person who doesn't take his responsibilities lightly." In the family, his somberness was seen as a virtue. Together, Frank's wrath and Hannah's sternness invested Nixon with an "ambivalent" view of how to handle his aggression, as his heroic efforts at self-control alternated with violent flare-ups.[29]

Hannah's selflessness toward outsiders also shortchanged her son, some psychobiographers concluded, of the love he needed. During his infancy, she failed, one biography argued, to be what the British psychoanalyst D. W. Winnicott called a "good-enough mother." While Richard was nursing, Hannah took in a nephew whom she breast-fed alongside him, instilling a primal insecurity and competitiveness. Soon after, she underwent a mastoid operation, compounding his sense of abandonment. The arrival the next year of another brother, Donald, and of Arthur four years later, multiplied Richard's rivals for his mother's affection. The upshot, David Abrahamsen suggested, was that Nixon felt "cheated out of love." It did not surprise the psychobiographers that Nixon wound up hostile and suspicious of his enemies even into adulthood. The Nixons' financial struggles amplified Richard's feelings of deprivation and resentment toward those he thought had it easy.[30]

This upbringing, the psychobiographers proposed, stunted Nixon's development of a healthy sense of self, leading him to hide his frail ego beneath his drive and aggression. "With Nixon," wrote Leo Rangell, "a chasm existed between insatiable wish and the always shaky feeling about its fulfillment." This classically narcissistic profile turned up in countless examples of childhood behavior recounted by his psychobiographers. The most fertile source of speculation was a letter Nixon wrote as part of a school assignment at age ten. In the note, Nixon described an adventure he fantasized he had when "his master" was away. "It is a tale," according to James Barber, "of hurt, panic, and depression":

My Dear Master:

The two boys that you left me with are very bad to me. Their dog, Jim, is very old and he will never talk or play with me.

One Saturday the boys went hunting. Jim and myself went with them. While going through the woods one of the boys triped [sic] and fell on me. I lost my temper and bit him. He kiked [sic] me in the side and we started on. While we were walking I saw a black round thing in a tree. I hit it with my paw. A swarm of black thing came out of it. I started to run and as both of my eyes were swelled shut I fell into a pond. When I got home I was very sore. I wish you would come home right now.

Your good dog,
Richard

Reprinting the note for the first time in his biography *The Real Nixon* (1960), the journalist Bela Kornitzer predicted, "Psychiatrists will undoubtedly have a field day." Indeed they did; practically every one of Nixon's psychobiographers meditated upon the letter.* One book, Frank DeHart's self-published *Traumatic Nixon* (1979)—either an example of psychobiography at its worst or an ingenious, unappreciated parody of the genre—went so far as to interpret Nixon's whole life through a peculiar reading of the letter, suggesting that Nixon had been forced to perform fellatio on a tramp he encountered in the woods. Michael Rogin and John Lottier suggested, in a more orthodox take, that "the imagery is anal; feces retaliate for the attack on the tree trunk's anus." David Abrahamsen, for his part, took the letter as an indication of Nixon's "oral fixation"—his tendency to respond to adver-

---

* Since Kornitzer, biographers have treated the document as an actual letter, to his mother, but the paper bears a strong resemblance to others that Nixon wrote as school assignments.

sity by lashing out orally (by biting)—and of his vulnerability, self-pity, and longing for his mother's comforts. Fawn Brodie saw in the note the seeds of Nixon's misbegotten sense of persecution, a sign of "how early he had begun to exaggerate the wrongs inflicted on him by others."[31]

Whatever their takes on the letter, Nixon's psychobiographers all detected a weak sense of self that spawned the traits that later became famous. Compensating for low self-esteem by seeking out adoration, Nixon gravitated to acting and politics. He had the makings, Blema Steinberg wrote, "of a narcissistic character with a fragile sense of self-worth who is driven to accomplish in order to replenish his emptiness." He concealed his neediness with a grandiose self-regard, hard-charging ambition, and hunger for power. In his youth, this ambition turned up in Nixon's determination to win debate contests and various student body presidencies; in his career, it appeared, for instance, when he insisted, in 1960, on campaigning in all fifty states—a foolish, counterproductive stunt.[32]

Nixon's grandiosity also entailed an outsized sense of entitlement, a belief that he could do no wrong because he was special. Several psychobiographers concluded that Nixon never developed an awareness of when he was crossing ethical boundaries. "Because of his deformed superego ... formation," wrote Abrahamsen, "Nixon had difficulty in making the connection between morality and his behavior." Brodie judged that Nixon was a pathological liar, whose need for love was so great that he developed "no emotional investment in the truth." Whether breaking into a dean's office to see his grades (as he had done at Duke Law School)* or cheating on his taxes (as he did as president),† Nixon's adult behavior proved to these psychobiographers that he had failed to develop a normal conscience.[33]

Psychobiographers also highlighted the childhood traumas that befell Nixon, which instilled, Mazlish wrote, an inordinate "threat and fear of

* The dean's office incident is not in dispute. Nixon himself told Bela Kornitzer about the incident in 1959. Both Nixon and the friends who joined him in the illegal entry downplayed it as an innocuous prank.

† During Watergate, it emerged that Nixon had paid virtually no taxes throughout his presidency. An investigation found that he owed nearly $467,000 to the government, which he agreed to pay. The House considered issuing an additional count of impeachment because of this tax evasion but declined to do so, concluding that such personal crimes did not rise to the level of impeachable behavior.

death." At age two, young Nixon was nearly trampled by horses. At three, he fell from a buggy, splitting open his head; he needed surgery to save his life. At four, he contracted severe pneumonia. Equally traumatic, two of his brothers died young. In 1925, Nixon's younger brother Arthur died from what is thought to have been meningitis or tuberculosis. Nixon resolved at that point, Hannah said, "to help make up for our loss by making us very proud of him." Two years later, Harold, Nixon's oldest brother, also contracted tuberculosis, and Hannah devoted the next five years to ministering to him (much of the time in Arizona) until he died. Fair-haired, jaunty, and easygoing, Harold had already seemed to Richard to be his parents' favorite, and the time Hannah lavished on her dying first-born, Nixon's psychobiographers concurred, exacerbated his feelings of neglect and resentment.[34]

The deaths of his brothers, along with his own mortal scares, warped Nixon's development, according to his psychobiographers. Besides resenting Harold's favored status, Nixon also felt guilty that he survived his brothers. That he then attended law school with the money earmarked for Harold's recovery reinforced a sense of "survivor guilt." These traumas also imbued in Nixon, his psychobiographers maintained, a sense that the world was dangerous. To gird himself against omnipresent threats, he developed an acute vigilance, a need to ward off enemies, a seedling of his later paranoia. "He would be able to grow," wrote Barber, "but there would always be that expectation of trouble ahead."[35]

The litany of Nixon's boyhood troubles suggested the roots of his sexual inhibitions. "It is hard to imagine," Rogin and Lottier wrote, "a set of circumstances more calculated to arouse a boy's anxiety over competition for the mother and to inhibit his capacity to experience genuine love and aggression." According to one anecdote, when Nixon washed dishes for his mother as a boy he closed the blinds to keep the neighbors from seeing him doing "women's work." Concerned with affirming his masculinity, he denigrated all things feminine. Childhood acquaintances remembered him proclaiming that he disliked girls and debating the topic "Resolved: Girls Are No Good." In adolescence, he showed no romantic side. Before marrying Pat, he had had only one girlfriend, and in Pat he found a reserved woman who demanded none of the shows of affection that made him self-conscious. Nixon rarely displayed any physical warmth toward her publicly, and, according to *The Final Days*, they had a sexless marriage for decades. Nixon's sexual inhibitions spilled out into other areas of his life as well, the psychobiographers noted. "The repression of his sexual desires," wrote Abrahamsen, "made him unknowing of himself to the point where he became secretive." His famous social awkwardness and his penchant for concealment were the result.[36]

Collectively, Nixon's psychobiographers sketched a portrait of his boyhood and character that, while dubious to those who rejected psychoanalysis altogether, did shed light on his behavior. If they overreached on individual points of interpretation, the project of exploring how his parents and traumas had shaped him was surely defensible and, indeed, often successful in reconciling Nixon's many paradoxes: the awkwardness alongside the ambition, the secrecy joined to the grandiosity, the anger mixed with the need to be liked. When the psychobiographers turned to analyzing Nixon's behavior as president, however, they were no longer relying on the neutral data of his early biography. Instead, they filtered his public actions through their own political judgments, which muddied their ostensibly non-ideological psychoanalytic readings. And while sometimes—as in explaining Watergate and Nixon's secret White House tapes—psychoanalytic theory could still offer valid and valuable answers, the supposedly dispassionate psychological readings could on other occasions seem hasty, glib, and crudely predicated on a political viewpoint that was simply different from Nixon's own.

Nixon's psychobiographers wasted little time in interpreting his presidency as an expression of his long-festering characterological traits. When Nixon pardoned Lieutenant William Calley for the My Lai Massacre, they saw an identification with the aggressor. When he lashed out at opponents of his Supreme Court nominees, they saw a response to humiliation. When he invaded Cambodia, they saw a need to replenish his self-esteem. As Nixon's controversial presidency rolled along, psychobiographers painted a picture not just of a neurotic but of a man unable to control his debilitating compulsions. By the time of the 1972 election, they were warning that

Nixon's unstable personality would produce a catastrophe in his second term. The apparent fulfillment of these predictions with Watergate only confirmed for psychobiographers the validity of their pursuits.

One of the first indications of Nixon's neuroses, his psychobiographers said, could be seen in his reaction to the trial of Lieutenant Calley, whose leadership of a 1968 massacre of Vietnamese civilians in the hamlet of My Lai had come to light in November 1969. When Calley was sentenced to life imprisonment in March 1971 by a U.S. Army tribunal, Nixon sided with many outraged Americans who felt the lieutenant was being scapegoated. The president ordered Calley to be released as he personally reviewed the case. Most liberals viewed the decision as a classic case of Nixonian opportunism: Calley enjoyed favor in the South, where Nixon was cultivating support. Psychobiographers Michael Rogin and John Lottier, however, saw unconscious motives at play. By intervening on Calley's behalf, they wrote, Nixon betrayed an "identification with a man who kills while experiencing himself as trapped." David Abrahamsen noted that Nixon repeatedly referred to Calley as if he were innocent. "By denying the killer's guilt," Abrahamsen wrote, "he seemed to deny his own criminal acts in Vietnam." In fact, the case of Calley was a difficult one, since the army officials who had covered up the massacre were spared punishment, and calling the lieutenant a scapegoat was a plausible stance. But Rogin and Lottier and Abrahamsen hardly viewed Nixon neutrally; they considered him a killer and a criminal—politically rooted judgments that influenced their psychoanalytic readings.[37]

Similarly, psychobiographers were quick to see Nixon's unconscious at work in the battles over two nominees to the Supreme Court, Southerners Clement Haynsworth and G. Harrold Carswell. After the Senate rejected Haynsworth in November 1969, Nixon refused to choose a more moderate candidate. "Like his unyielding father," psychiatrist Eli Chesen wrote in *President Nixon's Psychiatric Profile* (1973), "Nixon refused to give in to the face of reality." The stubbornness backfired when his second choice, Carswell, was defeated the following spring. On April 9, 1970, Nixon angrily accused the opposing senators of "character assassination." Commentators who viewed the actions through a traditional political lens saw the nominations as another effort to curry favor with the South and the outburst as an attempt to discredit the opposition. But psychobiographers focused again on hidden motives. The release of "pent-up emotions" at the press conference, Blema Steinberg wrote, revealed a "displacement of his own bitterness about the Senate's public act of defiance of his wishes and his corresponding humiliation." Nixon was not acting rationally, they agreed, but following his uncontrollable urges.[38]

Nixon's decision to invade Cambodia was also chalked up to unconscious motives. Many observers considered Cambodia, a neutral nation in the war, to be peripheral to the conflict, despite the existence there of sanctuaries for North Vietnamese soldiers. But Nixon, impelled by his grandiosity and enraged by North Vietnamese defiance, inflated the importance of the sanctuaries beyond reason. Steeling himself by watching his favorite movie, *Patton* (identifying with the protagonist who, like himself, defied those who humiliated him), Nixon overrode his advisers' counsel and delivered an overwrought speech announcing the invasion, determined to show that he was not a pushover. In declaring that the United States would not act like "a pitiful, helpless giant," Nixon revealed his own fears of being "powerless and humiliated—the opposite of his idealized grandiose self."[39]

With such speculative, even insupportable claims, the first batch of Nixon psychobiographies that appeared around 1972 were ripe targets for all manner of Nixon-watchers, and subsequent Nixon psychobiographies would meet the same unhappy fate. Liberals and conservatives, reporters, radicals, and loyalists—all attacked the psychobiographies for their leaps of inference, their disregard of non-psychological factors, their quick recourse to Freudian categories.* After David Abrahamsen wrote that Nixon's "fascination with potato-mashing apparently allowed this tense and moody child to express his unconscious anger," Richard Rovere quipped: "It makes one wonder what kind of unconscious anger Abraham Lincoln was working off when he was putting the axe to all those trees in Illinois. Was the rail-splitter getting ready to split the Union?" Examples of overreaching were easy to find and easier to mock.[40]

* The mainstream of the historical profession has remained resistant to psychohistory as well. Among Nixon biographers, historians as varied in their views of Nixon as Stephen Ambrose, Roger Morris, and Herbert Parmet have all been critical of the psychobiographies.

A more significant criticism was the argument that the biographers' politics distorted their judgments. Most of the writers, if not all, opposed Nixon politically. (James David Barber was among the Duke University faculty members who later stopped the university from housing Nixon's papers, and Fawn Brodie was writing op-ed pieces critical of Nixon in the *Los Angeles Times* as early as 1972.) Some reviewers argued that the psychobiographers' political biases undermined their efforts. Criticizing Barber, a fellow political scientist wrote, "Scratch Barber, and you will find a liberal Democratic partisan. Nixon is relegated to active-negative [one of Barber's four personality types] primarily because he was stubborn over Carswell and Cambodia." Nixon speechwriter Ray Price denigrated the work of David Abrahamsen because, he said, the psychiatrist "deemed 'irrational' anything that he happened to disagree with politically."[41]

Yet these criticisms, while valid, did not undermine all psychohistory, as some of its opponents liked to think. The reflexive detractors of psychohistory often simply refused to reckon with those instances—as in interpreting Nixon's night visit to the Lincoln Memorial—where psychoanalytic explanations made sense of what traditional political frameworks could not. The objections usually resulted from an unfamiliarity or uneasiness with psychoanalytic concepts. When Bob Haldeman dismissed all of the Nixon psychobiographies as "100 percent baloney," he clearly hadn't considered their relative merits at all. Equally close-minded was Gore Vidal, who wrote, "Do not inflict this Freudian horseshit on Nixon—*my* Nixon." The notoriously eccentric Vidal was himself surely a prime candidate for psychoanalytic investigation, but he apparently couldn't tolerate the notion that he might not always understand his own unconscious, let alone someone else's. Ignorant dismissals like his and Haldeman's did psychoanalysis the injustice of ignoring its genuine contributions.[42]

Watergate showed that psychoanalysis still had much to offer in the quest to understand Nixon. Suddenly, those psychobiographers who had warned of the president's unstable personality appeared prescient. During the 1972 elections, James Barber had expressed fear of "the possibility that Nixon . . . will become emotionally exhausted by compromise and criticism, fasten onto some cause, justify it in the name of principle, and use it to effect his personal salvation, whatever the social consequences."

As a second-term president, Barber predicted, Nixon would no longer need moderate support and might "transform a passing crisis into a permanent disaster." Similarly, journalist Arthur Woodstone argued that midway through Nixon's term it had become clear that "many of the president's assaults on his opponents . . . no longer seemed reasoned or pragmatic." A few reporters, Woodstone noted, had "stopped nodding incessantly at Machiavelli and began talking more in public of Freud." Woodstone elaborated the idea that many of Nixon's public actions stemmed from a need to punish enemies on whom he had projected his "early guilt." His book, *Nixon's Head*, published in May 1972, ended by warning that whatever Richard Milhous Nixon did next, "it would ultimately prove dangerous."[43]

The psychobiographers could also claim vindication on the matter of the White House tapes. In July 1973, former White House aide Alexander Butterfield revealed to Senate investigators something only a handful of people knew: that Nixon had been recording his White House conversations. Because some of those tapes would incriminate Nixon in the Watergate cover-up, the subpoenas for the tapes set off a year-long struggle. When Nixon finally released transcripts in April 1974, his remaining support crumbled. The tapes implicated Nixon in crimes, but, equally important, they gave many Americans their first look at what was taken to be the "real" Nixon. Here was Nixon speaking without his customary image-making pretenses, and the foul language, mean-spiritedness, and cold calculation shocked even his defenders. The tapes, the conservative *Chicago Tribune* editorialized, "stripped the man to his essential character, and that character could not stand that kind of scrubbing."[44]

Besides harming Nixon politically, the tapes also ratified a psychological reading. They confirmed that behind his public face lurked a congeries of primordial hates and fears. Why Nixon had recorded the tapes and why he refused to destroy them became the burning questions. Rationally speaking, those decisions made little sense. But it was in explaining irrational actions that psychoanalysis had the most to offer.

For the psychobiographers, the tapes symbolized Nixon's self-destructive tendencies. Nixon claimed he made the tapes to create a record for history. His psychobiographers accepted this explanation, but noted that, far from exculpatory, it was damning; grandiosely, he wanted to dictate how future generations would view him. Like the wiretapping of suspected enemies, the taping also showed Nixon's vigilance and paranoia, a determination not to let anyone else get the slightest edge. Besides, Nixon's explanation about making a record for history did not address the key questions. If he knew he was recording himself, why did he speak as he did with the machines rolling? Why did he preserve the recordings and release them despite knowing their incriminating contents? Here psychobiographers offered the idea that Nixon's unconscious guilt was manifesting itself. Len Garment, partaking himself in a bit of psychoanalysis, once said, metaphorically, that Nixon wanted everyone to see him going to the toilet; as Fawn Brodie elaborated, the president wanted "to exhibit his own nakedness, his ineffable dirtiness." Torn between entitlement and guilt, Nixon capitulated to his guilt, they surmised, and unconsciously sabotaged himself. When Nixon told David Frost in 1977, "I gave them a sword, and they stuck it [in], and they twisted it with relish," he was admitting to his own part in arranging his downfall.[45]

"At some point in the hot, muggy summer of 1973," Nixon recalled in his memoirs, "some of the more influential members of the Washington press corps concluded that I was starting to go off my rocker." During that summer, the disclosures of the Ervin Committee—the Enemies Lists, the tapes, details of the cover-up—were clearly taking a toll on the president. As Nixon entered what would be his final year in office, psychological interpretations of his behavior abounded. But now the nuanced readings of his childhood experiences and deep-seated character traits gave way, in the public discourse, to black-and-white, broad-brush pictures. If the psychobiographers' sketches of Nixon were overly elaborate, these popularized psychoportraits were reductive, rendering the president as little more than a paranoid lunatic cracking under Watergate's strains.[46]

Speculation about Nixon's behavior mounted when he visited New

Orleans on August 20. For a while he had appeared to be depressed, fitful, and short-tempered, but even by Nixon's usual standards his behavior in New Orleans was bizarre. As he entered the convention hall where he was to speak, the president grabbed Ron Ziegler, spun him around, and gave him a vigorous shove. He then delivered his speech poorly, rambling without his characteristic tightness, slurring his words. CBS cameraman Cal Marlin had caught the Ziegler incident on tape, and the network played the footage that night, as Dan Rather intoned ominously, "What you are about to see is a rare glimpse in public of presidential irritation. . . . The president's aides deny he is nervous or testy or anything." The Ziegler incident, along with commentary about Nixon's poor delivery of his speech, set "the Washington rumor mill grinding," wrote Stewart Alsop in *Newsweek*, "that he was on the naked edge of a nervous breakdown." Two days later, at a press conference, Nixon again seemed out of joint. He attacked his Democratic predecessors with startling bluntness,* and his voice trembled as he responded incoherently to questions. Reporters began making insinuations in print about Nixon's state of mind. Press critic Edwin Diamond, decrying an outbreak of "psychojournalism," faulted the media for being "frustratingly elliptical in what it was willing to share with its audience" while nonetheless hinting that Nixon was cracking up. He quoted a doctor who read *Time* magazine's account of Nixon's rambling New Orleans speech. "They're describing the symptoms of schizophrenia," the doctor objected, "without saying so!"[47]

The reporters' language concealed more than it disclosed. Rumors circulated that Nixon was on heavy medication, under psychiatric care, having a breakdown, or recovering from a stroke. White House correspondents eyed Nixon with extra care, feeling both trepidation and a frisson of excitement, *The New Republic*'s John Osborne later wrote, at the thought that "he might go bats in front of them at any time." Hunter S. Thompson reported in *Rolling Stone* that journalists were taking bets, "running at odds between two and three to one, . . . that Nixon will crack both physically and mentally under this pressure, and develop a serious psychosomatic illness of

---

* As described in chapter 4.

some kind.""* The mainstream press, in contrast, refrained from airing rumors, although many tried hard to verify them. *The New York Times*'s John Herbers spent weeks looking for a man (other than Hutschnecker) alleged to be Nixon's psychiatrist, flashing pictures to the guards at Nixon's San Clemente residence as if he were a private eye. Still, he published nothing. However much they gossiped, the press corps—the sui generis Thompson and maybe a few others excepted—felt they couldn't broach the subject of Nixon's health openly.[48]

Yet throughout October 1973—Nixon's most trying month in office since May 1970—the insinuations mounted. As war raged in the Middle East, the United States ratcheted its defense alert to Defcon III, edging closer to combat. Spiro Agnew resigned in the face of prosecution for tax evasion. Nixon, under order to surrender the tapes to Archibald Cox, continued to demur. Then, on October 20, came the Saturday Night Massacre, when he effectively fired Attorney General Elliot Richardson, his deputy William Ruckelshaus, and Cox in order not to give up the tapes. While some Americans worried that Nixon was planning to install himself as dictator, others saw the actions as proof of a fraying psyche. Nixon, wrote Abrahamsen, was "so fearful and defensive and angry that he was capable of destroying anyone who threatened him." The image of Nixon as unhinged took hold among both public figures (labor leader George Meany said that the president showed "dangerous emotional instability") and the man-on-the-street (a Buffalo Republican told *Time* magazine that Nixon was "liable to burst and push the red button"). These comments

---

* Thompson also wrote that nobody among the president corps believed reports of Nixon's pneumonia in July 1973. "High-powered journalists like Jack Germond and Jules Witcover immediately seized the phones to find out what was *really* wrong with Nixon... but the rest of us, no longer locked into deadlines or the fast-ringing terrors of some tomorrow's election day, merely shrugged at the news and kept on drinking." In 1976, he revisited the topic: "It is probably a good thing, in retrospect, that only a very few people in this country understood the gravity of Richard Nixon's mental condition during his last year in the White House. There were moments in that year when even his closest friends and advisers were convinced that the president of the United States was so crazy with rage and booze and suicidal despair that he was only two martinis away from losing his grip entirely and suddenly locking himself in his office long enough to make that single telephone call that would have launched enough missiles and bombers to blow the whole world off its axis or at least kill 100 million people."

finally gave reporters an excuse to print rumors of the president's break-down. "When George Meany spoke aloud of the President's 'emotional instability,'" explained *The New Yorker's* Elizabeth Drew, "he was saying something that others felt they could not say. And he was someone whom it was legitimate for the press to quote."[49]

The discussion grew more explicit. At Nixon's tension-filled October 26 press conference, a reporter asked him to address "how you are bearing up emotionally under the stress of recent events." The president insisted he was fine, but his comments reassured no one. In late November, *Newsweek* reported elliptically that Nixon's July illness, said to have been pneumonia, "was more serious than White House bulletins indicated"; the next week *The New York Times* noted that "for some time, Mr. Nixon's health and morale . . . have been a topic at Washington social gatherings, in conversations on Capitol Hill, in the departments and even in a number of White House offices." The deepening scandal and the growing calls for Nixon's removal fueled the debate. "Suddenly everyone and his uncle is raising the question of Mr. Nixon's fitness—as a person—to be president," wrote James Barber in a November 8 *New York Times* op-ed piece, gloating now that his predictions were coming true. Nixon's habit of repressing his emotions, Barber wrote, had created the president's typical "facade of humorless propriety." Now, though, "the barriers have dropped away" and the resentments flooded forth. It all seemed quite neat: a man hun-gering for control and omniscience created the Plumbers to oversee infor-mation-gathering efforts; a man who personalized conflict launched vendettas; a vigilant, secretive man recorded his conversations for poster-ity. A view was forming, Eli Chesen wrote, that "Watergate was a process of natural evolution—inevitable" given Nixon's character.[50]

Those who saw the president up close worried about his condition. At a White House dinner in December, Barry Goldwater was taken aback to hear Nixon talking "erratically." He sounded, Goldwater wrote (using a timely metaphor), "as if he were a tape with unexpected blank sections. . . . His mind seemed to halt abruptly and wander aimlessly away. . . . Nixon appeared to be cracking." Throughout the winter and spring, White House officials—Chief of Naval Operations Admiral Elmo Zumwalt, Defense Secretary James Schlesinger, Attorney General William Saxbe,

Vice President Ford—formed similar impressions. By the waning months
of the administration, Nixon's aides were panicking. In June and July
1974, the president ignored the advice of his doctor, Walter Tkach, not to
travel abroad because of his phlebitis, leading Tkach to conclude that
Nixon had a "death wish."[51]

Nixon left for an extended Middle East tour on June 9, to Tkach's dismay. Psychobiographers considered the phlebitis a form of self-punishment
that excused Nixon from consciously admitting his wrongdoing. "To his
ego, to his perception," wrote Abrahamsen, "it was an honorable illness."
Dubious though the proposition sounded to some, it was not far-fetched
to suggest that psychological factors contributed to the severity of
Nixon's phlebitis. Depression can alter the body's manufacture of hor-
mones, which affects the blood's ability to coagulate. As Len Garment put
it: "Someone who's in a calamitous state of anxiety, fear, rage, the death
throes of the presidency, is not going to have a vascular injury exacerbated
by it all?"[52]

Back in the United States in July after his trips to the Mideast and the
Soviet Union, Nixon entered a downward spiral, according to aides and
family members. The president's son-in-law, Ed Cox, saw Nixon talking to
the portraits on the White House walls and worried that he might take his
own life. Chief of Staff Al Haig developed similar fears after Nixon said to
him that military men had a way of handling crises like his, with someone
leaving a pistol in a drawer; Haig ordered the president's doctors to take
away his sleeping pills. Henry Kissinger, who entertained the thought that
Nixon might start a nuclear war, found himself kneeling in prayer with
the president while a "distraught" Nixon "bared his soul" over whether to
resign.[53]

On August 8, 1974, Nixon announced his decision to do so, and the
next day he gathered his aides in the East Room. His address would
become an emblem of authenticity to Nixon's loyalists, who saw the president at his best, and of arrant phoniness to liberals, who considered the
whole thing to have been another staged event. But to psychobiographers
it was a rare glimpse of Nixon's inner turmoil. In a free-associative ramble,
the president poured forth a stream of childhood memories and raw emotion as the television cameras rolled. Words tumbled out without his cus-

tomary planning. "This country needs good farmers, good businessmen, good plumbers . . . , " Nixon said, in another exquisite Freudian slip. He spoke, as he rarely did in public, of his father and his various hard-luck jobs, of his mother (as always, "a saint"), of the deaths of his brothers. Tears came to his eyes, sweat to his brow. Many viewers, Garment and David Eisenhower among them, thought he was unraveling live on national television. Catching himself, Nixon returned to his familiar mode of speechifying, before concluding: "Always remember," he said, "others may hate you, but those who hate you don't win unless you hate them, and then you destroy yourself." Unconsciously (or was it consciously?) Nixon seemed to be analyzing himself, admitting that his resentments had brought about his demise.[54]

The psychobiographers had another field day. They heard in the speech echoes of Nixon's shame over his father's failures and the idealization of his pious mother; they noted the projection of hatreds onto others. Non-professionals, too, reached for psychoanalytic language to describe the scene. "It was as if having kept himself in check all these years he had to put on display all the demons and dreams that had driven him to this point," wrote Kissinger. "He even wore glasses in public for the first time, symbolically forswearing the vanity and image-making of his career. . . . I was at the same time moved to tears and outraged at being put through the wringer again, so that even in his last public act Nixon managed to project his ambivalence onto those around him."[55]

Nixon's resignation did not halt talk about his mental health. Worsening phlebitis and the ordeal of his ouster left him depressed and, according to some reports, near suicidal. When Nixon gave his first post-resignation interviews in 1977, he confessed that although he never seriously considered suicide, he had felt that his life "nearly lost meaning." But in the fall of 1974, Ron Ziegler, still Nixon's loyal spokesman, denied that the deposed president was "having any psychiatric problems. . . . He feels like somebody would feel after going through a great and severe loss and after going through the uncertainty of the last 45 days." Ziegler's denials, alas, could not stanch the flood of conjecture.[56]

In 1975, a series of books appeared that dealt with Nixon's mental distress. In April, John Osborne published in *New York* magazine a preview of his forthcoming omnibus of White House columns. The lurid headline, WAS NIXON "SICK OF MIND"?, was splashed across the cover. Osborne quoted from Senate testimony by Alexander Butterfield, who said the president had behaved in "abnormal" ways. The aide reported that Nixon would obsess over details from the menus and music programs at state dinners to what gifts to give White House visitors or congressional leaders, even to "whether or not the curtains were closed or open." Osborne concluded that Nixon must have been "sick of mind" and was probably "suffering from some mental defect that preceded the Watergate affair by many years."[57]

Also that spring, Theodore H. White published *Breach of Faith*, which described Nixon as "an unstable personality," whose presidency might be assessed by future historians as "a study in psychiatric imbalance." White's publicists trumpeted the book's revelations of how Nixon "became unstable as the great forces of history bore down on his character flaws." Readers nodded. "The Nixon phenomenon is more easily explained in psychological rather than bare political terms," White's friend Julius Leetham wrote. Nixon's former speechwriter William Safire added to the speculation with his memoir, *Before the Fall*, in which he described the Lincoln Memorial excursion as "the strangest, most impulsive and perhaps most revealing night of Nixon's presidency." Reports surfaced too that Bob Woodward and Carl Bernstein were at work on their second book, on Nixon's last days in the White House, which would show the president cracking under the pressure of the crisis—as *The Final Days* did when it was published the following year.[58]

Commenting on this spate of books in May 1975, *New York Times* columnist James Reston wrote that Nixon's tenure raised the urgent question: "How is the nation to be protected from irrational presidents?" He proposed that "we need to look more carefully at presidential candidates before their 'Breach of Faith' and 'Before the Fall.' The flaws in Mr. Nixon's character were actually clear as far back as his original campaigns . . . but they were not examined." Reston worried that the political system lacked safeguards to protect the nation from a president who might bring on an even worse disaster.

Psychobiographers also addressed the question. "Is Nixon 'Dangerous'?" Eli Chesen asked. "Was Nixon as president capable of rationally discharging his responsibilities?" David Abrahamsen wondered. Abrahamsen refused to judge whether Nixon had had a breakdown, but he stated confidently that "Nixon was a deeply disturbed person whose prevailing symptoms intensified under the overwhelming pressure of his last two years in office." Chesen, writing in 1973, said that Nixon, although "overly stable, if not rigid, most of the time," was prone to outbursts, as in New Orleans; in such instances, "Nixon at least temporarily went beyond the limits of behavior that we label with the admittedly difficult-to-define word 'normal.'"[59]

These assessments by Reston and the others were relatively circumspect. Nevertheless, William Safire reacted angrily when he read his *Times* colleague's column. Writing the day after Reston, Safire derided attempts at "long-distance, amateur psychoanalysis" and insisted that the president was "a man harassed, tortured and torn, but of sound mind coming to a rational decision to resign." There existed no conclusive evidence that Nixon had suffered a breakdown (which is, in any event, a vague term without a specific diagnostic meaning). Still, Safire knew why the media's renderings of Nixon had taken a psychoanalytic turn. "There is a delicious inconsistency in the Nixon story: How could an intelligent man, a canny politician, blunder so egregiously in covering up a foolish crime—unless he had lost his marbles?" he wrote. "The historian who figures this out might earn a niche in history himself."[60]

Safire had identified a key question about Watergate, one that was more legitimate (and interesting) than the whispers about whether Nixon had gone crazy. Regardless of whether Nixon was "normal," something within his character had contributed to the behavior for which he was impeached. Nixon later admitted, to David Frost, that a self-destructive impulse had been at work; but that confession merely rephrased the question of why, when he was cruising toward reelection, he had felt the need to resort to criminal acts to ensure victory.

Again, psychobiographers were happy to provide answers where others could not. Nixon's Watergate activities were designed, they maintained, to exact revenge on enemies, real and imagined, onto whom Nixon projected his own hostile feelings. A rational observer might consider Nixon's dirty tricks and the cover-up to have been unnecessary, but the need for control generated by his gnawing insecurity prevented him from leaving anything to chance. "The Watergate saga," wrote Barber, ". . . took its shape from Nixon's old sense that nothing would be right unless he controlled the way of it." Lacking either external constraints on his power or the internal restraints of conscience, Nixon could not step back from the precipice. His famous explanation of his conduct—"When the president does it, that means it's not illegal"—revealed his sense of entitlement.[61]

An alternate theory was offered by the psychohistorian Peter Loewenberg, among others. Freud had observed that certain people suffered self-hatred for succeeding where others had failed, like those who experienced guilt after a sibling or loved one died. These individuals, "wrecked by success," as Freud put it, often inflicted misfortune upon themselves just at the moment they attained their goals. Loewenberg suggested that Nixon, who experienced the "survivor guilt" of outliving two of his brothers, "unconsciously needed to fail, in order to appease his guilt."[62]

Whatever the merits of the more complicated theories of Nixon's self-destruction, few would deny by the time of his resignation that his distinctive neuroses had harmed the country. The notion of Nixon as a madman, narcissist, or dangerous neurotic lived on in the political culture. After Nixon, Americans scrutinized the emotional fitness of all their potential leaders, at times ransacking their private lives in search of Nixonian demons. It became common to argue, as did for example Victor Navasky of *The Nation*, that Watergate established "some link between the private and public person." "Nixon made his way to the top in a particularly ruthless way," Navasky said, speaking for many, a quarter century after Nixon resigned. ". . . That had to do with questions of character in a very deep and profound way that eventually expressed themselves in his conduct of public affairs."[63]

The popularity of the notion that mental health influenced presidential performance could be seen as early as October 1973, when Gerald Ford came up for confirmation as vice president before the Senate. Ford's con-

firmation was relatively smooth sailing, but one of the main questions that
drew concern was whether the House Majority Leader had ever received
psychological treatment. A rumor was afloat that Ford had been a patient
of none other than Arnold Hutschnecker, and the House Judiciary Committee convened hearings to investigate that and other issues about Ford's
fitness for office. The committee called Hutschnecker to testify, and he
denied the rumor, as did Ford. The controversy was relegated to the newspapers' back pages by more pressing Watergate news, but not before a
New York Times reporter concluded that "consulting a psychiatrist or psychotherapist is still an unforgivable sin for an American politician."[64]

The debate about how to guard against unfit leaders continued.
Hutschnecker, never publicity shy, wrote an op-ed piece in *The New York
Times*, his second in five months, in which he bemoaned the stigma that
was still associated with seeking psychotherapy. Previously, Hutschnecker had urged the creation of an official "board of physicians and psychiatrists to make sure that [presidential candidates] are healthy in mind
and body"; now, in the wake of the Ford flap, he suggested that presidents
should receive ongoing psychiatric care. "I cannot help think[ing]," he
wrote, "that if an American president had a staff psychiatrist, perhaps a
case such as Watergate might not have had a chance to develop." The message, if stated obliquely, was clear: Nixon's untreated psychological debilities had led to Watergate. Many agreed. "There is little question that the
president's personality dynamics set the stage for the Watergate dynamics," Eli Chesen wrote. ". . . If the results of [a psychiatric] examination had
been made available to voters, Nixon could not have abused his presidential grandiosity as he did."[65]

Although Hutschnecker's Big Brother-ish (and impractical) idea of a
screening board met with fierce opposition, even some of those who
denounced it agreed that the experience of Nixon showed that the president's psychological makeup was of legitimate concern. Because of the
growth of the imperial presidency, Arthur Schlesinger wrote, "in recent
years we Americans have lived more than ever before at the mercy of presidential caprice and compulsion." Noting Johnson's neuroses as well as
Nixon's, he continued: "Whether it is disagreeable coincidence or
masochistic gratification, we have thereupon in quick succession elected

the two most capricious and compulsive presidents we have ever had." The playwright Arthur Miller, though a self-described "non-subscriber" to psychohistory, nonetheless agreed that "Richard Nixon's character is our history."[66]

It fell to Americans, especially the press, to police the newly fashionable issue of presidential "character." Candidates' personal traits had always mattered to voters, but after Nixon the collective focus on character intensified. The term itself previously referred to a vast range of attributes desirable in a leader: courage, generosity, honesty, decency. Now the word, as it got thrown about, took on a meaning that was at once both more narrow (in that it focused on the skeletons in one's closet) and more broad (in that it failed to distinguish between trivial and potentially dangerous shortcomings). The suspicion that any politician might be hiding Nixonian demons, whatever they might be, led journalists to scour the past behavior, private lives, and psyches of candidates for high office in search of warning signs. From Jimmy Carter's successful 1976 presidential bid onward, the character issue would dominate campaigns, as new and sometimes random elements of one's private life—past drug use, marital infidelity, military service—drew intense scrutiny with each election.

The post-Watergate policing of character was rooted in a wish to believe that disasters like Watergate couldn't arise under any presidency but grew out of the faulty character or warped mind of an individual. This was the same impulse that had made psychoanalytic readings of Nixon so popular and persuasive: Nixon was different from us, they implied, and his ouster had purged the system. As Fawn Brodie noted, those who craved a "psychiatric look" at Nixon really wanted "a brief answer, in a paragraph, something to reassure them of how separate they are from him . . . if we could just pin a psychiatric label on him—paranoid, sociopath— then we could dissociate ourselves from him . . . confident in our own integrity . . . [and] forget that we voted for him two-to-one in 1972. Those who voted for him would then be absolved, saying, 'He was mentally ill but we did not know it.'"[67]

Brodie herself resolved to avoid these balms by offering a more complex picture of Nixon's mental life. Yet her own judgments, and those of most of Nixon's psychobiographers, were sufficiently harsh toward the president to encourage the conclusion that Nixon was abnormal or deviant. It was impossible to find a psychobiography of Nixon that treated him as a relatively normal or healthy subject. Moreover, even if Nixon's neuroses did warrant special attention, the psychobiographers still neglected, as Peter Loewenberg noted, "Nixon's many ego strengths and adaptations in a long political career." They focused so unremittingly on his lying, his narcissism, his rage, and other shortcomings that they didn't adequately explain how he had risen as high as he did.[68]

Because so many of Nixon's psychobiographers disliked him, politically and personally, they often failed to appreciate their own lack of distance from him. The psychohistorical project was supposed to provide answers for a post-ideological age, to move beyond crude partisan interpretations. But Nixon's psychoanalysts were themselves captive to unrecognized assumptions and as a result their works often shaded into overdrawn studies in pathology. The journalist Godfrey Hodgson, in reviewing Fawn Brodie's Nixon biography, underscored the problems that books like hers posed for the viability of psychohistory. Was it even possible, he wondered, for psychobiographers, however adept, to overcome their own antipathies and analyze a controversial politician like Nixon as they would a private patient? "We are in danger of having the insights of psychotherapy," Hodgson wrote, "used as a tool for character destruction, certainly for libel, potentially for revenge."[69]

Not every psychobiographer succumbed to the impulse to separate Nixon from those who elected him. Leo Rangell, a former president of the International Psychoanalytic Congress and the author of *The Mind of Watergate* (1980), wrote that in the 1970s Americans were grappling with "compromises of integrity" in their own everyday lives. These concerns, he suggested, helped explain their fascination with Watergate. "While breakdowns at the top . . . receive the most dramatic attention, similar pressures weigh on every individual," he wrote. Modern American culture placed a premium on success, and people were struggling to reconcile their ambition and need for approval with their consciences. Nixon's case was much more extreme than most people's, Rangell suggested, but it resonated. Similarly, Kent State political scientist Steven R. Brown suggested that Americans were drawn to Nixon because of the obvious gulf between his public and private selves. In a culture that vaunted the elusive quality of authenticity, of being true to oneself, Nixon's ready assumption of public guises reminded people of their own daily deceptions and playing of roles; it made them suspect, he wrote, that "There is a 'Tricky Dick' within all of us, so to speak." In these explanations, it was not Nixon's difference but his similarity, at some level, to all conflicted Americans that was the most valuable lesson of the explorations of his psyche.[70]

Yet the psychological portrait of Nixon that survived was not as an exemplar of American neuroses but as an anomaly. Historian Jeffrey Kimball wrote about Nixon's Vietnam policy by treating the president metaphorically as a "madman." Len Garment, even as he defended his old patron, wrote of Nixon as "filled with a virtuoso collection of wounds and angers accumulated during childhood wars, political wars . . . and wars of survival." A Stanford University abnormal psychology class used Nixon's rambling 1962 "last press conference," in which he told reporters they would no longer have him to kick around, as course material. When the journalist Anthony Summers published his sensationalist biography, *The Arrogance of Power: The Secret World of Richard Nixon*, in 2000, early headlines focused on Summers's revelations about Nixon's relationship with Arnold Hutschnecker.* And when a batch of Oval Office tapes was released in 2002, the first news reports focused on a conversation in which Nixon talked maniacally of dropping a nuclear bomb on Vietnam. Whatever they thought of psychohistory, observers agreed that Nixon's character shaped his times.[71]

In popular culture, the image of Nixon as a madman could be seen, among other places, in Robert Altman's film *Secret Honor* (1984), which had been adapted from a stage play. Philip Baker Hall portrayed Nixon as possessed by childhood demons and long-standing resentments. Hall's

---

* Other press reports about the book focused on its claims that Nixon beat his wife and that, without a prescription, he took the drug Dilantin, which is intended for epileptics. Neither claim had any convincing evidence to support it. But Summers did interview Hutschnecker and revealed information about the doctor's relationship with Nixon—including that Nixon saw him during the 1952 fund crisis and stood with him at Pat's funeral.

Nixon spends an evening with a tape recorder, divulging for future generations the "true" Watergate story as he downs tumblers of Chivas Regal,
but his free-associative monologue constantly takes him back to reflect on
the death of his brother Harold, his rivalry with Jack Kennedy, and other
staples from the Nixon psychobiographical literature. Although the film
was marred by a strain of absurd conspiracism in the plot that marked it
as a radical leftist reading as much as a psychoanalytic one, its virtue lay
in its plumbing of Nixon's character.* Part Hunter S. Thompson, part Sigmund Freud, the film was, as *New Yorker* critic Pauline Kael wrote, a work
of "gonzo psychodocudrama." Hall depicted Nixon unraveling over the
course of an evening, portraying his self-destruction, psychoanalytically,
as a symptom of his divided self, the war between his ambition and his
guilt.[72]

In a similar vein, Mark Maxwell's novel *NixonCarver* (1998) ingen-
iously presents Nixon's life story as if recounted by the minimalist short
story writer Raymond Carver. Like Freud, Carver invested small, everyday acts and moments with meaning and portent; and Maxwell's mimicry
of Carver similarly makes use of the richly Freudian anecdotes about
Nixon's childhood, from the "Your good dog, Richard" letter to his closing
of the kitchen blinds when he washed dishes to the pleasure he took in
mashing potatoes. "I have a theory that when a boy needs love and can't
find it in his own immediate family," said one of Maxwell's Carverian nar-
rators, a (fictional) Whittier neighbor of the Nixons named Gordon, ". . . he
begins to look for it in other places. . . . Dick found the love he was looking for when he discovered the beautiful strength and responsiveness of
the Nixon family's farm equipment." Gordon goes on to recount a story of
how Hannah Nixon once discovered all her underwear to be missing, only
to have it returned the next day with hay and oil stains on it, suggesting
Nixon had used her underthings, while alone with the tractor, for auto-
erotic purposes.[73]

Neither *NixonCarver* nor *Secret Honor* was explicitly a work of psychohistory. Both avoided Freudian jargon, the recourse to diagnostic

---

* Turning the relatively benign "Committee of 100" from Nixon's 1946 campaign into a
  secret cabal of financial overlords, the movie posited that Nixon had deliberately brought
  about Watergate to free himself of their influence.

boxes, and the confident imputation of specific meanings to ambiguous episodes. Ironically, this was the strength of both works. As fiction, they enjoyed greater freedom to speculate about Nixon's mind than did his psychobiographers, who were constantly under fire for their wilder conjectures. They also bore no obligation to analyze explicitly, and thus they escaped the trap of reductive categories that never did justice to Nixon's complexity. Yet their psychoanalytic nature was clear.

The success of works like *NixonCarver* and *Secret Honor* suggested that although psychohistory was moribund as a genre by the 1980s and 1990s, its failure lay partly in its victory. Self-professed works of psychoanalytic biography were no longer the rage in academia—only one new Nixon psychobiography appeared in the 1990s—and Freud had continued to fall in the estimation of many academics. But the tacit influence of psychobiography, warts and all, was everywhere. Nixon, who had long derided psychoanalysis, helped, as a subject for its practitioners, to prove its worth.

7

The Foreign Policy Establishment: Nixon as Statesman

> He had lived a constructive life in his years out of the White House; he had written all these books; he tried to be a force in world affairs.
>
> —*Bill Clinton*[1]

"He went to China." Clare Boothe Luce predicted that this single sentence would someday mark Nixon's place in the history books. If the books written about him in his lifetime were any indication, she was mistaken. Even after two decades of working hard to rehabilitate himself, Nixon never elevated his foreign policy above Watergate in the assessments of his legacy. But Nixon's move to restore diplomatic relations with Communist China—and his international achievements more generally—did win recognition as a major if decidedly secondary hallmark of his presidency, among not only his devoted apologists but, more important, a crowd of Cold War–era commentators and policy hands for whom international affairs held a special mystique.[2]

As president, Nixon hoped to make his mark as a peacemaker who ended the Vietnam War and relaxed Cold War tensions, especially through his China initiative and the improved relations with the Soviet Union known as *détente*. With the equally ambitious Henry Kissinger as his national security adviser (and, after August 1973, also secretary of state), Nixon tried to build a lasting legacy in international affairs. Even after it became clear that Watergate would inevitably overshadow his diplomacy, he devoted his post-resignation career to building upon his reputation for foreign policy know-how. In a raft of books, speeches, dinners, op-ed pieces, and conversations with foreign policy hands, Nixon styled himself "an *homme sérieux*," as speechwriter Ray Price asserted, "a man of large vision who knows the world and whose views carry weight."[3]

This New Nixon—the statesman—never displaced Tricky Dick. When in 1990 Nixon published *In the Arena*, his third memoir, he groused that readers dwelled on the material about Watergate. "None of the other stuff in there, like on the Russians or the other personal stuff, made it into the news or even the reviews," he sighed to his assistant Monica Crowley. "Watergate—that's all anyone wants." His ideas themselves had minuscule impact; when Nixon's pronouncements attracted interest, it had little to do with the pronouncements and everything to do with Nixon. Still, praise for his leadership as president accrued. His aides and loyalists, besides considering him a victim, tirelessly extolled his record in memoirs, articles, and interviews. In particular, those who had contributed to his foreign policy, such as Kissinger, touted Nixon's performance as historic. Reflecting a common assessment of the 1970s and 1980s, the dean of diplomatic historians John Lewis Gaddis concluded that few nations ever "executed a more impressive or more rapid shift from defeat to dominance" than America did under Nixon. The public also rated him highly on world affairs, as polls continually showed. Nixon's late career profile, too, won recognition, as magazine articles ("The Sage of Saddle River" in *Newsweek*) and books (*Nixon's Ten Commandments of Statecraft*) celebrated him as an *éminence grise*. If never dominant, this new image won a place in the lengthening procession of Nixon's public identities.[4]

Nixon's wise man reputation won favor not only among his loyalists but also among an elite coterie of writers and officials sometimes called the foreign policy establishment. Many members of this coterie disliked Nixon and appreciated Watergate's gravity, yet they considered international affairs the ultimate measure of a president's performance; consequently, they tried to prevent Watergate from eclipsing his diplomatic accomplishments altogether. Journalists such as James Reston, Hugh Sidey, Theodore White, and Joseph and Stewart Alsop, younger counterparts such as Strobe Talbott, and a host of Washington foreign policy functionaries in and out of government spent their careers believing that geopolitics came first, and this assumption shaped their views of Nixon. "We didn't like the way Nixon looked; we didn't like the way he acted; we didn't like the way he talked," said Sidey, a longtime *Time* magazine writer. "But we couldn't deny his achievements in foreign policy." These foreign policy hands, as much as Nixon's apologists, succored the bid for redemption that he waged before his death.[5]

The story of Nixon's statesman image, no less than that of his early years, is also a story of image making. Of the many Nixons, the foreign policy sage is the face Nixon himself worked hardest to present to history. He believed that men attained greatness not through domestic governance but through leadership in world affairs. Like Winston Churchill, Charles de Gaulle, and Mao Zedong, about whom he loved to write and tell stories, Nixon aspired to be among the select few whose visions could alter the destiny of nations.

Nixon fancied himself a lonely visionary, tapped for leadership, endowed with uncommon skills to bring about peace. He styled himself the heavyweight who grappled with momentous issues of war and peace. "Foreign Policy = Strength," he wrote to himself in one of his many memos about his image. ". . . Must emphasize—Courage, Stands alone . . . Knows more than anyone else. Towers above advisers. World leader." As he told Theodore White in 1967, he thought America "could run itself domestically without a president. . . . All you need is a competent cabinet to run the country at home. . . . The president makes foreign policy." He was contemptuous of Congress, which he described in his memoirs as "cumbersome, undisciplined, isolationist, fiscally irresponsible, overly vulnerable to pressures from organized minorities, and too dominated by the media"— Lilliputians who would prevent him from realizing his grand designs. He made decisions alone. "You listen to everybody's argument, but then comes the moment of truth," he said in 1970. "I sit alone with my yellow pad," he explained, weighing competing arguments and summoning the judgment born of his experience.[6]

This grandiose conception contained an elitist strain at odds with Nixon's other self-portrait as an everyman. Nixon often talked of his common roots, but he aspired to transcend them. Garry Wills, who first observed the tension between Nixon's populist and elite personae, suggested that the reason Nixon admired Woodrow Wilson was that he identified with his predecessor as "a lonely misunderstood leader, . . . an introspective intellectual somewhat out of place in the glad-handing world of politics." Nixon once said that if he hadn't been a politician, he would have been an Oxford don. The comment made intellectuals chuckle, but it fit with this self-image. Nixon could imagine himself toiling in the solitude of scholarship, reading and writing tomes of history, philosophy, and world affairs. Indeed, in his post-resignation years of book writing and speechmaking, he lined his shelves with weighty works of philosophy and history, as awestruck visitors attested, although the books—Tolstoy's works, biographies of Napoleon and Churchill—were not the kind that intellectuals were reading in the 1980s or 1990s; they were tokens of an *image* of an intellectual, circa 1950.[7]

Nixon's self-image as a peacemaker and statesman may have had its roots in his childhood, when he idealized the values of his Quaker mother. From the start of his career, he showed an interest in international affairs. In his first year as a congressman he toured Europe, and the experience confirmed him as an internationalist who rejected the Republican Party's isolationist past. As vice president, he gained stature after debating Soviet leader Nikita Khrushchev at an exhibition of an American kitchen in Moscow. The performance helped him surmount his hatchet-man reputation and win confidence in his capacity for Cold War brinksmanship. He bolstered that image in 1958 when he stood up to crowds of anti-American protesters in Venezuela and Peru. In 1960, his international experience was the centerpiece of his presidential campaign.

Nixon's diplomat pose struck some observers as pure public relations. "Foremost among the roles that Nixon has consciously assumed is that of statesman-companion to the great," wrote Meg Greenfield in 1960. She mocked Nixon's "laundry-list approach" of rattling off the countries he visited and his clumsy name-dropping ("As Mr. Castro told me . . ."). Much of the public, however, accepted Nixon's self-portrait. Throughout his 1960s wilderness period, he traveled widely, and newspapers generously quoted his pronouncements on world affairs. The persona became part of the 1968 New Nixon, too: as a seasoned veteran, the candidate suggested, he would best be able to manage the Vietnam War and the coming international crises. To a large extent, Nixon delivered: until Watergate, foreign policy was the main focus of his presidency—apart, that is, from his concern with seeming like a statesman.[8]

Nixon's staff members agreed that his foreign policy would distinguish him in the history books—none more fervently than Kissinger. A German Jewish immigrant, former political science professor, and recent adviser to Nelson Rockefeller, Nixon's rival for the 1968 Republican nomination, Kissinger joined the Nixon administration in 1969 as national security adviser. The position had always been less important than that of secretary of state, but because Nixon meant to micromanage his own foreign policy, he generally bypassed his secretary of state, his longtime friend William Rogers, and entrusted Kissinger with his most sensitive tasks. Accordingly, Kissinger, who was as deft at cultivating the media as Nixon was inept, wound up reaping much credit for the administration's achievements; during Watergate, Kissinger wrote, "most critics seemed willing to spare me, even to protect me, from the mounting rancor, as if to preserve one public figure as a symbol of national continuity." But most historians of the Nixon administration agree that the president and not his aide was the driving force behind his most acclaimed initiatives.[9]

Kissinger agreed with that allocation of credit. In his memoirs and other writings, he consistently affirmed that the president devised and directed policy on China, Russia, and Vietnam (although when faced with Nixon foes who sought to "diminish his achievements by exalting my own," Kissinger conceded, ". . . there was no consistent record of my resisting" the claim). Behind this admiration, Kissinger's view of Nixon was complex. It was, he wrote, "compounded of aloofness and respect, of distrust and admiration." Like the president's critics, he believed that there was "no true Nixon" but rather that "several warring personalities struggled for prominence in the same individual." As a result, Kissinger explained, "None of us really knew the inner man. . . . Each member of his entourage was acquainted with a slightly different Nixon."[10]

That said, Kissinger described the Nixon he did come to know as alternately paranoid and visionary, disciplined and tawdry, courageous and devious, inspirational and calculating, and, in some sense, anti-Semitic. (For example, he wrote that Nixon believed Jews placed the interests of Israel above those of the United States and that "their control of the media made them dangerous adversaries.") But for all the rivalry and resentment Kissinger felt toward his superior, his bottom-line view was one of "a grudging respect and something akin to tender protectiveness toward him." Despite the insecurities, Kissinger admired Nixon as a visionary. The president, he wrote, "saw before him a vista of promise to which few statesmen have ever been blessed to aspire. He could envisage a new international order that would reduce lingering enmities, strengthen friendships, and give hope to emerging nations. It was a worthy goal for America and mankind."[11]

The chief exhibit in the case for Nixon's farsightedness—whether made by Kissinger, Nixon, or others—was his move to reopen ties with China. Those ties had been severed since Mao's Communists took power in 1949. As early as 1961, according to John Ehrlichman, Nixon concluded that a rapprochement with China would serve America's interest. In 1967, with the help of Ray Price, he wrote an article for *Foreign Affairs* entitled "Asia After Viet Nam" that argued for ending China's isolation from "the family of nations," lest it "nurture its fantasies . . . and threaten its neighbors." Nixon realized he could trade on his reputation as a Cold Warrior, and he saw a chance to exploit rifts between China and the USSR.[12]

Once in office, he reached out decisively. At first, the steps were small: referring to the "People's Republic of China" (a name previously shunned as an Orwellian euphemism) and easing travel and trade restrictions. Then, secretly, without telling even Secretary of State William Rogers, Nixon sent Kissinger to Beijing in July 1971 to begin negotiations. Days later the president dramatically announced the mission in a televised address from Burbank, California. The speech, recalled Helen Thomas, who covered it, "made the room rock." The nation was stunned and excited, and the press corps showered Nixon with praise.[13]

Belying his claims that the press was implacably hostile, Nixon almost always received accolades for his foreign policy, in his own time and afterward. His breakthroughs touched off an infectious giddiness among reporters, who were happy to find occasions to praise Nixon and prove their even-handedness. The reaction to his China announcement was typical. Labeling the venture "Nixon's Coup," *Time* endorsed Kissinger's claim that the administration was "turning a new page in history." Its account of Nixon's post-speech banquet lingered so adoringly over the filigree—the dinner at "Perino's, a fashionable Los Angeles restaurant," the "$40 bottle of Château Lafite Rothschild (1961)"—that one might have guessed the magazine's food critic had written the piece. *Newsweek*, only slightly less effusive, judged the move a "masterstroke."[14]

In February 1972, Nixon became the first American president to visit China. The trip burnished his statesman image to its highest gloss. Characteristically, he obsessed over the picture that he would project. Politics loomed large. The year before, Nixon and Haldeman had discussed the timing of a series of forthcoming initiatives. Haldeman noted that Nixon wanted to have "the Vietnam thing settled this summer, have a [U.S.-Soviet] Summit this fall, and wrap up the first SALT agreement; announce a China visit and have it in March or so of next year." They didn't hit their goals perfectly, but they were able to make Nixon's statesmanship the 1972 campaign's theme. For the China trip, Nixon pored over the details of the press coverage, handpicking the reporters who would accompany him. Enemies were excluded. The public relations focus didn't go unnoticed. One cartoonist drew a befuddled Nixon standing in a sea of reporters, cameras, and lights while his Chinese guide mused: "Just think, all this will have gone to waste if you're not reelected!" Yet awareness of the image making hardly diminished the excitement. For several nights running, network news broadcasts showcased a slate of cultural events, ceremonial banquets, and trips to the Great Wall and the Forbidden City. American viewers marveled. Reporters waited for hard news to seep out of the closed-door meetings. Never unafraid to nudge history's judgment,

Nixon declared it "the week that changed the world." His approval rating climbed seven points.[15]

Equally popular was Nixon's decision to work actively at improving U.S.-Soviet relations and halt the debilitating arms race. Summitry was not a departure from his predecessors' policies: the Kennedy administration had introduced the word *"détente"* into diplomatic parlance and signed a nuclear test-ban treaty, and Johnson's 1967 Glassboro summit had continued the process of nuclear arms control. The Soviet Union was sending signals that it was ready to talk further, and West Germany's moves to improve its own relations with Moscow made American intransigence unwise. Yet Nixon (after some initial hesitation) seized the moment to move the Strategic Arms Limitations Talks forward.

Again, Nixon's goals were fused to image making. Following the Beijing spectacle, he wanted another splashy, headline-grabbing, camera-pleasing event that would drive home his international successes. This time he planned a summit in Moscow in May 1972 that would be the first trip to the Soviet capital by an American president. The scheduling was artful: "close enough to the fall 1972 election campaign to be effective," William Safire explained, "far enough away not to be blatantly political." Even the trip's goals were cast in image making terms. "Our task is not to achieve greater public support for SALT," Colson noted, "but rather to strengthen the president's image as one of the great world leaders of this century."[16]

The summit succeeded in both respects. It dominated the news for several nights and was said to herald a new age. The nations agreed both to a SALT treaty that limited nuclear and defensive missiles and to a sweeping pledge of coexistence. Triumphantly, Nixon returned on June 1, dramatically arriving by helicopter from Andrews Air Force Base to a floodlit U.S. Capitol where he addressed a joint session of Congress. The speech, if not explicitly a "campaign kickoff" as Ehrlichman had envisioned, underscored the importance of keeping in office a master of foreign affairs. Advisers predicted, *Newsweek* wrote, that come November "the statesmanlike glow left over from Peking and Moscow," if accompanied by an end to the war, would carry Nixon to reelection.[17]

Once more, the press noted the image making. Since the summit's agreements were completed before Nixon's departure, the event itself was "window dressing," John Osborne wrote, "designed and arranged beforehand to further the impression that Nixon . . . [was] accomplishing a lot." A cartoonist drew a stage performance in which Nixon and Leonid Brezhnev locked arms amid rainbows, doves, and heavenly clouds: "Turn up the cloud machine, angels enter from the left," Kissinger, the conductor, instructed. Yet again awareness of the trip's PR benefits neither dampened the euphoria nor diluted the achievements. *Time* acknowledged that the signing of the accords was "stage-managed," but grasped that the symbolism—"the way in which they were signed and sealed"—nevertheless "gave them special import." It called the summit "the most important since Potsdam," likely to "change world diplomacy." The public concurred. Weary of nuclear anxieties, Cold War adventurism, and Vietnam, most Americans, especially swing voters, welcomed *détente*. Nixon's popularity surged again.[18]

Then there was Vietnam. Although some loyalists always pointed to Nixon's Vietnam policy as another example of his skilled diplomacy, that judgment enjoyed far less unanimity than did the praise for his China and Russia policies. Defenders of Nixon's conduct of the war noted that he ended the draft, replaced American soldiers with South Vietnamese, and (eventually) pulled American troops out of the quagmire. On the other hand, opposition to the war escalated all the while, as Nixon deferred the much-promised "peace with honor." The carnage continued; almost as many Americans died in Vietnam during Nixon's presidency as during all his predecessors' combined. Widening the war into Cambodia threw the country into turmoil. And although a treaty was struck in 1973—along lines similar to those Nixon could have obtained in 1969—the U.S. withdrawal allowed North Vietnam to overrun the South in short order, making the years of American bloodshed seem futile. Still, for those who lauded Nixon's foreign policy, the war's resolution was a feather in his cap. Nixon himself claimed it as one of his principal achievements.[19]

During Nixon's presidency, his foreign policy, even apart from Vietnam, was hardly uncontroversial. Criticisms of Nixon's Chile policy, for example—in which the United States supported the bloody overthrow of a democratically elected leader because of his Marxist politics—proved difficult to rebut; even most conservatives were hard-pressed to discern a threat to American security in the regime of Salvador Allende. In other parts of the globe, problems festered. Yet so resounding was the praise for the China and Russia overtures that these regional problems barely registered in assessments of Nixon's foreign policy. Even during Watergate, when his overall approval rating dipped to 26 percent, more than twice that portion of the electorate still praised his foreign policy. As Watergate worsened, Nixon would cling to this image as a foreign policy adept like a life raft in the rapids.[20]

The night of July 21, 1974, was, according to Ray Price, "a momentary respite" for the president. Three days earlier, the House Judiciary Committee had released five volumes of evidence about his role in Watergate; three days later, the Supreme Court would rule against him in the tapes case, forcing him to turn over more evidence still. But on this night, Nixon joined 150 guests at the Bel Air mansion of his budget director, Roy Ash, for a gala banquet. Although no one dared use the label, the dinner was clearly a farewell.[21]

After champagne and toasts, the president gave a speech, "extemporizing as usual," Price wrote, ". . . about America's role in the world, and about what America had done in the past five and a half years." Nixon was summarizing his achievements, offering his first draft of the history of his presidency. He praised the withdrawal from Vietnam, the improved relations with Russia and China, the headway toward peace in the Middle East. "As a result of these profound changes, the chance for peace to survive on a world basis is better now than it has been at any time in this century." He noted the fighting that had erupted between Greeks and Turks in Cyprus and that his own leadership had been necessary to resolve it. "Apart from the man," he said, "the office of the presidency must never be weakened, because a strong America and a strong American president is something which is absolutely indispensable if we are to build that peaceful world that we all want." The implications were clear: Impeaching Nixon could mean the collapse of world peace.[22]

Along with arguments about his victimization, the portrait of Nixon as a peacemaker constituted a key plank in his Watergate defense. But where the victim image smacked of defensiveness, the statesman image represented an offense; where the victim image was greeted cynically, the peacemaker was credible. Nonetheless, his diplomacy failed to salvage his presidency. On the contrary, so distrusted had Nixon become by 1974 that even his once-vaunted foreign policy ground to a halt.

It was natural that Nixon should use his foreign policy to try to deflect attention from Watergate. Indeed, his statesman and victim personae were, in their fullest elaboration, linked: both stemmed from Nixon's romantic self-conception as a misunderstood loner laid low by petty foes who couldn't appreciate his grand designs. Not everyone, obviously, who admired Nixon's diplomacy accepted his claims of persecution. But to Nixon these were two sides of a coin; and in practice the mavens who vaunted his statesmanship tended also to think that whatever his wrongs, he was, as Hugh Sidey said, being "driven from office."[23]

During the 1972 campaign, Watergate competed with Nixon's diplomacy for public attention. Diplomacy prevailed. The CREEP staff saturated the airwaves with commercials featuring footage from Beijing and Moscow. *Détente* introduced an optimistic note into a time of distress. By October, the prospect of an imminent end to the war sapped the McGovern campaign of its raison d'être. Nixon's statesman was on display, Tricky Dick apparently in remission. The president's apparent ability to rise above his former pettiness helped ensure his landslide.

The next year, however, the radiance of these triumphs dimmed. Soon Nixon and Kissinger's chessboard maneuverings seemed remote and inconsequential next to the constitutional questions raised by Watergate. To those who still prized geopolitics above all else, this development was unfortunate, attributable to narrow-minded Nixon-haters who wallowed in Watergate. It wasn't only loyal conservatives who warned that the Watergate inquiry would weaken Nixon's hand in negotiations; a number of veteran journalists, politicians, and Washington insiders who came to power with the Cold War also failed to grasp Watergate's import. More basically, they failed to appreciate the change in the zeitgeist, the displacement of great power politics as the nation's burning issue by concerns about the integrity of the American system.[24]

Many of these establishment figures were liberal. Few liked Nixon personally. Nixon, for his part, distrusted them so intensely that he couldn't see that they were lending him valuable support. "The establishment is dying," he said to John Dean in 1973, "and so . . . despite the success we've had in foreign policy and in the election, they've got to show that it is just wrong." In fact, the establishment generally revered Kissinger and clung to its view of the president as a master diplomat. Indeed, mainly in recognition of his foreign policy achievements, *Time* magazine named Nixon "Man of the Year" in 1971 and again in 1972, the second time bestowing the honor on Kissinger as well.[25]

Awe of Nixon's peacemaking gripped these Cold War journalists even as their younger colleagues were glimpsing Watergate's magnitude. In *The Making of the President 1972*, Teddy White veered between the scandal and Nixon's diplomacy, unsure which would prove more important. He concluded that a "national tragedy" would result if Americans "attempted to reverse the verdict of the people at the polls on the technicalities of a burglary, in a spasm of morality approaching the hysterical." James Reston also was caught flat-footed. When Senator Philip Hart of Michigan raised the prospect of impeachment in April 1973, the *Times* columnist scoffed that the "eminently rational" politician must be "smitten by the spring madness." Stewart Alsop wrote in May that Nixon's "historic turnabout in the relations between the United States and the two chief Communist powers" was "in danger of being smashed" because of an "idiotic exercise in political dirty work" by "a bunch of amateur James Bonds." His brother Joe argued the same thing almost until Nixon resigned. In July 1974, Joe invited to breakfast Congressman Tom Railsback, one of the wavering Judiciary Committee Republicans, to argue that ousting Nixon would leave the untested Gerald Ford to handle the Soviets and Chinese. Eventually, Alsop owned up to being "shocked by Nixon's transgressions," but he remained angry at the "hyenas around a corpse," as he described the president's critics. "After all," he wrote to Herblock, his colleague at *The Washington Post*, "he is our president, son of a bitch though he may be. And although nobody seems to remember the fact except myself, his misfortunes may very well be our misfortunes."[26]

Nixon made use of the regard for his foreign policy skills, even as he railed against the establishment. He timed Brezhnev's visit to the United States in June 1973 to overlap with John Dean's impending testimony before the Ervin Committee; despite some grumbles, the much-awaited sessions, with all their bombshells, were postponed as the media reveled again in heady talk of *détente*. By the spring of 1974, Nixon's arguments about his indispensability grew more deliberate. In May, in an eighty-minute interview with James Kilpatrick, Nixon said he wouldn't resign because he had to maintain world stability, to make sure everything turned out all right with China, Russia, and the Middle East. "We must seize the moment," Nixon asserted. "If we do not seize it, the world will inevitably move toward a conflagration that will destroy everything that we've made—everything this civilization has produced."[27]

Nixon matched the bombast with action. In April 1974, he took an unplanned trip to France for the funeral of President Georges Pompidou and found that he loved Paris in the springtime: he basked in flattering write-ups and cheering crowds, marred by none of the IMPEACH NIXON placards that had dotted his domestic audiences. Noting how warmly world leaders greeted Nixon, Chief of Staff Al Haig remarked that foreign heads of state considered the president "an essential factor" in building "a stable international environment." Upon his return in May, the White House announced that he would not only be visiting Moscow, as planned, but would also travel to the Middle East, Europe, and Japan. Nixon hoped to use his travels to regain moral authority, but the press scoffed. *Boston Globe* cartoonist Paul Szep drew Nixon boarding Air Force One with a suitcase stickered with tags from Egypt, Israel, Moscow, and Syria, and a caption reading, "When the going gets tough, the tough get going." Pessimistically, Nixon predicted to Ziegler that the press would dwell on "the minuscule problems involved in Watergate" rather than "the momentous stakes" in the Middle East.[28]

In fact, the trip, begun on June 10 after a send-off gala organized by Rabbi Korff, went exceedingly well for Nixon. In Cairo, he was embraced by Egyptian leader Anwar Sadat, who had recently broken with the Soviet Union, while Egyptian citizens climbed rooftops and treetops to watch his motorcade. Echoing the White House line, Sadat said that Nixon's personal diplomacy was "vital to promote peace and tranquility in the area."

In Israel, too, Nixon was cheered for having aided the Jewish state when it was attacked the previous fall during the Yom Kippur War. Journalists ingested a diet of parades and fanfare, and although some rued the sparse opportunities to ask Nixon about Watergate developments, they didn't deny him his customary good coverage. The president for his part stayed on message. In Moscow, he said in a toast to Brezhnev that *détente* stemmed from "a personal relationship" between the two leaders. "The agreement is only as good as the will of the parties to keep it."[29]

Ultimately, neither the trip nor foreign policy in general could rescue Nixon. On the contrary, his inveterate devotion to image making had made the motives behind all his actions suspect, and now many viewed even the once sacred realm of diplomacy as a PR ploy. Kissinger had first noted the toll the skepticism was taking in October 1973. Amid the Saturday Night Massacre, the military was put on high alert because of the Yom Kippur War, and the press gingerly questioned whether the unusual step might have been taken to bury Nixon's troubles. "We had a problem," an administration aide told *Newsweek* winkingly, "and we decided to make the most of it." The chatter infuriated Kissinger, who charged that the press had manufactured a "crisis of confidence." Yet Kissinger conceded that the administration's credibility was hurting. "It is a symptom of what is happening to our country," he said, "that it could even be suggested that the United States would alert its forces for domestic reasons."[30]

By Nixon's global tour the following June, newspapers were openly suggesting that he was trying to blot out Watergate with pseudo-events. As Nixon's stature collapsed, critics both left and right grew bold. The Democratic Congress, reasserting its primacy in international matters, cut off funding for the wars in Southeast Asia and passed the War Powers Act, which required congressional approval for any sustained use of armed force. The right seized on Nixon's weakness to prevent, as Kissinger wrote, the "full fruition" of *détente* and of Nixon's larger plan to build "a new structure of international relations." Nixon's ace had not only failed, it had backfired. Nixon understood why. Commenting years later on the struggles of another administration, he noted ruefully, "We tried to do what they are trying—to change the image during Watergate. It didn't work. Too phony."[31]

. . .

Whatever disfavor his foreign policy had fallen into, Nixon still took pride in it, and most Americans considered it a success. After Watergate, it remained his best weapon for supplanting the many negative images of him. Wasting little time, Nixon turned to promoting his elder-statesman image. He cultivated the journalists and mavens who had always written kindly about his global initiatives. Unlike other ex-presidents or presidential candidates—such as Adlai Stevenson in his day, or Jimmy Carter—Nixon was never formally enlisted in diplomatic missions on America's behalf. But the foreign policy crowd endorsed the elder statesman label, and that made it stick.

Not accidentally, Nixon's first major trip after his resignation was to the site of his greatest triumph: China. In February 1976, without President Ford's approval, he traveled to Beijing to meet with Mao Zedong, hoping to recapture the luster of his previous visit. Nixon spent almost two hours with Mao, dined with China's leaders, and addressed a crowd of three hundred in Beijing's Great Hall of the People.

The move set the media buzzing—though not because Nixon had regained their respect. His former triumphs were noted, and some called him "an old China hand." But the trip attracted attention because he remained the subject of fascination—and anger. Even the normally dispassionate David Broder savaged Nixon. Having praised Ford's pardon, Broder now blasted Nixon's "utter shamelessness" and willingness to do anything "to salvage for himself whatever scrap of significance he can find in the shambles of his life." Ford, too, was livid, knowing that Nixon's reemergence could only hurt him and the Republicans in the upcoming elections. Barry Goldwater suggested that Nixon had violated the Logan Act, which forbade private citizens from conducting foreign policy. "If he wants to do this country a favor," Goldwater added, "he might stay over there." Other commentators dwelled on Nixon's unflagging image-consciousness, with one account describing the trip as "the first step in a carefully planned campaign" to regain his popularity.[32]

Good or bad, Nixon loved the attention, and it whetted his appetite for more. "Tired of eating Watergate crow," wrote Robert Sam Anson, the

chronicler of his post-resignation life, Nixon spent the late Seventies looking for opportunities to travel. In 1978, Jonathan Aitken arranged for him
to speak at the prestigious Oxford Union debating society. Demonstrators
turned out to greet the ex-president, and at one point he found his limousine encircled by cursing protesters in a scene reminiscent of his 1958
South American trip. But once inside the hall, Nixon took heart from a
rousing ovation from a crowd that wanted to hear him hold forth on
world affairs. As he had during his 1960s wilderness period, Nixon
stepped up his travels, going to China, Pakistan, France, and elsewhere to
receive from foreigners the applause that was denied him at home.[33]

Soon, Nixon began finding friendly crowds in the United States as
well. Almost always he spoke about foreign policy, perfecting a *tour
d'horizon* of the crises on the global scene. He could extemporize without
notes for a half-hour or longer. At a time when Americans were becoming
glassy-eyed from political speeches stuffed with poll-tested platitudes
and delivered from prompters, the old-fashioned, square Nixon appeared
refreshingly self-reliant—and a far cry from the humbled, debilitated,
strung-out presence audiences remembered from 1974.

Ronald Reagan's election as president in 1980, although not an
unmixed blessing for Nixon, was on the whole a boon. Carter, who
loathed Nixon, had invited him to a White House dinner just once, to meet
visiting Chinese officials, and did so only because his foreign guests
insisted. When in the fall of 1980 Reagan appeared likely to reclaim the
White House for the GOP, Nixon thrilled to the prospect of wielding influence; he predicted publicly that he would be "a counselor or negotiator"
in a Reagan administration. He lobbied successfully to have Al Haig
named secretary of state, hoping that his old aide would serve as a
pipeline to the president. The reality was disappointing. Reagan, like
George Bush after him, would not risk the taint of too close an association
with his predecessor. His confidant Ed Meese pooh-poohed Nixon's contributions, implying that the president's team was indulging Nixon just to
make him feel good. When George Shultz replaced Haig, things got
worse. The new secretary of state, although also a Nixon administration
alumnus, "gave us nothing," Nixon fumed years later. But Reagan was
not entirely unhelpful. When Sadat was assassinated in 1981, Haig per-

suaded the president to let Nixon join Ford and Carter in a funeral dele-
gation, and despite some grumbling, the foreign policy hands, far more
than in 1976, cheered Nixon's return. *Time* called him "the world's unique
and ubiquitous elder statesman without portfolio," setting a tone that
would mark the magazine's coverage of Nixon for more than a decade.[34]

To influence the foreign policy crowd more directly, Nixon moved in
1980 from San Clemente to a town house in the heart of the establishment's favored district, Manhattan's tony Upper East Side—across the
back fence from Arthur Schlesinger, Jr. (who was less than thrilled with his
new neighbor) and across the street from Teddy White (who was much
more welcoming). There, and later in Saddle River and Park Ridge, New
Jersey, Nixon courted journalists and politicians. "I want to see some of
the young people that do writing," he said. "There are ten to fifteen. It's
difficult for them to come to California, but easy here." He hosted dinner
parties, sometimes twice a month. Stag affairs, they included old friends
and influential media figures: *New York Times* publisher Arthur
Sulzberger, ABC News president Roone Arledge, *Commentary* editor Norman Podhoretz, *Time* editor Henry Grunwald, anchorman David Brinkley,
Teddy White, High Sidey, William Safire, Pat Buchanan, Len Garment,
and scores of others. Feature writers detailed his activities, typically fas-
tening on the same items: Nixon mixing martinis, Nixon leading tours of
his residence, Nixon showing off gifts from foreign leaders (a Buddha
from the deposed Afghan king, a silk tapestry from Mao), Nixon guiding
the discussion over international affairs past and present. Few failed to
note that Nixon was trying to bolster his image as the sage. Visitors were
reminded everywhere of his China mission: the décor of the apartment,
the books on the shelves, the food and after-dinner drinks. Even his Mexican valet Manolo was gone, replaced by a Chinese couple. Nixon seemed
"carried away" by the motif, his editor at Simon & Schuster Michael
Korda commented. All of it evoked the piece of his legacy that he believed
held the best chance of someday overshadowing Watergate. And if perceptions about his presidency remained unalterable, he could still impress
others as an engaged and wise ex-president.[35]

Nixon wrote, too. He wrote op-ed pieces and essays for magazines
and newspapers, and after his memoirs sold well, publishers signed him

up to write more books. Nixon set up an office with various assistants where he produced volumes of commentary, mainly about foreign affairs. From 1980 onward, he published eight books in which he recited tales of his encounters with leaders like de Gaulle and Mao and dispensed advice on international problems. He warmed to the job of promoting the books, Korda wrote, "with all the enthusiasm of a born campaigner." As when he was president, he liked to appear live on television, where "he could appeal to his public over the heads of the reviewers." Nixon's loyalists also used the books to trumpet Nixon's rehabilitation. In Orange County, Korda noted, supporters would "cruise the local bookstores to check that his books were properly displayed, or, God forbid, out of stock," and would duly complain to the publisher, "often attributing any absence of books to liberal bias or to sabotage." Liberal bias or not, the books were widely reviewed and excerpted, often in *Time* magazine.[36]

Yet the travels and conversations, the dinners and writings, did not in themselves make Nixon influential. Reporters noted few instances in which Nixon's writings affected policymakers. Academic scholars rarely cited his works. Unlike articles by foreign policy thinkers such as Samuel Huntington or Francis Fukuyama, Nixon's ideas provoked no debate. His books bore nearly interchangeable names—*The Real War; Real Peace; 1999: Victory Without War; Beyond Peace*—and even devoted readers were unlikely to distinguish among them. Besides, Nixon's views, especially on Russia, fluctuated with the times. When Reagan took power with his old-fashioned, pre-*détente* view of Soviet communism, Nixon advocated Reaganesque toughness. When Reagan's militarism came under fire as too belligerent, Nixon backpedaled to a stance of "hard-headed *détente*." When the Iran-contra scandal purged the Reagan administration's hard-liners and empowered George Shultz and the moderates, Nixon got tough again, warning against embracing the new Soviet leader, Mikhail Gorbachev.[37]

Still, if less for their content than for their mere appearance, Nixon's voluminous writings fostered the impression that he was taken seriously as a savant. The Cold War journalists of Nixon's generation, along with some of their younger counterparts, repeated this claim. Some were genuinely charmed; others were still bending over backward to dispel any reputation of reflexive Nixon-hating. Teddy White had for years played

Liz Taylor to Nixon's Richard Burton, falling in and out of love, and when Nixon moved into the Upper East Side town house across the street, White felt ready to get hitched again. He wrote a flattering profile of his new neighbor for the Sunday newspaper supplement *Parade* and joined Nixon for a series of good-natured conversations on the *Today* show. White flattered Nixon in his private letters. "To have such praise from a master makes me glow," he wrote in reply to a note from Nixon. "There are many China scholars, but few who can make history with their perspectives. You did. Bravo! Some day, when all the froth and rancor have boiled away, some scholar will write a book on Nixon's foreign policy and give it all the honor it deserves."[38]

Cut from similar cloth was *Time's* Hugh Sidey. As president, Nixon used to rail about the correspondent and included him on a White House list of untrustworthy reporters. But Nixon also called Sidey an obsequious "sucker" who could be exploited. Sure enough, after a pilgrimage to Saddle River, Sidey returned awestruck. "He is absolutely amazing," the reporter gushed. "In my judgment he has a better grasp of world power than any man on the scene, except Kissinger. . . . He understands the personalities, the realities; sincerely, there is nobody who equals him in terms of his grasp of the world." Like White, Sidey built a working relationship with Nixon; into his final years Nixon would summon the aging journalist to discuss political and foreign affairs.[39]

Collectively, these men's endorsements certified Nixon's statesman image as something more than loyalist propaganda. So did a spate of articles about his "comeback." These pieces invariably followed a formula, tracing Nixon's ascent from the depths of disgrace to his newfound acclaim. They cited the same evidence: the books, speeches, and counsel to presidents. But instead of delving into Nixon's ideas or demonstrating their effects on policy, they usually just piled on the encomiums from a box of identical phrases: Nixon had an "undeniable" and "universally acknowledged expertise," *Newsweek* wrote; he was a "far-seeing foreign policy analyst whom Watergate, and Viet Nam, destroyed," said *Time*; he played "the international chessboard as adroitly as a grand master," according to *U.S. News & World Report*. In Nixon's last decade, such flattering references in the newsweeklies multiplied.[40]

The common explanation for Nixon's new status was that internationalists preferred his moderation to Reagan's bellicosity. He offered, *Newsweek* wrote, "pragmatism instead of dogmatism." In 1986, William Safire was delighted that Nixon had made a list of those who were "in" and Kissinger was among those "out"; Nixon was in with the in crowd, Safire said, because he was championing their "standard internationalism," which he dressed up in "harsh terms" by calling it "hard-headed *détente*." But Nixon's popularity with the establishment didn't really correlate with his statements on foreign affairs. He was just as much "in" when he was talking tough as when he was preaching restraint.[41]

Nixon chic among the foreign policy crowd had more to do with nostalgia. By the 1980s, Reagan's rhetoric notwithstanding, the Cold War was essentially over. The Soviet Union was crumbling from within, China was inching toward capitalism, and the old anti-Vietnam left was reduced to warning that Nicaragua or El Salvador could become another Vietnam. To old hands who had weathered the worst of the Cold War, Nixon's presidency seemed the last period when great statesmen walked the globe. Hugh Sidey fondly recalled standing with Teddy White and William F. Buckley at the back of Beijing's Great Hall of the People as Nixon drank champagne with Zhou Enlai. "No moment in my judgment," Sidey said, "has been as significant." Nixon had become, Len Garment commented, "the last of the old-timers." A certain amount of affection was inevitable. Accordingly, in stories about Nixon in the late 1980s and 1990s, Watergate was hardly absent, but it was no longer always front and center; increasingly it was challenged by the theme of Nixon as an elder sage.[42]

Two incidents in the last decade of Nixon's life—his appearance on a magazine cover and his circulation of a memo about Russia—demonstrated the process by which Nixon's statesman reputation took hold. Like Daniel Boorstin's pseudo-events, these episodes became news because reporters deemed them so. Each incident also illustrated Boorstin's corollary about self-fulfilling prophecies: once proclaimed newsworthy, they assumed a real significance.

By 1986, Nixon's statesman campaign was in high gear. His administrative assistant, John Taylor (later the director of his presidential library), updated reporters on the president's publications, speeches, and trips, and kept Nixon's name in the news. Often, relatively routine behavior landed Nixon in the papers: contracting the flu, making *Rolling Stone*'s list of "Who's Hot," raising money for his presidential library, patronizing a Burger King. What drew comment most often were his acts of seeming elder statesmanship: writing in *The New York Times* about espionage; opining on arms control in *Foreign Affairs*; speaking to the Los Angeles World Affairs Council on Soviet-American relations; meeting with Mikhail Gorbachev in Moscow. Merely appearing in the newspapers seemed to satisfy Nixon's craving for recognition.[43]

Amid this whirl of activity, Nixon spoke on April 21, 1986, at an Associated Press luncheon, during the 100th annual convention of the American Newspaper Publishers Association. He gave one of his dazzling overviews of the world scene. Watergate came up only when an audience member asked him what lesson he learned from the crisis. "Just destroy all the tapes," Nixon replied with a smirk. The publishers laughed. At the end, half the room gave him a standing ovation, and even his old nemesis Katharine Graham shook his hand, as flashbulbs flared.[*][44]

The speech wasn't any more or less newsworthy than the other activities for which Nixon had lately gained attention. News accounts, apart from noting the handshake with Graham, were perfunctory. But Graham considered the ovation to be significant, and although *Newsweek* (which The Washington Post Company owned) had already written about Nixon's "comeback" in recent years, she suggested that her reporters interview him. Roger Stone, a consultant who handled Nixon's media negotiations, said the ex-president would participate only if he appeared on the magazine's cover. The editors agreed.[45]

The issue was dated May 19. The glossy cover showed Nixon smiling, standing upright, dressed in suit and tie. The headline declared: "He's Back: The Rehabilitation of Richard Nixon." The contents page read like a

---

[*] The conciliation was superficial. Several years later, when a rumor swept Washington that Nixon had died, one reporter for *The Washington Post* trying to verify the story reached Nixon. He was told that the report was "wishful thinking" on the part of the *Post* and that "Mrs. Graham will go before I do."

press release. "Nixon has completed another of his resurrections," it said. ". . . He is a respected writer on foreign affairs, an adviser to Ronald Reagan and almost an elder statesman in his party." Inside, the main article and an interview with Nixon ("The Sage of Saddle River") ran for eight pages. *Newsweek* maintained that Nixon's "legacy of solid achievement, especially in foreign affairs," made him a natural consultant for presidents and politicians to turn to. The interview ranged over the world scene, from China to arms control to Libya to Nicaragua, although the reporters also saw fit to ask him about Watergate, the Pentagon Papers, and other topics that he wanted to avoid.[46]

The *Newsweek* cover took on a life of its own. It was hailed as definitive proof of Nixon's transformation from villain to visionary. In fact, the article was not nearly so unambiguous as the promotional aspects—the cover, the sprawling layout, and the headlines and subheads—suggested. The text was painstakingly even-handed, matching each pro-comeback quote or factoid with one that suggested the reverse. It noted that crowds turned out to see Nixon, but that they came "predictably" from Republican circles. Foreign policy hands praised his knowledge, but others questioned the long-term worth of his presidential policies. *Newsweek* reported that "nearly 4 in 10" Americans surveyed wanted him "back," but also that three quarters still believed his actions had warranted his ouster.[*] [47]

The discrepancy between the content of the piece and the ensuing declarations of rehabilitation testified to the power of hype; but they also showed that Nixon's statesman reputation was confined largely to the foreign policy pundits and news magazines. The celebrants of the sage of Saddle River were a specific and finite group whose assertions could be exposed as empty. In an unsigned editorial in *The New Yorker*, Jonathan Schell noted that *Newsweek* had based its judgment that Nixon was "back" on such unremarkable or frivolous feats as writing for *Foreign Affairs* or visiting a Burger King, "signs that he's acceptable again to the public in some way or other, and hence to the mass media—including, above all, *Newsweek*. . . . The statement in this context makes itself true: if *Newsweek*

---

* Historians continued to give Nixon low marks as president. One poll ranked him as the second all-time worst, behind Harding, another as third worst, behind Harding and Grant.

says he's back, he is." Schell's commentary underscored the problematic nature of the judgment that Nixon was "back": To what, exactly, had he returned, other than the spotlight's glare? It was not at all certain that the approbation of the foreign policy mavens reached outside their own hermetic circle.[48]

All the same, the *Newsweek* extravaganza mattered symbolically, if only because it became a prime exhibit for those who deemed Nixon recovered. To expose the self-supporting nature of the comeback proclamations was not to deter them; on the contrary, the logical circle became an accelerating wheel. "His reputation in history," said Stephen Ambrose, "is going to go up and up." "A third resurrection, if not a complete rehabilitation, is under way," agreed Herbert Parmet. "A new set of judges apparently is ready to leave behind the old Herblock caricatures." Such judgments from respected Nixon-watchers gave the comeback claims new heft.[49]

Five years after the *Newsweek* cover, in 1991, Nixon "came back" yet again. The Soviet Union was breaking up, and Nixon was eager to join the debate about how the United States should respond. At first he inclined toward a hawkish stance. When prominent Russia hands urged the United States to help its old rival progress toward democracy and capitalism with targeted economic aid, Nixon called the idea a "grand con job." But after Boris Yeltsin's election as Russian president in July 1991, Nixon reversed himself. Six months later, when he hit the talk show circuit to promote a new book, he championed aid to Russia as part of his pitch, arguing the case in forums from CNN's *Larry King Live* to *Time* magazine.[50]

Nixon's appearances attracted notice, but this time the attention passed quickly. By now the story of his comeback was old news, and Nixon's points about Russia, though sensible, were being made by others. Still hungering for the limelight, however, Nixon played another card: In the past, he had sometimes written "confidential" memos to policymakers that he then "leaked" to friendly journalists, who would obligingly report his comments with an air of discovery. After meeting with Gorbachev in 1986, Nixon had recounted the visit in a memo to Reagan—and then promptly gave the memo to *Time*'s Strobe Talbott, Nixon's self-described "case officer" at the news weekly. Talbott published it alongside an interview with Nixon. In 1990, a similarly "secret" memo to George Bush about

Nixon's latest China trip also surfaced in *Time*. So, in February 1992, Nixon tried the same trick. "I am going to write a secret memo and distribute it, if you know what I mean," he told Monica Crowley. He set down his by now well-known ideas about Russia in a memo, which he springloaded with sharp, attention-getting lines: he called Bush's response to changes in Russia "pathetically inadequate," and, borrowing a recent coinage from *Washington Post* columnist Charles Krauthammer, predicted that Bush's hesitance would lead future historians to ask: "Who lost Russia?" Nixon sent the memo to journalists and foreign policy experts. He hoped not just to affect policy, Crowley noted, but to "reinforce" what she considered his position "as the country's preeminent elder statesman."[51]

At first, few seemed to care. Most recipients ignored the memo or noted it in passing. *USA Today* gave it a 200-word write-up. The *Los Angeles Times* ran an item from the Reuters news service. But at least two influential people thought differently. Daniel Schorr, who had heard about the memo through the journalistic grapevine, mentioned the memo in a conversation with Mitchell Levitas, the editor of *The New York Times* op-ed page. Levitas thought it could make a splash and asked Schorr to write about it. Schorr agreed. Moreover, since the op-ed page had a policy of not scooping the paper's reporters, Levitas gave the memo to the news desk. Diplomatic correspondent Thomas Friedman was assigned to write a regular article for the next day's paper. "It landed on my desk at three o'clock and the editor said, 'Write it up,'" Friedman recalled. Though hardly an inexperienced reporter, Friedman hyped the "confidential" memo as if he were divulging the contents of the Pentagon Papers. Friedman framed his story as a fight between Nixon and Bush—"president against president, mentor against protégé"—and it ran on the front page. Taking their cue from the *Times*, television networks and other papers stepped up their coverage of the memo.[52]

Nixon had deliberately released the memo just as a Nixon Library conference on global politics was getting underway. The hype was still fresh on March 11, 1991, when Nixon delivered his argument to some two hundred former aides, foreign policy buffs, and conference goers. His reception could hardly have been warmer. His former defense secretary, James Schlesinger, introduced him as a man whose "place in history" would be "undergirded by his acknowledged skills in foreign policy." For many of the older observers, the pleasure came not from seeing Nixon fêted but from reliving old memories. Roaming the cocktail hour in his tuxedo, Schorr regaled reporters with Watergate war stories. *The Washington Post*'s veteran diplomatic correspondent Don Oberdorfer wrote in his diary that he enjoyed "wallowing a bit in what for me was a nostalgic occasion." Some reporters felt they had played into Nixon's hands by treating his commonplace advice as a blockbuster—although Friedman continued to insist that he had been right to sensationalize the criticism of Bush. Schorr in contrast concluded that he'd been used. "It was really the Nixon campaign all over again," he said afterward. Reflecting on the episode, Len Garment agreed that the memo incident was "stagecraft" and "public theater," calling Nixon "much more Machiavelli than he is Woodrow Wilson."[53]

Again, however, a pseudo-event became real; image created reality. The buzz about the Russia memo not only enhanced Nixon's wise man reputation but actually shifted the terms of the Russian aid debate. It elevated the aid issue to prominence, and "Nixon's position" became a reference point in the debate. The *Los Angeles Times* said the former president had "performed a service to his country" by emphasizing foreign aid. PBS's nightly news program opened its broadcast with "Richard Nixon's call for help." Strobe Talbott arranged for Nixon to publish another foreign policy essay in *Time*. For the first time since he resigned, pundits discussed Nixon's advice in the context of not just his own image making but policy. Claims for his influence still rested on circular logic. "First they quoted him on foreign policy, ran interviews with him regarding arms control," wrote a critic in the *Columbia Journalism Review*. "Then they cited those very quotations and interviews as evidence that Nixon had been rehabilitated." But saying it did make it so—at least to an extent. The flood of articles trumpeting Nixon's return and hailing his sagacity left some readers accepting these developments as fact.[54]

Not all who praised Nixon for global expertise downplayed Tricky Dick. Unlike Nixon's loyalists, the establishment types who most visibly championed Nixon's statesman image were in no hurry to forget Watergate or soft-pedal Nixon's ruthlessness. Many Nixon-watchers tried to reconcile the two personae. A common solution was to call Nixon a "tragic" figure, to see his career a classical drama and his life "the stuff of Shakespeare," as his former communications aide David Gergen wrote. The stress on the Shakespearean and the tragic was meant to honor Nixon's complexity, to suggest, as *The Washington Post*'s Bob Kaiser wrote, that Nixon's character contained "the seed of his own destruction." But the "tragic" and "Shakespearean" labels, if intended to deepen the understanding, served mainly to simplify Nixon's image, as they reduced his deeply embedded traits to unfortunate foibles.[55]

In the past Nixon had been called Shakespearean, but usually in reference to one of the playwright's larger-than-life villains. In the early 1970s, comparisons to the scheming, malevolent, and megalomaniacal Richard III of Shakespeare's play were so frequent as to border on cliché. In *The Bearding of the President* (1969), Rip Torn conflated the two Richards, enacting the drama of Richard III as he skulked around the White House with televised images of 1960s carnage and chaos flickering in the background. In the musical *Dick Deterred* (1974), a ferociously ambitious King Richard had his "Committee to Re-elect the King" kidnap the Prince of Wales (George McGovern) and the Duke of York (Ed Muskie) and imprison them in the Watergate Tower. Even Barbara Garson, author of the vicious LBJ-as-Macbeth play *Macbird*, undertook a Nixon-as-Richard III sequel that she considered calling *MacDick*. Other dastardly Shakespearean monarchs furnished comparisons, too. In *The Tragical History of Samlet, Prince of Denmark*, performed as part of the Yale School of Drama's 1974 *Watergate Classics* revue, Nixon was Samlet's "Uncle Claudickus," who murdered the prince's father to usurp the throne. "O! My offence is rank, it smells to heaven: A brother's bugging! A nation's rape," he confesses in a soliloquy. "But enough of that. . . ."[56]

In contrast to these parodic villains, the later claims for Nixon's Shakespearean propensities fashioned him as a tragically imperfect hero whose whole personality—greatness and flaws—had to be understood as of a piece. "'He was a man, take him for all in all,'" said Henry Kissinger at Nixon's funeral in 1994. "'I shall not look upon his like again.'" The quote,

from Hamlet's own lament for his slain father, cast Nixon not as the murderous uncle Claudius but as the legitimate king who was robbed of his
throne—perhaps a subtle reference to Watergate.[57]

Previously, to speak of Nixon's tragic nature had been to argue, as had
the psychohistorians, that a disaster like Watergate was virtually bound to
occur under Nixon, since the same white-hot resentment that fueled his
rise also brought him down. But the new conception of Nixon's "tragic
flaw," like the new conception of his Shakespearean nature, was gentler,
more forgiving. The word "flaw" has at least two meanings. The classical
definition refers to a deeply rooted core trait that unavoidably leads to
one's undoing; the modern sense indicates a near-trivial shortcoming that
slightly mars an otherwise noble figure. When applied to Nixon, the classical and modern meanings were blurred. Instead of some profound character strain—amorality, paranoia, vindictiveness, ambition—Nixon's flaw
now meant an Achilles' heel, a spot of weakness that just happened to trip
him up.

While purportedly offering a "complete" picture of Nixon, the tragic
view actually bolstered the statesman persona by making his diplomacy
the key to his ostensible greatness. One of the many who wrote of Nixon's
"Shakespearean complexity," Jonathan Aitken elaborated the concept in
his sympathetic biography. "'If it hadn't been for Watergate,'" Aitken
wrote, echoing Nixon's own lament. "What an ocean of sorrows and dis-
appointments lie behind those six words. For Nixon was planning a series
of global and domestic initiatives which would have made his second
term even richer in achievement than his first four years. . . . The 'if onlys'
can be made to resonate on and on like the tolling of a church bell." This
line of thinking implied that Watergate was an avoidable blunder, a case
of neglect or misjudgment, not an unconstitutional abuse of power. It
resembled Nixon's own self-portrait as guilty of only minor infractions.
The new "tragic" Nixon was not a prisoner of destiny but a man who
made a mistake.[58]

In *Star Trek VI: The Undiscovered Country* (1991), set in the distant future,
Mr. Spock of the planet Vulcan is trying to convince his friend earthling

James Kirk, longtime commander of the *Starship Enterprise*, to make peace with the alien Klingons, a people Kirk has spent his career fighting. "There is an old Vulcan proverb," Spock says: "'Only Nixon could go to China.'"

Nixon's China initiative never eclipsed Watergate, but it did contribute a concept to political analysis, that of the politician leveraging his hard-line reputation to effect a major policy reversal. "Nixon going to China" not only entered the vernacular as a phrase; it entered the larger culture. Although Watergate still provided the backdrop for most representations of Nixon, in a handful of works China instead provided the setting.

Most significantly, Nixon's trip provided the storyline for the opera *Nixon in China* (1987). Within the music world, *Nixon in China* drew notice because of the reputations of its director, Peter Sellars, considered an *enfant terrible* within the profession, and of its composer, John Adams, and librettist, Alice Goodman. But the reason the show drew attention beyond fans of minimalist opera was its subject matter. To focus a Nixon drama on China—not Watergate—was controversial; some said it played into his rehabilitation. "Nobody trills [an aria called] *Watergate*," one reviewer sniped. To such criticisms, Sellars insisted that he and his collaborators weren't ranking the China overture as more important than Watergate. They simply assumed that "everybody dragged that [knowledge of Watergate] in with them, so we could leave that offstage."[59]

That Sellars and company did not consider Nixon a wise man was borne out by the portrayal of Nixon. Far from the cagey diplomat of *Time* and *Newsweek* profiles, the operatic character borders on the cartoonish, a parody of the striver of liberal demonology. Devoid of suavity, he fawns before Mao and rises at a banquet to speak banalities. "Never have I so enjoyed/A dinner," he sings. ". . . A vote of thanks to one and all/Whose efforts made this possible." Diplomacy itself fares poorly. Nixon's "grand design" is rendered as a blundering exercise undertaken by rubes and buffoons. Kissinger blows hot air and wanders around cluelessly ("Premier, /Please, where's the toilet?"). Mao's koans sound like pretentious pap designed to cow his guests. Nixon's negotiating skills are unmasked as poker tricks he learned in the navy. "Five-card stud/Taught me a lot about mankind," he says. "Speak softly and don't show your hand/Became my motto."[60]

The opera's Nixon also exhibits hallmarks of the old manipulator bent on swaying history's judgment. He states self-importantly that "the eyes and ears of history" are upon him and likens his touchdown in Beijing to the moon landing—an analogy that Sellars claimed was meant to express "a certain poignancy and heroism" about Nixon but seemed like a swipe at his ego. Moreover, as what John Adams called "the first opera ever to use a staged 'media event' as the basis for its dramatic structure," *Nixon in China* commented on the role of media politics in modern diplomacy. Nixon is hyperaware of his image making and savors his chance to project his peacemaker persona to Middle Americans; his people, he sings, "watch us now;/The three main networks' colors glow/Livid through drapes onto the lawn./Dishes are washed and homework is done/. . . I know America is good/at heart." The opera's Nixon grasps that image making creates its own reality.[61]

Another artist, if not quite of Sellars's caliber, who considered the China opening significant enough to write about was John Ehrlichman. In his post-prison career as a pulp novelist, Ehrlichman wrote two potboilers set in Washington; for his third, he turned to foreign affairs. Published in 1986, *The China Card* recounts how Zhou Enlai secretly enlisted a (fictional) young Nixon aide named Matt Thompson to bring about the reconciliation between the countries. But like *Nixon in China*, *The China Card* also ironically denied glory to Nixon for what the pundits hailed as his signal achievement: In the book, it is not Nixon but Matt Thompson—and the Chinese—to whom Ehrlichman assigns credit. Other works of art in the Eighties and Nineties also challenged the supposedly ascendant peacemaker image. The case for including Vietnam among Nixon's accomplishments had always been weak, but even so, one might have expected a television movie called *Kissinger and Nixon* airing in 1995 to purvey the claims of statesmanship. Instead, it showed Nixon (played by Beau Bridges) as a near-incompetent drunk—anti-Semitic, paranoid, and incorrigibly concerned about the political implications of Vietnam.[62]

Coincidentally, a new wave of scholarship in the 1990s was coming to similarly unflattering conclusions about Nixon's diplomacy. Although left-leaning reporters such as Tad Szulc and Seymour Hersh had written scathing critiques of Nixon's foreign policy, they were works of journalism more than history, insofar as such distinctions are meaningful; they were sallies into ongoing political debates more than attempts to impart new perspectives borne of emotional distance. In the 1990s, with greater access to archives, historians such as Jeffrey Kimball and Larry Berman entered the debate, arguing that Nixon had achieved neither peace nor honor in Vietnam. Similarly, in *Nixon Reconsidered*, Joan Hoff concluded that Nixon's "diplomatic legacy is weaker than he and many others have maintained." Most influential was the publication in 1998 of *A Tangled Web*, a mammoth survey of Nixon's foreign policy by William Bundy. Unlike Berman, Kimball, or Hoff, Bundy was a charter member of the American foreign policy establishment. A former Kennedy and Johnson official and editor of *Foreign Affairs*, Bundy was exactly the type of insider whom Nixon sought to cultivate in his final years. Thick with evidence, and argued without the moral outrage that had animated previous critiques, *A Tangled Web* challenged the long-standing claims of innovation and brilliance in Nixon's international policy. In Bundy's telling, the gains Nixon made in relations with China and Russia dissipated after he left office; more important, they were reached through unconscionable deceptions of the public and Congress. Bundy's title (an allusion to Walter Scott's couplet, "O what a tangled web we weave/When first we practice to deceive!") made clear that Nixon's trickery was his dominant theme. In Bundy's book, as in much of the emergent scholarship, Nixon the liar or the manipulator outshone Nixon the sage.[63]

A final challenge to Nixon's reputation as a wise man came, ironically, from a book that aspired to showcase Nixon's acumen. In 1996 and 1998, Nixon's former assistant Monica Crowley published two volumes of her conversations with her old boss as she recollected them. Crowley understood that Americans still craved a glimpse of the "real" Nixon behind his public facades; by reprinting Nixon's comments to her about Watergate, politics, and world affairs, she hoped both to humanize him and to show off his wisdom. But to many readers Nixon's undifferentiated remarks, from everyday chatter about the 1992 election to freshman-level musings about various political philosophers, came across as embarrassingly banal. Instead of peeking into the mind of a visionary, readers found themselves eavesdropping on an elderly kibitzer. If Crowley had hoped to highlight Nixon's mastery of geopolitics, the president's old friend Len Garment thought, her gambit backfired. Her books, he said, showed Nixon "at his worst: . . . craven, pompous, vain, vindictive, and, most unforgivably, silly. After years of struggle to redeem his posterity . . . once again we see Nixon wallowing in the mud." Turning psychoanalytic, Garment suggested that Nixon perhaps had an unconscious compulsion to repeat the embarrassment of the Watergate tapes, to commit "a final uncontrolled act of self-revelation: Richard Nixon's self-activated last tape."[64]

Nixon's statesman identity could not be easily separated from his deceitful, even villainous, side, and it required more than clichés about his tragic flaw to explain them conjointly. Nixon's admirers saw his potential for greatness on the world stage as having been undone by his foibles; in contrast, the recent challenges to his reputation reversed the equation. As they viewed it, Nixon's devious nature was inseparable not just from the crimes of Watergate but from the foreign policy triumphs for which he was long extolled.

Where Nixon's victim persona remained popular mostly among Republican die-hards, his statesman image entered the wider culture. When *Entertainment Weekly* surveyed actors and singers asking for their favorite presidents, a pop star named Mark McGrath replied: "You know who got a bad knock? Nixon. That Watergate thing was a real black eye, but the U.S. is still benefiting from the good international relations he fostered." How much the lead singer of the late-Nineties group Sugar Ray knew about the long-term benefits of Nixon's diplomacy was not the point; the remark showed a wish to seem iconoclastic by bucking a received consensus. It also showed that this New Nixon trickled down to the point where even a fleetingly famous pop star could tweak the readers of a movie magazine by parroting it.[65]

A more surprising and more influential subscriber to the wise-man image was President Bill Clinton. Nixon had skillfully won Clinton's favor. After the 1992 election, Nixon sent the president-elect a lengthy congratulatory note and then flattered him in op-ed pieces in *The New York Times*. Bob Dole, Democratic operative Bob Strauss, Strobe Talbott (whom Clinton appointed to oversee his Russia policy), and others lobbied Clinton to seek out Nixon's advice. In March 1993, Clinton agreed. He telephoned the ex-president and they talked for forty minutes. The call thrilled Nixon, who phoned Crowley to share the news. "It was the best conversation with a president I've had since I was president," he bubbled. ". . . It was never a dialogue with the others. I used to have to force things into the conversation with Reagan and Bush. This was a different cup of tea."[66]

Clinton, too, was impressed. He told Strauss (according to Nixon) that the talk was the best he'd had since entering office, and he invited Nixon to the White House for a private meeting. There he enlisted his predecessor in lobbying congressional Republicans to support his Russia policy. Nixon, who had been planning to stay in Washington for a meeting with Talbott and a ninetieth birthday party for Strom Thurmond, agreed. Although Washington Republicans and Democrats alike scratched their heads—Nixon consultant Roger Stone and Clinton aide Paul Begala joked about a "Friends of Bill and Dick" club—the odd couple flourished. For the next year, Clinton sporadically telephoned Nixon to solicit his advice on Russia and a range of other issues, while Nixon entertained feelings of grandeur. "As long as he is talking to me," he said, "he'll be OK."[67]

Clinton, who suffered his own political battering even before assuming the presidency, clearly identified with his bloodied predecessor. He claimed the feeling was mutual. "He told me he identified with me because he thought the press had been too hard on me in '92 and that I had refused to die," Clinton said, "and he liked that." More than any of his predecessors, the baby-boom Democrat showed interest in Nixon's advice. "I had him back to the White House," he recalled. "I just thought I ought to do it. He had lived a constructive life in his years out of the White House; he had written all these books; he tried to be a force in world affairs."[68]

The Nixon whom Clinton described in these comments was not a man striving for respectability but one genuinely concerned with the state of the world in the winter of his life. Like *The Washington Post* veteran Don Oberdorfer enjoying feelings of nostalgia in watching Nixon speak in 1992, Clinton seemed to enjoy his talks with his predecessor the way one enjoyed watching an old-timers' game. From this perspective, Nixon's age and experience—and his battle scars and weathered ignominy—made him less menacing, almost grandfatherly. They conferred on him an elder's stature. This was, after all, the Nixon who still donned a suit and tie for his morning walks; who gave his speeches the old-fashioned way; whose personal library contained the fusty books of a bygone era; who came from a time when globe-straddling statesmen believed they could change the world. He was a throwback, and therein lay his appeal. Square and stodgy to the last, Nixon seemed to have been bypassed by the past decades' cultural changes, even by the spread of the fast-paced, savvy image culture that he had done so much to promote. Joan Hoff declared it a "post-modern moment" when Nixon, "who had to deal with charges of inauthenticity all his public life, became more real and more authentic than the totally packaged variety of modern politician."[69]

Seeing Nixon as authentic, of course, depended on seeing him in a context that was indeed postmodern—in which everyone understood that it was all a simulacrum, a show. If Nixon had returned to actual power, people might have felt threatened and the glow of imputed wisdom would have vanished. But by merely joining a club of iconic celebrities, he remained an appealing curiosity, harmless fun to watch. The election-year comeback jokes—"tanned, rested and ready," "Nixon in '92"—elicited smiles because they had it backwards: the pleasure in hearing Nixon hold forth was based not on a wish that he return to influence but on the safety of knowing that he would not.

What the pundits who anointed Nixon an elder statesman failed to grasp was that the interest that he attracted was morally neutral. In some cases, it might reflect newfound respect; in others—the 1976 return to China or the Frost interview—it signaled a continuing hostility; usually, it meant simply an enduring fascination with the most enigmatic leader of recent times. "We are suckers for a good show," wrote *The Washington Post*'s Bob Kaiser ten years after Watergate; Nixon's journey was "America's longest-running soap opera," filled with "pathos, bathos, intrigue, surprise." Bob Woodward was more blunt. "In my view, candidly, he's a freak—an oddity." People wanted to hear his views because he was America's chief villain, or at best a figure of bewitching inscrutability, but not because they expected or wanted him to solve the world's ills.[70]

Many who interviewed or dined with Nixon felt similarly. David Frost called him "the most intriguing man in the world." Bob Greene of the *Chicago Sun-Times*, who landed one of the early post-resignation interviews, wanted to talk to him for the same reason "an eight-year-old wants to go to Disney World." Nixon had become a celebrity, well known for his well-knownness, a human pseudo-event. Nixon himself accepted this fact. Of his audiences, he said to *Newsweek*, "They're here because they want to hear what I have to say, but they're [also] here because they say, 'What makes this guy tick?'" To Nixon, what mattered was that they wanted to hear from him. Toward the end of his life he was heard to ask anxiously, "Do you think the interest in me is down?"[71]

The conditions that gave rise to Nixon's statesman image, ironically, undermined the legitimacy of the image itself. From the 1986 *Newsweek* stories onward, Michael Schudson has written, "rehabilitation, not Richard Nixon, became even more prominently the main subject for public discussion of Nixon." Wittingly or not, journalists framed the elder statesman stories as tales of Nixon's battle to replace Watergate's legacy with that of China and *détente*. As a result, Watergate and the flight from it remained central, if submerged, themes of Nixon's late career.

The persistence of Watergate didn't mean that Nixon's statesman image lacked substance. Through its promotion, it *became* substantive in people's minds. But the promotion was understood as promotion, as Nixonian reinvention. The rehabilitation saga revealed not only another New Nixon but, more important, the pertinacity of the old Nixon—a man keen on courting history's judgment, sometimes surprisingly adept, sometimes clumsy. Whatever the authenticity of his new statesman persona, his labors mainly reinforced what Americans now saw as the preeminence of image making in postwar political life.[72]

8

The Historians:
Nixon as Liberal

Ultimately, [Nixon's] domestic programs may . . . minimize
his negative Watergate image. . . . In fact, the Age of Nixon
that would end in the denouement of disgrace actually
reached its climax in the area of domestic reform.
—*Joan Hoff*, Nixon Reconsidered[1]

The twenty-fifth anniversary of Richard Nixon's resignation arrived in
August 1999 with a stream of television interviews, newspaper features,
opinion pieces—even an exhibit of Watergate photographs at the Smith-
sonian Institution's Museum of American History. Once more, Nixon was
vigorously debated, and the cacophonous commentary rehearsed the
many images of him that had been assimilated into the culture: reminders
of his villainy, psychologizing about his personality, pronouncements
about his quintessential Americanness. But beside these familiar images
there now emerged yet a final new view of Nixon, one that few of either
his old enemies or his boosters would likely recognize. In this new portrait, rendered by professional historians and serious-minded journalists,
Nixon appeared, improbably, as an innovator in domestic policy, an
activist steward of the Great Society, the last of the big-spending liberal
presidents.[2]

One had only to pick up a newspaper or magazine that summer to see how deeply this image had penetrated into the public discourse. In *The Washington Post*, E. J. Dionne commemorated Nixon's departure from office by calling attention to his progressive environmental record and generous spending on social services. In *U.S. News & World Report*, Michael Barone rhapsodized about Nixon's far-sighted policies toward American Indians, worker safety, and the arts. Even Nixon's old adversary Daniel Schorr—who on the twentieth anniversary of the resignation had called for an end to the "moratorium on Nixon-bashing occasioned by his [recent] death"—now, just five years later, saluted "the other Nixon" who fought hunger and bequeathed a legacy of desegregated schools.[3] Not just the press fostered this image. The pundits' commentary rested on a bed of new scholarship that delved into Nixon's domestic policies and judged them surprisingly substantive. That same August, for example, Melvin Small published *The Presidency of Richard Nixon*, an overview of Nixon's administration that included a persuasive case for the president as a reformer. As a synthesis of the existing Nixon scholarship, Small's work capped a decade of other historians' labors along similar lines.[4]

This was a qualified image. Most of the Nixon revisionists (as they, more accurately than the Watergate deniers, were being called) noted that Nixon had advanced his policies with a Democratic Congress and a liberal political climate that all but required him to compromise with the left. He was elected in 1968 with only a plurality, not a majority, of the vote, and his determination to improve his showing forced him to cultivate the political center. Once he was reelected, many pointed out, his domestic policy veered rightward. Nor by any means did this newest Nixon supplant other, earlier Nixons, who remained vivid and alive. But to the surprise, and outrage, of many, it did now jostle alongside them in the public consciousness, testifying if nothing else to Nixon's continuing mutability.

It was tempting to write off this newest Nixon as the creation of a wave of Nixon scholars eager to win notice with an unconventional thesis. But the sheer number of instances of Nixon's liberalism that the historians adduced made such dismissal impossible. Setting aside foreign policy, where Nixon had long been known for playing against type, his liberal legacies, in the revisionists' count, numbered at least five. Heading the list, typically, were his social policies. Historians noted that although Nixon vowed to shrink the government and cut taxes, as president he proposed or signed some of the most expansive legislation of the postwar era. Most prominently, the Family Assistance Plan, a welfare reform blueprint that Nixon unveiled in 1969, would have delivered cash payments to every poor family in America had Congress not killed it. But even the consolation-prize program, Supplemental Security Income (SSI), was Rooseveltian in scope, showering aid on the disabled and the elderly. Under Nixon, too, Social Security benefits were increased (and indexed to inflation so they would rise each year), universal health insurance was proposed, a war on cancer was declared, and the Food Stamps program was expanded. Over-all, domestic expenditures jumped 44 percent between the 1968–69 and 1971–72 federal budgets, while defense spending ebbed—a reversal of the priorities of every other postwar president.[5]

Historians of the 1990s also gave Nixon a makeover on issues of race. Past observers had cast him as a maestro of racial resentment, who pitted blacks against whites for political advantage. Now his base motives took a backseat to his administration's real gains in extending the Great Soci-ety's civil rights revolution. No one denied that, as his contemporaneous critics had charged, Nixon opposed busing and quotas and pandered to white Southerners by nominating latter-day Dixiecrats for the Supreme Court. But in other ways—more important ways, these historians argued—the Nixon presidency witnessed and even helped attain greater equality. For all his anti-busing rhetoric, Nixon's civil rights division over-saw the desegregation of Southern schools; between 1968 and 1972, the share of Southern black children attending all-black schools fell from 68 to 8 percent. Nor did his denunciation of quotas stop him from reviving Lyn-don Johnson's "Philadelphia Plan" to make federal contractors act affir-matively in hiring minorities. With regard to Native Americans, moreover, Nixon bolstered the Bureau of Indian Affairs, endorsed the Indians' pre-ferred policy of self-determination, and settled several land disputes in the tribes' favor.[6]

Macroeconomics marked a third area in which historians came to regard Nixon as an unsung liberal. Nixon, they acknowledged, open-mindedly jettisoned his allegiance to laissez-faire economics in the face of the twin perils of inflation and stagnation, going so far as to declare himself a Keynesian. Even if moved by reelection hopes, Nixon, they agreed, acted boldly (if also, many thought in retrospect, ill-advisedly) to impose controls on wages, prices, and corporate profits. Further, he proposed a "full employment budget"—in essence, deficit spending—to create jobs and, more consequentially, canceled the long-standing promise to redeem American dollars in gold bullion, meaning the dollar would thereafter "float," its value determined only by the market.

Nixon's economic liberalism ranged into regulatory policy as well. Once considered a servant of business, Nixon reemerged as a protector of the environment, workers, consumers, and motorists. His government, historians noted, established the Environmental Protection Agency, the Occupational Safety and Health Administration, the National Transportation Safety Board, and other regulatory bodies. The number of federal regulations tripled during his term in office. "Probably more new regulation was imposed on the economy during the Nixon administration than in any other presidency since the New Deal," wrote Herb Stein, Nixon's chief economic adviser.[7]

Finally, the Nixon whom sophisticates once labeled a philistine and a square was reconstructed as a high-minded supporter of the arts and sciences and even an exemplar of cultural toleration. Historians downplayed his hatred of refined liberals, focusing instead on his support for the National Endowments for the Arts and Humanities. They saw past his tirades against public broadcasting and efforts to slash its funding to acknowledge his establishment of National Public Radio and the flourishing of the Public Broadcasting System under his watch. On science and technology, they credited him with supporting costly federal projects from the supersonic transport plane to space exploration. On inflammatory cultural issues such as drugs, they minimized the scolding, moralistic rhetoric for which the hippie counterculture had scorned him and the creation of the martial Drug Enforcement Agency and retrospectively judged his policies, especially his promotion of methadone use for heroin addiction, as the most progressive of recent times.

A minister to the poor, a proponent of racial justice, a Keynesian, a watchdog against predatory capitalism, a patron of the arts—this, truly, was a new Nixon. In the late 1990s, the image seemed to have sprung suddenly into ubiquity, the apparent product of a coincidental, collective change of mind. In fact, it had always been lurking around in vague form. It now stepped forward not just because of the cooling of Watergate-era passions but also because of the nation's rightward surge after Nixon left office—and because of the assumptions and methods of the historians themselves.

In 1972, someone describing Richard Nixon as liberal in domestic policy would have been laughed at. For one thing, almost everyone believed that he barely cared about domestic matters, certainly not the way he relished international diplomacy. On the heels of his Moscow and China summits in 1972, pundits routinely observed, in the words of *Time* magazine, that "it does not seem to be Nixon's nature to offer bold leadership at home." A political cartoon in the magazine asked when Nixon would be "coming to *this* summit"—showing a picture of the Capitol rotunda and a sign wistfully announcing: "Welfare Reform, Formerly #1 Priority." No one expected Nixon to leave a mark on social programs at home.[8]

When Nixon did tackle social and economic problems, his proposals almost always fell far short of what liberals and Democrats were endorsing. The president routinely described himself as a conservative, in favor of a smaller federal government, traditional values, and private business, and pitted himself in direct contrast to the liberals. His aides were presumed to situate themselves similarly; at the start of his term, his Attorney General, John Mitchell, promised a reporter, "This country is going so far to the right you won't recognize it." The left agreed that his administration was, as *The New Yorker*'s Richard Rovere wrote, "stridently right wing." Liberal journalists attacked him weekly over not just Vietnam but also social spending, black civil rights, women's rights, the environment, and indeed practically every item on their legislative agenda. ("My God, he's dismembering the Great Society before the Texan's boots are cold!" wrote Robert Kuttner in *The Village Voice*. "Right-wing advisers surround him in the White House," warned *The Nation*.) Undoubtedly, Nixon's positions on all these issues represented the conservative position in the dominant discourse of the time. Indeed, even most Americans on the right agreed, admiring him as a champion of the conservative values of the Silent Majority and an opponent of increased federal spending. "The Great Society, R.I.P.," Pat Buchanan wrote hopefully in a policy memo to the president. Theodore White, characteristically, voiced the consensus: Nixon's domestic policy was "an area of blur," he wrote, guided by, if anything, "a conservative impulse, which distrusted government [and] abhorred Washington's increasing intrusion into the private lives of ordinary people." A Republican president and a partisan one, Nixon's political orientation seemed clear.[9]

But even during Nixon's presidency, two cliques of dissenters challenged these orthodoxies. Although they made little impact at the time, their views provided the outlines for the portrait of a liberal Nixon that historians would later complete. The first of these groups was a crowd of conservatives who had long since stopped thinking of Nixon as one of their own. These "movement conservatives," as they would later be known, paid fealty less to the Republican Party than to a set of principles—extreme anti-communism, devotion to the free market—and to charismatic leaders such as Barry Goldwater and Ronald Reagan. At the outset of Nixon's career, these ideologically exacting conservatives backed him happily. But as early as his 1954 upbraiding of their hero Joe McCarthy they had begun to suspect (with many liberals) that Nixon was less a true believer than an opportunist. They distrusted his loyalty to Eisenhower and his so-called modern Republicanism. After Nixon consummated his "Compact of Fifth Avenue" with Nelson Rockefeller—an agreement to adopt the liberal Republican governor's planks in his 1960 presidential campaign in exchange for an uncontested nomination at the GOP convention—these conservatives were embittered. In 1968, many rallied behind Reagan for president, though not enough to threaten Nixon's selection.

These charter members of the New Right first charged that since Nixon did not share their passion for repealing the previous decade's social programs, he must have been a crypto-liberal. Nixon had not been in office a month before the conservative commentator James J. Kilpatrick said that he and his fellow conservatives "have had precious little to smile about." L. Brent Bozell, a New Right mandarin, told conservatives that

Nixon had "repudiated" them; he "rejected," Bozell said, their "campaigns against big government, against Keynesian economics, against compulsory welfare; [their] defense of states' rights and the constitutional prerogatives of Congress"—in short, all that defined their movement domestically.[10]

During Nixon's presidency, conservatives would continue their love-hate relationship with him. Watergate, as noted, split them into two camps: some rushed to defend the president and the conservative agenda from an imagined liberal putsch, while others believed that the unprincipled opportunist was getting his due. Afterward, many turned out at Republican fund-raisers to hear him speak, as others purposefully boycotted the occasions. Later, as growing numbers of the far right came to reconceive of Nixon as a fallen martyr, its critique of his domestic policies would nonetheless endure.

Apart from Nixon's policies toward Russia and China, which offended the right most of all, it was probably Nixon's Family Assistance Plan (FAP) that finally dashed conservatives' hopes of a Nixon-led right-wing revival. Originally conceived by former Rockefeller aide Richard Nathan, pushed on Nixon by Kennedy and Johnson administration alumnus Daniel Patrick Moynihan, FAP promised to provide minimum incomes to all Americans—with a work requirement attached at the suggestion of Labor Secretary George Shultz. Like other conservatives in the 1960s, Nixon had fulminated against rising welfare rolls and the "custodial" mentality that saw government payments as permanent sustenance for the poor instead of short-term relief. But once in office, Nixon eyed a chance to steal the Democrats' thunder and grew convinced of the political benefits of the plan, which he announced with much to-do on August 8, 1969. Although FAP never passed the Congress, it outranked all other policies as "the source of [Nixon's] self-conception as a reformer," wrote the conservative newspaper columnists Rowland Evans and Robert Novak in *Nixon in the White House: The Frustration of Power* (1971).[11]

FAP was also the source of the right's conception of Nixon as a sellout. Ironically, for a brief moment many Republicans backed FAP. Loosely based on the conservative economist Milton Friedman's idea for a "negative income tax"—a substitution of cash payments for social services for the very poor—the program promised to prune the federal bureaucratic thicket that conservatives abhorred by scuttling wasteful services and agencies. Nixon's own support for the program rested largely on his expectation that it would not only alleviate poverty but also shrink the government. (When he asked Moynihan if FAP would "get rid of social workers," he was delighted to hear his aide reply, "It will wipe them out.") Yet the right's support for FAP was precarious, and eventually the anti-statism of the *National Review* and other conservative redoubts prevailed. Henry Hazlitt, a writer for the magazine, called FAP "a giant step deeper into the quagmire of the welfare state." William F. Buckley, who after vigorous courtship by Moynihan had initially ventured support for the program, reversed himself and assailed it as "yet another federal prop, to be added to a house already jerry-built." Milton Friedman distanced himself from it, too. Eventually, mounting conservative opposition helped to sink the plan. Nixon himself showed declining enthusiasm for it, and his own virtual abandonment of the plan sealed its fate. (Haldeman noted in 1970 that the president "wants to be sure it's killed by Democrats and that we make big play for it, but don't let it pass.") But despite Nixon's reversal, FAP still served to convince conservatives that Nixon was, if not a liberal, then far too willing to act like one. Indeed, for decades afterward, the incomes policy would remain the prime exhibit for not just the right but virtually all who came to view Nixon as a Great Society reformer.[12]

Some ultraconservatives fashioned a view of Nixon as a faux conservative—either a liberal who spouted conservative rhetoric or, more often, a man whose ambition allowed him to adopt whatever policies served his popularity. The far-right magazine *Human Events* accused Nixon of jettisoning his entire 1968 agenda: "Instead of ruthlessly examining existing domestic legislation and eliminating the unnecessary, he kept all the Kennedy-Johnson programs [and] called for increased funding of them." Nixon's old friend Ralph de Toledano felt that "conservatives won the election for Richard Nixon and they are losing the election *to* him." And the *Manchester Union-Leader*'s William Loeb (who came to support Nixon only when he believed the liberals were planning a "coup") agreed that Nixon was "favoring his enemies and offending his friends." In July 1971, William F. Buckley convened a group of conservative activists in his Manhattan home to proclaim that they were "suspending" their support for Nixon, and he later persuaded Ohio congressman John Ashbrook to challenge the president in the 1972 primaries.[13]

But if ultraconservatives were convinced of Nixon's crypto-liberalism, a more tenable case for Nixon as a liberal by default—a president whose canny political sense led him to accept liberal policies—was advanced by Evans and Novak in *Nixon in the White House*. The authors did not build their book around the Nixon-as-liberal claim; with his policies still changing and the political climate in flux, it was too early to situate Nixon's agenda in the stream of postwar history. But they did devote a good part of the book to their cogent and unconventional case that Nixon in his first three years had confounded expectations and governed as a steward of the Great Society.[14]

Evans and Novak argued that in several areas—notably civil rights and social welfare—Nixon reversed the course he laid out in the 1968 campaign and even quietly contradicted his presidential rhetoric. Citing a September 1969 *Newsweek* article, they noted that Nixon had been comparing himself around the White House to Benjamin Disraeli, the Tory British prime minister who in the 1880s introduced far-reaching reforms, gaining unprecedented support for his party from the working class. The idea of emulating Disraeli, they reported, was suggested by Pat Moynihan, who had gained the president's favor for a spell at the start of his administration. Moynihan, later a Democratic U.S. senator from New York, was a former Harvard professor whose academic pedigree and experience in the administrations of Nixon's Democratic predecessors made him seem at first blush an unlikely Nixonite. But Moynihan was also a contrarian liberal, and in the late 1960s he joined with other disaffected liberal intellectuals such as Irving Kristol and Nathan Glazer to offer what became known as the neoconservative critique of the Great Society. Personally, Moynihan seethed with scorn for much of the liberal intelligentsia, who had savaged him over a controversial 1965 report he wrote on what he injudiciously called the "pathology" of black families. Nixon, of course, shared this scorn (and then some). Moreover, the president's dislike of the intelligentsia was born of a long-standing sense of inferiority, and he hoped that the presence of a liberal academic in his administration would give him the cachet he had always lacked. Moynihan thus joined his administration as resident Democrat, intellectual at large, and domestic policy guru.[15]

For the first years of the administration, Novak recalled, Moynihan exerted "an enormous amount of influence." Having gotten the president's ear, Moynihan planted the Disraeli bug. He commended to Nixon a popular biography of the English statesman, which Nixon read and began quoting. But although reporters, like those for *Newsweek*, picked up the Disraeli theme, it never framed the way they thought about Nixon, since it didn't accord with the images of Nixon then prevalent. "It was obvious but ignored," Novak recalled. In Novak's assessment, the "extremely non-ideological" Nixon had entered the White House with a thin agenda and was thus highly suggestible. Moynihan exploited this weakness. "Moynihan was a beguiling personality," said Novak, "and a liberal. Not a George McGovern liberal, but a liberal." He used his influence to promote FAP, to increase aid for higher education, and to preserve (if in some cases briefly) Lyndon Johnson's anti-poverty Office of Economic Opportunity, the "Model Cities" urban aid program, and other Great Society staples.[16]

On civil rights, too, Evans and Novak were among the first to peg Nixon as a mover behind desegregation rather than an obstacle to it. They reported that although many in the administration opposed desegregation because they wanted to woo Southern whites, Nixon in fact took "a middle way" between such conservatives and the administration's pro-integration moderates, including longtime aide Robert Finch, and Leon Panetta, a young Californian whom Nixon appointed as director of the administration's civil rights office. Nixon ended up, the journalists wrote, "strongly upholding what had been national policy based on Supreme Court doctrine for sixteen years and strongly opposing new departures—such as busing." To preserve Southern goodwill, Nixon ducked behind the Supreme Court rulings that required desegregation so he could profess that his hands were tied. The policy worked, Evans and Novak said; in districts "where the white power structure had shouted 'Never!' a few years before," schools were integrating. Evans and Novak also reported briefly on Nixon's Philadelphia Plan, which they called "his one major innovation," and on his funding of black colleges. On the whole they cred-

ited Nixon with a progressive record on race. They ascribed black ingrati-
tude to the general propensity to focus on "his style, his rhetoric and his
tone" rather than his actual policies. "Nixon may have been an ogre,"
Novak later said, "but he was not an ideologically conservative ogre." It
was an observation with which many historians, not least liberal ones,
would eventually agree.[17]

Besides the dedicated conservatives, a second group also adopted the
unfashionable view of the Nixon administration as a hotbed of liberalism.
These were the policymakers themselves, from upper-level White House
aides and cabinet members, such as Finch and Moynihan, to lower-tier
analysts and bureaucrats. The workers who performed the technical tasks
of analyzing data and devising the specifics of policy did not generally
debate the legitimacy of the welfare state. They took it as a given that helping the poor, caring for the sick, tending the environment, protecting consumers, and otherwise providing for the general welfare was part of the
federal government's charge; after all, that was their charge.

The use of analytically refined policy as a tool for social improvement
came of age during the Kennedy and Johnson administrations. In the
1960s, society broadly endorsed federal efforts to extend the good life to
all Americans. The country was rich, its economy humming, its universities burgeoning, its mood confident. It could now dedicate itself, as Arthur
Schlesinger, Jr., prescribed in a 1956 article setting out an agenda of "qual-
itative" liberalism, "to the bettering of people's lives and opportunities."
Though objectors existed on the left and right, a quasi-consensus formed
behind the premise that the state, especially a wealthy state, had a duty to
act. With Democrats controlling the Congress and the White House, the
government embarked on a sweeping agenda of reform. Aid to schools,
community development projects, ecological protection measures, Head
Start, Medicare and Medicaid—a fleet of social improvement programs
sailed through the Congress in the mid-Sixties. The Eighty-ninth Congress, which took its seats in January 1965 after Johnson's record-breaking
election victory, accomplished as much as any legislative session in American history.[18]

As central to the Great Society's character as its liberalism was its technocratic creed. The liberal doubts about democracy and the masses that became so pronounced in the 1950s led them to embrace wholeheartedly the faith in expertise that since the Progressive Era had informed liberal thought. The best policies would arise from social science, they believed; non-partisan experts could conduct research and derive dispassionate conclusions about how to proceed. In 1960, the sociologist Daniel Bell popularized, in *The End of Ideology*, the idea that philosophical differences were passé, that a rough consensus now backed the welfare state and a mixed economy. Society's current problems, Bell wrote, needed technical, not ideological answers. Bell's ideas became de rigueur. "The central domestic problems of our time," President Kennedy declared at Yale's commencement in 1962, ". . . do not relate to basic clashes of philosophy and ideology, but to ways and means of recasting common goals— to research for sophisticated solutions to complex and obstinate issues. . . . political beliefs and ideological approaches are irrelevant." The advent of sophisticated computers and software allowed number-crunching social scientists to claim additional authority. Kennedy and Johnson stocked their administrations with academics and backed the use of social science in creating and assessing programs.[19]

With businesses prospering, the public reaping the social programs' dividends and leaders hailing academic know-how, policy wonks thrived. New programs sprang up in each session of Congress. The laws authorizing them required funding for research and evaluation—which meant more opportunities for the analysts. At America's research universities— now advanced, complex "multiversities," as the educator Clark Kerr put it—public policy and applied social science programs proliferated, and their graduates marched eagerly to Washington. Think tanks, particularly the prestigious Brookings Institution, wielded clout up and down Pennsylvania Avenue. At Brookings's fiftieth anniversary celebration in September 1966, Lyndon Johnson delivered the keynote address, lauding the explosion of research taking place at the think tanks. "Without the tide of new proposals that periodically sweeps into this city," Johnson declared, "the climate of our government would be very arid indeed."[20]

The technocratic assumptions of the Great Society were not as ideologically neutral as many liked to think. Like much of the political think-ing of the day, they contained a built-in liberal premise: that government policy could work. Practitioners of social science, wrote Moynihan in *Maximum Feasible Understanding*, a book about the travails of LBJ's Com-munity Action Program, had in the 1960s attained "quite extraordinary access to power" and used it "to promote social change in directions *they* deem[ed] necessary and desirable." That social scientists and policy ana-lysts were overwhelmingly liberal in their politics was not coincidental.* If you favored state policy as an instrument for addressing social ills, you got involved; if you opposed government intervention, you made your way elsewhere, probably in the private sector. At the high tide of federal activism, the thought of a government full of bureaucrats striving to dis-mantle the government would have seemed paradoxical.[21]

So when Nixon took office, it was only natural that many Kennedy and Johnson hands and certainly many civil servants should stay aboard. Nixon himself railed against federal bureaucrats, frequently making such comments to his aides as that "96 percent of the bureaucracy are against us; they're bastards who are out to screw us." In his memoirs, he com-plained that he "urged, exhorted and finally pleaded with my Cabinet and other appointed officials to replace holdover Democrats with Republicans who would be loyal," but that his appointees refused, justifying the reten-tion of the holdovers "for reasons of 'morale' or in order to avoid contro-versy or unfavorable publicity." During Nixon's presidency (and Ford's), a concerted effort to weed out liberals did raise the percentage of Republi-cans among high-level career executives from 15 to 24 percent and low-ered the percentage of Democrats from 54 to 24 percent (the majority claimed to be independents). But as the still low number of Republicans indicated, for Nixon to have staffed his administration from top to bottom with conservatives would have been impossible.[22]

---

* Surveys have shown most policy analysts, civil servants, and social scientists to be liberal, supportive of government activism, and Democratic (even during the Nixon administra-tion). For example, according to a 1969 survey of 100,000 academics (with 60,000 respond-ing) by the Carnegie Commission on Higher Education and the American Council on Education, 75 percent of social science professors voted for Hubert Humphrey in 1968, 20 percent for Nixon, compared to 42.7 and 43.4 percent of the electorate. A later study showed scholars of politics in the 1980s still to be predominantly liberal.

Although Nixon took pains to move the locus of policymaking from cabinet departments to his White House staff, the bureaucrats still had an enormous role to play. For them, the Nixon years were a heady time. Despite an incipient backlash against the welfare state, public opinion still supported federal spending on a host of social problems, especially those like Medicare and Social Security that cushioned a growing middle class. A sense of possibility suffused the warrens where analysts hashed out the nitty-gritty of programs. One analyst in the Nixon administration, Jodie Allen, later a prominent journalist, recalled that "it was an extremely exciting time for anyone in policy," and that "Health, Education and Welfare was the hot place to work." Allen did computer modeling on FAP, while her husband worked at the newly created Environmental Protection Agency. To both of them, working for Nixon was an expression less of partisan loyalty than of professional interest.[23]

If the infrastructure of workers in the Nixon administration supported policy innovation, so did many of Nixon's top aides. Nixon chose a cabinet whose politics were to his left. His presidency, indeed, marked the last time that a significant contingent of liberals flourished within the Republican Party—the so-called Rockefeller Republicans. Generally well-to-do Northeastern patricians moved by a sense of noblesse oblige, they had long abounded within the GOP, and in the late Sixties and early Seventies still constituted a sizable minority of the party. Nixon, nominated in 1968 because he appealed to both liberal and conservative Republicans, placed many of them in top administration posts and allowed them a free hand in shaping the administration's plans. As Nixon told Teddy White, he preferred to focus on foreign policy and leave domestic concerns to "a competent cabinet." This deference empowered the welfare-state Republicans running departments and agencies in the administration, who operated as if the promulgation of policy should continue as it had been for some years. "We just didn't have a new conventional wisdom," Richard Nathan said. "We accepted the paradigm of the Great Society."[24]

The liberal minions of the Nixon administration, whether policy analysts or top-tier officials, found nothing unusual about regarding Nixon as a reformer. Some of them, to be sure, such as Leon Panetta, left the administration in anger over its lethargic progress on the causes they valued. But others looked back on their service with pride. John Whitaker, one of Nixon's environmental aides, conceded in his book *Striking a Balance* that the administration never did as much as activists would have liked, but he commended its "comprehensive" and "progressive" action during a critical time. Ehrlichman, never accused of liberal tendencies while serving as Nixon's domestic policy chief, later attributed to the administration "creditable domestic work" on race and environmental issues—work that went unnoticed afterward, he said, because of Watergate. Richard Nathan, Len Garment, Elliot Richardson, Maurice Stans, Herb Stein, and George Shultz all offered similar sentiments.[25]

Of all those who remembered their service to Nixon as a period of liberal achievement, the most celebrated—and the most influential to later historians—was Daniel Patrick Moynihan. Writing in 1973 as a self-described "participant-historian," Moynihan detailed the career of FAP in *The Politics of a Guaranteed Income*. Thorough and provocative, this chronicle became (along with Vincent J. and Vee Burke's *Nixon's Good Deed: Welfare Reform*)[26] the first text to which subsequent historians of FAP turned—usually leading them to accept Moynihan's interpretations along with his account of events. And because Moynihan remained in Washington from 1977 until 2001 as a New York senator with a taste for the capital's social life and a reputation for policy expertise, he had easy access to journalists, most of whom found him as beguiling as Nixon had. Jodie Allen, Michael Barone, and Tom Wicker were among the Nixon revisionists who cited his influence. For these reasons, Moynihan's portrayal of FAP as far-sighted and heroic came to be widely accepted.

As Moynihan explained it for posterity, FAP fell victim to an unholy alliance of left and right. The bill's liberal foes claimed to oppose it because it was too parsimonious; the head of the left-wing National Welfare Rights Organization called the plan's allotment of $1,600 per family "anti-poor and anti-black" and insisted on $5,500. In fact, Moynihan contended, the liberals had darker motives. "Accustomed to introducing vast visionary legislation by way of staking out a claim on the future . . . when the Nation would finally catch up," he wrote, "[all] of a sudden they found themselves behind. Behind *Richard Nixon!*" Angered at having been upstaged, they determined to sink Nixon's project, even though ideological consistency would have dictated they lend their support.[27]

Conservatives, Moynihan continued, accurately sized up FAP as "the work of men for the most part strangers to Nixon's political cadres"—not the Haldemans and Zieglers but men like Nathan and Moynihan himself. Accordingly, they too distrusted it. Moynihan recognized early that conservatives construed FAP as proof of Nixon's opportunism, if not his apostasy. Viewing it as of a piece with "school desegregation in the South, massive 'full employment' deficits, arms-control talks with the Soviets and the failure to dismantle the Great Society," they believed FAP showed Nixon in thrall to the left. Hence, they prepared to use it as ammunition in an intraparty assault on him. "This might have seemed fantasy to the president's Democratic critics," Moynihan added, "but the prospect was extraordinarily vivid to the men who met in the Roosevelt Room at 7:30 each morning to plan the administration's day." The need to guard Nixon's right flank, Moynihan suggested—to fend off a potential challenge for the 1972 GOP nomination, perhaps by Ronald Reagan—forced the administration to temper its enthusiasm for FAP. "From the right," Moynihan wrote, "Nixon's record looked consistently left."[28]

Moynihan was correct in perceiving that most observers in 1970 could not take seriously the picture of Nixon as a reformer. With the Vietnam War raging, the White House denouncing "radiclibs," and Nixon cultivating the Silent Majority, no one on the left would see Nixon as a kindred soul. In Nixon's second term, polarization worsened, making it all the more unlikely that anyone would cross party lines to proclaim him a kinsman. The image of Nixon as a liberal would take time to gain adherents.

After Nixon's resignation, his reformer image all but vanished. Liberals had no wish to credit him with any good on behalf of their cause, while Republican leaders, recently embracing anti-government ideology, had just as little desire to remind the public of a legacy they now considered embarrassing. The country was still reeling from Watergate, which dominated discussions of Nixon's presidency, and it seemed impossible to classify him as anything other than a man of the right.

Beginning in the 1980s, however, the resistance to crediting (or blaming) Nixon for progressive policies eroded.* The reasons were several. First, there were professional imperatives. History writing is, by its nature, revisionist. New scholarship depends on new interpretations, informed by new concerns; as Oscar Wilde quipped, the one duty we owe to history is to rewrite it. But a historian studying Nixon in the 1980s had little room to rewrite, if Watergate and the "White House horrors" were to remain the focus of his life and presidency. Stanley Kutler amplified that well-known story with *The Wars of Watergate* (1990), delving deep into the documentary record, and journalists and documentarians turned in creditable work along the same line. Others, as noted, revisited Watergate in order to rewrite it entirely. Most historians, however, found that after the flood of Watergate memoirs and journalistic accounts of the late 1970s, it was hard if not impossible to reexamine the central event of Nixon's presidency with much claim of originality. To make a scholarly contribution, it seemed, one had to turn elsewhere.[29]

Supply constrained Nixon scholars as much as demand. For many academic historians, archival documents—more than other sources of information—are presumed to provide access to historical truth.† Academics who held fast to that assumption could evaluate Nixon "historically" only when they had access to his hallowed presidential papers, which the federal government was making available very slowly (largely because of legal disputes with Nixon himself). Since key foreign policy materials

---

* The first step toward revising the image was to argue, as Alonzo Hamby did in *Liberalism and Its Challengers* (1985), that Nixon was a neoconservative president. Nixon, Hamby noted, shared with these rightward-moving intellectuals a resentment of the elite "New Class" that supported government policy planning. His policies, Hamby argued, marked a path between liberalism and conservatism.

† A 1993 survey of the Organization of American Historians (OAH), which elicited 1,047 responses, found this assumption widespread. David Thelen, editor of the OAH's *Journal of American History*, wrote: "Respondents revealed a deeply empirical strain. Historians seem to believe that wisdom emerges, not from theory, but from experience that is best approached and distilled through primary sources. Like non-historians, we like to hold out a document or an experience from the past and explore what it might teach us for the present."

remained closed, ostensibly for national security reasons, and since Nixon was blocking the release of new Watergate material, the first documents opened to the public included mainly records about his domestic policy. That, then, was where archivally oriented historians first had to conduct their revisionist labors.[30]

Nixon-as-liberal revisionism stemmed not just from historians' professional concerns but also from the times in which they wrote. Perhaps more than any other group of Americans, intellectuals and academics experienced the election of 1980 as a thunderclap. Unexpectedly broad and deep in their scope, the victories of Ronald Reagan and his upstart infantrymen in congressional districts across the country signaled that conservatism was surging. Among intellectuals—still predominantly people of the left—reactions ranged from dismay to hysteria. "The election of 1980 may mark one of the great calamities of American history," opined the political theorist Sheldon Wolin in *The New York Review of Books* just after Reagan's win, citing it as a triumph of "moral indignation and political despair." Used to treating Reagan contemptuously, intellectuals now warned of the dangers he posed. From his martial Cold War rhetoric, they conjured nuclear nightmares; in his coziness with Christian fundamentalists, they detected a dawning repression; behind his recital of far-out economic theories, they saw sinister plans to demolish a half century of safety-net programs and regulations. "The next time you see a picture postcard of Old Faithful," prophesied one left-wing journalist, Nicholas von Hoffman, only half in jest, "the geyser will be surrounded by oil derricks." Liberals braced for doom.[31]

The retrenchment of the Reagan years, as it turned out, did not live up to the liberals' worst concerns. Reagan shifted from confrontation to conciliation with a crumbling Soviet Union; toleration largely prevailed over fundamentalism on social issues; and bedrock government protections, though eroded, stood strong. Reagan's presidency in the end mattered most in that it marked a turning point away from support for federal activism and toward an unabashed embrace of laissez-faire, as an anti-government ethos took firm hold in both parties. Over the next two decades, no matter which party held the White House, the Reaganized climate (and the massive budget deficits he ran up) would thwart practically every effort to pass or even entertain seriously any far-reaching programs of the Great Society stripe.

For scholars writing about the recent past, the anti-government ethos of the late twentieth century could not but color their choice and treatment of their subjects. Arthur Schlesinger, Jr., writing about the newfound popularity of Presidents Hoover and Eisenhower, noted that "Every generation of historians has its distinctive worries about the present, and consequently its distinctive demands on the past." The conservative revival led some historians to explore the neglected history of the right; others sought to make sense of where and how liberalism went awry. For Nixonologists in the academy (most of whom, left or liberal in their politics, had opposed the Vietnam War and voted against him), reassessment consisted of situating Nixon in a narrative whose contours now seemed different and whose terminus now seemed to be Reaganism.[32]

It was not an easy fit. There were both continuities and changes between Nixon and Reagan. Nixon had mastered anti-government rhetoric and planned an executive branch overhaul that would have shifted power to state governments. Drawing on his career-long populist conservatism, he rhetorically associated government activism with an effete, out-of-touch, and profligate Democratic Party—a formula for future Republican triumphs. Reagan, however, surpassed Nixon in both these regards. He ratcheted up the anti-government oratory and cemented the negative associations with liberalism, successfully transforming the word "liberal" into an epithet. In the flamboyantly conservative Reagan era, Nixon appeared progressive.

Whatever their conscious intent, the revisionists made an implicit argument on behalf of the welfare state. To remind the public that Nixon had espoused many favorite liberal ideas (even if he had done so opportunistically) underscored that not only liberal Democrats but presidents of both parties had built the Great Society. Such a realization might decouple welfare-state programs from their tight association with the tarnished Democratic elite—and, perhaps, restore the possibility of bipartisan support for a progressive agenda.

. . .

The first article to make the case for Nixon as a liberal appeared in *The Washington Post* on February 24, 1983, squarely in the middle of the Reagan ascendancy. Titled "Last of the Big Spenders," it was written by Jodie Allen, the former Nixon administration policy analyst who had gone to work at the *Post*'s editorial page. Allen was inspired by a conversation she had had over lunch with some fellow alumni from the Nixon administration. At the lunch, Allen recalled, they waxed nostalgic for the excitement of those days. In the Carter years, it seemed to her, the enthusiasm among policy analysts had diminished, and with Reagan's anti-government mandate it ground to a halt. The Nixon administration, Allen and her former colleagues agreed, now seemed a veritable incubator of social innovation; at the time, they hadn't realized how good they had it. "We ticked off all the things Nixon did," she said. "I made a long list." Allen told her idea to Meg Greenfield, the *Post*'s longtime Nixon-watching editorial page editor, who agreed to run it. Mostly an inventory of the Nixon administration's most progressive policies—FAP, Social Security hikes, Food Stamps, low-income housing, child nutrition policies—Allen's piece concluded with the verdict that it was "an admirable record of social accomplishment . . . [of which] Lyndon Johnson must have been envious."[33]

It is impossible to say precisely what impact Allen's piece made. Certainly, it did not spark an overnight revision of Nixon's legacy, yet many influential people did read it. Among them was Joan Hoff of Indiana University, the author of, among other books, a revisionist study of Herbert Hoover. Hoff was in the middle of examining what she called "another discredited Republican Quaker president" for a book she planned to title *Nixon Without Watergate*. She had been working in the Nixon presidential papers, but because most of the material relating to his foreign policy was still closed to scholars, Hoff said, "from the very beginning I was forced to work on domestic policy." As she began pulling together the material, she read Allen's piece—"the first time," Hoff said, "I had seen this argument anywhere. It confirmed what I was finding in the papers." Armed with her research, Hoff began formulating a more thoroughly documented version of the argument, which she presented in papers around the country.[34]

She delivered one paper in 1987 at Hofstra University in Hempstead, Long Island. The occasion was a conference held from November 19 to 21, which convened 150 historians, political scientists, journalists, Nixon administration officials, and political activists from the Nixon years to discuss his presidency. Covered by an enthusiastic press corps that never seemed to tire of Nixon stories, the conference emphasized domestic policy issues as much as foreign policy or Watergate. Supplementing the Moynihan and Burke accounts of the Family Assistance Plan with her research, Hoff's paper recounted in detail the plan's genesis and judged it "the most comprehensive welfare reform ever proposed by a U.S. president."[35]

Hoff was hardly the only presenter at Hofstra who had come to praise Nixon. "What several scholars called 'upward revisionism,'" wrote E. J. Dionne, then at *The New York Times*, was ". . . prevalent in the view that many took toward Mr. Nixon's domestic program." Leading the reassessment were the former officials who attended. John Whitaker said Nixon "produced the best conservation and environmental record since Theodore Roosevelt." Former commerce secretary Maurice Stans claimed Nixon made strides on behalf of minority businessmen. More important, scholars were sharing this view. Longtime Nixon critic Arthur Schlesinger, Jr., stressed Nixon's highly illiberal record on civil liberties yet conceded that his domestic record had been "underrated."[36]

The job of tying these disparate strands together fell, by chance, to a young scholar named Barry Riccio, who presented his paper, "Richard Nixon Reconsidered: The Conservative as Liberal?" at the conference's final session. A recent PhD from the University of California at Berkeley, Riccio had read Moynihan's *Politics of a Guaranteed Income* and Evans and Novak's *Nixon in the White House*, both of which had made him doubt the view of Nixon as a right-winger. Considering himself neither "an unabashed Nixon revisionist" nor "a professional Nixon hater," Riccio was a student of liberalism (he later wrote a book on Walter Lippmann), and he looked at Nixon through that lens. Reaganism, he realized, had changed the valence of the term "liberal" from its early Seventies McGovernite connotations. "I very much had Ronald Reagan on my mind as I was writing the paper," he remembered. The nation's rightward turn gave new coloration to events as near as the Nixon years. "I wasn't trying to romanticize Nixon," Riccio recalled. "I really was struck by the irony."[37]

Riccio consolidated a pithy case for Nixon as a liberal, braiding together accounts of Nixon's enlargement of social spending, his imposition of regulations, his experiments with wage and price controls, and his promotion of FAP. But, in a caveat that would become familiar, Riccio also noted that Nixon "operated under rather severe constraints": the first president in more than a century elected with the opposition party controlling Congress, he served amid a climate of broad, if waning, support for activist government. In most cases, Democrats had led the fight for reform, and Nixon followed. These factors, along with Nixon's frequently expressed hostility to bureaucrats, regulations, and deficit spending, persuaded Riccio that he could not in the end declare Nixon a man of the left. Of his paper's subtitle, "The Conservative as Liberal?", Riccio noted: "I didn't mean to go too far with that. I put in a question mark."[38]

Some participants at the Hofstra conference were dismayed at the reinvention of Nixon taking place before their eyes. In the context of recent declarations that Nixon had "come back," his critics feared that the conference would give a scholarly patina to what they felt was a cynical whitewash—fears that mounted when news articles declared that the Hofstra conferees were rehabilitating Nixon's image.[39]

Dyed-in-the-wool Nixon-haters used their allotted time to turn back the revisionist tide. When Roger Wilkins of George Mason University, a veteran of the civil rights movement, arrived to discuss Nixon's record on race, he affirmed: "I've been told that there's a lot of revisionism going on and a lot of rehabilitation of Richard Nixon. . . . What I want to tell you is that I am not here to rehabilitate Richard Nixon; I am here to bury him." (Nixon was not yet dead.) The fervor was no less strong from many of those who spoke about Nixon's record on civil liberties, his abuses of executive power, and the secrecy in which his administration operated.[40]

Others confronted the revisionists on their own turf of social and economic policy, offering evidence that Nixon was indeed the conservative they had always taken him to be. For every liberal program the revision-

ists named, Nixon's detractors could point to a conservative one: his gut-
ting of the Office of Economic Opportunity or his impoundment of funds
for a clean water bill that had passed over his veto. Liberal critics also reaffirmed their view of Nixon as an opportunist. When he tacked leftward,
he had done so either to aid his reelection (as when he agreed to let Social
Security benefits rise with inflation) or to hamstring his opponents (as
when he tried to pit blacks against organized labor by forcing unions with
federal contracts to integrate). In such cases, said the anti-revisionists,
Nixon's "liberalism" was solely instrumental; to group it with the agendas
of Kennedy and Johnson was specious.[41]

More profoundly, advocates of the liberal Nixon image failed to
acknowledge that, like the Nixon-watchers whose assessments they were
revising, they too were captive to cultural biases. Historians in general—
and, for that matter, their readers—share a conceit that time cools passions
and brings keener judgments that draw us closer to the truth. But that conceit, although a prerequisite for choosing to study history, must be
defended with humility. It logically implies that future historians will
revise the very judgments current scholars now deem clear-eyed and
detached. As the historian David Lowenthal has written:

> In vain do ever more rigorous techniques of retrieving ever more of
> the past heighten hopes of objectivity. Historians who abjure former
> biases now fancy themselves less prone to bias; recognizing forerun-
> ners' flaws, they suppose their own less serious. But this is an illusion
> common to every generation. We readily spot the outgrown motives
> and circumstances that shaped past historians' views; we remain
> blind to conditions that only our successors will be able to detect and
> correct.

Historians cannot, of course, relinquish their aspirations to understand
the past with new clarity; we can't treat the images we form of figures
from the past as *nothing but* cultural constructions, without objective basis.
But the tenor of the revisionism at Hofstra erred in the opposite direction,
presenting the picture of Nixon-as-liberal as an almost scientific improvement over previous, emotion-laden and distorted Nixons, certifiably truer
and more accurate than the Nixons of the past.[42]

Stanley Kutler of the University of Wisconsin was among those in attendance who addressed the fallacy that time and distance automatically bring perspective and wisdom. In Nixon's case, Kutler warned, historians were losing touch with what made him so controversial and larger than life—with the very reasons Nixon had occasioned events like the grand conference they were attending. "We are, to some extent, in danger of forgetting—not forgetting Richard Nixon, but forgetting what he did and what he symbolized to his contemporaries," Kutler chided. "History is, after all, not just what the present wishes to make of the past for its own purposes. . . . Historians must judge the past by the standards of that past, not their own." In their embrace of the perspective of the Eighties, the revisionists, for all the new insight they gained, were letting the experience of the Sixties and Seventies, as the participants understood it, slip through their fingers.[43]

Not everyone shares the conceit that time's passage brings with it automatic progress toward truth. Whereas historians believe the participants in history to be irredeemably biased, the participants themselves claim a purchase on the truth precisely because they were there. They argue that historians, however able, can never really know what it was like. (Some historians agree: Fawn Brodie, for one, wrote that the definitive judgment of a figure is always rendered during his lifetime.) Time can bring forgetfulness as well as perspective, distortion as easily as clarification. When Kutler spoke of what Nixon "symbolized to his contemporaries," he was recognizing the substance and historical significance of earlier perceptions of Nixon. He grasped that the ways denizens of the past understood the worlds they inhabited—including what they thought about controversial figures like Nixon—constitute, as much as the filigree of policymaking, the subjects with which history should be dutifully concerned.[44]

Kutler's dissent notwithstanding, the main picture of Nixon that emerged from the Hofstra weekend was the revisionist one of the unlikely liberal. The papers by Hoff, Riccio, and others not only shaped the news coverage, which was extensive, but also influenced three participants who were writing biographies of Nixon : Stephen Ambrose of the University of New

Orleans; Herbert Parmet of the City University of New York; and Tom Wicker of *The New York Times*. None of these men's books turned out to be an apologia; insisting that they did not believe Nixon was a victim in Watergate, the authors were partway revisionists only. Yet neither could any of their books be called an exercise in Nixon-hating. Each gave Nixon abundant credit for his performance as president—far more than might have been the case a decade earlier.

Stephen Ambrose was a military historian who had written a well-regarded popular biography of Eisenhower when his editor at Simon & Schuster, Alice Mayhew, suggested he turn next to Nixon. An unrepentant Nixon-hater since his college days, Ambrose said he didn't want to spend so much time studying a man he still detested. He also questioned whether he could write about Nixon fairly. But, he recounted, Mayhew prevailed on him, arguing: "Where else will you find such a challenge as this?" Ambrose accepted the challenge and tried hard not to be unfair. "I started off looking for things to admire in Nixon," he recalled, "because I knew I was going to be critical about an awful lot in his career." By the Hofstra weekend, Ambrose, several years into his work, was finding what he set out to find. "Nixon accepted the Great Society and indeed proposed a welfare reform more sweeping than anything the Democrats had dared to try," the historian told one Hofstra audience. "A great deal that happened in the Nixon administration was positive, innovative, forward-looking, and imaginative," he told another. But if Ambrose was already leaning toward such partial revisionism, he later wrote, the Hofstra conference was nonetheless "an invaluable experience" that pushed him further in that direction.[45]

As it turned out, Ambrose's three-volume biography didn't deal with Nixon's social policies much at all. Useful for having gathered and set forth the wealth of known facts about Nixon's life, it smoothly recapitulated the public record of his career. But Ambrose did not reinterpret Nixon. His volumes, which appeared between 1987 and 1991, followed the well-trodden path of previous accounts. They won praise for their even-handedness and scope, not for originality. Hewing to the familiar narrative, Ambrose emphasized Watergate and foreign policy more than domestic affairs. And despite his comments at Hofstra, his judgment of

Nixon's domestic policies echoed the journalists of Nixon's own day. "On the domestic side, Nixon has no claim to greatness," Ambrose wrote. ". . . Nixon might have achieved that level of accomplishment in a number of areas, such as welfare reform, or national health insurance for all, or government reorganization, or revenue sharing, but in each case he failed."[46]

In the closing paragraphs of his final volume, Ambrose turned sentimental. Although he had barely discussed Nixon's relationship to American conservatism, Ambrose concluded his trilogy with a ringing endorsement of Nixon's presidency that was informed by the conservatism of the Reagan years. "Because Nixon resigned," Ambrose wrote of the man he once hated, "what the country got was not the Nixon Revolution but the Reagan Revolution. It got massive, unbelievable deficits. It got Iran-contra. It got the savings and loans scandals. It got millions of homeless and gross favoritism for the rich. . . . When Nixon resigned, we lost more than we gained." This peroration revealed an opposition to Reaganism more than any analysis of the likely results of Nixon's unfulfilled agenda (it simply doesn't follow, for example, that the savings and loan scandals wouldn't have happened if Nixon had stayed in office). It also revealed Ambrose's profound ambivalence. A few pages earlier he had called Watergate "that spot that will not out" (appropriating a Shakespearian reference that Kutler had used at Hofstra) and stated that future textbooks would mention Nixon's scandals and resignation above all else. But Ambrose seemed disinclined to end his biography on a bitter note and, by appending his fond summary, inched his judgment toward the revisionist camp.[47]

Another Nixon biographer present at Hofstra who came away more charitably disposed toward Nixon was Herbert Parmet, the author of books about Roosevelt, Eisenhower, and Kennedy. The focus of Parmet's own book, which was published in 1991 as *Richard Nixon and His America*, was the man's populist conservatism and lifelong affinities with his "forgotten Americans." Parmet remembered being struck that the conference's tenor was "not a great emphasis on Nixon's conservatism" but emphasized his pragmatism and sophistication. Parmet did not come away persuaded that Nixon was a liberal or wind up dwelling on Nixon's domestic policies any more than Ambrose did (he also largely avoided

Watergate). But in focusing on Nixon's populism, Parmet rendered Nixon as something of an accidental liberal, one whose Main Street conservatism often pointed toward goals that dovetailed with those of his liberal foes. "His populist instincts were strong enough," Parmet wrote, "to appreciate the injustice of programs that shifted responsibility onto those already resentful of being ignored by government. . . . All too often, and Nixon had seen it over and over again, the 'leadership class' got its privileges for no better reason than the accident of birth and the advantages of wealth."[48]

Reagan's triumph, Parmet said, had made it plain that conservatism comprised multiple strands. Nixon's variety "contained more of the essence of populism than of the pristine ideological right." Parmet's Nixon was no Reaganite. The author quoted Herb Stein as saying that while Nixon did not "bleed for the poor" like a knee-jerk liberal, neither did he "send them into the streets"—a comment Parmet considered "an obvious reference to the then-current Reagan presidency." The Reagan administration's staunch opposition to social services and its perceived callousness made Nixon seem comparatively tenderhearted. Nixon himself supported this claim, telling Parmet in a 1988 interview that FAP, the Philadelphia Plan, his minority business initiative, and his "impeccable civil rights record" amounted to "progressive ideas," and that he was "not on the far right on social issues." While stopping short of retrofitting Nixon as a man of the left, Parmet's portrayal, like Ambrose's, paved the way for more wholesale revisions.[49]

Tom Wicker, who was also "in the thick of writing my book" at the time of the Hofstra conference, found the weekend on Long Island most illuminating of all. In his book *One of Us* (1991), he cited Riccio and Hoff's papers as having influenced him. He later added that the panel on Nixon's environmental policies opened his eyes to a realm he hadn't considered. Having interviewed Ehrlichman, Garment, and Moynihan, Wicker, like Ambrose and Parmet, found his old hatreds withering. "When I began to study the record," he said, "I saw it was a good deal more impressive than I'd thought at the time." *One of Us* included a comprehensive synthesis of Nixon's domestic policies. "This strange and reclusive figure," Wicker concluded, ". . . was not personally an activist or progressive *man*; but— vastly more significant—in his first term he was both an activist and a progressive *president*, mostly because he had to be." The acknowledgment of the political forces and motives behind Nixon's liberalism seemed less notable than that he promulgated a liberal agenda at all.[50]

In the reviews of Wicker's book, critics singled out his claim that "in certain respects Nixon was the last liberal president we've had." Even some longtime Nixon-haters accepted this judgment, if only for the purpose of invidiously comparing Wicker's Nixon with the incumbent, George Bush. "Why was it," Wicker's fellow *Times* columnist Anthony Lewis asked, "that Richard Nixon tried to meet some of the pressing domestic needs of the day, while George Bush runs away from them?" Others, in contrast, argued that Nixon revisionism was going overboard, as he was being judged by the standards of a different era. Kutler, keeping alive the anti-revisionist flame, charged that Wicker had been taken in by Ehrlichman and others with an interest in repairing Nixon's legacy.[51]

The reassessments of Ambrose, Parmet, and Wicker all rested, in part, on a testament of personal conversion or revelation that was penitent— almost religious—in tone. The authors weren't just reevaluating Nixon; they were absolving him. Former Nixon-haters all, they had experienced a period of confusion and doubt, emerging from their years of study having seen the light. They had undergone not just an intellectual excursion but an awakening, a change of heart as well as mind. "In volume one," wrote Ambrose, "I developed a grudging admiration for the man; . . . in volume two I came to have a quite genuine and deep admiration for many of his policies . . . and in volume three I found, to my astonishment, that I had developed a liking for him." It was as if, stricken by guilt for roughing up Nixon during his presidency, they now wished to make amends. And their confessions of past error and dogmatism, they implied, gave them credibility.[52]

But while atonement for past injustices might appease their consciences, it didn't guarantee that the new judgments would be more accurate than the old. Second opinions, too, can be beholden to assumptions of the moment. "The aim of history," Arthur Schlesinger, Jr., noted, "is to reconstruct the past according to its own pattern, not according to ours." But that goal, he added, is never quite attainable. "The historian, like everyone else, is forever trapped in the egocentric predicament. . . . His profes-

sional obligation is to transcend the present. He can never quite succeed."
Just as the unsparing Watergate-era judgments of Nixon reflected the spirit
of those embattled years, so the verdicts of the Reagan-era Nixon revisionists reflected, if unconsciously, the temper of their own times.[53]

The reassessments of Ambrose, Parmet, and Wicker were not anomalies.
During the 1990s, a slew of historians and journalists endorsed the Nixon-
as-liberal image. Proponents included civil rights historian Hugh Davis
Graham, sociologist Barry Schwartz, journalist-historians Michael Barone,
E. J. Dionne, Nicholas Lemann, and Martin Walker, Nixon loyalist
Jonathan Aitken, and even the anti-Nixon conservative writers Jonathan
Rauch and George Will, the latter of whom called Nixon's presidency
"more liberal than any, other than Lyndon Johnson's, since the Second
World War."[54]

The liberal Nixon image benefited from the country's continued rightward drift. If the Reagan years had made Nixon scholars wistful for more
progressive times, the Clinton administration, dashing early hopes for a
liberal renaissance, wound up whetting their nostalgia and bolstering
Nixon's reformer image. Clinton won election by appealing both to traditional liberal constituencies and to the conservative "New Democrats"
who had coalesced in the Eighties, and he governed as a moderate—often
disappointing both camps. Those who had hoped for more progressive
policies—many historians included—now came to see Nixon's domestic
policies as lost to a bygone era. Nixon himself looked more like a liberal
than ever.

This shift from the Nixon era's fundamental liberalism to the Clinton
era's underlying conservatism revealed itself particularly during Clinton's initial struggles over health care and welfare reform. After the president proposed a moderate national health insurance plan in his first term,
The New Republic reprinted a 1971 speech of Nixon's under the headline
"Health Care Now," as if to taunt the shortsighted Democratic powerbro-
kers who back in the liberal heyday had rejected the ambitious plan as too
parsimonious. When Clinton delivered on his plan to "end welfare as we
know it," commentators noted, some bitterly, that his proposal was far

more austere than Nixon's FAP. Under the Democrat who declared big government to be over, Monday-morning liberal quarterbacks rued that they or their ideological forerunners had not seized Nixon's reforms when they had the chance.[55]

In this climate Hoff published, in August 1994, *Nixon Reconsidered*, the book she had planned to call *Nixon Without Watergate*. Hoff advanced the most comprehensive and passionately argued case to date for Nixon as a liberal. A former New Leftist who voted for Eldridge Cleaver in 1968 and later joked that she had been "too busy protesting the war to notice" Nixon's achievements, Hoff also evinced a trace of the personal conversion narrative in her account. She argued that previous Nixonologists had gotten everything backward. Where most ranked Watergate as his most lasting legacy, followed by international and then domestic affairs, Hoff upended those priorities, hailing his domestic achievements, downgrading his diplomacy (she remained scornful of his handling of Vietnam), and relegating Watergate—a "distracting melodrama" that may have been all John Dean and Al Haig's fault—to the bottom rung.[56]

The demotion of Watergate drew the most flak. Partway revisionists such as Tom Wicker had taken pains to assert they were not depreciating Watergate even as they applauded Nixon's programs. But for Hoff, reaching the conclusion that Nixon deserved praise on the home front seemed to pluck a prop from a house of cards. The realization appeared to trigger, almost inexorably, a complete reshuffling of his whole image. Hoff severed what many considered the necessary link between Nixon and Watergate: she rejected the claim that Watergate was constitutive of the Nixon presidency, thus making it possible to conclude not just that (in her words) "Nixon is more than Watergate" but also that "Watergate is more than Nixon." The very act of locating the heart of Nixon's legacy outside his presidency's most momentous episode entailed a shift to a new paradigm for understanding his import. Ipso facto, it rendered Watergate a secondary or tertiary consideration. Such a reconceptualization may have explained why a diligent scholar who had sifted through archival boxes when assessing Nixon's policies could, on Watergate, entertain speculative flights of fancy. Although Hoff insisted that she thought Nixon indeed "should have been impeached" for obstructing justice in Watergate, that

statement was hard to square with other achievements such as her ranking of the constitutional crisis as less significant than Nixon's achievements in, say, Native American affairs.[57]

Hoff's signal contribution, however, consisted not in her assessment
of Watergate but in building, through what biographer Richard Norton
Smith, in reviewing her book, judged "exhaustive research and [a]
provocative intellectual framework," the most solid case so far for Nixon's
liberalism. Delving into such areas as the environment, American Indians,
civil rights, welfare, health care, and macroeconomics, Hoff marshaled a
mass of documentary evidence to put to rest the Watergate-era notion of a
reactionary Nixon—an image, she argued, that persisted only because of
the disproportionate influence of an aging band of Nixon-hating journalists and intellectuals. "Nixon remains the only modern president," she
averred, "whose personality, rhetoric and image can be used with
impunity to dismiss or ignore his concrete achievements, especially in the
area of expanding civil rights enforcement in particular and domestic
reform in general."[58]

Hoff presented her case with verve and an air of certitude bordering
on cockiness. Scathing references to Nixon-haters littered her book. But if
her animosity toward anti-Nixon liberals echoed that of Nixon's apologists, her motives differed. Hoff in fact seemed to pine for the heyday of
government activism. Her conclusions reflected the zeitgeist of a conservative age, as seen from the left. In a passage reminiscent of Ambrose's
verdict on Nixon, Hoff speculated that if not for Watergate,

> Nixon would probably have been succeeded by another middle-of-
> the-road Republican. Without Watergate and the "stagflation" caused
> by the impact of the war on the economy, there would not have been
> a Carter administration to further discredit the presidency (and liber-
> alism). This perceived "failure" of Carter allowed fundamentalism
> and neoconservative Reaganism to dominate the 1980s, giving nei-
> ther substance nor sustenance to a dying political system. Watergate,
> in essence, perverted what should have been a fairly progressive
> period of conservatism following the end of the war into a regressive
> one under Reagan and Bush.

Like the partway revisionists, Hoff was revealing that her unhappiness with the nation's recent rightward thrust shaped her assessment of Nixon. Like them, too, Hoff suggested that her archival labors, and her intellectual conversion had led her nearer to truth. And like the others, finally, she showed little awareness that her conclusions were themselves products of her times and of her own predilections. This New Nixon, she implied, was closer to the truth than that of those who were still refighting the wars of Watergate.[59]

Hoff proselytized. She wrote newspaper editorials and book reviews about the New Nixon. As special editor of the journal *Presidential Studies Quarterly*, she devoted an issue to Nixon, emphasizing his liberalism. A protégé of hers wrote a dissertation (later a book) that portrayed Nixon's civil rights policies in a flattering light. In his 1999 survey of Nixon's presidency, Melvin Small (another Vietnam-era peace activist who came to appreciate Nixon's domestic liberalism) drew amply on Hoff's work for his chapter called "Disraeli Redux." Michael Barone of *U.S. News & World Report*, who had already advanced the Nixon-as-liberal thesis in a history of postwar America called *Our Country* (1990), quoted Hoff at length in a 1999 article for the newsweekly. By the decade's end, the liberal Nixon image had insinuated itself into much of what was written about the man, even if only as another New Nixon with which others had to contend.[60]

In the end, however, this newest Nixon did not supplant images of Tricky Dick any more than had Nixon's victim or statesman personae. Its advocates failed to acknowledge the extent to which it was shaped by the conservative tenor of the times and by the teleological fallacy that revision brings us greater clarity about the past. The liberal Nixon image also came across as arid, incomplete, even one-dimensional; it failed to reckon with the matter of Nixon's meaning. Privileging matters of budgets, laws, and regulations, it diminished Nixon as a person and stripped him of his importance as a symbol.

If Nixon's psychobiographers overemphasized the personal—saddling one man's psyche with the burden of Watergate—the policy-minded historians of the Eighties and Nineties committed the opposite sin. They located authenticity exclusively in the realm of policy and sought the "real" Nixon in his programs. But while the list of Nixon's progressive programs ran to several pages, it still read like a laundry list; Nixon as a person hardly entered the picture. Richard Norton Smith had criticized *Nixon Reconsidered* because "process crowds out personality" in the book. "Instead of biographical context," he wrote, ". . . we get eye-glazing accounts of White House policy toward American Indians, and of turf wars between the Council on Economic Policy and the Commission on International Trade and Investment Policy." Smith's boredom notwithstanding, the book's problem was not so much its purported tediousness as its sacrifice of context, flavor, and meaning. No president, especially not Nixon, can be adequately measured as the sum total of his policy decisions, and to dwell only on policy is to reduce the president to just that. "In pursuing her vision of Nixon without Watergate," Smith wrote, "Ms. Hoff comes dangerously close to giving us Nixon without Nixon." Her Nixon was a shadow of his former self.[61]

Smith leveled this critique at Hoff, but it applied to all who promoted the liberal Nixon. For instance, Tom Wicker's distinction between Nixon the *man* and Nixon the *president*, a distinction endorsed by other historians, was ultimately untenable. History has to consider people—their personalities, their motives, their achievements, their images—as whole, three-dimensional beings. Nixon's personal qualities influenced his governance; both influenced his image. The brief for Nixon as a liberal assumed that the results of Nixon's presidential policies were what counted above all. It censored questions about Nixon's character, motives, and public identity, mistakenly deeming them epiphenomena, passing passions of little concern to truth-seeking historians.

The legacy of a president lies not just in the laws he passed or the policies he favored but also in how people felt about him. "From the Depression to Watergate," historian Bruce Kuklick has noted, "the resolution of substantive problems was not central to politics. What actually made leaders effective was their ability to convey to Americans that the world made sense, that the state had moral authority. . . . The problem of leadership was to inculcate a positive temper in the electorate, not to gain specific ends." Understanding a president's importance requires reaching beyond policy to appreciate the feelings and reactions he inspired from the people he led. Those feelings and reactions are what invest a public figure with meaning, and meaning is what historians are trying to find.[62]

The historians' image of a liberal Nixon had some validity. Seen from the vantage of the 1990s, Nixon's presidency certainly did seem to be the high-water mark of post–New Deal federal activism. But this latest New Nixon, like the other Nixons that preceded it, also had to be recognized as a culturally influenced construct. It reflected the nation's post-1960s rightward drift. It also, more subtly, revealed another new assumption: the newly prevalent suspicion that all politicians are equally opportunistic. For in focusing relentlessly on policy, historians were foregoing questions about character, motive, and image as peripheral to the "real" Nixon legacy. Accepting the claim that all politicians act cynically, they suggested that the instrumentalism underlying Nixon's liberalism carried no more historical weight than any other politician's compromises. Far from central to Nixon's character and image, that instrumentalism was for historians a secondary concern, a distraction, a residue of passions past.

Yet those passions matter. Nixon continues to attract interest, to confound simple images of him, and to invite reinterpretation precisely because he remains capable of exciting strong feelings. There will never be an end to the search for the "real" Nixon. Nixon was too elusive to be so easily pigeonholed, too controversial to allow for agreement about what he really meant. What's more, it is in the nature of history to revise, as we realize the limitations and biases of earlier interpretations and stay vainly vigilant about our own. If history can help us to understand Nixon better, it will do so not by stripping away and discarding the many images of him that have proliferated over the years, but by gathering and assembling them into a strange, irregular mosaic. In the collage and collisions of perspectives from the past, a satisfying meaning might at last be found.

EPILOGUE

Nixon as Comeback Artist

Do you remember/Your president Nixon?

—*David Bowie*

Shortly after Nixon's death in 1994, a security guard at the Nixon Library witnessed a series of unusual phenomena, according to the *L.A. Weekly*. One night he saw a phosphorescent green cloud floating above Nixon's headstone. Another night he observed a figure entering the old Nixon clapboard house, which is preserved on the grounds, only to find the doors locked when he inspected it. On other occasions he would hear knocking noises coming from the museum's Watergate exhibit, and the next day the machines that play the White House tapes wouldn't be working right. Some visitors also claimed to have seen what might have been Nixon's ghost in their peripheral view, or to have felt a sudden chill while strolling the grounds. The *L.A. Weekly* journalist was himself dubious about these purported instantiations of Nixon's shadow, but he noted that "Oliver Stone has based movies on less." And he recalled a comment that Nixon had made to *Newsweek* in 1986: "They see me and they think, 'He's come back,' or 'He's risen from the dead.'"[1]

Nixon's gift for resurrecting himself, for staging comebacks—like a phoenix, it was said, or Lazarus, or Dracula—was evident throughout his career. The alleged ghost-sightings merited mention in an alternative paper only because a lighthearted reporter appreciated them as a literalization of the late president's gift for (metaphorically) remaining alive. "It's like Elvis. Nixon isn't dead either," said John Sears, an old Nixon aide, making the same point.[2] The reference to Elvis Presley was apt: The King, like the president, enjoyed a reputation as a comeback artist nonpareil, and in his case too the idea was made literal after his death in the form of imagined glimpses of his ghost.

Perhaps it was more than a cultural oddity that the most requested Nixon items from the National Archives—and the best-selling Nixon image at the Nixon Library and in souvenir shops elsewhere—were those bearing photographic images of Nixon and Elvis together on the occasion of the rock star's self-arranged visit to the White House in December 1970. The pictures taken at the meeting appeared on T-shirts, ashtrays, screensavers, and the like, and even inspired a small corpus of bad art, including a novel and a made-for-cable-TV movie. Those attempts to imagine a narrative behind the meeting fell flat because they stood no chance of improving on the deliciously bizarre image itself: The two men awkwardly facing the camera, a row of five drooping flags arrayed behind them like synthetic Christmas trees. Nixon is wearing an American flag pin in his lapel, Elvis an enormous gold belt buckle that makes him look like a professional wrestling champion. They are clasping hands firmly, forming a bond. They could be wax replicas wheeled over from Madame Tussaud's.[3]

To the culturally attuned liberal cognoscenti, the photograph's appeal lay in its hilarious incongruity: the epitome of Republican squareness forcing a smile with a bloated, over-the-hill, and quite possibly stoned rock star who was petitioning the president to join the war on drugs. For them, the image was a classic of irony, the two men taking seriously a moment that later generations would view with detached amusement. But such attitudes toward the picture can't account for its popularity. Other Americans—heirs to the Silent Majority who voted for Nixon in 1972 and who made Elvis's 1968 comeback concert a smash success—liked the picture, too. They saw in it two admirable, even great men fortuitously thrown together. The irony, for them, was that there was no irony.

Yet there was a third option besides viewing the photograph condescendingly or viewing it reverentially. Though mass-produced and badly appropriated, the image itself was more than kitsch. For all their surface ridiculousness, the late-career Elvis and the early-1970s Nixon (as seen from a post-Watergate vantage point) both exuded a certain stature. Just as Elvis, however pathetic, still mattered to anyone who cared about rock 'n' roll, so Nixon, for all his disgrace, insisted on mattering to anyone who cared about politics. Loved or hated, Nixon had made a difference. He had to be reckoned with.

At Nixon's funeral on April 27, 1994, in Yorba Linda, California, President Bill Clinton stood on the dais with Gerald Ford, Jimmy Carter, Ronald Reagan, and George Bush—the four other men who had succeeded Nixon in the nation's highest office. Before a crowd that included Gordon Liddy and George McGovern, before cameras that beamed his speech around the world, Clinton extolled the late president and admonished the reporters, who were every bit as much his own enemies as Nixon's: "May the day of judging President Nixon on anything less than his entire life and career come to a close."[4]

Like the funeral coverage as a whole, Clinton's words were construed as official certification of Nixon's last comeback. For the former McGovern campaign worker whose wife served on the Watergate Committee's legal team to call for a fairer reassessment of Nixon surely indicated a turn in opinion: that hatreds were fading, passions cooling, more objective assessments imminent. In fact, Clinton's words, typically, said less than they appeared to say. Judging Nixon—judging anyone—on less than his entire life and career is inherently unfair. The question of *how* to judge Nixon's life Clinton left unanswered. Fittingly, it remained a matter of contention.

Some eulogists took the occasion to try to rehabilitate Nixon, painting his career as a model of statesmanship: Clinton himself stressed Nixon's skill in "working his way back into the arena by writing and thinking." Henry Kissinger called his boss "one of the seminal presidents" in foreign affairs, citing not only *détente* and the China opening, but long-forgotten deeds from the creation of the European Security Conference to improved relations with Arab nations. Nixon, too, promoted the statesman image even in death. Thumbing his nose at those who detested him for prolonging Vietnam, he had decreed that his headstone bear as an epitaph a line from his first inaugural address: "The greatest honor history can bestow is the title of peacemaker."[5]

The paeans to Nixon's diplomacy, however, showed but one of Nixon's many faces. For the droves of well-wishers converging on Yorba Linda—the forty thousand citizens who had in recent days braved crackling thunder and pelting hail, bumper-to-bumper freeways and swarming crowds, to pay him tribute—the Anti-Ballistic Missile Treaty or the European Security Conference mattered little next to Nixon's stubborn defense of their conservative values. It wasn't Kissinger's sonorous eulogy that moved these legions but Bob Dole's lachrymose requiem for Nixon the fighting populist. "To tens of millions of his countrymen, Richard Nixon was an American hero," Dole said, before sobbing, "a hero who shared and honored their belief in working hard, worshiping God, loving their families and saluting the flag, . . . truly one of us."[6]

Yet Dole's Norman Rockwell image wasn't the end of the story either. In the newspapers, and in the assessments of historians trotted out to comment, a different picture emerged: a man who established agencies to protect the environment and worker safety, who sought to expand welfare, who adopted Keynesian economic policies. A *Newsday* article entitled "Richard Nixon's Liberal Legacy" suggested that history might yet "come to enshrine him in the pantheon of liberal saints," or at least view him with "a greater ambivalence than his detractors might ever have imagined."[7]

De mortuis nil nisi bonum, says a Latin proverb: of the dead say nothing unless it is kind. The funeral eulogists, unsurprisingly, omitted or downplayed Watergate. Yet a few guests dared to broach the subject, if only to defend their late leader as the target of runaway liberal wrath. Ben Stein reminisced about the speech he wished Nixon had given in August 1974 instead of resigning: "Yes, I made mistakes," Stein imagined a defiant Nixon saying, "but I didn't have call girls in the White House and I didn't have Mafia pals. . . . I didn't build a TV empire completely on peddling influence." Nixon's old "everyone does it" argument still gripped some. "He goofed, but I didn't see any halos above anybody else's head then in Washington or around here tonight," said Jim Schiffman, a Southern Californian who came to the funeral.[8]

Statesman and everyman, domestic innovator and scapegoat—the parade of sympathetic Nixons was deemed proof of a change of heart toward Tricky Dick. But countervailing opinions, just offstage and just as loud, argued otherwise. The distinguished Nixon-hater Philip Roth—who once claimed he chose to write political satire because of his longtime nemesis—captured the spirit of the dissenters, who despite their relative silence during the marathon of fond funeral tributes did not stay muzzled for long. In Roth's novel *I Married a Communist* (1998), Murray Ringold, a survivor of the Red Scare who has sat through the "barely endurable" spectacle of Nixon's interment, looses a frenetic, eloquent tirade against "the man who turned a whole country's morale inside out, the generator of an enormous national disaster, the first and only president of the United States of America to have gained from a handpicked successor a full and unconditional pardon for all the breaking and entering he committed while in office." Murray wasn't alone.[9]

They may not have been visible on the news networks broadcasting from Yorba Linda, but in the following days and weeks, unsentimental remembrances came from real-life Murray Ringolds. *The New Republic* reprinted choice excerpts from past anti-Nixon tirades by Irving Howe, Arthur Schlesinger, Jr., and William Costello, among others. Some former Nixon allies, still feeling betrayed, joined the critics. Barry Goldwater boycotted the funeral, as did former Attorney General William Saxbe, who explained that he stayed away because Nixon "had lied to me as he lied to everyone, and . . . I can never forgive him." Others dissented from the love-in more creatively: One night a Los Angeles artist postered Yorba Linda's freeways with images of Nixon and Checkers beneath the title "Richard M. Nixon Memorial Pet Peeve"—explaining to a reporter that Nixon "set the standard for smarmy opportunism . . . and ruined many people's lives in the process."[10]

Other assessments of Nixon's life also refused to give him a free pass upon his passing. The psychologically inclined returned to the "tangled personality," as *U.S. News & World Report* called it, that spawned so many tortured controversies. Some observers, like *The Washington Post*'s Jonathan Yardley, felt it enough simply to dismiss Nixon as a "psychological basket case" or to speak off-handedly of his paranoia. Others rehearsed in detail the boyhood traumas and trials that shaped his character. *New York Times* reporter John Herbers, who had crisscrossed the country in 1973 searching for Nixon's psychiatrist, quoted in the paper of record's obituary an assessment from James David Barber: "'Out of his childhood Nixon brought a persistent bent toward life as painful, difficult, and, perhaps as significant, uncertain.'"[11]

On the far left, ambivalence prevailed. Some New Left die-hards like the *Los Angeles Times* columnist Robert Scheer insisted that Nixon had been "hounded out of office . . . subjected to a double standard, being judged much more harshly because he was, by virtue of personality, the anti-Teflon president." Others remained proudly unreconstructed in their Nixon-hating: Hunter S. Thompson called Nixon "a swine of a man and a jabbering dupe of a president," possessed of an "ugly, Nazi spirit," whose body "should have been burned in a trash bin." A headline in the alternative *Chicago Reader* imagined "Nixon in Hell." In the *Radical History Review*'s special issue of "Counter-Obituaries," vilification of Nixon coexisted with indictments of America as a whole. Contributors dwelled less on Watergate than on Vietnam, Cambodia, Kent State, Chile, and other crimes of "the American imperialist system," as they branded Nixon a war criminal, a murderer of civilians, and "the enthusiastic 'Commander-in-Chief' in prosecuting the genocide for six years."[12]

Characteristically ambivalent, too, were White House reporters, who veered between canned funeral-ready reverence and a felt duty to point out the phoniness of the event. Battle-scarred old-timers scolded their younger colleagues for being "a polite and timid bunch," as Russell Baker wrote in *The New York Times*, "too delicate to utter truly rude noises over newly filled coffins." The postmortem heraldings of a New Nixon, argued four-star journalists from Garry Wills to David Halberstam, showed only that Nixon was, in the words of a *New York* magazine headline, "spinning from his grave." Weighing in with impertinent refreshers on Nixon's dark deeds, other columnists and cartoonists sought to strip away the puff and PR. Pithiest of all, the *Los Angeles Times*'s Paul Conrad drew a tombstone with a double entendre for an epitaph: "Here Lies Richard M. Nixon."[13]

That so many images of Nixon still coexisted in the culture even at his death, vying for prominence and dominance, was telling. Deep divisions remained in American life, and Nixon continued to serve as a repository for different people's values and visions, hopes and fears. The persistence of clashing political and cultural predilections among dissimilar groups worked against any neat resolution of his meaning. Besides, Nixon was too protean, too controversial, too enigmatic for that.

Still, it was only natural that Nixon-watchers, professional and amateur, should look to judge which, if any, of Nixon's many images had prevailed. Survey numbers, the most obvious gauge, may not have yielded any unanimity of opinion, but they showed that most Americans still associated Nixon with corruption and dishonesty. A March 2002 Gallup poll found that 54 percent of Americans "disapproved" of Nixon's performance as president, while 34 percent approved—an improvement over some past surveys but still the worst showing among the eight presidents from Kennedy to Clinton.* Polls of historians also showed Nixon to have modestly bettered his lot in recent years but still to have fared poorly overall. Even conservative scholars, on balance, continued to judge him unfavorably compared to other presidents.[14]

Quantitative measures, of course, are blunt and inadequate instruments. What they fail to convey, cultural indices often better relate. Nixon's effect on the language, for instance, spoke to his enduring meaning: "Nixonian" has become a synonym for Machiavellian. The "gate" suffix, appended like laundry tags to the names of new scandals, testifies to Watergate's secure place as the benchmark of political wrongdoing. Nixon going to China has also entered the lexicon, evoking his creative foreign policies—although the phrase speaks not just to his diplomatic bravura but also to his slightly untrustworthy political resourcefulness.

Popular culture—frequently a better barometer and more powerful shaper of public opinion than newspaper commentary—still portrays Nixon in an array of guises: Oliver Stone's conspirator and Robert Altman's psycho; James Taylor's shifty little opportunist and Peter Sellars's media-obsessed China traveler; the unglamorous hero to a young conser-

---

* Only once after his resignation—immediately after the funeral—did Nixon win approval from a majority of Americans.

vative in *Family Ties* and the pitiable campaigner of Neil Young's dirge; the railroaded victim of John Updike's plainspoken heartlanders and the figure of fun lampooned in *Dick*. Yet here too the villainous images dominate. For Philip Roth, among others, Nixon represented nothing less than the subversion of American democracy, not just in *I Married a Communist* but also in his previous novel, *American Pastoral* (1997), in which Lou Levov, watching the Watergate Hearings in 1973, figures that if the investigators could just "Get Nixon," then "America will be America again, without everything loathsome and lawless that's crept in, without all this violence and malice and madness and hate. . . . Cage the crook!" On the popular cartoon show *The Simpsons*, Nixon was a common punching bag: in one episode, Homer tells his son, Bart, that Checkers went to doggy hell, and in another Moe the Bartender uses a Nixonian Enemies List to plot acts of revenge. "If you would have told me twenty-five years ago that I'd be making a living by making fun of Richard Nixon," said the show's creator, Matt Groening, "I would have been so happy."[15]

In the end, the polls and the historians and the purveyors of culture all revealed that the dark Nixon—whether seen as crook or conspirator, liar or Machiavellian, or some combination of the above—remained his most enduring identity. Other images—the populist, the victim, the statesman, the liberal—were not without basis in reality, or without decided adherents, even as the years rolled on. But the effort to judge Nixon on his entire life and career had to accept that no other president directed a criminal conspiracy from the White House; that none so grievously traduced the Constitution; that none so eagerly abused his power; that none resigned under duress because of the magnitude and scope of his wrongdoing. Above all, Nixon remained a symbol of thrusting ambition gone amok, of a powerlust and concern for image and reputation so deep and unquenchable that neither death nor dishonor could deter their eruption. Nixon's career spanned more than the Watergate years and embraced more than these bitter realities. But even amid the fine and fulsome eulogies that rang out from Yorba Linda in April 1994, these were the inescapable first facts of any reckoning with Nixon. Obituaries did not start with his trip to China, his crusades for forgotten Americans, his victimization, or his Great Society agenda. They did start with Watergate.

Nonetheless, if Nixon was destined to be remembered most often as Tricky Dick, it was not necessarily as the crudest of caricatures. Many Nixon-haters appreciated subtle dimensions to Nixon that could be applauded as well as scorned. Matt Groening and the comedy writers he worked with recognized something in Nixon beyond arrant villainy. On Groening's cartoon show *Futurama*, set in a distant century, Nixon's head is preserved in a jar and, in one episode titled "A Head in the Polls," runs for president. Groening and company aren't just mocking Nixon's ruthless drive; they're also admiring—or admiring in the guise of mocking—his resilience and relevance. Even Philip Roth, in his scathing satire *Our Gang*, paid homage to Nixon's doggedness. After Trick E. Dixon is assassinated while seeking to have the sweat glands removed from his upper lip, he surfaces in Hell, where "On the Comeback Trail" he challenges Satan for leadership of the underworld. Though murdered and consigned for eternity to blackest oblivion, Nixon/Dixon remains undaunted, attacking Satan for letting Job off the hook, and asserting: "It's our whole lives that you should be judging here tonight. It's what we stand for."[16]

As sure as Bill Clinton unintentionally echoed Trick E. Dixon in his eulogy, so life perchance imitated art. If fictional Nixons continued to pursue office from a perch in Hades or a cryogenic jar, Nixon too seemed to be refashioning his image from the beyond (no matter how unreliable the sightings of his shadow). For running through the varied swatches of obituarial commentary was a single uniting thread: Critics and defenders—those who denounced Nixon's cynicism and those who praised his grit—concurred that he had remade his identity yet again. But the ubiquity of such assertions showed precisely the reverse: that everyone remained acutely aware of Nixon's resolve to control how others would regard him. The common denominator to the postmortem analyses, the consensus within the dissensus, was that Nixon was again constructing and doctoring his public identity: coming back, fighting for rehabilitation, rolling out this year's model of the New Nixon.

But whether it was new or used, most Americans weren't buying another persona from this man, at least not for long. What the funeral affirmed, finally, wasn't a New Nixon but a change in public consciousness that had been brewing for fifty years. The prevalent talk of Nixon's reinvention indicated only that a new blanket awareness had taken hold: an awareness that all politicians—Nixon being in this regard the most extreme and single-minded—routinely manipulate images. In bringing image craft to the forefront of American political culture and consciousness, Nixon was a pioneering figure of the postwar age. If nothing else, his funeral made that plain.

Notes

Abbreviations

Archives

CSF Cal-State Fullerton

CU Columbia University

CUOHP Columbia University Oral History Program

GRFPL Gerald R. Ford Presidential Library

HIA Hoover Institution Archives

HU Harvard University

LCMD Library of Congress Manuscripts Division

MC Microfilm Collection

NA National Archives.

NALN National Archives, Laguna Niguel

NPL Nathan Pusey Library

NPMP Nixon Presidential Materials Project

OH Oral History

PE Herman Perry Papers

POF President's Office Files

PPF President's Personal Files

PPS Pre-Presidential Series

RMNOH Richard M. Nixon Project Oral History Program

RNL Richard Nixon Library

SAVF Social Action Vertical File

SHSW State Historical Society of Wisconsin

SM Dana Smith Papers

SMOF Staff Member and Office Files

SP Herbert Spencer Papers
SPP Sidney Peck Papers
THWP Theodore H. White Papers
UCB University of California Berkeley
VPP Vice Presidential Papers
WHCF White House Central Files
WHSF White House Special Files

Books

Ambrose 1—Stephen Ambrose, *Nixon* Vol. I: *The Education of a Politician, 1913–1962*

Ambrose 2—Stephen Ambrose, *Nixon*, Vol. II: *The Triumph of a Politician, 1962–1972*

Ambrose 3—Stephen Ambrose, *Nixon*, Vol. III: *Ruin and Recovery, 1973–1990*

AP—Stanley Kutler, ed., *Abuse of Power: The New Nixon Tapes*

FRSC—Final Report of the Select Committee on Presidential Campaign Activities (Ervin Committee)

HD—The Haldeman Diaries

Hofstra 1—Leon Friedman and William Levantrosser, eds., *Richard M. Nixon: Politician, President, Administrator*

Hofstra 2—Leon Friedman and William Levantrosser, eds., *Watergate and Afterward: The Legacy of Richard M. Nixon*

Hofstra 3—Leon Friedman and William Levantrosser, eds., *Cold War Patriot and Statesman*

NP—Kenneth W. Thompson, ed., *The Nixon Presidency*

NPPC—The Nixon Presidential Press Conferences

PP—The Public Papers of the Presidents, 1963, 1969–74

PT—Washington Post, ed., *The Presidential Transcripts*

WH—New York Times, ed., *The Watergate Hearings*

Periodicals

CJR Columbia Journalism Review
LAT Los Angeles Times
NR National Review
NYP New York Post
NYT The New York Times
TNR The New Republic
UNSWR U.S. News & World Report
WDN Whittier Daily News or Whittier News
WSJ Wall Street Journal
WP The Washington Post

Introduction

1. Stanley Kutler, *The Wars of Watergate: The Last Crisis of Richard Nixon* (New York: Norton, 1992), 33.

2. Quoted in Fawn Brodie, *Richard Nixon: The Shaping of His Character* (New York: Norton, 1981), 306.

3. See James Schamus, *The Ice Storm: The Shooting Script* (London: Nick Hern Books, 1997). The endnote at the conclusion of each paragraph includes citations for material mentioned throughout that paragraph. If there are footnotes in the text, sources for the material in that footnote are also cited in the endnote for the corresponding paragraph.

4. Ibid.; author's interview with James Schamus, February 22, 2001.

5. *Morning Edition*, National Public Radio, October 30, 2000; *Time*, November 12, 1973; *Boston Globe*, December 23, 1990, W3; *St. Petersburg Times*, March 7, 1993, 3F; *Seattle Times*, October 22, 1993, B2; *Omaha World-Herald*, October 22, 1998, 20.

6. Stewart Alsop, interview with Nixon, 13–18, Papers of Joseph and Stewart Alsop, Box 47, Folder "Richard Nixon: The Mystery and the Man," LCMD.

7. Murray Kempton, *America Comes of Middle Age: Columns 1950–1962* (Boston: Little, Brown, 1963), 255; "Nixon as Literary Artifact," *Raritan*, vol. 15, no. 2 (Fall 1995), 83–96; Paul Johnson, "In Praise of Richard Nixon," *Commentary* (October 1988), 50.

8. Theodore H. White, *The Making of the President 1972* (New York: Atheneum, 1973), 18; *NYT*, August 19, 1974, 29; Joan Hoff, *Nixon Reconsidered* (New York: Basic Books, 1994), 346; Herbert Parmet, *Richard Nixon and His America* (Boston: Little, Brown, 1990), 620–46; Melvin Small, *The Presidency of Richard Nixon* (Lawrence: University of Kansas Press, 1999), 311.

9. Robert K. Murray and Tim H. Blessing, "The Presidential Performance Study: A Progress Report," *Journal of American History*, vol. 70, no. 3 (December 1983), 543; Reuven Frank, *Out of Thin Air: The Brief Wonderful Life of Network News* (New York: Simon & Schuster, 1991), 339; David Wallechinsky, Irving Wallace, and Amy Wallace, *The Book of Lists* (New York: Bantam Books, 1977), 1; Michael Korda, *Another Life: A Memoir of Other People* (New York: Random House, 1999), 462.

10. Daniel J. Boorstin, *The Image: A Guide to Pseudo-Events in America* (New York: Vintage, 1992 [1961]), 265, 254; Stephen J. Whitfield, "*The Image*: The Lost World of Daniel Boorstin," *Reviews in American History*, vol. 19, no. 2 (June 1991), 305. As Whitfield notes, the subtitle of Boorstin's book was changed on its publication in paperback in 1964.

11. Boorstin, *The Image*, 204, 41–43, 36.

12. Whitfield, "*The Image*," 303.

13. On Henry Tudor, see Brendan Bruce, *Images of Power: How the Image Makers Shape Our Leaders* (London: Kogan Page, 1992), 9–10; on American politics, see Kathleen Hall Jamieson, *Packaging the Presidency: A History and Criticism*

of Presidential Campaign Advertising, 3rd edn. rev. (New York: Oxford University Press, 1996 [1984]), 8–12, and Gil Troy, *See How They Ran*, 2nd edn. rev. (Cambridge: Harvard University Press, 1996 [1991]), 149. The Hearst anecdote is probably apocryphal, but it dates to the turn of the century, suggesting that pseudo-eventfulness was not unknown at that time. David Nasaw cites it in *The Chief: The Life of William Randolph Hearst* (Boston: Houghton Mifflin, 2000), 127. The case for the tale's spuriousness is argued in W. Joseph Campbell, "Not Likely Sent: The Remington-Hearst 'Telegrams,' " *Journalism and Mass Communication Quarterly*, vol. 77, no. 2 (Summer 2000), 405–22.

14. Boorstin, *The Image*, 194.

15. David Riesman, with Nathan Glazer and Reuel Denney, *The Lonely Crowd: A Study of the Changing American Character*, 3rd edn. rev. (New Haven: Yale University Press, 2000 [1950]), 180–81; David Halberstam, *The Powers That Be* (New York: Knopf, 1979), 29.

16. Richard Nixon, *RN: The Memoirs of Richard Nixon* (New York: Grosset & Dunlap, 1978; cited hereafter as *RN*), 354.

17. Jamieson, *Packaging the Presidency*, 521.

18. Kiku Adatto, *Picture Perfect: The Art and Artifice of Public Image Making* (New York: Basic Books, 1993), 24–60; Daniel C. Hallin, *We Keep America on Top of the World: Television and Journalism in the Public Sphere* (New York: Routledge, 1994), 133–52.

19. Boorstin, *The Image*, 44; the cartoon appeared in *NYT*, March 8, 1992, E4, and is described in Adatto, *Picture Perfect*, 2.

20. Peter Sloterdijk, *Critique of Cynical Reason* (Minneapolis: University of Minnesota Press, 1987), 5; the joke is attributed to comedian Lily Tomlin in William Chaloupka, *Everybody Knows: Cynicism in America* (Minneapolis: University of Minnesota Press, 1999), 27.

21. Kiku Adatto has called images "bearers of meanings, enduring carriers of ideals and myths"—Adatto, *Picture Perfect*, 167; Daniel Bell, *The End of Ideology: On the Exhaustion of Political Ideas in the Fifties*, 2nd edn. rev. (Cambridge, MA: Harvard University Press, 1988 [1960]), 38.

22. Marc Bloch, *The Historian's Craft* (New York: Knopf, 1953), 151. Michael Walzer adds that "The image provides a starting point for political thinking"; "matters of feeling" as well as logic, they "shape our whole sensibility." "On the Role of Symbolism in Political Thought," *Political Science Quarterly*, vol. 81, no. 2 (June 1967), 191–204.

23. The pioneer in this work is Fred I. Greenstein of Princeton University. On children and politics, see his "The Benevolent Leader: Children's Images of Political Authority," *American Political Science Review*, 54 (1960), 934–43; and Robert D. Hess and David Easton, "The Child's Changing Image of the President," *Public Opinion Quarterly*, 24 (1960), 632–44; on psychosomatic responses to presidential deaths, see Fred I. Greenstein, "What the President Means to Americans," in James David Barber, ed., *Choosing the President*

(Englewood, NJ: Prentice-Hall, 1974), 123-24. On Dean, see *Blind Ambition: The White House Years* (New York: Simon & Schuster, 1976), 193.

24. I have been influenced by many predecessors. A number of notable historians have studied the meanings imparted to a historical figure or event, including Peter Burke, *The Fabrication of Louis XIV* (New Haven: Yale University Press, 1992); Michael Kammen, *A Machine That Would Go of Itself: The Constitution in American Culture* (New York: Knopf, 1986); Merrill D. Peterson, *The Jefferson Image in the American Mind* (New York: Oxford University Press, 1962), and *Lincoln in American Memory* (New York: Oxford University Press, 1994); Barry Schwartz, *George Washington: The Making of an American Symbol* (New York: Free Press, 1987); and, most influential to this book, Michael Schudson, *Watergate in American Memory: How We Remember, Forget, and Reconstruct the Past* (New York: Basic Books, 1992). Of slightly different approach but also great influence in arguing for the importance of "explaining the explainers" is Ron Rosenbaum, *Explaining Hitler: The Search for the Origins of His Evil* (New York: Random House, 1998), a forerunner to which might be Peter Geyl, *Napoleon: For and Against* (New Haven: Yale University Press, 1949). I also owe a debt to those who have used multiple perspectives to expand our knowledge of history, including James Goodman, *Stories of Scottsboro* (New York: Pantheon, 1994); Eric Foner, *The Story of American Freedom* (New York: Norton, 1999); and Richard Wightman Fox, *Trials of Intimacy: Love and Loss in the Beecher-Tilton Scandal* (Chicago: University of Chicago Press, 1999). On Nixon's interest in popular culture, see Charles McWhorter, "Memorandum for File," NALN, VPP, Series 320, Box 667, Folder "Sahl, Mort"; Kutler, *Wars of Watergate*, 168; Dean, *Blind Ambition*, 31.

25. The line has often been attributed to Mort Sahl, but without certainty. Having tried to trace it, Stephen Whitfield calls the joke's source "obscure." "Richard Nixon as a Comic Figure," *American Quarterly*, vol. 37, no. 1 (Spring 1985), 116.

26. Stewart Alsop, interview with Nixon, 17, Papers of Joseph and Stewart Alsop, Box 47, Folder "Richard Nixon: The Mystery and the Man," LCMD; David Wise, "Are You Worried About Your Image, Mr. President?" *Esquire* (May 1973), 119ff.; Kutler, *Wars of Watergate*, 167; Richard Nixon, *Leaders* (New York: Warner, 1982), 4.

27. John Ehrlichman, *Witness to Power: The Nixon Years* (New York: Simon & Schuster, 1982), 275; Richard W. Waterman, Robert Wright, and Gilbert St. Clair, *The Image-Is-Everything Presidency: Dilemmas in American Leadership* (Boulder, CO: Westview, 1999); Lawrence R. Jacobs and Robert Y. Shapiro, "The Rise of Presidential Polling: The Nixon White House in Historical Perspective," *Public Opinion Quarterly*, vol. 59, no. 2 (Summer 1995), 163–95; Small, *Presidency*, 230–33; Kutler, *Wars of Watergate*, 167; Stephen Ambrose, *Nixon*, Vol. II: *The Triumph of a Politician, 1962–1972* (New York: Simon & Schuster, 1989; cited hereafter as *Ambrose 2*), 314; "Copied from Printer's Ink," NALN, VPP, Series 320, Box 311, Folder "Haldeman."

28. H. R. Haldeman, with Joseph DiMona, *The Ends of Power* (New York: Times Books, 1978), 70; Walter Cronkite, *A Reporter's Life* (New York: Knopf, 1996),

227; Dan Rather and Gary Paul Gates, *The Palace Guard* (New York: Harper, 1974), 283–85.

29. Haldeman, *Ends of Power*, 62; William Safire, *Before the Fall: An Inside View of the Pre-Watergate White House* (Garden City, NY: Doubleday, 1975), 603; Gene Marine, "What's Wrong with Nixon?: Public Life of a Cardboard Hero," *Nation*, August 16, 1956, 134; Bruce Mazlish, *In Search of Nixon* (New York: Basic Books, 1972), 74–76; Henry Spalding, *The Nixon Nobody Knows* (Middle Village, NJ: J. David, 1972); Gary Allen, *Richard Nixon: The Man Behind the Mask* (Boston: Western Islands, 1971); Bela Kornitzer, *The Real Nixon* (New York: Rand McNally, 1960); William Appleman Williams, "Excelsior!" *New York Review of Books*, February 24, 1972.

30. Earl Mazo, *Richard Nixon: A Political and Personal Portrait* (New York: Harper, 1959), 136; *NYT*, October 18, 1955, 41; David C. Williams, "Is There a New Nixon?" *ADA World* (October 1957), 3; Americans for Democratic Action Papers (ADA), Series 6, No. 64, CU, MC; Ronald Steel, *Walter Lippmann and the American Century* (Boston: Little, Brown, 1980), 589.

31. *NYP*, May 21, 1974, 41.

32. "The earliest construction of an historical object limits the range of things subsequent generations can do with it," notes sociologist Barry Schwartz, who has written about images of George Washington and Abraham Lincoln; in other words, though susceptible to revision, a public image can't be remade at will. Barry Schwartz, "Social Change and Collective Memory: The Democratization of George Washington," *American Sociological Review*, vol. 56, no. 2 (April 1991), 232.

Chapter 1: The California Conservatives: Nixon as Populist

1. RNL, PPS 1.224.

2. Roger Morris, *Richard Milhous Nixon: The Rise of an American Politician* (New York: Holt, 1990), 276; *WDN*, November 2, 1945, 1.

3. Morris, *Richard Milhous*, 276; *WDN*, November 2, 1945, 1.

4. Jorgensen OH, UCB, 8, 12; *WDN*, November 3, 1945, 1; *RN*, 35.

5. *WDN*, November 3, 1945; Herbert Parmet, interview with Nixon, June 4, 1984; Roy McLaughlin to Perry, RNL, PE 141. See also Parmet, *Richard Nixon*, 93–94; *RN*, 35; Morris, *Richard Milhous*, 280.

6. *WDN*, November 29, 1945, 1; RN to Perry, October 6, 1945, RNL, PE 147; Jorgensen OH, UCB, 12; Irwin F. Gellman, *The Contender: Richard Nixon, The Congress Years, 1946–1952* (New York: Free Press, 1999), 34–35; Kornitzer, *Real Nixon*, 154; Morris, *Richard Milhous*, 281–82.

7. Day OH, UCB; Carey McWilliams, *California: The Great Exception* (New York: Current, 1949), 193–96.

8. Stanley Kelley, *Professional Public Relations and Political Power* (Baltimore: Johns Hopkins University Press, 1956), 50.

9. On populism, see Michael Kazin, *The Populist Persuasion: An American History* (New York: Basic Books, 1995); Kevin Phillips, *The Emerging Republican Majority* (New Rochelle: Arlington House, 1969); *WP*, December 2, 1993, A21.

10. Jerry Voorhis, *Confessions of a Congressman* (Garden City, NY: Doubleday, 1947), 331; Ernest Brashear, "Who Is Richard Nixon?" *TNR*, September 1, 1952, 9–12, and September 8, 1952, 9–11; William Costello, *The Facts About Nixon: An Unauthorized Biography* (New York: Viking, 1960), 51; Stephen Ambrose, *Nixon*, Vol. I: *The Education of a Politician, 1913–1962* (New York: Simon & Schuster, 1989; cited hereafter as *Ambrose 1*), 126–27; Gellman, *Contender*, 84–85, 281.

11. Kevin P. Phillips, *Post-Conservative America: People, Politics, and Ideology in a Time of Crisis* (New York: Random House, 1982), 53–72; E. J. Dionne, *Why Americans Hate Politics* (New York: Simon & Schuster, 1991), 200–05; Godfrey Hodgson, *The World Turned Rightside Up: A History of the Conservative Ascendancy in America* (Boston: Houghton Mifflin, 1996), 123–27.

12. Clinton Rossiter, *Conservatism: The Thankless Persuasion*, 2nd edn. rev. (New York: Vintage, 1962 [1955]), 165–75.

13. On Southern California at midcentury, see John Gunther, *Inside U.S.A.* (New York: Harper, 1947), 1–63; Carey McWilliams, *California* and *Southern California Country: An Island on the Land* (New York: Duell, Sloan & Pearce, 1946); and Kevin Starr, *Material Dreams: Southern California Through the 1920s; Endangered Dreams: The Great Depression in California; The Dream Endures: California Enters the 1940s;* and *Embattled Dreams: California in War and Peace, 1940–1950* (New York: Oxford University Press, 1990, 1996, 1997, 2002, respectively).

14. McWilliams, *California*, 9; Lisa McGirr, *Suburban Warriors: Grass-Roots Conservatism in the 1960s*, unpublished dissertation, Columbia University, 1995, 33.

15. Gunther, *Inside U.S.A.*, 42; Starr, *Material Dreams*, 132.

16. Starr, *Material Dreams*, 120–50; Morris, *Richard Milhous*, 184.

17. Robert Gottlieb and Irene Wolt, *Thinking Big: The Story of the Los Angeles Times, Its Publishers and Their Influence on Southern California* (New York: Putnam, 1977), 83–105.

18. Gunther, *Inside U.S.A.*, 13–14, 53–54; McWilliams, *California*, 180ff.; see also Starr, *Endangered Dreams;* and Greg Mitchell, *The Campaign of the Century: Upton Sinclair's Race for Governor and the Birth of Media Politics* (New York: Random House, 1992).

19. Alan Brinkley, *Liberalism and Its Discontents* (Cambridge, MA: Harvard University Press, 1998), 285; Roger W. Lotchin, ed., *The Way We Really Were: The Golden State in the Second Great War* (Chicago: University of Chicago Press, 2000).

20. Morris, *Richard Milhous*, 186; James T. Patterson, *Congressional Conservatism and the New Deal* (Lexington: University of Kentucky Press, 1967); Clyde Weed, *The Nemesis of Reform: The Republican Party During the New Deal* (New

York: Columbia University Press, 1994); and Albert Fried, *F.D.R. and His Enemies* (New York: St. Martin's Press, 1999).

21. "The Best of American Life," NALN, VPP, Series 433, Box 1, Folder 1.

22. Roy Day OH, UCB; 4*RN*, 42; Gunther, *Inside U.S.A.*, 6; Parmet, *Richard Nixon*, 90.

23. Gerald Kepple OH, CSF, 6; Herbert L. Spencer to RN, December 17, 1945, RNL, PPS 1.29; Day to Fact-Finding Committee, November 15, 1945, RNL, PPS 1.10.

24. Costello, *Facts About Nixon*, 38; Frank Jorgensen OH, UCB, 5; McIntyre Faries, *Rememb'ring* (Glendale, CA: Griffin, 1993), 201; James Keogh, *This Is Nixon* (New York: Putnam, 1956), 33; Herman L. Perry to RN, September 29, 1945, RNL, PE 142; *RN*, 34.

25. Cabell Phillips, *The 1940s: Decade of Triumph and Trouble* (New York: Macmillan, 1975), 274–77; Frederick F. Siegel, *Troubled Journey: From Pearl Harbor to Ronald Reagan* (New York: Hill & Wang, 1984), 86–90.

26. Phillips, *The 1940s*, 278–85; Siegel, *Troubled Journey*, 90–92; Gunther, *Inside U.S.A.*, 5.

27. RN to Day, November 29, 1945, RNL, PPS 1.3.

28. RN to Perry, December 17, 1945, RNL, PPS 1.28; Day OH, 9; *WDN*, January 15, 1946, 3; *WDN*, January 16, 1946, 3; Calendar, RNL, PPS 212(1946).1; Wallace Black OH, 18; Kepple, OH, 5.

29. Day OH, 9; Speech, 1946, RNL, PPS 208.

30. Speech, RNL, PPS 208.2; Speech notes, March 1, 1946, RNL, PPS 208.3A; *WDN*, November 29, 1945, 10; RN to Day, December 4, 1945, RNL, PPS 1.17(1).

31. *LAT*, February 10, 1946, 1; Speech, February 12, 1946, RNL, PPS 208.3.

32. Speech notes, RNL, PPS 208.24.

33. Speech notes, RNL, PPS 208.13.

34. Parmet, *Richard Nixon*, 46–49; Speech, May 13, 1946, RNL, PPS 208.5.

35. Paul Bullock, *Jerry Voorhis: The Idealist as Politician* (New York: Vantage, 1978), 244.

36. *WDN*, January 15, 1946, 3.

37. Day to Sam Jackson, April 29, 1946, RNL, PPS 1.91; Day to Jackson, undated, RNL, PPS 1.159.

38. Day OH, 4; "Newsgram for All Nixon-for-Congress Campaign Chairmen," RNL, PPS 1.104; "Richard M. Nixon Is One of Us," RNL, PPS 1.224; Lester David, *The Lonely Lady of San Clemente: The Story of Pat Nixon* (New York: Thomas Crowell, 1978), 65. On conservative populism among postwar veterans, see Kazin, *Populist Persuasion*, 178–83.

39. Perry to Lance D. Smith, October 3, 1945, RNL, PE 145; Bruce Mazlish, "Towards a Psychohistorical Inquiry: The 'Real' Richard Nixon," in his *The Leader, the Led and the Psyche: Essays in Psychohistory* (Hanover, NH: Univer-

sity of New England Press, 1990), 207; *NYT,* January 26, 1969, 54; "News-gram for All Nixon-for-Congress Campaign Chairmen," RNL, PPS 1.104; Thomas W. Bewley to Rev. Walter Brown Murray, October 19, 1946, NALN, VPP, Series 433, Box 1, Folder 9; "How Much Experience Should a Congressman Have?", NALN, VPP, Series 434, Box 2, Folder 2; Campaign Ad, RNL, PPS 1.225.

40. Day OH, 9; Bullock, *Jerry Voorhis,* 244; *WDN,* March 6, 1946, 7; RN to John Cassidy, March 29, 1946. NALN, VPP, Series 433, Box 2, Folder 9.

41. "Richard M. Nixon Is One of Us," RNL, PPS 1.224. Tom Wicker used the phrase as the title of his 1991 book, *One of Us: Richard Nixon and the American Dream* (New York: Random House, 1991).

42. Lillian Amberson to RN, February 8, 1946, RNL, PPS 1.38; Hector M. Powell to RN, February 27, 1946, RNL, PPS 1.49; Notes, NALN, VPP, Series 433, Box 2, Folder 1; Calendar 1946, RNL, PPS 212(1946).1; Gellman, *Contender,* 44.

43. Kornitzer, *Real Nixon,* 160–61; Herbert G. Klein, *Making It Perfectly Clear* (New York: Doubleday, 1980), 77; Murray Chotiner to RN, March 4, 1946, NALN, VPP, Series 433, Box 2, Folder 2.

44. Day memo, May 17, 1946, RNL, PE 188; Carlos G. Stratton to John W. Anderson, April 29, 1946, RNL, PPS 1.103; Kenneth Spencer, et al., to "Fellow Dentist," October 22, 1946, RNL, PPS 1.207; Ron Stevens to "Fellow Members of the Insurance Business," October 21, 1946, RNL, PPS 1.206a; Advertisement, NALN, VPP, Series 433, Box 1, Folder 2.

45. Gellman, *Contender,* 58–59; Morris, *Richard Milhous,* 303; Day memo, June 11, 1946, RNL, PE 189.

46. James Boylan, *The New Deal Coalition and the Election of 1946* (New York: Garland, 1981), 121–28; Phillips, *The 1940s,* 289–90.

47. Siegel, *Troubled Journey,* 35–47; Boylan, *New Deal Coalition,* 135–40.

48. Faries, *Rememb'ring,* 204; Gellman, *Contender,* 61, 63.

49. Gellman, *Contender,* 36; Morris, *Richard Milhous,* 259–60; Voorhis, *Confessions,* 187–92.

50. Jorgensen OH, 13. On the populist element of anti-communism, see Peter Viereck, "The Revolt Against the Elite," in Daniel Bell, ed., *The Radical Right (The New American Right, Expanded and Updated)* (Garden City, NY: Doubleday, 1963), 135–54; and Kazin, *Populist Persuasion,* 165–93.

51. *WDN,* April 24, 1946, 6; *RN,* 39.

52. RNL, PE 219; *WDN,* September 17, 1946, 6; Bullock, *Jerry Voorhis,* 266; *WDN,* October 22, 1946, 1.

53. Black OH, 17; *LAT,* February 16, 1946; *Ambrose 1,* 123.

54. *RN,* 41.

55. Day OH, 10; Lyle Otterman OH, CSF 27.

56. Otterman OH, 27; Spencer to RN, September 14, 1946, RNL, SP 12; *LAT,* September 14, 1946, §III, 3; Holifield OH, 181.

57. Political advertisement, NALN, VPP, Series 433, Box 1, Folder 4; Political advertisement, NALN, VPP, Series 433, Box 1, Folder 3; "How Much Experience Should a Congressman Have?", NALN, VPP, Series 434, Box 2, Folder 2; *Alhambra Post-Advocate*, October 8, 1946, quoted in Morris, *Richard Milhous*, 325; *Alhambra Post-Advocate*, October 29, 1946, quoted in ibid., 331.

58. Holifield OH, 181; *WDN*, October 8, 1946, 1; *Alhambra Post-Advocate*, October 29, 1946; Gellman, *Contender*, 80; Morris, *Richard Milhous*, 330–31; Faries, *Rememb'ring*, 204.

59. Black OH, 20; Kepple OH, 8; Lynn Bowers and Dorothy Blair, "How to Pick a Congressman," *Saturday Evening Post*, March 19, 1949, 133.

60. Sara H. Morelock to RN, October 29, 1946, NALN, VPP, Series 433, Box 2, Folder 9; Hubert C. Perry to RN, October 29, 1946, RNL, PPS 1.169; Bowers and Blair, "How to Pick," 133; Kepple OH, 9.

61. "The People's Way," *Time*, November 18, 1946, 21.

62. *WDN*, November 7, 1946, 1; *WDN*, November 14, 1946, 1; "Nixon Letters—12th district," RNL, PPS 1.206; R. H. Poole to RN, November 6, 1946, RNL, PPS 1.330; Talmadge V. Burke to RN, November 11, 1946, RNL, PPS 1.252; Mr. and Mrs. Walter C. Ray to RN, November 17, 1946, RNL, PPS 1.336; Carl P. Miller to RN, November 8, 1946, RNL, PPS 1.317; Leland S. Poage to RN, November 7, 1946, RNL, PPS 1.329; Robert T. Radford to RN, November 11, 1946, RNL, PPS 1.334; RNL, PPS 1.235–1.391.

63. Kepple OH, 8; Black OH 14; Voorhis, *Confessions*, 334.

64. *Washington Times-Herald*, January 21, 1947; RN to Perry, April 2, 1947, RNL, PE 257; *LAT*, August 24, 1947, 7.

65. *LAT*, May 18, 1948, §II, 2; *LAT*, January 21, 1948, §I, 16.

66. Whittaker Chambers, *Witness* (New York: Random House, 1952), 793n.

67. Itinerary, NALN, VPP, Series 207, Box 1, Folder 2; Advertisement, RNL, PPS .205? Scrapbook; *LAT*, September 8, 1948, 18.

68. Quoted in Morris, *Richard Milhous*, 606; *WP*, December 5, 1948, 2M; Bowers and Blair, "How to Pick," 31ff.; Gellman, *Contender*, 335; *LAT*, November 8, 1950.

69. Mazo, *Nixon*, 85; Kornitzer, *Real Nixon*, 209; Hillings OH, 31; *Ambrose 1*, 256; Gellman, *Contender*, 346–47; Morris, *Richard Milhous*, 632–39.

70. Dwight D. Eisenhower, *Mandate for Change: The White House Years, 1953–56* (Garden City, NY: Doubleday, 1963), 46.

71. Boyd H. Gibbons to RN, August 18, 1952, NALN, VPP, Series 320, Box 287, Folder "Boyd Gibbons"; "Why It's Nixon," *USNWR*, July 18, 1952, 36; Eleanor Harris, "The Nixons," *American Weekly*, August 24, 1952, 4–5.

72. Series RNL, PPS 9.

73. Morris, *Richard Milhous*, 845; Jeanne Wells to RN, September 24, 1952, RNL, PPS 9(CA).1068; Bill Hanna to RN, September 23, 1952, RNL, PPS 9(CA).3202; Halderman, *Ends of Power*, 48–49. On responses to Checkers, see series RNL, PPS 9.

74. Lawrence Wright, "Why We Liked Dick," *Washington Monthly* (December 1986), 17–20.

75. Garry Wills, *Nixon Agonistes: The Crisis of the Self-Made Man* (New York: Signet, 1969), 140.

Chapter 2: The Fifties Liberals:
Nixon as Tricky Dick

1. Kempton, *America Comes of Middle Age*, 126.

2. Stewart Alsop, "The Mystery of Richard Nixon," *Saturday Evening Post*, July 12, 1958, 29; Alsop, interview with Nixon, 15, Papers of Joseph and Stewart Alsop, Box 47, Folder "Richard Nixon: The Mystery and the Man," LCMD.

3. Truman's other nemesis was former Missouri governor Lloyd C. Stark. Merle Miller, *Plain Speaking: An Oral Biography of Harry S. Truman* (New York: Putnam, 1974), 135, 178; John Bartlow Martin, *Adlai Stevenson of Illinois: The Life of Adlai E. Stevenson*, Vol. 1 (Garden City, NY: Doubleday, 1976), 693; Allida M. Black, *Casting Her Own Shadow: Eleanor Roosevelt and the Shaping of Postwar Liberalism* (New York: Columbia University Press, 1996), 187; Douglas Brinkley, *Dean Acheson: The Cold War Years, 1953–71* (New Haven: Yale University Press, 1992), 263; Brodie, *Richard Nixon*, 244; Richard Rovere, *Arrivals and Departures: A Journalist's Memoirs* (New York: Macmillan, 1979), 114.

4. Lippmann quoted in "What About Nixon," *TNR*, March 12, 1956, 5; Arthur Schlesinger, Jr., "What McCarthyism Is," *ADA World* (November 1950), 4, ADA Papers, Series 6, No. 64, CU MC; Costello, *Facts About Nixon*, 282; Robert W. Merry, *Taking On the World: Joseph and Stewart Alsop—Guardians of the American Century* (New York: Viking, 1996), 236.

5. *NYT*, April 24, 1994; Robert Coover, *The Public Burning* (New York: Viking, 1977); William F. Buckley, "The Nixonites on the Road," *NR*, April 11, 1975, 415.

6. D. B. Hardeman and Donald C. Bacon, *Rayburn: A Biography* (Austin: Texas Monthly Press, 1987), 382; Miller, *Plain Speaking*, 178; Kempton, *America Comes of Middle Age*, 256.

7. William Lee Miller, "The Debating Career of Richard M. Nixon," *Reporter*, April 19, 1956, 11.

8. On 1950s liberalism, see Robert Booth Fowler, *Believing Skeptics: American Political Intellectuals, 1945–1964* (Westport: Greenwood Press, 1978); Richard Pells, *The Liberal Mind in a Conservative Age: American Intellectuals in the 1940s and 1950s* (New York: Harper, 1985); Steven Gillon, *Politics and Vision: The ADA and American Liberalism, 1947–1985* (New York: Oxford University Press, 1987); and Kent M. Beck, "What Was Liberalism in the 1950s?", *Political Science Quarterly*, vol. 102, no. 2 (Summer 1987), 233–58.

9. Vance Packard, *The Hidden Persuaders* (New York: D. McKay, 1957), 155–72;

Sidney Blumenthal, *The Permanent Campaign: Inside the World of Elite Political Operatives* (Boston: Beacon Press, 1980); Jamieson, *Packaging the Presidency,* 39–121.

10. Lippmann, *Essays in the Public Philosophy* (Boston: Little, Brown, 1955), 20; Schumpeter quoted in Fowler, *Skeptics,* 149-75; Lionel Trilling, *The Liberal Imagination: Essays on Literature and Society* (New York: Viking, 1950); Dwight Macdonald, "Masscult & Midcult," in *Against the American Grain* (New York: Random House, 1962).

11. Irving Howe, "Stevenson and the Intellectuals," *Dissent,* Winter, 1954, 13; *WP,* October 23, 1952, 10; Adlai Stevenson, *The New America,* Seymour E. Harris, John Bartlow Martin, and Arthur Schlesinger, eds. (New York: Harper, 1957); Pells, *The Liberal Mind,* 392–96.

12. August Hecksher, "The Future of 'The Party of the Future': The Nixon Problem is Not Yet Settled," *Reporter,* September 20, 1956, 21–24.

13. TRB, "Washington Wire," *TNR,* October 13, 1958, 2; Carey McWilliams, "Bungling in California," *Nation,* November 4, 1950, 411; *WP,* October 28, 1950, 15B; Costello, *Facts About Nixon,* 283. On 1950, see Morris, *Richard Milhous,* 606–13; *Ambrose 1,* 215–23; Mitchell, *Campaign of the Century, passim.*

14. *NYP,* October 18, 1955, 4; *NYP,* October 20, 1955, 42; Richard Rovere, "Nixon: Most Likely to Succeed," *Harper's,* September 1955, 60; Alsop quoted in Brodie, *Richard Nixon,* 336; Selig Harrison, "Nixon: The Old Guard's Young Pretender," *TNR,* August 20, 1956, 9. On Voorhis's view of the 1946 race, see Voorhis, *Confessions,* 342, 347–49. On liberals against Hiss, see *NYP,* October 17, 1955, 1; Alistair Cooke, *A Generation on Trial: U.S.A. v. Alger Hiss* (New York: Knopf, 1950); and Kenneth O'Reilly, "Liberal Values, the Cold War, and American Intellectuals: The Trauma of the Alger Hiss Case, 1950–1978," in Athan Theoharis, ed., *Beyond the Hiss Case: The FBI, Congress and the Cold War* (Philadelphia: Temple University Press, 1982), 309–35.

15. Houston quoted in Arthur Schlesinger, Jr., *Kennedy or Nixon: Does It Make Any Difference?* (New York: Macmillan, 1960), 14.

16. *NYP,* October 20, 1955, 42; Schlesinger, *Kennedy or Nixon,* 16.

17. *NYP,* October 3, 1956, 50; Morris H. Rubin, "The Trouble with Nixon: A Documented Report," *Progressive* (October 1956), 6.

18. Meg Greenfield, "The Prose of Richard M. Nixon," *Reporter,* September 29, 1960, 15–20. For similar exegeses, see Miller, "The Debating Career," 11–17; Lynn Hinds and Carolyn Smith, "Rhetoric of Opposites: Nixspeak," *Nation,* February 16, 1970, 172–74; and Jeff Greenfield, "A Short Course in Nixon's Rhetoric," *Village Voice,* January 13, 1972, 1.

19. Ralph M. Blagden and Robert K. Bingham, "Who Is Richard Nixon?", *Reporter,* August 19, 1952, 16; Brashear, "Who Is Richard Nixon?", Parts I & II, *TNR,* September 1, 1952, 9–12, and September 8, 1952, 9–11; Willard Shelton, "The Number One Number Two Man," *Progressive* (September 1952), 9–12.

20. Jamieson, *Packaging the Presidency*, 54–55.

21. Helen Gahagan Douglas, *A Full Life* (Garden City, NY: Doubleday, 1982), 326; Greg Mitchell, *Tricky Dick and the Pink Lady: Richard Nixon vs. Helen Gahagan Douglas—Sexual Politics and the Red Scare, 1950* (New York: Random House, 1998), 138–39, 234; Costello, *Facts About Nixon*, 70–71; Morris, *Richard Milhous*, 550, 599–600. On the Malek incident, see *WP*, September 11, 1988, A1; *WP*, June 5, 1991, A1; *NYT*, October 7, 1999, A21.

22. Murray Chotiner to Mendel B. Silberberg, July 25, 1952; Chotiner memo, "Bare Gentleman's Agreement—Nixon home and others covered," October 9, 1952; Ralph E. Becker to Chotiner, August 13, 1952; Bernard Katzen telegram to Tom Stephens, August 13, 1952; Katzen to Chotiner, September 2, 1952; Chotiner to McIntyre Faries, October 8, 1952; RN to Edgar L. Strauss, August 8, 1952, NALN, VPP, Series 320, Box 46, Folder "Anti-Semitic"; Arnold Forster to ADL Regional Directories, August 19, 1952, NALN, VPP, Series 320, Box 45, Folder "Anti-Defamation League."

23. Faries to Chotiner, October 6, 1952, NALN, VPP, Series 320, Box 46, Folder "Anti-Semitic"; Press release, September 3, 1960, NALN, VPP, Series 320, Box 384, Folder "Jewish Problem (political)"; Al S. Waxman, "Nixon's Anti-Semitic Record," *Beverly Hills Reporter*, August 29, 1956, 1, NALN, VPP, Series 320, Box 80, Folder "Beverly Hills Reporter"; Raymond Moley, "Nixon and Anti-Semitism," *Newsweek*, September 5, 1960, 76.

24. Brashear Part I, 12; Blagden and Bingham, "Who Is Richard Nixon?", 1616; "Pearson Reports on His Investigation of Nixon's Life," *Radio Reports*, October 5, 1952, RNL, SM 58; *WP*, October 6, 1952, 27; *WP*, October 30, 1952, 3, 41; Costello, *Facts About Nixon*, 114; *RN*, 108–9.

25. "Pearson Discusses Nixon's Relations with His Law Firm," *Radio Reports*, September 28, 1952, RNL, SM 54; "Says Celler Asks Nixon to Explain Aid to Malaxa," *Radio Reports*, October 12, 1952, RNL, SM 59; "Nixon Writes Ambassador to Aid Smith in Gambling Debt, Says Pearson," *Radio Reports*, October 26, 1952, RNL, SM 61; *WP*, September 29, 1952, B25; *WP*, October 10, 1952, B55; *WP*, October 30, 1952, 3, 41; *WP*, November 3, 1952, B27; NALN, VPP, Series 320, Box 702, Folder "Forgeries"; NALN, VPP, Series 320, Box 702, Folder "Malaxa Case"; Drew Pearson, *Diaries, 1949–1959* (New York: Holt, 1974), 227, 229, 238, 239.

26. Oliver Pilat, *Drew Pearson: An Unauthorized Biography* (New York: Harper's Magazine Press, 1973), 303; Jack Anderson, with James Boyd, *Confessions of a Muckraker: The Inside Story of Life in Washington During the Truman, Eisenhower, Kennedy and Johnson Years* (New York: Random House, 1979), 326; Morris, *Richard Milhous*, 812; *NYP*, September 18, 1952, 1. See also Richard J. Donovan, "Birth of a Salesman," *Reporter*, October 14, 1952, 29–33; "Richard Nixon's Secret Income," *TNR*, September 29, 1952, 10ff.

27. Mazo, *Nixon*, 112–18; Morris, *Richard Milhous*, 785–90; Richard Nixon, *Six Crises* (Garden City, NY: Doubleday, 1962), 83; *RN*, 96; *NYT*, September 20, 1952, 1, 8; *NYP*, September 21, 1952, 1.

28. Jean Begeman, "Nixon: How the Press Suppressed the News," *TNR*, Octo-

ber 6, 1952, 11–13; "Nixon Incident Jolts GOP; Alters Campaign Strategy," *Newsweek*, September 29, 1952, 25; "Sir Mordred," *TNR*, September 29, 1952, 6.

29. Alsop, "Mystery," 66.

30. "Richard Nixon's Secret Income," *TNR*, September 29, 1952, 10; *NYP*, September 24, 1952, 48.

31. Schlesinger, *Kennedy or Nixon*, 12–13; *NYP*, September 24, 1952, 44.

32. *NYP*, September 24, 1952, 44.

33. *NYT*, September 28, 1952, E5; *NYP*, September 25, 1952, 26.

34. *NYP*, September 26, 1952; for a similar view, held by the Alsop brothers, see *WP*, October 19, 1952, 5B.

35. Richard Rovere, *Final Reports: Personal Reflections on Politics and History in Our Time* (Garden City, NY: Doubleday, 1984), 33.

36. Drew Pearson and Jack Anderson, *U.S.A—Second Class Power?* (New York: Simon & Schuster, 1958), 277; Brodie, *Richard Nixon*, 292–93; Costello, *Facts About Nixon*, 117.

37. John Bartlow Martin, *Adlai Stevenson and the World: The Life of Adlai E. Stevenson*, Vol. 2 (Garden City, NY: Doubleday, 1977), 105.

38. *NYT*, March 14, 1954.

39. *NYP*, March 15, 1954, 22; *NYT*, March 14, 1954, 46; *NYP*, March 15, 1954, 22.

40. Rubin, "Trouble with Nixon," 8; Parmet, *Richard Nixon*, 262.

41. Stephen Edward Kercher, "The Limits of Irreverence: 'Sick' Humor and Satire in America, 1950–1964," PhD dissertation, Indiana University, 2000, 34, 59.

42. Whitfield, "Richard Nixon as a Comic Figure," 116; Kercher, "Limits of Irreverence," 30; Parmet, *Richard Nixon*, 262; Herbert Block, *Herblock Special Report* (New York: Norton, 1974), 34, 38–40; *WP*, October 23, 1954, 9; *Ambrose 1*, 357; Halberstam, *The Powers That Be*, 842–43.

43. John Bartlow Martin, *Stevenson and the World*, 129; Irving Howe, "Poor Richard Nixon," *TNR*, May 7, 1956, 8.

44. Howe, "Poor Richard Nixon," 9; Hecksher, "The Future of 'The Party of the Future,'" 23; Lippmann quoted in "What About Nixon," *TNR*, March 12, 1956, 5.

45. *Nixon: The Second Man* (pamphlet), 7. Americans for Democratic Action Papers, Series 6, No. 64, CU, MC.

46. Robert Coughlan, "A Debate, Pro and Con. Subject: Richard M. Nixon," *Life*, July 16, 1956, 93.

47. TRB, "Washington Wire," *TNR*, November 5, 1958, 2.

48. Susan E. Tifft and Alex S. Jones, *The Trust: The Private and Powerful Family Behind the New York Times* (Boston: Little, Brown, 1999), 289.

49. *Nixon: The Second Man*, 1; Franklin A. Moss to Violet Gunther, September 11, 1956, Americans for Democratic Action Papers, Series 6, No. 64, CU, MC; Ben Mandel to RN, March 16, 1956; Robert C. McManus to Robert

Humphreys, April 24, 1956, NALN, VPP, Series 320, Box 700, Folder "Smears (Ballad of Richard Nixon)"; Advertisement, *Progressive* (October 1956), 40.

50. "How Fit Is Nixon for President?", NALN, VPP, Series 320, Box 45, Folder "Anti-Nixon"; Alsop, "Mystery," 66; "The Vice-Presidency: Target: The Issue," *Time*, January 24, 1955; "After Chicago," *Newsweek*, August 27, 1956; *NYT*, October 9, 1956, 12; *NYT*, October 24, 1956, 8; *NYT*, October 31, 1956, 10; Jamieson, *Packaging the Presidency*, 103; "The 'Different' Nixon of '56," *Newsweek*, October 1, 1956, 25–31.

51. Stevenson, *The New America*, 193, xxiv; John Kenneth Galbraith, *A Life in Our Times: Memoirs* (Boston: Houghton Mifflin, 1981), 346; Jeff Broadwater, *Adlai Stevenson and American Politics: The Odyssey of a Cold War Liberal* (New York: Twayne, 1994), 171; Stevenson, *The New America*, 249; Brodie, *Richard Nixon*, 357; Jamieson, *Packaging the Presidency*, 104–05.

52. *NYP*, October 10, 1956, 48; Martin, *Stevenson and the World*, 390.

53. Martin, *Stevenson and the World*, 390; Jamieson, *Packaging the Presidency*, 103–04; William Lee Miller, "'Should We Fight Dirty Too?' A Democrat Gives His Answer," *Reporter*, October 21, 1954, 19.

54. *NYT*, October 18, 1956; Alsop, "Mystery," 70; Gerald Gardner, *The Mocking of the President: A History of Campaign Humor from Ike to Ronnie* (Detroit: Wayne State University Press, 1988), 105; *NYP*, October 20, 1955. On the New Nixon, see also Richard L. Wilson, "The Big Change in Richard Nixon," *Look*, September 3, 1957; Cabell Phillips, "Nixon in '58—and Nixon in '60," *NYT Magazine*, October 24, 1958.

55. Brodie, *Richard Nixon*, 357; Kenneth S. Davis, *The Politics of Honor: A Biography of Adlai E. Stevenson* (New York: Putnam, 1972), 347; Pearson and Anderson, *U.S.A.*, 298.

56. *WP*, October 26, 1956; *WP*, February 15, 1956; Block, *Special Report*, 43–44.

57. *NYP*, October 21, 1955, 5; Rovere, "Nixon," 57–63; R.T. McKenzie, "Ike: Stuck with Dick," *Nation*, September 1, 1956, 171; *Ambrose 1*, 297. See also Robert Bendiner, "All Things to All Republicans," *Reporter*, November 4, 1954, 15–17; Robert Riggs, "Flexible Dick Nixon: Still the Man to Beat," *Progressive* (November 1955), 5–8; Marine, "Cardboard Hero," 131–34.

58. Greenfield, "Prose of Richard M. Nixon," 19; "*Reporter's* Notes," *Reporter*, December 12, 1957, 2; *NYP*, October 3, 1956, 50; Kornitzer, *Real Nixon*, 107.

59. Miller, "The Debating Career," 11, 12.

60. *NYP*, October 20, 1955, 42. The phrase was California senator William Knowland's, but liberals quoted it.

61. Rubin, "Trouble with Nixon," 8; Rovere, "Nixon," 61; Howe, "Poor Richard Nixon," 9; Marine, "Cardboard Hero," 131; "Salesman's Progress," *Reporter*, February 16, 1954, 4.

62. *Nixon: The Second Man*, 8.

63. Stevenson, *The New America*, 5; Douglass Cater, "Who Is Nixon, What Is He?" *Reporter*, November 27, 1958, 10; Costello, *Facts About Nixon*, 265.

64. Packard, *Hidden Persuaders*, 155, 164.

65. Ibid., 200; Schlesinger, *Kennedy or Nixon*, 10.

66. Eisenhower quoted in Siegel, *Troubled Journey*, 105.

67. *NYP*, October 19, 1956; Schlesinger, *Kennedy or Nixon*, 4, 18; Howe, "Poor Richard Nixon," 9.

68. Costello, *Facts About Nixon*, 283, 290; Pearson and Anderson, *U.S.A.*, 300.

69. Sevareid quoted in Schlesinger, *Kennedy or Nixon*, 1; Dwight Macdonald, "The Candidates and I," *Commentary* (April 1960), 288–93.

70. Martin, *Stevenson and the World*, 469; Schlesinger, *Kennedy or Nixon*, 4, 8–9; Kercher, "Limits of Irreverence," 253, 258.

71. Theodore H. White, *The Making of the President, 1960* (New York: Atheneum, 1961), 293; Brodie, *Richard Nixon*, 427.

72. Boorstin, *The Image*, 44.

73. Cater, "Who Is Nixon," 13.

74. Meg Greenfield, *Washington* (New York: Public Affairs, 2001), 79.

Chapter 3: The New Left Radicals: Nixon as Conspirator

1. Hunter S. Thompson, *The Great Shark Hunt: Strange Tales from a Strange Time* (New York: Summit, 1979), 19, 24.

2. John Ehrlichman, "The White House and Policy Making," in *NP*, 138; Nicholas Lemann, *The Promised Land: The Great Migration and How It Changed America* (New York: Knopf, 1991), 208. On Nixon's inaugural, see *Ambrose 2*, 243–45; Small, *Presidency*, 35–36; *RN*, 365–67.

3. *WDN*, January 18, 1969, 1; *NYT*, January 21, 1969, 23; *NYT*, January 21, 1969, 22; Stew Albert, "The Dream Is Dead: Inhoguration Daze," *Berkeley Barb*, January 24, 1969, 5; "A Call to Come to Washington, D.C. January 19," SHSW, SPP.

4. Rennie Davis and Ruth Gallo to "Friends," November 27, 1968, SHSW, SPP; *Berkeley Barb*, January 24, 1969, 5; Steve Lerner, ". . . And Chicago Was Last Summer," *Village Voice*, January 23, 1969, 1; Thompson, *Great Shark Hunt*, 179.

5. *Berkeley Barb*, January 24, 1969, 5; *Liberation* (February 1969), 27; Fred Halstead, *Out Now!: A Participant's Account of the American Movement Against the Vietnam War* (New York: Monad, 1978), 441–46.

6. *RN*, 366.

7. Ibid.; *NYT*, January 21, 1969; Nancy Zaroulis and Gerald Sullivan, *Who Spoke Up?: American Protest Against the War in Vietnam, 1963–1975* (Garden City, NY: Doubleday, 1984), 210.

8. Zaroulis and Sullivan, *Who Spoke Up?*, 210; Allan Brick to "New Mobe Key Contacts," undated, SHSW, SAVF, Box 31; David Dellinger, *More Power Than*

We Know: The People's Movement Toward Democracy (Garden City, NY: Doubleday, Anchor Books, 1975), 66–69; Sidney Lens, *Unrepentant Radical: An American Activist's Account of Five Turbulent Decades* (Boston: Beacon Press, 1980), 341–43; *NYT*, May 31, 1973, 1.

9. I. F. Stone, "Nixon's Blitzkrieg," *New York Review of Books*, January 25, 1973, 13.

10. The terms were coined by Daniel Pipes in *Conspiracy: How the Paranoid Style Flourishes and Where It Comes From* (New York: Free Press, 1997), and Richard Hofstadter in *The Paranoid Style in American Politics* (New York: Knopf, 1965).

11. Pamphlet, New Left Collection, HIA, Stanford University, Box 59; Hunter S. Thompson, *Fear and Loathing on the Campaign Trail '72* (San Francisco: Straight Arrow, 1973), 140; Todd Gitlin, *The Sixties: Years of Hope, Days of Rage* (New York: Bantam Books, 1997), 339.

12. On Nixon's comeback, see *Ambrose 2*, 1–222; Jules Witcover, *The Resurrection of Richard Nixon* (New York: Putnam, 1970).

13. David Mixner, *Stranger Among Friends* (New York: Bantam Books, 1996), 56; Thompson, *Fear and Loathing*, 397, 20; *NYT*, October 11, 1968, 53; Milton Viorst, *Fire in the Streets: America in the 1960s* (New York: Simon & Schuster, 1979), 511–12; John Heineman, "Look Out Kid, You're Gonna Get Hit!: Kent State and the Vietnam Antiwar Movement," in Melvin Small and William D. Hoover, eds., *Give Peace a Chance: Exploring the Vietnam Antiwar Movement* (Syracuse: Syracuse University Press, 1992), 212–13; *NYT*, October 2, 1968, 28; Mobe memo, SHSW, SPP.

14. Waskow to the Mobilization Administrative Committee, November 8, 1968, SHSW, SPP; Gitlin, *Sixties*, 340.

15. *NYT*, May 20, 1977; *NYT*, February 12, 1998; Fred Emery, *Watergate: The Corruption of American Politics and the Fall of Richard Nixon* (New York: Times Books, 1994), 426; Small, *Presidency*, 310; Michael Genovese, *The Nixon Presidency: Power and Politics in Turbulent Times* (Westport: Greenwood Press, 1990) 231; Arthur M. Schlesinger, Jr., "The Evolution of the Nixon Legacy: Discussant," in Leon Friedman and William Levantrosser, eds., *Watergate and Afterward: The Legacy of Richard M. Nixon* (Westport: Greenwood Press, 1992; cited hereafter as *Hofstra 2*), 327; Kutler, *Wars of Watergate*, 617.

16. C. Wright Mills, *The Power Elite* (New York: Oxford University Press, 1956); William Appleman Williams, *The Tragedy of American Diplomacy* (Cleveland: World, 1959).

17. *United States v. United States District Court for the Eastern District of Michigan* 407 U.S. 297 (1972).

18. Christopher Pyle, "CONUS Intelligence: The Army Watches Civilian Politics," *Washington Monthly* (January 1970), 4–16; *NYT*, March 10, 1971, 7; *NYT*, March 29, 1971, 20; *NYT*, April 17, 1971, 1; Christopher Pyle, "Military Surveillance of Civilian Politics, 1967–1970," PhD dissertation, Columbia University, 1974; *NYT*, January 16, 1970, 21; *NYT*, February 25, 1971, 14. See also David Wise, *The American Police State: The Government Against the People* (New York: Random House, 1976), 4–106; Frank J. Donner, *The Age of Sur-*

veillance: The Aims and Methods of America's Political Intelligence System (New York: Knopf, 1980), 241–86; and Athan Theoharis, "Thirty Years of Wiretapping," *Nation*, June 14, 1971, 744–50. On the so-called Kissinger taps, see Emery, *Watergate*, 9–13; J. Anthony Lukas, *Nightmare: The Underside of the Nixon Years* (New York: Viking, 1976), 40–67; and the pages in Wise cited just above. For Kissinger's self-defense, see Henry Kissinger, *Years of Upheaval* (Boston: Little, Brown, 1982), 118–22.

19. Mixner, *Stranger*, 106–10; *NYT*, May 5, 1969, 30.

20. *Report of the President's Commission on Campus Unrest* (Washington, DC: Government Printing Office, 1970), 1, 38; Brown quoted in Gitlin, *Sixties*, 316. Other sources quote Brown as saying violence is as American as cherry pie, but this does not make much sense, since cherry pie is not commonly thought of as a classic American dessert.

21. Huston to Haldeman, March 12, 1970, NPMP, WHSF, H. R. Haldeman Papers (HRH), Box 152, quoted in Tom Wells, *The War Within: America's Battle Over Vietnam* (Berkeley: University of California Press, 1994), 413; Jeb Stuart Magruder, *An American Life: One Man's Road to Watergate* (New York: Atheneum, 1974), 196–97; Lukas, *Nightmare*, 9–40; Moynihan to Haldeman, March 12, 1970, NPMP, WHSF, HRH, Box 152, in Wells, *War Within*, 413–14; Lemann, *Promised Land*, 204–05; *NYT*, September 24, 1981, 1; Genovese, *Presidency*, 128. On administration figures fearing retribution, see Spiro Agnew, *Go Quietly . . . Or Else* (New York: Morrow, 1980), 189; Dean, *Blind Ambition*, 272–73, 292, 309.

22. On journalists' fears, see Wise, *Police State*, 161–72; Katharine Graham, *Personal History* (New York: Knopf, 1997), 483; Howard Bray, *The Pillars of the Post: The Making of a News Empire in Washington* (New York: Norton, 1980), 132; Bob Woodward and Carl Bernstein, *All the President's Men* (New York: Simon & Schuster, 1974), 317. On the Jack Anderson incident, see G. Gordon Liddy, *Will: The Autobiography of G. Gordon Liddy* (New York: St. Martin's Press, 1996 [1980]), 207–10, 213–14.

23. David, "1984 Is Alive and Well in Amerika," *Berkeley Barb*, December 5, 1969, 15.

24. Wells, *War Within*, 311; Judith Clavir Albert and Stewart Edward Albert, *The Sixties Papers: Documents of a Rebellious Decade* (New York: Praeger, 1984), 37; Wise, *Police State*, 408; Donner, *Age of Surveillance*, 22–30. On the campaign against black nationalists, see Donner, *Surveillance*, 212–37; Sidney Blumenthal, "Cointelpro: How the FBI Tried to Destroy the Black Panthers," in Sidney Blumenthal and Harvey Yazijian, eds., *Government by Gunplay: Assassination Conspiracy Theories from Dallas to Today* (New York: Signet, 1976), 68–92.

25. Geoffrey Rips, *The Campaign Against the Underground Press* (San Francisco: City Lights, 1981); Muhammad Khan I, "Draft Shaft from Dick," *Berkeley Barb*, September 5, 1969, 2; Bill Biggin, "Nixon's Plan for Amerikkka," *Philadelphia Free Press*, April 20, 1970, 3.

26. Hofstadter quoted in "The Spirit of '70: Six Historians Reflect on What Ails the American Spirit," *Newsweek*, July 6, 1970, 23.

27. Jacob Cohen, "Conspiracy Fever," *Commentary*, vol. 60, no. 4 (October 1975), 33–42; Hofstadter, "Spirit," 3–40; Bernard Bailyn, *The Ideological Origins of the American Revolution* (Cambridge, MA: Harvard University Press, 1967); David Brion Davis, ed., *The Fear of Conspiracy: Images of Un-American Subversion from the Revolution to the Present* (Ithaca: Cornell University Press, 1971), xiii–xiv; David Brion Davis, *The Slave Power Conspiracy and the Paranoid Style* (Baton Rouge: Louisiana State University Press, 1969); James Hitchcock, "The McCarthyism of the Left," in Richard O. Curry and Thomas M. Brown, eds., *Conspiracy: The Fear of Subversion in American History* (New York: Holt, 1972), 239–51. See also Alan F. Westin, "Radical Left and Radical Right: The Deadly Parallels," *Harper's* (April 1962), 25–32.

28. Tony Tanner, *City of Words* (New York: Harper & Row, 1971), 15; Thomas Pynchon, *Gravity's Rainbow* (New York: Viking, 1973), 754–57; Ishmael Reed, "D Hexorcism of Noxon D Awful," in John A. Williams and Charles F. Harris, eds., *Amistad I: Writings on Black History and Culture* (New York: Vintage, 1970).

29. Lou Rossetto, *The Take-Over* (Seacaucus, NJ: Lyle Stuart, 1974); J. E. Vacha, "It Could Happen Here: The Rise of the Political Scenario Novel," *American Quarterly*, vol. 29, no. 2 (Summer 1977), 194–206; Philip K. Dick, *Radio Free Albemuth* (New York: Arbor House, 1985). Published posthumously, *Albemuth* was written around the time of Nixon's presidency.

30. Irving Howe, "Watergate: The Z Connection," *Dissent* (Summer 1973), 276.

31. On conspiracy films, see Fredric Jameson, *The Geopolitical Aesthetic: Cinema and Space in the World System* (Bloomington: Indiana University Press, 1992), 11–84; Peter Lev, *American Films of the '70s* (Austin: University of Texas Press, 2000), 49–68. *Klute* was made before Nixon's taping system came to light.

32. Bruce Wiegl, "Nixon," *American Poetry Review*, vol. 29, no. 3 (May–June 2000), 33.

33. Elizabeth Drew, "Silent Spring," *Atlantic* (April 1969), 14; Todd Gitlin, Foreword, in Wells, *War Within*, xiv.

34. Sid Lens, "Editorial: Nixon's Peace Plan," *Liberation* (June 1969), 2–3; I. F. Stone, "Lessons for Nixon," *New York Review of Books*, December 4, 1969; *WP*, October 7, 1969, A19; Lukas, *Nightmare*, 11.

35. Mixner, *Stranger*, 99; Lens, *Unrepentant Radical*, 356.

36. Lukas, *Nightmare*, 9; Melvin Small, *Johnson, Nixon and the Doves* (New Brunswick: Rutgers University Press, 1988), 202; Zaroulis and Sullivan, *Who Spoke Up?*, 320; Flyer, SHSW, SAVF, Box 5; Charles DeBenedetti, with Charles Chatfield, *An American Ordeal: The Antiwar Movement of the Vietnam Era* (Syracuse, NY: Syracuse University Press, 1990), 280; Wells, *War Within*, 443.

37. Wells, *War Within*, 431–36; Bill Gulley with Mary Ellen Reese, *Breaking Cover* (New York: Simon & Schuster, 1978), 166–67.

38. "Tin Soldiers & Nixon Coming," *Rolling Stone*, June 25, 1970, 3; "The Politics of Manslaughter," *Nation*, May 18, 1970, 578–79; John Morthland, "Nixon in

Public: He Was Mumbling at His Feet," *Rolling Stone,* June 11, 1970, 10; Poster, SHSW, SAVF, Box 31; Whitfield, "Richard Nixon as a Comic Figure," 122.

39. "More Flimflam," *Nation,* May 4, 1970, 515; Morthland, "Nixon in Public," 11.

40. Daniel Berrigan, "Street Without Joy," *Berkeley Barb,* July 28, 1972, 2; Norman Mailer, *St. George and the Godfather* (New York: New American Library, 1972), 168, 217; Pablo Neruda, "The Song of Punishment," in *A Call for the Destruction of Nixon and Praise for the Revolution,* trans. Teresa Anderson (Cambridge, MA: West End, 1980); Sanford Levinson, "Responsibility for Crimes of War," *Philosophy and Public Affairs,* vol. 2, no. 3 (Spring 1973), 244–73; Richard Falk, Gabriel Kolko, and Robert Jay Lifton, eds., *Crimes of War* (New York: Random House, 1971); Neil Sheehan, "Should We Have War Crimes Trials?" *NYT Book Review,* March 28, 1971, 1.

41. Thomas Monsell, *Nixon on Stage and Screen: The Thirty-seventh President as Depicted in Films, Television, Plays and Opera* (Jefferson, NC: McFarland, 1998), 92–94; Andor Skotnes, "Hearts and Minds," *Radical History Review,* 60 (Fall 1994), 186–88; Gerald S. and Deborah H. Strober, *Nixon: An Oral History of His Presidency* (New York: Harper, 1994), 195, 200.

42. Ron Rosenbaum, "The '72 Election May Be Held as Scheduled," *Village Voice,* April 16, 1970, 3.

43. Ron Rosenbaum, "Anatomy of a Rumor," *Village Voice,* November 5, 1970, 5ff.; Dick Gregory, "The Party's Over," [Richmond, CA] *Freedom News,* July 1970, 2–3; "Infrastructure of Repression," *Nation,* April 27, 1970, 482–83; Art Kunin, "Will Nixon Cancel the Elections?", *Los Angeles Free Press,* May 8–14, 1970, 1.

44. Rosenbaum, "Anatomy of a Rumor," 5ff.; James Keogh, *President Nixon and the Press* (New York: Funk & Wagnalls, 1972), 148; *Scanlan's Monthly* (August 1970), 1, advertisement; "The Famous Agnew Memo," *NYT,* July 30, 1970, 34; *NYT,* July 22, 1970, 23; *NYT,* July 30, 1970, 15; Dean, *Blind Ambition,* 24–26. For the hard-hat incident, see Wells, *War Within,* 426–27; Zaroulis and Sullivan, *Who Spoke Up?,* 334–35.

45. "Infrastructure of Repression," *Nation,* April 27, 1970, 482–83; Rosenbaum, "Anatomy of a Rumor," 5ff.

46. *RN,* 492–93; "Nixon Came to San Jose," *San Jose Red Eye,* November 12–25, 1970, 3; Safire, *Before the Fall,* 327–34; *HD,* October 29, 1970, 245.

47. "Nixon Came to San Jose," *San Jose Red Eye,* November 12–25, 1970, 3; "What Really Happened," *Free You,* November 4, 1970, 13–14; "San Jose: 'V' for Victim," *Kudzu,* November 1970, 3; Tom DeVries, "Nixon Wasn't Stoned," *Village Voice,* November 5, 1970, 3; Donald Freed, "Gemstone: The Bottom Line," in Steve Weissman, ed., *Big Brother and the Holding Company: The World Behind Watergate* (Palo Alto, CA: Ramparts, 1974), 95.

48. "The Anatomy of San Jose," *Nation,* November 16, 1970, 482; Mel Wax, "Incident at San Jose," *CJR* (Winter 1970–71), 47–52; Safire, *Before the Fall,* 331–32.

49. Gulley, *Breaking Cover*, 198; *HD*, October 29, 1970, 245.

50. Lawrence Ferlinghetti, "Tyrannus Nix?", *Ramparts* (December 1969), 45–50.

51. Garry Trudeau, *Doonesbury*, *WP*, June 19, 1972; June 26, 1972; Edward Sorel, *Unauthorized Portraits* (New York: Knopf, 1997), 129, 131.

52. *Berkeley Barb*, November 10, 1972; SAVF, SHSW, Box 17; "What It Was," *Nation*, June 4, 1973, 709; *Los Angeles Free Press*, June 12, 1970.

53. Bella S. Abzug, *Bella!: Ms. Abzug Goes to Washington* (New York: Saturday Review, 1972), 134; *NYT*, August 16, 1972, 20; *NYT*, October 23, 1972, 25; *NYT*, August 17, 1972, 24. Boasted Hunter Thompson: "I was, after all, the only accredited journalist covering the 1972 campaign to compare Nixon with Adolf Hitler." Thompson, *Great Shark Hunt*, 239.

54. *NYT*, August 31, 1971, 33; "The Dick Nixon Show," *Nation*, January 24, 1972, 98; *NYT*, May 9, 1972, 41; Robert Lowell, "George III," in Tom Paulin, ed., *The Faber Book of Political Verse* (Boston: Faber & Faber, 1986), 404–06.

55. Wells, *War Within*, 524–27.

56. *NYT*, November 10, 1968, 1; *NYT*, August 21, 1973, 1.

57. David Hilliard, *This Side of Glory: The Autobiography of David Hilliard and the Story of the Black Panther Party* (Boston: Little, Brown, 1973), 265–66, 272, 335; *NYT*, May 5, 1971, 1.

58. *Berkeley Barb*, May 28, 1971; Paul Krassner, *Confessions of a Raving, Unconfined Nut: Misadventures in the Counter-Culture* (New York: Simon & Schuster, 1993), 124–25.

59. Kutler, *Wars of Watergate*, 442; *NR*, February 1, 1974, 123; Lens, *Unrepentant Radical*, 358; Wells, *War Within*, 421; Abzug, *Bella!*, 295.

60. *NYT*, June 1, 1972, 27.

61. Thompson, *Great Shark Hunt*, 24; Bo Burlingham, "To Our Newsstand Readers," *Ramparts* (November 1973); David Armstrong, "Opened Watergate," *Berkeley Barb*, February 1–7, 1974, 8.

62. Herbert S. Levine, "Watergate: Surreptitious Entry: The Hitler Analogy," *Nation*, September 10, 1973, 199–202; Levine, "The Culture of Fascism," *Nation*, August 17, 1974, 103–07; *WP*, May 31, 1973; Elizabeth Drew, *Washington Journal: The Events of 1973–1974* (New York: Random House, 1974), 53; *RN*, 935; I. F. Stone, "Impeachment," *New York Review of Books*, June 28, 1973, 12–19; Stone, "Why Nixon Fears to Resign," *New York Review of Books*, November 29, 1973, 14; Ramsey Clark, "Watergate: Brush with Tyranny," *Nation*, June 4, 1973, 712–14; James David Barber, "The Nixon Brush with Tyranny," *Political Science Quarterly*, vol. 92, no. 4 (Winter 1977–78), 581–605.

63. John Herbers, *No Thank You, Mr. President* (New York: Norton, 1976), 48–51; *NYT*, March 4–7, 1973; RN to Ehrlichman, March 4, 1973, WHSF, PPF, Box 4; Arthur M. Schlesinger, Jr., *The Imperial Presidency* (Boston: Houghton Mifflin, 1973), ix, 417–18, 378.

64. Schlesinger, *Imperial Presidency*, 378; George McGovern, *Grassroots: The Autobiography of George McGovern* (New York: Random House, 1977), 254; Noam Chomsky, "Watergate and Other Crimes," *Ramparts* (June 1974), 32.

65. Chomsky, "Watergate and Other Crimes," 32; "The First Word," *Ramparts* (June 1973), 2.

66. Dellinger, *More Power*, 37.

67. Chomsky, "Watergate and Other Crimes," 35.

68. Dellinger, *More Power*, 65.

69. The two main anthologies are Sidney Blumenthal and Harvey Yazijian, eds., *Government by Gunplay: Assassination Conspiracy Theories from Dallas to Today* (New York: Signet Books, 1976), and Steve Weissman, ed., *Big Brother and the Holding Company: The World Behind Watergate* (Palo Alto, CA: Ramparts, 1974).

70. Blumenthal and Yazijian, eds., *Gunplay*, 130–35; Weissman, *Big Brother*, 251–75.

71. "Sundance Links Dick and Mob," *Berkeley Barb*, October 27, 1972; "The Mafia Metaphor," *Nation*, July 10, 1972; "Gang War Erupts Over Burglary," *Ramparts* (August–September 1973).

72. Paul Hoffman, "Don't Read This Unless You're Paranoid," *Village Voice*, June 7, 1973, 5–7, 13; Barboura Morris Freed, "Flight 533: The Watergate Murder?" in Weissman, ed., *Big Brother*, 127–58; "Colson's Weird Scenario," *Time*, July 8, 1974, 16. According to private detective Richard Lee Bast, Colson said of the CIA, "I don't say this to my people. They'd think I'm nuts. I think they killed Dorothy Hunt." For more on CIA theories, see chapter 5.

73. The Editors, "A Decade of Unanswered Questions," *Ramparts* (December 1973), 43.

74. Small, *Presidency*, 22. Key conspiracist works include Harrison E. Livingstone and Robert J. Groden, *The Assassination of JFK and the Case for Conspiracy* (New York: Carroll & Graf, 1998 [1980]); Carl Oglesby, *The Yankee and Cowboy War: Conspiracies from Dallas to Watergate* (Kansas City: Sheed Andrews & McMeel, 1976); L. Fletcher Prouty, *The Secret Team: The CIA and Its Allies in Control of the United States and the World* (Englewood Cliffs, NJ: Prentice-Hall, 1973) and *JFK: The CIA, Vietnam and the Plot to Assassinate John F. Kennedy* (New York: Carol, 1996); Peter Dale Scott, *Crime and Cover-Up: The CIA, the Mafia and the Dallas-Watergate Connection* (Berkeley: Westworks, 1977) and *Deep Politics and the Death of JFK* (Berkeley: University of California Press, 1993); and Scott, Paul L. Hoch, and Russell Stetler, eds., *The Assassinations: Dallas and Beyond* (New York: Random House, 1976).

75. Peter Dale Scott, "From Dallas to Watergate: The Longest Cover-Up," *Ramparts* (November 1973), 12–54; Mae Brussell, "Why Was Martha Mitchell Kidnapped?", *The Realist* (August 1972); "Mae Brussell's Conspiracy Newsletter," published by *The Realist*, undated; Krassner, *Confessions*, 199–215.

76. Oglesby, *Yankee and Cowboy War*, 357.

77. Ibid., 4.

78. Ibid., 232, 264; Ron Dorfman, "The Truth Is Bad Enough," *Nation*, July 30,

1973, 73–75; Carl Oglesby, "Conspiracy or Miasma?", *Nation*, September 3, 1973, 162, 180.

79. Kirkpatrick Sale, "Yankees and Cowboys—The World Behind Watergate," in Weissman, ed., *Big Brother*, 277–96, adapted from Sale, "The World Behind Watergate," *New York Review of Books*, May 3, 1973; Oglesby, *Yankee and Cowboy War*, 23.

80. Chris Salewicz, *Oliver Stone* (London: Orion, 1997), 112; Fred Barnes, "Not the One: Nixon's Inaccuracies," *TNR*, January 22, 1996, 10; *San Francisco Chronicle*, December 22, 1995, A29; *WP*, December 18, 1995, G01; *NYT*, December 17, 1995, §2, 1; *Chicago Sun-Times*, December 17, 1995, Show 1; Kathryn S. Olmstead, *Challenging the Secret Government: The Post-Watergate Investigations of the CIA and FBI* (Chapel Hill: University of North Carolina Press, 1996), 77–79; Robert Brent Toplin, *History by Hollywood: The Use and Abuse of the American Past* (Urbana: University of Illinois Press, 1996), 50–51; *Boston Globe*, November 16, 1991, §3, 10; *Boston Globe*, December 19, 1991, 1; *Boston Globe*, December 22, 1991, A19; Eric Hamburg, ed., *Nixon: An Oliver Stone Film* (New York: Hyperion, 1995); *LAT*, December 22, 1995, F1.

81. Hamburg, ed., *Nixon*, 190–92.

82. Ibid., 263, 183; *LAT*, December 22, 1995, F1. For a refutation of Stone's theories about Nixon's role in the Kennedy assassination, see Evan Thomas, "Whose Obsession Is It, Anyway?", *Newsweek*, December 11, 1995, 68.

83. Hamburg, ed., *Nixon*, 221–22, 59.

84. Charles McWhorter, "Memorandum for File," NALN, VPP, Series 320, Box 667, Folder "Sahl, Mort"; *Berkeley Barb*, May 24–30, 1974, 7; *Los Angeles Free Press*, March 27, 1970, 35; Wise, *Police State*, 131, 333.

85. Monsell, *Nixon on Stage and Screen*, 52, 80–81; Dean, *Blind Ambition*, 29; John B. Judis, "The Porn Broker," *TNR*, June 5, 1995, 14–16; Sidney Blumenthal, "Gramm, the Movie!", *TNR*, May 19, 1995, 12–13.

86. Debra Bicker Balken, *Philip Guston's Poor Richard* (Chicago: University of Chicago Press, 2001); Nick Kazan, "My Affair with Tricia Nixon," *Realist* (May–June 1971), 14–21.

87. Krassner, *Confessions*, 312–13.

88. Tony Hendra, *Going Too Far* (New York: Doubleday, 1987), 364–65.

89. "The Final Days," *The Best of Dan Aykroyd* (Broadway Video, 1986); Doug Hill and Jeff Weingrad, *Saturday Night: A Backstage History of Saturday Night Live* (New York: Beech Tree, 1986), 140–42.

90. Philip Roth, "The President Addresses the Nation," *New York Review of Books*, June 14, 1973, 11.

91. "Nixon Coup: Planned 1969," *Berkeley Barb*, December 14, 1973, 4; *NYP*, May 13, 1974, 29.

92. Kissinger, *Years of Upheaval*, 1199; *NYT*, September 1, 1974, §4, 15; *NYT*, August 25, 1974, 1.

93. *New York Observer*, February 2, 1998.

94. Ibid.; Gitlin, *Sixties*, 415; Tom Hayden, "The Protest Movement: Discussant," in *Hofstra 2*, 138.

95. Carl Oglesby and David Horowitz, "In Defense of Paranoia: An Exchange," *Ramparts* (March 1975), 15–20.

96. Ibid.

Chapter 4: The Washington Press Corps: Nixon as News Manager

1. Ben Bradlee, *A Good Life: Newspapering and Other Adventures* (New York: Simon & Schuster, 1995), 352.

2. *Congressional Quarterly*, October 2, 1971, 2046–47, October 9, 1971, 2094, October 16, 1971, 2142, October 23, 1971, 2190–91, October 30, 1971, 2239; *NYT*, September 28, 1971, 16; *NYT*, September 29, 1971, 66.

3. *NYT*, October 1, 1971, 24.

4. For the press in the Nixon years, see William L. Rivers, *The Adversaries: Politics and the Press* (Boston: Beacon Press, 1970); Fred Powledge, *The Engineering of Restraint: The Nixon Administration and the Press* (Washington, DC: Public Affairs, 1971); James Aronson, *Deadline for the Media: Today's Challenges to Press, TV and Radio* (Indianapolis: Bobbs-Merrill, 1972); William J. Small, *Political Power and the Press* (New York: Norton, 1972); David Wise, *The Politics of Lying: Government Deception, Secrecy and Power* (New York: Random House, 1973); Lewis W. Wolfson, ed., *The Press Covers Government: The Nixon Years from 1969 to Watergate* (Washington, DC: American University Press, 1973); Timothy Crouse, *The Boys on the Bus* (New York: Ballantine, 1974 [1973]); William E. Porter, *Assault on the Media* (Ann Arbor: University of Michigan Press, 1976); Michael Baruch Grossman and Martha Joynt Kumar, *Portraying the President* (Baltimore: Johns Hopkins University Press, 1981); Marilyn Lashner, *The Chilling Effect in TV News: Intimidation by the Nixon White House* (New York: Praeger, 1984); Joseph C. Spear, *Presidents and the Press: The Nixon Legacy* (Cambridge, MA: MIT Press, 1984); and John Anthony Maltese, *Spin Control: The White House Office of Communications and the Management of Presidential News* (Chapel Hill: University of North Carolina Press, 1992).

5. Gary Paul Gates, *Air Time: The Inside Story of CBS News* (New York: Berkeley Books, 1979 [1978]), 320; Spear, *Presidents*, 191; Wolfson, ed., *The Press*, 34.

6. Colson OH, 39; Raymond K. Price, *With Nixon* (New York: Viking, 1976), 175; Safire, *Before the Fall*, 342–43; *RN*, 355.

7. Grossman and Kumar, *Portraying*, 257; C. Richard Hofstetter, *Bias in the News: Network Television Coverage of the 1972 Election Campaign* (Columbus: Ohio State University Press, 1976); John Orman, "Covering the American Presidency," *Presidential Studies Quarterly*, vol. 14, no. 3 (Summer 1984), 381–90.

8. Arguments for the administration's view of an anti-Nixon media include Daniel Patrick Moynihan, "The Presidency and the Press," *Commentary*, 51 (March 1971), 41–52; Keogh, *President Nixon*; Price, *With Nixon*, 175–91.

9. Jim Deakin of the *St. Louis Post-Dispatch* quoted in J. Anthony Lukas, "The White House Press 'Club,'" *NYT Magazine*, May 15, 1977, 65.

10. Douglass Cater, *The Fourth Branch of Government* (New York: Vintage, 1965 [1959]).

11. Jules Witcover, "Washington: The News Explosion," *CJR* (Spring 1969), 23.

12. Cater, *Fourth Branch*, 75–88; John Tebbel and Sarah Miles Watts, *The Press and the Presidency: From George Washington to Ronald Reagan* (New York: Oxford University Press, 1985), 319, 332–33.

13. Blair Atherton French, *The Presidential Press Conference* (Lanham, MD: University Press of America, 1982), 4–16.

14. Reston quoted in Edwin R. Bayley, *Joe McCarthy and the Press* (Madison: University of Wisconsin Press, 1981); Cater, *Fourth Branch*, 107 (Sevareid quote), vii.

15. Rivers, *Adversaries*, 8; Tebbel and Watts, *The Press*, 489–500; Small, *Political Power*, 119.

16. Witcover, "News Explosion," 23.

17. Buchanan's views are expressed in *The New Majority: President Nixon at Mid-Passage* (n.p.: Girard Bank, 1973) and Julius Duscha, "The White House Watch Over TV and the Press," *NYT Magazine*, August 20, 1972, 9ff. Moynihan's are found in "The Presidency and the Press."

18. Keogh, *President Nixon*; 10; Robert Miraldi, *Muckraking and Objectivity: Journalism's Colliding Traditions* (Westport: Greenwood Press, 1990), 155; Stanford Sesser, "Journalists: Objectivity and Activism," *The Quill* (December 1969), 6–7; David Halberstam, "Press and Prejudice," *Esquire* (April 1974), 111; David S. Broder, *Behind the Front Page: A Candid Look at How News Is Made* (New York: Simon & Schuster, 1987), 332. For a critique of Moynihan's positions, see Michael Schudson, *Discovering the News: A Social History of American Newspapers* (New York: Basic Books, 1978), 176–83.

19. On New Journalism, see Crouse, *Boys on the Bus*, 321–38; Morris Dickstein, *Gates of Eden: American Culture in the Sixties* (Cambridge, MA: Harvard University Press, 1997 [1977]), 128–53; Leonard Downie, Jr., *The New Muckrakers* (Washington, DC: New Republic Books, 1976), 236–42; and Tom Wolfe, *The New Journalism* (New York: Harper & Row, 1973).

20. On investigative journalism, see Schudson, *Discovering the News*, 176–94.

21. On advocacy journalism, see Dickstein, *Gates*, 138; Downie, *New Muckrakers*, *passim*; Carey McWilliams, "Is Muckraking Coming Back?", *CJR* (Fall 1970), 8–15.

22. Aronson, *Deadline*, 102; Bray, *Pillars*, 94; Broder, *Front Page*, 338; Grossman and Kumar, *Portraying*, 9; "Journalism's In-House Critics," *Time*, December 6, 1971, 74; "Judging the Fourth Estate," *Time*, September 5, 1969, 38–39;

McWilliams, "Is Muckraking Coming Back?"; Chalmers Roberts, *The Washington Post: The First 100 Years* (Boston: Houghton Mifflin, 1977), 411; Jules Witcover, "The Press and Chicago: The Truth Hurt," *CJR* (Fall 1968), 5–9.

23. Price, *With Nixon*, 178.

24. Hedley Donovan, *Roosevelt to Reagan: A Reporter's Encounters with Nine Presidents* (New York: Harper & Row, 1985), 109. Robert Coughlan, "A Debate, Pro and Con. Subject: Richard M. Nixon," *Life*, July 16, 1956, was typical of the balanced coverage of Nixon in the 1950s.

25. Earl Mazo OH, CU, 31–34.

26. Safire, *Before the Fall*, 345; Halberstam, *Powers That Be*, 465.

27. Jack Germond, *Fat Man in a Middle Seat: Forty Years of Covering Politics* (New York: Random House, 1999), 89; Carl T. Rowan, *Breaking Barriers: A Memoir* (Boston: Little, Brown, 1991), 167.

28. Bill Lawrence, *Six Presidents, Too Many Wars* (New York: Saturday Review Press, 1972), 289.

29. Nixon, *Six Crises*, 107.

30. Herbers, *No Thank You*, 36; Witcover, *Resurrection*, 151–52.

31. Germond, *Fat Man*, 93.

32. Broder, *Front Page*, 86–87; Theodore H. White, *The Making of the President 1968* (New York: Atheneum, 1969), 403; Norman Mailer, *Miami and the Siege of Chicago* (New York: New American Library, 1968), 41–44.

33. Thompson, *Great Shark Hunt*, 185; Whitfield, "Richard Nixon as a Comic Figure," 118.

34. Crouse, *Boys on the Bus*, 269–74; Harrison Salisbury, *Without Fear of Favor: The New York Times and Its Times* (New York: Times Books, 1980), 415–17; Robert B. Semple, Jr., "It's Time Again for the Nixon Phenomenon," *NYT Magazine*, January 21, 1968, 24ff.

35. Salisbury, *Without Fear*, 415–16; *RN*, 303. Nixon's 1968 press strategy is described in McGinniss's *Selling of the President* (New York: Trident, 1969), which is discussed at length later in this chapter.

36. *NYT*, June 24, 1968, 16; Adatto, *Picture Perfect*, 23–60; Hallin, *We Keep America On Top of the World*, 133–52.

37. Price, *With Nixon*, 177–78; John Osborne, *The Nixon Watch* (New York: Liveright, 1970), 4.

38. *WP*, October 1, 1968, A19.

39. Roberts, *The Washington Post*, 408.

40. Block, *Special Report*, 85; Jack Anderson with Daryl Gibson, *Peace, War and Politics: An Eyewitness Account* (New York: Tom Doherty, 1999), 177; David Schoenbrun, *America Inside Out* (New York: McGraw-Hill, 1984), 398; White to Nixon, June 27, 1969, THWP, NPL, HU, Box 49, Folder 14.

41. Wicker, *One of Us*, 437; Germond, *Fat Man*, 90–91; *NYT*, December 20, 1969, 14; Max Frankel, *The Times of My Life and My Life with The Times* (New York:

Notes to pages 140–150   375

Random House, 1999), 313–14; Orman, "Covering the American Presidency," 387; Edwin Diamond, "Tape Shock: the Nixon Transcripts," *CJR* (July–August 1974), 9.

42. "The Communications Gap," *Newsweek*, August 18, 1969, 22–23.

43. Alistair Cooke, "An M.A. in Political Cosmetics," *WP Book World*, October 5, 1969, 1.

44. McGinniss, *Selling*, 19; Leonard Garment, *Crazy Rhythm: My Journey from Brooklyn, Jazz and Wall Street to Nixon's White House, Watergate and Beyond . . .* (New York: Times Books, 1997), 136–39; Victor Gold, "Gate Crasher Tells All," *NR*, November 18, 1969, 1173–74; Jamieson, *Packaging the Presidency*, 262–64; "Technicians for Rent," *Newsweek*, October 13, 1969, 119–20.

45. McGinniss, *Selling*, 31, 23, 20.

46. Ibid., 190–99.

47. Richard J. Whalen, *Catch the Falling Flag: A Republican's Challenge to His Party* (Boston: Houghton Mifflin, 1972), 212; Adatto, *Picture Perfect*, 43, 64; Jamieson, *Packaging the Presidency*, 262.

48. Crouse, *Boys on the Bus*, 197–99; White, *1968*, 164–67.

49. "Understanding Nixon," *NR*, December 16, 1969, 1287.

50. John Osborne, "Nixon Through the Tube," *TNR*, October 11, 1969, 26–28.

51. Osborne, *The Nixon Watch*, 6.

52. Klein, *Making It Perfectly Clear*, 172.

53. Keogh, *President Nixon*, 171–90.

54. Haldeman notes, November 3, 1969, NPMP, WHSF, SMOF, HRH, Box 40; Lawrence, *Six Presidents*, 285–86; *HD*, 128; Porter, *Assault*, 44; *RN*, 411; Safire, *Before the Fall*, 352.

55. *NYT*, November 24, 1969, 24.

56. Halberstam, "Press and Prejudice," 230; *NYT*, November 14, 1969, 25; Keogh, *President Nixon*, 138; Klein, *Making It Perfectly Clear*, 171; Martin F. Nolan, "The Re-Selling of the President," *Atlantic Monthly* (November 1972), 81; Safire, *Before the Fall*, 362; "Judging the Fourth Estate," *Time*, September 5, 1969, 38–39.

57. Spear, *Presidents*, 120; Small, *Political Power*, 130; *HD*, 130, 131; Agnew's speech is reprinted in Keogh, *President Nixon*, 199–204.

58. Frank, *Out of Thin Air*, 296; author's interview with Martin Plissner, October 25, 2001; *NYT*, November 14, 1969, 24, 25; Klein, *Making It Perfectly Clear*, 172.

59. Cronkite, *Reporter's Life*, 223; Aronson, *Deadline*, 9–10.

60. *NYT*, November 24, 1969, 24; Safire, *Before the Fall*, 353.

61. Marvin Barrett, ed., *The Alfred I. DuPont-Columbia University Survey of Broadcast Journalism 1969–1970* (New York: Grosset & Dunlap, 1970), 33.

62. Alfred Balk, "Beyond Agnewism," *CJR* (Winter 1969–70), 15; Keogh, *Presi-*

dent Nixon, 8; Roberts, *The Washington Post*, 412–13; Wolfson, *The Press*, 8. See also Joseph Kraft, "The Imperial Media," *Commentary* (May 1981), 36–47.

63. Keogh, *President Nixon*, 132; John Osborne, "Agnew's Effect," *TNR*, February 28, 1970.

64. Marvin Kalb, *The Nixon Memo: Political Respectability, Russia, and the Press* (Chicago: University of Chicago Press, 1994), 198; Herbers, *No Thank You*, 36; Strober and Strober, *Nixon*, 493; Dan Rather, *The Camera Never Blinks* (New York: Morrow, 1978), 217.

65. "Watergate—Now the Movie," *Newsweek*, June 2, 1975, 73; "Mr. Pakula Goes to Washington," *Film Comment* (September–October 1976), 16.

66. "Mr. Pakula Goes to Washington," 16; Art Buchwald, *"I Am Not a Crook"* (New York: Putnam, 1974), 79–80; Jules Feiffer, *Feiffer on Nixon: The Cartoon Presidency* (New York: Random House, 1974).

67. Helen Thomas, *Dateline: White House* (New York: Macmillan, 1975), 137; Herbers, *No Thank You*, 34; Max Frankel, "Presidential News Conferences Quietly Dying of Nixon Disuse," *NYT*, June 19, 1972, 19; *NYT*, September 24, 1969, 24; Wolfson, *The Press*, 15–16; *NPPC*, 269, 298.

68. *NYT*, June 15, 1972, 52; Safire, *Before the Fall*, 362. See also *WSJ*, August 5, 1970, 14; Vermont Royster, "Presidential Press Conferences: Somewhere Along the Line the Idea Has Gotten Lost," *The Quill* (February 1971), 9–11; Hugh Sidey, "Neither Questions nor Answers," *Time*, November 5, 1973, 23; Jules Witcover, "How Well Does the White House Press Perform?", *CJR* (November–December 1973), 39–43. Cartoon reprinted in John Osborne, *The Fourth Year of the Nixon Watch* (New York: Liveright, 1973), 112.

69. Hedrick Smith, "When the President Meets the Press," *Atlantic* (August 1970), 65–67; Jules Witcover, "Salvaging the Presidential Press Conference," *CJR* (Fall 1970), 27–34; Herbers, *No Thank You*, 94–97.

70. *WP*, April 7, 1971, B15; Duscha, "White House Watch," 96; "How Nixon's White House Works," *Time*, June 8, 1970, 17; "How Nixon Gets News," *Christian Science Monitor*, December 16, 1972.

71. Magruder, *An American Life*, 101; Maltese, *Spin Control*, 11–12, 58–63.

72. Bradlee, *Good Life*, 358.

73. Spear, *Presidents*, 75; Robert Walters, "What Did Ziegler Say and When Did He Say It?" *CJR* (September–October 1974), 30–35; Wolfson, *The Press*, 21–23.

74. Spear, *Presidents*, 148–49; Daniel Schorr, *Clearing the Air* (Boston: Houghton Mifflin, 1973), 70–86; *FRSC*, 144; author's interview with Daniel Schorr, October 11, 2002.

75. Haldeman, *Ends of Power*, 110; Small, *Presidency*, 236–37. Kissinger's role in stoking Nixon's outrage over the Pentagon Papers' publication was reported in *The New York Times*, December 9, 1973, p. 1. Haldeman recounted Kissinger's "weakling" remark in his memoir. The account has been accepted by well-known works on Watergate, including Lukas, *Nightmare*, 68–69, and *Ambrose 2*, 447. One of the most thorough accounts of the

White House reaction, including Kissinger's, appears in Tom Wells, *Wild Man: The Life and Times of Daniel Ellsberg* (New York: Palgrave, 2001), 459–61. Wells cites, among other sources, an affidavit by Chuck Colson, who said, "Dr. Kissinger was even more alarmed over the leaks than the president. He believed that the leaks must be stopped at all costs, that Ellsberg must be stopped from making further disclosures of classified information." The Colson affidavit, of April 29, 1974, is found in NPMP, WHSF, Fielding, Box 2, according to Wells's notes. Kissinger does not mention Ellsberg by name in his memoirs, but he does write, "I not only supported Nixon in his opposition to this wholesale theft and unauthorized disclosure; I encouraged him." *White House Years* (Boston: Little, Brown, 1979), 730.

76. Frankel, *Times of My Life*, 333; Graham, *Personal History*, 457–58.

77. Wolfson, *The Press*, 34; Crouse, *Boys on the Bus*, 192; Wise, *Lying*, 17.

78. Wolfson, *The Press*, 2, 7, 8, 34.

79. Ibid., 11; Maltese, *Spin Control*, 3.

80. Richard Reeves, *President Nixon: Alone in the White House* (New York: Simon & Schuster, 2001), 502–11; Ben Bagdikian, "Watergate and the Press: Success and Failure," in Walter Lubars and John Wicklein, eds. *Investigative Reporting: The Lessons of Watergate* (Boston: Boston University Press, 1975), 5; *NYT*, July 23, 1972, 31; *NYT*, August 10, 1972, 24; Safire, *Before the Fall*, 363. In an earlier article, Bagdikian had counted only some four hundred White House reporters, of whom perhaps fifteen had investigated Watergate. "The Fruits of Agnewism," *CJR* (January–February 1973), 9–21.

81. Jules Witcover, "The Trials of a One-Candidate Campaign," *CJR* (January–February 1973), 25–28; Spear, *Presidents*, 171–83; Crouse, *Boys on the Bus*, 263–70; *WP*, October 1, 1972, C7.

82. RN to HRH, January 9, 1970, NPMP, WHSF, SMOF, HRH, Box 229; *WP*, October 12, 1972, A18; Crouse, *Boys on the Bus*, 250–56.

83. *AP*, 52; Gates, *Air Time*, 320–25; Halberstam, *Powers*, 908–25.

84. Colson OH, June 15, 1988, NPMP, 39–41; Cronkite, *Reporter's Life*, 311; Gates, *Air Time*, 320–25; Halberstam, *Powers*, 908–25; *HD*, 639; William S. Paley, *As It Happened: A Memoir* (Garden City, NY: Doubleday, 1979), 318-27; Sally Bedell Smith, *In All His Glory: The Life of William S. Paley* (New York: Simon & Schuster, 1990), 477–78.

85. Frankel, *Times of My Life*, 345; Salisbury, *Without Fear*, 419–33; Germond, *Fat Man*, 98.

86. Henry Grunwald, *One Man's America: A Journalist's Search for the Heart of His Country* (New York: Doubleday, 1997), 433; Herbers, *No Thank You*, 43; Rather, *Camera Never Blinks*, 234.

87. Edward Jay Epstein, "Did the Press Uncover Watergate?" *Commentary* (July 1974), 21–24. For a critique of Epstein's position and others who downplay the role of the press in Watergate, see Schudson, *Watergate in American Memory*, 21–24, 104–10. Here and elsewhere, Schudson's thinking has informed my own.

88. Bradlee, *Good Life*, 363; Bagdikian, "Watergate and the Press," 4; James McCartney, "The *Washington Post* and Watergate: How Two Davids Slew Goliath," *CJR* (July–August 1973), 8; "Mr. Pakula Goes to Washington," 18. Schudson deals with the "mythology" of Watergate in *Discovering the News*, 188–91, and in *Watergate in American Memory* (New York: Basic Books, 1992), 20–23, 103–26.

89. Woodward and Bernstein, *President's Men*; see also Downie, *The New Muckrakers*, 1–53; Barry Sussman, *The Great Cover-Up: Nixon and the Scandal of Watergate* (New York: Crowell, 1974); Jack Hirshberg, *A Portrait of All the President's Men* (New York: Warner Books, 1976).

90. *WP*, June 14, 1992, G1; William Goldman, *Adventures in the Screen Trade: A Personal View of Hollywood and Screenwriting* (New York: Warner Books, 1984), 216; William Goldman, *Which Lie Did I Tell?: More Adventures in the Screen Trade* (New York: Pantheon, 2000), 179.

91. Bray, *Pillars*, 126; Salisbury, *Without Fear*, 419; "What Did the Media Learn from Watergate?", in *Investigative Reporting*, 15–17.

92. Carl Bernstein, "Remarks on Acceptance of Honorary Degree at Boston University," in *Investigative Reporting*, 10; Strober and Strober, *Nixon*, 494, 493.

93. Broder, *Front Page*, 141; Strober and Strober, *Nixon*, 493–94.

94. Alexander M. Haig, with Charles McCarry, *Inner Circles: How America Changed the World* (New York: Warner, 1992), 348; Richard M. Nixon, "Statement About Watergate Investigations," August 15, 1973, *PP*, 1973, no. 234.

95. Spear, *Presidents*, 226.

96. "What Did the Media Learn from Watergate?", 24; Lukas, *Nightmare*, 491; Helen Thomas, *Front Row at the White House: My Life and Times* (New York: Simon & Schuster, 1999), 315; James Jackson Kilpatrick, "He Lied," *NR*, August 30, 1974, 965; *WP*, May 20, 1977, A27. See also Bradlee, *Good Life*, 352; Lou Cannon, "The Press and the Nixon Presidency," in *NP*, 193.

97. *USA Today*, September 3, 1998, 15A; David Gergen, *Eyewitness to Power: The Essence of Leadership, Nixon to Clinton* (New York: Simon & Schuster, 2000), 91; *Newsday*, April 24, 1994, A6; "A Day That Will Live in Infamy," *Newsweek*, June 25, 1973, 21; Whitfield, "Richard Nixon as a Comic Figure," 126.

98. Witcover, "How Well?", 39–40.

99. Bray, *Pillars*, 131; Roberts, *Post*, 441; Wolfson, *The Press,* 1; Bernstein, "Remarks," 9.

100. Osborn Elliot, *The World of Oz* (New York: Viking, 1980), 163; Grunwald, *One Man's America*, 438; Orman, "Covering the American Presidency," 385; Grossman and Kumar, *Portraying the President*, 257; Cannon, "The Press," 197; Charles W. Colson, "The Georgetown Blacking Factory," *NYT*, January 30, 1973, 37; Joseph Kraft, "On Being Bugged," *The New York Review of Books*, October 4, 1973, 32–36; Tifft and Jones, *The Trust*, 504.

101. Donovan, *Roosevelt to Reagan*, 123; Grunwald, *One Man's America*, 433; Herbers, *No Thank You*, 59.

102. Finlay Lewis, "Some Errors and Puzzles in the Watergate Coverage," *CJR* (November–December 1973), 26–33; Laurence I. Barrett, "The Dark Side of Competition," *CJR* (July–August 1974), 14–15; *NYT* November 16, 1973, 26.

103. Gergen, *Eyewitness to Power*, 91; Lukas, "The White House Press 'Club,'" 64; "The Long Trail of Denials to Credibility Gap," *Newsweek*, April 30, 1973, 20; Clark Mollenhoff, *Game Plan for Disaster: An Ombudsman's Report on the Nixon Years* (New York: Norton, 1976), 193; "The Roughriders," *Newsweek*, June 18, 1973, 74; Witcover, "How Well?", 40; Robert Pierpoint, *At the White House: Assignment to Six Presidents* (New York: Putnam, 1981), 139.

104. *RN*, 851, 855; "The Roughriders," 74; Downie, *New Muckrakers*, 252; Barrett, *Survey*, 14.

105. *NPCC*, 303; Howard K. Smith, *Events Leading up to My Death: The Life of a Twentieth-Century Reporter* (New York: St. Martin's Press, 1996), 352.

106. *NPCC*, 336, 339, 353.

107. Donovan, *Roosevelt to Reagan*, 126; "The President Should Resign," *Time*, November 12, 1973, 2; Thomas, *Front Row*, 108.

108. Spear, *Presidents*, 200, 356–74.

109. Sidey, "The Man in Foreign Policy," NP, 23; *NYT*, November 1, 1973, 43; "Capital Bulletin," *NR*, November 16, 1973, B173.

110. "Has the Press Done a Job on Nixon?" *CJR* (January–February 1974), 58; Donovan, *Roosevelt to Reagan*, 128.

111. Gates, *Air Time*, 390–92; Halberstam, *Powers*, 974–79; Aaron Latham, "The Reporter the President Hates," *New York*, January 21, 1974, 34–42; Rather, *Camera Never Blinks*, 11–24, 214; Wise, "The President and the Press," *Atlantic* (April 1973), 60–61; *WP*, January 20, 1974.

112. Gates, *Air Time*, 390–92; Halberstam, *Powers*, 974–79; "Adversary Relationship," *Newsweek*, April 1, 1974, 66–67; Rather, *Camera Never Blinks*, 20.

113. Schorr, *Clearing the Air*, 108, 113, 119.

114. Ibid., 114–15; Gates, *Air Time*, 410–12; Halberstam, *Powers*, 979–82; Sidey, "The Man," 308.

115. Downie, *New Muckrakers*, 7–11; Lukas, "The White House Press 'Club,'" 67; Fallows quoted in Michael Janeway, *Republic of Denial: Press, Politics and Public Life* (New Haven: Yale University Press, 1999), 161. As Michael Schudson has noted, the trend of growing interest in journalism and journalism schools began before Watergate. Schudson, *Watergate*, 110–11.

116. *WP*, August 1, 1999, G1.

Chapter 5: The Loyalists: Nixon as Victim

1. Jonathan Rieder, *Canarsie: The Jews and Italians of Brooklyn Against Liberalism* (Cambridge, MA: Harvard University Press, 1985), 159.

2. Baruch Korff, *The President and I* (Providence, RI: Baruch Korff Foundation, 1995), 3–4; "Nixon's Rabbi," *Newsweek*, October 1, 1973, 32–33.

3. Korff, *President*, 6–8; "An Appeal for Fairness," advertisement, *NYT*, July 29, 1973, §4, 14.

4. Korff, *President*, 8, 21, 156; "Source of Strength," *Time*, July 29, 1974, 27; *LAT*, July 18, 1995, A22.

5. Korff, *President*, 11–17; "The Rape of America," advertisement, *NYT*, December 2, 1973, §4, 18; "The Assassins," *NYT*, November 7, 1973, 34.

6. Korff, *President*, 7–9, 25–27; Bob Woodward and Carl Bernstein, *The Final Days* (New York: Simon & Schuster, 1976), 101–02.

7. Korff, *President*, 31–33, 48–56, 75–78, 154; Korff, *The Personal Nixon: Staying on the Summit* (Washington, DC: National Citizens' Committee for Fairness to the Presidency, 1974), 58, 60–61, 64, *passim*; *WP*, July 19, 1974, E1; Woodward and Bernstein, *Final Days*, 208–09, 379; Drew, *Washington Journal*, 290, 414.

8. Paul Johnson, *Modern Times: The World from the Twenties to the Nineties* (New York: Harper, 1992 [1984]), 649.

9. Victor Lasky, *It Didn't Start with Watergate* (New York: Dial, 1977), 1; Stephen Ambrose, *Nixon*, Vol. III: *Ruin and Recovery, 1973–1990* (New York: Simon & Schuster, 1991; cited hereafter as *Ambrose 3*), 592; Korff, *President*, 154–55.

10. Many of the detailed books on Watergate written by journalists remain trustworthy and valuable, including Anthony Lukas's *Nightmare*, Theodore H. White's *Breach of Faith*, and Woodward and Bernstein's *The Final Days*. Volumes 2 and 3 of Stephen Ambrose's Nixon biography also tell the standard Watergate story. The first history by an academic scholar was Stanley Kutler's *The Wars of Watergate*, which made extensive use of primary documents. In 1994, journalist Fred Emery published *Watergate: The Corruption of American Politics and the Fall of Richard Nixon*, a shorter account that included some new information but did not substantially change the contours of the story.

11. Richard M. Scammon and Ben J. Wattenberg, *The Real Majority* (New York: Coward-McCann, 1970).

12. Samuel G. Freedman, *The Inheritance: How Three Families Moved from Roosevelt to Reagan and Beyond* (New York: Simon & Schuster, 1996), 265–91; Buchanan, *The New Majority*, 62.

13. Buchanan, *The New Majority*, 63–64.

14. "Watergate as Power Struggle," *NR*, June 29, 1973, B89.

15. "Is the Press Living by a Double Standard?", *USNWR*, October 10, 1977, 29; Spear, *Presidents*, 214; *Newsweek*, November 12, 1973, 87.

16. *Ambrose 1*, 605; *RN*, 254; *NYT*, November 12, 1960; *NYT*, November 19, 1960; *NYT*, November 24, 1960; *NYT*, November 25, 1960; *NYT*, November 26, 1960; *NYT*, December 2, 1960; *NYT*, December 4, 1960; *NYT*, December 7, 1960; *NYT*, December 11, 1960; *NYT*, December 12, 1960; *NYT*, December 13, 1960; Thruston B. Morton OH, University of Kentucky Library, Thruston B. Morton OH Project, 17; Brodie, *Richard Nixon*, 433. See also Edmund F. Kal-

lina, Jr., *Courthouse over White House: Chicago and the Presidential Election of 1960* (Orlando: University of Central Florida Press, 1988); Kallina, "Was the 1960 Presidential Election Stolen? The Case of Illinois," *Presidential Studies Quarterly* (Winter 1985), 113–18; David Greenberg, "Was Nixon Robbed?", *Slate*, October 16, 2000; *LAT*, November 10, 2000, B9; and "Gracious Loser? Hardly," *Brill's Content*, February 2001, 106ff.

17. Wicker, *One of Us*, 256.

18. *RN*, 773; *HD*, June 20, 1972, 473, September 11, 1972, 611; Haldeman notes, September 11, 1972, NPMP, quoted in *Ambrose 2*, 607.

19. Emery, *Watergate*, 159, 176, 223; White, *1972*, 427–28; *NPPC*, 281.

20. *HD*, October 15, 1972, 632, October 16, 1972, 634; Kutler, *Wars of Watergate*, 238.

21. Dean, *Blind Ambition*, 135–40; Emery, *Watergate*, 216–221; *HD*, September 15, 1972, 613; Kutler, *Wars of Watergate*, 232–36; *RN*, 681; *PT*, 41; Ford to Brown, September 28, 1972, and Charles F. C. Ruff to Elizabeth Holtzman, October 15, 1976, both in GRFPL, Philip Buchen Files, Box 55, Folder "President-Wright Patman Investigation."

22. *RN*, 710.

23. Herbers, *No Thank You*, 81; Sarah McClendon, *My Eight Presidents* (New York: Wyden Books, 1978), 177.

24. "Watergate as Power Struggle," *NR*, July 6, 1973, 720–21; George F. Will, "Ring in the Old," *NR*, January 4, 1974, 20; George F. Will, "Menacing Words," *NR*, June 7, 1974, 639; "A Will of His Own," *Newsweek*, September 30, 1974, 56.

25. "Watergate as Power Struggle," *NR*, July 6, 1973, 720–21; John B. Judis, *William F. Buckley, Jr.: Patron Saint of the Conservatives* (New York: Simon & Schuster, 1988), 359; *NYT*, November 13, 1973, 45.

26. www.lynyrdskynyrd.com.

27. *RN*, 774.

28. Korff, *Personal Nixon*, 64; "The Man Who Bugged Nixon," *Time*, August 13, 1973, 16–17; Haldeman testimony, July 30, 1973, *WH*, 555.

29. *HD*, 576.

30. News Summary, June 20, 1972, quoted in *Ambrose 2*, 565; *RN*, 630–31; W. Richard Howard to Pat Buchanan, June 22, 1972, and Pat Buchanan to Chuck Colson, June 25, 1972, both in NPMP, WHSF, SMOF, Buchanan, Box 10, Folder "Bugging DNC HQ."

31. *RN*, 636–37 (italics in original); *AP*, 75, 92; *PT*, 34.

32. Kutler, *Wars of Watergate*, 256–58, 272; Dean testimony, June 25, 1973, *WH*, 283; *PT*, 71.

33. Dean, *Blind Ambition*, 184–85; Dean testimony, June 25, 1973, *WH*, 286–88; *PT*, 66, 70–71; Lukas, *Nightmare*, 284–87; "Past Dirty Tricks," *Time*, August 27, 1973, 15–16.

34. *AP*, 424, 453–54, 541, 561; RN to Haig, July 7, 1973, in Bruce Oudes, ed., *From the President: Richard Nixon's Secret Files* (New York: Harper, 1989), 591–94.

35. *NPPC*, 340–43.

36. "Paranoia," *TNR*, September 1, 1973, 9–11; "Past Dirty Tricks," *Time*, August 27, 1973, 15–16; Lukas, *Nightmare*, 286; *NYT*, August 24, 1973, 1; *NYT*, August 25, 1973, 22.

37. Thompson, *Great Shark Hunt*, 247; "The Jury of the People Weighs Nixon," *Time*, November 12, 1973, 27.

38. Schudson, *Watergate*, 35; Art Buchwald, "Instant Answers," in *Yale/Theater*, 5 (Winter 1974), 124–26; *WP*, February 6, 1974; Don Novello, *The Lazlo Letters: The Amazing, Real-Life, Actual Correspondence of Lazlo Toth, American!* (New York: Workman, 1977). Novello took the name of the man who in 1972 attacked the *Mona Lisa*.

39. *NPCC*, 339.

40. Jack Hoffman and Daniel Simon, *Run, Run, Run* (New York: Putnam, 1994), 207; "Main Street Revisited: Changing Views on Watergate," *Time*, November 12, 1973, 21; "Vox Pop: 'Get It Over With,'" *Newsweek*, January 14, 1974, 16.

41. Howard Phillips, "The Plot to Get Nixon," *Human Events*, December 15, 1973, 9; NPMP, WHSF, SMOF, Ronald Ziegler Papers, Box 17, Folder "Watergate, August 1, 1973"; Strober and Strober, *Nixon*, 109, 469.

42. William B. Saxbe, with Peter D. Franklin, *I've Seen the Elephant* (Kent, OH: Kent State University Press, 2000), 125; "President Agnew," *NR*, June 8, 1973, 616; *HD*, 756; Robert Alan Goldberg, *Barry Goldwater* (New Haven: Yale University Press, 1995), 273–83; "Nixon Presses His Counterattack," *Time*, November 26, 1973, 16.

43. "Nixon Presses His Counterattack," 16; *NYP*, May 13, 1974, 29; Kutler, *Wars of Watergate*, 451, 498–504, 538–40; Goldberg, *Goldwater*, 283.

44. Colson to Nixon, May 7, 1973, NPMP, WHSF, SMOF, PPF, Box 7, Folder "Colson, Charles"; see also Colson to Nixon, November 12, 1973, in Oudes, ed., *From the President*, 605–06; Charles Colson, *Born Again* (Old Tappan, NJ: Chosen, 1976), 181, 213; Charles W. Colson and John W. Dean, "The Specter of Richard Nixon," *USNWR*, December 21, 1998, 28; *USA Today*, April 27, 1994, 10A.

45. *NYT*, August 2, 1973, 35; Woodward and Bernstein, *Final Days*, 340.

46. William F. Buckley, "The Resignation Proposal," *NR*, April 26, 1974, 499. George Will agreed, saying that conservative apologists for Nixon, "worse than . . . dogmatic," were beholden to a reflexive loyalty that "lets the *New York Times* run your life." "A Will of His Own," *Newsweek*, September 30, 1974, 56.

47. Kissinger, *Years of Upheaval*, 1178.

48. *NYT*, May 19, 1974, 1.

49. *NYP*, May 15, 1974, 44; "The President's Priest," *Newsweek*, May 20, 1974, 71; Kutler, *Wars of Watergate*, 454; Maltese, *Spin Control*, 105–06.

50. Spear, *Presidents*, 223; Maltese, *Spin Control*, 105–06; *NYT*, May 27, 1974, 22; *WP*, August 9, 1979, D1; Woodward and Bernstein, *Final Days*, 229–30; Price, *With Nixon*, 311, 321–22.

51. Memo to Karl Rove, undated, HIA, Stanford University; College National Republicans Collection, Box 24, Folder "July–September 24"; Drew, *Washington Journal*, 325.

52. Woodward and Bernstein, *Final Days*, 149.

53. Henry Tobias, "Hang in There, Mr. President," RNL, SM124; Herbers, *No Thank You*, 110, 83; Hugh Sidey, "Richard Nixon's Morale Booster," *Time*, April 8, 1974, 11.

54. *NYT*, May 19, 1974, 1; Rieder, *Canarsie*, 158–59.

55. John Updike, *Rabbit Is Rich* (New York: Knopf, 1979), 103.

56. John Updike, *Memories of the Ford Administration* (New York: Knopf, 1991), 12, 14; Freedman, *Inheritance*, 290–91; Woodward and Bernstein, *Final Days*, 455; Jonathan Aitken, *Nixon: A Life* (London: Weidenfeld & Nicolson, 1993), 525.

57. *WP*, October 27, 1974.

58. Haldeman, *Ends of Power*, xii, xiii, 318; Robert Sam Anson, *Exile: The Unquiet Oblivion of Richard M. Nixon* (New York: Simon & Schuster, 1984), 205.

59. Sandra Salmans, "Ghosts in the Hall," *Newsweek*, August 30, 1976, 40; Lasky, *It Didn't Start*, 3; Schudson, *Watergate*, 133; Rudy Maxa, "As a Writer for the Right, He Makes a Killing Watching the Left," *WP Magazine*, October 23, 1977, 4.

60. *NYT*, April 25, 1977, 31; William Safire, *Safire's Washington* (New York: Times Books, 1980), 102; *NYT*, January 2, 1975, 33; *NYT*, June 5, 1975, 37. For a good discussion of Safire, see Schudson, *Watergate*, 70–73.

61. Schudson, *Watergate*, 73–82.

62. *NYT*, December 8, 1975, 31.

63. *WP*, May 20, 1977, A27; Wicker, *One of Us*, 675.

64. *WP*, August 9, 1984, A23.

65. David Frost, *"I Gave Them a Sword": Behind the Scenes of the Nixon Interviews* (New York: Morrow, 1978), 69 ff.; *NYT*, May 1, 1977, 27; "Nixon Talks," *Time*, May 9, 1977, 22; David M. Alpern, "Nixon Speaks," *Newsweek*, May 9, 1977, 25–39.

66. *WP*, May 1, 1977, A1; Alpern, "Nixon Speaks," 25–39; Frost, *Sword*, 203–04.

67. *NYT*, May 5, 1977, B10; Frost, *Sword*, 242.

68. *NYT*, May 11, 1977, C22; David Alpern, "Watching Nixon," *Newsweek*, May 16, 1977, 29; "'No One Knows How It Feels," *Time*, June 6, 1977, 11; *WP*, May 14, 1977, A2; *NYT*, June 6, 1977, 51; "Nixon: Once More, with Feeling," *Time*, May 16, 1977, 22; *NYT*, May 27, 1977, A23; Haldeman, *Ends of Power*, 65; *NYT*, May 5, 1977, A27.

69. *NYT*, May 29, 1977, 30; "Nixon: Once More, with Feeling," *Time*, May 16, 1977, 21; *NYT*, July 23, 1977, 17; "The People's Verdict: Guilty," *Newsweek*, May 16, 1977, 31; George H. Gallup, *The Gallup Poll 1977* (Wilmington: Scholarly Resources, 1978), 1100; Peter Goldman with Hal Bruno, "Nixon on His Fall," *Newsweek*, June 6, 1977, 33.

70. *NYT*, May 5, 1977, A27.

71. David Obst, *Too Good to Be Forgotten: Changing America in the '60s and '70s* (New York: Wiley, 1998), 242.

72. Cameron Crowe, "Neil Young: The Last American Hero," *Rolling Stone*, February 8, 1979; Alpern, "Nixon Speaks," 25–39; "Nixon Talks," 27.

73. Bob Woodward, "Gerald Ford," in Caroline Kennedy, ed., *Profiles in Courage for Our Time* (New York: Hyperion, 2002), 293; *NYT*, May 22, 2001, A14; Joseph Carroll, "Americans Grew to Accept Nixon's Pardon," *Gallup News Service*, May 21, 2002.

74. James A. Nuecheterlein, "Watergate: Toward a Revisionist View," *Commentary* (August 1979), 38–45.

75. Edward J. Epstein and John Berendt, "Did There Come a Point in Time When There Were 43 Different Theories of How Watergate Happened?", *Esquire* (November 1973), 127–32.

76. Salisbury, *Without Fear*, 420–21.

77. *AP*, 61, 67–68; transcript of June 23 conversation, NPMP, quoted in *Ambrose* 2, 568.

78. *AP*, 67–69.

79. Lukas, *Nightmare*, 231–35; *HD*, 785.

80. *AP*, 629; *NYT*, May 9, 1973, 28.

81. Trevor F. Swoyer to Theodore H. White, March 15, 1974, HU, NPL, THWP, Box 35, Folder 9; Miles Copeland, "The Unmentionable Uses of a CIA," *NR*, September 14, 1973, 996; Lasky, *It Didn't Start*, 239–49.

82. Frost, *Sword*, 242; Michael Beschloss, "How Nixon Came in from the Cold," *Vanity Fair* (June 1992), 148; Price, *With Nixon*, 360–69; Haldeman, *Ends of Power*, 33–40, 109, 133–47; "Colson Saga: CIA," *NR*, July 19, 1974, 794–95; "Colson's Weird Scenario," *Time*, July 8, 1974, 16; Dean, *Blind Ambition*, 392–97. On Howard Baker, see *AP*, 631, 633–34; *FRSC*, 1105–65; Fred D. Thompson, *At That Point in Time: The Inside Story of the Senate Watergate Committee* (New York: Quadrangle, 1975), esp. 145–82. See also *NYT*, January 5, 1975, 1; *NYT*, January 17, 1975, 9.

83. Wise, *Police State*, 226–57; Lasky, *It Didn't Start*, 239–53; Oglesby, *Yankee and Cowboy War*, 265–302; Renata Adler, "Searching for the Real Nixon Scandal: A Last Inference," *Atlantic* (December 1976), 76–95.

84. Author's interview with Jim Hougan, February 28, 2002.

85. Jim Hougan, *Secret Agenda: Watergate, Deep Throat, and the CIA* (New York: Random House, 1984), 202, *passim*. On Silbert, see *NYT*, November 6, 1984, D24.

86. Hougan, *Secret Agenda*, 212. See Aaron Latham, "Mixed Nuts," *Nation*, February 2, 1985, 117–18; J. Anthony Lukas, "A New Explanation of Watergate," *NYT Book Review*, November 11, 1984, 7; Anthony Marro, "Deep Throat, Phone Home," *WP Book World*, November 25, 1984, 5.

87. Michelle Slung, "New Look at an Old Burglary," *WP Book World*, January 1, 1984, 15; Hougan, *Secret Agenda*, 206, 269.

88. Phil Stanford, "Watergate Revisited," *CJR* (March–April 1986), 46–49; *CSM*, March 5, 1990, 18; Len Colodny and Robert Gettlin, *Silent Coup: The Removal of a President* (New York: St. Martin's Press, 1991), viii. See also Brian Lamb interview with Colodny and Gettlin on "Booknotes," August 11, 1991, at www.booknotes.org.

89. *WP*, July 23, 1997, C1; *Tampa Tribune*, January 31, 2000, 2; Mark Davis, "Liddy and Dean Fight to a Draw," *Insight*, vol. 16, no. 31 (August 21, 2000), 24ff; J. Anthony Lukas, review of *Silent Coup* and *Watergate* in *Washington Monthly* (July 1994), 44; *NYT*, May 16, 1994, C13; *LAT*, August 7, 1994, §Home, 4; Anthony Summers, *The Arrogance of Power: The Secret World of Richard Nixon* (New York: Viking, 2000), 525–26n, 529n, 530n.

90. Hoff, *Nixon Reconsidered*, 311; Joan Hoff, *Watergate Revisited* (Greenville, NC: East Carolina University Press, 1993); Parmet, "Tricking Dick," 46; Morris, Foreword, in *Silent Coup*, xiv. The introduction to *Silent Coup* appeared to mark the start of Morris's descent into conspiracist thought. His own 1990 book on Nixon, *Richard Milhous Nixon: The Rise of an American Politician*— the sequels to which have never appeared—had taken a dim view of Nixon but was a thoroughly researched and beautifully shaped work and was nominated for a National Book Award. Afterward, however, Morris's books became increasingly unreliable. One subscribed to far-fetched theories about Bill and Hillary Clinton and the next traced the secret history of Las Vegas as a center of an all-powerful, sinister underworld. Moreover, he and his wife and co-author Sally Denton asserted that Peter Dale Scott's "historic book *Deep Politics* has revolutionized the writing of recent American history for us and for others." Sally Denton and Roger Morris, *The Money and the Power: The Making of Las Vegas and Its Hold on America, 1947–2000* (New York: Knopf, 2001), 459.

91. Monica Crowley, *Nixon in Winter* (New York: Random House, 1998), 295. See also Aitken, *Nixon*, 471; "Watergate Investigated," *NR*, July 6, 1992, 39–42; "Anniversary Gate," *NR*, July 14, 1997, 40; "Overrating Watergate," *NR*, October 12, 1998, 30.

92. Aitken, *Nixon*, 473, 477, 467; Michael R. Beschloss, "The Remaking of a President," *WP Book World*, April 24, 1994, X, 1. On Aitken's perjury, see Jonathan Aitken, *Pride and Perjury* (London: Harper, 2000); Luke Harding, David Leigh, and David Pallister, *The Liar: The Fall of Jonathan Aitken* (London: Penguin, 1997). On Johnson and Aitken, see Julie Baumgold, "Nixon's New Life in New York," *New York*, June 9, 1980, 27; *Sunday Telegraph*, January 10, 1993, 11; "Source Notes," in Paul Johnson, *A History of the American People* (New York: Harper, 1998), 1052–53; Aitken, *Nixon*, 571.

93. Crowley, *Winter*, 299.

94. *NYT*, June 1, 1975, 60.

95. *NYT*, September 9, 1992, A15; *WP*, October 21, 1992, B1; e-mail correspondence, John Taylor to author, June 30, 1999, July 1, 1999. Ben Stein, a bit older than Kristol but also a second-generation Nixonite, similarly relished being alone in his Yale Law School class in supporting Nixon and in recoiling from the extremist actions of anti-Nixon college kids at the University of California at Santa Cruz. Benjamin Stein, "Au Revoir, Mr. President," *American Spectator* (July 1994).

96. Crowley, *Winter*, *passim*.

97. Anson, *Exile*, 242; David M. Alpern with John J. Lindsay, "Nixon in Prime Time," *Newsweek*, April 16, 1984, 34; Monica Crowley, *Nixon off the Record* (New York: Random House, 1996).

98. "The Elder Statesman," *USNWR*, February 8, 1988, 57; *NYT*, March 25, 1996, B5.

99. *WP*, July 20, 1990, D1; *WP*, July 20, 1990, A5.

100. *LAT*, July 8, 1990, A1; *LAT*, July 10, 1990, A3; *WP*, July 19, 1990, A18; *LAT*, July 19, 1990, A3; *LAT*, July 21, 1990, A5.

101. Aitken, *Nixon*, 569, 572.

Chapter 6: The Psychobiographers: Nixon as Madman

1. *NYT*, November 20, 1973, 39.

2. Memo, NPMP, WHSF, SMOF, PPF, Box 11, Folder "Memorandum of Events, May 1 [sic], 1970"; *Ambrose 2*, 354–57; Parmet, *Richard Nixon*, 3–13; Safire, *Before the Fall*, 205–09.

3. *Berkeley Barb*, May 15–21, 1970, 10; White, *Breach of Faith*, 131. Moynihan statement in HU, NPL, THWP, Box 139, Folder 8.

4. Mazlish, *In Search of Nixon*, 132–34; David Abrahamsen, *Nixon vs. Nixon: An Emotional Tragedy* (New York: Farrar, Straus & Giroux, 1977), 236, 186; James David Barber, "The Question of Presidential Character," *Saturday Review*, September 23, 1972, 62–66.

5. The slips are cited in Brodie, *Richard Nixon*, 428, 458.

6. Haldeman, *Ends of Power*, 83 (italics in the original).

7. Strober and Strober, *Nixon*, 39; *Ambrose 3*, 588; *WP*, August 9, 1979, D1.

8. The earliest articles were Bruce Mazlish, "Towards a Psychohistorical Inquiry: The 'Real' Richard Nixon," *Journal of Interdisciplinary History*, 1 (Autumn 1970), reprinted in *The Leader, the Led and the Psyche: Essays in Psychohistory*, 198–246; and Michael Rogin and John Lottier, "The Inner History of Richard Milhous Nixon," *Transaction*, vol. 9, nos. 1–2 (November–

December 1971), 21. Among the other significant works of Nixon psychobi-
ography are those by Abrahamsen and Brodie, as well as James David Barber, *The Presidential Character: Predicting Performance in the White House*, 3rd
edn. rev. (Englewood Cliffs, NJ: Prentice-Hall, 1985 [1972]); Eli S. Chesen,
President Nixon's Psychiatric Profile: A Psychodynamic-Genetic Interpretation
(New York: Peter H. Wyden, 1973); Leo Rangell, *The Mind of Watergate* (New
York: Norton, 1980); Blema S. Steinberg, *Shame and Humiliation: Presidential
Decision Making on Vietnam* (Pittsburgh: University of Pittsburgh Press,
1996), 124–206; Vamik D. Volkan, Norman Itzkowitz, and Andrew W. Dod,
Richard Nixon: A Psychobiography (New York: Columbia University Press,
1997); and Arthur Woodstone, *Nixon's Head* (New York: St. Martin's Press,
1972). Significant articles include Steven R. Brown, "Richard Nixon and the
Public Conscience: The Struggle for Authenticity," *Journal of Psychohistory*,
vol. 5, no. 4 (Spring 1978), 93–111; James W. Hamilton, "Some Reflections on
Richard Nixon in the Light of His Resignation and Farewell Speeches," *Journal of Psychohistory*, vol. 4, no. 4 (Spring 1977), 491–511; James P. Johnson,
"Nixon's Use of Metaphor: The Real Nixon Tapes," *Psychoanalytic Review*,
vol. 66, no. 2 (1979), 263–74; Henry W. Lawton, "Milhous Rising," *Journal of
Psychohistory*, vol. 6, no. 4 (Spring 1979), 519–42; Jules Levey, "Richard
Nixon as Elder Statesman," *Journal of Psychohistory*, vol. 13, no. 4 (Spring
1986), 27–48; Peter Loewenberg, "Nixon, Hitler and Power: An Ego Psychol-
ogy Study," *Psychoanalytic Inquiry*, vol. 6, no. 1 (1986), 27–48; Leo Rangell,
"Lessons from Watergate: A Derivative for Psychoanalysis," *Psychoanalytic
Quarterly*, vol. 45, no. 1 (1976), 37–61; Stanley Allen Renshon, "Psychological
Analysis of Presidential Personality: The Case of Richard Nixon," *History of
Childhood Quarterly: The Journal of Psychohistory*, vol. 2, no. 3 (Winter 1975),
415–50; and Alan B. Rothenberg, "Why Nixon Taped Himself," *Psychoana-
lytic Review*, vol. 62, no. 2 (Summer 1975), 201–23.

9. Mazlish, *The Leader*, 98–99.

10. Arnold A. Rogow, *The Psychiatrists* (New York: Putnam, 1970), 15; Nathan
G. Hale, Jr., *The Rise and Crisis of Psychoanalysis in the United States: Freud and
the Americans, 1917–1985* (New York: Oxford University Press, 1995), 302;
David Frum, *How We Got Here: The 70s: The Decade That Brought You Modern
Life* (New York: Basic Books, 2000), 101.

11. Christopher Lasch, *The Culture of Narcissism* (New York: Norton, 1978), 29,
22; Daniel Yankelovich, *New Rules: Searching for Self-Fulfillment in a World
Turned Upside Down* (New York: Random House, 1981), *passim*; Edwin
Schur, *The Awareness Trap: Self-Absorption Instead of Social Change* (New York:
McGraw-Hill, 1976), 1. The term the "Me" Decade was likely coined by the
journalist Tom Wolfe in "The 'Me' Decade and the Third Great Awakening,"
New York, August 23, 1976. See also Peter Marin, "The New Narcissism,"
Harper's (October 1975), 45–56, and Richard Sennett, *The Fall of Public Man*
(New York: Knopf, 1977).

12. Hale, *Rise and Crisis*, 276–99.

13. Sigmund Freud and William C. Bullitt, *Thomas Woodrow Wilson, Twenty-
Eighth President of the United States: A Psychological Study* (Boston: Houghton

Mifflin, 1966); Nixon, *Leaders*, 16–17; William L. Langer, "The Next Assignment," *American Historical Review*, 63 (January 1958), 286; Erik Erikson, *Young Man Luther: A Study in Psychoanalysis and History* (New York: Norton, 1958); *NYT*, April 26, 1971, 37.

14. Important books include Jacques Barzun, *Clio and the Doctors: Psycho-History, Quanto-History and History* (Chicago: University of Chicago Press, 1973); Saul Friedlander, *History and Psychoanalysis: An Inquiry into the Possibilities and Limits of Psychohistory* (New York: Holmes & Meier, 1978); Peter Gay, *Freud for Historians* (New York: Oxford University Press, 1985); Peter Loewenberg, *Decoding the Past: The Psychohistorical Approach* (New Brunswick: Transaction, 1996); Mazlish, ed., *Psychoanalysis and History*; Mazlish, *The Leader*; David E. Stannard, *Shrinking History: On Freud and the Failure of Psychohistory* (New York: Oxford University Press, 1980).

15. Important articles: Jacques Barzun, "History: The Muse and Her Doctors," *American Historical Review*, 77 (February 1972), 36–64; Robert Coles, "Shrinking History" (parts one and two), *The New York Review of Books*, February 22, 1973, 15–21, and March 8, 1973, 25–30; Coles and Bruce Mazlish, "An Exchange on Psychohistory," *The New York Review of Books*, May 3, 1973, 36–38; Marcus Cunliffe, "From the Facts to the Feelings," *Times Literary Supplement*, October 23, 1981, 1241–42; John J. Fitzpatrick, William L. Langer, and Peter Loewenberg, "Communications," *American Historical Review*, 77 (October 1972), 1194–97; Gertrude Himmelfarb, "The 'New' History," *Commentary* (January 1975), 72–78; Kenneth S. Lynn, "History's Reckless Psychologizing," *Chronicle of Higher Education*, January 16, 1978, 48; and Barbara W. Tuchman, "Can History Use Freud?", *Atlantic* (January 1967), 39–45.

16. On TR, see Stanley Allen Renshon, *The Psychological Assessment of Presidential Candidates* (New York: New York University Press, 1996), 1–4. On Wilson, see Alexander L. and Juliette L. George, *Woodrow Wilson and Colonel House: A Personality Study* (New York: J. Day, 1956); William Bayard Hale, *The Story of a Style* (New York: B. W. Huebsch, 1920); and Freud and Bullitt, *Thomas Woodrow Wilson*.

17. On Goldwater, see Rogow, *Psychiatrists*, 125–28; Renshon, *Psychological Assessment*, 29. On Muskie, see Broder, *Behind the Front Page*, 23–49; on Eagleton, see Renshon, *Psychological Assessment*, 146–76; White, *1972*, 183–217.

18. Mazlish, "History, Psychology and Leadership," in Barbara Kellerman, ed., *Leadership: Multidisciplinary Perspectives* (Englewood Cliffs, NJ: Prentice-Hall, 1984), 16; Mazlish, *In Search of Nixon*, vi; James David Barber, "A Summary of Predictions of Richard M. Nixon as President," Paper at Center for Advanced Study in the Behavioral Sciences, Stanford University, January 19, 1969, quoted in Barber, "Brush with Tyranny," 592.

19. Witcover, *Resurrection*, 212; McGinniss, *Selling*, 100–01; *Ottawa Citizen*, March 20, 1998, A9; Chesen, *Profile*, 167–71.

20. Garment, *Crazy Rhythm*, 85, 299; Nixon, *Six Crises*, 8.

21. Arnold A. Hutschnecker, *The Drive for Power* (New York: M. Evans, 1974), 3; Summers, *Arrogance*, xiv, 40, 456.

22. John Ehrlichman, Meeting notes, HIA, Stanford University, John Ehrlichman Papers, Box 2, Folder "1/9/71"; on Nixon's relationship with Hutschnecker, see Aitken, *Nixon*, 196–97; Brodie, *Richard Nixon*, 331–35; Helen W. Erskine, "Dick and Pat Nixon: The Team on Ike's Team," *Collier's*, July 9, 1954, 35; Hutschnecker, *Drive*, 3–10, 82–85; Summers, *Arrogance*, 88–94.

23. Hutschnecker, *Drive*, 3–4, 6–9, 311–14 (Drew Pearson, Address to National Press Club, November 14, 1968, reprinted); *NYT*, November 14, 1968, 34; "The Pearson Syndrome," *Newsweek*, November 25, 1968, 36; Robert G. Sherrill, "Drew Pearson: An Interview," *Nation*, July 7, 1969, 8; Steinberg, *Shame*, 334–45n.

24. Ibid. (all references).

25. Arnold A. Hutschnecker, "The Mental Health of Our Leaders," *Look*, July 15, 1969, 51–54.

26. *Ambrose 3*, 543–44.

27. Brodie, *Richard Nixon*, 36; *Real Nixon*, Kornitzer, 79; Brodie interview with Tom Bewley, June 15, 1976, Fawn Brodie Research Collection, Marriott Library, Special Collections, University of Utah, Salt Lake City; Barber, *Presidential Character*, 354–55; Steinberg, *Shame*, 133; Gerald Shaw OH, CSF, 3, quoted in Brodie, *Richard Nixon*, 25; Mazlish, *The Leader*, 214.

28. Brodie, *Richard Nixon*, 59–60; Barber, *Presidential Character*, 348.

29. Brodie, *Richard Nixon*, 57; Kornitzer, *Real Nixon*, 46–47.

30. Volkan et al., *Psychobiography*, 32; Abrahamsen, *Nixon vs. Nixon*, 25.

31. Rangell, *Mind*, 214; Barber, *Presidential Character*, 348; Kornitzer, *Real Nixon*, 56–57; Frank DeHart, *Traumatic Nixon* (self-published, 1979); Rogin and Lottier, "Inner History," 21; Abrahamsen, *Nixon vs. Nixon*, 60–61; Brodie, *Richard M. Nixon*, 77. Nixon Library archivist Susan Naultry pointed out to me that the letter was written as a school assignment.

32. Steinberg, *Shame*, 133.

33. Abrahamsen, *Nixon vs. Nixon*, 116–19, 231; Brodie, *Richard Nixon*, 131, 502. On the dean's office incident, see Kornitzer, *Real Nixon*, 120; *Ambrose 1*, 79. On Nixon's personal financial scandals, see Lukas, *Nightmare*, 343–68.

34. Mazlish, *In Search of Nixon*, 204; Hannah Milhous Nixon, as told to Flora Rheta Schreiber, "Richard Nixon: A Mother's Story," *Good Housekeeping* (June 1960), 212.

35. Mazlish, *In Search of Nixon*, 204; Barber, *Presidential Character*, 348.

36. Rogin and Lottier, "Inner History," 21; Abrahamsen, *Nixon vs. Nixon*, 101; Woodward and Bernstein, *Final Days*, 32, 165–66.

37. Rogin and Lottier, "Inner History," 27–28; Abrahamsen, *Nixon vs. Nixon*, 188–89.

38. Barber, "The Question of Presidential Character," 65; Chesen, *Profile*, 97–98; Volkan et al., *Psychobiography*, 121; Steinberg, *Shame*, 181–85.

39. Abrahamsen, *Nixon vs. Nixon*, 184-88; Barber, "The Question of Presidential Character," 65; Rothenberg, "Why Nixon Taped Himself," 209–10; Steinberg, *Shame*, 169–206; Volkan et al., *Psychobiography*, 129–33.

40. Rovere, *Final Reports*, n4.

41. Arnold A. Rogow, review of *In Search of Nixon*, in *Political Science Quarterly*, vol. 87, no. 4 (December 1972), 676; Price, *With Nixon*, 19–20.

42. H. R. Haldeman, "The Evolution of the Nixon Legacy: Discussant," in *Hofstra 2*, 319; Gore Vidal, "Nixon Without Knives," in Lee Eisenberg, ed., *Fifty Who Made a Difference* (New York: Villard, 1986), 30. Parmet, "Nixon Biographers: Discussant," in *Hofstra 2*; Morris, *Richard Milhous*, xiii; *Ambrose 3*, 589.

43. Barber, "The Question of Presidential Character," 66; Woodstone, *Nixon's Head*, vi, 248.

44. *Ambrose 3*, 336.

45. Abrahamsen, *Nixon vs. Nixon*, 200–20; Brodie, *Richard Nixon*, 510–12; Chesen, *Profile*, 182–88; Rothenberg, "Why Nixon Taped Himself," 216–20; Volkan et al., *Psychobiography*, 95–96; Rangell, *Mind*, 62 and *passim*; author's interview with Leonard Garment, March 16, 2000; Woodward and Bernstein, *Final Days*, 146.

46. *RN*, 961.

47. *NYT*, August 21, 1973, 1; Rather, *Camera Never Blinks*, 243–44; Stewart Alsop, "The President and His Enemies," *Newsweek*, September 3, 1973, 92; *NYT*, August 23, 1973, 1; Edwin Diamond, "Psychojournalism: Nixon on the Couch," *CJR* (March–April 1974), 8.

48. Agnew, *Go Quietly*, 130; Thompson, *Shark Hunt*, 281, 249, 460; Herbers, *No Thank You*, 90–99; John Osborne, *The Last Nixon Watch* (Washington, DC: New Republic Books, 1975), 5.

49. Abrahamsen, *Nixon vs. Nixon*, 196–97; Drew, *Washington Journal*, 69; "The Jury of the People Weighs Nixon," *Time*, November 12, 1973, 27.

50. *NYT*, December 4, 1973, 36; *NYT*, November 8, 1973, 47; Chesen, *Profile*, 160.

51. Barry M. Goldwater, with Jack Casserly, *Goldwater* (New York: Doubleday, 1988), 267–71; *Ambrose 3*, 320, 339; *NYT*, April 24, 1974, 20; *TNR*, April 13, 1974.

52. Abrahamsen, *Nixon vs. Nixon*, 242; Volkan et al., *Psychobiography*, 104; Anson, *Exile*, 75n; author's interview with Garment, March 16, 2000.

53. Woodward and Bernstein, *Final Days*, 395, 403–04, 422–23; Kissinger, *Years of Upheaval*, 1207–10.

54. Abrahamsen, *Nixon vs. Nixon*, 244–45; Brodie, *Richard Nixon*, 30–32; Hamilton, "Farewell Speeches," 502–06; Johnson, "Nixon's Use of Metaphor: The Real Nixon Tapes," *Psychoanalytic Review*, vol. 66, no. 2 (1979), 267–68; Woodward and Bernstein, *Final Days*, 455; author interview with Garment, March 16, 2000.

55. Kissinger, *Years of Upheaval*, 1213; *RN*, 1088; Woodward and Bernstein, *Final Days*, 455.

56. *NYT*, September 12, 1974, 1; *NYT*, September 14, 1974, 1; Anson, *Exile*, 46.

57. John Osborne, "Was Nixon 'Sick of Mind'?", *New York*, April 21, 1975.

58. White, *Breach of Faith*, 34; "The Dell Reporter," May 1976, HU, NPL, THWP, Box 145, Folder 4; Julius A. Leetham to White, September 30, 1974; see also Mrs. Clifton Fadiman to White, September 23, 1974, HU, NPL, THWP, Box 35, Folder 10; Safire, *Before the Fall*, 202.

59. *NYT*, May 7, 1975, 43; Abrahamsen, *Nixon vs. Nixon*, 224–38; Chesen, *Profile*, 226–30.

60. *NYT*, May 8, 1975, 39; Safire, *Before the Fall*, 39. Haig, Ziegler, Price, and others shared Reston's view. Author's interview with Ray Price, March 11, 1999; Strober and Strober, *Nixon*, 471–72.

61. Barber, *Presidential Character*, 349. For psychoanalytic explanations of Watergate, see Abrahamsen, *Nixon vs. Nixon*, 225–42; Barber, *Presidential Character*, 364-88; Brodie, *Richard Nixon*, 500–17; Chesen, *Profile*, 159–95; Lawton, "Milhous," 535–37; Rangell, *Mind, passim*; Volkan et al., *Psychobiography*, 133–39.

62. Peter Loewenberg, "Nixon, Hitler and Power," 29. Freud's essay, written in 1916, was called "Those Wrecked by Success," part of a longer article entitled "Some Character Types Met with in Psychoanalytic Work," in *The Standard Edition of the Complete Psychological Works of Sigmund Freud*, ed. James Strachey (London: Hogarth Press, 1957), 316–32. A similar interpretation is advanced by Johnson, "Nixon's Use of Metaphor," 263–74. David Abrahamsen, not incompatibly, suggested the guilt stemmed from Nixon's yearning for his mother. Since his brothers' deaths allowed him that much more of his mother's attention, the Oedipal guilt over that yearning may have been of a piece with the "survivor guilt."

63. *LAT*, August 9, 1999, A1.

64. *NYT*, October 21, 193, §4, 2; *NYT*, November 2, 1973, 23; *NYT*, November 21, 1973, 1, 18.

65. *NYT*, October 17, 1973, 29; *NYT*, July 4, 1973, 15; *NYT*, November 20, 1973, 39; Chesen, *Profile*, 233–34.

66. Arthur Schlesinger, Jr., "Can Psychiatry Save the Republic?", *Saturday Review*, September 7, 1974, 10–11, 15; Arthur Miller, "The Limited Hang-Out," *Harper's* (September 1974), 14, 18. See also Michael J. Halberstam, "Who's Medically Fit for the White House?" *NYT Magazine*, October 22, 1972, 102; *NYT*, July 16, 1973, 28; *NYT*, August 5, 1973, §IV, 15.

67. Brodie, *Richard Nixon*, 20.

68. Loewenberg, "Nixon, Hitler and Power," 29.

69. Ibid.; Newell G. Bringhurst, *Fawn McKay Brodie: A Biographer's Life* (Norman, OK: University of Oklahoma Press, 1999), 223–41; Godfrey Hodgson, "The Liar on the Couch," *TNR*, September 9, 1981, 25–27.

70. Rangell, *Mind of Watergate*, 21–25; Brown, "Richard Nixon," 102.

71. Jeffrey P. Kimball, *Nixon's Vietnam War* (Lawrence: University Press of Kansas, 1998); Garment, *Crazy Rhythm*, 298; Herbers, *No Thank You*, 95; Sum-

mers, *Arrogance*, xiv–xv, 40, 88–89, 456, and *passim*; *NYT*, August 27, 2000, 26; *NYT*, August 31, 2000, 22; *NYT*, September 3, 2000, §4, 3; *Newsday*, August 28, 2000, A15.

72. Pauline Kael, "The Current Cinema," *New Yorker*, July 15, 1985, 70–73.

73. Mark Maxwell, *NixonCarver: A Novel* (New York: St. Martin's Press, 1998), 53–55.

Chapter 7: The Foreign Policy Establishment: Nixon as Statesman

1. Jann S. Wenner, "Bill Clinton: The *Rolling Stone* Interview," *Rolling Stone*, December 28, 2000–January 4, 2001, 91–92.

2. Korff, *Personal Nixon*, 54.

3. Ray Price, "Nixon's Reassessment Comes Early," *NP*, 389; *NYT*, April 28, 1994, A1.

4. Crowley, *Winter*, 286; John Lewis Gaddis, *Strategies of Containment: A Critical Appraisal of Postwar American National Security Policy* (New York: Oxford University Press, 1982), 343; Harris survey, January 19, 1981; Harris survey, April 15, 1985; Gallup survey, December 1998; Tony Fuller, Morton M. Kondracke, and John J. Lindsay, "The Sage of Saddle River," *Newsweek*, May 19, 1986, 32; James C. Humes, *Nixon's Ten Commandments of Statecraft* (New York: Scribner's, 1997).

5. Hugh Sidey, "The Man and Foreign Policy," *NP*, 305.

6. Reeves, *President Nixon*, 22; White, *1968*, 171; *RN*, 770; Small, *Presidency*, 216.

7. Wills, *Nixon Agonistes*, 140, 395.

8. Meg Greenfield, "The Prose of Richard M. Nixon," *Reporter*, September 29, 1960, 18.

9. Kissinger, *Years of Upheaval*, 416.

10. Ibid., 7, 73–74, 1182.

11. Ibid., 88, 102–03, 202–03, 1183; Henry A. Kissinger, *White House Years* (Boston: Little, Brown, 1979), 1475–76.

12. Strober and Strober, *Nixon*, 129; Richard Nixon, "Asia After Viet Nam," *Foreign Affairs* (October 1967), 111–25.

13. Thomas, *Front Row*, 186.

14. "Nixon's Coup: To Peking with Peace," *Time*, 11–17; "Nixon: I Will Go to China," *Newsweek*, July 26, 1971, 16–22.

15. *HD*, May 28, 1971, 356; "From Russia with Hope," *Newsweek*, June 5, 1972, 26; *Time*, March 6, 1972, 12; Small, *Presidency*, 124; Elmer Plischke, "Nixon as Summit Diplomat," in Leon Friedman and William Levantrosser, eds., *Cold War Patriot and Statesman* (Westport: Greenwood Press, 1993; cited hereafter as *Hofstra 3*), 233.

16. Safire, *Before the Fall*, 442, 443, 458; Reeves, *President Nixon*, 494.

17. *HD*, 567; "After the Moscow Primary," *Newsweek*, June 12, 1972, 21.

18. Osborne, *Fourth Year*, 81, 88, 100; *Newsweek*, June 12, 1972, 22; "What Nixon Brings Home from Moscow," *Time*, June 5, 1972, 13; *HD*, 568; Plischke, "Nixon as Summit Diplomat," 233.

19. *RN*, 390.

20. *Ambrose 3*, 365.

21. Price, *With Nixon*, 312–14.

22. Ibid.; Richard M. Nixon, "Remarks at a Dinner in Bel Air, California, Honoring the President," *PP 1974* (Washington, DC: Government Printing Office, 1975), no. 227.

23. Sidey, "The Man and Foreign Policy," *NP*, 307.

24. *NYT*, May 14, 1974, 22.

25. *PT*, 88.

26. White, *1972*, 493–94; Kutler, *Wars of Watergate*, 471; Stewart Alsop, "Poor Mr. Nixon," *Newsweek*, May 7, 1973, 112; Woodward and Bernstein, *Final Days*, 231; Joseph W. Alsop, with Adam Platt, *I've Seen the Best of It: Memoirs* (New York: Norton, 1992), 478–79.

27. *NYT*, May 17, 1974, 24; James J. Kilpatrick, "A Stout If Rambling Defense," *Time*, May 27, 1974, 16; "Nixon Interview," *NR*, July 16, 1974, 632.

28. *NYT*, May 27, 1974, 27; Herbers, *No Thank You*, 123; *NYT*, May 26, 1974, §4, 4; Osborne, *Last Nixon Watch*, 149.

29. Woodward and Bernstein, *Final Days*, 216; Herbers, *No Thank You*, 120–31; Raymond L. Garthoff, *Détente and Confrontation: American-Soviet Relations from Nixon to Reagan* (Washington, DC: Brookings Institution, 1985), 481.

30. Kutler, *Wars of Watergate*, 411.

31. William P. Bundy, *A Tangled Web* (New York: Hill & Wang, 1998), 398–99; Kissinger, *White House Years*, 1254; Crowley, *Record*, 65.

32. "An Old China Hand," *Newsweek*, March 8, 1976, 38; *NYT*, February 26, 1976, 3; *WP*, February 25, 1976, A15; *NYT*, February 26, 1976, 3; "Nixon Comes Back into the Limelight—and Controversy," *USNWR*, March 1, 1976, 24.

33. Anson, *Exile*, 195, 199–200.

34. *St. Louis Post-Dispatch*, October 3, 1980, 2A; Jennifer Allen, "Richard Nixon Is Making Something of a Comeback," *Manhattan*, January 19, 1981, 1–3; Crowley, *Winter*, 149; Anson, *Exile*, 250; "The Private Travels of Nixon," *Time*, November 2, 1981, 30.

35. Julie Baumgold, "Nixon's New Life in New York," *New York*, June 9, 1980, 24; Allen, "Richard Nixon Is," 1–3; *WSJ*, July 2, 1981, 1; Michael Beschloss, "How Nixon Came In from the Cold," *Vanity Fair* (June 1992), 114ff.; Korda, *Another Life*, 451–62; Grunwald, *One Man's America*, 451–53.

36. Korda, *Another Life*, 453.

37. Kalb, *Nixon Memo*, 34–39; *Ambrose 3*, 522–23, 530–31, 550, 563–64.

38. White to RN, October 14, 1983, HU, NPL, THWP, Box 49, Folder 14.

39. Reeves, *President Nixon*, 297, 517; Sidey, "The Man and Foreign Policy," *NP*, 308; Brian Lamb interview with Monica Crowley, *Booknotes*, C-SPAN, September 29, 1996, www.booknotes.org; Crowley, *Record*, 61–62.

40. Russ Witcher, *After Watergate: Nixon and the Newsweeklies* (Lanham, MD: University Press of America, 2000), 44, 51–57.

41. David M. Alpern with John J. Lindsay, "Nixon in Prime Time," *Newsweek*, April 16, 1984, 34; *NYT*, January 12, 1986, §4, 27.

42. Sidey, "Perspectives on Richard Nixon," in Leon Friedman and William Levantrosser, eds., *Richard M. Nixon: Politician, President, Administrator* (Westport: Greenwood Press, 1991; cited hereafter as *Hofstra 1*), 12; Kalb, *Nixon Memo*, 103.

43. *Ambrose 3*, 558–60; *NYT*, January 12, 1986, §4, 27; *NYT*, February 28, 1986, B4; Larry Martz, et al., "The Road Back," *Newsweek*, May 19, 1986, 26; *NYT*, September 29, 1986, B8; *NYT*, April 4, 1986, D20; *NYT*, January 8, 1986, A23; Nixon, "Superpower Summitry," *Foreign Affairs* (Fall 1985), 1–11; Martz et al., "The Road Back," 26; Richard M. Nixon, "The Pillars of Peace," *Vital Speeches*, July 15, 1986, 585–89.

44. *NYT*, April 22, 1986, A17; *Chicago Tribune*, April 22, 1986, C5.

45. *NYT*, April 22, 1986, A17; *LAT*, April 22, 1986, A18; Reuters News Service, April 22, 1986; Malcolm S. Forbes, "Fact and Comment," *Forbes*, June 16, 1986, 17; *Ambrose 3*, 561; Kalb, *Nixon Memo*, 31; Beschloss, "How Nixon Came In," 148.

46. "Nixon's Long Road Back," *Newsweek*, May 19, 1986, 3ff.

47. Schudson, *Watergate*, 193; Thomas J. Johnson, *The Rehabilitation of Richard Nixon: The Media's Effect on Collective Memory* (New York: Garland, 1995), 6; *Hofstra 2*, 34; *NYT*, July 13, 1986, §3, 1; Martz et al., "The Road Back," 26ff.; Arthur B. Murphy, "Evaluating the Presidents of the United States," *Presidential Studies Quarterly*, vol. 14, no. 1 (Winter 1984), 126.

48. "Notes and Comment," *The New Yorker*, May 26, 1986, 23.

49. "The Best and Worst of Presidents," *USNWR*, May 4, 1987; Herbert Parmet, "Book Reviews," *The New Leader*, May 4, 1987, 23.

50. Kalb, *Nixon Memo*, 41–42; Richard Nixon, "The Time Has Come to Help," *Time*, January 13, 1992, 27; David Postman, "He's Back Again," *TNR*, April 6, 1992, 10; Kalb, *Nixon Memo*, 58–59.

51. *Ambrose 3*, 562, 569; Kalb, *Nixon Memo*, 74–76; Crowley, *Winter*, 77–82.

52. *USA Today*, March 10, 1992, 6A; *LAT*, March 10, 1992, A3; Kalb, *Nixon Memo*, 84–89; Postman, "He's Back Again," *TNR*, 10; *NYT*, March 10, 1992, A1.

53. Kalb, *Nixon Memo*, 77, 98, 104; *WP*, March 12, 1992, C4; Kalb, *Nixon Memo*, 104; Postman, "He's Back Again," 11.

54. Kalb, *Nixon Memo*, 116, 122; Richard Nixon, "We Are Ignoring Our World

Role," *Time*, March 16, 1992, 74; William Boot, "Nixon Resurrectus," *CJR* (September–October 1987), 20.

55. Gergen, *Eyewitness to Power*, 21; *WP*, August 5, 1984, C1.

56. Monsell, *Nixon on Stage and Screen*, 41, 83–87; Jeremy Geidt and Jonathan Marks, "The Tragical History of Samlet, Prince of Denmark," *Watergate Classics, Yale/Theatre*, 5 (Winter 1974), 24–51; Barbara Garson, "MacDick?" *Village Voice*, November 29, 1973, 34.

57. Small, *Presidency*, 308.

58. Aitken, *Nixon*, 577, 465–66.

59. Monsell, *Nixon on Stage and Screen*, 157; *LAT* Calendar, December 13, 1987, 4.

60. John Adams, *Nixon in China: An Opera in Three Acts*, libretto Alice Goodman (Amsterdam: De Nedelandse Opera, 1988), 47, 58, 62.

61. www.earbox.com; Adams, *Nixon in China*, 38.

62. John Ehrlichman, *The China Card* (New York: Simon & Schuster, 1986).

63. Kimball, *Nixon's Vietnam War*; Larry Berman, *No Peace, No Honor: Nixon, Kissinger, and Betrayal in Vietnam* (New York: Free Press, 2001); Hoff, *Nixon Reconsidered*, 147; Bundy, *Tangled Web, passim*.

64. Garment, *Crazy Rhythm*, 387.

65. "Flashes," *Entertainment Weekly*, February 11, 2000.

66. Crowley, *Winter*, 127–29.

67. Kalb, *Nixon Memo*, 144–59; Crowley, *Winter*, 127–29.

68. Wenner, "Bill Clinton," 91–92.

69. Hoff, *Nixon Reconsidered*, 346.

70. Kaiser, "What Power Does He Hold Over Us?", C1; Strober and Strober, *Nixon*, 518.

71. Frost, *Sword*, 13; *Ambrose 3*, 535; "The Sage of Saddle River," 33; Crowley, *Winter*, 308.

72. Schudson, *Watergate*, 194–96.

Chapter 8: The Historians: Nixon as Liberal

1. Hoff, *Nixon Reconsidered*, 144.

2. *NYT*, August 9, 1999, A1.

3. *WP*, August 20, 1999, A35; Michael Barone, "Nixon's America," *USNWR*, September 20, 1999, 26; *WP*, August 7, 1994, C1; *CSM*, August 13, 1999, 11; see also *WP*, December 28, 1995, A1; *Atlanta Journal-Constitution*, January 14, 1996, C7; *NYT*, September 29, 1996, §4, 1; *WP*, February 2, 1997, C7; David A. Bell, "Richard Milhous Clinton," *TNR*, January 18, 1999, 22; Ramesh Ponnuru, "A Conservative No More," *NR*, October 11, 1999; *NYT*, November 16, 1999, A27.

4. Books advancing this idea include the previously cited works by Melvin
    Small, Joan Hoff, Tom Wicker, and Herbert Parmet, as well as Michael Barone,
    Our Country: The Shaping of America from Roosevelt to Reagan (New York: Free
    Press, 1990), and Alonzo Hamby, *Liberalism and Its Challengers: From F.D.R. to
    Bush*, 2nd edn. (New York: Oxford University Press, 1992 [1985]).

5. Barone, *Our Country*, 486.

6. Hoff, *Nixon Reconsidered*, 90.

7. Herbert Stein, *Presidential Economics* (Washington, DC: American Enterprise
    Institute, 1988), 190.

8. "And Now, Why Not a Domestic Summit," *Time*, June 12, 1972, 13.

9. Rovere quoted in Daniel Patrick Moynihan, *The Politics of a Guaranteed
    Income: The Nixon Administration and the Family Assistance Plan* (New York:
    Random House, 1973), 368; Bob Kuttner, "Trimming the Meat and Keeping
    the Fat: Nixon vs. the Great Society," *Village Voice*, February 22, 1973; "Fight
    or Switch?" *Nation*, November 23, 1970, 514. Buchanan to Nixon, November
    10, 1972, in Oudes, ed., *From the President*, 560; White, *Breach of Faith*, 110–11.

10. Parmet, *Richard Nixon*, 543; William F. Buckley, Jr., *Inveighing We Will Go*
    (New York: Putnam, 1972), 68–69.

11. Rowland Evans, Jr., and Robert Novak, *Nixon in the White House: The Frus-
    tration of Power* (New York: Random House, 1971), 223–32.

12. Small, *Presidency*, 187; Jeffrey Bell, "Mr. Nixon's Sometime Friends," *Nation*,
    July 24, 1972, 43–46; Buckley, *Inveighing*, 284; *HD*, 181.

13. Bell, "Mr. Nixon's," 43; Gary Allen's *Richard Nixon: The Man Behind the Mask*
    represents a quintessential expression of the extreme right's view of Nixon
    as a rank opportunist who posed as a conservative but governed as a lib-
    eral. *Human Events*, Toledano, and Loeb are all quoted in Allen, 20–21.

14. Evans and Novak, *Nixon in the White House, passim.*

15. Ibid., 211–14.

16. Author's interview with Robert Novak, May 6, 2000; Parmet, *Richard Nixon*,
    550; Evans and Novak, *Nixon in the White House*, 40–43.

17. Evans and Novak, *Nixon in the White House*, 172, 175–76; author's interview
    with Novak, May 6, 2000.

18. Arthur Schlesinger, Jr., "The Challenge of Abundance," *The Reporter*, May 3,
    1956, 8–11; Irwin Unger, *The Best of Intentions: The Triumphs and Failures of the
    Great Society Under Kennedy, Johnson, and Nixon* (New York: Doubleday,
    1996), 104–47.

19. Bell, *End of Ideology*; John F. Kennedy, "Commencement Address at Yale
    University, June 11, 1962," *PP* 1963, no. 234.

20. James Allen Smith, *Brookings at Seventy-Five* (Washington, DC: Brookings
    Institution, 1991), 1–4. For more on the rising influence of policy analysts
    during the Great Society, see Smith, *The Idea Brokers* (New York: Free Press,
    1991).

21. Daniel Patrick Moynihan, *Maximum Feasible Misunderstanding: Community*

Action in the War on Poverty (New York: Free Press, 1969), 177 (his italics). On the politics of social scientists, see Everett Carll Ladd and Seymour Martin Lipset, *The Divided Academy: Professors and Politics* (New York: McGraw-Hill, 1975), 3–4, 62; Joel D. Aberbach and Bert A. Rockman, "Clashing Beliefs Within the Executive Branch: The Nixon Administration Bureaucracy," *American Political Science Review*, vol. 70, no. 2 (June 1976), 456–68; Christopher J. Bosso, "Congressional and Presidential Scholars: Some Basic Traits," *PS: Political Science and Politics* (December 1989), 839–48.

22. *HD*, 309; *RN*, 355–56; Small, *Presidency*, 41.

23. Author's interview with Jodie Allen, April 12, 2000.

24. White, *1968*, 171; *RN*, 339; Lemann, *Promised Land*, 207.

25. John C. Whitaker, *Striking a Balance: Environment and Natural Resources Policy in the Nixon-Ford Years* (Washington, DC: American Enterprise Institute, 1976), *passim*; Ehrlichman, *Witness to Power*, 243.

26. Vincent J. and Vee Burke, *Nixon's Good Deed: Welfare Reform* (New York: Columbia University Press, 1974).

27. Unger, *Best of Intentions*, 319; Moynihan, *Guaranteed Income*, 353 (his italics).

28. Moynihan, *Guaranteed Income*, 368, 371, 374–75.

29. Hamby, *Liberalism*, 298–331.

30. David Thelen, "The Practice of American History," *Journal of American History*, vol. 81, no. 3 (December 1994), 958.

31. Sheldon S. Wolin, "Reagan Country," *New York Review of Books*, December 18, 1980, 11; Nicholas von Hoffman, "Know Thy President," *New York Review of Books*, June 25, 1981, 27.

32. Arthur Schlesinger, Jr., *The Cycles of American History* (Boston: Houghton Mifflin, 1986), 373.

33. Author's interview with Jodie Allen, April 12, 2000; *WP*, February 24, 1983, A15.

34. Author's interview with Joan Hoff, May 4, 2000; e-mail from Hoff to the author, May 29, 2000.

35. Joan Hoff-Wilson, "Outflanking the Liberals on Welfare," in *Hofstra 1*, 86–106.

36. *NYT*, November 23, 1987, A14; John C. Whitaker, "The Environment: Discussant," in *Hofstra 1*, 203; Maurice H. Stans, "Nixon's Economic Policy Toward Minorities," in ibid., 2408–48; Robert H. Finch, "Social Welfare: Discussant" in ibid., 132–33; Elliot L. Richardson, "The Capacity for Greatness," in ibid., 4–5; Carl Lieberman, "Legislative Successes and Failure: The Social Welfare Policies of the Nixon Administration," in ibid., 107–31; Hugh D. Graham, "The Incoherence of Civil Rights Policy in the Nixon Administration," in ibid., 159–72; Arthur M. Schlesinger, Jr., "The Evolution of the Nixon Legacy: Discussant," in *Hofstra 2*, 326.

37. Barry Riccio, "Richard Nixon Reconsidered: The Conservative as Liberal?", in *Hofstra 2*, 279–94; author's interview with Barry Riccio, April 13, 2000.

38. Ibid.

39. *San Diego Union-Tribune,* November 20, 1987, A10.

40. *Hofstra 2,* 186, and *passim.*

41. On the impoundment, see e.g. Charles S. Warren, "The Nixon Environmental Record: A Mixed Picture," in *Hofstra 1,* 198–99; on the OEO, see Small, *Presidency,* 190–91.

42. David Lowenthal, *The Heritage Crusade and the Spoils of History* (Cambridge, UK: Cambridge University Press, 1998 [1996]), 111.

43. Stanley I. Kutler, "Watergate Reexamined: Discussant," in *Hofstra 2,* 35–36; Hoff, *Nixon Reconsidered,* 337.

44. Brodie, *Richard Nixon,* 500; Kutler in *Hofstra 2,* 35–36.

45. Brian Lamb interview with Stephen Ambrose, *Booknotes,* C-SPAN, June 5, 1994, available at www.booknotes.org; *Ambrose 1,* 722; *Hofstra 1,* 16; *Hofstra 2,* 236; *Ambrose 2,* 705.

46. *Ambrose 3,* 591; see also *LAT,* July 20, 1990, B1. On reviews of Ambrose, see (for vol. 1) *NYT Book Review,* April 26, 1987, 3; *LAT,* June 21, 1987, 12; *The New York Review of Books,* July 16, 1987, 10–13; *Reviews in American History* (December 1988), 662–67; (for vol. 2) *LAT,* October 15, 1989; *Newsday,* October 12, 1989, 22; *WP,* November 12, 1989, X1; (for vol. 3) *NYT,* November 25, 1991, C20; *NYT Book Review,* November 24, 1991, 3; *Reviews in American History* (March 1993), 135–38.

47. *Ambrose 3,* 597; Kutler in *Hofstra 2,* 38.

48. Author's interview with Herbert Parmet, April 14, 2000; Parmet, *Richard Nixon,* 530–31.

49. Parmet, *Richard Nixon,* 642, 530; Herbert Parmet interview with Richard Nixon, November 16, 1988, in author's possession.

50. *Booknotes,* C-SPAN, April, 7, 1991; transcript available at www.booknotes.org; Wicker, *One of Us,* 703, 541 (his italics); author's interview with Tom Wicker, May 5, 2000.

51. *Boston Globe* March 10, 1991, B17; *NYT,* June 7, 1991, A35; *Christian Science Monitor,* March 27, 1991, 13.

52. *Ambrose 3,* 635–36.

53. Schlesinger, *Cycles,* 373.

54. Barry Schwartz, "Our Nixon: The Presidency in a Culture of Ridicule," *Newsletter of the Sociology of Culture,* vol. 14., no. 3 (Spring–Summer 2000), 1–3; Hugh D. Graham, *The Civil Rights Era: Origins and Development of National Policy, 1960–1972* (New York: Oxford University Press, 1990), 301–475; Barone, *Our Country,* 473–97; Dionne, *Why Americans Hate Politics,* 193–200; Lemann, *Promised Land,* 202–21; Martin Walker, *America Reborn: A Twentieth-Century Narrative in Twenty-Six Lives* (New York: Knopf, 2000); Aitken, *Nixon,* 395–400; *WP,* April 24, 1994, C7; Jonathan Rauch, "What Nixon Wrought," TNR, May 16, 1994, 28.

55. "Health Care Now," *TNR,* September 19 and 26, 1994, 11; see also *LAT,* June 14, 1994, A5; *WP,* July 27, 1996, A23.

56. Author's interview with Hoff, May 4, 2000; *LAT,* July 17, 1990, E1; Hoff, *Nixon Reconsidered,* 9.

57. Hoff, *Nixon Reconsidered,* 1, 329, 341.

58. Richard Norton Smith, "The Nixon Watch Continues," *NYT Book Review,* October 30, 1994, 9; Hoff, *Nixon Reconsidered,* 113.

59. Hoff, *Nixon Reconsidered,* 335.

60. Dean J. Kotlowski, "Politics and Principle: The Nixon Administration and Civil Rights Policy," PhD dissertation, Indiana University, 1998; Small, *Doves,* ix; Barone, "Nixon's America," 26. For other books on Nixon's liberal domestic policies, see Dan Baum, *Smoke and Mirrors: The War on Drugs and the Politics of Failure* (Boston: Little, Brown, 1996); Michael Massing, *The Fix* (New York: Simon & Schuster, 1998), 97–131; James T. Patterson, *Grand Expectations: The United States 1945–1974* (New York: Oxford University Press, 1996), 718–29; Jacob Weisberg, *In Defense of Government: The Fall and Rise of Public Trust* (New York: Scribner's, 1996), 88–90; Paul F. Boller, *Not So!: Popular Myths About America from Columbus to Clinton* (New York: Oxford University Press, 1995), 183–87; Unger, *Best of Intentions,* 301–45.

61. Smith, "The Nixon Watch Continues," 9.

62. Bruce Kuklick, *The Good Ruler: From Herbert Hoover to Richard Nixon* (New Brunswick: Rutgers University Press, 1988), 26–30.

Epilogue: Nixon as Comeback Artist

1. Jeffrey Vallance, "The Nix Files: 'I Am Not a Spook!'", *Nixco News,* vol. 4, no. 1 (January 1998), 21.

2. Sears quoted in Sidney Blumenthal, "Ghost in the Machine," *New Yorker,* October 2, 1995, 46.

3. The story of Nixon and Elvis is told by former White House Plumber Egil "Bud" Krogh in *The Day Elvis Met Nixon* (Bellevue, WA: Pejama Press, 1994). Fictional versions include Jonathan Lowy, *Elvis and Nixon: A Novel* (New York: Crown, 1991), and Alan Arkush, *Elvis Meets Nixon,* Showtime, 1998. See also www.gwu.edu/~nsarchiv/nsa/elvis/elnix.html.

4. *NYT,* April 28, 1994, A1.

5. Ibid., A20.

6. Ibid.

7. *Newsday,* April 24, 1994, A4. See also Rauch, "What Nixon Wrought," *TNR,* May 16, 1994, 28.

8. Benjamin J. Stein, "Au Revoir, Mr. President," American Spectator (July 1994); *NYT,* April 28, 1994, A21.

9. Philip Roth, *I Married a Communist* (Boston: Houghton Mifflin, 1998) 277–80.

10. Saxbe, *I've Seen the Elephant*, 179; *LAT*, May 30, 1998, A1; *Newsday*, May 1, 1994, A37; "Nixon-Hating: An Anthology," *TNR*, May 16, 1994, 24; *LAT*, May 13, 1994, F21.

11. Mel Elfin and Gary Cohen, "Richard M. Nixon," *USNWR*, May 2, 1994, 24; *NYT*, April 24, 1994, 29.

12. *LAT*, April 25, 1994, B7; Hunter S. Thompson, "Redbaiter, Liar, Warmonger, Crook," *Rolling Stone*, June 16, 1994; *Radical History Review*, 60 (Fall 1994), 134, 188, 198.

13. *NYT*, April 26, 1994, A23; Garry Wills, "Nixon in Heaven," *Esquire* (July 1994), 38ff.; David Halberstam, "Richard Nixon's Last Campaign," *CJR* (July/August 1994), 35ff.; Jacob Weisberg, "Spinning from His Grave," *New York*, May 9, 1994, 39ff.; *LAT*, April 25, 1994.

14. On public opinion polls, see, among others, the Gallup polls of April 8 (conducted March 18–20), and June 17, 2002, cited at www.gallup.com. Of the eight presidents from Kennedy to Clinton, Nixon repeatedly fared the worst. On historians' polls, see Arthur M. Schlesinger, Jr., "The Ultimate Approval Rating," *NYT Magazine*, December 15, 1996, 46; and "C-SPAN Survey of Presidential Leadership," at www.americanpresidents.org/survey/historians .overall.asp. On conservatives' polls, see the Intercollegiate Studies Institute poll of 1997, cited in Gary L. Gregg, "Liberals, Conservatives, and the Presidency," *The Intercollegiate Review* (Spring 1998), 26–31; and the Federalist Society poll of November 2000, cited in *Chicago Sun-Times*, November 17, 2000, 5.

15. Philip Roth, *American Pastoral* (Boston: Houghton Mifflin, 1997), 299–300; www.revolutionsf.com.

16. Philip Roth, *Our Gang, Starring Tricky and His Friends* (New York: Random House, 1971), 200.

Select Bibliography

Archival Collections

David Abrahamsen Papers, Rare Book and Manuscript Library, CU, New York, NY

Joseph and Stewart Alsop Papers, LCMD, Washington, DC

Alternative Newspaper Collection, CU, MC, New York, NY

Americans for Democratic Action Papers, CU, MC, New York, NY

Fawn Brodie Research Collection, Marriott Library, Special Collections, University of Utah, Salt Lake City, UT

John Ehrlichman Papers, HIA, Stanford University, Stanford, CA

Gerald R. Ford Vice Presidential Papers, GRFPL, Ann Arbor, MI

Herbert H. Lehman Papers, Lehman Suite, CU, New York, NY

Thruston Morton Papers, University of Kentucky Library, Lexington, KY.

New Left Collection, HIA, Stanford University, Stanford, CA

Richard Nixon Pre-Presidential Papers, RNL, Yorba Linda, CA

Richard Nixon Vice Presidential Papers, NARA, Pacific Branch, Laguna Niguel, CA

Sidney Peck Papers, SHSW, Madison, WI

A. James Reichely Research Interviews, GRFPL, Ann Arbor, MI

Social Action Vertical File, SHSW, Madison, WI

Ralph de Toledano Papers, HIA, Stanford University, Stanford, CA

White House Central Files, RNPLP, NARA II, College Park, MD

White House Special Files, RNPLP, NARA II, College Park, MD

Theodore H. White Papers, Nathan Pusey Library, Harvard University Archives, Cambridge, MA

Author's Interviews

Jodie Allen, Sidney Blumenthal, Benjamin Bradlee, Adam Clymer, John W. Dean III,

Leonard Garment, Todd Gitlin, Seymour Hersh, Joan Hoff, Jim Hougan, Charles
Lichtenstein, Bruce Mazlish, Robert Novak, Herbert Parmet, Martin Plissner,
Raymond Price, Barry Riccio, Ron Rosenbaum, James Schamus, Daniel Schorr,
Tom Wicker.

Other Interviews and Oral Histories

Stephen Ambrose, by Brian Lamb. *Booknotes*, C-SPAN, June 5, 1994

Kenneth Ball. RMNOH, CSF, Fullerton, CA

Wallace Black. RMNOH, CSF, Fullerton, CA

Roy Day. Earl Warren OH Program, BL, UCB, Berkeley, CA

Patrick J. Hillings. OH Program, UCLA, Los Angeles, CA

Chet Holifield. Helen Gahagan Douglas OH Program, BL, UCB, Berkeley, CA

Frank Jorgensen. Earl Warren OH Program, BL, UCB, Berkeley, CA

Gerald Kepple. RMNOH, CSF, Fullerton, CA

Earl Mazo. CUOHP, New York, NY

Thruston Morton. University of Kentucky Library, Lexington, KY

A. C. Newsom. RMNOH, CSF, Fullerton, CA

Richard Nixon, by Herbert Parmet. November 16, 1988

Lyle Otterman. RMNOH, CSF, Fullerton, CA

Gerald Shaw. RMNOH, CSF, Fullerton, CA

Tom Wicker, by Brian Lamb. *Booknotes*, C-SPAN, April 7, 1991

Government Documents and Published Compilations of Primary Sources

Haldeman, H. R. *The Haldeman Diaries: Inside the Nixon White House*. New York:
Berkeley Books, 1994.

Johnson, George W., ed. *The Nixon Presidential Press Conferences*. New York: Earl
M. Coleman, 1978.

Kutler, Stanley, ed. *Abuse of Power: The New Nixon Tapes*. New York: Free Press,
1997.

Maxwell, Bruce, ed. *Historic Documents of 1994*. Washington, DC: Congressional
Quarterly, 1995.

New York Times, ed. *The Watergate Hearings: Break-in and Cover-Up*. New York:
Bantam Books, 1973.

President's Commission on Campus Unrest. *The Report of the President's Commission on Campus Unrest*. Washington, DC: Government Printing Office, 1970.

Public Papers of the Presidents, 1963, 1969–74. Washington, DC: Government Printing Office, 1964, 1971–75.

Schulte, Renee, ed. *The Young Nixon: An Oral Inquiry*. Fullerton, CA: California State University Press, 1978.

Strober, Gerald S., and Deborah H. *Nixon: An Oral History of His Presidency*. New York: Harper, 1994.

Thompson, Kenneth W., ed. *The Nixon Presidency: Twenty-Two Intimate Perspectives of Richard M. Nixon*. Lanham, MD: University Press of America, 1982.

U.S. Congress, Senate. *Final Report of the Select Committee on Presidential Campaign Activities*. 93rd Congress, 2nd Session. Washington, DC: Government Printing Office, 1974.

Washington Post, ed. *The Presidential Transcripts*. New York: Dell, 1974.

Articles, Books, and Dissertations

Aaron, Daniel. "Nixon as Literary Artifact," *Raritan* (Fall 1995).

Aberbach, Joel D., and Bert A. Rockman. "Clashing Beliefs Within the Executive Branch: The Nixon Administration Bureaucracy," *American Political Science Review*, vol. 70, no. 2 (June 1976).

Abrahamsen, David. *Nixon vs. Nixon: An Emotional Tragedy*. New York: Farrar, Straus & Giroux, 1977.

Abzug, Bella S. *Bella!: Ms. Abzug Goes to Washington*. New York: Saturday Review, 1972.

Adatto, Kiku. *Picture Perfect: The Art and Artifice of Public Image Making*. New York: Basic Books, 1993.

Adler, Renata. *Canaries in the Mineshaft: Essays on Politics and Media*. New York: St. Martin's Press, 2001.

Agnew, Spiro. *Go Quietly . . . Or Else*. New York: William Morrow, 1980.

Aitken, Jonathan. *Nixon: A Life*. London: Weidenfeld & Nicolson, 1993.

———. *Pride and Perjury*. London: Harper, 2000.

Albert, Judith Clavir, and Stewart Edward Albert. *The Sixties Papers: Documents of a Rebellious Decade*. New York: Praeger, 1984.

Allen, Gary. *Richard Nixon: The Man Behind the Mask*. Boston: Western Islands, 1971.

Alsop, Joseph W., with Adam Platt. *I've Seen the Best of It: Memoirs*. New York: W. W. Norton, 1992.

Ambrose, Stephen E. *Nixon*. Vol. I: *The Education of a Politician, 1913–1962*. New York: Simon & Schuster, 1987 (cited in text as *Ambrose 1*).

———. *Nixon*. Vol. II: *The Triumph of a Politician, 1962–1972*. New York: Simon & Schuster, 1989 (*Ambrose 2*).

———. *Nixon*. Vol. III: *Ruin and Recovery, 1973–1990*. New York: Simon & Schuster, 1991 (*Ambrose 3*).

Anderson, Jack, with James Boyd. *Confessions of a Muckraker: The Inside Story of*

Life in Washington During the Truman, Eisenhower, Kennedy and Johnson Years. New York: Random House, 1979.

———, with Daryl Gibson. *Peace, War and Politics: An Eyewitness Account.* New York: Tom Doherty, 1999.

Anson, Robert Sam. *Exile: The Unquiet Oblivion of Richard M. Nixon.* New York: Simon & Schuster, 1984.

Aronson, James. *Deadline for the Media: Today's Challenges to Press, TV and Radio.* Indianapolis: Bobbs-Merrill, 1972.

Arterton, F. Christopher. "The Impact of Watergate on Children's Attitudes Toward Political Authority," *Political Science Quarterly*, vol. 89, no. 2 (June 1974).

———. "Watergate and Children's Attitudes Toward Political Authority Revisited," *Political Science Quarterly*, vol. 90, no. 3 (Autumn 1975).

Bagdikian, Ben. *The Effete Conspiracy: And Other Crimes by the Press.* New York: Harper, 1972.

Bailyn, Bernard. *The Ideological Origins of the American Revolution.* Cambridge, MA: Harvard University Press, 1967.

———, ed. *Pamphlets of the American Revolution, 1750–1776.* Cambridge, MA: Harvard University Press, 1965.

Barber, James David, ed. *Choosing the President.* Englewood Cliffs, NJ: Prentice-Hall, 1974.

———. "The Nixon Brush with Tyranny," *Political Science Quarterly*, vol. 92, no. 4 (Winter 1977–78).

———. *The Presidential Character: Predicting Performance in the White House.* 3rd edn. rev. Englewood Cliffs, NJ: Prentice-Hall, 1985 (1972).

Barone, Michael. *Our Country: The Shaping of America from Roosevelt to Reagan.* New York: Free Press, 1990.

Barrett, Marvin, ed. *The Alfred I. DuPont–Columbia University Survey of Broadcast Journalism.* New York: Grosset & Dunlap, 1970.

Barzun, Jacques. *Clio and the Doctors: Psycho-History, Quanto-History and History.* Chicago: University of Chicago Press, 1973.

———. "History: The Muse and Her Doctors," *American Historical Review*, vol. 77, no. 1 (February 1972).

Baughman, James L. *The Republic of Mass Culture: Journalism, Filmmaking and Broadcasting in America Since 1941.* Baltimore: Johns Hopkins University Press, 1997.

Baum, Dan. *Smoke and Mirrors: The War on Drugs and the Politics of Failure.* Boston: Little, Brown, 1996.

Bayley, Edwin R. *Joe McCarthy and the Press.* Madison: University of Wisconsin Press, 1981.

Beck, Kent M. "What Was Liberalism in the 1950s?", *Political Science Quarterly*, vol. 102, no. 2 (Summer 1987).

Bell, Daniel. *The End of Ideology: On the Exhaustion of Political Ideas in the Fifties.* Cambridge, MA: Harvard University Press, 1988 (1960).

————, ed. *The Radical Right: The New American Right.* Expanded and updated. Garden City, NY: Doubleday, 1963.

Bender, Thomas. *Intellect in Public Life.* Baltimore: Johns Hopkins University Press, 1993.

Berman, Larry. *No Peace, No Honor: Nixon, Kissinger, and Betrayal in Vietnam.* New York: Free Press, 2001.

Berman, Marshall. *The Politics of Authenticity: Radical Individualism and the Emergence of Modern Society.* New York: Atheneum, 1970.

Berthoff, Warner. *A Literature Without Qualities: American Writing Since 1945.* Berkeley: University of California Press, 1979.

Black, Allida M. *Casting Her Own Shadow: Eleanor Roosevelt and the Shaping of Postwar Liberalism.* New York: Columbia University Press, 1996.

Bloch, Marc. *The Historian's Craft.* New York: Knopf, 1953.

Blumenthal, Sidney. *The Permanent Campaign: Inside the World of Elite Political Operatives.* Boston: Beacon Press, 1980.

————, and Harvey Yazijian, eds. *Government by Gunplay: Assassination Conspiracy Theories from Dallas to Today.* New York: Signet, 1976.

Boller, Paul F. *Not So!: Popular Myths About America from Columbus to Clinton.* New York: Oxford University Press, 1995.

Bonastia, Chris. "Why Did Affirmative Action in Housing Fail During the Nixon Era?" *Social Problems*, vol. 47, no. 4 (November 2000).

Boorstin, Daniel J. *The Image: A Guide to Pseudo-Events in America.* New York: Vintage Books, 1992 (1961).

Bosso, Christopher J. "Congressional and Presidential Scholars: Some Basic Traits," *PS: Political Science and Politics*, vol. 22, no. 4 (December 1989).

Boyer, Peter J. *Who Killed CBS? The Undoing of America's Number One News Network.* New York: Random House, 1988.

Boylan, James. *The New Deal Coalition and the Election of 1946.* New York: Garland, 1981.

Bradlee, Benjamin C. *A Good Life: Newspapering and Other Adventures.* New York: Simon & Schuster, 1995.

Bray, Howard. *The Pillars of the Post: The Making of a News Empire in Washington.* New York: W. W. Norton, 1980.

Bringhurst, Newell G. *Fawn McKay Brodie: A Biographer's Life.* Norman: University of Oklahoma Press, 1999.

Brinkley, Alan. *Liberalism and Its Discontents.* Cambridge, MA: Harvard University Press, 1998.

Brinkley, Douglas. *Dean Acheson: The Cold War Years, 1953–71.* New Haven: Yale University Press, 1992.

Broadwater, Jeff. *Adlai Stevenson and American Politics: The Odyssey of a Cold War Liberal*. New York: Twayne, 1994.

Broder, David S. *Behind the Front Page: A Candid Look at How News Is Made*. New York: Simon & Schuster, 1987.

Brodie, Fawn. *Richard Nixon: The Shaping of His Character*. New York: W. W. Norton, 1981.

Brown, Steven R. "Richard Nixon and the Public Conscience: The Struggle for Authenticity," *Journal of Psychohistory*, vol. 5, no. 4 (Spring 1978).

Bruce, Brendan. *Images of Power: How the Image Makers Shape Our Leaders*. London: Kogan Page, 1992.

Buchanan, Patrick J. *The New Majority: President Nixon at Mid-Passage*. N.p.: Girard Bank, 1973.

———. *Right from the Beginning*. Boston: Little, Brown, 1988.

Buckley, William F. *Inveighing We Will Go*. New York: Putnam, 1972.

Bullock, Paul. *Jerry Voorhis: The Idealist as Politician*. New York: Vantage, 1978.

Bundy, William P. *A Tangled Web: The Making of Foreign Policy in the Nixon Presidency*. New York: Hill & Wang, 1998.

Burke, Peter. *The Fabrication of Louis XIV*. New Haven: Yale University Press, 1992.

Burke, Vincent J., and Vee Burke. *Nixon's Good Deed: Welfare Reform*. New York: Columbia University Press, 1974.

Campbell, W. Joseph. "Not Likely Sent: The Remington-Hearst 'Telegrams,'" *Journalism and Mass Communications Quarterly*, vol. 77, no. 2 (Summer 2000).

Cappella, Joseph N., and Kathleen Hall Jamieson. *Spiral of Cynicism: The Press and the Public Good*. New York: Oxford University Press, 1997.

Carnes, Mark C., ed. *Past Imperfect: History According to the Movies*. New York: Holt, 1995.

Cater, Douglass. *The Fourth Branch of Government*. New York: Vintage, 1965 (1959).

Cavan, Sherri. *20th-Century Gothic: America's Nixon*. San Francisco: Wigan Pier, 1979.

Chaloupka, William. *Everybody Knows: Cynicism in America*. Minneapolis: University of Minnesota Press, 1999.

Chambers, Whittaker. *Witness*. New York: Random House, 1952.

Chesen, Eli S. *President Nixon's Psychiatric Profile: A Psychodynamic-Genetic Interpretation*. New York: Peter H. Wyden, 1973.

Colodny, Len, and Robert Gettlin. *Silent Coup: The Removal of a President*. New York: St. Martin's Press, 1991.

Colson, Charles. *Born Again*. Old Tappan, NJ: Chosen Books, 1976.

Cooke, Alistair. *A Generation on Trial: U.S.A. v. Alger Hiss*. New York: Knopf, 1950.

Costello, William. *The Facts About Nixon: An Unauthorized Biography*. New York: Viking, 1960.

Cronkite, Walter. *A Reporter's Life*. New York: Knopf, 1996.

Crouse, Timothy. *The Boys on the Bus*. New York: Ballantine, 1974 (1973).

Crowley, Monica. *Nixon in Winter*. New York: Random House, 1998.

———. *Nixon Off the Record*. New York: Random House, 1996.

Curry, Richard O., and Thomas M. Brown. *Conspiracy: The Fear of Subversion in American History*. New York: Holt, 1972.

David, Lester. *The Lonely Lady of San Clemente: The Story of Pat Nixon*. New York: Thomas Crowell, 1978.

Davis, David Brion. *The Slave Power Conspiracy and the Paranoid Style*. Baton Rouge: Louisiana State University Press, 1969.

———, ed. *The Fear of Conspiracy: Images of Un-American Subversion from the Revolution to the Present*. Ithaca, NY: Cornell University Press, 1971.

Davis, Kenneth S. *The Politics of Honor: A Biography of Adlai E. Stevenson*. New York: Putnam, 1972.

Dean, John W. III. *Blind Ambition*. New York: Simon & Schuster, 1976.

Deakin, Jim. *Straight Stuff: The Reporters, the White House and the Truth*. New York: William Morrow, 1984.

DeBenedetti, Charles, with Charles Chatfield. *An American Ordeal: The Antiwar Movement of the Vietnam Era*. Syracuse, NY: Syracuse University Press, 1990.

DeHart, Frank. *Traumatic Nixon*. Self-published, 1979.

Dellinger, David. *More Power Than We Know: The People's Movement Toward Democracy*. Garden City, NY: Anchor, 1975.

Diamond, Edwin. *Behind the Times: Inside the "New" New York Times*. New York: Villard, 1993.

———, and Stephen Bates. *The Spot: The Rise of Political Advertising on Television*. Cambridge, MA: Harvard University Press, 1992.

Dickstein, Morris. *Gates of Eden: American Culture in the Sixties*. Cambridge, MA: Harvard University Press, 1997 (1977).

Dionne, E. J. *Why Americans Hate Politics*. New York: Simon & Schuster, 1991.

Dodden, Arthur Power. "The Record of Political Humor," *American Quarterly*, vol. 37, no. 1 (1985).

Donner, Frank J. *The Age of Surveillance: The Aims and Methods of America's Political Intelligence System*. New York: Knopf, 1980.

Donovan, Hedley. *Roosevelt to Reagan: A Reporter's Encounters with Nine Presidents*. New York: Harper, 1979.

Douglas, Helen Gahagan. *A Full Life*. Garden City, NY: Doubleday, 1982.

Douglass, Wayne J. "Tricky Dick: Richard Nixon as Literary Character," *Lamar Journal of the Humanities*, vol. 7, no. 2 (1981).

Downie, Leonard. *The New Muckrakers*. Washington, DC: New Republic Books, 1976.

Drew, Elizabeth. *Washington Journal: The Events of 1973–1974*. New York: Random House, 1974.

Edelman, Murray J. *Constructing the Political Spectacle*. Chicago: University of Chicago Press, 1988.

Edmundson, Mark. *Nightmare on Main Street: Angels, Sadomasochism, and the Culture of Gothic*. Cambridge, MA: Harvard University Press, 1997.

Edwards, Lee. *The Conservative Revolution: The Movement That Remade America*. New York: Free Press, 1999.

Efron, Edith. *The News Twisters*. Los Angeles: Nash, 1971.

Ehrhart, W. D. *Busted: A Vietnam Veteran in Nixon's America*. Amherst: University of Massachusetts Press, 1994.

Ehrlichman, John. *Witness to Power: The Nixon Years*. New York: Simon & Schuster, 1982.

Eisenberg, Lee, ed. *Fifty Who Made a Difference*. New York: Villard, 1986.

Eisenhower, Dwight D. *Mandate for Change: The White House Years, 1953–56*. Garden City, NY: Doubleday, 1963.

Elliot, Osborne. *The World of Oz*. New York: Viking, 1980.

Emery, Fred. *Watergate: The Corruption of American Politics and the Fall of Richard Nixon*. New York: Times Books, 1994.

Endicott, David. "Spectacular Fictions: The Cold War and the Making of Historical Knowledge," PhD dissertation, Ball State University, 1998.

Epstein, Edward Jay. *Agency of Fear: Opiates and Political Power in America*. London: Verso, 1990 (1977).

Erikson, Erik. *Young Man Luther: A Study in Psychoanalysis and History*. New York: W. W. Norton, 1958.

Evans, Rowland, Jr., and Robert Novak. *Nixon in the White House: The Frustration of Power*. New York: Random House, 1971.

Ewen, Stewart. *PR!: A Social History of Spin*. New York: Basic Books, 1996.

Falk, Richard, Gabriel Kolko, and Robert Jay Lifton, eds. *Crimes of War*. New York: Random House, 1971.

Fallows, James. *Breaking the News: How the Media Undermine American Democracy*. New York: Pantheon, 1996.

Faries, McIntyre. *Rememb'ring*. Glendale, CA: Griffin, 1993.

Farrell, James. *Spirit of the Sixties: Making Postwar Radicalism*. New York: Routledge, 1997.

Fenno, Richard. *Homestyle: House Members in Their Districts*. Boston: Little, Brown, 1978.

Fitzpatrick, John J., William L. Langer, and Peter Loewenberg. "Communications," *American Historical Review*, vol. 77, no. 4 (October 1972).

Flippen, Brooks. *Nixon and the Environment*. Albuquerque: University of New Mexico Press, 2000.

Foner, Eric. *The Story of American Freedom*. New York: W. W. Norton, 1999.

Ford, Gerald. *A Time to Heal: The Autobiography of Gerald R. Ford*. New York: Harper, 1979.

Fowler, Robert Booth. *Believing Skeptics: American Political Intellectuals, 1945–1964*. Westport: Greenwood Press, 1978.

Fox, Richard Wightman. *Trials of Intimacy: Love and Loss in the Beecher-Tilton Scandal*. Chicago: University of Chicago Press, 1999.

Frank, Reuven. *Out of Thin Air: The Brief Wonderful Life of Network News*. New York: Simon & Schuster, 1991.

Frankel, Max. *The Times of My Life and My Life with The Times*. New York: Random House, 1999.

Fraser, Steve, and Gary Gerstle, eds. *The Rise and Fall of the New Deal Order, 1930–1980*. Princeton: Princeton University Press, 1989.

Freedman, Samuel G. *The Inheritance: How Three Families Moved from Roosevelt to Reagan and Beyond*. New York: Simon & Schuster, 1996.

French, Blaire Atherton. *The Presidential Press Conference: Its History and Role in the American Political System*. Lanham, MD: University Press of America, 1982.

Freud, Sigmund. "Some Character Types Met with in Psychoanalytic Work," in *The Standard Edition of the Complete Psychological Works of Sigmund Freud*, ed. James Strachey. London: Hogarth Press, 1957.

———, and William C. Bullitt. *Thomas Woodrow Wilson, Twenty-Eighth President of the United States: A Psychological Study*. Boston: Houghton Mifflin, 1966.

Frick, Daniel E. "Richard Nixon in Fact and in Fictions: Myth and Ideology in Contemporary American Literature and Popular Culture," PhD dissertation, Indiana University, 1991.

———. "Coover's Secret Sharer?: Richard Nixon in *The Public Burning*," *Critique*, vol. 37 (Winter 1996).

Fried, Albert. *FDR and His Enemies*. New York: St. Martin's Press, 1999.

Friedlander, Saul. *History and Psychoanalysis: An Inquiry into the Possibilities and Limits of Psychohistory*. New York: Holmes & Meier, 1978.

Friedman, Leon, and William Levantrosser, eds. *Cold War Patriot and Statesman*. Westport: Greenwood Press, 1993 (cited in text as *Hofstra 3*).

———. *Richard M. Nixon: Politician, President, Administrator*. Westport: Greenwood Press, 1991 (*Hofstra 1*).

———. *Watergate and Afterward: The Legacy of Richard M. Nixon*. Westport: Greenwood Press, 1992 (*Hofstra 2*).

Frost, David. *"I Gave Them a Sword": Behind the Scenes of the Nixon Interviews*. New York: William Morrow, 1978.

Frum, David. *How We Got Here: The 70s: The Decade That Brought You Modern Life. For Better or Worse*. New York: Basic Books, 2000.

Fry, William F. "The Power of Political Humor," *Journal of Popular Culture*, vol. 10, no. 1 (1976).

Gabler, Neal. *Life, the Movie: How Entertainment Conquered Reality*. New York: Knopf, 1998.

Gaddis, John Lewis. *Strategies of Containment: A Critical Appraisal of Postwar American National Security Policy*. New York: Oxford University Press, 1982.

Galbraith, John Kenneth. *A Life in Our Times: Memoirs*. Boston: Houghton Mifflin, 1981.

Gardner, Gerald. *The Mocking of the President: A History of Campaign Humor from Ike to Ronnie*. Detroit: Wayne State University Press, 1988.

Garment, Leonard. *Crazy Rhythm: My Journey from Brooklyn, Jazz and Wall Street to Nixon's White House, Watergate and Beyond* . . . New York: Times Books, 1997.

———. *In Search of Deep Throat: The Greatest Political Mystery of Our Time*. New York: Basic Books, 2000.

Garment, Suzanne. *Scandal: The Crisis of Mistrust in American Politics*. New York: Random House, 1991.

Garthoff, Raymond L. *Détente and Confrontation: American-Soviet Relations from Nixon to Reagan*. Washington, DC: Brookings Institution, 1985.

Gates, Gary Paul. *Air Time: The Inside Story of CBS News*. New York: Harper, 1978.

Gay, Peter. *Freud for Historians*. New York: Oxford University Press, 1985.

Gellman, Irwin F. *The Contender: Richard Nixon, The Congress Years, 1946–1952*. New York: Free Press, 1999.

Genovese, Michael. *The Nixon Presidency: Power and Politics in Turbulent Times*. Westport: Greenwood Press, 1990.

George, Alexander L., and Juliette L. George. *Woodrow Wilson and Colonel House: A Personality Study*. New York: J. Day, 1956.

Gergen, David. *Eyewitness to Power: The Essence of Leadership, Nixon to Clinton*. New York: Simon & Schuster, 2000.

Germond, Jack. *Fat Man in a Middle Seat: Forty Years of Covering Politics*. New York: Random House, 1999.

Gerstle, Gary. "The Protean Character of American Liberalism," *American Historical Review*, vol. 99, no. 4 (October 1994).

Geyl, Peter. *Napoleon: For and Against*. New Haven: Yale University Press, 1949.

Gillon, Steven. *Politics and Vision: The ADA and American Liberalism, 1947–1985*. New York: Oxford University Press, 1987.

Gitlin, Todd. *The Sixties: Years of Hope, Days of Rage*. New York: Bantam Books, 1987.

Goldberg, Benjamin J. "The Vice Presidency of Richard M. Nixon: One Man's Quest for National Respect, an International Reputation, and the Presidency," PhD dissertation, College of William and Mary, 1998.

Goldman, William. *Adventures in the Screen Trade: A Personal View of Hollywood and Screenwriting*. New York: Warner Books, 1984.

———. *Which Lie Did I Tell?: More Adventures in the Screen Trade*. New York: Pantheon, 2000.

Goldwater, Barry M., with Jack Casserly. *Goldwater.* New York: Doubleday, 1988.

Goodman, James. *Stories of Scottsboro.* New York: Pantheon, 1994.

Gottfried, Paul, and Thomas Fleming. *The Conservative Movement.* Boston: Twayne, 1988.

Gottlieb, Robert, and Irene Wolt. *Thinking Big: The Story of the Los Angeles Times, Its Publishers and Their Influence on Southern California.* New York: Putnam, 1977.

Graham, Hugh Davis. *The Civil Rights Era: Origins and Development of National Policy, 1960–1972.* New York: Oxford University Press, 1990.

Graham, Katharine. *Personal History.* New York: Knopf, 1997.

Greenfield, Meg. *Washington.* New York: Public Affairs, 2001.

Greenstein, Fred I. "The Benevolent Leader: Children's Images of Political Authority," *American Political Science Review,* vol. 54, no. 4 (December 1960).

———. *The Presidential Difference: Leadership Style from FDR to Clinton.* New York: Free Press, 2000.

Grofman, Bernard. "Richard Nixon as Pinocchio, Richard II, and Santa Claus: The Use of Allusion in Political Satire," *Journal of Politics,* vol. 51, no. 1 (February 1989).

Grossman, Michael Baruch, and Martha Joynt Kumar. *Portraying the President.* Baltimore: Johns Hopkins University Press, 1981.

Grunwald, Henry. *One Man's America: A Journalist's Search for the Heart of His Country.* New York: Doubleday, 1997.

Gulley, Bill, with Mary Ellen Reese. *Breaking Cover.* New York: Simon & Schuster, 1978.

Gunther, John. *Inside U.S.A.* New York: Harper, 1947.

Haig, Alexander M., with Charles McCarry. *Inner Circles: How America Changed the World.* New York: Warner, 1992.

Halberstam, David. *The Fifties.* New York: Villard, 1993.

———. *The Powers That Be.* New York: Knopf, 1979.

Haldeman, H. R., with Joseph DiMona. *The Ends of Power.* New York: Times Books, 1978.

Hale, Nathan G., Jr. *The Rise and Crisis of Psychoanalysis in the United States: Freud and the Americans, 1917–1985.* New York: Oxford University Press, 1995.

Hale, William Bayard. *The Story of a Style.* New York: W. B. Huebsch, 1920.

Hallin, Daniel C. *We Keep America on Top of the World: Television and Journalism in the Public Sphere.* New York: Routledge, 1994.

Halstead, Fred. *Out Now!: A Participant's Account of the American Movement Against the Vietnam War.* New York: Monad, 1978.

Hamburg, Eric, ed. *Nixon: An Oliver Stone Film.* New York: Hyperion, 1995.

Hamby, Alonzo. *Liberalism and Its Challengers: From F.D.R. to Bush.* 2nd edn. New York: Oxford University Press, 1992 (1985).

Hamilton, James W. "Some Reflections on Richard Nixon in the Light of His Resignation and Farewell Speeches," *Journal of Psychohistory*, vol. 4, no. 4 (Spring 1977).

Hardeman, D. B., and Donald C. Bacon. *Rayburn: A Biography*. Austin: Texas Monthly Press, 1987.

Harding, Luke, David Leigh, and David Pallister. *The Liar: The Fall of Jonathan Aitken*. London: Penguin, 1997.

Hendra, Tony. *Going Too Far*. New York: Doubleday, 1987.

Herbers, John. *No Thank You, Mr. President*. New York: W. W. Norton, 1976.

Hertsgaard, Mark. *On Bended Knee: The Press and the Reagan Presidency*. New York: Farrar, Straus & Giroux, 1988.

Hess, Robert D., and David Easton. "The Child's Changing Image of the President," *Public Opinion Quarterly*, vol. 24, no. 4 (Winter, 1960).

Hill, Doug, and Jeff Weingrad. *Saturday Night: A Backstage History of Saturday Night Live*. New York: Beech Tree Books, 1986.

Hilliard, David. *This Side of Glory: The Autobiography of David Hilliard and the Story of the Black Panther Party*. Boston: Little, Brown, 1973.

Himmelstein, Jerome. *To the Right: The Transformation of American Conservatism*. Berkeley: University of California Press, 1990.

Hirshberg, Jack. *A Portrait of All the President's Men*. New York: Warner, 1976.

Hodgson, Godfrey. *The World Turned Rightside Up: A History of the Conservative Ascendancy in America*. Boston: Houghton Mifflin, 1996.

Hoff, Joan. *Nixon Reconsidered*. New York: Basic Books, 1994.

———. *Watergate Revisited*. Greenville, NC: East Carolina University Press, 1993.

Hoffman, Jack, and Daniel Simon. *Run, Run, Run: The Lives of Abbie Hoffman*. New York: Putnam, 1994.

Hofstadter, Richard. *The Paranoid Style in American Politics*. New York: Knopf, 1965.

Hofstetter, C. Richard. *Bias in the News*. Columbus: Ohio State University Press, 1976.

Hollinger, David. "Ethnic Diversity, Cosmopolitanism, and the Emergence of the American Liberal Intelligentsia," *American Quarterly*, vol. 27, no. 2 (May, 1975).

Hougan, Jim. *Secret Agenda: Watergate, Deep Throat, and the CIA*. New York: Random House, 1984.

Howe, Irving. *Politics and the Novel*. New York: Horizon, 1957.

Hume, Brit. *Inside Story*. Garden City, NY: Doubleday, 1974.

Humes, James C. *Nixon's Ten Commandments of Statecraft*. New York: Scribner's, 1997.

Hutschnecker, Arnold A. *The Drive for Power*. New York: M. Evans, 1974.

Jacobs, Lawrence R., and Robert Y. Shapiro. "The Rise of Presidential Polling: The Nixon White House in Historical Perspective," *Public Opinion Quarterly*, vol. 59, no. 2 (Summer 1995).

Jameson, Fredric. *The Geopolitical Aesthetic: Cinema and Space in the World System.* Bloomington: University of Indiana Press, 1992.

Jamieson, Kathleen Hall. *Packaging the Presidency: A History and Criticism of Presidential Campaign Advertising.* 3rd edn. rev. New York: Oxford University Press, 1996 (1984).

Janeway, Michael. *Republic of Denial: Press, Politics and Public Life.* New Haven: Yale University Press, 1999.

Johnson, James P. "Nixon's Use of Metaphor: The Real Nixon Tapes," *Psychoanalytic Review,* vol. 66, no. 2 (1979).

Johnson, Paul. *A History of the American People.* New York: Harper, 1998.

———. *Modern Times: The World from the Twenties to the Nineties.* New York: Harper, 1992.

Johnson, Thomas J. *The Rehabilitation of Richard Nixon: The Media's Effect on Collective Memory.* New York: Garland, 1995.

Judis, John B. *William F. Buckley, Jr.: Patron Saint of the Conservatives.* New York: Simon & Schuster, 1988.

Julian, Patrick. "So Many Limitations and Trammels of Historical Fact: Mythmaking in the Portrayal of the President in 20th-Century American Drama," PhD dissertation, Bowling Green State University, 1996.

Kalb, Marvin. *The Nixon Memo: Political Respectability, Russia, and the Press.* Chicago: University of Chicago Press, 1994.

Kallina, Edmund F., Jr. *Courthouse over White House: Chicago and the Presidential Election of 1960.* Orlando: University of Central Florida Press, 1988.

———. "Was the 1960 Election Stolen?: The Case of Illinois," *Presidential Studies Quarterly,* vol. 15, no. 1 (Winter 1985).

Kalman, Laura. *The Strange Career of Legal Liberalism.* New Haven: Yale University Press, 1996.

Kammen, Michael. *A Machine That Would Go of Itself: The Constitution in American Culture.* New York: Knopf, 1986.

Kazin, Michael. *The Populist Persuasion: An American History.* New York: Basic Books, 1995.

Keener, John F. "Magical Disturbances: Biographical Narrative and the Historical Figure in Contemporary Fiction," PhD dissertation, University of Kentucky, 1997.

———. "Writing the Vacuum: Richard Nixon as Literary Figure," *Critique,* vol. 41, no. 2 (Winter 2000).

Kellerman, Barbara, ed., *Leadership: Multidisciplinary Perspectives.* Englewood Cliffs, NJ: Prentice-Hall, 1984.

Kelley, Stanley. *Professional Public Relations and Political Power.* Baltimore: Johns Hopkins University Press, 1956.

Kempton, Murray. *America Comes of Middle Age: Columns 1950–1962.* Boston: Little, Brown, 1963.

Keogh, James. *President Nixon and the Press*. New York: Funk & Wagnalls, 1972.

———. *This Is Nixon*. New York: Putnam, 1956.

Kerbel, Matthew Robert. *Remote and Controlled: Media Politics in a Cynical Age*. Boulder, CO: Westview, 1990.

Kercher, Stephen Edward. "The Limits of Irreverence: 'Sick' Humor and Satire in America, 1950–1964," PhD dissertation, Indiana University, 1998.

Kimball, Jeffrey P. *Nixon's Vietnam War*. Lawrence: University Press of Kansas, 1998.

Kissinger, Henry. *White House Years*. Boston: Little, Brown, 1979.

———. *Years of Upheaval*. Boston: Little, Brown, 1982.

Klein, Herbert G. *Making It Perfectly Clear*. New York: Doubleday, 1980.

Korda, Michael. *Another Life: A Memoir of Other People*. New York: Random House, 1999.

Korff, Baruch. *The Personal Nixon: Staying on the Summit*. Washington, DC: National Citizens' Committee for Fairness to the Presidency, Inc., 1974.

———. *The President and I: Richard Nixon's Rabbi Reveals His Role in the Saga That Traumatized the Nation*. Providence, RI: Baruch Korff Foundation, 1995.

Kornitzer, Bela. *The Real Nixon*. New York: Rand McNally, 1960.

Kotlowski, Dean J. "Politics and Principle: The Nixon Administration and Civil Rights Policy," PhD dissertation, Indiana University, 2000.

Krassner, Paul. *Confessions of a Raving, Unconfined Nut: Misadventures in the Counter-Culture*. New York: Simon & Schuster, 1993.

Krogh, Egil. *The Day Elvis Met Nixon*. Bellevue, WA: Pejama Press, 1994.

Kuklick, Bruce. *The Good Ruler: From Herbert Hoover to Richard Nixon*. New Brunswick: Rutgers University Press, 1988.

Kurtz, Howard. *Spin Cycle: Inside the Clinton Propaganda Machine*. New York: Free Press, 1988.

Kutler, Stanley I. *The Wars of Watergate: The Last Crisis of Richard Nixon*. New York: Knopf, 1990.

Ladd, Everett Carll, and Seymour Martin Lipset. *The Divided Academy: Professors and Politics*. New York: McGraw-Hill, 1975.

Langer, William L. "The Next Assignment," *American Historical Review*, vol. 63, no. 2 (January 1958).

Lasch, Christopher. *The Culture of Narcissism*. New York: W. W. Norton, 1978.

Lashner, Marilyn A. *The Chilling Effect in TV News: Intimidation by the Nixon White House*. New York: Praeger, 1984.

Lasky, Victor. *It Didn't Start with Watergate*. New York: Dial Press, 1977.

Lawrence, Bill. *Six Presidents, Too Many Wars*. New York: Saturday Review Press, 1972.

Lawton, Henry W. "Milhous Rising," *Journal of Psychohistory*, vol. 6, no. 4 (Spring 1979).

Lazarowitz, Arlene. *Years in Exile: The Liberal Democrats, 1950–1959*. New York: Garland, 1988.

Leff, Mark H. "Revisioning U.S. Political History," *American Historical Review*, vol. 100, no. 3 (June 1995).

LeGoff, Jacques. "Is Politics Still the Backbone of History?", in Felix Gilbert and Stephen R. Graubard, eds., *Historical Studies Today*. New York: W. W. Norton, 1972.

Lemann, Nicholas. *The Promised Land: The Great Black Migration and How It Changed America*. New York: Knopf, 1991.

Lens, Sidney. *Unrepentant Radical: An American Activist's Account of Five Turbulent Decades*. Boston: Beacon Press, 1980.

Leuchtenberg, William E. *In the Shadow of FDR: From Harry Truman to Bill Clinton*. 2nd edn. rev. Ithaca, NY: Cornell University Press, 1993.

———. "The Persistence of Political History: Reflections on the Significance of the State in America," *Journal of American History*, vol. 73, no. 3 (December 1986).

———. *A Troubled Feast: American Society Since 1945*. Boston: Little, Brown, 1979.

Lev, Peter. *American Films of the '70s*. Austin: University of Texas Press, 2000.

Levey, Jules. "Richard Nixon as Elder Statesman," *Journal of Psychohistory*, vol. 13, no. 4 (Spring 1986).

Levinson, Sanford. "Responsibility for Crimes of War," *Philosophy and Public Affairs*, vol. 2, no. 3 (Spring 1973).

Liddy, G. Gordon. *Will: The Autobiography of G. Gordon Liddy*. New York: St. Martin's Press, 1980.

Lippmann, Walter. *Essays in the Public Philosophy*. Boston: Little, Brown, 1955.

———. *Public Opinion*. New York: Harcourt, 1922.

Livingstone, Harrison E., and Robert J. Groden. *The Assassination of JFK and the Case for Conspiracy*. New York: Carroll & Graf, 1998 (1980).

Loewenberg, Peter. *Decoding the Past: The Psychohistorical Approach*. New Brunswick, NJ: Transaction, 1996.

———. "Nixon, Hitler and Power: An Ego Psychology Study," *Psychoanalytic Inquiry*, vol. 6, no. 1 (1986).

Lotchin, Roger W., ed. *The Way We Really Were: The Golden State in the Second Great War*. Urbana: University of Illinois Press, 2000.

Lubars, Walter, and John Wicklein, eds. *Investigative Reporting: The Lessons of Watergate*. Boston: Boston University Press, 1975.

Lukas, J. Anthony. *Nightmare: The Underside of the Nixon Years*. New York: Viking, 1976.

Macdonald, Dwight. *Against the American Grain*. New York: Random House, 1962.

Magruder, Jeb Stuart. *An American Life: One Man's Road to Watergate*. New York: Atheneum, 1974.

Mailer, Norman. *Miami and the Siege of Chicago*. New York: New American Library, 1968.

———. *St. George and the Godfather*. New York: New American Library, 1972.

Maltese, John Anthony. *Spin Control: The White House Office of Communications and the Management of Presidential News*. Chapel Hill: University of North Carolina Press, 1992.

Maravillas, Anthony Rama. "Nixon in the Fifties," PhD dissertation, University of Illinois, Chicago, 2001.

Martin, John Bartlow. *Adlai Stevenson and the World: The Life of Adlai E. Stevenson*. Vol. 2. Garden City, NY: Doubleday, 1977.

———. *Adlai Stevenson of Illinois: The Life of Adlai E. Stevenson*, Vol. 1. Garden City, NY: Doubleday, 1976.

Martin, John Frederick. *Civil Rights and the Crisis of Liberalism: The Democratic Party, 1945–1976*. Boulder, CO: Westview, 1979.

Massing, Michael. *The Fix*. New York: Simon & Schuster, 1998.

Matusow, Allen J. *Nixon's Economy: Booms, Busts, Dollars, and Votes*. Lawrence: University Press of Kansas, 1998.

———. *The Unraveling of America: A History of Liberalism in the 1960s*. New York: Harper, 1984

Mazlish, Bruce. *In Search of Nixon: A Psychohistorical Inquiry*. New York: Basic Books, 1972.

———. *The Leader, the Led and the Psyche: Essays in Psychohistory*. Hanover, NH: University Press of New England, 1990.

———. "Towards a Psychohistorical Inquiry: The 'Real' Richard Nixon," *Journal of Interdisciplinary History*, vol. 1, no. 1 (Autumn 1970).

———, ed. *Psychoanalysis and History*. Englewood Cliffs, NJ: Prentice-Hall, 1963.

Mazo, Earl. *Richard Nixon: A Political and Personal Portrait*. New York: Harper, 1959.

McClendon, Sarah. *My Eight Presidents*. New York: Wyden Books, 1978.

McCord, James W. *A Piece of Tape: The Watergate Story: Fact and Fiction*. Rockville, MD: Washington Media Services, 1974.

McGinniss, Joe. *The Selling of the President 1968*. New York: Trident, 1969.

McGirr, Lisa. "Suburban Warriors: Grass-Roots Conservatism in the 1960s," PhD dissertation, Columbia University, 1995.

McGovern, George. *Grassroots: The Autobiography of George McGovern*. New York: Random House, 1977.

McWilliams, Carey. *California: The Great Exception*. New York: Current, 1949.

———. *Southern California Country: An Island on the Land*. New York: Duell, Sloan & Pearce, 1946.

Merry, Robert W. *Taking On the World: Joseph and Stewart Alsop—Guardians of the American Century*. New York: Viking, 1996.

Miller, James. *Democracy Is in the Streets: From Port Huron to the Siege of Chicago.* New York: Simon & Schuster, 1987.

Miller, Merle. *Plain Speaking: An Oral Biography of Harry S. Truman.* New York: Putnam, 1974.

Mills, C. Wright. *The Power Elite.* New York: Oxford University Press, 1956.

Minow, Newton N., John Bartlow Marlin, and Lee M. Mitchell. *Presidential Television.* New York: Basic Books, 1973.

Miraldi, Robert. *Muckraking and Objectivity: Journalism's Colliding Traditions.* Westport: Greenwood Press, 1990.

Mitchell, Greg. *The Campaign of the Century: Upton Sinclair's Race for Governor and the Birth of Media Politics.* New York: Random House, 1992.

———. *Tricky Dick and The Pink Lady: Richard Nixon vs. Helen Gahagan Douglas— Sexual Politics and the Red Scare, 1950.* New York: Random House, 1998.

Mixner, David. *Stranger Among Friends.* New York: Bantam Books, 1996.

Mollenhoff, Clark. *Game Plan for Disaster: An Ombudsman's Report on the Nixon Years.* New York: W. W. Norton, 1976.

Monsell, Thomas. *Nixon on Stage and Screen: The Thirty-Seventh President as Depicted in Films, Television, Plays and Opera.* Jefferson, NC: McFarland, 1998.

Morris, Roger. *Richard Milhous Nixon: The Rise of an American Politician.* New York: Holt, 1990.

Moynihan, Daniel Patrick. *Maximum Feasible Misunderstanding: Community Action in the War on Poverty.* New York: Free Press, 1969.

———. *The Politics of a Guaranteed Income: The Nixon Administration and the Family Assistance Plan.* New York: Random House, 1973.

Murphy, Arthur B. "Evaluating the Presidents of the United States," *Presidential Studies Quarterly,* vol. 14, no. 1 (Winter 1984).

Murray, Robert K., and Tim H. Blessing. "The Presidential Performance Study: A Progress Report," *Journal of American History,* vol. 70, no. 3 (December 1983).

Nash, George H. *The Conservative Intellectual Movement in America Since 1945.* New York: Basic Books, 1976.

Nasaw, David. *The Chief: The Life of William Randolph Hearst.* Boston: Houghton Mifflin, 2000.

New York Times. *The End of a Presidency.* New York: Holt, 1974.

Nixon, Richard. "Asia After Viet Nam," *Foreign Affairs* (October 1967).

———. *Beyond Peace.* New York: Random House, 1994.

———. *In the Arena: A Memoir of Victory, Defeat and Renewal.* New York: Simon & Schuster, 1990.

———. *Leaders.* New York: Warner Books, 1982.

———. *1999: Victory Without War.* New York: Simon & Schuster, 1988.

———. *No More Vietnams.* New York: Arbor House, 1985.

———. *Real Peace.* New York: Warner Books, 1984.

———. *The Real War.* New York: Warner Books, 1980.

———. *RN: The Memoirs of Richard Nixon.* New York: Grosset & Dunlap, 1978.

———. *Seize the Moment.* New York: Simon & Schuster, 1992.

———. *Six Crises.* Garden City, NY: Doubleday, 1962.

———. "Superpower Summitry," *Foreign Affairs* (Fall 1985).

Norton, Anne. *Republic of Signs: Liberal Theory and American Popular Culture.* Chicago: University of Chicago Press, 1993.

Obst, David. *Too Good to Be Forgotten: Changing America in the '60s and '70s.* New York: John Wiley, 1998.

Oglesby, Carl. *The Yankee and Cowboy War: Conspiracies from Dallas to Watergate.* Kansas City, KS: Sheed Andrews & McMeel, 1976.

Olmstead, Kathryn S. *Challenging the Secret Government: The Post-Watergate Investigations of the CIA and FBI.* Chapel Hill: University of North Carolina Press, 1996.

Orman, John. "Covering the American Presidency," *Presidential Studies Quarterly,* vol. 14, no. 3 (Summer 1984).

Osborne, John. *The Fourth Year of the Nixon Watch.* New York: Liveright, 1973.

———. *The Last Nixon Watch.* Washington, DC: New Republic, 1975.

———. *The Nixon Watch.* New York: Liveright, 1970.

———. *The Second Year of the Nixon Watch.* New York: Liveright, 1971.

———. *The Third Year of the Nixon Watch.* New York: Liveright, 1972.

Packard, Vance. *The Hidden Persuaders.* New York: D. McKay, 1957.

Paley, William S. *As It Happened: A Memoir.* Garden City, NY: Doubleday, 1979.

Parmet, Herbert S. *The Democrats: The Years After FDR.* New York: Macmillan, 1976.

———. *Richard Nixon and His America.* Boston: Little, Brown, 1990.

Patterson, James T. *Congressional Conservatism and the New Deal.* Lexington: University of Kentucky Press, 1967.

———. *Grand Expectations: The United States, 1945–1974.* New York: Oxford University Press, 1996.

Pearson, Drew. *Diaries, 1949–1959.* New York: Holt, 1974.

———, and Jack Anderson. *U.S.A.—Second Class Power?* New York: Simon & Schuster, 1958.

Pells, Richard. *The Liberal Mind in a Conservative Age: American Intellectuals in the 1940s and 1950s.* New York: Harper, 1985.

Peterson, Merrill D. *The Jefferson Image in the American Mind.* New York: Oxford University Press, 1962.

———. *Lincoln in American Memory.* New York: Oxford University Press, 1994.

Phillips, Cabell, ed. *Dateline: Washington: The Story of National Affairs Journalism in the Life and Times of the National Press Club.* Garden City, NY: Doubleday, 1949.

———. *The 1940s: Decade of Triumph and Trouble*. New York: Macmillan, 1975.

Phillips, Kevin. *The Emerging Republican Majority*. New Rochelle, NY: Arlington, 1969.

———. *Post-Conservative America: People, Politics, and Ideology in a Time of Crisis*. New York: Random House, 1982.

Pierpont, Robert. *At the White House: Assignment to Six Presidents*. New York: Putnam, 1981.

Pilat, Oliver. *Drew Pearson: An Unauthorized Biography*. New York: Harper's Magazine Press, 1973.

Pipes, Daniel. *Conspiracy: How the Paranoid Style Flourishes and Where It Comes From*. New York: Free Press, 1997.

Plissner, Martin. *The Control Room: How Television Calls the Shots in Presidential Elections*. New York: Free Press, 1999.

Porter, William E. *Assault on the Media: The Nixon Years*. Ann Arbor: University of Michigan Press, 1976.

Powledge, Fred. *The Engineering of Restraint: The Nixon Administration and the Press*. Washington, DC: Public Affairs, 1971.

Price, Raymond K. *With Nixon*. New York: Viking, 1977.

Prouty, L. Fletcher. *JFK: The CIA, Vietnam and the Plot to Assassinate John F. Kennedy*. New York: Carol, 1996.

———. *The Secret Team: The CIA and Its Allies in Control of the United States and the World*. Englewood Cliffs, NJ: Prentice-Hall, 1973.

Pyle, Christopher. "Military Surveillance of Civilian Politics, 1967–1970," PhD dissertation, Columbia University, 1974.

Rangell, Leo. "Lessons from Watergate: A Derivative for Psychoanalysis," *Psychoanalytic Quarterly*, vol. 45, no. 1, 1976.

———. *The Mind of Watergate*. New York: W. W. Norton, 1980.

Rather, Dan. *The Camera Never Blinks*. New York: William Morrow, 1978.

———, and Gary Paul Gates. *The Palace Guard*. New York: Harper, 1974.

Reeves, Richard. *President Nixon: Alone in the White House*. New York: Simon & Schuster, 2001.

Renshon, Stanley Allen. "Psychological Analysis of Presidential Personality: The Case of Richard Nixon," *History of Childhood Quarterly: The Journal of Psychohistory*, vol. 2, no. 3 (Winter 1975).

———. *The Psychological Assessment of Presidential Candidates*. New York: New York University Press, 1996.

Reston, James. *Deadline: A Memoir*. New York: Random House, 1991.

Reuben, William A. *The Honorable Mr. Nixon*. New York: Action, 1958.

Rieder, Jonathan. *Canarsie: The Jews and Italians of Brooklyn Against Liberalism*. Cambridge, MA: Harvard University Press, 1985.

Riesman, David. *The Lonely Crowd: A Study of the Changing American Character*. New Haven: Yale University Press, 1950.

Ripon Society and Clifford W. Brown, Jr. *Jaws of Victory: The Game-Plan Politics of 1972, the Crisis of the Republican Party, and the Future of the Constitution*. Boston: Little, Brown, 1973.

Rips, Geoffrey. *The Campaign Against the Underground Press*. San Francisco: City Lights, 1981.

Rivers, William L. *The Adversaries: Politics and the Press*. Boston: Beacon Press, 1970.

Roberts, Chalmers M. *First Rough Draft: A Journalist's Journal of Our Times*. New York: Praeger, 1973.

———. *The Washington Post: The First 100 Years*. Boston: Houghton Mifflin, 1977.

Rogin, Michael, and John Lottier. "The Inner History of Richard Milhous Nixon," *Transaction*, vol. 9, no. 1–2 (November–December 1971).

Rogow, Arnold A. *The Psychiatrists*. New York: Putnam, 1970.

Rosenbaum, Ron. *Explaining Hitler: The Search for the Origins of His Evil*. New York: Random House, 1998.

Rosenberg, Bernard, and David White, eds. *Mass Culture: The Popular Arts in America*. Glencoe, IL: Free Press, 1957.

Rossinow, Douglas. *The Politics of Authenticity: Liberalism, Christianity, and the New Left in America*. New York: Columbia University Press, 1998.

Rossiter, Clinton. *The American Presidency*. New York: Harcourt, 1956.

———. *Conservatism: The Thankless Persuasion*. 2nd. edn. rev. New York: Vintage, 1962 (1955).

Roth, Philip. *Reading Myself and Others*. New York: Farrar, Straus & Giroux, 1975.

Rothenberg, Alan B. "Why Nixon Taped Himself," *Psychoanalytic Review*, vol. 62, no. 2 (Summer 1975).

Rovere, Richard. *Arrivals and Departures: A Journalist's Memoirs*. New York: Macmillan, 1979.

———. *Final Reports: Personal Reflections on Politics and History in Our Time*. Garden City, NY: Doubleday, 1984.

Rowan, Carl T. *Breaking Barriers: A Memoir*. Boston: Little, Brown, 1991.

Rowen, Hobart. *Self-Inflicted Wounds: From LBJ's Guns and Butter to Reagan's Voodoo Economics*. New York: Times Books, 1994.

Rudenstine, David. *The Day the Presses Stopped: A History of the Pentagon Papers Case*. Berkeley: University of California Press, 1996.

Rusher, William. *The Rise of the Right*. New York: William Morrow, 1984.

Sabato, Larry. *Feeding Frenzy: How Attack Journalism Has Transformed American Politics*. New York: Free Press, 1991.

Safire, William. *Before the Fall: An Inside View of the Pre-Watergate White House*. Garden City, NY: Doubleday, 1975.

———. *Safire's Washington*. New York: Times Books, 1980.

Salewicz, Chris. *Oliver Stone*. London: Orion, 1997.

Salisbury, Harrison. *Without Fear of Favor: The New York Times and Its Times*. New York: Times Books, 1980.

Saxbe, William B., with Peter D. Franklin. *I've Seen the Elephant: An Autobiography*. Kent, OH: Kent State University Press, 2000.

Scammon, Richard M., and Ben J. Wattenberg. *The Real Majority*. New York: Coward-McCann, 1970.

Schell, Jonathan. *The Time of Illusion*. New York: Knopf, 1976.

Schlesinger, Arthur, Jr. *The Cycles of American History*. Boston: Houghton Mifflin, 1986.

———. *The Imperial Presidency*. Boston: Houghton Mifflin, 1973.

———. *Kennedy or Nixon: Does It Make Any Difference?* New York: Macmillan, 1960.

Schmitz, Neil. "Telling the Truth: Richard Nixon and American Political Fiction," *American Studies*, vol. 18, no. 1 (Spring 1977).

Schoenbrun, David. *America Inside Out*. New York: McGraw-Hill, 1984.

Schorr, Daniel. *Clearing the Air*. Boston: Houghton Mifflin, 1977.

———. *Staying Tuned: A Life in Journalism*. New York: Pocket Books, 2001.

Schudson, Michael. *Discovering the News: A Social History of American Newspapers*. New York: Basic Books, 1978.

———. *The Good Citizen: A History of American Civic Life*. New York: Free Press, 1998.

———. "The Present in the Past Versus the Past in the Present," *Communication*, vol. 11, no. 2 (1989).

———. *Watergate in American Memory: How We Remember, Forget, and Reconstruct the Past*. New York: Basic Books, 1992.

Schur, Edwin. *The Awareness Trap: Self-Absorption Instead of Social Change*. New York: McGraw-Hill, 1976.

Schwartz, Barry. *George Washington: The Making of an American Symbol*. New York: Free Press, 1987.

———. "Social Change and Collective Memory: The Democratization of George Washington," *American Sociological Review*, vol. 56, no. 2 (April 1991).

Siegel, Frederick F. *Troubled Journey: From Pearl Harbor to Ronald Reagan*. New York: Hill & Wang, 1984.

Scott, Peter Dale. *Crime and Cover-Up: The CIA, the Mafia and the Dallas-Watergate Connection*. Berkeley, CA: Westworks, 1977.

———. *Deep Politics and the Death of JFK*. Berkeley: University of California Press, 1993.

———, Paul L. Hoch, and Russell Stetler, eds. *The Assassinations: Dallas and Beyond*. New York: Random House, 1976.

Seelye, John. "The Clay Foot of the Social Climber: Richard M. Nixon in Perspective," in William L. Andrews, ed., *Literary Romanticism in America*. Baton Rouge: Louisiana State University Press, 1981.

Sennett, Richard. *The Fall of Public Man*. New York: Knopf, 1977.

Skotnes, Adnor. "Hearts and Minds," *Radical History Review*, vol. 60 (Autumn 1994).

Sloterdijk, Peter. *Critique of Cynical Reason*. Minneapolis: University of Minnesota Press, 1987.

Small, Melvin. *Johnson, Nixon and the Doves*. New Brunswick: Rutgers University Press, 1988.

———. *The Presidency of Richard Nixon*. Lawrence: University Press of Kansas, 1999.

———, and William D. Hoover, eds. *Give Peace a Chance: Exploring the Vietnam Antiwar Movement*. Syracuse, NY: Syracuse University Press, 1992.

Small, William J. *Political Power and the Press*. New York: W. W. Norton, 1972.

Smith, Franklin B. *The Assassination of Richard Nixon*. Rutland, VT: Academy Press, 1976.

Smith, Howard K. *Events Leading Up to My Death: The Life of a Twentieth-Century Reporter*. New York: St. Martin's Press, 1996.

Smith, James Allen. *Brookings at Seventy-Five*. Washington, DC: Brookings Institution, 1991.

———. *The Idea Brokers*. New York: Free Press, 1991.

Smith, Sally Bedell. *In All His Glory: The Life of William S. Paley*. New York: Simon & Schuster, 1990.

Spalding, Henry. *The Nixon Nobody Knows*. Middle Village, NJ: J. David, 1972.

Spear, Joseph C. *Presidents and the Press: The Nixon Legacy*. Cambridge, MA: MIT Press, 1984.

Stannard, David E. *Shrinking History: On Freud and the Failure of Psychohistory*. New York: Oxford University Press, 1980.

Starr, Kevin. *The Dream Endures: California Enters the 1940s*. New York: Oxford University Press, 1997.

———. *Embattled Dreams: California in War and Peace, 1940–1950*. New York: Oxford University Press, 2002.

———. *Endangered Dreams: The Great Depression in California*. New York: Oxford University Press, 1996.

———. *Material Dreams: Southern California Through the 1920s*. New York: Oxford University Press, 1990.

Steel, Ronald. *Walter Lippmann and the American Century*. Boston: Little, Brown, 1980.

Steck, Joan Orr. "Press Commentary and the 1972 Presidential Election: An Analysis of Selected Columnists," PhD dissertation, University of Wisconsin, Madison, 1980.

Stein, Herbert. *Presidential Economics*. Washington, DC: American Enterprise Institute, 1988.

Steinberg, Blema S. *Shame and Humiliation: Presidential Decision Making on Vietnam.* Pittsburgh: Pittsburgh University Press, 1996.

Stevenson, Adlai. *The New America,* ed. Seymour E. Harris, John Bartlow Martin, and Arthur Schlesinger. New York: Harper, 1957.

Summers, Anthony. *The Arrogance of Power: The Secret World of Richard Nixon.* New York: Viking, 2000.

Sussman, Barry. *The Great Cover-Up: Nixon and the Scandal of Watergate.* New York: Thomas Crowell, 1974.

Tanner, Tony. *City of Words: American Fiction, 1950–1970.* New York: Harper, 1971.

Tebbel, John, and Sarah Miles Watts. *The Press and the Presidency: From George Washington to Ronald Reagan.* New York: Oxford University Press, 1985.

Thelen, David. "The Practice of American History," *Journal of American History,* vol. 81, no. 3 (December 1994).

Theoharis, Athan, ed. *Beyond the Hiss Case: The FBI, Congress and the Cold War.* Philadelphia: Temple University Press, 1982.

———. *Spying on Americans: Political Surveillance from Hoover to the Huston Plan.* Philadelphia: Temple University Press, 1978.

Thomas, Helen. *Dateline: White House.* New York: Macmillan, 1975.

———. *Front Row at the White House: My Life and Times.* New York: Simon & Schuster, 1999.

Thompson, Fred D. *At That Point in Time: The Inside Story of the Senate Watergate Committee.* New York: Quadrangle, 1975.

Thompson, Hunter S. *Fear and Loathing on the Campaign Trail '72.* San Francisco: Straight Arrow, 1973.

———. *The Great Shark Hunt: Strange Tales from a Strange Time.* New York: Summit, 1979.

Tifft, Susan E., and Alex S. Jones. *The Trust: The Private and Powerful Family Behind The New York Times.* Boston: Little, Brown, 1999.

Toplin, Robert Brent. *History by Hollywood: The Use and Abuse of the American Past.* Urbana: University of Illinois Press, 1996.

Trilling, Lionel. *The Liberal Imagination: Essays on Literature and Society.* New York: Viking, 1950.

———. *Sincerity and Authenticity.* Cambridge, MA: Harvard University Press, 1972.

Troy, Gil. *See How They Ran.* 2nd edn. rev. Cambridge, MA: Harvard University Press, 1996 (1991).

Ungar, Sanford. *The Papers and the Papers: An Account of the Legal and Political Battle Over the Pentagon Papers.* New York: Dutton, 1972.

Unger, Irwin. *The Best of Intentions: The Triumphs and Failures of the Great Society Under Kennedy, Johnson, and Nixon.* New York: Doubleday, 1996.

Utley, Garrick. *You Should Have Been Here Yesterday: A Life in Television News.* New York: Public Affairs, 2000.

Vacha, J. E. "It Could Happen Here: The Rise of the Political Scenario Novel," *American Quarterly*, vol. 29, no. 2. (Summer 1977).

Viorst, Milton. *Fire in the Streets: America in the 1960s*. New York: Simon & Schuster, 1979.

Volkan, Vamik D., Norman Itzkowitz, and Andrew W. Dod. *Richard Nixon: A Psychobiography*. New York: Columbia University Press, 1997.

Voorhis, Jerry. *Confessions of a Congressman*. Garden City, NY: Doubleday, 1947.

Walker, Martin. *America Reborn: A Twentieth-Century Narrative in Twenty-six Lives*. New York: Knopf, 2000.

Walters, Vernon. *Silent Missions*. Garden City, NY: Doubleday, 1978.

Walzer, Michael. "On the Role of Symbolism in Political Thought," *Political Science Quarterly*, vol. 81, no. 2 (June 1967).

Waterman, Richard W., Robert Wright, and Gilbert St. Clair. *The Image-Is-Everything Presidency: Dilemmas in American Leadership*. Boulder, CO: Westview, 1999.

Weed, Clyde. *The Nemesis of Reform: The Republican Party During the New Deal*. New York: Columbia University Press, 1994.

Weisberg, Jacob. *In Defense of Government: The Fall and Rise of Public Trust*. New York: Scribner's, 1996.

Wells, Tom. *The War Within: America's Battle Over Vietnam*. Berkeley: University of California Press, 1994.

———. *Wild Man: The Life and Times of Daniel Ellsberg*. New York: St. Martin's Press, 2001.

Whalen, Richard J. *Catch the Falling Flag: A Republican's Challenge to His Party*. Boston: Houghton Mifflin, 1972.

Whitaker, John C. *Striking a Balance: Environment and Natural Resources Policy in the Nixon-Ford Years*. Washington, DC: American Enterprise Institute, 1976.

White, Theodore H. *America in Search of Itself: The Making of the President, 1956–1980*. New York: Warner Books, 1982.

———. *Breach of Faith: The Fall of Richard Nixon*. New York: Atheneum, 1975.

———. *The Making of the President, 1960*. New York: Atheneum, 1961.

———. *The Making of the President, 1968*. New York: Atheneum, 1969.

———. *The Making of the President, 1972*. New York: Atheneum, 1973.

Whitfield, Stephen J. "*The Image*: The Lost World of Daniel Boorstin," *Reviews in American History*, vol. 19, no. 2 (June 1991).

———. "Richard Nixon as a Comic Figure," *American Quarterly*, vol. 37, no. 1 (Spring 1985).

Wicker, Tom. *One of Us: Richard Nixon and the American Dream*. New York: Random House, 1991.

Wiebe, Robert. *Self-Rule: A Cultural History of American Democracy*. Chicago: University of Chicago Press, 1995.

Wiessman, Steve, ed. *Big Brother and the Holding Company: The World Behind Watergate*. Palo Alto, CA: Ramparts, 1974.

Williams, William Appleman. *The Tragedy of American Diplomacy*. Cleveland: World, 1959.

Wills, Garry. *Nixon Agonistes: The Crisis of the Self-Made Man*. New York: Signet, 1969.

Wise, David. *The American Police State: The Government Against the People*. New York: Random House, 1976.

———. *The Politics of Lying: Government Deception, Secrecy, and Power*. New York: Random House, 1973.

Witcher, Robert. *After Watergate*. Lanham, MD: University Press of America, 2000.

Witcover, Jules. *The Resurrection of Richard Nixon*. New York: Putnam, 1970.

Wolfe, Tom. *The New Journalism*. New York: Harper & Row, 1973.

Wolfson, Lewis W., ed. *The Press Covers Government: The Nixon Years from 1969 to Watergate*. Washington, DC: American University, 1973.

Woodstone, Arthur. *Nixon's Head*. New York: St. Martin's Press, 1972.

Woodward, Bob, and Carl Bernstein. *All the President's Men*. New York: Simon & Schuster, 1974.

———. *The Final Days*. New York: Simon & Schuster, 1976.

Woodward, C. Vann. *Responses of the Presidents to Charges of Misconduct*. New York: Delacorte, 1974.

Yankelovich, Daniel. *New Rules: Searching for Self-Fulfillment in a World Turned Upside Down*. New York: Random House, 1981.

Zaroulis, Nancy, and Gerald Sullivan. *Who Spoke Up?: American Protest Against the War in Vietnam, 1963–1975*. Garden City, NY: Doubleday, 1984.

Cartoons

Auth, Tony. *Behind the Lines: Cartoons*. Boston: Houghton Mifflin, 1977.

Balken, Debra Bicker. *Philip Guston's Poor Richard*. Chicago: University of Chicago Press, 2001.

Block, Herbert. *Herblock Special Report*. New York: W. W. Norton, 1974.

Conrad, Paul. *The King and Us: Editorial Cartoons*. Los Angeles: Clymer, 1974.

Feiffer, Jules. *Feiffer on Nixon: The Cartoon Presidency*. New York: Random House, 1974.

MacNelly, Jeff. *MacNelly: The Pulitzer Prize Winning Cartoonist*. Richmond, VA: Westover, 1972.

Marlette, Doug. *Garden of Eight*. Boston: Faber & Faber, 1985.

Oliphant, Pat. *Four More Years*. New York: Simon & Schuster, 1973.

———. *The Jellybean Society*. Kansas City, KS: Andrews & McMeel, 1981.

Sorel, Edward. *Superpen: The Cartoons and Caricatures of Edward Sorel*. New York: Random House, 1978.

———. *Unauthorized Portraits*. New York: Knopf, 1997.

Trudeau, Garry. *The Doonesbury Chronicles*. New York: Holt, 1975.

Fiction and Humor

Agnew, Spiro. *The Canfield Decision*. Chicago: Playboy, 1976.

Bishop, Michael. *The Secret Ascension, or Philip K. Dick Is Dead, Alas*. New York: Tom Doherty, 1987.

Coover, Robert. *The Public Burning*. New York: Viking, 1977.

———. *Whatever Happened to Gloomy Gus of the Chicago Bears?* New York: Linden, 1987.

Dick, Philip K. *Radio Free Albemuth*. New York: Arbor House, 1986.

Ehrlichman, John. *The China Card*. New York: Simon & Schuster, 1986.

———. *The Company*. New York: Simon & Schuster, 1976.

———. *The Whole Truth*. New York: Simon & Schuster, 1979.

Heberlein, L. A. *Sixteen Reasons Why I Killed Richard M. Nixon*. Livingston, AL: Livingston, 1996.

Lowy, Jonathan. *Elvis and Nixon: A Novel*. New York: Crown, 2001.

Maxwell, Mark. *NixonCarver*. New York: St. Martin's Press, 1998.

Novello, Don. *The Lazlo Letters: The Amazing, Real-Life, Actual Correspondence of Lazlo Toth, American!* New York: Workman, 1977.

Pynchon, Thomas. *Gravity's Rainbow*. New York: Viking, 1973.

Reed, Ishmael. *Cab Calloway Stands in for the Moon*. Flint, MI: Bamberger, 1986.

———. "D Hexorcism of Noxon D Awful," in John A. Williams and Charles F. Harris, eds., *Amistad I: Writings on Black History and Culture*. New York: Vintage, 1970.

———. *The Freelance Pallbearers*. Garden City, NY: Doubleday, 1967.

Rosetto, Lou. *The Take-Over*. Secaucus, NJ: Lyle Stuart, 1974.

Roth, Philip. *American Pastoral*. Boston: Houghton Mifflin, 1997.

———. *I Married a Communist*. Boston: Houghton Mifflin, 1998.

———. *Our Gang (Starring Tricky and His Friends)*. New York: Random House, 1971.

Seelye, John. *Dirty Tricks, or, Nick Noxin's Natural Nobility*. New York: Liveright, 1973.

Spark, Muriel. *The Abbess of Crewe*. New York: Viking, 1974.

Updike, John. *Memories of the Ford Administration*. New York: Knopf, 1992.

———. *Rabbit Is Rich*. New York: Knopf, 1979.

Films (Cinematic and Television)

Allen, Woody. *Sleeper*. New Yorker Films, 1973.

Altman, Robert. *Secret Honor*. Sandcastle, 1984.

Arkush, Alan. *Elvis Meets Nixon*. Showtime, 1998.

Ashby, Hal. *Shampoo*. Columbia, 1975.

Bigelow, Kathryn. *Point Break*. Twentieth-Century Fox, 1991.

Costa-Gavras, Constantin. *Missing*. Universal, 1982.

———. *Z*. Fox Lorber, 1969.

De Antonio, Emile. *Millhouse: A White Comedy*. New Yorker Films, 1971.

Fleming, Andrew. *Dick*. Columbia, 1999.

Flicker, Theodore J. *The President's Analyst*. Paramount, 1967.

Frankenheimer, John. *Seven Days in May*. Warner, 1964.

Gold, Mick. *Watergate*. Brian Lapping Associates/Discovery Channel, 1994.

Joffe, Roland. *The Killing Fields*. Warner, 1984.

Lee, Ang. *The Ice Storm*. Twentieth-Century Fox, 1997.

Lindsay-Hogg, Michael. *Nasty Habits*. Bowden, 1977.

Linson, Arthur. *Where the Buffalo Roam*. Universal, 1980.

Meyer, Nicholas. *Star Trek VI: The Undiscovered Country*. Paramount, 1991.

Nelson, Gary. *Washington: Behind Closed Doors*. Paramount/ABC, 1977.

Pakula, Alan J. *All the President's Men*. Warner, 1976.

———. *Klute*. Warner, 1971.

———. *The Parallax View*. Paramount, 1974.

Petrie, Daniel. *Kissinger and Nixon*. Turner, 1995.

Stone, Oliver. *Born on the Fourth of July*. Universal, 1989.

———. *JFK*. Warner, 1991.

———. *Nixon*. Buena Vista, 1995.

Zemeckis, Robert. *Forrest Gump*. Paramount, 1994.

Musicals, Operas, and Plays

Adams, John. *Nixon in China: An Opera in Three Acts*, libretto Alice Goodman. Amsterdam: De Nedelandse Opera, 1988.

Bramwell, Dana Glenn. *The Tragedy of King Richard: Shakespearean Watergate*. Salina, KS: Survey, 1974.

Brustein, Robert, et al., eds. *The Tragical History of Samlet, Prince of Denmark, Watergate Classics*, November 1973–January 1974, Yale Repertory Theater, New Haven. Published in *Yale/Theatre*, vol. 5 (Winter 1974).

Edgar, David. *Dick Deterred: A Play in Two Acts.* New York: Monthly Review Press, 1974.

Freed, Donald, and Arnold M. Stone. "Secret Honor: The Last Testament of Richard M. Nixon: A Political Myth," in Elizabeth Osborn and Gillian Richards, eds., *New Plays U.S.A. 2.* New York: Theatre Communications Group, 1984.

Lees, Russell. *Nixon's Nixon.* New York: Dramatists Play Service, 1996.

Myers, Robert John. *The Tragedie of King Richard, the Second.* Washington, DC: Acropolis Books, 1973.

Reddin, Keith. *But Not for Me,* South Coast Repertory Theater, November 3, 1998.

Vidal, Gore. *The Best Man: A Play About Politics.* Boston: Little, Brown, 1960.

———. *An Evening with Richard Nixon.* New York: Random House, 1972.

Wolfe, Burton H. *The Devil and Dr. Noxin.* San Francisco: Wild West, 1973.

Poems

Ferlinghetti, Lawrence. *Tyrannus Nix?* New York: New Directions, 1969.

Lindsay, Vachel. "Bryan, Bryan, Bryan," *Nebraska History,* vol. 77, nos. 3 & 4, (Fall/Winter 1996).

Lowell, Robert. "George III," *The Faber Book of Political Verse,* Tom Paulin, ed. Boston: Faber & Faber, 1986.

Margolis, Jack S., comp. *The Poetry of Richard Milhous Nixon.* Los Angeles: Cliff House, 1974.

Merriam, Eve. *The Nixon Poems.* Illustrated by John Gerbino. New York: Atheneum, 1970.

Neruda, Pablo. *A Call for the Destruction of Nixon and Praise for the Chilean Revolution.* Translated by Teresa Anderson. Cambridge, MA: West End Press, 1980.

Wiegl, Bruce. "Nixon," *American Poetry Review,* vol. 29, no. 3, (May/June 2000).

Records and Songs

Bowie, David. "Young Americans." *Young Americans.* RCA, 1975.

Crosby, Stills, Nash & Young. "Ohio." *Four-Way Street.* Atlantic, 1971.

Guthrie, Arlo. "Presidential Rag." *Arlo Guthrie.* Reprise, 1974.

Lynyrd Skynyrd. "Sweet Home Alabama." *Second Helping.* MCA, 1974.

McDonald, Joe. "Tricky Dicky." *Resist! Sings Country Joe.* Rag Baby, 1971.

Ochs, Phil. "Here's to the State of Richard Nixon." *Chords of Fame.* A&M, 1976.

Scott-Heron, Gil. "H20 Gate Blues." *The Mind of Gil Scott-Heron.* Arista, 1979.

Taylor, James. "Line 'Em Up." *Hourglass.* Columbia/Sony, 1997.

Young, Neil. "Campaigner." *Decade.* Reprise, 1977.

Television Shows

Family Ties
Futurama
Laugh-In
Saturday Night Live
The Simpsons
The X-Files

Acknowledgments

Nixon's Shadow began as my dissertation at Columbia University, and so my many debts for help on this book begin there. My adviser, Alan Brinkley, known as one of this country's premier historians, is also a mentor without peer. He assisted me at every stage of this book—addressing conceptual challenges, reading drafts, offering constructive criticism. He guided me through fellowship applications, job talks, and the hurdles of academic life. His own exemplary work showed me that scholarly rigor need not come at the expense of literary grace.

Several other terrific advisers also have my great appreciation: Eric Foner, for hard-headed, cut-to-the-core advice; Ann Douglas, for brilliant streams of ideas and unflagging encouragement; Ira Katznelson, for introducing me to questions and literatures to broaden the book's scope and pertinence; and Casey Blake, for helping me enrich the book's cultural dimension. Thanks also, for many kinds of assistance, to Columbia professors Richard Bushman, Sam Freedman, Ken Jackson, Mike Janeway, Alice Kessler-Harris, Bill McAllister, Bob Shapiro, and Anders Stephanson.

I'm fortunate to have a wildly talented group of friends, many of whom measurably improved the manuscript. Warren Bass, Mark Brilliant, Matt Dallek, and Sharon Musher read nearly all of the book's chapters and offered valuable comments along the way, as well as moral support. Warren gets double credit for expertly line-editing the manuscript. Mike McCaughan and Eric Liu also provided loyal friendship and intelligent, incisive, and helpful thoughts on the penultimate draft. Chris Capozzola, Dave Ekbladh, Blake Eskin, Rob Genter, Michael Kimmage, Anne Kornhauser, Andy

McStay, Rick Perlstein, Jack Shafer, Jeff Shesol, and Sam Tanenhaus all read selected chapters and made valuable suggestions.

I have relied heavily on the work of other Nixon scholars. Whatever comments I offer on their books—and every new work on a subject implicitly critiques its forerunners—I owe a debt to Stephen Ambrose, Robert Sam Anson, Rowland Evans and Robert Novak, Irv Gellman, Joan Hoff, Stanley Kutler, Anthony Lukas, Roger Morris, Michael Schudson, Melvin Small, Tom Wicker, Garry Wills, and Bob Woodward and Carl Bernstein. Along with books by Richard Bradley and Thomas Monsell, Schudson's *Watergate in American Memory* furnished me with examples of Nixon's appearance in popular culture. Michael was also a source of ideas and stimulation, both in conversation and through his book, which has informed my thinking on many points. I cite several historians' works as models of the kind of history I'm attempting, but I must credit Ron Rosenbaum's *Explaining Hitler* with showing me the virtues of "explaining the explainers." I thank Ron, too, for sharing his experiences covering Nixon and for batting around ideas.

Bob Woodward, an early mentor, has taught me volumes about being a writer. Acclaimed for his reporting skills, Bob is also an astute analyst of Nixon, politics, and journalism; our conversations constantly challenged me and enriched the book. He and Elsa Walsh remain cherished friends. Bob also planted the idea for the book's title. On that subject, thanks to my estimable editor at *Slate*, Jacob Weisberg, for the subtitle, which he tossed out over Chinese food with his characteristic effortlessness.

The book's bibliography names subjects who sat for interviews, to whom I offer thanks, and it lists the archives I've consulted, whose archivists, librarians, and assistants also have my gratitude. I want to thank especially Susan Naulty and Beverly Lindy at the Nixon Library; Paul Wormser at the National Archives in Laguna Niguel; Carol Leadenham at the Hoover Institution; and Bob Scott and the superb library staff at Columbia. Kat Aaron, Andrew Dennington, Michelle Godwin, Erica Toth, and Eric Yellin were first-rate research assistants. Critical help with the photo research came from Marty Baldessari, Paul and Kay Conrad, Allan Goodrich at the Kennedy Library, Steve Greene at the National Archives, Ruth Mandel, Brian Montopoli, Photofest, and Michele Urton at the Center for the Study of Political Graphics. Thanks, too, for favors large and small, to Jon Finck, Charlie Forcey, Larry Friedman, James Goodman, Ken Hughes, Stephen Kercher, Nina Kushner, Nick Lemann, Jonathan Mahler, Maritsa Poros, Zachary Schrag, and the crew at *Slate*.

I am grateful to the institutions that gave me grants and fellowships: the Mrs. Giles R. Whiting Foundation, the Josephine de Karman Foundation, the Gerald R. Ford Presidential Library, the White House Historical Association, and Columbia University. I also extend my deep appreciation to Barbara Locurto, Kirsten Olsen, and the Columbia History Department staff for countless assists over the years; to Peter Bearman and the Institute for Social and Economic Research and Policy for office space; and to everyone at the American Academy of Arts & Sciences, especially the saintly James Carroll and my splendid companions Joseph Entin, Page Fortna, Jay Grossman, Andy Jewett, Ann Mikkelsen, and Eric Bettinger.

A heartfelt thanks to my agent, Peter Matson of Sterling Lord Literistic. Peter understood intuitively what I hoped to achieve with this book and found it the right home. He shepherded me, with humor, savvy, and confidence, through the unfamiliar terrain of publishing. Saskia Cornes and Jim Rutman at Sterling Lord were also indispensable. Starling Lawrence at W. W. Norton has also been a strong guiding hand. He shared my vision of what this book should be, gave critical advice in the early going, and, when necessary, flipped over his hourglass to give me the extra time I needed. Morgen Van Vorst has been an industrious and dependable project editor. Georgia Liebman produced the fantastic cover. I had the pleasure to work with Ann Adelman again after eight years and remembered why she is so highly esteemed as a copy editor. Louise Brockett and Rachel Salzman have worked to find the book an appreciative audience. Many others at Norton have my thanks for all those tasks that went on outside my ken.

I'm also lucky to have what I only late in life realized was the rare gift of a family with whom I share my intellectual work. I have dedicated this book to my parents, Robert and Maida Greenberg. They have always nurtured my intellectual aspirations, taken a serious interest in my work, and given me boundless love and sustenance. They are also a lot of fun. My father brought his philosopher's sharp mind to bear on the manuscript. My brother, Jonathan, read chapters and gave constructive advice, especially on the themes of image and authenticity, with which his own scholarly work is also concerned. Judith, my sister, offered loving humor and tireless encouragement and got me to read Baudrillard. My brother-in-law, Ira Joseph, eagerly talked about Nixon and politics with me and was a big help all around, even if the interview with Adnan Khashoggi never did come to fruition. Renee, Deon, and Ilana Nossel, David Bernstein and Kathleen Restifo, and Megan Blumenreich provided support and enthusiasm as *Nixon's Shadow* progressed from idea to dissertation to book.

Suzanne Nossel has lived with this project since its inception. When I met Suzanne, I was trying to find both a book topic and (with rather less intensity) a woman to spend my life with. As it turned out, I found both at once. For the last four years, Suzanne has struck the perfect balance of patience and prodding, bearing with me through times of uncertainty, sharing with me in times of excitement. She weathered my departures to visit archives, bouts of writer's block, and fluctuating income. She read drafts of the chapters and offered comments with love and enthusiasm. She has been my biggest booster, sharpest critic, and best friend. When the frustrations of writing were lessened, or its joys heightened, it was because Suzanne was at my side.

Permissions

Index